Procedural Content Generation for Games

Automate 3D Asset and Environment Creation with Blender Python and Geometry Nodes

Isabel Lupiani

Apress®

Procedural Content Generation for Games: Automate 3D Asset and Environment Creation with Blender Python and Geometry Nodes

Isabel Lupiani
Orlando, FL, USA

ISBN-13 (pbk): 979-8-8688-1786-1 ISBN-13 (electronic): 979-8-8688-1787-8
https://doi.org/10.1007/979-8-8688-1787-8

Managing Director, Apress Media LLC: Welmoed Spahr
Acquisitions Editor: Spandana Chatterjee
Coordinating Editor: Gryffin Winkler

Cover designed by eStudioCalamar

Cover image designed by Freepik (www.freepik.com)

Distributed to the book trade worldwide by Springer Science+Business Media New York, 1 New York Plaza, New York, NY 10004. Phone 1-800-SPRINGER, fax (201) 348-4505, e-mail orders-ny@springer-sbm.com, or visit www.springeronline.com. Apress Media, LLC is a Delaware LLC and the sole member (owner) is Springer Science + Business Media Finance Inc (SSBM Finance Inc). SSBM Finance Inc is a **Delaware** corporation.

For information on translations, please e-mail booktranslations@springernature.com; for reprint, paperback, or audio rights, please e-mail bookpermissions@springernature.com.

Apress titles may be purchased in bulk for academic, corporate, or promotional use. eBook versions and licenses are also available for most titles. For more information, reference our Print and eBook Bulk Sales web page at http://www.apress.com/bulk-sales.

Any source code or other supplementary material referenced by the author in this book is available to readers on GitHub (https://link.springer.com/book/9798868817861). For more detailed information, please visit https://www.apress.com/gp/services/source-code.

If disposing of this product, please recycle the paper

For James, Zoe, and Caleb

Table of Contents

About the Author

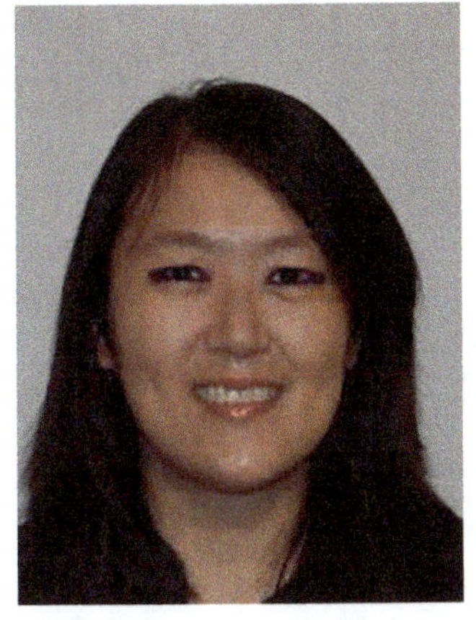

Isabel Lupiani is a software engineer by day and maker by night, who enjoys handcrafting 3D models as much as procedurally generating them. She received her MS in Computer Science from Georgia Tech and has worked at several game studios in the past as an AI engineer for PC/Xbox games. Her book credits include *Blender Scripting with Python: Automate Tasks, Write Helper Tools, and Procedurally Generate Models in Blender 4*. Isabel most recently worked as a Lead AI Engineer in the simulation industry.

About the Technical Reviewer

Ajit Deolikar is a mechanical engineer from Pune, India, with experience in new product design and development. He is currently working on designing next-generation accessories, power parts for four-wheelers and two-wheelers. His ongoing projects also include designing equipment used in the manufacturing of automotive parts, as well as for the construction and agriculture sectors.

Alongside his engineering work, he is passionate about art. He began using Blender many years ago as a hobby to create short animations and educational videos. Over time, he has integrated Blender into his professional workflow for product styling, CAD construction with hard surface modeling, and simulating complex mechanical motions. Using Blender's Python scripting, he has developed custom add-ons to automate tasks, improve product quality, and shorten delivery schedules. His Blender-based marketing videos and brochures help him stand out in the industry.

In his spare time, he enjoys playing chess and analyzing the strategies used by the world's great grandmasters. One day, he hopes to write a book on these approaches.

Acknowledgments

A big thank you to all the readers out there—your support allows me to keep writing! I'd also like to express gratitude to Spandana Chatterjee, Nirmal Selvaraj, Gryffin Winkler, Kripa Joseph, Joseph Quatela, and the rest of the Apress team for your support and guidance throughout the writing and publishing process. Special thanks to the technical reviewer Ajit Deolikar for tirelessly checking everything and making the book the best it can be. Last but not least, thank you to my husband James, my daughter Zoe, and my son Caleb for your eternal love and support.

Introduction

My first memory of an art class is folding origami cranes in kindergarten. The idea of transforming a single, uncut sheet of paper into a 3D object through clever manipulation is sheer genius. *Procedural Content Generation* (PCG) has the same kind of allure—all you need is an idea and some helpful tools like Blender Python and geometry nodes, to make complex 3D meshes appear as if out of thin air. In this book, I hope to share that magic with you.

The book opens with an overview of PCG methods, then takes you through eight different PCG "workshops," and concludes with a tutorial on how to import your Blender assets into Unreal Engine 5. By the time you reach the end of the book, you'll have created Blender Python scripts, geometry node trees, and shader node trees that procedurally generate everything from weapons, terrain, plants, to cities.

Who the Book Is For

This book is for developers who want to procedurally generate 3D assets and environments to use in their game, film, or simulation projects. It is also for anyone who wants to generate 3D meshes for any purpose, such as makers creating 3D printable parts or researchers producing scientific visualizations. The reader is assumed to have a high-level understanding of the 3D content pipeline, such as the basic structure of a mesh and what it means to unwrap and apply materials to a model.

You'll get the most out of the book if you already use Blender or are interested in learning the basics on your own, although many of the PCG techniques in the book are transferable at the conceptual level. Since the book makes heavy use of the Blender Python API, ideally you already know some basic Python or are willing to catch up by using resources outside the book.

Chapter Outline

Chapter 1 explains what PCG is and why it is useful. It also provides a survey of different PCG methods and the scenarios for which each method is suitable, along with historical examples of games that have used these techniques and the author's own examples.

Chapters 2 to 9 take you through eight different PCG workshops. Chapters 2 and 3 give you a quick start on Blender Python and guide you through designing and implementing a gun generator with parametric controls for varying the number of barrels, shape and size of the grip, etc. You'll also learn how to structure the generator to maintain relative proportions between components automatically.

In Chapter 4, you'll use shader nodes to generate materials such as colored metals with brushed and grid patterns for the guns from Chapters 2 and 3. You'll also use geometry nodes to create "bump" arrays of various shapes, from primitives to custom motifs, then bake them into normal maps with Blender Python to create 3D surface details for the gun grips. To wrap up the chapter, you'll modify the gun generator to unwrap and apply materials to the meshes automatically.

In Chapter 5, you'll continue to build on your geometry node skills. The first half of the chapter demonstrates clever uses of built-in textures for creating complex 3D details on meshes, such as Voronoi cracks, gem facets, ripples, and rocks. In the second half of the chapter, you'll design and build a node tree to transform any mesh into a "sliceform" version with two sets of interlocking cross-section plates, reminiscent of modern architecture. Along the way, you'll learn how to use advanced features such as Topology nodes for deriving relationships between neighboring geometry and Repeat blocks for creating `for` loops.

Chapter 6 demonstrates how to implement noise and fractal terrain generators in Blender Python. The first part of the chapter discusses noise-based methods, such as value noise with uniform sampling, value noise with noise basis functions, fBm, and the diamond-square algorithm. The second part of the chapter covers fractal-based methods, like hybrid multi fractal, multi fractal, and hetero terrain.

Chapter 7 shows you how L-System works from the ground up, starting with a pen-and-paper example, followed by a 2D then 3D turtle graphics-based system in Python that interprets L-System grammars and generates tree meshes. Along the way, you'll learn how to modify existing grammar sets as well as come up with your own to encode rules for generating custom meshes.

Chapters 8 and 9 teach you how to generate geometry from GIS (Geographic Information System) data. In Chapter 8, you'll learn how to find free building footprint datasets, preprocess them in the open source software QGIS, then write Blender Python code to generate city skyline meshes from them. In Chapter 9, you'll find out where to source free Digital Elevation Model (DEM) sets for places on Earth (or other planets), then write Python code to generate terrain meshes from them.

Chapter 10 opens with a step-by-step tutorial on how to export geometry you've created in Blender to FBX and glTF 2.0 formats with embedded materials. The second part of the chapter shows you how to automate the export process in Python. The final part of the chapter demonstrates how to import geometry into Unreal Engine 5.

Suggested Roadmap

The first five chapters are designed to be read in linear order, with Chapter 1 providing an overview, Chapters 2 and 3 a Blender Python quick start, and Chapters 4 and 5 tutorials on geometry nodes and shader nodes. In Chapters 2 and 3, you'll build your first procedural generator, then in Chapter 4, you'll generate normal maps and materials for the generated models. Chapters 6 through 9 are stand-alone PCG workshops that can be read in any order. Once you've read Chapters 1–5, you can read Chapter 10 to learn how to export and import geometry into Unreal Engine 5.

If you are experienced in Blender Python but new to geometry nodes and/or shader nodes, you can read Chapters 1, 4, and 5, then the rest of the book in any order. If you are only interested in Blender Python but not shader or geometry nodes, you can skip most of Chapter 4 and all of Chapter 5, except the sections on baking normal maps and modifying the gun generator to unwrap and apply materials in Python. If you do not care for generating geometry from GIS (real world) data, you can skip Chapters 8 and 9. You can pass over Chapter 10 if you do not use Unreal Engine. However, parts of Chapter 10 on how to develop a custom export script may still be useful.

CHAPTER 1

Overview of Procedural Content Generation Methods

Welcome to the world of Procedural Content Generation (PCG). In this chapter, we'll approach the subject from a high level, starting with a discussion on what PCG is and the motivations and benefits behind using it. We'll then survey a plethora of PCG techniques and learn about how each one works and what you might use it for. Along the way, we'll attempt to categorize these generation methods in different ways, based on characteristics such as what kinds of inputs they take, whether contents are generated offline or online, or if error checking is done during or after generation. You'll also learn about the computational techniques that drive some of these generation methodologies behind the scenes. To wrap up the chapter, we'll discuss the types of assets that can be produced with PCG methods and how they are used in games.

Downloading This Chapter's Figures

The source code and color figures for this book are available on GitHub via the book's product page, located at `https://link.springer.com/book/9798868817861`.

What Is Procedural Content Generation (PCG)?

If I am given one sentence to define *Procedural Content Generation (PCG)*, I would say it is "*writing programs to generate meshes*," which is arguably the most popular way PCG is used in practice and the first thing that comes to mind for most people–and it is for good

I. Lupiani, *Procedural Content Generation for Games*, https://doi.org/10.1007/979-8-8688-1787-8_1

reason. 3D content is usually the one bottleneck most teams have trouble with. You need art to make games, lots of it!

If I'm able to elaborate, I would go on to tell you that there are many types of assets you can generate besides meshes, such as textures, materials, rigs, particles, and so on. In fact, it is possible to procedurally generate both visual and nonvisual content for games, including sounds, level maps, or even missions. Contrary to popular belief, not all PCG systems generate content from scratch, many of which utilize input data of various forms to their advantage, anywhere from control parameters to real-world data such as building footprints or point clouds. A PCG system may draw from a library of modular parts, then either assemble them like Lego pieces or combine them with scratch-generated content, for example, a system that creates a city by assembling road mesh tiles into a map, then generating buildings on top of it. You may even have a PCG system that takes existing models and modifies them in an automated way—for instance, the sliceform models in Figure 1-1 are produced by a PCG system written by the author that takes existing meshes as input and based on which generates the given number of slices cut at specific angles.

A much better definition of PCG, I believe, is "*writing programs to generate, assemble, or edit digital content in an automated way*." Automation is the key here, as it sets a procedural generation system apart from an editing tool.

Figure 1-1. *Example of meshes generated by a PCG system that takes an existing mesh as input and based on which generates another mesh. Pictured here are two "sliceform" models output by a generator written by the author. The generator takes an input mesh and computes its cross-sections at the specified angle and spacing. The input mesh for the model on the left is the Stanford bunny, and on the right is the Utah teapot (both are well-known sample models from computer graphics research).*

Why Use Procedural Content Generation?

Now that you have a general understanding of what PCG is, in this section, we'll discuss the motivations that drive developers to opt for PCG in their production.

From the Content Creator's Standpoint

We'll first talk about the benefits of using PCG from the content creators' standpoint. Here, content creators refer to game and film devs, as well as anyone that uses digital art in their projects, such as simulation developers, researchers, educators, and so on.

More Art

The first and foremost reason to use procedural generation is to get *more art* than you have human artists to create. This could happen if the nature of your project requires a large amount of art, like an open-world game with a focus on exploration. Maybe your team has a limited budget that prevents you from hiring more artists, or perhaps you are just a couple of programmers who want to work on a project but don't know any artists to collaborate with. In these cases, it might make sense to invest the resources to develop a PCG system, with which you are able to produce many variations, or even reuse between projects.

Faster Production Speed

With careful planning, and a PCG system producing art that only involve limited or no postprocessing to be production ready, you could speed up a project substantially by filling in areas that draw little attention from players or viewers with generated assets, such as set dressings that are below the eye level or at a distance. There are many tried and true PCG techniques for generating natural-looking terrain that cover a large area (like the fractal terrain method we'll see in Chapter 6). In addition, PCG methods excel at generating a large number of similar but varied objects, such as crowds in a stadium, or trees framing a road. Instead of wasting precious production resources at modeling 50 trees and 100 spectators then placing them one by one, you'll be much better off generating these meshes then writing a program to automatically place them. We'll see how to generate plants with L-Systems in Chapter 7.

Cheaper Production

Assuming your PCG system is working well and not continuing to incur overhead like requiring constant manual error checking or repairs of generated output, once you've offset the cost of acquiring the PCG system in the first place, the rest of your production will be cheaper since you can scale up the amount of usable art without having to bring on more artists.

Ability to Evaluate Many Variations at Once

In addition to churning out assets during production, a PCG system can serve as a prototyping tool in the design stage, which is a practice architects and industrial designers refer to as *Form Finding*. *Form Finding* means using PCG to create variations of a model representing different possibilities of a design that you would lay out side by side and compare, like the example shown in Figure 1-2. You repeat the generate-and-compare process many times, until you arrive at a final design. Form Finding is similar to painters doing studies in hand sketches before starting to paint, or game artists making alternative versions of concept arts for a weapon before starting to model. The difference is, with Form Finding, a PCG system creates the variations, either on its own or from the range of parameter values set by the designer.

Form Finding goes hand in hand with *Parametric Modeling*, a 3D design technique with which the artist structures a mesh as a hierarchy of interrelated parts, such that the property of one part constrains that of another. When you modify one part, the parametric system automatically adjusts other part(s) constrained by it based on the relationship between them. For example, if a parametric tire model is set up to always have a height that is twice its width, scaling its height from 5 to 10 will scale its width from 2.5 to 5. Therefore, if you set up a parametric model so the key qualities of a design are preserved through relationships between parts, no matter how you edit the components, all the variations produced will remain valid and meaningful. You will work through examples of Parametric Modeling as you implement your own procedural game weapon generator in Blender Python in Chapters 2 and 3. Since the purpose of *Form Finding* is to evaluate candidates for a design, you want the candidates to be functionally valid as well as aesthetically pleasing—which a parametric model will produce as long as proper limits are set up on argument values. We'll go over additional examples of Parametric Modeling in Chapter 5.

Form Finding can also be used to iterate on the design of the PCG system itself. As you experiment with different parameter values and observe the generated outcomes, you may notice a part of a mesh that's fixed should instead be exposed to parametric control to make the variations more interesting. You may also notice if certain proportions between parts of the model are off and should be adjusted.

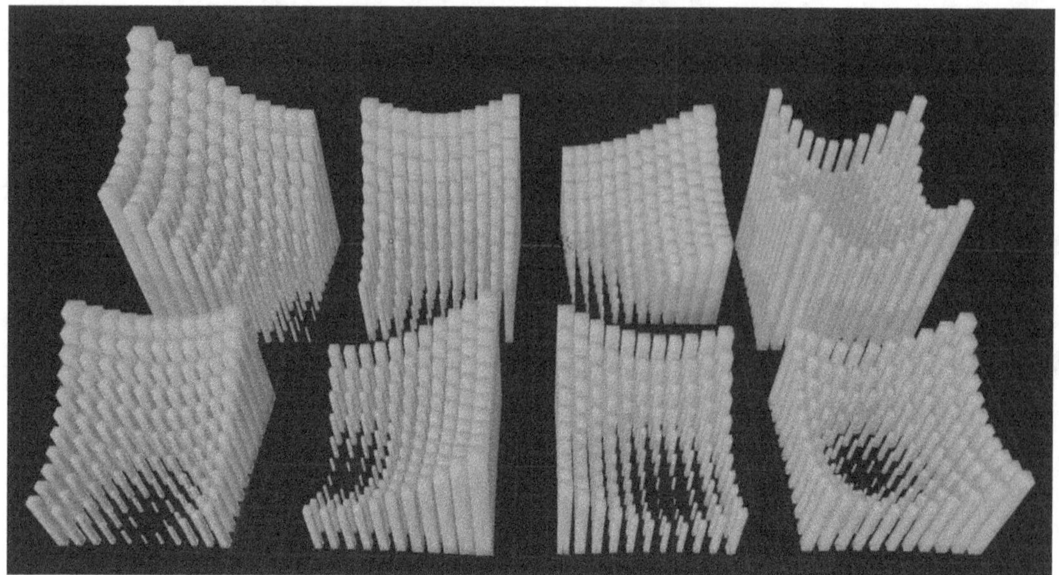

Figure 1-2. *Example of Form Finding by generating multiple variations of a design at a time, by varying the combinations of input values for a parametric model*

As Tools to Help Artists Create

We often consider the purpose of procedural generation as creating content that can be used directly in some product. However, a PCG system does *not* have to output final content that requires no further editing. Instead, it can be used as a tool to help artists create. For example, many game artists start their models by blocking out primitives that roughly resemble the shape they are going for, then refine the mesh over time. A PCG system can output partial models that have gone through these beginning stages which the artist can then take over and finish by hand. Looking at it another way, if you are unable to implement a PCG system that could output models of high enough quality to be used directly, the system could still be useful as a helper tool.

The *Form Finding* process described in the previous section can also be used as an artist's creative tool. Instead of picking a final design from the candidates produced by the generator, an artist can treat the variations as inspirations and create another design from it altogether.

Creating Something Mathematical or Scientific

Perhaps something that's less on game or film devs' radar, PCG can also be used for generating models that need to be mathematically precise. For example, if you are a researcher or educator, you can easily write PCG programs to generate curves or surfaces based on math formulas, faster and more accurately than any human artist could (doing so would equally spare the artist the agonizing tedium). The same goes for any meshes that require precise measurements or proportions, such as models that are scientific in nature.

In addition to using models generated from math formulas as they are, you can use them to form the bases of more complex designs. We will see an example of this in Chapter 3, where we use a partial parabolic curve as the basis for generating the trigger pull on a handgun. Some objects in nature have inherent frameworks that can be modeled mathematically, for example, seashells can be closely approximated from spiral curves. Figure 1-3 shows examples of seashell meshes generated by a program written by the author, which bridges circular cross-sections along a spiral curve with decreasing sizes and distances to the central axis.

Some organic objects have self-repeating structures that lend themselves well to grammar-based representations. You will learn how to generate meshes using L-Systems in Chapter 7, where you formulate your own rule sets for describing plant structures and use them to generate curves and meshes in Blender Python. For now, just know that in grammar-based PCG systems, you encode the structure of meshes as a few strings (which can be thought of as rules for generation), then write programs that interpret these strings to create models.

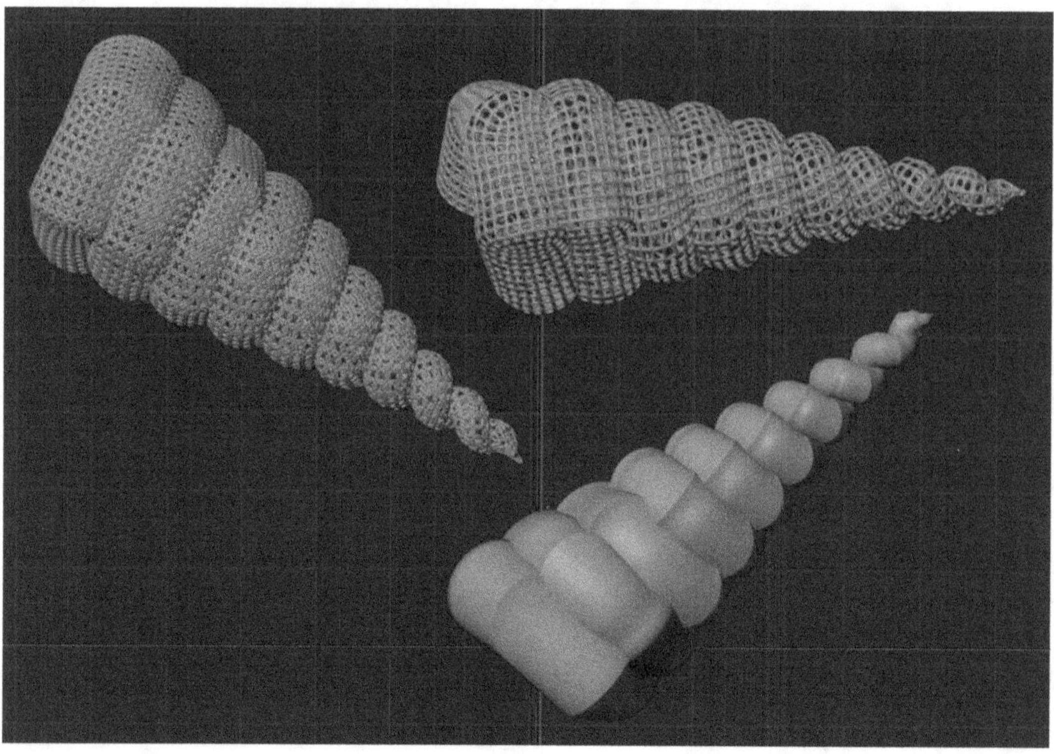

Figure 1-3. *Examples of seashell meshes generated from bridging circles along a spiral curve at decreasing sizes and distances to the central axis (by the author, 2022)*

Creating Something Accurate to Real-World Data

It's become a trend in recent years for simulation developers to advertise their 3D maps as "digital twins." Painstakingly hand modeled, some from scratch, and others after point clouds, the term boasts the companies' virtual environments as bona fide reproductions of their real-world counterparts.

Procedural generation is a very effective way to create environments based on Geographic Information System (GIS) data. For example, you can generate meshes to create a skyline from building footprint data, which encompass shapefiles (`*.shp`) that represent 2D cross-sections of buildings accompanied by spreadsheets containing building height, ground elevation, etc., which we'll see examples of in Chapter 8. The building meshes generated this way will be true to their real-world measurements. An example of New York's Battery Park generated from building footprint data by the author is shown in Figure 1-4, whereas a portion of San Jose, California's downtown skyline generated from building footprint data is shown in Figure 1-5.

Another example of GIS-based PCG is generating terrain from Digital Elevation Model (DEM) data, which are digital representations of the earth's surface minus buildings, vegetables, etc., which you'll see examples of in Chapter 9. The terrain generated from DEM can be textured using other real-world data such as satellite imagery of the corresponding area.

Other GIS data could also be used to generate environments, such as lidar point clouds, although this is beyond the scope of the book. Point clouds of a large area like a city are often taken aerially from a plane. A smaller area like a few buildings or roads may be scanned by a ground vehicle. The point clouds are cleaned up (denoised) then subsampled, before being triangulated into meshes. An example of a mesh over an area in San Jose, California, generated by the author from point clouds is shown in Figure 1-6.

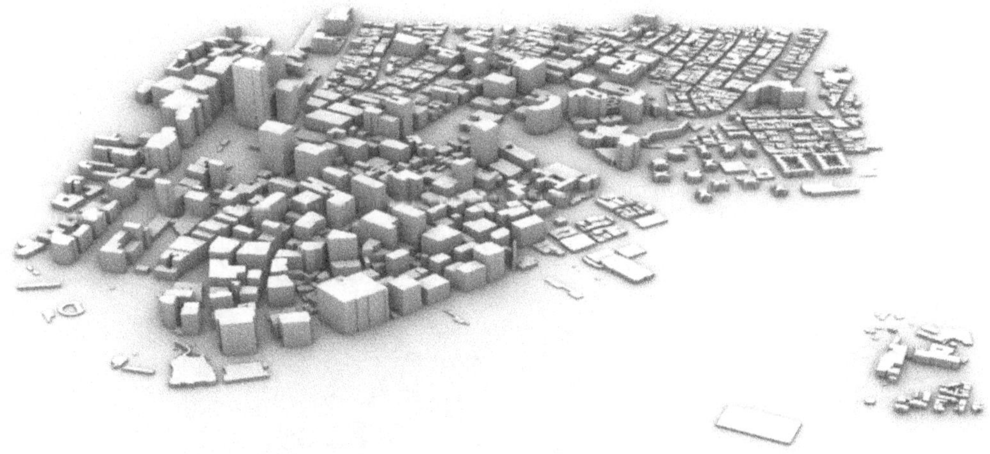

Figure 1-4. *Example of a cityscape mesh procedurally generated by the author from building footprint data (a type of Geographic Information System (GIS) data). The skyline pictured is part of Battery Park, New York City, New York.*

***Figure 1-5.** Example of a cityscape mesh procedurally generated by the author from building footprint data (a type of GIS data). The skyline pictured is part of downtown San Jose, California.*

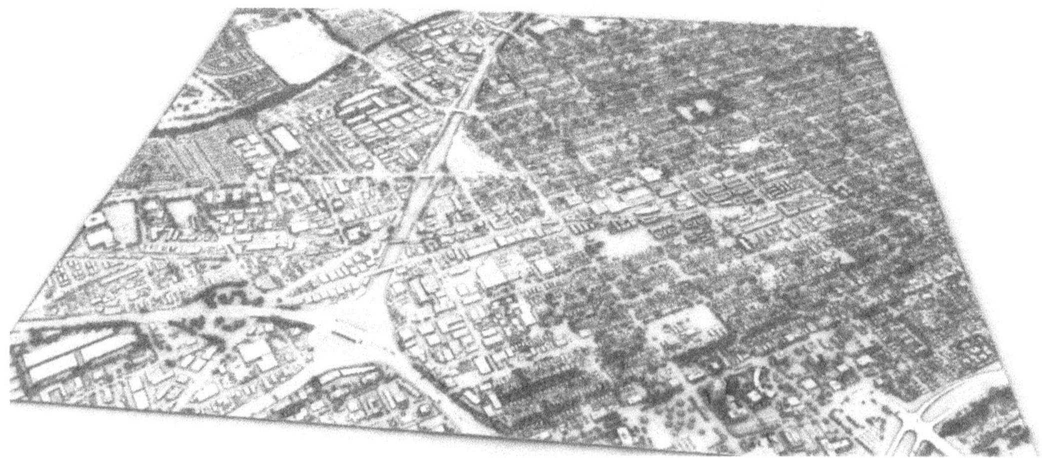

***Figure 1-6.** Example of a cityscape mesh procedurally generated by the author based on lidar point clouds (a type of GIS data). The skyline pictured is part of downtown San Jose, California. Lidar point clouds of a large area (as in this example) are usually taken aerially by plane.*

Creating Something Impossibly Complex to Model by Hand

As we've deliberated earlier, procedural generation is writing programs to generate or manipulate content like meshes. What are computer programs good at? Crunching calculations, repeating sequences of steps, and editing things precisely to a fault at impossible resolutions. Taking advantage of this, you can procedurally generate meshes that are so complex or involve so many steps that make them impossible or downright impractical for humans to model by hand. For instance, the mesh shown in Figure 1-7 is generated by a PCG program written by the author which takes meshes as input and generates woven versions of them. The input for the particular example in Figure 1-7 is the Utah teapot, which is a computer graphics classic. The output mesh has the same silhouette as the input but is formed from an over-under basket weave. To model a mesh like Figure 1-7 by hand would be impossibly tedious for humans.

Procedurally generating seemingly impossible objects can also be used to create moody or abstract game environments, for an Alice in Wonderland or alien planet sort of feel. Making this type of PCG system parametric can make iterating abstract designs easier, since you can dial sliders up and down until something "feels right."

Figure 1-7. *Example of procedurally generated "basket woven" mesh (by the author) that would be impossibly complex to model by hand. The PCG system takes a mesh as input (in this case, the famous Utah teapot from computer graphics), then generates an over-under basket weave structure from it (see zoomed portion on the lower right), according to the input mesh's topology.*

Novelty (Creating Unexpected Variations)

Occasionally, a generator could output a model that is unexpected but in a good way, perhaps emerging from a combination of parameter values the human designer hasn't thought of, or as an accident due to a bug in the generator code. In any case, it is a nice surprise when it happens. Although an example like this is usually an unintended side effect, it is possible to make a PCG system do this on purpose, for example, by giving a parameter an unusual range or lifting the limit altogether. You will not find most teams do this in production, since novel but positive variations are few and far between, although it is a fun thing to try, and can potentially get you out of a creative rut.

Lower Storage Requirement

In the early days, game developers didn't have much storage to work with. When they wanted to pack more content into a game, they had to get creative. One way to utilize PCG in games is to not ship with or store the contents for the entire span of the game–instead, generate the contents needed as they come up, for example, during loading for the next level, or in the background during gameplay if processing power permits.

Some early examples of games using PCG to expand content but reduce space requirements include the 1980's dungeon crawler Rogue, which generated a new level every time a player descended a set of stairs, and Elite (1984), which used procedural generation to make a vast game world of 8 galaxies and 256 planets for a rich space trading and combat experience.

Rogue influenced many MMOs and roguelike games after it, such as Diablo and War of Warcraft. Elite defined the genre for space exploration games, including the recent No Man's Sky, which, despite having been built by just three programmers and one artist, was able to create a diverse and almost infinite-feel game world from a mix of procedurally generated planets, ships, creatures, etc., and hand-crafted models.

Less demand for storage opens a game up to more platforms, like mobile devices or handhelds. It also allows the game to be downloaded or streamed more easily by the players, which is always nice.

From the Content Consumer's Standpoint

So far we've talked about incentives for using PCG from the developers' perspective. In this section, we'll put ourselves in the players' shoes (or anyone that consumes content) and consider how PCG could make a game more appealing.

Ability to Extend the Game (Almost) Infinitely

For a player, a PCG game that generates content *online* (during loading or gameplay) greatly increases replay value. Imagine an infinite runner or side scroller that keeps going, an RPG that gives a not-before-seen quest each time you pick it up, or an open-world game that seemingly doesn't run out of new areas to explore. In reality, PCG games do *not* truly have infinite variations. However, they could keep things fresh for a long time.

Customization

A PCG system could generate content collaboratively with a player, in the form of avatar creators or level modders. For example, in the Sims games and Spore Creature Creator, the player could assemble a 3D avatar from body parts of their choice which is then automatically animated and deployed in the game. This lets players customize the avatars to their personal liking and makes the game more engaging.

The customization could happen post world generation as well, for example, in Minecraft, the worlds are generated from noise functions, after which the players are able to come in and build their houses and craft items, which is not unlike a level designer refining a procedurally generated level by hand and putting in finishing touches.

The immensely popular Townscaper is a procedural world building game in which the player "grows" land and buildings in an intuitive way by dragging and clicking with their mouse. The game automatically generates aesthetically pleasing pieces of appropriate dimensions based on the context set by the player, for example, a row of houses with variations for visual interest that are sized to fit the portion of land the cursor is currently over. Even though there is no real "gameplay" in Townscaper (no points, enemies, or objectives, etc.), it provides a simple Lego-like experience where you just build and let your mind wander in a zen-like flow, that really connects with a lot of players.

Having the Content Adapt to Your Preference and Style

PCG could generate the same content given the same input for all players, which is called *generic* PCG, or adapt what is generated to the player's interaction with the game, for example, what the player selects in the preferences, what items the player picks up, which areas (or types of areas) the player frequents, and so on. The PCG adaptation could also be based on a player's playing style, for instance, what kinds of weapons the player opts for, against what types of enemies? How does the player move toward the target–does the player go for it in the open, or take cover? The PCG system could tally stats on player behaviors, then adjust the types of contents, or the characteristics of the contents it generates. For example, if the player prefers multibarrel guns over single-barrel ones, the PCG system could generate more of those types of weapons. If the player tends to take cover behind boulders, the PCG system could generate more rocks in new levels.

Instead of adaptation based on playing style, a PCG game could adjust its generation purely based on visual elements, such as display options the player specifies through preferences (e.g., color scheme), or the type of skins or armors the player chooses (those that are purely decorative and don't serve a purpose in the game). Level-wise, the PCG system could generate more of certain types of buildings or terrains if a player explores those areas more.

Lower Storage Requirement

Just as a lower storage requirement benefits developers, a PCG game that does not ship with all the contents up front is nice for players since it takes up less space on disk, though it does tend to have longer loading time (the space-time trade-off). A smaller game size also means a faster download and possibly the ability to be streamed.

Ability to Share Generated Contents with Friends

Many well-known procedurally generated games on the market utilize noise function (e.g., Perlin noise) driven approaches under the hood, such as Minecraft and No Man's Sky. These approaches generate worlds deterministically, such that the same seed value always generates the same environment. A popular thing for Minecrafters to do is share the seed that generated a world they like with a friend, who can then use the same seed to generate the same world on their machine. You will work through practical examples of how to use noise functions to generate terrains in Chapter 6.

Who Uses Procedural Content Generation (and How)?

In this section, we'll take a brief detour and think about the "who" instead of the what and the how in PCG. We'll look beyond game and film developers and brainstorm who uses procedural generation—what fields they are in and what kinds of applications they use it for. Laying out all the possibilities is a good way to remind us of all the ways that PCG is useful. If you are a developer looking to create PCG middleware, an exercise like this also helps you identify any market sectors you may have missed.

Many simulation developers (a.k.a. serious games) make heavy use of 3D environments in their products, such as flight simulators and the America's Army military training game. These developers are motivated to use PCG in very much the same way as game developers. Simulation developers in particular often need to replicate large real-world environments, for which PCG methods that generate terrain or cityscapes based on GIS data are particularly beneficial. A military training game can also take advantage of PCG to produce near infinite combinations of training levels and missions, or adapt difficulty levels or styles of gameplay based on player progress.

As discussed earlier, PCG methods inherently lend themselves well to models that need to be numerically or dimensionally accurate. Researchers could use PCG to generate scientific renderings to use in papers and presentations. Educators could use PCG to prepare models for lectures, such as hard-surface parts for engineering with exact dimensions. Students studying digital art, game development, and computer science may also use procedural generation as a way of exploring certain topics.

3D printing enthusiasts also use PCG to generate meshes. Some (like the author) use PCG to create geometric art pieces based on fractals or tessellations. A friend of the author routinely writes programs in the open source CAD software OpenSCAD to create parametric models for mechanical parts and enclosures used in electronic projects. A popular trend for a while among makers is to generate lithophane models from images by turning them into height maps based on pixel values, then 3D print them using light colored filaments or resin so light can shine through.

Many architects and industrial designers use parametric models for *Form Finding* as part of their design process, as discussed earlier in the chapter. They typically generate many variations of a model surrounding a central design and iterate on them.

What Kinds of Software Are Used for PCG?

Most CAD software have a scripting API which can be used to procedurally generate meshes, materials, and so on, including Blender, Rhino, Maya, 3Ds Max, Houdini, etc. Some CAD software also have node editors (graphical scripting interfaces), such as Blender's Shader Editor and Geometry Nodes (which we'll discuss in Chapters 4 and 5), Houdini Nodes, Rhino's Grasshopper, etc.

For game developers that produce a lot of procedurally generated meshes, Houdini is a popular choice since its workflow centers around PCG. Rhino Grasshopper is popular among architects and industrial designers, for its intuitive use of parametric modeling. Hobbyists opt for the likes of Blender and OpenSCAD for their low cost of entry. Some developers choose to do PCG directly in the game engine of their preference (Unreal, Unity, etc.), while others write something proprietary as part of their pipeline.

Types of Procedurally Generated Contents

In this section, we'll think about PCG systems in terms of the types of content they produce. We'll approach the topic at a high level, based on where they fit in a production workflow and how they are used in game.

Visual vs. Nonvisual

PCG systems could output visual content, which is any data in game that adds to the viewing interest, or nonvisual content, which covers anything you can't see. Examples of visual contents include meshes used for player avatars, weapons, pickups (usable or collectable), level geometry, etc. Visual contents also include textures, materials, particles, and so on. Nonvisual contents may be logical, like maps, navmeshes, missions, quests, game rules, and so on. Nonvisual content also includes sound effects (e.g., footsteps, weapon sounds) or music. In this book, we will only cover the generation of visual content.

Necessary or Auxiliary

Necessary contents are those that are required for a player to advance through a game, for example, a key to the door connected to the next level, an artifact required to solve a puzzle, a weapon needed to beat the end boss, and so on. *Auxiliary contents* are those that are optional but add to the visual richness or enjoyment of the game, such as bonus items you can collect, extra side quests you can partake to earn points or achievements, armors you can use to decorate your avatar but don't provide extra protection, etc.

It naturally follows that necessary game contents produced by procedural generation systems must undergo error checking to ensure their validity, which, at the minimum, means they can be used in game for their intended purposes and allow the player to advance. Ideally, they should be free of visual defects as well, since they are under close scrutiny of the players and any oddness will seem very obvious and detract from the experience. If the PCG system generates contents *online*, i.e., after the game has shipped, during loading or gameplay, its error checking for necessary contents must have some kind of fallback, to ensure that the player can go on—for example, reject the functionally invalid output but allow those with visual defects, or substitute bad output with a canned version of the item shipped with the game, etc.

Requirements for generated auxiliary contents are much more relaxed since they are icing on the cake and not necessary for getting through the game. An occasional error by the PCG system on an auxiliary item may actually be perceived as humorous by the players and sought after as Easter eggs. Less emphasis is put on auxiliary contents also because on average, players do not pay much attention to them, for example, auxiliary contents in the form of extra items placed in relatively hidden areas of a level that the player could collect to get an achievement. Unless you go out of your way to look for them, some players may go through the whole game without ever noticing these items. Although in general it is still best to strive for your PCG system to be as error-free as possible for the overall quality of the game, even for optional content.

Level of Completion

Does the generator produce complete assets that are ready to use? Do the generated contents require human refinement or error correction? These are both good questions to ask yourself in the design phase of a generator as well as during implementation and after deployment.

The completeness of a PCG system's generated contents (or the lack thereof) could be the nature of the system's design, or a measurement of how well the system is doing, sometimes both. A procedural system's purpose may be helping an artist create as opposed to producing final content, for example, a system designed to generate roughly blocked-out meshes that have gone through the beginning stages of modeling ready for the artist to take over and refine, or a tool that automates part of the mesh editing process that is difficult to do by hand. This type of PCG system does *not* produce complete pieces of content *on purpose*. The system is performing well as long as it realizes the level of completeness you planned for.

Another possibility is you manage to implement a PCG system that does most of the work, i.e., generate a piece of content that is mostly there, but it is immensely difficult or impractical to automate that last 10% of the process. If you are able to allocate enough man hours to do the final tweaking by hand, sometimes it can still be a perfectly usable system.

If you must have a PCG system that generates final, ready-to-use content, for example, a system that ships with the game and generates contents online, possibly adapting to the player's behavior or style, care must be taken to ensure the generated content is valid, particularly necessary contents.

Types of PCG Methods (the How)

Now that you're familiar with the motivations behind using PCG and how it's useful in various applications, in this section, we'll categorize PCG methods from an implementation perspective, based on the types of input data, where and how in the generation process it interacts with the designer, as well as the computational techniques that drive them.

Level of User Involvement

The level of user involvement called for in PCG systems varies greatly, ranging from fully automatic (no user input) to fully interactive, where users must provide feedback between runs or select pieces during generation (e.g., an avatar creator). Many PCG systems fall somewhere in between, where users provide values for generation parameters (e.g., size of door, number of appendages, etc.) and/or other forms of input data.

Types of Input Data

We've discussed a few different types of input data to procedural generation systems already when we went over the motivations behind using PCG for developers. We'll summarize them here in one place, along with the chapters in which you'll see examples of throughout the book:

PCG systems could take real-world data as input, such as Geographic Information System (GIS) data like building footprints, Digital Elevation Models (DEM), satellite photos, lidar point clouds, etc. We'll work through examples of this type in Chapters 8 and 9.

Generation systems set up as parametric models need user-supplied values for their parameters, optionally with default values to fall back on. We'll see this in action in Chapters 2 and 3.

Approaches using gradient noise functions will typically use a predefined set of noise that's been tested to work well but take a seed value per generation, which we'll see examples of in Chapter 6.

PCG systems could take premade 2D or 3D mesh tiles as input, then tessellate or assemble the tiles using predefined rules (which themselves could have arguments). Contents generated from tiles could be combined with other types of generation, for example, a L-System tree that consists of premade leaf meshes placed on branches generated from scratch, which we'll see examples of in Chapter 7. Another example is placing premodeled building meshes on 3D terrain generated from GIS data. Instead of taking the tiles as input, the PCG system could also store a pool of tiles to draw from.

A generation system could take mathematical formulas or coefficients for these formulas as input. For example, a seashell can be generated from a conical surface created by a circle traveling up a spiral curve with decreasing radii and distances to the central axis, as the examples shown in Figure 1-3. The generation system could take coefficients for the spiral curve as inputs to vary the generated shells. In Chapter 3, you will learn how to procedurally generate a trigger pull for a handgun model using a partial parabolic curve.

A PCG system may base its generation on user-supplied grammars or generation rules. For example, the system could expect instances of a certain class of grammar to be passed in (e.g., L-System, shape grammar, etc.), then based on the interpretation of these rules generate meshes from it. In Chapter 7, we'll build a turtle-style L-System interpreter and generate 3D meshes from the passed in axiom (starting string) and rewriting rules. For this type of generation systems, the interpretation part of the workflow is typically fixed regardless of the arguments passed in. However, it is possible to inject some pseudo randomness to create more variations. For example, upon reading a rule to create a branch to the right, instead of branching at a fixed angle each time, the interpreter could choose an angle from a range. If the system mixes premade tiles as part of the generation, for instance, placing premade leaf meshes on a generated branch, the interpreter could pick among several different leaves compatible with the rule instead of always using the same one.

A PCG system could take images as input, then based on which generate other contents. For example, the system may use the images passed in as sampling sources for generating procedural textures or materials, or create height maps from the inverse of the images' pixel values for generating lithophanes (where darker pixels are taller), as the example shown in Figure 1-8. In the context of deep learning, the input images may be used for style transfer.

Procedural generation programs could take meshes as input, then based on which generate other meshes, like the sliceform generator example shown in Figure 1-1 and the woven mesh generator in Figure 1-7. Simpler examples of this style of generation, such as a generator that takes a mesh as input then creates a wireframe version of it, can be seen as a form of "postprocessing," though in reality, the input models are usually unaltered, and a new mesh is constructed and output by the generator.

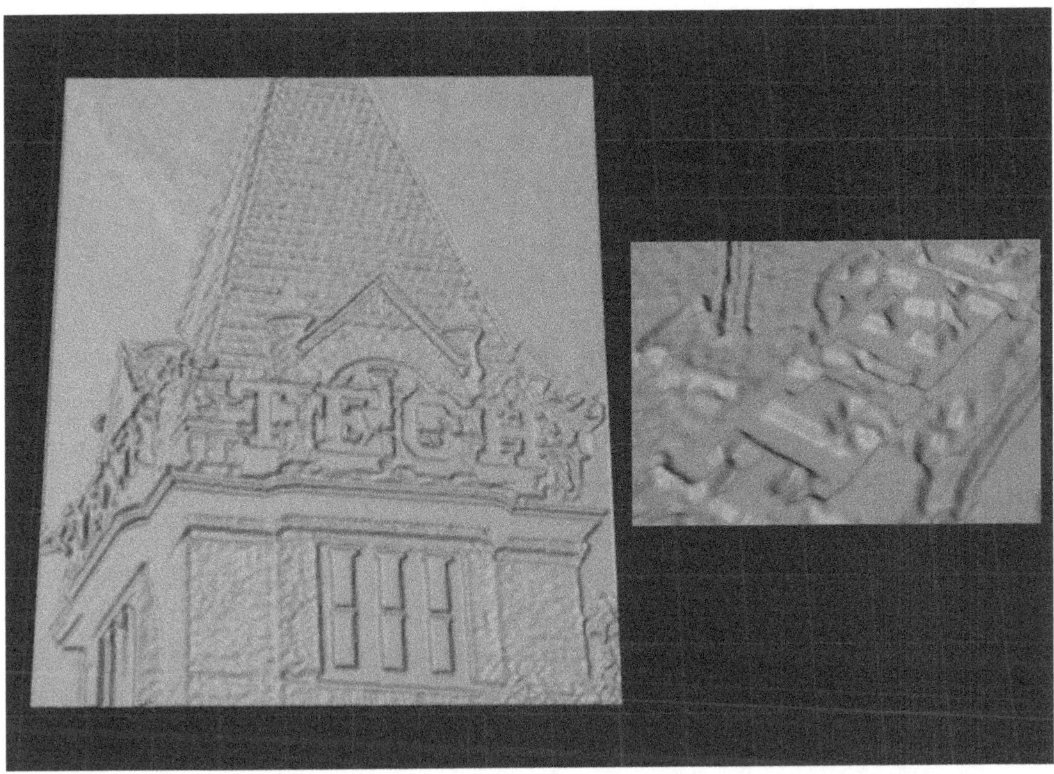

***Figure 1-8.** Example of procedurally generated lithophane mesh by the author. The generator takes an image as input, creates a height map inverse of the pixel values (darker is taller), then generates a mesh based on that. The zoomed-in portion of the mesh on the right shows the mesh height at the "TECH" portion (which is white) lower than its surrounding areas. The image is of the Tech Tower on the Georgia Tech campus, the author's alma mater.*

Online vs. Offline

A PCG system can generate content *online* while the game is loading or gameplay is in session. *Offline* means generating content during development or while the player is *not* interacting with the game.

Generic vs. Adaptive

A *generic* PCG system does *not* change its behavior over time, whereas an *adaptive* PCG system learns and adjusts what it generates based on factors such as the player's playing style, in-game behavior, or preferences.

Deterministic vs. Nondeterministic

A *deterministic* PCG system always produces the same output given the same input. For example, given the same seed, Minecraft always generates the same world, regardless of which player triggered the generation or on whose machine. A *nondeterministic* PCG system may generate something different from run to run even with the same input. Deterministic PCG must be used for generating necessary game content, as the player must always have a consistent and predictable way to advance through the game. While you can theoretically use nondeterministic PCG for generating auxiliary content, it is tricky to do so while ensuring a fair and quality-assured experience for players across the board. Since you can't tell what the PCG system will generate based on its input, a nondeterministic system is also very difficult to debug, if not impossible.

Error Checking (During or After Generation)

A PCG system, like any other software, can have bugs. Those among us that are modelers also know that you can approach a mesh with the best intentions and do everything right, but still have it come out with errors, like flipped normals. Therefore, the output of a procedural generator must always be checked. For a generator operating offline, you have the option to error check automatically using a program or manually by a human. On the other hand, an online generator has no choice but to have automated error checking in place, to ensure that only valid content is deployed into the game.

Error checking can be done during generation and rectified by the generator as they come up, which is known as *constructive* PCG. When error checking is done postgeneration, the bad output is usually either discarded or fixed manually by a human artist. An approach known as generate and test repeats generation and error checking in a loop until a good outcome is produced.

Type of Algorithms

In this section, we'll discuss PCG systems in terms of the type of algorithms or computational techniques driving the generation behind the scenes.

Proprietary Code

Instead of using known algorithms from literature, many PCG systems are written based on a developer's own design, for example, by automating a manual modeling process and turning the mesh into a parametric model such that the dimensions and other properties of one part constrain that of another–for example, making the radius of a gun's grip proportional to the width of its slide. Some of these properties can then be exposed to the user as arguments to the generator, therefore allowing the user to get different variations. A PCG system of this type can be written entirely in code using the CAD software's scripting API (e.g., Blender Python), or created via the CAD software's node editor (e.g., Blender geometry nodes). You will learn to implement your own game weapon generator in Blender Python in Chapters 2 and 3. You'll also find out how to create parametric models with geometry nodes in Chapters 4 and 5.

Node System

A node editor is a graphical scripting interface where one drags and drops premade nodes (which are like code modules) onto a canvas and connect them into a tree to create a program. In the context of a modeling software, a node editor lets you write programs to procedurally generate contents like meshes (e.g., Blender geometry nodes) and materials (Blender shader nodes). Node editors lend themselves well to parametric modeling since nodes (or groups of nodes) can be set up to correspond to parts of a mesh and the relationship between parts created by connections between nodes. You will learn to generate models using Blender geometry nodes in Chapters 4 and 5.

You might wonder, if I have access to a node editor, why would I still want to write code? It is because no matter how great a node editor is, chances are when you try to design a model complex enough, sooner or later you run into the situation where no node will do what you want. In that case, you either have to change your design to avoid having to do that thing, or write a script to do it instead. The advantage of code is that you are not limited to what nodes are available—you can pretty much generate whatever you want, as long as you can find a way to write it.

Don't get me wrong—nodes are great; I use them all the time. They are more intuitive than code to set up and faster to get going for simpler projects. Node editors are more interactive than code, allowing you to change the value of a node and preview the effect in real time, vs. having to rerun a script to generate another model to visualize the change. On the other hand, when you try to do something complicated with nodes, it tends to balloon quickly into a ball of incomprehensible spaghetti. I also find it hard to annotate a complex node tree and keep it organized.

Some node editors allow you to define your own custom nodes, therefore freely mixing nodes and source code in the same tree. For example, Rhino's Grasshopper lets you define your own Python script nodes that can be connected like any other node.

Rule-Based

Rule-based generators take a certain class of grammar strings as input (e.g., L-System, shape grammar) and interpret them, then based on which generate meshes or other content. For example, an L-System generator takes as input an axiom (a starting string) and a set of rewriting rules that tell how to expand the axiom into a string which encodes generation steps for the given number of iterations. In Chapter 7, you'll learn to implement your own L-System generator in Blender Python that, when given the proper axiom and rewriting rules, is capable of generating any type of mesh with a self-similar structure, like the fractal meshes shown in Figure 1-9 and the shrub mesh shown in Figure 1-10.

Search-Based

Search-based PCG uses path finding algorithms such as A* to generate content. It is typically used to generate something with defined start and end points, such as map topology (i.e., road structures, how rooms are connected by hallways, etc.) or mission logic (e.g., "defeat the wizard with magic staff to obtain the key and go to the castle behind the locked gate"). Search-based PCG is beyond the scope of this book, since our focus is on generating meshes and materials in Blender. It is nonetheless an interesting class of PCG methods.

Noise-Based

Noise-based PCG is made famous by popular games like Minecraft and No Man's Sky that are known for their procedural worlds generated using these methods. "Noise" usually refers to the fractal terrain method, with which a noise function like Perlin noise is used to generate gradients (the rates of change) of mountain or valley slopes over a grid that represents the span of the world. The same process is repeated at multiple resolutions, or "frequencies" (which just means the grid is divided from coarse to fine). The gradients from all the frequencies are summed together, based on which a terrain is generated.

This method is called "fractal" terrain because terrains in the real world exhibit self-similarity, meaning that when you zoom in on a terrain at multiple levels, they all have hills and valleys and look similar to one another. Therefore, by dividing the grid at multiple resolutions, generating gradients, and summing them together, you are mimicking this natural self-similarity, which is why terrain generated this way looks more natural than other methods. You will build your own fractal terrain generator in Blender Python in Chapter 6.

Math-Based

By design, PCG systems can generate surfaces and curves from formulas as they are, or use these mathematical constructs as the bases for generating something else, like how artists use primitives to block out models. For example, the seashell meshes in Figure 1-3 are generated by forming circular cross-sections upward along a spiral curve with decreasing radii and distance to the central axis. In Chapter 3, you will also see an example where a partial parabolic curve is used to generate the trigger pull on a handgun mesh.

Deep Learning

Generative Adversarial Networks (GANs), a type of deep learning method, are all the rage these days. GANs are typically trained on massive amounts of images and themselves generate images, though it is possible to train GANs on other types of media as well. A GAN learns by having two deep neural networks compete with one another, with one acting like an art forger and the other an art authenticator. The forger has to get better and better at making fake art to not get caught, while the authenticator has to improve over time at spotting forgery to not be fooled by the forger. Deep learning is usually too resource-hungry to be used by game developers and beyond the scope of this book. However, it is an interesting technique to look out for. As it continues to mature, perhaps one day, we'll see GANs used in some capacity in the game industry.

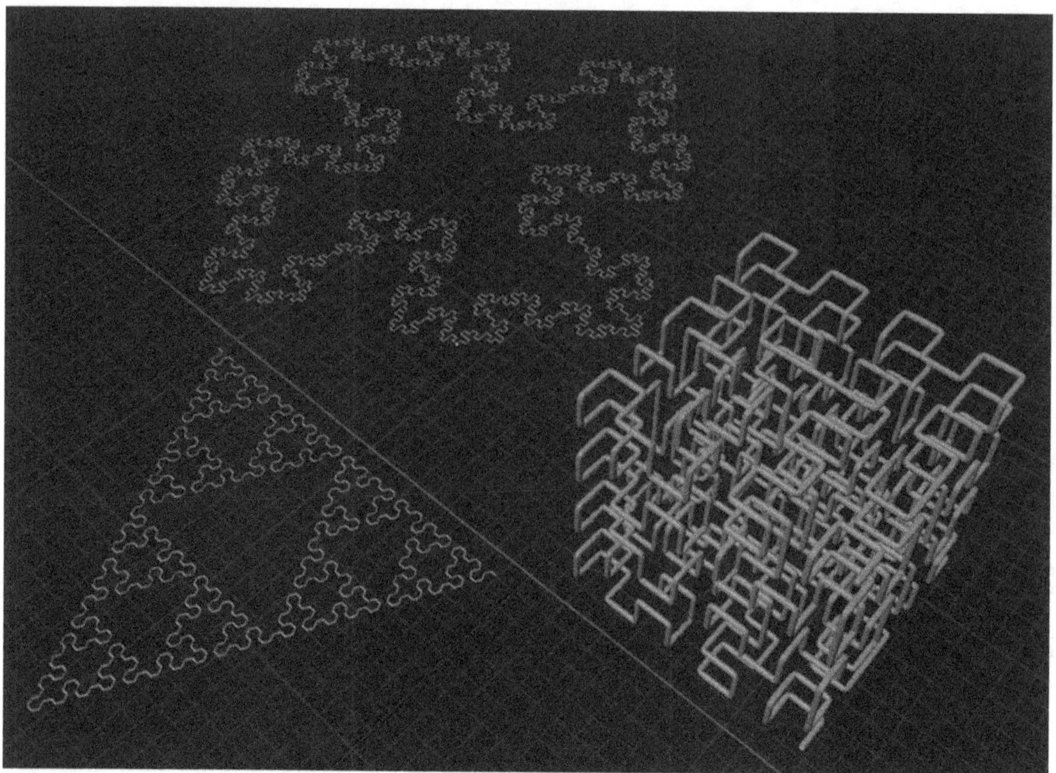

Figure 1-9. *Examples of fractal meshes generated using the L-System implementation from Chapter 7. The generator takes an axiom (a starting string) and a set of rewriting rules, then expands the axiom for the given number of iterations and based on which generates a mesh. Fractals are self-similar objects, which perfectly align with L-System grammar's recursive nature. Clockwise from the top: Quad Koch curve, 3D Hilbert space-filling curve, and Sierpinski gasket.*

Figure 1-10. *Example of shrub mesh generated using the L-System implementation from Chapter 7. The generator takes an axiom (a starting string) and a set of rewriting rules, then expands the axiom for the given number of iterations and generates a mesh from it. Plants naturally have a self-similar structure, which lends itself well to this type of generation.*

Summary

In this chapter, you embarked on a whirlwind tour of Procedural Content Generation (PCG). You learned that PCG means writing programs to automate the process of creating, editing, and assembling digital content, most often in the form of 3D meshes. You then learned about the motivations behind using PCG, both from the content creator's (developer) and content consumer's (player) standpoint.

The developers benefit from the ability to produce more art than they have manpower for, at a potentially higher speed, resulting in a cheaper production. When PCG is used in conjunction with *Parametric Modeling*, the 3D design technique where a mesh is structured as a system of interrelated parts whose properties constrain one another, designers can evaluate many variations at once in a process called *Form Finding*. Other benefits of PCG include the ability to create numerically accurate models for scientific purposes, as well as 3D environments based on GIS data that are faithful to their real-world counterparts ("digital twins"). In addition, PCG can be used to produce models that are impossibly complex to model by hand. Sometimes, PCG even creates novel variations that humans do not think of, from surprising combinations of parameter values or bugs in the generation code. When PCG is used to generate contents online (e.g., during game loading), the game's storage requirements are lowered as it does not need to ship with all the contents up front, benefiting both developers and players.

The players of a procedurally generated game that generates content *online* benefit from (almost) infinite replayability. Games that utilize PCG in the form of avatar or weapon creators provide their players extra levels of customization, while games that adapt the generated contents to the player's in-game behaviors could adjust difficulties in line with the player's playing style. Games that generate their worlds deterministically using noise functions allow players to share the seed values with their friends to get the same environments.

After deliberating the benefits of using PCG, we took a detour and brainstormed who might utilize PCG to produce contents outside the game and film industries, such as simulation developers, researchers, hobbyists, etc., in an attempt to broaden our understanding of all the ways that PCG is useful. We also touched on the type of applications each group uses PCG for.

We then discussed PCG systems in terms of the type of content they produce, which could be *visual* (e.g., meshes) or *nonvisual* (e.g., mission logic, sound effects, etc.). Another way to classify generated content is whether it is *necessary*, i.e., required for players to advance through the game, or *auxiliary*, which is nice to have but optional, like items that are decorative or grant extra points. Necessary content must be valid and ideally free of visual defects, while auxiliary contents are more relaxed. In addition, PCG systems could differ by the level of completion in the contents they produce. By design, a PCG system could output final, production-ready content, or produce partial content meant for human artists to take over and refine.

Last but not least, we discussed the different types of PCG methods available and categorized them in terms of the types of input data they expect (e.g., GIS, mesh tiles, etc.), whether the generated contents are *generic* (i.e., static) or *adaptive*, and the types of computational methods that drive them, such as nodes, search, and grammars, etc.

CHAPTER 2

Blender Python Game Weapon Generator: Part 1

In this chapter and the next, we'll dive right in and implement a game weapon generator with parametric controls. In case you are new to Blender Python, we'll first take a tour of the Scripting workspace, which includes a built-in *Text Editor* for editing and running scripts, a custom *Python Console* streamlined for accessing the Blender Python API, and an *Info Editor* that (with developer configs) logs every operator call whether invoked interactively by the user via hot keys/menus or through Python. We'll then do a high-level overview of `bpy` and `bmesh`, which are Blender Python's built-in modules for mesh editing, and experiment with manipulating the startup cube by calling operators in the console and watching the mesh change in real time in the 3D Viewport.

Once you are familiar with mesh editing basics, we'll kick off our game weapon generator project by first creating a concept design based on reference photos, followed by hand modeling a hard surface prototype to inform which part(s) of the weapon to break out into separate mesh objects. After that, we'll brainstorm which aspects of the prototype to expose via parametric controls to create interesting and meaningful variations. With a plan in place, we'll start to implement the weapon generator in Python step by step.

A Tour of Blender's Scripting Workspace and Blender Python Quick Start

Workspaces are presets of open editor types in Blender, each designed for the purpose of performing a particular task. For example, the built-in UV Editing workspace has a 3D Viewport and UV Editor side by side, which make it easy to iteratively edit a model and see the effects on its UVs. An active or selected object in one workspace is also active

I. Lupiani, *Procedural Content Generation for Games*, https://doi.org/10.1007/979-8-8688-1787-8_2

or selected in others. Therefore, users can easily jump between workspaces (via tabs) as they iterate on different aspects of the same model, such as mesh, UVs, textures, etc. The built-in Scripting workspace, which is accessible via the "Scripting" tab at the top, consists of a 3D Viewport, Python Console, Info Editor, and Text Editor, as shown in Figure 2-1.

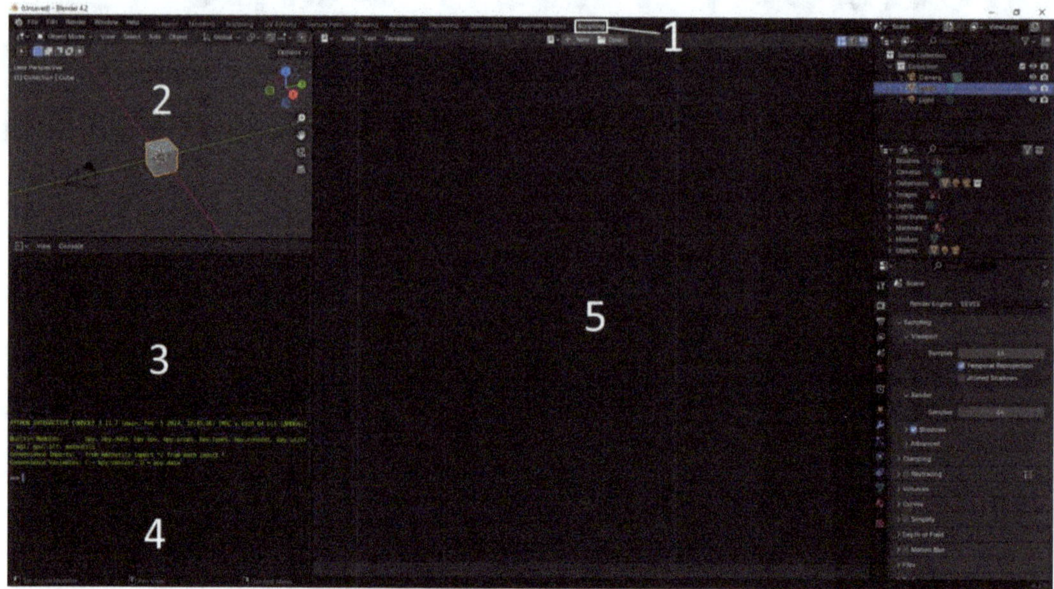

***Figure 2-1.** Blender's built-in Scripting workspace is accessible via the (1) "Scripting" tab at the top and consists of a (2) 3D Viewport, (3) Python Console, (4) Info Editor, and (5) Text Editor.*

Python Console

At the top of the Python Console, you'll see a message similar to the following that tells you which Python version it is running (which in this example is 3.11.11 for Blender 4.4):

```
PYTHON INTERACTIVE CONSOLE 3.11.11 (main, Feb 11 2025, 07:53:58) [MSC
v.1929 64 bit (AMD64)]
Builtin Modules:       bpy, bpy.data, bpy.ops, bpy.props, bpy.types, bpy.
context, bpy.utils, bgl, gpu, blf, mathutils
Convenience Imports:  from mathutils import *; from math import *
Convenience Variables: C = bpy.context, D = bpy.data
```

Note that the Python Console runs the Python version bundled with your Blender installation (under `C:\Program Files\Blender Foundation\Blender 4.4\4.4\python` for a default 4.4 installation on Windows). Paying attention to which Python version your Blender runs is important as it informs you what other built-in Python modules are available and which version of third-party libraries (e.g., `numpy`) will work.

Some of the commonly used Blender Python API modules are automatically imported for you in the console, such as `bpy` (the root module that most everything inherits from), `bpy.data` (data block types), `bpy.ops` (operators), `mathutils` (3D math related types, e.g., `Vector`), and so on, which makes the console very convenient for experimentation, as you can type in or copy a call from the Info Editor and run it directly without worrying about dependencies. If you are writing a script in the Text Editor (or an external IDE), you will have to import these Blender Python API modules yourself, for example, `import bpy`.

To reduce typing, the console provides some *Convenience Variables*, which are aliases of common expressions, like `C = bpy.context` (you can type `C` instead of `bpy.context` wherever it is expected).

Tip It is possible to `pip install` third-party Python libraries to the Python bundled with Blender. I will show you how to do this in the Appendix.

Autocomplete

My favorite feature of the console is *Autocomplete*. If you are unsure what a function or variable is called, you can type in a partial expression at the prompt, then click *Console* ➤ *Autocomplete* to look up a list of options for completing that line of code. In addition to code completion, you can use *Autocomplete* to explore what functions or variables are available under a Blender Python type.

Let's try this in an example. Inside the Python Console, type `import bmesh` at the prompt and hit *enter* to import the `bmesh` module, which is a built-in Blender Python module for mesh editing that we will use extensively for the weapon generator. At the next prompt, type `bmesh.ops.` (be sure to include the dot at the end). Then, without hitting *enter*, click *Console* ➤ *Autocomplete*. You should see the list of available functions under `bmesh.ops.` automatically brought up, like this:

```
>>> import bmesh
>>> bmesh.ops.
              average_vert_facedata(
              beautify_fill(
              bevel(
              bisect_edges(
              bisect_plane(
              bmesh_to_mesh(
              bridge_loops(
< ------------ SNIPPED ------------ >
```

If you type out the full name of a function (or variable) and click *Console* ➤ *Autocomplete*, the console will retrieve that function's (or variable's) entry in the Blender Python documentation, where available. For example, try typing `bmesh.ops.bridge_loops` at the next prompt, then without hitting *enter*, click *Console* ➤ *Autocomplete*. You will see the doc string for the function `bridge_loops()` brought up, like this:

```
>>> bmesh.ops.bridge_loops(
bridge_loops()
BMeshOpFunc bmesh.ops.bridge_loops(bmesh, edges=[], use_pairs=False,
use_cyclic=False, use_merge=False, merge_factor=0.0, twist_offset=0)
-> dict(faces=[], edges=[])
```

Note that for *Console* ➤ *Autocomplete* to search successfully, both a partial term's capitalization and the ordering of words in an expression must be correct. In the above example, if you had typed `bmesh.ops.bridge_Loop` instead of `bmesh.ops.bridge_loops`, *Autocomplete* would fail to return any results.

Converting Console Contents into a Script

The *Console* ➤ *Copy as Script* (***Shift-Ctrl-C***) feature will copy your console session thus far in its entirety, with the lines formatted to Python syntax and the prompt symbols ">>>" removed. The console output lines (e.g., from calling a function or searching with autocomplete) are automatically prepended with "#~" and converted to Python comments. You can paste (***Ctrl-V***) the content copied with Copy as Script anywhere you write a Python script, including the Text Editor under the Scripting workspace.

Info Editor

When you click menus or use hot keys anywhere in Blender, the corresponding Blender Python API calls are logged in the Info Editor, which can then be copied and pasted into the Python Console to experiment with or Text Editor to start a script. Errors stemming from Blender Python API calls are logged in the Info Editor as well. Output of print statements, native Python errors, and full stack traces are not echoed to the Info Editor, but instead to *Window ➤ Toggle System Console.*

Tip The Python System Console can also be summoned via `bpy.ops.wm.console_toggle()` from the Python Console or a script.

Editing the Startup Cube with bpy.ops Operators

A great way to experiment with and discover what functions are available in Blender Python is to hand edit a mesh in the viewport, capture the corresponding Blender Python call in the Info Editor, then copy and paste the call in the console. You can then change the argument value, call the function again from the console, and get real-time feedback in the viewport. We will try this in an example next, where we alternate editing the startup cube mesh by hand and via the Python Console.

With the default startup `.blend` file open and the cube selected in the Layout workspace, tab into Edit mode. Change the Mesh Selection mode to Face, left-click to deselect all, and select the top face of the cube. Hit the E key to extrude (which will default to extrude in Z), then the one key for one unit, and left-click to confirm. The top of the cube should now be extruded one unit upward, as shown in Figure 2-2.

Switch to the Scripting workspace. You should see the following calls logged in the Info Editor as the results of the previous extrusion (I've abridged the arguments to `bpy.ops.mesh.extrude_region_move` for space):

```
bpy.ops.object.editmode_toggle()
bpy.ops.mesh.select_mode(use_extend=False, ↩
    use_expand=False, ↩
    type='FACE')
bpy.ops.mesh.extrude_region_move(, ↩
    MESH_OT_extrude_region={...}, ↩
    TRANSFORM_OT_translate={...})
```

You can easily tell from the names which function call corresponds to which action—the first line toggles between Edit and Object mode, the second line changes Mesh Select to Face, and the third line extrudes. Now, try copying the first call by left-clicking it in the Info Editor to select, right-click ➤ Copy (or Ctrl-C) to copy, then Ctrl-V to paste it into the console. You'll notice that the console calls the function as soon as it's pasted, without you hitting enter. You should see the viewport has changed to Object mode.

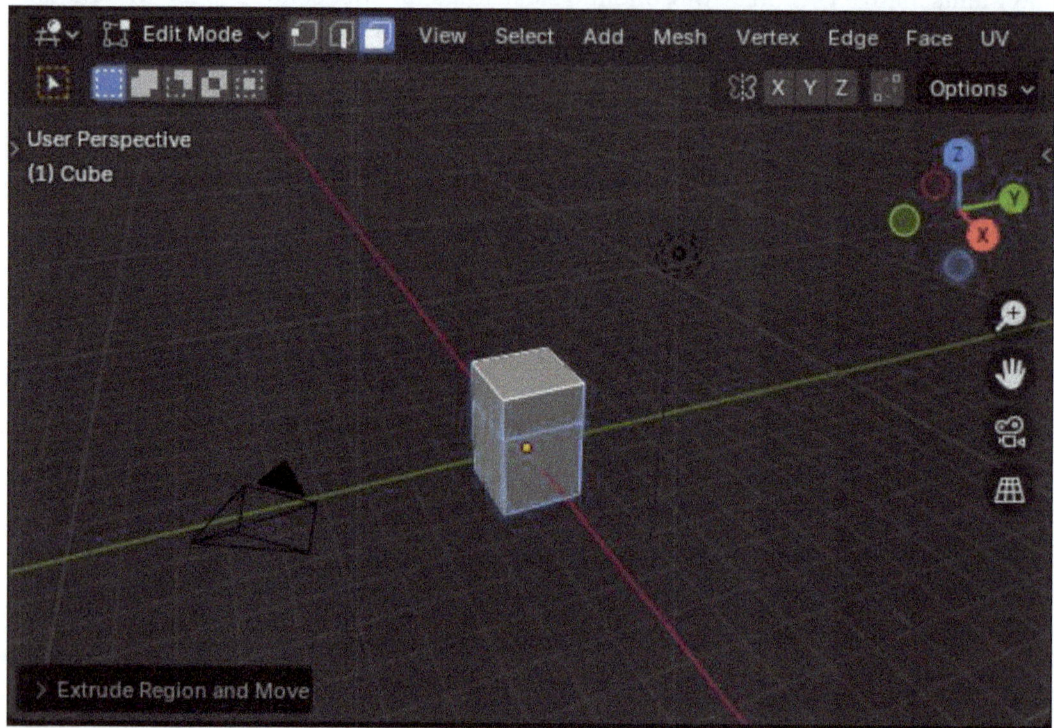

***Figure 2-2.** Results of extruding the top face of the startup cube by one unit along + Z*

Now copy the second call from the Info Editor and paste it in the console. Unlike toggle, calling `bpy.ops.mesh.select_mode` with the same arguments a second time does nothing since it tries to set Mesh Selection to the same mode as before. We'll change the argument and try again. Press the up arrow key in the console to bring up the call again (which is the last line entered at the prompt), then change the type to `'EDGE'` and press enter. You should now see the Mesh Select mode change to Edge.

Extrude is a little trickier. You might've noticed that the call to `bpy.ops.mesh.extrude_region_move` does *not* specify which mesh, or what part of a mesh to extrude. This is because operators under the `bpy.ops` module act upon an existing selection, made either by a user or a Python script, unlike bmesh operators, which typically take the geometry to edit as an argument. We'll be using both bpy.ops.mesh and bmesh operators extensively for mesh editing when we implement the game weapon generator later in this chapter.

Note An *operator* is a tool that does one unit of work. When you click a menu item or use a hot key in Blender, you are usually invoking an operator behind the scenes.

---

bpy.ops.mesh.extrude_region_move takes two (very long) Python dictionaries as arguments, MESH_OT_extrude_region and TRANSFORM_OT_translate. The good news is that both dictionaries have default values for all of their entries, so you can skip most of them when calling this operator and only specify the ones that matter. With the cube in Edit mode with the top face selected, type the following truncated call to bpy.ops.mesh.extrude_region_move where only the extrusion amount is specified into the console and press enter. You should see the top of the cube extruded upward along Z by another unit:

```
bpy.ops.mesh.extrude_region_move( ↩
    TRANSFORM_OT_translate={"value":(0, 0, 1)})
```

Note In the Blender Python API, you will see many parameter values expressed in the form of a three-tuple, which is a sequence of three values enclosed by parentheses. The three values usually correspond to settings for the X, Y, and Z axes, respectively.

Editing the Startup Cube with bmesh Operators

In this section, we'll again practice editing the startup cube from the Python Console, this time using the bmesh module. Starting with the startup .blend file, we'll import bmesh by entering the following line at the prompt:

```
>>> import bmesh
```

Next, we'll look up the cube object by name ("Cube") from the current list of scene objects and store a reference to it in the variable cube:

```
>>> cube = bpy.context.scene.objects["Cube"]
```

To get ready for editing, we'll switch cube to *Edit mode*:

```
>>> bpy.ops.object.mode_set(mode='EDIT')
{'FINISHED'}
```

Then create a bmesh instance bm based on the cube object's mesh data, cube.data, like this:

```
>>> bm = bmesh.from_edit_mesh(cube.data)
```

We can now make edits to cube by calling bmesh.ops operators with bm. We can also access the cube's verts, edges, and faces via bm.verts, bm.edges, and bm.faces, respectively. Note that switching cube to Object mode will invalidate bm; therefore, the cube must stay in Edit mode for the duration we are using bm.

Next, we'll check the number of edges in cube with len(), which is Python's built-in function for measuring the length of a container:

```
>>> len(bm.edges)
12
```

Since Python uses zero-based indexing, the first item in a container has index 0. Therefore, the first edge is bm.edges[0], the second bm.edges[1], ..., and the last bm.edges[11], which has index 1 less than the length of the container. The numerical indices of vertices, edges, and faces in Blender reflect the order in which they are created (elements with smaller indices are created first). Let's get a reference to the edge with index 7 and save it in a variable e, through which we'll edit that edge later:

```
>>> e = bm.edges[7]
>>> e.index
7
```

Unlike bpy.ops operators, which require an existing selection to act upon, bmesh operators allow you to specify which mesh and what portion of the mesh to edit through their arguments. We'll try this next. Type the following line at the prompt, then *without* hitting enter, click *Console* ➤ *Autocomplete* to pull up the list of functions under bmesh.ops:

```
>>> bmesh.ops.
              average_vert_facedata(
              beautify_fill(
              bevel(
< ------------- SNIPPED ------------- >
```

bmesh.ops.bevel looks interesting. Let's look up its doc string to see how we can use it. Type bmesh.ops.bevel at the prompt (without the parentheses), then *without* hitting enter, click *Console* ➤ *Autocomplete* (note that a "(" will appear after bmesh.ops.bevel after the click):

```
>>> bmesh.ops.bevel(
bevel()
BMeshOpFunc bmesh.ops.bevel(bmesh, geom=[], offset=0.0, offset_
type='OFFSET', profile_type='SUPERELLIPSE', segments=0, profile=0.0,
affect='VERTICES', clamp_overlap=False, material=0, loop_slide=False,
mark_seam=False, mark_sharp=False, harden_normals=False, face_strength_
mode='NONE', miter_outer='SHARP', miter_inner='SHARP', spread=0.0, custom_
profile=None, vmesh_method='ADJ')
-> dict(faces=[], edges=[], verts=[])
```

The doc string tells us that **bmesh**, the first argument to bmesh.ops.bevel, is a bmesh instance created from the mesh we intend to edit. **geom** is the list of vertices, edges, or faces to be beveled. You'll likely recognize that **segments** is the number of segments to bevel and **affect** is whether to bevel verts or edges. The last line of the doc string, -> dict(faces=[], edges=[], verts=[]), tells us that bmesh.ops.bevel returns a dictionary containing the bmesh instance's faces, edges, and verts postbeveling. Note that Autocomplete will only work on a library that has been imported—in this example, you must have imported bmesh before using Autocomplete for it to work on anything under bmesh.

We'll now call bmesh.ops.bevel with bm to bevel the edge on the cube with index 7 which we previously retrieved, with offset 0.5 and 3 segments:

```
>>> bmesh.ops.bevel(bm, geom=[e], offset=0.5, segments=3, affect='EDGES')
{'faces': [<BMFace(0x000001EABED30FA0), index=5, totverts=4>,
<BMFace(0x000001EABED30FD8), index=6, totverts=4>,
< ------------ SNIPPED ------------ >
<BMVert(0x000001EABED270D8), index=13>]}
```

But wait—nothing's happened in the viewport. This is because edits made to bm are queued up on bm until you flush them through to cube's mesh data. We'll do so by entering the following line in the console:

```
>>> bmesh.update_edit_mesh(cube.data)
```

Check the viewport again. You should now see edge #7 of the cube beveled, as shown in Figure 2-3.

Tip You can temporarily maximize an editor inside a workspace (such as the 3D Viewport inside the Scripting workspace), via View ➤ Area ➤ Toggle Maximize Area (Ctrl-Spacebar). Just click the "Back to Previous" button at the top when you are ready to go back.

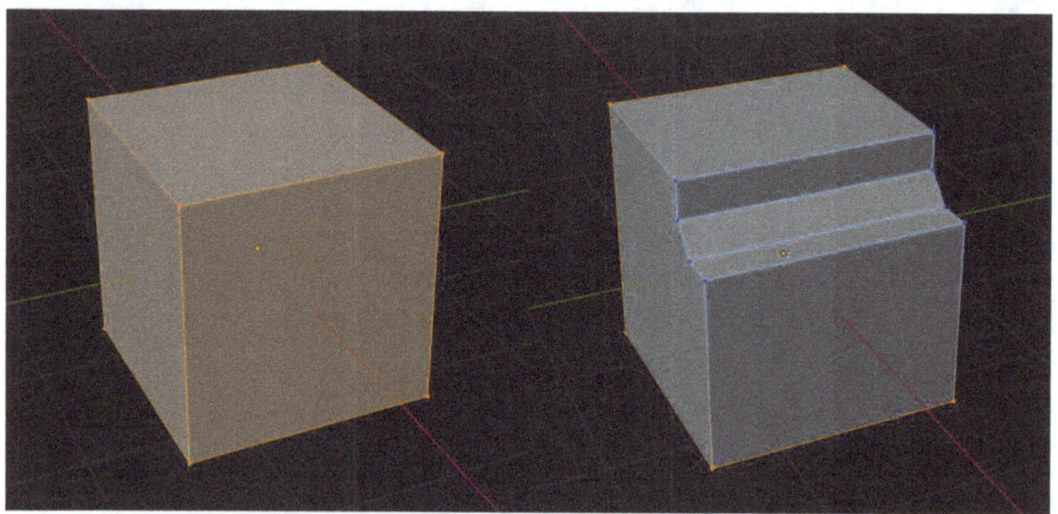

Figure 2-3. *Left: the startup cube mesh before editing. Right: results of beveling edge #7 by calling bmesh.ops.bevel with a bmesh instance created from the cube's mesh data*

An important thing to note is that the beveling has added new geometry to the cube. Every time you add or remove geometry, you must call `ensure_lookup_table()` on the `bmesh` instance to refresh mesh element indices before iterating through them (e.g., `for v in bm.verts`) or indexing them (e.g., `bm.edges[5]`) once again:

```
>>> bm.verts.ensure_lookup_table()
>>> bm.edges.ensure_lookup_table()
>>> bm.faces.ensure_lookup_table()
```

You might be wondering—in reality, there is no way to tell which edge is which by index in Python (not to mention the indices change when geometry is added or deleted), so how could you possibly derive the list of geometry to call `bmesh.ops` operators with? Turns out there are many ways, such as inferring from neighboring geometry, which I will show you as we implement the game weapon generator later in this chapter and the next chapter.

Instead of using an operator, you can also manipulate individual vertex, edge, or face directly, just as you could when editing a mesh by hand. We will try this next. Let's deselect all, then check the cube object's number of vertices:

```
>>> bpy.ops.mesh.select_all(action='DESELECT')
{'FINISHED'}

>>> len(bm.verts)
14
```

As an experiment, we'll randomly pick a vertex to edit. Let's say vertex #11:

```
>>> v = bm.verts[11]
>>> v.index
11
```

We'll select v by setting `v.select` to `True`, so it is easier to see which vertex we're editing. Note that we also have to call `bmesh.update_edit_mesh` to see the selection reflected in the viewport:

```
>>> v.select = True
>>> bmesh.update_edit_mesh(cube.data)
```

We've discussed that the absolute index of a mesh element isn't crucial, since it's arbitrary and becomes outdated constantly. Nonetheless, there is a developer's option you can enable to display a selected vert, edge, or face's index. First, go to *Edit* ➤ *Preferences...* ➤ *Interface* ➤ *Display*, and check the *Developer Extras* box. Then in Edit mode, expand the Mesh Edit Mode Overlays menu, and check the Developer ➤ *Indices* checkbox, as shown in Figure 2-4. Once this option is enabled, you'll see the number "11" show up in the viewport beside the vertex we've just selected.

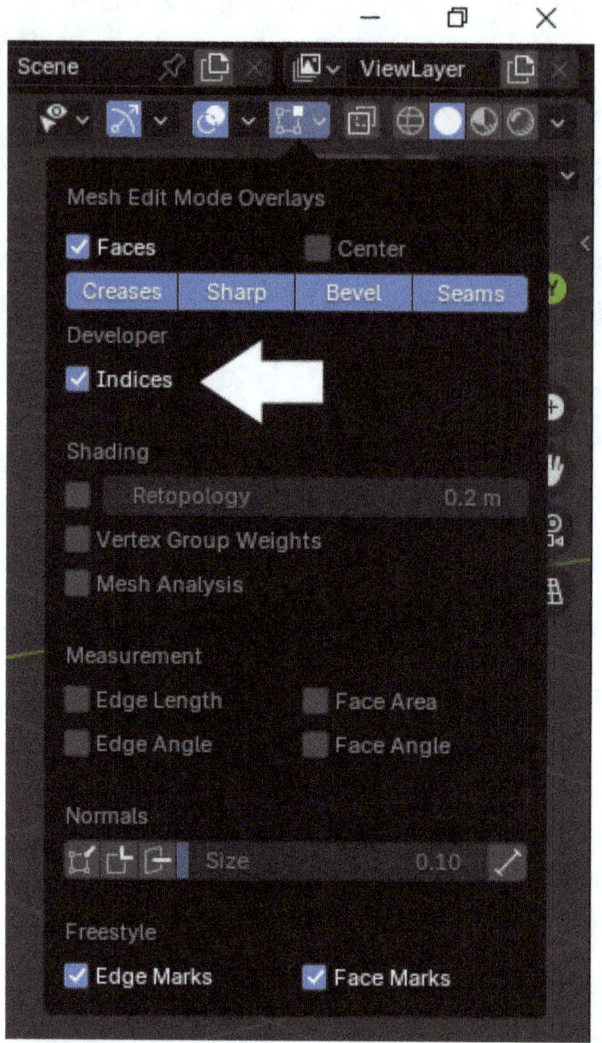

Figure 2-4. *After checking the Edit ➤ Preferences... ➤ Interface ➤ Display ➤ Developer Extras box, the "Indices" checkbox will appear under the Mesh Edit Mode Overlays menu in Edit mode in the viewport. Checking the "Indices" box will enable the display of selected mesh element indices in the viewport.*

You can check `v`'s current position via `v.co`, which is a `mathutils.Vector` instance, with its three values denoting the X, Y, Z coordinates, respectively. Note that a vertex's position is *relative* to the mesh object's origin—which, in this case, happens to be the global origin, at (0, 0, 0). Therefore, `v.co` is the same as its corresponding global coordinates. However, if the cube object had been moved to (x, y, z), `v.co` would still be `Vector((0.5, -1.0, 1.0))`, but would now correspond to the global coordinates (x+0.5, y-1.0, z+1.0).

```
>>> v.co
Vector((0.5, -1.0, 1.0))
```

You can move v simply by doing arithmetic on `v.co`. For example, you can move v one unit along +Y, by adding 1 to `v.co[1]`, which will look like Figure 2-5:

```
>>> v.co[1] += 1
>>> bmesh.update_edit_mesh(cube.data)
```

Which has the same effect as `v.co += Vector((0, 1, 0))`.

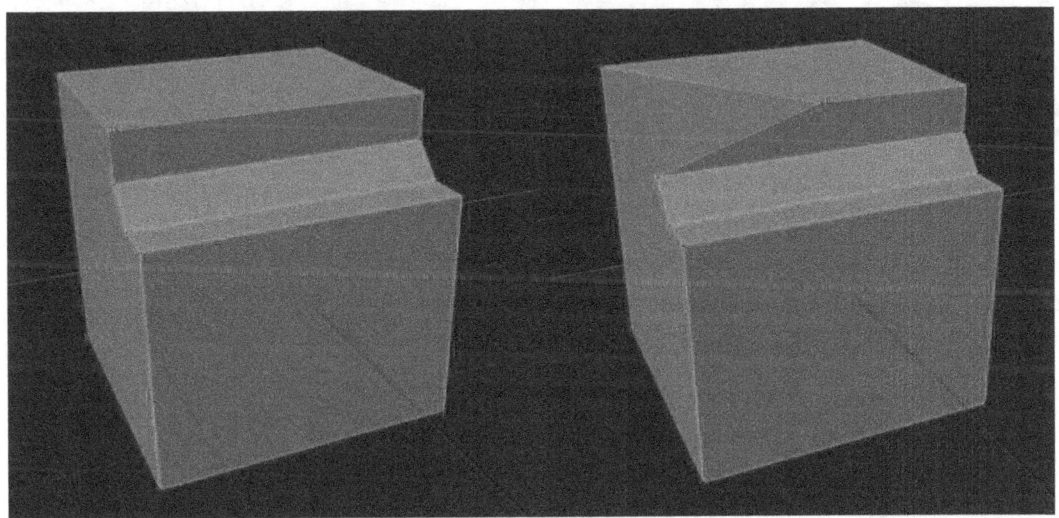

***Figure 2-5.** Before (left) and after (right) moving vertex #11 one unit along +Y*

Text Editor

The Text Editor under the Scripting workspace is a basic Python IDE that lets you edit and run scripts directly in Blender. With the Text Editor, you can iterate on a procedural generator quickly as you can modify a script, run it, and see what impact the change has on the mesh, and repeat, without having to reload the scripts or switch back and forth between Blender and an external editor. In this section, we'll download and run the game weapon generator script in the Text Editor to get comfortable with its interface and to get a taste of the variety of guns the generator can produce.

Before we start, let's take a look at the Text Editor interface, which differs depending on whether a script's been loaded. Before a script is open, the interface has three buttons at the top, which are for selecting a script data block as active, creating a new data block ("+New"), and opening a file on disk ("Open"), respectively, as shown in Figure 2-6. Note that script data blocks are not packed into the `*.blend` file before Blender 4.3, so you must save them separately as *.py files.

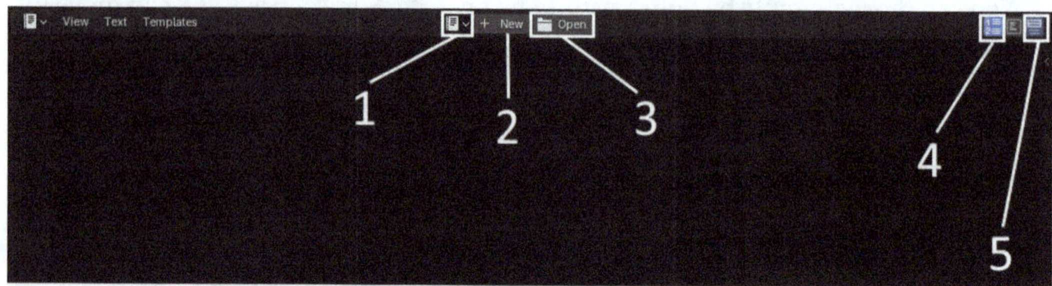

***Figure 2-6.** Text Editor interface before a file is loaded. (1) Button to expand the list of script data blocks, which may have been loaded from disk, or created but not yet saved. (2) Button to create a new script data block. (3) Button to open a *.py file on disk. (4) Toggle display of line numbers. (5) Toggle syntax highlighting*

Let's load the game weapon generator script and take a look. **The source code and color figures for this book are available on GitHub via the book's product page, located at `https://link.springer.com/book/9798868817861`.** In the Text Editor, click "Open," and select `/Ch2/gun_generator.py` from the downloaded source. You'll see the Text Editor's interface change to the one shown in Figure 2-7, where the "+New" button is replaced by the active script's name and a "Run Script" button appears as well as a Word Wrap button.

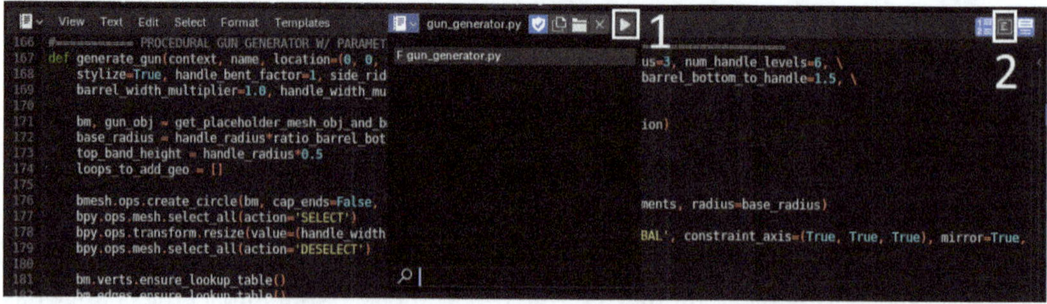

***Figure 2-7.** After opening gun_generator.py in the Text Editor, a (1) Run Script button appears, along with a (2) Word Wrap button. The "+New" button is replaced by the name of the active block, which also appears in the list of all blocks in memory.*

A `__main__` block has been set up at the bottom of `gun_generator.py`, which automatically calls the function `test_gen_gun_row` when you click the "Run Script" button. Go ahead and try it! You'll see nine gun mesh variations generated in the viewport, as shown in Figure 2-8.

```
if __name__ == "__main__":
    test_gen_gun_row(bpy.context)
```

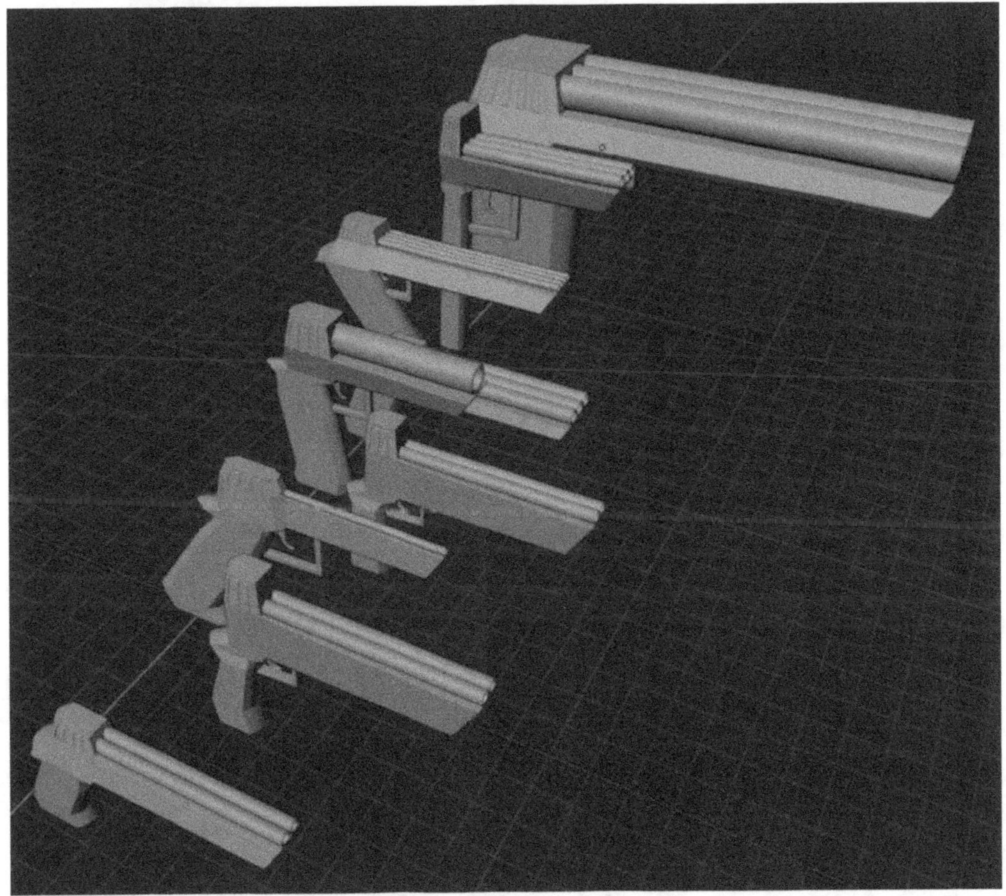

***Figure 2-8.** A selection of gun variations generated by calling test_gen_gun_row(bpy.context) in /Ch2/gun_generator.py*

You can try calling `test_gen_gun_grid(bpy.context)` in the `__main__` block instead, which generates the same nine gun variations, but with the meshes arranged into a grid on the XZ plane, as shown in Figure 2-9. It is easy to see the differences between the variations in this view, which include handle length, handle tilt direction, handle width, the number of barrels, and so on.

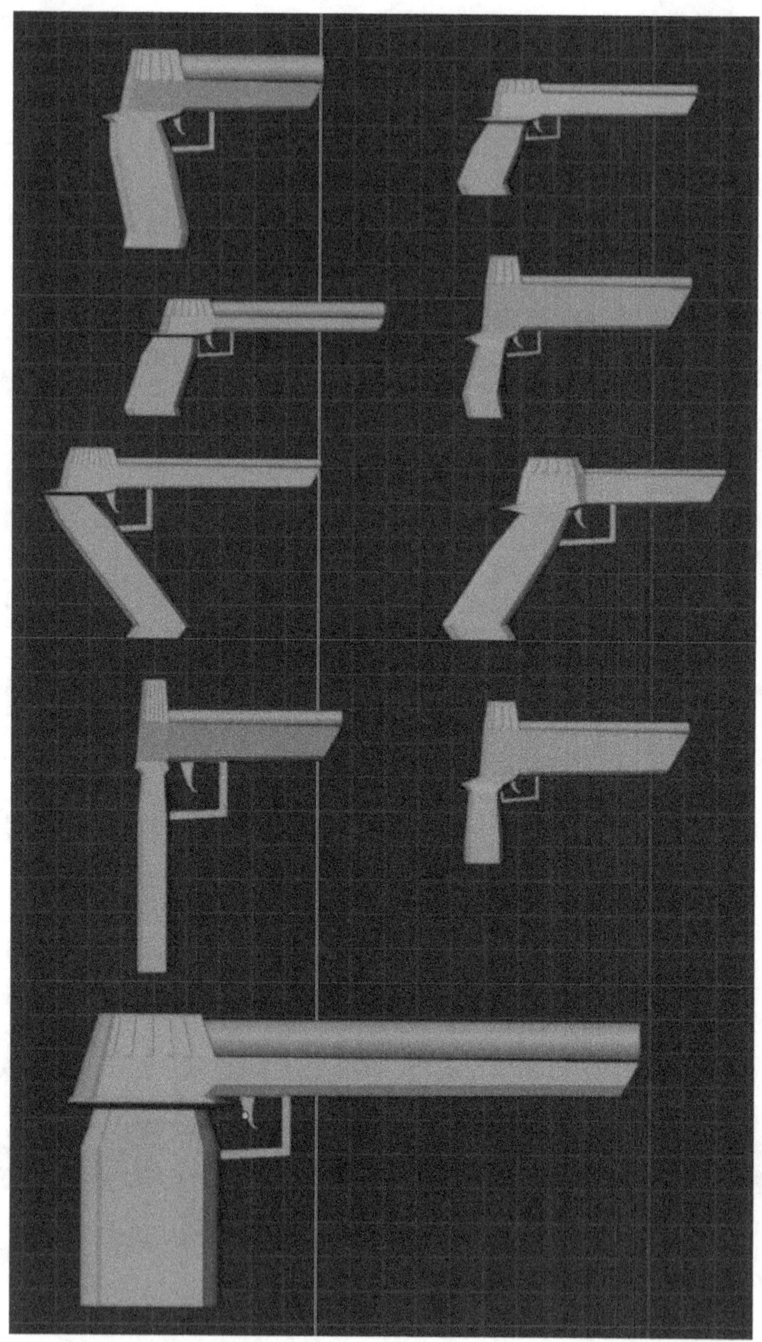

***Figure 2-9.** A selection of gun variations generated by calling test_gen_gun_grid(bpy.context) in /Ch2/gun_generator.py, which are arranged into a grid for side-by-side comparison*

Creating a Procedural Game Weapon Generator

Now that you've familiarized yourself with the Scripting workspace and tried your hand at editing meshes via the Python Console, in the second half of the chapter, we'll begin to design and implement a procedural game weapon generator, inspired by Lara Croft-esque handguns from the Tomb Raider game series.

We'll start by analyzing a few reference photos and deciding which features to incorporate and which to abstract away. Once we arrive at a preliminary design, we'll hand model a prototype to investigate how to logically break down the model into parts and derive the possible steps for generating each part. The prototype will also help us understand the dependencies between the gun's components and how their properties constrain one another. With a plan sketched out, we'll discuss what aspects of the gun to expose to parametric controls along with the range of values that will create the most meaningful and aesthetically pleasing variations.

Analyzing References and Creating a Preliminary Design

The most iconic of Lara Croft-esque handguns are the Desert Eagle and Colt Mark pistols, several variations of which are shown in Figure 2-10. To compare the two brands systematically, let's write down a list of their similarities and differences:

Similarities:

1. Both have a single barrel.
2. Both have a grip that tilts back to front.
3. Both have a textured covering over the sides of the grip (grip panels).
4. Both have ribbed areas behind the barrel and above the grip.
5. Both have a thumb safety behind and above the grip (which looks like a lip).
6. Both have a slant below the muzzle, with the top protruding more.

Differences:

1. Some Desert Eagles have interchangeable barrels of different lengths that you can swap out.
2. Some Desert Eagles have an additional detail where a short segment at the bottom of the grip tilts the opposite way.

A rule of thumb is to try and incorporate as many features common between the different reference photos as possible, since those will make your design the most recognizable as the subject you're modeling after. The features included in the weapon generator in this chapter and the next are underlined above. The textured covering on the grip is foregone since it does not contribute to the gun's silhouette in a significant way. The ribbed sidings behind the barrel are kept since they are seen in all the reference photos. Even though the detail at the bottom of the grip (where a segment tilts the opposite way) is only seen on Desert Eagles, I liked the look so I kept it in the design. To reduce the complexity of the model, I omitted some of the smaller parts such as the front/rear sights and the hammer, which likely won't be noticeable from a distance. To produce more interesting variations, I decided to let users specify the number of barrels. In the case of multiple barrels, all the barrels will have equal size and length and be laid out horizontally across the frame.

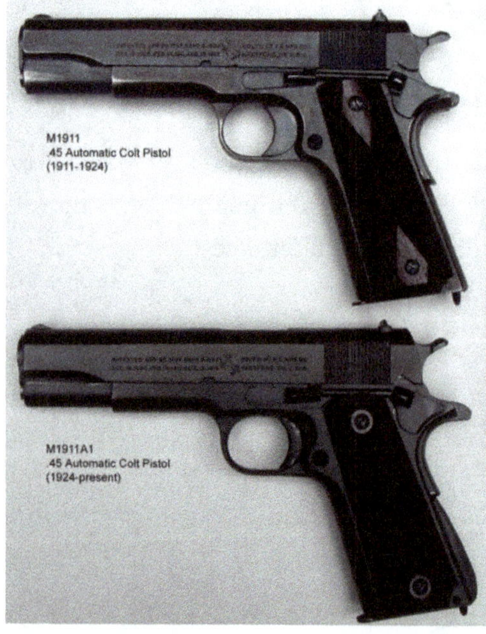

Figure 2-10. *Reference photos for handgun mesh generation. Left: government-issue M1911 and M1911A1 pistols, by Dkamm at English Wikipedia, Public domain, via Wikimedia Commons. Right: an IWI Desert Eagle with an aftermarket magazine surrounded by Magnum Research 50AE JHP bullets, By Bobbfwed–own work, CC BY-SA 3.0, `https://commons.wikimedia.org/w/index.php?curid=14937606`*

Overview of Parametric Modeling

Parametric Modeling is a 3D design technique with which a mesh is structured as a hierarchy of interrelated parts, such that properties of some parts affect or constrain the properties of others. For example, the barrel on a pistol is set up to be the same length as the slide over it, so when you scale one, the other scales with it. You will typically expose some of a parametric model's properties for user editing (*Parametric Controls*). For example, let users drag a slider to adjust the barrel radius or length. To ensure the generated models are valid, functional, and aesthetically pleasing, you will usually restrict the range of values the exposed properties are allowed to take on. For example, you might decide the length of the barrel needs to be between four and eight inches, so the size of the generated gun meshes works with the characters in your game and makes sense as handguns.

In a traditional workflow where the final mesh is handcrafted, after the preliminary sketch, you'll likely create concept arts and iterate on them, so you have a clear vision of the design by the time you start the modeling process. For a parametric procedural generator, however, since the appearance of the models is partially controlled by the user at generation time (imagine dragging a slider to make the gun handle tilt more or less), you can be much less "final" on the design at this stage, since the modeling becomes a "Form Finding" process where you explore the range of generated models and sometimes discover variations you like that you have not anticipated.

Converting Hand Modeling Steps into Generation Steps

In this section, we'll discuss general strategies for converting hand modeling steps into procedural generation steps at a high level, so you know what to look for and think about when you manually model the prototypes.

Extruding Cross-Sections into a 3D Silhouette

You can create a wide range of 3D silhouettes in Python by continuously extruding edge loops while shaping them, just as you would modeling a mesh by hand. As an added bonus, since edge loops cannot form in the presence of poles, this approach also creates clean topology with mostly quads that is easy to unwrap and animate later.

Choosing a Direction to Grow a Mesh

When hand modeling, many artists opt for "tracing over" a front and a side reference photo by creating a 2D vert and edge outline to frame the subject, then cross reference the two views to create depth. This is *not* usually how you would procedurally generate the same mesh, however, since the 2D outline of the model is far more complex this way than extruding from a narrower end of the model (which could be bottom to top, or tail to head, etc.).

For example, imagine trying to generate a handgun in Python by creating an outline of the gun's side view, then extrude and shape the outline somehow to create depth, which would be impossibly complicated, vs. starting at the bottom of the grip (which has a roughly flattened oval shape) and extruding upward, scaling and tilting the cross-section along the way to create the desired contour, then growing the barrel lengthwise sideways—the latter approach has far simpler edge loops overall.

In general, when deciding which way to generate a mesh, look for the direction with the simplest cross-section and a straightforward central axis, e.g., one that can be described by summing a series of vectors, or computed from a mathematical curve. With this strategy, you can grow the mesh from one end by extruding edge loops (cross-sections) along this axis. Whenever you get multiple such axes crossing one another in the model, those become natural partitions where you'd break into separate meshes. For example, for our handgun, the grip would be one mesh (since it grows roughly along Z from bottom to top), the barrel and slide would be a second mesh (since it grows laterally, say along X), and the trigger/trigger guard would be a third mesh (since it conforms to neither the first nor the second mesh's axis). The frame (the part below the barrel) can be integrated into the grip mesh, since it is at a right angle to the grip and can be relatively easily redirected.

Using Primitives to Create the Starting Cross-Section

To create the initial cross-section edge loop for a hard surface model, oftentimes you could start with a primitive (i.e., circle, grid, etc.) and strategically scale portions of it along various directions to create the shape you want. For example, to create the bottom cross-section of the handgun grip, as shown in Figure 2-11, we start with a circle with the desired number of segments and scale it along one axis to stretch it into an oval, then squaring it off by scaling its sides to 0, and finally scaling the front and back to create detail.

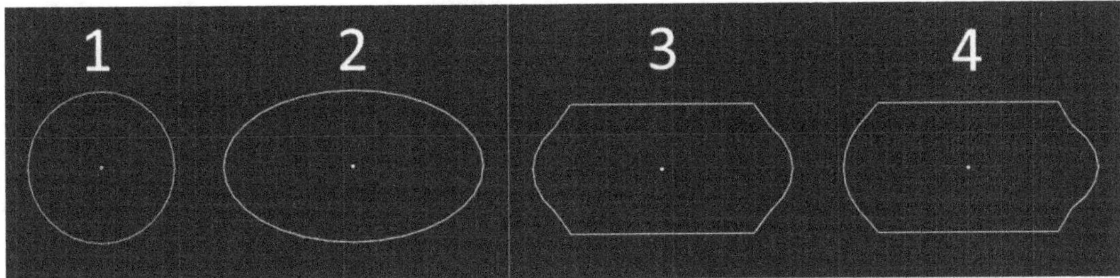

Figure 2-11. *Generating the bottom cross-section of the handgun grip for the weapon generator. (1) Generate a circle with the desired number of segments, (2) scale the circle to create an oval, (3) flatten out the sides of the oval (by scaling to 0 along Y), and (4) scale the front and back of the grip to create detail.*

Inferring Data from Neighboring Geometry

One of the biggest differences between hand modeling and procedural generation is that since you can't be there to look at the mesh to select what to edit next, the script must have a logical way to infer data from neighboring geometry. The inference must be invariant, meaning whatever values the generation parameters might take on, the script must be able to draw the same conclusion from the context (e.g., no matter the size and shape of the grip, the script is able to calculate the position for the trigger based on an offset from where the grip meets the frame). Much of this may sound abstract unless you've already had some experience generating meshes—don't worry, you will work through many examples in Python as we implement the game weapon generator later in this chapter and continuing into the next.

Without getting into mathematical detail yet, here are some high-level examples of how you could infer data from neighboring geometry:

- Using dot product to tell if two face normals point in roughly the same (or opposite) direction. You might use this to
    - Tell which side to attach an appendage or continue to grow a mesh.
    - Check if a group of faces are parallel or facing the same way, e.g., which faces are on the sides of the gun behind the barrel to create the ribbed detail (you may need additional checks to tell multiple groups of parallel faces apart).

- Using dot product to calculate the angle between two edges or two faces. You might use this to
    - Tell where to bevel and by how much.
    - Find which edges to mark sharp.
    - Identify where to cut extra edge loops to preserve hard edges under the influence of a subsurf modifier.
    - Determine how to rotate an edge or a face to align with another edge/face or rotate it to face in a certain direction.
- Finding the midpoint of an edge by averaging the coordinates of the edge's two end verts, to tell where to do a loop cut.
    - Instead of the midpoint, you might interpolate between the two end verts of an edge to calculate how to evenly space multiple loop cuts.
- Interpolating between "landmarks" or offsetting from a landmark on a mesh to tell where to generate a part or add detail. For example, offsetting from the muzzle backward to tell where to add a sight.
- Using edges' lengths to tell them apart. You'll see an example of this in the game weapon generator where I use edges' lengths along with their end vertices' Zs to tell which edges are at the bottom of the frame to create beveled detail.
- Using the areas of faces to differentiate between them. There is an example of this in the game weapon generator where I use the faces' areas to pick out the two faces on the front and back of the trigger finger pull.
- Using edge/face connectivity combined with edge directions to trace edge/face loops. For example, an edge along an edge loop would have end vertices with two outgoing edges that are *not* parallel.
    - In some cases, you might look for the opposite—edges along an edge *ring*, which have end verts with parallel outgoing edges. To make a loop cut or loop cut and slide, you'll need an edge from the edge ring where the cut should be made to call the appropriate operators.

As you've seen in previous sections where we experimented with `bmesh` operators in the Python Console, adding or removing geometry often invalidates references to verts, edges, and faces set up previously in the script. Therefore, inferences to neighboring geometry are best made (and used) immediately after their creation.

Generating Shapes with Math

Not everyone likes math; however, it is a necessary evil when it comes to procedural content generation. The good news is in many cases; you need not fully comprehend the theory to use the formulas—just enough to tinker with parameters to get what you want. It does help though to understand the math, especially if you want to move beyond modifying someone else's code and come up with your own.

As shown in Figure 2-12, the trigger pull that you'll see in Chapter 3 is generated by creating an edge chain in the shape of a partial parabola, then duplicating and rotating the chain to form a face with the original, and extruding the face for thickness. The equation for the parabola is the same regardless of other generation parameters:

$$z = 0.35 * x^2 - 2$$

while the range of x values is adjusted based on the grip height.

Iterating on Hand Modeled Prototypes

Now that you're familiar with strategies for converting hand modeling steps to procedural generation, while working on mesh prototypes for a generator, think about how you create cross-sections and how they can be edited from primitives. Take note of which edge loops are scaled and by how much along the way. Decide how to logically break up the model into multiple meshes, if doing so makes generation easier (e.g., if there are abrupt changes in topology, like intersecting flows of edge loops). Think about the best direction for generating each mesh for the simplest cross-sections and axes.

You'll likely iterate on the mesh prototype a few times to work out kinks and try out different ideas. Figure 2-13 shows one of my prototypes for the game weapon generator. I decided to break up the model into three meshes:

- The grip (which includes the frame, back of the slide, and the safety)
- The barrel(s)
- The trigger

The grip will be extruded bottom-up, starting with an edge loop modified from a circle, as described in Figure 2-11. Once the grip height is reached, the edge loop atop the grip is scaled and the back of which is extruded upward to create the safety, followed by the back of the slide with ribbed detail. The front side of the loop atop the grip will be extruded sideways into the frame, which is the part the barrels sit on.

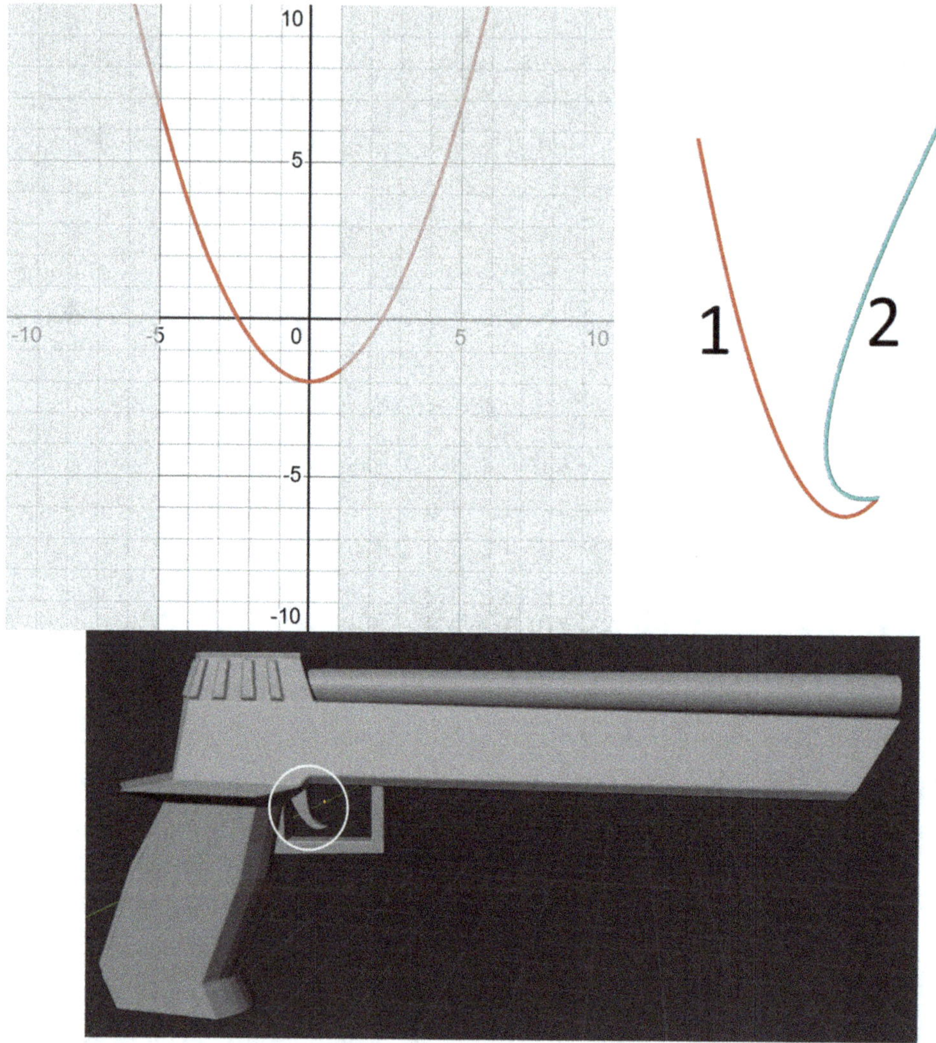

Figure 2-12. *Upper left: creating a partial parabolic curve by limiting the range of its X value. Upper right: duplicating and rotating the curve (2), then forming a face between the original (1) and the duplicate (2). Lower: extruding the face from the previous step into a trigger pull. Graph in the upper left is created using the Desmos Quadratic Equation/Parabola Grapher at* `https://www.desmos.com/calculator/ox38qwb5ek`.

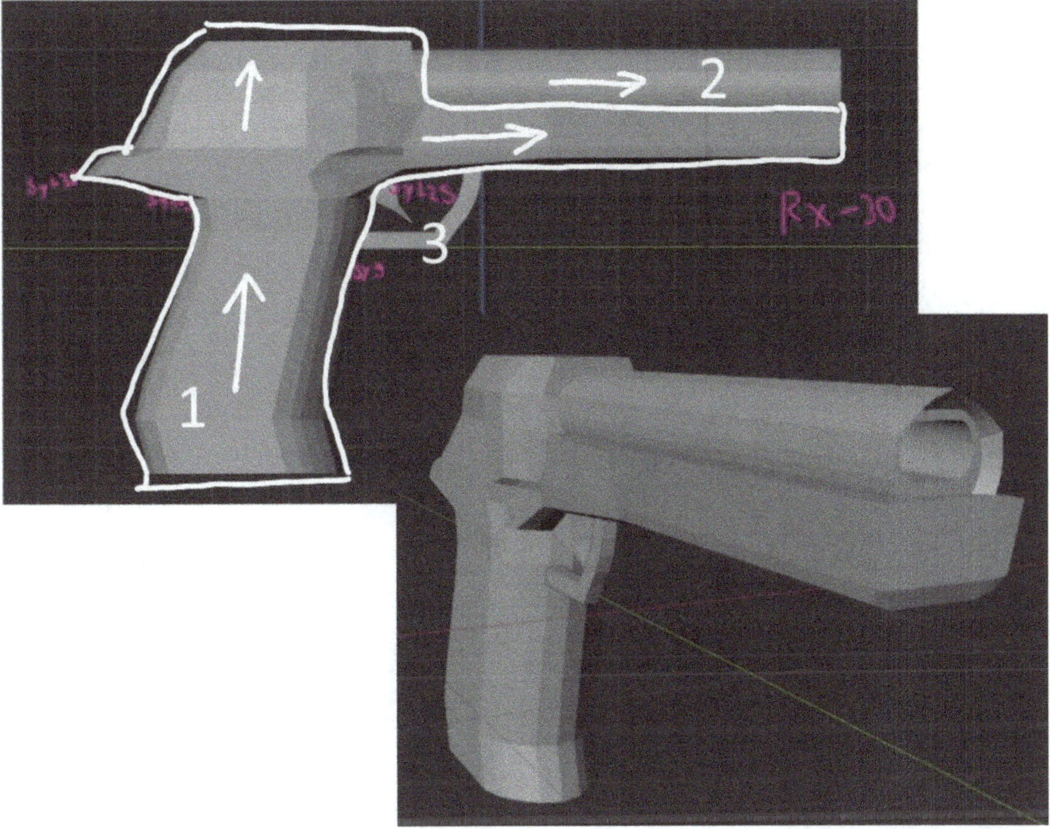

Figure 2-13. *One iteration of the hand-modeled pistol prototype. The model is broken into three mesh objects (marked 1, 2, and 3), with their respective extrusion directions shown. The ribbed detail at the back of the slide is not modeled in this iteration.*

Implementing the Gun Generator in Python

In this section, we'll start implementing the gun generator in Blender Python. First, we'll write a utility function called `get_placeholder_mesh_obj_and_bm`, as shown in Listing 2-1, which creates a placeholder mesh object with empty mesh data and initializes a `bmesh` instance for editing it. We'll be calling this function to create the three mesh objects making up the gun model as described in Figure 2-13. You can find `get_placeholder_mesh_obj_and_bm` in the file `/Ch2/mesh_editing_utils.py`.

Listing 2-1. Util function for creating a placeholder mesh object with empty mesh data, plus a bmesh instance for editing it (see /Ch2/mesh_editing_utils.py)

```
def get_placeholder_mesh_obj_and_bm(context, name, location):
    mesh_placeholder = bpy.data.meshes.new(name=name)
    obj_placeholder = bpy.data.objects.new(name=name, ↩
        object_data=mesh_placeholder)
    obj_placeholder.location = location
    context.collection.objects.link(obj_placeholder)
    for o in context.scene.objects:
        o.select_set(False)
    context.view_layer.objects.active = obj_placeholder
    bpy.ops.object.mode_set(mode='EDIT')
    bm = bmesh.from_edit_mesh(mesh_placeholder)
    return bm, obj_placeholder
```

get_placeholder_mesh_obj_and_bm takes three arguments—the current context, name for the mesh object and data to be created, and the object's location (we'll discuss what "context" means shortly). The function starts by creating a new mesh data block mesh_placeholder, then a new mesh object obj_placeholder with mesh_placeholder as its mesh data and the passed-in location (e.g., (1, 2, 3)) as its location. Next, the function links obj_placeholder to the scene collection, deselects all (by iterating through all objects in the scene and calling select_set(False) on each object), sets obj_placeholder as active, and switches it to Edit mode. Finally, a bmesh instance bm is created from obj_placeholder's mesh data by calling bmesh.from_edit_mesh so obj_placeholder can be edited through bm.

Context and Context Override

Many Blender operators, such as those under bpy.ops, perform tasks based on the current ***context***, which is an object keeping track of where and how the user is interacting with Blender. A context contains info such as the current active screen area, what the user has selected, the active object, etc.

If such operator is called from the console or a Python script, there are two possibilities: The first being the script is purposed as an interactive tool which expects users to make a selection for it to act upon (e.g., a beveling tool that expects users to select which edges to bevel). The second possibility is the script will automate some task without human input, in which case, it will need to create a "fake" context object for the operator to act upon, for example, pretending that an UV unwrap operator is called from the UV Editor. "Faking" the context in which an operator runs in Python is called ***context override***, which we'll see many examples of throughout the book.

"Having the right context" could mean many different things depending on the nature of the operator. Some examples include having the appropriate type of object selected in a certain area (e.g., a mesh object selected in the viewport), having the active object in a particular mode (e.g., Edit mode), or having a certain editor type as the focused screen area (e.g., an UV Editor).

Handling Imports for Scripts to Run in the Text Editor

The code for Chapters 2 and 3 is organized into two files: the first file `/Ch2/mesh_editing_utils.py` contains utility functions that we'll reuse throughout the book. The second file `/Ch2/gun_generator.py` contains code specific to the weapon generator. In this section, we'll look at how `gun_generator.py` imports functions from `mesh_editing_utils.py`. When running in the Text Editor, by default, Blender does *not* look for imports in the directory where your active `*.py` file is. You have to add the directory to the list of paths Blender will scan, as shown in Listing 2-2.

Listing 2-2. Importing functions from other *.py files in the same folder to run in the Text Editor (see /Ch2/gun_generator.py)

```
import os, sys
script_dir = ""
if bpy.context.space_data and bpy.context.space_data.text:
    script_filepath = bpy.context.space_data.text.filepath
    if script_filepath:
        script_dir = os.path.dirname(script_filepath)
        if not script_dir in sys.path:
            sys.path.append(script_dir)

from mesh_editing_utils import ↩
    get_placeholder_mesh_obj_and_bm, ↩
    select_edge_loops, extrude_edge_loop_copy_move
```

Since you're running the script in the Text Editor, `bpy.context.space_data` is the Text Editor, `bpy.context.space_data.text` is the active text data block, and `bpy.context.space_data.text.filepath` is the active block's path—note that if the block is newly created and not yet saved to disk, this path will be invalid (a zero-length string), hence the null check. If the path is valid, we proceed to extract the directory from it with `os.path.dirname` and append it to `sys.path`, which is the list of folders Blender Python will look for imports.

With the active block's directory appended to `sys.path`, you can import functions from any `*.py` file in that directory via `from <module> import <function>`, then call the imported function as if it's in the active block itself.

Creating the Initial Cross-Section for the Grip Mesh

We will start the gun generation at the bottom of the grip and extrude upward. Listing 2-3 shows the function generate_gun's signature plus its initial code block. Since the number of arguments to generate_gun is numerous, I will explain them as they come up in the code block in which they are used throughout the remainder of this chapter and the next. The arguments used in Listing 2-3 are shown in **bold**.

Listing 2-3. The signature and first code block of generate_gun, where a grip mesh object is created with an initial oval edge loop (see /Ch2/gun_generator.py)

```
def generate_gun(context, name, location=(0,0,0), ↩
    num_cir_segments=32, grip_radius=3, num_grip_levels=6, ↩
    stylize=True, grip_bent_factor=1, side_rib_only=False, ↩
    num_barrels=2, ratio_frame_to_grip=1.5, ↩
    slide_back_width_multiplier=1.0, ↩
    grip_width_multiplier=1.75):

    bm, grip_obj = get_placeholder_mesh_obj_and_bm( ↩
        context, name=name, location=location)
    base_radius = grip_radius*ratio_frame_to_grip
    bmesh.ops.create_circle(bm, cap_ends=False, ↩
        cap_tris=False, segments=num_cir_segments, ↩
        radius=base_radius)
    bpy.ops.mesh.select_all(action='SELECT')
```

```
bpy.ops.transform.resize( ↩
    value=(grip_width_multiplier,1,1), ↩
    orient_type='GLOBAL', ↩
    constraint_axis=(True, True, True), ↩
    mirror=True, snap_target='CLOSEST', ↩
    use_snap_self=True, ↩
    use_snap_edit=True, use_snap_nonedit=True)
bpy.ops.mesh.select_all(action='DESELECT')
```

The code starts by calling `get_placeholder_mesh_obj_and_bm` (Listing 2-1) to create a mesh object for the grip (`grip_obj`) and a `bmesh` instance `bm` for editing it. It then calls `bmesh.ops.create_circle` with `num_cir_segments` to create the starting cross-section and adds it to `grip_obj` through `bm`. An example of the circle is shown as (1) in Figure 2-11.

The radius of the circle (`base_radius`) is computed from `grip_radius` times `ratio_frame_to_grip`. The argument `ratio_frame_to_grip` specifies the ratio of the frame length to the grip width. We make the circle proportional to `ratio_frame_to_grip` so that the bigger the frame (or the longer the barrel), the wider the grip—which makes the gun look more balanced as a whole.

Next, we turn the circle into an oval by selecting all, scaling with `grip_width_multiplier` along X, and deselecting all. An example of the oval is shown as (2) in Figure 2-11. Note that `generate_gun` makes the gun axes aligned with global X and Y, such that the barrel aligns with global X and points toward –X, which makes the generation process simpler as a whole.

Flattening Out the Sides of the Oval

Next, in Listing 2-4, we'll flatten out the oval created by Listing 2-3 to shape the sides of the grip (an example of which is shown as (3) in Figures 2-11 and 2-14).

Listing 2-4. Second block of generate_gun, where the sides of the oval edge loop at the bottom of the grip are flattened (see /Ch2/gun_generator.py)

```
bm.verts.ensure_lookup_table()
base_front_verts = []
base_back_verts = []
curvature_threshold = ↩
    (grip_width_multiplier*base_radius)*0.8
```

```
verts_to_straighten_y = []
for v in bm.verts:
    x_dist_from_center = abs(v.co[0])
    if v.co[0] >= 0:
        if x_dist_from_center > curvature_threshold:
            base_front_verts.append(v)
        else:
            verts_to_straighten_y.append(v)
    else:
        if x_dist_from_center > curvature_threshold:
            base_back_verts.append(v)
        else:
            verts_to_straighten_y.append(v)

for v in verts_to_straighten_y:
    if v.co[1] > 0:
        v.select = True
bpy.ops.transform.resize(value=(1,0,1), ↩
    orient_type='GLOBAL', ↩
    constraint_axis=(False, True, False), mirror=True, ↩
    use_snap_self=True, use_snap_edit=True, ↩
    use_snap_nonedit=True)
bpy.ops.mesh.select_all(action='DESELECT')

for v in verts_to_straighten_y:
    if v.co[1] <= 0:
        v.select = True
bpy.ops.transform.resize(value=(1,0,1), ↩
    orient_type='GLOBAL', ↩
    constraint_axis=(False, True, False), mirror=True, ↩
    use_snap_self=True, use_snap_edit=True, ↩
    use_snap_nonedit=True)
bpy.ops.mesh.select_all(action='DESELECT')
```

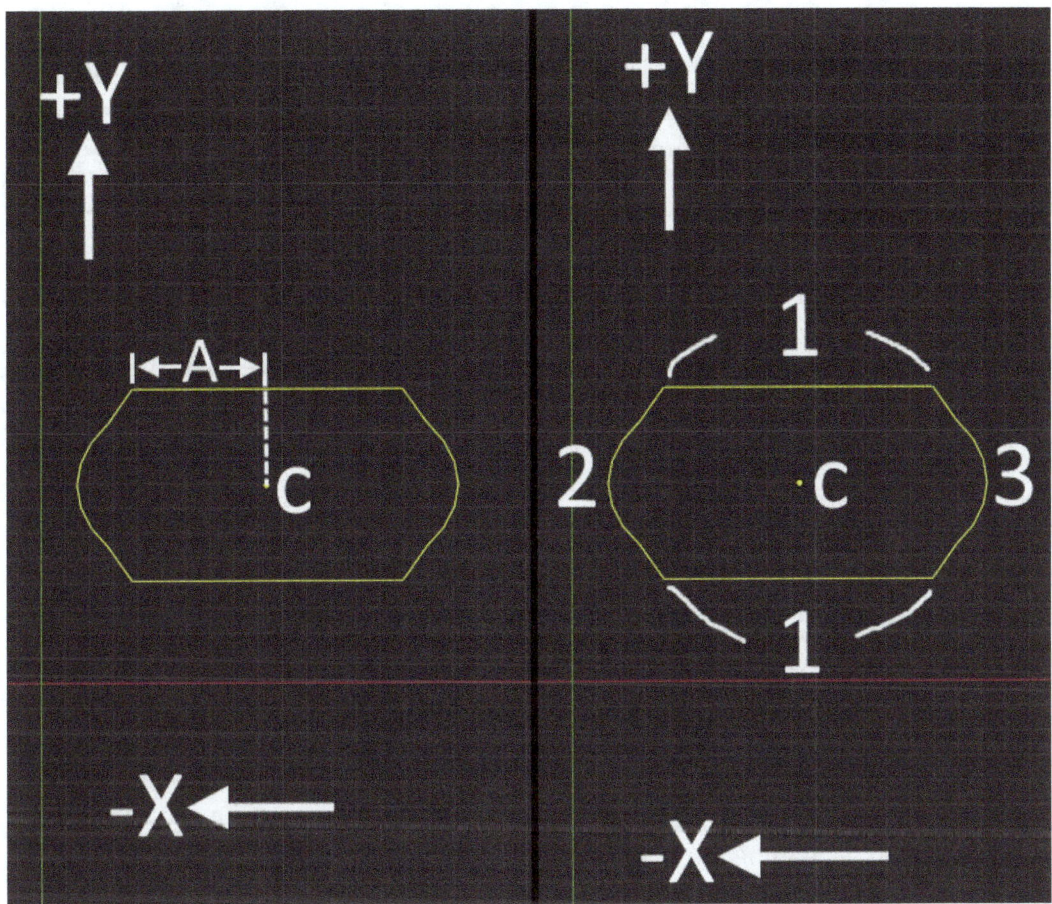

Figure 2-14. *Left: A =* `curvature_threshold` *and c =* `grip_obj.location`*. Right: (1)* `verts_to_straighten_y`*, which are the vertices in the oval edge loop to scale to 0 along Y; (2)* `base_front_verts`*, which are the verts at the front of the grip (trigger side); and (3)* `base_back_verts`*, which are the verts at the back of the grip*

The objective of Listing 2-4 is to divide the oval loop's verts into three lists (as shown in Figure 2-14):

1. `verts_to_straighten_y` contains verts that will be scaled to 0 along Y and become the sides of the grip.
2. `base_front_verts` contains verts that will become the front of the grip (trigger side).
3. `base_back_verts` contains verts that will become the back of the grip.

We divide the verts up such that those with an X distance `abs(v.co[0])` from the loop center within `curvature_threshold` belong to `verts_to_straighten`. Outside the threshold, those on the –X side belong to `base_front_verts`, and those on the +X side belong to `base_back_verts`. Here, the loop center coincides with `grip_obj.location`. Note that a vertex's coordinates are based on the mesh object's local coordinate system, which has its origin at the object's location.

With the verts divided, we'll flatten the verts in `verts_to_straighten_y` by selecting them and calling `bpy.ops.transform.resize` with `value=(1,0,1)`and `constraint_axis=(False, True, False)` (scaling to 0 along Y). We cannot scale all the verts at once, since this would collapse them into a line. To get the effect we want, where each side of the oval is flattened, we need to select the half of the verts with Y less than the center (`v.co[1] <= 0`) first, scale them, then scale the other half (`v.co[1] > 0`).

Shaping the Initial Grip Cross-Section at the Front and Back

In Listing 2-5, we'll continue shaping the front and back of the initial grip cross-section. We shape the front by selecting the verts in `base_front_verts`, scaling them to 1.25 along X, then deselecting all. We then shape the back by selecting the verts in `base_back_verts`, scaling them to 0.7 along X, then deselecting all. Here, the scale factors are hardcoded and not user controllable, since they don't contribute to the gun silhouette much overall. After shaping the front and back, we fill the loop with a n-gon by selecting all and calling `bpy.ops.mesh.edge_face_add()`. We then call `bm.edges.ensure_lookup_table()` to update the `bmesh` instance's internal edge lookup table, so we can grab the first edge to use as reference for extruding the grip next. An example of the state of the mesh at the end of Listing 2-5 is shown as (4) in Figure 2-11, with the more flattened side as the front.

Listing 2-5. Third block of generate_gun, where the front and back of the initial grip cross-section are shaped (see /Ch2/gun_generator.py)

```
for v in base_front_verts:
    v.select = True
base_front_scale = 1.25
bpy.ops.transform.resize( ↩
    value=(base_front_scale,1,1), ↩
    orient_type='GLOBAL', ↩
```

```
        constraint_axis=(True,False,False), ↩
        mirror=True)
    bpy.ops.mesh.select_all(action='DESELECT')

    for v in base_back_verts:
        v.select = True
    base_back_scale = 0.7
    bpy.ops.transform.resize(value=(base_back_scale,1,1), ↩
        orient_type='GLOBAL', ↩
        constraint_axis=(True,False,False), ↩
        mirror=True)

    bpy.ops.mesh.select_all(action='SELECT')
    bpy.ops.mesh.edge_face_add()
    bm.edges.ensure_lookup_table()
    ref_edge = bm.edges[0]
```

Extruding the Grip

With the initial cross-section formed, we're ready to extrude it upward into the grip. In Listing 2-6, we begin at the bottom, extrude upward, and pause at the point just after the thumb safety. Parameters exposed to user control are shown in **bold**.

Listing 2-6. Fourth block of generate_gun, where the initial cross-section loop is extruded upward into the grip (see /Ch2/gun_generator.py)

```
    context.tool_settings.mesh_select_mode = ↩
        [False, False, True]
    grip_level_height = grip_radius*1.15
    face_loop_grip_top = []
    num_grip_levels = max(1, num_grip_levels)
    total_levels = num_grip_levels+3
    safety_loops = []
    for i in range(total_levels):
        z_offset = grip_level_height

        if i == total_levels-1:
            z_offset *= 2
```

```
        elif i >= total_levels-3 and i < total_levels-1:
            z_offset = grip_level_height*0.35

        if stylize:
            skew = 5 if i==total_levels-2 else ↩
                grip_radius*0.5*grip_bent_factor
            direction = Vector((-skew, 0, z_offset))
            if i==0 or i==total_levels-3:
                direction = Vector((skew, 0, z_offset))
            elif i==total_levels-1:
                direction = Vector((0, 0, z_offset))
        else:
            direction = Vector((0, 0, z_offset))

        sx = slide_back_multiplier if i==(total_levels-1) ↩
            else 1
        if i >= (num_grip_levels-2):
            sx = 0.9 if i < num_grip_levels else 1.05
        sy = slide_back_multiplier if i==(total_levels-1) ↩
            else 1

        scale = Vector((sx, sy, 1))
        extrusion = extrude_edge_loop_copy_move( ↩
            bm, ref_edge, direction, scale)
        ref_edge = extrusion[0]

        if i==total_levels-1:
            face_idx = 0
            for f in bm.faces:
                if f.select:
                    face_loop_grip_top.append(f)
                face_idx += 1

        if i==total_levels-2 or i==total_levels-3:
            safety_loops.append(extrusion)
```

```
bpy.ops.mesh.select_all(action='DESELECT')
for e in safety_loops[-1]:
    for v in e.verts:
        v.select = True
bpy.ops.transform.resize(value=(1.25, ↩
    ratio_frame_to_grip, 1), orient_type='GLOBAL')
bpy.ops.mesh.select_all(action='DESELECT')
for e in safety_loops[-2]:
    for v in e.verts:
        v.select = True
bpy.ops.transform.resize(value=(1.45, ↩
    ratio_frame_to_grip, 1), orient_type='GLOBAL')
bpy.ops.mesh.select_all(action='DESELECT')
bmesh.update_edit_mesh(grip_obj.data)
```

We'll start by changing Mesh Select Mode to Face via `context.tool_settings.mesh_select_mode = [False, False, True]`, where the list of bools on the right corresponds to vert, edge, and face, respectively (you can have more than one `True` value in the list, which will set multiple select modes at a time, e.g., vert and edge). We calculate a `grip_level_height` that is 115% of `grip_radius` to extrude the `num_grip_levels` that form the actual grip (A in Figure 2-15). Two levels above that form the safety (B in Figure 2-15), with each "B" level at 35% the height of an "A" level. Another level above forms the back of the slide (C in Figure 2-15), which also doubles as the transition into the frame. This last level (C) has 200% the height of an "A" level. Therefore, the total number of extrusions is `num_grip_levels` plus 3.

Typically, you don't want to expose every generation parameter to the user, since it becomes impossible to understand how to adjust parameter values to get the outcome that you want. Instead, make only the most important parameters user configurable and the rest constrained by them. For example, to simplify parametric controls for the grip dimension, only `num_grip_levels` is directly set by the user, with `grip_level_height` constrained by `grip_radius` (a user param).

The `stylize` argument when `True` applies a X offset to the "A" grip levels, which makes the grip tilt forward or backward. The argument `grip_bent_factor` can be used by the user to control the amount of tilt (the larger the factor, the more pronounced the tilt). When `grip_bent_factor` is positive, the grip tilts backward, as the example shown in Figure 2-15; when grip_bent_factor is negative, the grip tilts forward. The bottom-most level of the grip is skewed the opposite direction as the remaining (num_grip_levels-1) levels above it. When stylize=False, no X offset is applied, only Z, which makes a straight grip, like the examples shown in Figure 2-16.

The argument slide_back_multiplier scales the back of the slide uniformly (the ribbed part). Since the top portion of the grip ("C" in Figure 2-15) connects to the back of the slide, we want to scale it proportionally to create a smooth transition. Therefore, we'll scale the "C" extrusion (which starts at index total_levels-1) by slide_back_multiplier along X and Y. We'll also apply a minor shaping on the "A" levels along X to make the grip taper slightly toward the top.

Once the direction and scale are determined for a level, we call the function extrude_edge_loop_copy_move (discussed in Listing 2-7) to extrude it. We keep a reference to an edge (any edge) that is part of the loop atop the most recent extrusion, so we can use it to select the loop to extrude from next.

If we've just extruded the very last level (i==total_levels-1, "C" in Figure 2-15), we want to keep a reference to its face loop, so we can continue extruding the frame from it next. Since the newly formed faces stay selected immediately postextrusion, we can find the face loop by iterating through bm.faces and picking out the faces that are selected.

If we've just extruded the levels that form the safety (i==total_levels-2 or i==total_levels-3, "B" in Figure 2-15), we'll also want to keep references to their top edge loops, so we can scale them shortly once we're finished extruding all the grip levels.

Right after the for loop, we select the safety levels ("B" in Figure 2-15) and scale them with fixed scale factors along X and ratio_frame_to_grip (user specified) along Y. We've finished the grip generation at this point, so we call bmesh.update_edit_mesh(grip_obj.data) to flush the edits through to grip_obj's mesh data. We will pick up from here and continue generating the rest of the gun in Chapter 3.

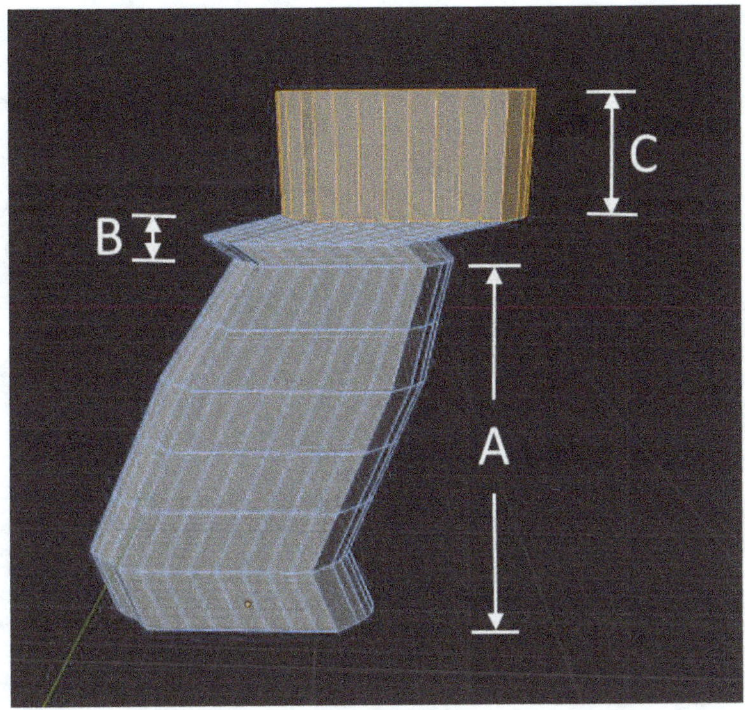

Figure 2-15. *One possible example of the state of the gun at the end of Listing 2-6. (A) The grip, formed by `num_grip_levels` extrusions (input by user). All extrusions in this part have the same Z height (which is 115% of the `grip_radius`). (B) Two additional levels above A form the safety. Each extrusion in this part has 35% the height of an A level. (C) A third additional level forms the back of the slide, which also transitions into the frame. This level has 200% the height of an A level.*

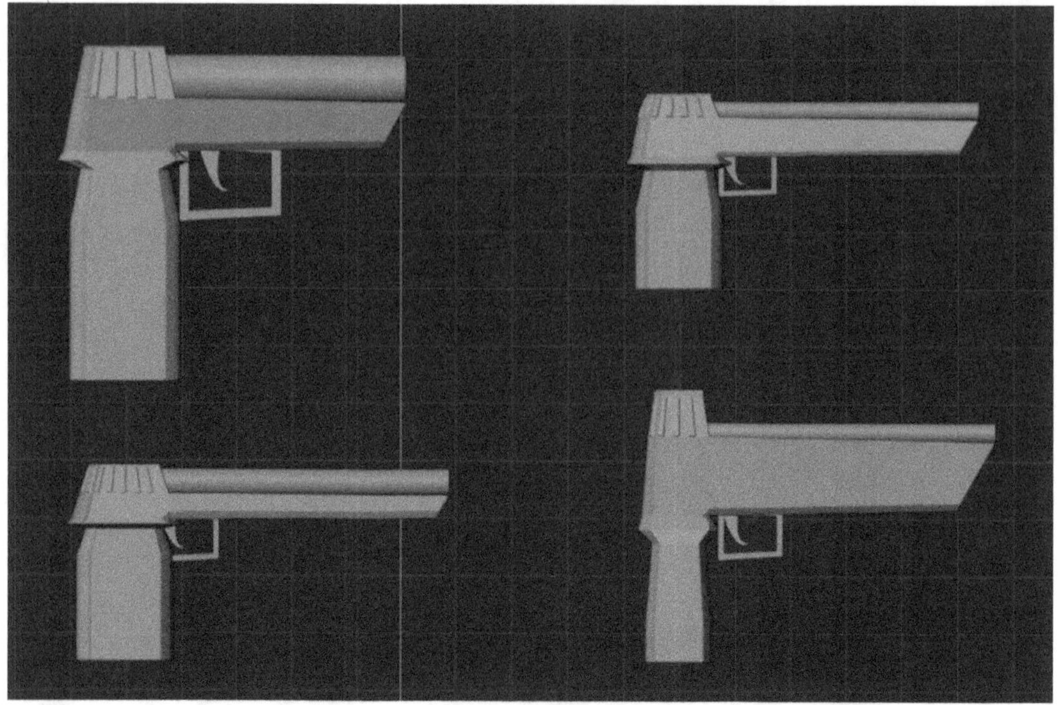

Figure 2-16. *Examples of guns generated with* `stylize=False`*, which have straight grips*

Util: Extrude by Copy-Move Edge Loop and Bridge

Listing 2-7 shows the utility function `extrude_edge_loop_copy_move` that we've seen previously in Listing 2-6. You can find the function in the file `/Ch2/mesh_editing_utils.py`.

Listing 2-7. Util function for extruding the edge loop containing the given reference edge along the given direction. The top of the extrusion is scaled by the given scale_factor (see /Ch2/mesh_editing_utils.py)

```
def extrude_edge_loop_copy_move(bm, ref_edge, direction, ↩
    scale_factor):
    select_edge_loops(bm, [ref_edge], select_rings=False)
    bpy.ops.mesh.duplicate()
    bpy.ops.transform.translate(value=direction)
    bpy.ops.transform.resize(value=scale_factor)
```

```
    new_edge_loop = []
    for e in bm.edges:
        if e.select:
            new_edge_loop.append(e)

    select_edge_loops(bm, [new_edge_loop[0], ref_edge])
    bpy.ops.mesh.bridge_edge_loops()
    for e in new_edge_loop:
        e.select = False
    return new_edge_loop
```

extrude_edge_loop_copy_move takes a reference edge (ref_edge) to call select_edge_loops with (discussed next in Listing 2-8) to select any edge loop ref_edge might be a part of. It then calls bpy.ops.mesh.duplicate() to make a copy of the selected edge loop, moves the copy with bpy.ops.transform.translate along the given direction, and scales the copy via bpy.ops.transform.resize with the given scale_factor.

Since bpy.ops operators do not return a copy of the geometry they operated on, we find the duplicate edge loop by iterating through bm.edges and picking out edges that are still selected postscaling.

Next, we select both the original and the duplicate edge loops and call bpy.ops.mesh.bridge_edge_loops() to bridge the two. We finish by deselecting the duplicate loop and returning it.

Util: Select Edge Loops (or Rings)

Listing 2-8 shows the utility function select_edge_loops that we've previously seen in Listing 2-7. You can find the function in the file /Ch2/mesh_editing_utils.py.

Listing 2-8. Util function for selecting the edge loop containing the given reference edge (see /Ch2/mesh_editing_utils.py)

```
def select_edge_loops(bm, ref_edges, select_rings=False):
    bpy.ops.mesh.select_all(action='DESELECT')
    for re in ref_edges:
        re.select = True
    bpy.ops.mesh.loop_multi_select(ring=select_rings)

    loop_edges = []
```

```
    for e in bm.edges:
        if e.select:
            loop_edges.append(e)
    return loop_edges
```

select_edge_loops takes a list of reference edges (ref_edges) and selects any edge loops those edges are a part of. Since you'd only want the loops you intend to select to become selected, we first deselect all, then select the edges in ref_edges in a for loop before calling bpy.ops.mesh.loop_multi_select with the given select_rings value to select the edge loops (or rings) encompassing the edges already selected. The last block of select_edge_loops accumulates the selected edge loops (or rings) in a list (loop_edges) and returns it.

Summary

In this chapter, you started implementing your first procedural game weapon generator in Blender Python. You began with a tour of the Scripting workspace and learned how to play with Blender Python operators in the built-in Python Console and use Autocomplete as a way to explore API functions and access documentation. You also learned that when you access any menu item or hot key in Blender, the corresponding Blender Python API call gets logged in the Info Editor, which can then be copied and pasted into the console for experimentation. In addition, you practiced editing the startup cube with Blender Python from the console, first by calling bpy operators to extrude, then using bmesh to bevel edges and select and move vertices. Lastly, you learned how to navigate the built-in Text Editor, a basic Python IDE with syntax highlighting with which you can edit and run scripts, then see results applied instantly in Blender.

In the second half of the chapter, you planned and formulated a design for the game weapon generator. First, you analyzed reference photos and created a preliminary design. Then you learned about Parametric Modeling, a 3D design technique with which you structure a mesh as a hierarchy of interrelated parts, such that one part's properties constrain those of another. We discussed how you can utilize Parametric Modeling to plan out the weapon generator such that the user has stylistic control over the variations produced. With that in mind, you hand modeled a handgun prototype to research which direction has the simplest cross-sections and therefore is the easiest to grow the mesh.

You also thought about how to divide the model into separate mesh objects to simplify the generation process. Along the way, you learned about various techniques to infer data from neighboring geometry, such as using the dot product to check if two face normals point in the same direction, which can be used to tell which side of a mesh to attach an appendage or continue to grow a mesh.

With a design in place, you kicked off the implementation for the weapon generator by editing a circle primitive to create the initial cross-section and extruding it upward to form the grip. Along the way, you learned how to perform many types of mesh edits in Blender Python, such as how to create a mesh object and a `bmesh` instance for adding geometry to it; how to select, deselect, and scale mesh elements; how to change Mesh Selection Mode; and how to select, extrude, and bridge edge loops.

CHAPTER 3

Blender Python Game Weapon Generator: Part 2

In this chapter, we'll continue to implement the procedural game weapon generator in Blender Python. Picking up where we left off in Chapter 2, we'll start at the top of the grip, continuing forward along –X to build the frame and upward along Z to form the back of the slide with ribbed detail, at which point we'll have completed the first part of the gun. After that, we'll create a new mesh object to organize the number of barrel meshes requested by the user, which are automatically resized by the generator to fit the frame and the back of the slide. Last but not least, we'll add a third mesh object to house the trigger and generate the finger pull through the clever use of a partial parabolic curve.

Creating the Frame

Recall that at the end of Chapter 2, we extruded and shaped an extra face loop atop the grip mesh in preparation of transitioning into the frame (shown as "C" in Figure 2-15). In this section, we'll locate the front center faces of the aforementioned face loop and extrude them forward along –X to create the frame (the part of the gun underneath the barrel(s)).

Extruding the Front Faces of the Grip's Top Face Loop

In Listing 3-1, we filter the grip's topmost face loop (shown as "C" in Figure 2-15) to locate the faces that are at the front of the gun (barrel-side). We'll extrude these faces along –X to form the frame and clean up the mesh by removing doubles.

I. Lupiani, *Procedural Content Generation for Games*, https://doi.org/10.1007/979-8-8688-1787-8_3

Listing 3-1. Fifth block of generate_gun, where the front center faces of the grip's top face loop are extruded along –X to form the frame (see /Ch2/gun_generator.py)

```
bpy.ops.mesh.select_all(action='SELECT')
bpy.ops.mesh.normals_make_consistent(inside=False)
if bm.faces[0].normal[2] > 0:
    bpy.ops.mesh.flip_normals()
bpy.ops.mesh.select_all(action='DESELECT')

num_front_faces = 0
for f in face_loop_grip_top:
    if f.normal.normalized().dot(-unit_x) > ↩
        cos(radians(45)):
        f.select = True
        num_front_faces += 1

_, _, grip_top_y_span = get_y_span(face_loop_grip_top, ↩
    Side.Top, num_front_faces)
barrel_locs_center, barrel_loc_list, barrel_radius = ↩
    get_pos_inside_face_loop(face_loop_grip_top, ↩
    num_barrels, grip_top_y_span)

bpy.ops.transform.resize(value=(0, 1, 1), ↩
    orient_type='GLOBAL')
frame_len = grip_radius*2*ratio_frame_to_grip * 5
bpy.ops.mesh.extrude_region_move( ↩
    TRANSFORM_OT_translate={"value": ↩
        (-frame_len, -0, -0), "orient_type":'GLOBAL'})

bpy.ops.mesh.select_all(action='SELECT')
bpy.ops.mesh.remove_doubles()
bpy.ops.mesh.select_all(action='DESELECT')
```

Since we need to use normals to identify face directions, we'll first ensure that they are correct by selecting all and calling `bpy.ops.mesh.normals_make_consistent(inside=False)` to recalculate outside normals (Mesh ➤ Normals ➤ Recalculate Outside). Since the mesh is not yet closed at this point, sometimes Blender confuses which side of the mesh is outside. To see if this is the case, we add a sanity check for the normal direction at the bottom of the grip (`bm.faces[0].normal`)—if it's pointing up (with its Z coordinate > 0), then normals are inside out, as shown in Figure 3-1. In which case, we flip the normals by calling `bpy.ops.mesh.flip_normals()`. We finish working with the normals by deselecting all.

Next, we iterate through the face loop atop the grip to find the faces in the front (–X). To do so, we check the *dot product* between each face's normalized normal vector and the negative unit X vector, to see if it is *greater than* `cos(radians(45))`. If so, it indicates that the face normal is *less than* 45 degrees from –X, or the face is roughly pointing toward –X, as shown in Figure 3-2 (don't worry–we'll break down this math step by step in the next section). As we select the front faces, we also keep count of how many there are.

Since the barrel meshes will originate about where we are—at the back of the slide, above the grip—we'll look ahead and calculate the barrel position(s) and radius. We call the function `get_y_span`[1] to find the two outermost verts of the front faces and the distance between them. After that, we call the function `get_pos_inside_face_loop`[2] to interpolate between these two points to find the user-specified number of positions for generating the barrels (`num_barrels`). `get_pos_inside_face_loop`[2] also calculates the radius of each barrel and the origin for the barrel object.

In the last part of the listing, we extrude the front faces of the loop into the frame, by scaling them to 0 along X to flatten (Figure 3-2), then calling `bpy.ops.mesh.extrude_region_move` with `(-frame_len, -0, -0)` to extrude a length of `frame_len` along –X (Figure 3-3). Here, we constrain `frame_len` with the user-specified parameters `grip_radius` and `ratio_frame_to_grip`, then multiply it with a fixed factor found through experimentation.

[1] Utility function discussed two sections ahead, in "Util: Finding the Widest Part of a List of Faces in Terms of Y."

[2] Utility function discussed three sections ahead, in "Util: Finding the Center, Approximate Radius, and List of Interpolated Positions Across a Face Loop."

We clean up the mesh generated thus far, by selecting all, removing doubles (`bpy.ops.mesh.remove_doubles()`), and deselecting all.

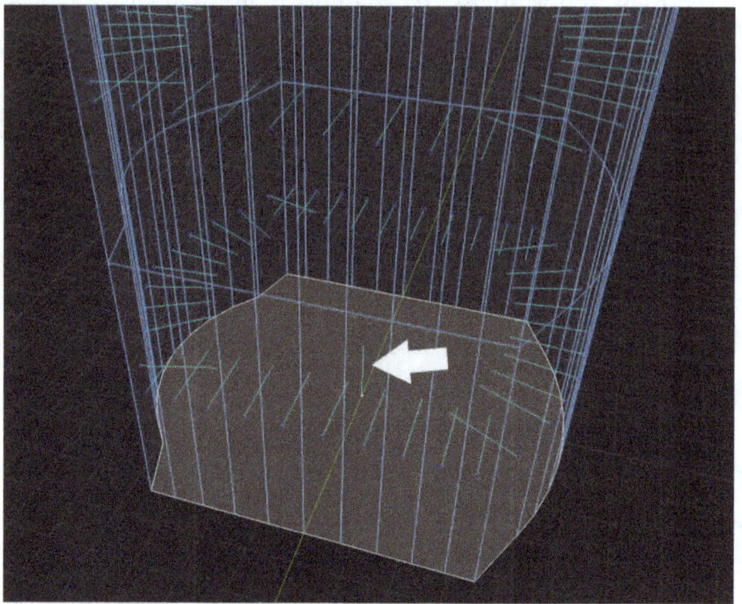

Figure 3-1. *Since the generated mesh is not yet closed at this point, occasionally Blender confuses the inside and outside of the mesh. As a fail-safe, we check the normal of the first face of the mesh (`bm.faces[0]`)—if it's pointing up (with a Z > 0), then the normals are inside out (as shown).*

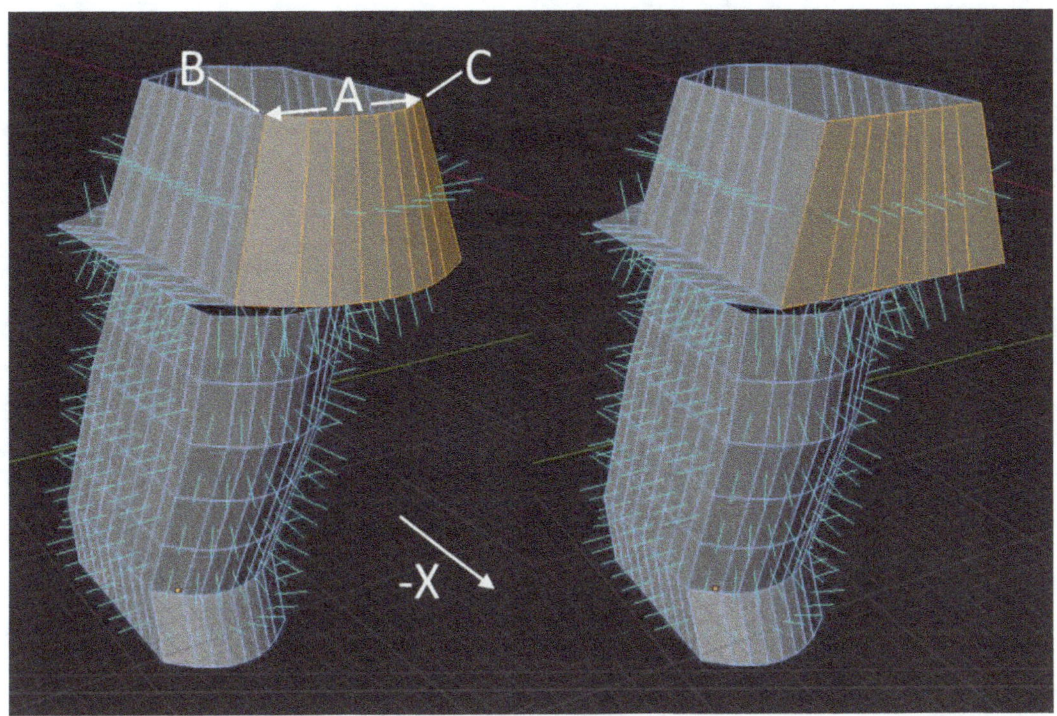

Figure 3-2. *Left: front faces of the loop atop the grip (as selected). A, B, and C correspond to the three return values of* `get_y_span` *in Listing 3-1, which are* `grip_top_y_span`*,* `grip_top_end_1`*, and* `grip_top_end_2`*. Right: the front faces scaled to 0 along X.*

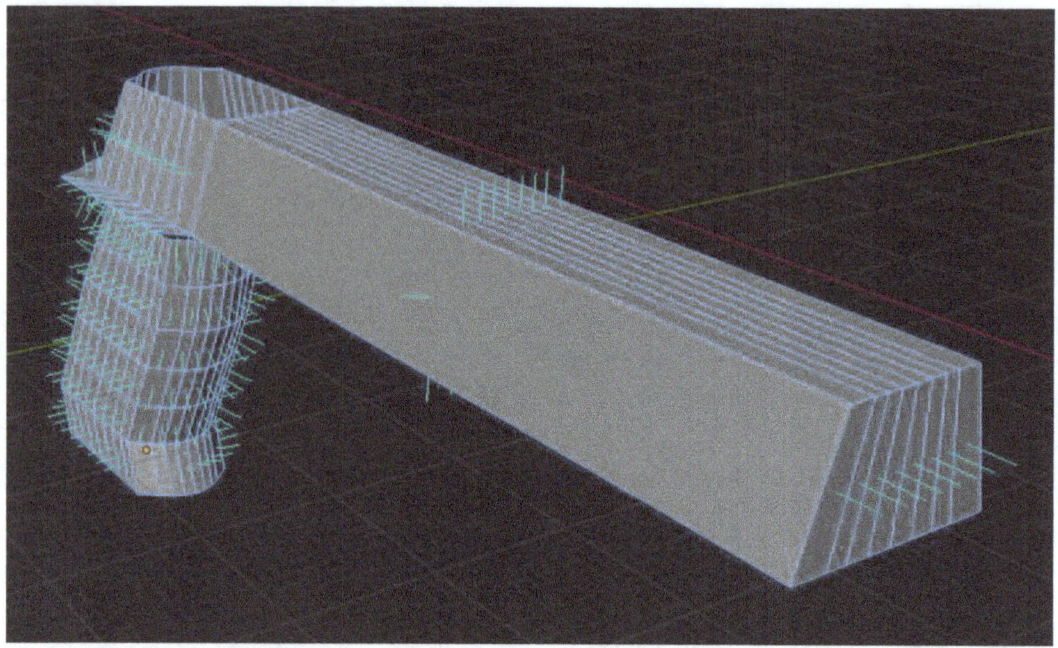

Figure 3-3. *The front faces of the loop atop the grip, scaled to 0 along X, then extruded along –X to form the frame*

Using Dot Product to Check If Two Vectors Point in the Same Direction (or to Find the Angle Between Them)

To see if a face is pointing toward a certain direction, you can check if the dot product between the face' normalized normal and the normalized direction vector is close to 1. Recall that the dot product of two vectors v1 and v2 is

$$dot(v1,v2) = |v1| \cdot |v2| \cdot \cos(\theta)$$

where

$$|v1| \; and \; |v2|$$

are the lengths of the two vectors and theta is the angle between them.

If v1 and v2 are pointing in roughly the same direction, theta will be small; therefore,

$$\cos(\theta)$$

is close to 1. If you normalize v1 and v2 (maintain their directions but make their lengths 1), then the previous dot product formula simplifies to

$$dot(v1,v2)=cos(\theta)$$

You can then find θ by taking arc cosine on both sides:

$$\arccos(dot(v1,v2))=\theta$$

The good news is that Blender Python's `mathutils.Vector` type as well as Python's built-in `math` module both have functions that will perform the calculations in the above formula for you. Let's open the Scripting workspace and try this in the Python Console. We'll import the relevant functions from `mathutils` and `math`, then create two `Vector` instances, `v1` and `v2`:

```
>>> from mathutils import Vector
>>> from math import acos, cos, degrees, radians
>>> v1 = Vector((1, 2, 3))
>>> v2 = Vector((4, 5, 6))
```

You can calculate the dot product between the normalized copies of `v1` and `v2` like this:

```
>>> dot_v1_v2 = v1.normalized().dot(v2.normalized())
```

You can type `dot_v1_v2` at the next prompt, then hit enter to print the value of `dot_v1_v2` in the console:

```
>>> dot_v1_v2
0.9746318235993385
```

which is close to 1, indicating that the angle between `v1` and `v2` is small. To print the value of `dot_v1_v2` in the Text Editor instead, you'd need to add the following line to the Python script:

```
print("dot_v1_v2 = " + str(dot_v1_v2))
```

The value of the `print` statement will be displayed in the System Console window (Window ➤ Toggle System Console).

To calculate the angle θ (theta) between v1 and v2, you'd take the arc cosine of their dot product, like this:

```
>>> theta_v1_v2 = acos(dot_v1_v2)
>>> theta_v1_v2
0.22572622951924962
```

By default, both Blender Python and Python use radians. To get a more intuitive sense of how large theta_v1_v2 is, we can call the function degrees under the math module (which we imported above) to convert it into degrees:

```
>>> degrees(theta_v1_v2)
12.933160276854341
```

As expected, the angle between v1 and v2 is small (about 13 degrees); in other words, v1 and v2 face mostly the same way. Finding whether two vectors (or two face normals, or a face normal and a vector, etc.) point in roughly the same direction, but not exactly the same, is something we'll see again and again in procedural generation. We've seen an example already in the previous section, where we find the front side of the face loop atop of the grip by checking whether the dot product between the face normals and the unit –X vector is *above* a threshold.

Let's see if the angle between v1 and v2 is *less than* 30 degrees, by checking if *dot_v1_v2* is *greater than* cosine of 30 degrees:

```
>>> cos(radians(30))
0.8660254037844387

>>> dot_v1_v2 > cos(radians(30))
True
```

The value of cosine theta is 1 to –1 for theta from 0 to 180 degrees. Cosine theta is 0 when theta is 90 degrees. In other words, cosine theta *decreases* as theta *increases.* Therefore, if the angle between v1 and v2 needs to be less than 30 degrees, their dot product must be greater than cos(radians(30)).

Here are some examples of how you can utilize dot products for deriving relationships between mesh elements, some of which are visualized in Figure 3-4:

- Check if two faces point in roughly the same direction, by checking if the dot product of their normalized normals is *greater than* a positive threshold, for example, cos(radians(30)), if you want the angle between the normals to be *less than* 30 degrees.
    - Similarly, you can check if two faces are orthogonal, by checking if the dot product of their normalized normals is almost 0.
    - Or see if the two faces are pointing in opposite directions, by checking that the dot product of their normalized normals is close to −1.
    - You might use this strategy to find the correct side of the mesh to attach an appendage, or to continue extruding a mesh.
    - You could also use this method to find the angle between two faces, for example:
        - To see if the edge between them should be beveled or smoothed and by how much.
        - To mark edges as sharp.
        - To determine how to rotate one mesh to align with another so they can be stitched together, for example, attaching an arm to a torso.
- Check if two edges are parallel, by checking that the two edges' direction vectors point in either the same or opposite directions (in which case, the dot product of their normalized direction vectors would be either 1 or −1, so you can check that the absolute value is close to 1). If you have a `bmesh` instance `bm`, you can get an edge's direction vector by subtracting one of the edge's end vertex from the other, like this:

  ```
  e = bm.edges[0]
  dir = e.verts[1] - e.verts[0]
  ```

  If you subtract the end vertices the other way, i.e.,

  ```
  dir_opposite = e.verts[0] - e.verts[1]
  ```

The resulting directional vector would point in the opposite direction.

- This could be used in part for analyzing topology, for example, locating edge loops or rings.
- If you use the dot product to calculate the angle between two edges, that could tell you if a face corner is too sharp.
- You can also check if two edges are orthogonal, by checking if the dot product of their (normalized) direction vectors is close to 0.

- You can check if a face is pointing in a certain direction, for example, the global X, Y, or Z, by checking if the dot product of the face's normalized normal vector and the unit vector in that direction is close to 1.
  - The unit vector that aligns with
    - Global X is `Vector((1, 0, 0))`.
    - Global –X is `Vector((-1, 0, 0))`.
    - Global Y is `Vector((0, 1, 0))`.
    - Global –Y is `Vector((0, -1, 0))`.
    - Global Z is `Vector((0, 0, 1))`.
    - Global –Z is `Vector((0, 0, -1))`.

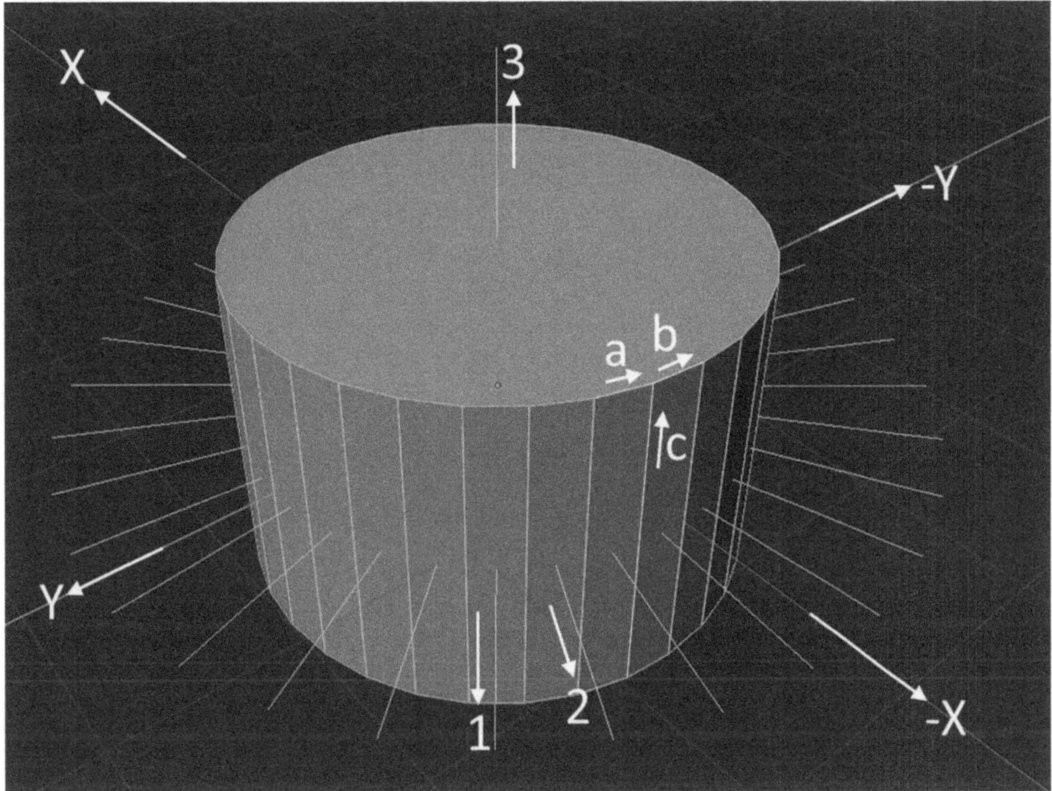

Figure 3-4. *A few sample scenarios where you could use the dot product. The faces 1 and 2 face roughly the same direction, so the dot product of their normalized normals would be close to 1. Face 3 is orthogonal to face 1, so the dot product of their normalized normals would be 0. Edges a and b are roughly parallel, so the dot product of their normalized direction vectors would be close to 1 (or −1). Edges a and c are orthogonal, so the dot product of their normalized direction vectors would be 0. You could also check the dot product between any of these vectors with a global unit vector (e.g., unit X, unit Y, etc.) to see if they align with a global axis.*

Util: Finding the Widest Part of a List of Faces in Terms of Y

In this section, we'll discuss the function `get_y_span` (Listing 3-2), which, when given a face loop (or any list of faces), returns the two vertices at the widest part of the faces in terms of Y and the distance between them. `get_y_span` was previously called in Listing 3-1 to find the Y span of the face loop atop the grip, as part of the process for finding the positions to generate the barrel meshes.

Listing 3-2. Given a face loop (or a list of faces), find the two points at the loop's widest part in terms of Y and the distance between them (see /Ch2/gun_generator.py)

```
def get_y_span(faces, side, num_front_faces):
    ref_faces = sorted(faces, key=lambda f: ↩
        max([f.verts[i].co[0] for i in range(4)]))

    end_verts = set()
    forward_most_faces = ref_faces[:num_front_faces]
    for f in forward_most_faces:
        end_verts.update(f.verts)

    to_reverse = True if side.value==Side.Top.value ↩
        else False
    end_verts = sorted(list(end_verts), ↩
        key=lambda v: v.co[2], ↩
        reverse=to_reverse)[:num_front_faces+1]
    end_verts = sorted(end_verts, key=lambda v: v.co[1], ↩
        reverse=to_reverse)
    span = abs(end_verts[0].co[1]-end_verts[-1].co[1])
    return end_verts[0], end_verts[-1], span
```

get_y_span starts by sorting the input faces by the maximum X of their verts, with Python's built-in sorted function and a custom lambda. Recall that in Listing 3-1, we selected and counted the front faces of the loop atop the grip (num_front_faces). Since the gun points toward –X, the front faces have the *smallest* X—therefore, we slice the list sorted by X to only retain num_front_faces faces from the *beginning*. Since neighboring faces have overlapping verts, we use a set to prune the list to get rid of duplicates—what remains is the set of unique verts that belong to the front faces.

get_y_span takes an additional argument, side, which is of type Side, an IntEnum class defined in /Ch2/gun_generator.py:

```
@unique
class Side(IntEnum):
    Top = 0
    Bottom = 1
```

The value of side tells get_y_span whether to look for the outermost verts at the *top* or *bottom* of the front faces. In either case, we'll continue to sort the verts by Z, then again by Y. For Side.Top, we want the verts with the largest Z values, for Side.Bottom the smallest. After sorting by Y, if we take the verts at the beginning and end of the list (which would have the extreme Y values—smallest and largest), we'll get the outermost verts along Y. The difference between the Y coordinates of these two verts gives you the Y span (abs(end_verts[0].co[1]-end_verts[-1].co[1])). Note that we take the absolute value of the Y coordinate difference since we want the distance, not the displacement.

Note Lambdas are short anonymous functions that can be used as arguments to other functions, for example, as we've done in Listing 3-2 with sorted. Under the hood, Python calls the given lambda with each element of the container, then uses the results of these calls to sort the container.

Util: Finding the Center, Approximate Radius, and List of Interpolated Positions Across a Face Loop

In this section, we'll look at the function get_pos_inside_face_loop (Listing 3-3), which interpolates evenly spaced positions across the widest part of a given face loop and calculates the radius of circles that could center at these positions and be tangent with one another. We called get_pos_inside_face_loop with the face loop atop the grip in Listing 3-1 to find the list of interpolations across its widest part across Y that would become barrel centers.

Listing 3-3. Given a face loop, compute the loop center, the list of evenly spaced positions across the widest part along Y, and the radius of hypothetical circles centered at these positions (see /Ch2/gun_generator.py)

```
def get_pos_inside_face_loop(faces, num_pos, y_width):
    ref_faces = sorted(faces, key=lambda f: ↩
        max([f.verts[i].co[0] for i in range(4)]))

    verts_far_ends = list(ref_faces[0].verts)
    verts_far_ends.extend(ref_faces[-1].verts)
```

```
    verts_far_ends = sorted(verts_far_ends, ↩
        key=lambda v: abs(v.co[1]))[:4]
    verts_far_ends = sorted(verts_far_ends, ↩
        key=lambda v: v.co[2], reverse=True)
    center = (verts_far_ends[0].co+verts_far_ends[1].co)/2

    circle_radius = y_width/(num_pos*2)
    start = center - Vector((0, y_width/2-circle_radius, 0))
    pos_list = [start + Vector((0, circle_radius*2*i, 0)) ↩
        for i in range(num_pos)]

    return center, pos_list, circle_radius
```

Our first goal is to figure out the center of the given face loop. To do so, we sort the faces by their verts' max X. We then take the faces at the two X extremes, sort their verts by Y, and take the first four verts, which are the four verts closest to the origin, as shown in Figure 3-5. We narrow down the four verts further by sorting them descendingly by Z and taking the first two, which are the verts at the top of the faces. We then calculate the center as the midpoint of these two verts. An example of this process is shown in Figure 3-5. Notice that since a vertex's coordinates are in the object's local coordinate system, you could move or rotate the object and the relative max and min between the vertices' coordinates in Listing 3-3 will still hold.

Our second goal is to interpolate the given number of positions (`num_pos`) across the faces' Y span through `center` (as shown in Figure 3-6). Since this function is called in Listing 3-3 right after `get_y_span` (Listing 3-2), which already calculates the Y span, we pass it in as an argument (`y_width`) instead of calculating it again. Each interpolated position is meant to be the center of a circle (future barrel cross-section); therefore, the radius of each circle is `y_width/(num_pos*2)`. The start of the axis through `center` is `center` offsetted by `y_width/2` along Y. The center of the first circle is then `circle_radius` back toward `center`. Since the circles are tangent, each subsequent circle is `circle_radius*2` offset in Y from the previous, as shown in Figure 3-6.

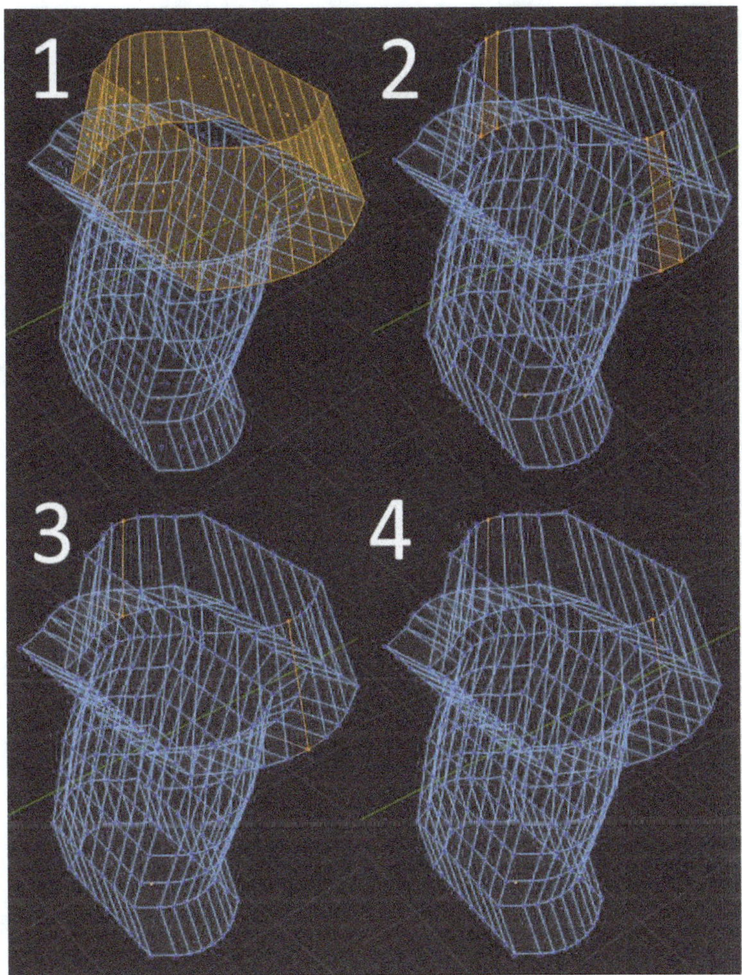

Figure 3-5. *Finding the center of a face loop (first half of Listing 3-3). (1) The face loop (selected). (2) The faces at the loop's two X extremes. (3) The verts of these two faces further narrowed down to four verts closest to the origin along Y. (4) The four verts narrowed to two verts with the largest Z.*

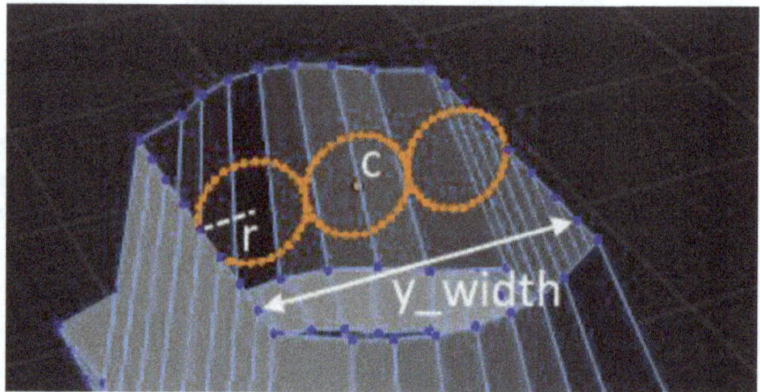

Figure 3-6. *Results of the second half of Listing 3-3. The circles shown are those that would be centered at the interpolated positions when num_pos=3 (r is `circle_radius`, and c is `center`)*

Cleaning Up and Rotating the Tip of the Frame

Next, we'll rotate the tip of the frame in Listing 3-4 so its bottom tilts inward. Since we removed doubles just before, the geometry may have changed; therefore, we call `bmesh.update_edit_mesh` to flush the changes through to `grip_obj`'s mesh data and `bm.faces.ensure_lookup_table()` to update `bm`'s internal face lookup table, so we can look up the faces at the tip of the frame again.

We search for the front faces here differently than Listing 3-1—instead of sorting the faces by their verts' max X, which will no longer uniquely identify them since some faces on the frame's side overlap the front, we sort the faces by the *sum* of their verts' X coordinates, then take the first `num_front_faces` faces as the front (recall that the frame is extruded along –X; therefore, the faces at the tip have the smallest X). We select the front faces by iterating through them and setting each face's `select` variable to `True`, then call `bpy.ops.transform.rotate` to rotate them 30 degrees around Y and deselect all. Remember to call `radians` (`math` module built-in function) to convert 30 degrees to radians first, since `bpy` operators use radians.

Listing 3-4. Sixth block of generate_gun, where the tip of the frame is rotated such that the bottom is recessed (see /Ch2/gun_generator.py)

```
bmesh.update_edit_mesh(grip_obj.data)
bm.faces.ensure_lookup_table()
frame_front_faces = sorted(bm.faces, ↩
```

```
    key=lambda f: sum([f.verts[i].co[0] for i in ↩
    range(len(f.verts))]))[:num_front_faces]

frame_front_rot = 30
for f in frame_front_faces:
    f.select = True
bpy.ops.transform.rotate( ↩
    value=radians(frame_front_rot), ↩
    orient_axis='Y', orient_type='GLOBAL')
bpy.ops.mesh.select_all(action='DESELECT')
```

Beveling the Outer Bottom Edges of the Frame and Deriving Trigger Location and Radius

Next, in Listing 3-5 we'll finish generating the frame by beveling its outer bottom edges. The trigger position needs to be derived from where the frame meets the grip and the trigger dimension from the size of the frame. Since beveling creates additional geometry, it'd be much easier to do the trigger-related calculations *right before* the beveling rather than after, which is what we'll do.

Listing 3-5. Seventh block of generate_gun, where we locate and bevel the outer bottom edges of the frame and derive the trigger location and radius (see /Ch2/gun_generator.py)

```
context.tool_settings.mesh_select_mode = ↩
    [False, True, False]
frame_bot_v1, frame_bot_v2, _ = get_y_span( ↩
    frame_front_faces, Side.Bottom, num_front_faces)
frame_side_faces = [f for f in bm.faces if ↩
    ((frame_bot_v1 in f.verts) or ↩
        (frame_bot_v2 in f.verts)) and ↩
    abs(f.normal.normalized().dot(unit_y)) > ↩
        cos(radians(30))]

frame_bot_start_verts = []
for f in frame_side_faces:
    for e in f.edges:
```

```
        for i in range(2):
            v = e.verts[i]
            if frame_bot_v1==v or frame_bot_v2==v:
                if abs(e.verts[0].co[2] - ↩
                    e.verts[1].co[2]) < 1:
                    e.select = True
                    frame_bot_start_verts.append( ↩
                        e.verts[1-i])

frame_top_v1, _, _ = get_y_span(frame_front_faces, ↩
    Side.Top, num_front_faces)
frame_x_extent = frame_top_v1.co[0]
frame_top_z = frame_top_v1.co[2]
for i in range(len(barrel_loc_list)):
    barrel_loc_list[i][2] = frame_top_z
frame_height = abs(frame_top_z - frame_bot_v1.co[2])
grip_height = frame_bot_start_verts[0].co[2]
trigger_radius = min(grip_height, abs(frame_x_extent))/8
trigger_loc = (frame_bot_start_verts[0].co + ↩
    frame_bot_start_verts[1].co)/2
trigger_loc[2] -= trigger_radius
if not stylize:
    trigger_loc[0]-=(grip_radius*grip_width_multiplier)

frame_bevel_offset = ↩
    (grip_top_y_span/num_front_faces)*0.9
bpy.ops.mesh.bevel(offset=frame_bevel_offset, ↩
    segments=1, loop_slide=False)
bpy.ops.mesh.select_all(action='DESELECT')
```

We start by setting Mesh Select Mode to Edge since ultimately we want to select the frame's outer bottom edges for beveling. We then call `get_y_span` (Listing 3-2) to locate the bottom outermost verts at the tip of the frame (`frame_bot_v1` and `frame_bot_v2`)—with which, plus the help of the dot product, we can search for the frame's side faces. We do so by iterating through `bm.faces` and finding faces that have either `frame_bot_v1` or `frame_bot_v2` as a vertex, plus a normal *less than* 30 degrees from the Y axis (in the code, we write this check as follows: the absolute value of the dot product between the face's normalized normal and the unit Y vector is *greater than* `cos(radians(30))`).

Once we find the side faces of the frame, we can iterate through their edges and pick out the bottom edges as having either `frame_bot_v1` or `frame_bot_v2` as a vertex and two end vertices with almost the same Z (`abs(e.verts[0].co[2]-e.verts[1].co[2])<1`). We select each edge found and keep a reference to its *other* end vertex (in the list `frame_bot_start_verts`), as shown in Figure 3-7, which we'll use to find the trigger location shortly.

As discussed earlier, we derive the trigger position and size *before* beveling since it's simpler (beveling adds additional geometry). First, we find the frame's dimension so we can use it to constrain barrel and trigger sizes. To do so, we call `get_y_span` with the frame's front faces and `Side.Top` to get one of its *top corner* verts at the tip (`frame_top_v1`)—this tells us the frame's extent along X (`frame_x_extent`) and Z (`frame_top_z`), which we use to update the barrel centers (`barrel_loc_list`). The `frame_height` is the difference between a top and bottom corner Z, whereas `grip_height` is a bottom corner Z. Later in the generation process, we will be creating the trigger box from a *circle* of four segments (since it's the simplest way); therefore, we derive a `trigger_radius` here. Since the trigger is nestled between the grip and the frame, the trigger size is constrained by both; therefore, we calculate it from a ratio of the *smaller* of the two (`min(grip_height, abs(frame_x_extent))/8`).

If you imagine the midpoint of `frame_bot_start_verts` as the upper left corner of the trigger box (which centers on the intersection of the frame and the grip), the trigger Z is offsetted `trigger_radius` downward from there. In the case that `stylize` (user parameter) is `False`, the grip is straight and the trigger box needs to shift about half the grip width over toward the frame so it does not overlap the grip (`trigger_loc[0]-=(grip_radius*grip_width_multiplier)`).

With the trigger dimension and location derived, we'll now bevel the frame's outer bottom edges by calling `bpy.ops.mesh.bevel`, with an offset proportional to the Y span (thickness) of the grip and inversely proportional to the number of faces at the frame's tip. We bevel only one segment here to create the tapered styling and finish by deselecting all. Two examples of generation stopping at the end of Listing 3-5 are shown in Figure 3-8.

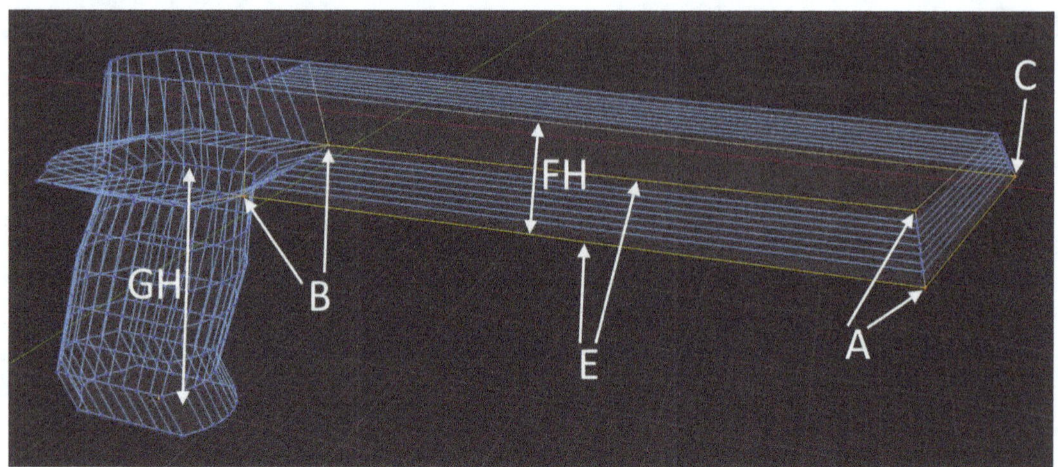

Figure 3-7. *Components of Listing 3-5 visualized. (A)* `frame_bot_v1` *and* `frame_bot_v2`*. (B)* `frame_bot_start_verts`*. (C)* `frame_top_v1`*. (E) Edges to bevel. (FH)* `frame_height`*. (GH)* `grip_height`

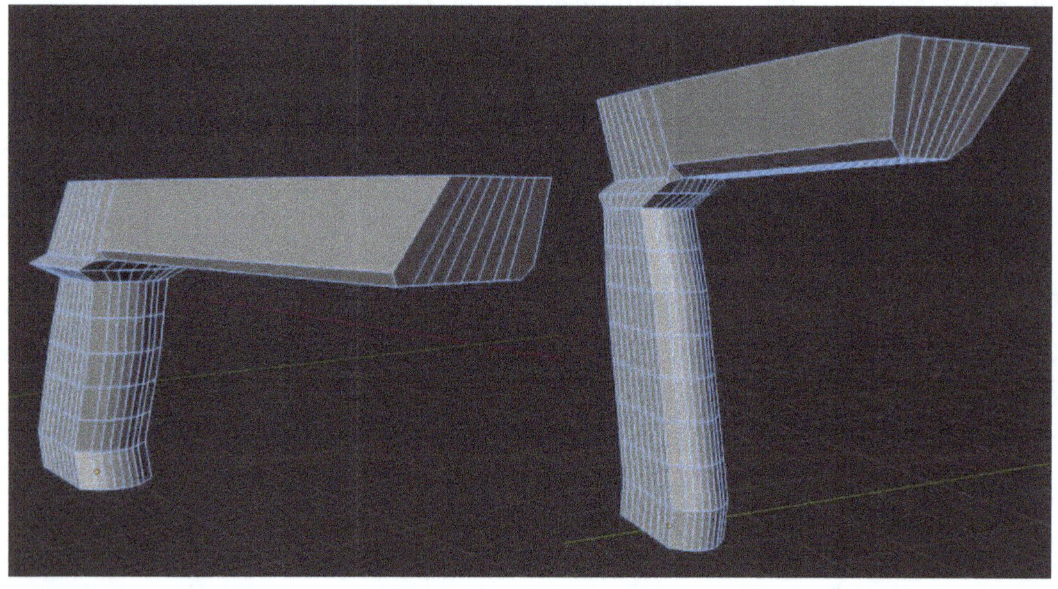

Figure 3-8. *Two examples of mesh generation stopping at the end of Listing 3-5, where the outer bottom edges of the frames are beveled*

Creating the Back of the Slide

In this section, we'll continue extruding upward from the grip to create the back of the slide with ribbed sidings and cap detail.

Extruding Upward to Form the Back of the Slide

We'll start by extruding two levels, with the first forming the back of the slide and the second a cap detail above it, as shown in Figure 3-9.

Listing 3-6. Eighth block of generate_gun, where we create the back of the slide and the cap detail above it (see /Ch2/gun_generator.py)

```
slide_back_face_loops = []
slide_back_main_loop = []
slide_back_radius = grip_radius
pcrt_of_sphere = 0.6

z_offset = slide_back_radius*pcrt_of_sphere
theta = asin(z_offset/slide_back_radius)
r_at_level = slide_back_radius*cos(theta)
level_scale_factor = r_at_level/slide_back_radius
scale = Vector((level_scale_factor, ↩
    level_scale_factor, 1))
direction = Vector((0,0,grip_level_height * ↩
    slide_back_multiplier))
extrusion = extrude_edge_loop_copy_move( ↩
    bm, ref_edge, direction, scale)
ref_edge = extrusion[0]
slide_back_height = direction[2]*scale[2]
bm.faces.ensure_lookup_table()
for f in bm.faces:
    if f.select:
        f_normal_dot_unit_x = ↩
            f.normal.normalized().dot(-unit_x)
```

```
            if side_rib_only:
                if abs(f_normal_dot_unit_x) < 0.1:
                    slide_back_face_loops.append(f)
            else:
                if f_normal_dot_unit_x < 0.1:
                    slide_back_face_loops.append(f)
            slide_back_main_loop.append(f)

    _, _, barrel_back_y_span = ↩
        get_y_span(slide_back_main_loop, Side.Top, ↩
            num_front_faces)

    direction = Vector((0, 0, slide_back_radius*0.2))
    extrusion = extrude_edge_loop_copy_move( ↩
        bm, ref_edge, direction, Vector((1,1,1)))
    ref_edge = extrusion[0]
    bpy.ops.mesh.extrude_region_move( ↩
        TRANSFORM_OT_translate={"value": Vector((0, 0, 0))})

    bpy.ops.mesh.select_all(action='DESELECT')
    select_edge_loops(bm, [ref_edge], select_rings=False)
    bpy.ops.mesh.edge_collapse()
```

We start by creating two lists, slide_back_face_loops and slide_back_main_loop, to keep references of faces as we extrude them (we'll discuss how these faces are relevant as they come up in context). Since this part of the mesh is a continuation of the grip, we'll use the same radius. We also keep track of the extrusions' total height as we'll need it later to constrain the barrel height.

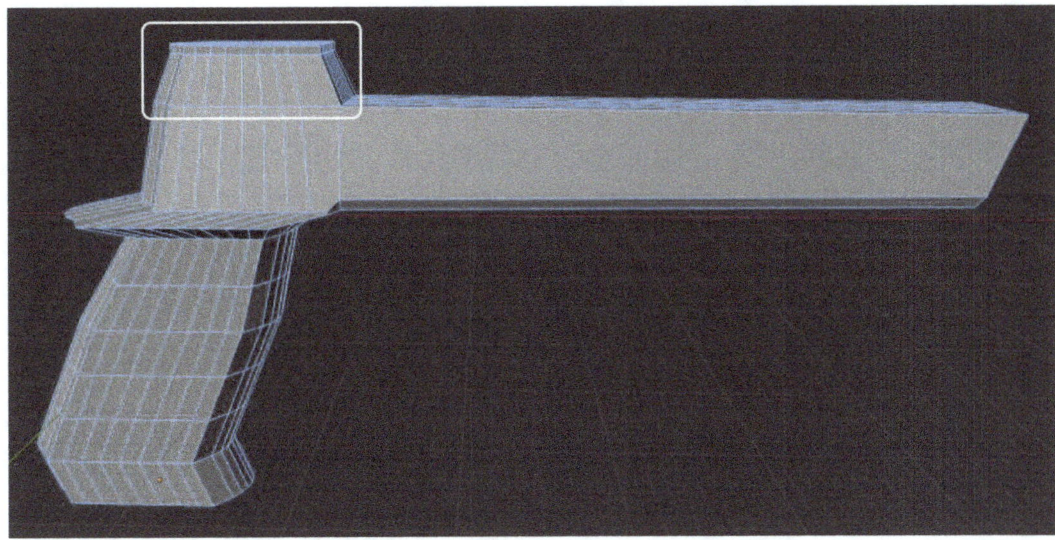

Figure 3-9. *Sample mesh with generation stopping at the end of Listing 3-6. The back of the slide has been created but no ribbed detail is added yet*

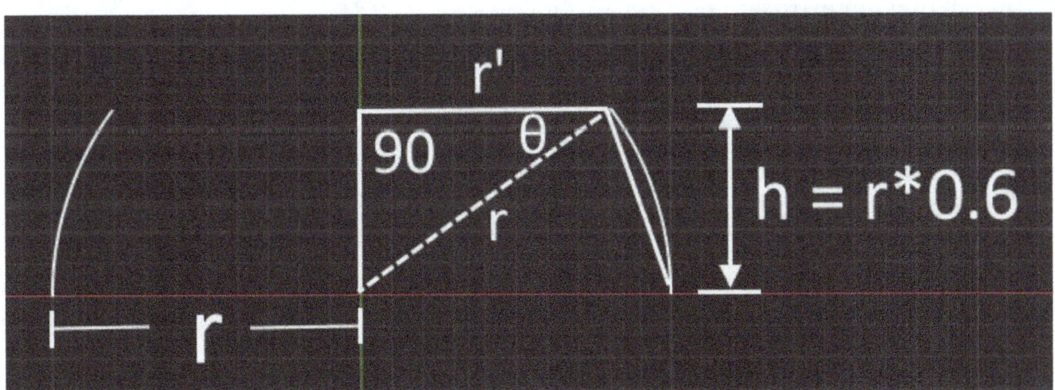

Figure 3-10. *Calculating the scale factor for extruding the back of the slide*

The back of the slide is generated using an incomplete dome. Intuitively, as you travel up a dome from the bottom, the horizontal cross-sections get smaller. Therefore, we need to find how much to scale the extrusion along XY (`level_scale_factor`). Since we're not restricting the dome height to the dome radius at the bottom, the dome may be a squashed or elongated hemisphere. We can still perform our calculations for the XY scale factor as if the dome is a true hemisphere, however, then add a Z offset in the extrusion `direction Vector` to account for the height discrepancy.

If the dome is a true hemisphere with radius r, then from Figure 3-10:

```
h = r*pcrt_of_sphere = r*0.6
```

Let's call the angle opposite h theta (θ). It follows that sin(θ) = h/r. We're then able to calculate θ = arcsin(h/r). Therefore, r', the radius of the level cross-section, can be calculated as r' = r * cos(theta).

Let's revisit Listing 3-6 and see which step of our derivation above corresponds to which line of code. In Listing 3-6, h is calculated as `z_offset` at this line:

```
z_offset = slide_back_radius*pcrt_of_sphere
```

θ is calculated as `theta` at this line:

```
theta = asin(z_offset/slide_back_radius)
```

r' at each extrusion level is calculated as `r_at_level`, at this line:

```
r_at_level = slide_back_radius*cos(theta)
```

Recall that our extrusion process is as follows:

1. Make a copy of the topmost loop of the previous extrusion.
2. Calculate the XY scale factor and use it to scale the copy to match the current level's cross-section size.
3. Move the scaled copy to the right position (updated level height, plus any horizontal skew).
4. Bridge the current level cross-section to the previous level.

In other words, each level is copied and scaled from the level just before it. Since we're only extruding one level to form the back of the slide, the XY scale factor is just the ratio of the cross-section radius (`r_at_level`) to the "dome bottom" radius (`slide_back_radius`):

```
level_scale_factor = r_at_level/slide_back_radius
```

The same factor is applied to both X and Y:

```
scale = Vector((level_scale_factor, level_scale_factor, 1))
```

The extrusion height is specified through the Z component of the direction vector, which is proportional to grip_level_height and scaled by the user parameter slide_back_multiplier:

```
direction = ↩
    Vector((0,0,grip_level_height*slide_back_multiplier))
```

We call extrude_edge_loop_copy_move (Listing 2-7) with ref_edge and the direction and scale vectors we just derived to extrude the back of the slide (recall that ref_edge is an edge that is part of the grip's topmost loop from Listing 2-6). We save an edge from this extrusion with which to continue extruding the cap detail next. We also record the slide height in slide_back_height so it can be used to constrain the barrel height later and call bm.faces.ensure_lookup_table() to refresh the internal face indices.

Next, taking advantage of the fact that new geometry stays selected right after extrusion, we iterate through the selected faces to pick out the ones that will be used to create the rib detail. If side_rib_only is True, ribs are created only on the sides. If False, ribs will wrap around the back as well. Since we generate the gun axis aligned with the barrels pointing toward global –X, to determine which face is on the back of the slide, we check the face normal's dot product with -unit_x (which is Vector((-1, 0, 0))):

```
f_normal_dot_unit_x = f.normal.normalized().dot(-unit_x)
```

If side_rib_only is True, we want only the faces on the side, which are roughly perpendicular to –X and have dot products with -unit_x that're almost 0:

```
if side_rib_only:
    if abs(f_normal_dot_unit_x) < 0.1:
        slide_back_face_loops.append(f)
```

Otherwise, we want to include both faces on the sides and on the back (that point away from the barrels). Faces on the back roughly oppose -X and therefore have their dot products with -unit_x close to –1. By setting the threshold to < 0.1, we'll include both dot products close to 0 (side faces) and close to –1 (back faces):

```
    else:
        if f_normal_dot_unit_x < 0.1:
            slide_back_face_loops.append(f)
```

While iterating, we'll also accumulate all selected faces in the list `slide_back_main_loop`, so we can call `get_y_span` (Listing 3-2) to get their width across Y (`barrel_back_y_span`), which we'll use to constrain the barrel generation later.

In the next block, we call `extrude_edge_loop_copy_move` (Listing 2-7) to extrude the cap. We then extrude again in place by calling `bpy.ops.mesh.extrude_region_move` with a zero translation, which is like hitting E, then enter without moving the extrusion, so there is extra geometry to close the top with while keeping it flat. In the following block, we select the top edge loop by calling `select_edge_loops` (Listing 2-8), then `bpy.ops.mesh.edge_collapse()` to close it.

Creating the Ribbed Detail

In Listing 3-7, we'll create the ribbed detail on the back of the slide. If the user-controlled parameter `side_rib_only` is `True`, the ribs are created only on the sides. If `False`, the ribs will wrap around the back as well.

Listing 3-7. Ninth block of generate_gun, where we create the ribbed detail on the back of the slide (see /Ch2/gun_generator.py)

```
fl = sorted(slide_back_face_loops, ↩
    key=lambda f: max([f.verts[i].co[1] for ↩
        i in range(4)]))
num_half = int(len(fl)/2)
fl_first_half = sorted(fl[:num_half], ↩
    key=lambda f: max([f.verts[i].co[0] for ↩
        i in range(4)]))
fl_sec_half = sorted(fl[num_half:], ↩
    key=lambda f: max([f.verts[i].co[0] for ↩
        i in range(4)]))
fl_first_half_to_inset = [fl_first_half[i] for ↩
        i in range(num_half) if i%2==1]
bmesh.ops.inset_region(bm, ↩
    faces=fl_first_half_to_inset, ↩
    thickness=0.2, depth=0.3)
fl_sec_half_to_inset = [fl_sec_half[i] for i in ↩
    range(num_half) if i%2==1]
```

```
bmesh.ops.inset_region(bm, ↩
    faces=fl_sec_half_to_inset, ↩
    thickness=0.2, depth=0.3)

bpy.ops.mesh.select_all(action='SELECT')
bpy.ops.mesh.remove_doubles()
bmesh.ops.recalc_face_normals(bm, faces=bm.faces)
bmesh.update_edit_mesh(grip_obj.data)
bpy.ops.object.mode_set(mode='OBJECT')
```

The list of faces we gathered in Listing 3-6 for creating ribs on the back of the slide (`slide_back_face_loops`) is not in order. Therefore, to outset *every other face* to create the ribs, we have to sort them first. We start by sorting the faces by their verts' largest Y. Since the gun is symmetrical across Y, doing so allows us to divide the faces in half, with each half on either side of the gun. Next, we sort each half of the faces by their verts' max X ascendingly—since the barrels point toward –X, this will sort them from front to back. We filter each ordered half to retain only every other face (the ones with odd indices) and *outset* them by calling `bmesh.ops.inset_region` with a *positive* `depth`. Since Python uses zero-based indexing, the second, fourth, sixth... faces with indices 1, 3, 5, ... and so on (counting from the barrel-side of the gun) will get outset, as shown on the right (A) of Figure 3-11. If we were to use a negative `depth` for `bmesh.ops.inset_region`, the faces will inset instead, which creates the effects shown on the left (B) of Figure 3-11.

We finish generating the rib detail by selecting all, removing doubles, recalculating normals, flushing mesh edits from `bm` to `grip_obj`, and switching to Object mode.

Figure 3-11. Creating the ribbed detail on the back of the slide. (A) Every other face is outset and wrapped around the back when `side_rib_only=False` (when True, the ribs are on the sides only). (B) If the faces are inset instead.

Generating the Barrels

In Listing 3-8, we'll create a new barrel object (`barrel_obj`), then generate and add the user-specified number of barrel meshes (`num_barrels`) to it via a `bmesh` instance (`bm2`). Recall that we previously derived the `barrel_obj` location (`barrel_locs_center`) along with the list of barrel centers (`barrel_loc_list`) and each barrel's radius (`barrel_radius`) in Listing 3-1, by calling `get_pos_inside_face_loop` (which is discussed in Listing 3-3 and illustrated in Figure 3-6).

Listing 3-8. Tenth block of generate_gun, where we create the barrel object (see /Ch2/gun_generator.py)

```
bm2, barrel_obj = get_placeholder_mesh_obj_and_bm( ↩
    context, name=name+"_barrel", ↩
    location=barrel_locs_center+Vector(location))
barrel_thickness_pcrt = 0.3

for barrel_loc in barrel_loc_list:
    bpy.ops.mesh.select_all(action='DESELECT')
```

```
    bmesh.ops.create_circle(bm2, cap_ends=False, ↩
        cap_tris=False, segments=num_cir_segments, ↩
        radius=barrel_radius)
    context.tool_settings.mesh_select_mode = ↩
        [True, False, False]
    bm2.verts.ensure_lookup_table()
    bm2.verts[-1].select = True
    bpy.ops.mesh.select_linked()
    offset = barrel_loc - barrel_locs_center
    bpy.ops.transform.translate( ↩
        value=(offset[0],offset[1],offset[2]), ↩
        orient_type='GLOBAL')
    bpy.ops.transform.rotate(value=1.5708, ↩
        orient_axis='Y', orient_type='LOCAL', ↩
        constraint_axis=(False,True,False), mirror=True)
    this_barrel_len = abs(frame_x_extent - barrel_loc[0])
    bpy.ops.mesh.extrude_region_move( ↩
        TRANSFORM_OT_translate={ ↩
            "value":(-this_barrel_len,0,0)})
    bm2.faces.ensure_lookup_table()
    bm2.faces[-1].select = True
    bpy.ops.mesh.select_linked()
    context.tool_settings.mesh_select_mode = ↩
        [False, False, True]
    barrel_thickness=barrel_thickness_pcrt*barrel_radius
    bpy.ops.mesh.extrude_region_shrink_fatten( ↩
        TRANSFORM_OT_shrink_fatten={ ↩
            "value":-barrel_thickness, ↩
            "use_even_offset":False, "mirror":False})

bm2.faces.ensure_lookup_table()
bpy.ops.mesh.select_all(action='SELECT')
raw_barrel_width = barrel_radius*2*num_barrels
raw_barrel_height = barrel_radius*2
target_height = min(max(raw_barrel_height, ↩
    slide_back_height), slide_back_height)
```

```
    height_scale = target_height/raw_barrel_height
    target_width = min(1, height_scale) * ↩
        (barrel_back_y_span-grip_top_y_span) ↩
        + grip_top_y_span
    width_scale = target_width/raw_barrel_width
    barrel_scale = min(height_scale, width_scale)

    bpy.ops.transform.translate( ↩
        value=(0,0,barrel_radius*barrel_scale), ↩
        orient_type='GLOBAL')
    bpy.ops.transform.resize(value= ↩
        (1,barrel_scale,barrel_scale), ↩
        orient_type='GLOBAL')

    bpy.ops.mesh.remove_doubles()
    bmesh.ops.recalc_face_normals(bm2, faces=bm2.faces)
    bmesh.update_edit_mesh(barrel_obj.data)
    bpy.ops.object.mode_set(mode='OBJECT')
```

We start by creating a mesh object for the barrels (`barrel_obj`) with empty mesh data and a `bmesh` instance (`bm2`) for editing it, by calling `get_placeholder_mesh_obj_and_bm` (Listing 2-1). Recall that the barrel object location `barrel_locs_center` we derived is in terms of `grip_obj`'s face loop (therefore in `grip_obj`'s local coordinate system). To get the barrel object location in the global coordinate system, we have to add `grip_obj`'s location (`location`).

We iterate through the list of barrel centers (`barrel_loc_list`) and extrude the barrels one by one from circular cross-sections. For each barrel, we call `bmesh.ops.create_circle` with `cap_tris=False` (do not fill in with face) to create a circle as its cross-section. Since `bmesh.ops.create_circle` does *not* let you specify a location, we must move the circle into place postcreation. To do so, we select the circle by selecting its last vertex (`bm.verts[-1]`) and select linked. Then call `bpy.ops.transform.translate` to move it based on its offset from `barrel_locs_center`. At this point, the circle is on the XY plane, but we need it on the YZ plane, so we call `bpy.ops.transform.rotate` to rotate it 90 degrees around Y (1.5708 radians). With the circle in place, we extrude it along –X into a tube by calling `bpy.ops.mesh.extrude_region_move`. Next, we give the barrel thickness by extruding inward along normals. To do so, we select the tube by selecting its last face (`bm.faces[-1]`) and select linked, change to Face select mode, then call bpy.ops.mesh.extrude_region_shrink_fatten to extrude along normals. We set the extrusion amount (barrel thickness) to 30% of the barrel radius. Note that since we're extruding *inward*, the extrusion amount needs to be *negative*.

Since the barrel centers we previously derived are at the top of the grip, we need to move them upward into place and scale them to fit inside the back of the slide, as shown in Figure 3-12. The barrels are laid out side by side; therefore, the overall barrel height is simply twice the barrel radius. The height_scale will then be at most the ratio to scale the barrels to the height of the back of the slide (slide_back_height). The width limit is more complicated, however, since the width of the back of the slide tapers toward the top, so we must interpolate based on how high the barrels come up (imagine going up a trapezoid from the bottom, as shown in Figure 3-12):

```
target_width = min(1, height_scale)* ↩
    (barrel_back_y_span-grip_top_y_span)+grip_top_y_span
```

The width at the bottom of the trapezoid is grip_top_y_span and at the top is barrel_back_y_span. To find the width limit, we start at the bottom, then interpolate by scaling the range (the difference between the top and bottom) with height_scale. We then calculate width_scale by dividing the width limit (target_width) by the total barrel width, which is the number of barrels times each barrel's diameter (barrel radius * 2). Since we want to maintain the barrels' aspect ratio and keep them cylindrical, the overall scale factor, barrel_scale, is the minimum of height_scale and width_scale.

With the scaling factors computed, we move the barrels into place by calling bpy.ops.transform.translate with a Z offset of barrel_radius*barrel_scale so the bottom of the barrels sit level with the back of the slide and scale the barrels by calling bpy.ops.transform.resize with barrel_scale along Y and Z. We wrap up the barrel generation by removing doubles, recalculating normals, flushing mesh edits from bm2 to barrel_obj, and switching to Object mode.

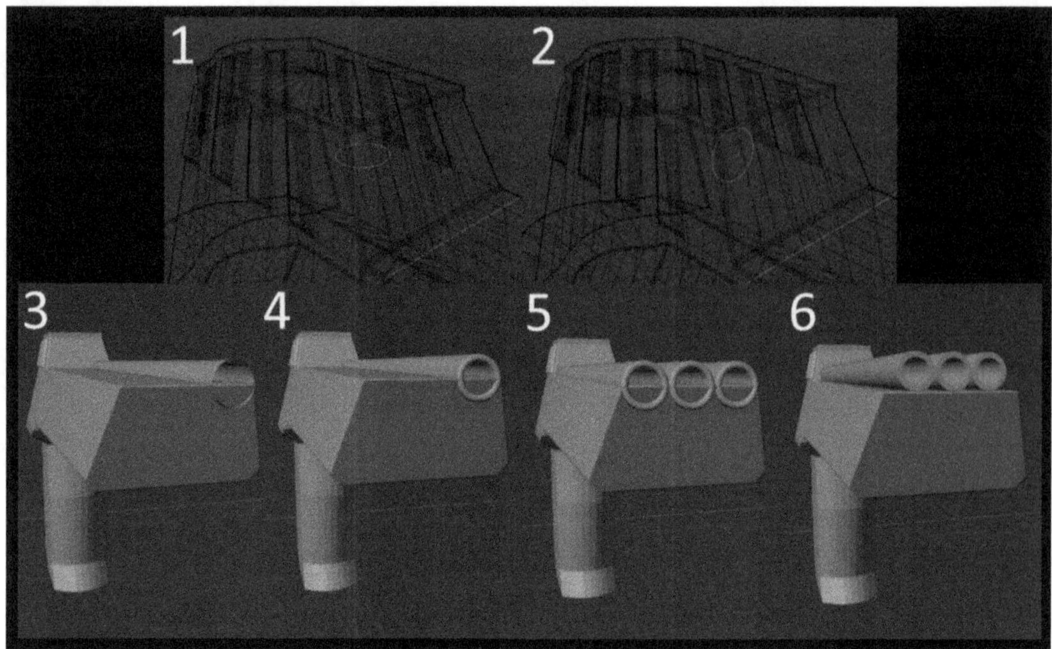

Figure 3-12. *Steps for generating the barrel object. (1) Each barrel mesh starts out as a circle primitive that is moved into place relative to the object origin. (2) The circle is rotated 90 degrees around Y so it lies on the YZ plane. (3) The circle is extruded into an open-ended cylinder. (4) The cylinder is extruded inward along normals (negative extrusion amount) to create thickness for the barrel. (5) All barrel meshes generated. (6) Barrels moved into place and scaled relative to the back of the slide.*

Generating the Trigger

In Listing 3-9, we'll create a trigger object (`trigger_obj`), then add the frame and pull pieces to its mesh data via a `bmesh` instance (`bm3`). Recall that we derived the `trigger_obj`'s location (`trigger_loc`) and radius (`trigger_radius`) in Listing 3-5.

Listing 3-9. Eleventh block of generate_gun, where we create the trigger object (see /Ch2/gun_generator.py)

```
bm3, trigger_obj = get_placeholder_mesh_obj_and_bm( ↩
    context, name=name+"_trigger", ↩
    location=trigger_loc+Vector(location))
cir_radius = trigger_radius*(1/cos(radians(45)))
```

```
trigger_frame_thickness = base_radius/2
bmesh.ops.create_cone(bm3, cap_ends=False, ↩
    cap_tris=False, segments=4, radius1=cir_radius, ↩
    radius2=cir_radius, depth=trigger_frame_thickness)
bpy.ops.mesh.select_all(action='SELECT')
bpy.ops.transform.rotate(value=radians(45), ↩
    orient_axis='Z', orient_type='GLOBAL')
bpy.ops.transform.rotate(value=radians(90), ↩
    orient_axis='X', orient_type='GLOBAL')
bpy.ops.transform.resize(value=(1.5,1,1), ↩
    orient_type='GLOBAL', ↩
    constraint_axis=(True,False,False), ↩
    mirror=True)
bpy.ops.mesh.extrude_region_shrink_fatten( ↩
    TRANSFORM_OT_shrink_fatten={ ↩
        "value":trigger_radius*0.5, ↩
        "use_even_offset":False, "mirror":False})
bpy.ops.mesh.select_all(action='DESELECT')

pull_z_tolerance = frame_height
x_start = sqrt((trigger_radius+pull_z_tolerance+2)/0.35)
x_end = -(x_start/5)
finger_pull_thickness = trigger_frame_thickness/2
x_offset = 0 if stylize else -0.5*trigger_radius
create_finger_pull_xz(context, x_start, x_end, bm3, ↩
    x_offset, finger_pull_thickness)

bpy.ops.mesh.remove_doubles()
bmesh.ops.recalc_face_normals(bm3, faces=bm3.faces)
bmesh.update_edit_mesh(trigger_obj.data)
bpy.ops.object.mode_set(mode='OBJECT')
```

We start by creating a mesh object for the trigger (`trigger_obj`) with empty mesh data and a bmesh instance (`bm3`) for editing it, by calling `get_placeholder_mesh_obj_and_bm` (Listing 2-1). Recall that the `trigger_loc` we derived is in terms of `grip_obj`'s vertices (therefore in `grip_obj`'s local coordinate system). To get the trigger location in the global coordinate system, we have to add `grip_obj`'s location transform (`location`).

Next, we generate a four-segment tube as the start of the trigger frame and add it to `trigger_obj` via `bm3`. Since the `trigger_radius` we computed before is half the side of a square, we convert it to a circle radius (`cir_radius`) by dividing it with cos(45 deg), as shown in Figure 3-13. We call `bmesh.ops.create_cone` with the same value for `radius1` and `radius2` to make a cylindrical shape, `cap_tris=False` to make it open on both ends so it's a tube, and `segments=4` so the cross-section is a square. The tube height (`depth`), which becomes the trigger thickness, is constrained to half the grip thickness. At creation, the tube is on the XY plane, but we need it on the XZ plane instead, so we rotate it 45 degrees around Z and 90 degrees around X, as shown in Figure 3-13. We then scale it 1.5 along X to make it rectangular and extrude along normals by calling `bpy.ops.mesh.extrude_region_shrink_fatten` to give it thickness.

Next, we'll create the finger pull using the parabolic curve:

$$z = 0.35 \cdot x^2 - 2$$

(which is explained in detail in the next section). We know the pull height needs to be the `trigger_radius` (half the side of the square) along Z, since it sits on the XZ plane. We also want the top of the pull to embed into the trigger frame, so we add a tolerance to the Z value (`pull_z_tolerance`). We then rearrange the parabolic equation and work out the starting X value as follows:

$$z = 0.35 \cdot x^2 - 2$$

$$(z+2) = 0.35 \cdot x^2$$

$$\frac{(z+2)}{0.35} = x^2$$

$$x = \sqrt{\frac{(z+2)}{0.35}}$$

Plugging in `z=trigger_radius+pull_z_tolerance` in the last step of the above derivation, we get

```
x_start = sqrt((trigger_radius+pull_z_tolerance+2)/0.35)
```

where `sqrt` is a built-in function under Python's `math` module, which calculates the square root of a number.

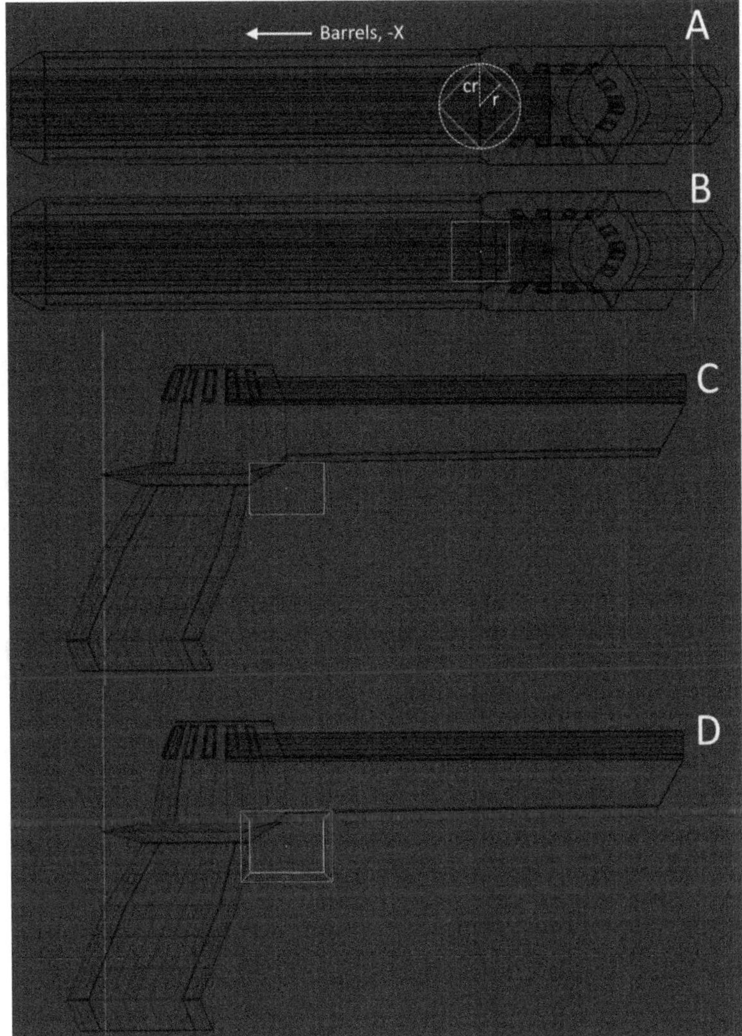

Figure 3-13. *Steps for generating the trigger frame. (A) Generation starts with a tube mesh with square (four-segment circle) cross-sections. The cross-section radius cr (`cir_radius` in Listing 3-9) is equal to r/cos(45 deg), where r is `trigger_radius` in Listing 3-9. (B) The tube mesh is rotated 45 degrees around Z, (C) 90 degrees around X, then scaled 1.5 along X. (D) Finally, the tube mesh is extruded along normals to create thickness.*

As shown in Figure 3-14, `x_end` is the amount that you want the parabolic curve to go over the "center line" (therefore, how pronounced you want the "hook" for the pull to be). I find that using a fifth the width of `x_start` for `x_end` works well (`x_end = -(x_start/5)`). As for the pull thickness, constraining it to half the trigger frame thickness looks reasonable. With the pull params decided, we can now call the helper function `create_finger_pull_xz` (Listing 3-10) to generate the pull, which is explained step by step in the next section.

We wrap up the trigger generation by removing doubles, recalculating normals, flushing mesh edits from `bm3` to `trigger_obj`, and switching to Object mode.

Generating the Trigger Pull Using a Parabola

In Listing 3-10, we'll take a closer look at the helper function `create_finger_pull_xz` we used to generate the trigger pull in Listing 3-9. At a glance, the function creates an edge chain from a parabolic curve with given start and end X values, then duplicates the chain, and rotates it to form the outline of the pull shape with the original chain. The two chains are then merged and filled in with a n-gon and extruded to create thickness.

Listing 3-10. Generating a trigger pull mesh using a parabola and adding it to the object via the given bmesh instance (see /Ch2/gun_generator.py)

```
def create_finger_pull_xz(context, x_start, x_end, bm, ↩
    x_offset=0, pull_thickness=1):
    num_divs = 10
    x_step = (x_end-x_start)/num_divs
    x_steps = [x_start+x_step*i for i in range(num_divs+1)]
    for x in x_steps:
        bmesh.ops.create_vert(bm, co= ↩
            Vector((x+x_offset, 0, 0.35*x*x-2)))
    bm.verts.ensure_lookup_table()
    start_v_idx = len(bm.verts)-(num_divs+1)
    for i in range(start_v_idx, start_v_idx+num_divs, 1):
        bmesh.ops.contextual_create(bm, geom=[bm.verts[i], ↩
            bm.verts[i+1]], mat_nr=0, use_smooth=False)

    context.tool_settings.mesh_select_mode = ↩
        [True, False, False]
    bm.verts.ensure_lookup_table()
    bm.verts[-1].select = True
    bpy.ops.mesh.select_linked()
```

```
bpy.ops.mesh.duplicate_move( ↩
    MESH_OT_duplicate={"mode":1}, ↩
    TRANSFORM_OT_translate={"value":(0,0,0)})

bpy.ops.mesh.select_all(action='DESELECT')
bm.verts.ensure_lookup_table()
bm.verts[-1].select = True
bpy.ops.mesh.select_linked()
rot = Matrix.Rotation(radians(-30.0), 3, 'Y')
bmesh.ops.rotate(bm, cent=bm.verts[-1].co, matrix=rot, ↩
    verts=bm.verts[len(bm.verts)-(num_divs+1):])

bm.verts[len(bm.verts)-(num_divs+1)-1].select = True
bpy.ops.mesh.select_linked()

bpy.ops.mesh.bridge_edge_loops()
bpy.ops.mesh.dissolve_faces()
bpy.ops.mesh.remove_doubles()

half_pull_thickness = pull_thickness/2
bpy.ops.mesh.extrude_region_move( ↩
    TRANSFORM_OT_translate={"value": ↩
        (0,0,half_pull_thickness), ↩
        "orient_type":'NORMAL', ↩
        "orient_matrix_type":'NORMAL', ↩
        "constraint_axis":(False,False,True)})

context.tool_settings.mesh_select_mode = ↩
    [False, False, True]
bm.faces.ensure_lookup_table()
sel_f_normal = None
selected_f_area = 0
for f in bm.faces:
    if f.select:
        sel_f_normal = f.normal.normalized()
        selected_f_area = f.calc_area()
        break
```

```
cos_150 = cos(radians(150))
if sel_f_normal:
    for f in bm.faces:
        if not f.select:
            if isclose(f.calc_area(), ↩
                selected_f_area, rel_tol=0.05) and ↩
                f.normal.normalized().dot(sel_f_normal)
                    < cos_150:

                bpy.ops.mesh.select_all( ↩
                    action='DESELECT')
                f.select = True
                bpy.ops.mesh.extrude_region_move( ↩
                    TRANSFORM_OT_translate={ ↩
                        "value": ↩
                            (0,0,half_pull_thickness),
                        "orient_type":'NORMAL', ↩
                        "orient_matrix_type":'NORMAL',↩
                        "constraint_axis": ↩
                            (False,False,True)})

                bpy.ops.mesh.select_all( ↩
                    action='DESELECT')
                break
```

The parabolic curve we'll use as the template for the pull shape is

$$z = 0.35 \cdot x^2 - 2$$

as shown in Figure 3-14. Imagine using this formula to create verts on the XZ plane, with X values ranging from x_start to x_end (inclusive), at 10% X increments (step size of (x_end-x_start)/10). At each X value, we call bmesh.ops.create_vert to add a new vert with zero Y and Z at

$$0.35 \cdot x^2 - 2$$

to the passed in bmesh instance bm and use bmesh.ops.contextual_create to connect adjacent verts pairwise with an edge. Note that the caller can pass in an x_offset to offset each X value, thus shifting all the verts by x_offset. An example of the resulting edge chain is shown as (1) on the right side of Figure 3-14. Recall that bmesh verts are indexed in the order of their creation. Therefore, the 11 verts we've just created are at the 11 slots at the end of bm.verts.

Tip bmesh.ops.contextual_create will create geometry in the context of the list of geometry passed in. For example, if you give it a list of edges, it will fill them with faces. If you give it a list of verts, it will create edges between them.

Next, we set Mesh Select Mode to Vert, then select the edge chain we just formed, by selecting its last vertex (bm.verts[-1]) and calling bpy.ops.mesh.select_linked() to select linked (Ctrl-L or Select ➤ Select Linked ➤ Linked). We then duplicate the chain by calling bpy.ops.mesh.duplicate_move. Right after duplication, the copy will be at the same location as the original. We want to rotate the copy pivoting at its "hook end," so afterward it forms the trigger pull shape with the original, as shown in Figure 3-14. To do so, we deselect all, then select the copy by selecting its last vert (bm.verts[-1]) followed by select linked (bpy.ops.mesh.select_linked()). We then create a rotation matrix rot for rotating –30 degrees around Y (Matrix.Rotation(radians(-30.0), 3, 'Y')) and use it to call bmesh.ops.rotate to rotate the duplicate with the center of rotation at the chain's last vert (cent=bm.verts[-1].co). The duplicate chain is passed to bmesh.ops.rotate as the last 11 verts of bm.verts. Note that when the edge chain is duplicated, the copy is added as new geometry at the end of bm.verts and bm.edges. Therefore, the duplicate's verts are the last 11 verts in bm.verts. After the rotation, the two chains (original and copy) will look like the right side of Figure 3-14 and form a trigger pull shape.

With the duplicate chain still selected, we want to now also select the original chain. We'll do so by selecting the 12th vert counting back from the end of bm.verts (skipping the 11 that belong to the duplicate), then select linked. With both chains selected, we call bpy.ops.mesh.bridge_edge_loops() to fill the area between the two chains with a n-gon, then bpy.ops.mesh.dissolve_faces() and bpy.ops.mesh.remove_doubles() to clean up (recall that the two chains overlapped at one end by a vertex). The result of this step is shown in Figure 3-15.

Next, we'll create thickness for the pull. Since the pull face is centered on the gun along Y, we'll extrude it outward along both Y and –Y, as shown in Figure 3-16. With the pull face still selected, we call bpy.ops.mesh.extrude_region_move with half the thickness passed in to extrude the first half along normals, constrained to Z.

To extrude the second half, we need to go back and select the pull face on the *opposite side* of the first extrusion. Since many faces on the trigger frame have normals in that direction, normal alone won't uniquely identify it. However, we *can* look for a combination of a face area matching the first pull face, *plus* a normal that's in the opposite direction.

Let's walk through this process in Python. We call `bm.faces.ensure_lookup_table()` to refresh `bm`'s face indices, then iterate through `bm.faces` to find the selected face (that's the pull face atop the first extrusion). We compute its normalized normal and area (`selected_f_area = f.calc_area()`) and break out of the loop.

Next, we iterate through `bm.faces` again, this time looking for an *unselected* face with an area almost identical to `selected_f_area` and a normal in the opposite direction. We compare two face areas using Python's built-in function `is_close`:

```
isclose(f.calc_area(), selected_f_area, rel_tol=0.05)
```

`isclose` compares its first two arguments to see if the difference is at most `rel_tol`; if so, it returns `True`, and `False` otherwise. Here, we use `isclose` to check if a face's area is within 0.05 of `selected_f_area`.

To see if a face is on the opposite side of the first extrusion, we check if the dot product of its normalized normal and `sel_f_normal` is close to −1:

```
f.normal.normalized().dot(sel_f_normal) < cos_150
```

where `cos_150 = cos(radians(150))`. In other words, a face qualifies if the angle between its normal and `sel_f_normal` is > 150 degrees. Once the face is found, we select it and call `bpy.ops.mesh.extrude_region_move` to extrude it half the thickness along normals constrained to Z. Since this face's normal points in the opposite direction of the first extrusion, it extrudes the other way, which is what we want. The result of the extrusion is shown in Figure 3-16.

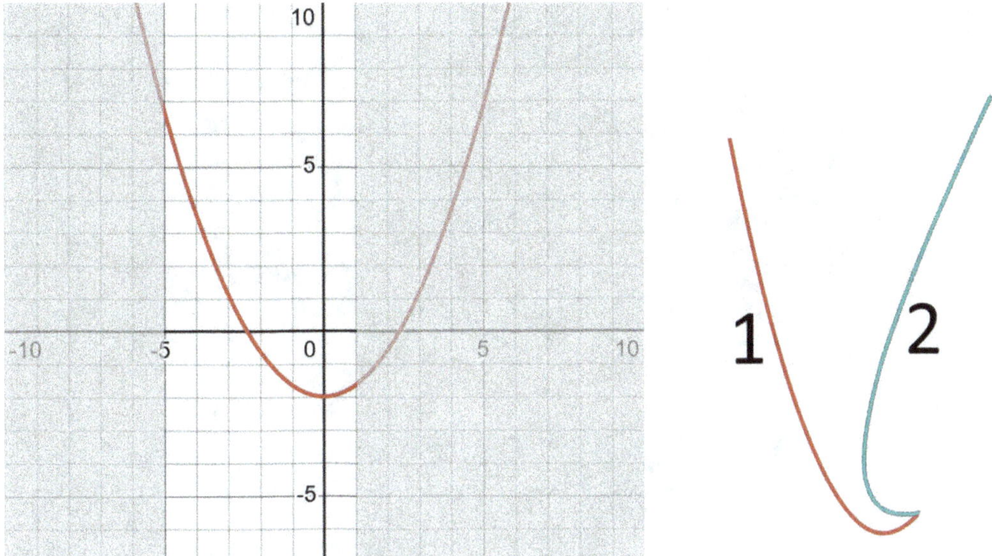

Figure 3-14. *Creating edge chains to outline the trigger pull. Left: red curve is $z = 0.35 \cdot x^2 - 2$ which is the parabola used in Listing 3-10. The window framed by the gray portions has x_start = -5 and x_end = 1. Right: (1) An edge chain is created based on the partial parabola from the left and (2) duplicated, with the copy rotated with the end point of (1) as the pivot. Together (1) and (2) form the outline of the trigger pull.*

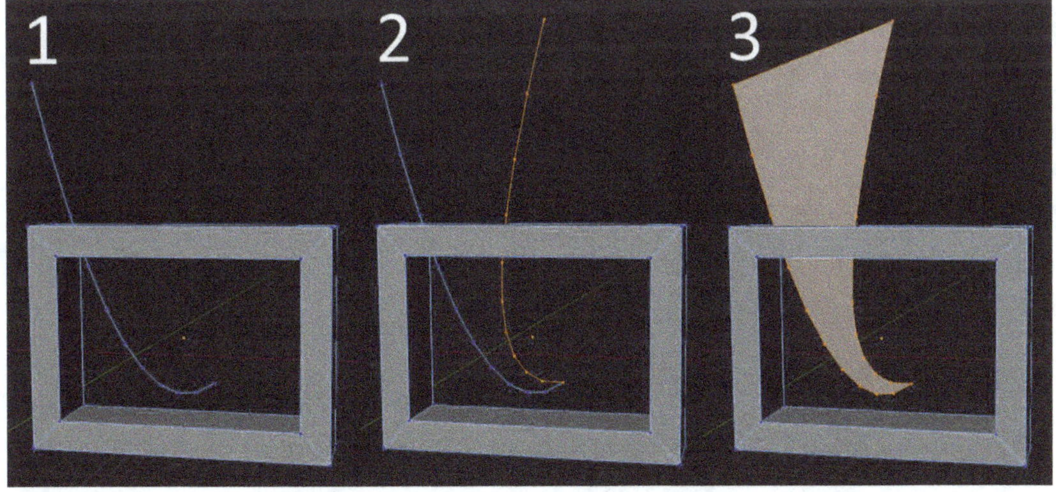

Figure 3-15. *(1) Creating an edge chain using $z = 0.35 \cdot x^2 - 2$ with the given X range (x_start to x_end). (2) Duplicating (1) and rotating the copy, pivoting on its last vert. (3) Using Bridge Edge Loops to fill the space between the two edge chains with an n-gon, to create the flat pull piece.*

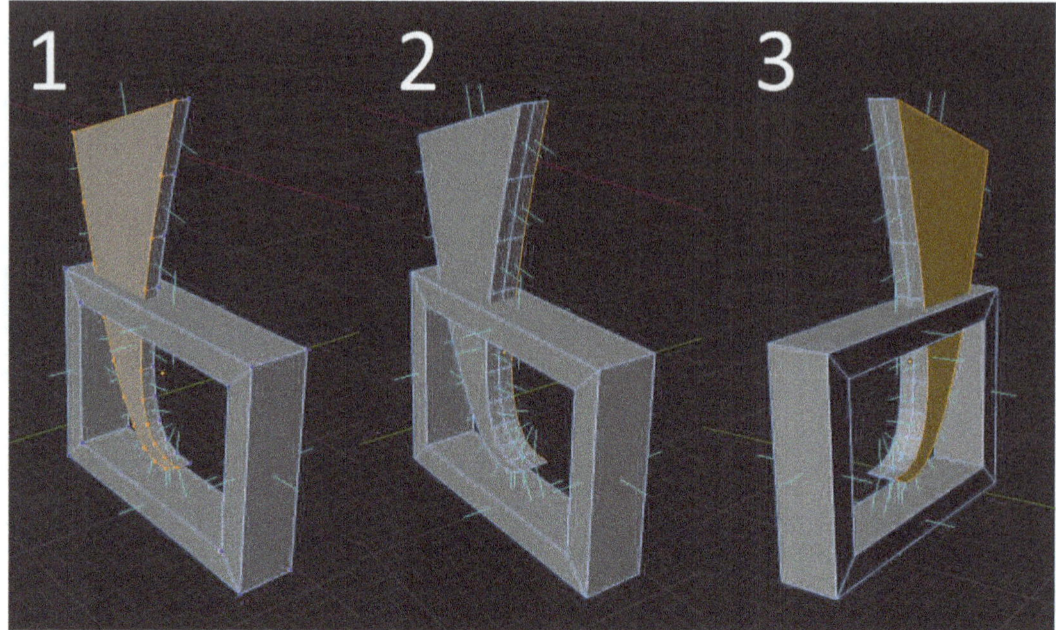

Figure 3-16. *(1) Extruding the first half of the thickness for the trigger pull. (2) Extruding the second half of the thickness in the opposite direction. (3) Alternative view of (2)*

Applying Transforms and Adding Modifiers

At this point, we've finished generating all the meshes for the gun. Woot! In this section, we'll wrap up by applying transforms and adding modifiers, as shown in Listing 3-11.

Listing 3-11. Twelfth block of generate_gun, where we apply transforms and add modifiers to all mesh objects that constitute the gun model (see /Ch2/gun_generator.py)

```
bpy.ops.object.select_all(action='DESELECT')
gun_objs = [grip_obj, barrel_obj, trigger_obj]
bevel_width = [2, 2, 1]
for i in range(len(gun_objs)):
    obj = gun_objs[i]
    obj.select_set(True)
    add_bevel_modifier(obj, width=bevel_width[i], ↩
        segments=3)
```

```
    bpy.ops.object.transform_apply(location=True, ↩
        rotation=False, scale=False)
    bpy.ops.object.origin_set( ↩
        type='ORIGIN_CENTER_OF_VOLUME', center='MEDIAN')
    add_simple_deform_taper_modifier(trigger_obj)

    bpy.ops.object.select_all(action='DESELECT')
```

We start by deselecting all. Then set up the three mesh objects comprising the gun model in a list, with a corresponding list of bevel widths, for easy iteration. We then iterate through these objects, selecting and adding a bevel modifier to each by calling the helper function add_bevel_modifier (discussed next in Listing 3-12).

With the three objects selected, we apply location transform next by calling bpy.ops.object.transform_apply with location=True (which is equivalent to Ctrl-A ➤ Location in the viewport). After that, we set the objects' origin to center of volume via bpy.ops.object.origin_set with type='ORIGIN_CENTER_OF_VOLUME' (which is the same as Object ➤ Set Origin ➤ Object to Center of Mass (Volume)). These two steps are necessary to ensure that the Simple Deform modifier we're adding to trigger_obj next (via add_simple_deform_taper_modifier in Listing 3-13) will behave correctly. We finish by deselecting all.

Adding a Bevel Modifier to a Mesh Object

If you need to add a modifier to multiple objects, it's easier to write a helper function to do so, like add_bevel_modifier in Listing 3-12, which adds a Bevel modifier to a given mesh object with the specified width and number of segments. Here, the modifier is always set up to bevel edges ('EDGES'); you can change it to bevel verts ('VERTICES') instead.

Listing 3-12. Helper function to add a Bevel modifier to a given mesh object (see /Ch2/gun_generator.py)

```
def add_bevel_modifier(obj, width=2, segments=3):
    bevel_mod = obj.modifiers.new(obj.name+"_bevel_mod", ↩
        'BEVEL')
    bevel_mod.affect = 'EDGES'
    bevel_mod.width = width
    bevel_mod.segments = segments
    return bevel_mod
```

In general, you can add a modifier of `<type>` to a mesh object `<obj>` via the following line:

```
mod = <obj>.modifiers.new(<name>, <type>)
```

You can find a modifier's `<type>` Enum string by adding it to a test object and checking the corresponding call logged in the Info Editor. Likewise, to find the variable for a modifier's property (e.g., `segments` for segments for Bevel), you can change that property's value through the UI and see what gets logged in the Info Editor (e.g., `bpy.context.object.modifiers["1_bevel_mod"].segments = 4`).

Another way to find the Python equivalent of Blender menu options and hot keys is through Python Tooltips, which can be enabled by checking the User Tooltips and Python Tooltips boxes under Edit ➤ Preferences... ➤ Interface ➤ Display, as shown in Figure 3-17 (ensure that both boxes are checked–the first checkbox enables tooltips in general, while the second shows the Python value inside the tooltip). Once Python Tooltips is enabled, you can go to Properties Editor ➤ Modifier tab, click the Add Modifier button as if you are going to add a modifier, then hover over a modifier in the menu—in the tooltip that appears, you'll see a line at the bottom that shows its Python equivalent, as shown in Figure 3-18. Once a modifier is added, you can hover over any of its properties to find out that property's Python equivalent as well, as shown in Figure 3-19 (ensure that you hover over the property's widget (e.g., slider), not its text label).

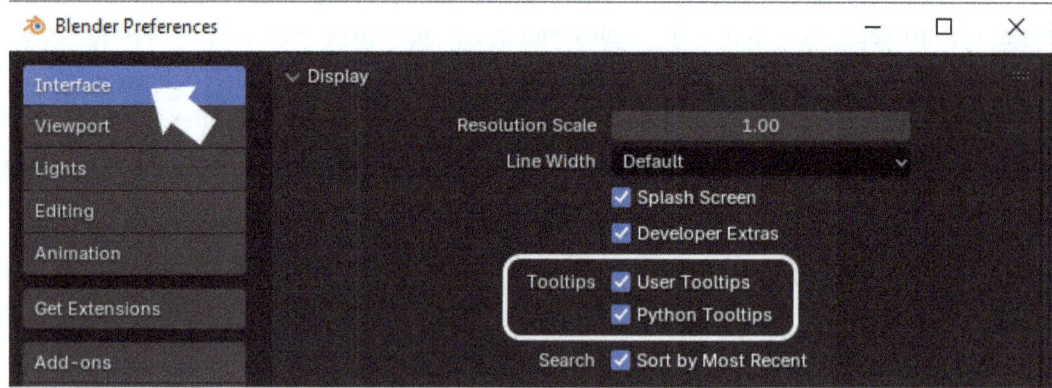

Figure 3-17. *You can enable Python Tooltips by going to Edit ➤ Preferences... ➤ Interface; then under Display ➤ Tooltips, check both the User Tooltips and Python Tooltips checkboxes.*

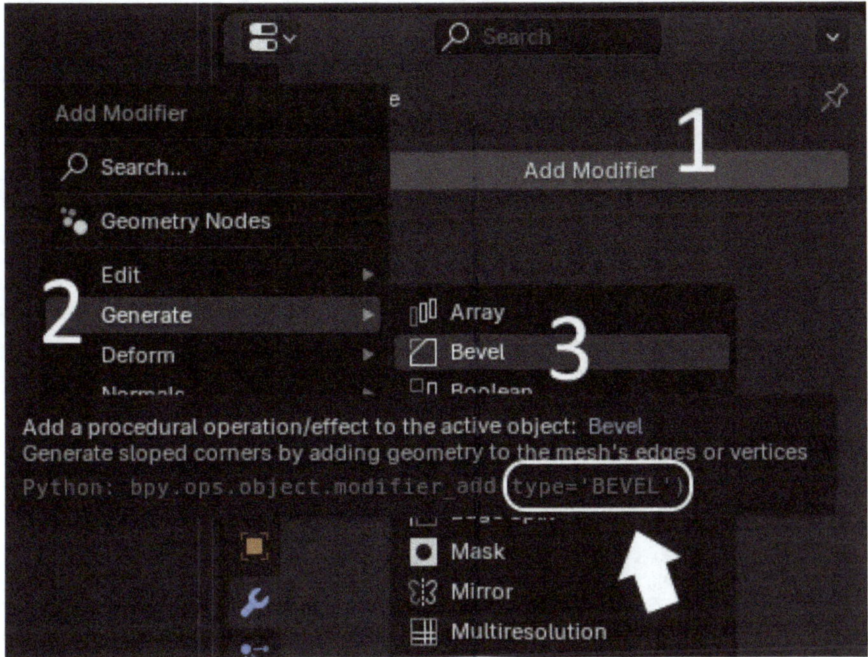

Figure 3-18. *Once Python Tooltips is enabled (Figure 3-17), you can find a modifier's corresponding Python Enum value in the tooltip that appears when you hover over it in the menu. For example, to find the Enum value for the Bevel modifier, go to Properties Editor ➤ Modifier tab ➤ (1) Add Modifier ➤ (2) Generate, then (3) hover over Bevel in the menu with your mouse, in the tooltip that appears you'll find the type is 'BEVEL' (circled).*

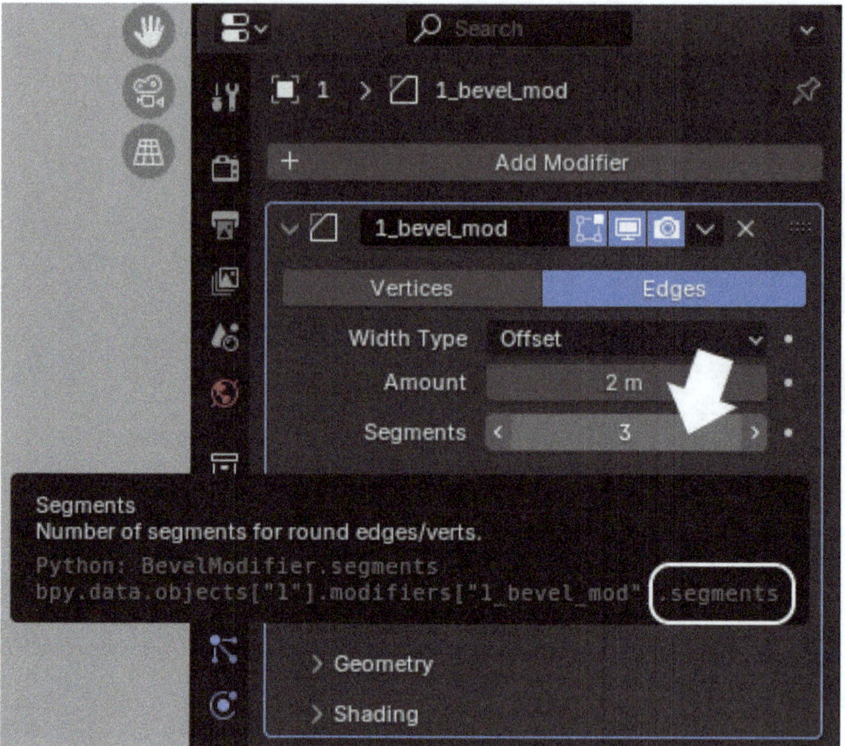

Figure 3-19. *Once Python Tooltips is enabled (Figure 3-17), you can find a modifier property's corresponding Python variable in the tooltip that pops up when you hover over the property's UI widget with your mouse.*

Note Blender follows PEP8 for styling Python code with some customizations, one of which being string literals for specifying `Enum` values need to be enclosed by single quotes, while all other strings by double quotes. For example, in Listing 3-12, the value `'EDGES'` assigned to the Bevel modifier instance's `affect` variable is one of several `Enum` values, therefore should be surrounded by single quotes. The `"_bevel_mod"` value used in part as the modifier's name is a non-`Enum` string literal, therefore should be enclosed by double quotes.

Adding a Simple Deform Modifier to Taper a Mesh Object

`add_simple_deform_taper_modifier` in Listing 3-13 is called in Listing 3-11 to give the trigger object a slight taper so it doesn't appear as boxy. The code is structured in a similar way as Listing 3-12.

Listing 3-13. Helper function to add a Simple Deform modifier and set it to taper a given mesh object (see /Ch2/gun_generator.py)

```
def add_simple_deform_taper_modifier(obj):
    taper_deform_mod = obj.modifiers.new( ↩
        obj.name+"_taper_simple_deform_mod", 'SIMPLE_DEFORM')
    taper_deform_mod.deform_method = 'TAPER'
    taper_deform_mod.factor = 0.135
    taper_deform_mod.deform_axis = 'X'
    return taper_deform_mod
```

Summary

In this chapter, you continued to implement the procedural game weapon generator in Blender Python. Picking up where you left off in Chapter 2, you extruded from the top of the grip to form the transition into the frame. You then wrote two utility functions to analyze the face loop atop the grip to locate the faces at the front to extrude into the frame and calculated the positions and dimensions for the barrel(s). To refine the frame, you rotated its tip to recess it inward and searched for its outer bottom edges to bevel. After that, you extruded upward to build the back of the slide and analyzed its face loops with dot products to outset every other face to create the ribbed detail.

With the first part of the gun generated, next you created a separate mesh object and `bmesh` instance to generate the barrels. You created each barrel mesh by generating a circle primitive, moving it into place, extruding it lengthwise to form a cylinder, then extruding along normals inward to give it thickness. Finally, you created a third and final mesh object to generate the trigger and learned to use a parabolic curve to create the basis for a finger pull. To finish up, you cleaned up by correcting normals, removing doubles, and applying transforms. You then added Bevel modifiers to soften the edges and a Simple Deform modifier to taper the trigger so it looks less boxy.

CHAPTER 4

Generating Materials with Geometry Nodes, Python, and Shader Nodes

In this chapter, you'll continue to build on the game weapon generator you've created in Chapters 2 and 3, by adding code to unwrap and generate materials for different parts of the gun. We'll begin by using geometry nodes to create a circular bump grid, then write Python code to bake a normal map from it to build the gun grip's shader node tree, to emulate 3D detail without the expense of actual geometry. After that, we'll build a second geometry node tree to generate a custom cross-motif grid to bake a more complex normal map for the gun's grip. With these two projects under your belt, you'll have developed the skills necessary to generate normal maps for any project.

In the second part of the chapter, we'll generate shader node trees for various metallic materials using Blender Python, including shiny, brushed, and a fine-gridded pattern that can be colored gold, silver, copper, or any color of your choice. Finally, we'll adapt the weapon generator code to automatically unwrap and assign the procedural materials to various parts of the gun.

Running This Chapter's Examples

This chapter's examples consist of Python scripts (`*.py` files) as well as `*.blend` files that include geometry node trees and shader node trees. **The source code and color figures for this book are available on GitHub via the book's product page, located at**

I. Lupiani, *Procedural Content Generation for Games*, https://doi.org/10.1007/979-8-8688-1787-8_4

https://link.springer.com/book/9798868817861. Navigate to the /Ch4 folder in the downloaded files, and when prompted by the text, open each *.blend file with File ➤ Open...(Ctrl-O) and each *.py file in the Text Editor under the Scripting workspace. At the bottom of each script, you'll find an `if __name__ == "__main__"` block already set up with calls to the code listings with sample arguments, which you can easily modify to experiment with.

Scripts Overview

This chapter's Python examples are implemented across three scripts. The first is /Ch4/gun_generator.py, which is a modified version of the game weapon generator from Chapters 2 and 3 that unwraps and generates material for each part of the gun; the second is /Ch4/texture_material_generation.py, which contains functions that generate various normal maps and shader node trees used by /Ch4/gun_generator.py; the third is /Ch4/material_and_image_utils.py, which provides utility functions for saving images, creating materials, and editing nodes used by /Ch4/texture_material_generation.py. The imports in these scripts have been set up for you. You can refer to the section "Handling Imports for Scripts to Run in the Text Editor" in Chapter 2 for more detail on how to set up imports for scripts run from the Text Editor.

Blend and Other Files Overview

Here is an overview of the *.blend and other files supplied in the downloaded source. The usage of each file will be detailed throughout the chapter.

- /Ch4/round_bumps.blend
    - Use in conjunction with /Ch4/texture_material_generation.py to generate a normal map as part of the material for the gun grip.
    - /Ch4/round_bumps_normal_map_generated.blend shows the state of the file after the normal map is generated.
    - /Ch4/round_bumps_normal_map.png is a copy of the generated normal map saved to disk as image.

- /Ch4/cross_motif_grid.blend
    - Use in conjunction with /Ch4/texture_material_generation.py to generate a normal map as part of the material for the gun grip.
    - The file /Ch4/cross_motif_grid_normal_map_generated.blend shows the state of the file after the normal map is generated.
    - /Ch4/cross_motif_grid_normal_map.png is a copy of the generated normal map saved to disk as image.
- pcg_mats_for_guns_demo.blend contains the five sample procedural gun models shown in Figure 4-27.

Installing Dependencies

Some of the util functions for material generation that we'll implement later in this chapter require NumPy, an open source Python library for scientific computing. Please refer to the Appendix for instructions on how to install numpy and other third-party Python packages under Blender Python.

Baking a Normal Map from a Procedural Mesh

In this section, we'll use geometry nodes to generate a bump grid mesh, which we'll utilize in conjunction with Python code to bake a normal map for simulating 3D detail on the gun grip, as shown in Figure 4-1. We'll start with an overview of geometry nodes, then build the tree to generate the grid mesh. Along the way, we'll learn how to write the normal map as a *.png file to disk.

Figure 4-1. *Example of a gun model produced by the game weapon generator (Chapters 2, 3, and 4) with a procedural normal map applied to the grip to simulate surface bumps*

Generating a Circular Bump Grid Mesh Using Geometry Nodes

Geometry nodes is Blender's visual scripting system for generating and editing 3D geometry. You build up a geometry node tree by adding and connecting one node's output(s) to the next node's input(s). A geometry node tree is created as a modifier on an existing mesh object. In addition to the object it is set up with, a geometry node tree can access other curve or mesh objects in the 3D viewport as well as materials from shader trees. You can set up user inputs for a geometry node tree to control its behavior, as we'll see shortly.

Generating a Single Circular Bump

I believe the best way to learn geometry nodes is to make something with them, which is what we'll do. In this section, we'll jump right in and generate a circular bump mesh that will serve as a single unit in the grid mesh we'll create next.

Start with a default startup `*.blend` file and head to the Geometry Nodes workspace. Select the Cube object, then click the +New button at the top of the geometry nodes editor to create a new tree, which is automatically added to Cube as a modifier, as shown in Figure 4-2. Upon its creation, a tree has two nodes—a Group Input node and a Group Output node. The Group Input node's "Geometry" socket is set up with the data of the object you added the tree to by default, which in this case is Cube's mesh data. When you add input parameters to the tree, they'll show up in the Group Input node as well. The Group Output node has one socket called "Geometry"—which is the tree output preview that will display in the viewport. Initially, the Group Input node's "Geometry" output is connected to the Group Output node's "Geometry" input; therefore, the Cube shows up as the preview.

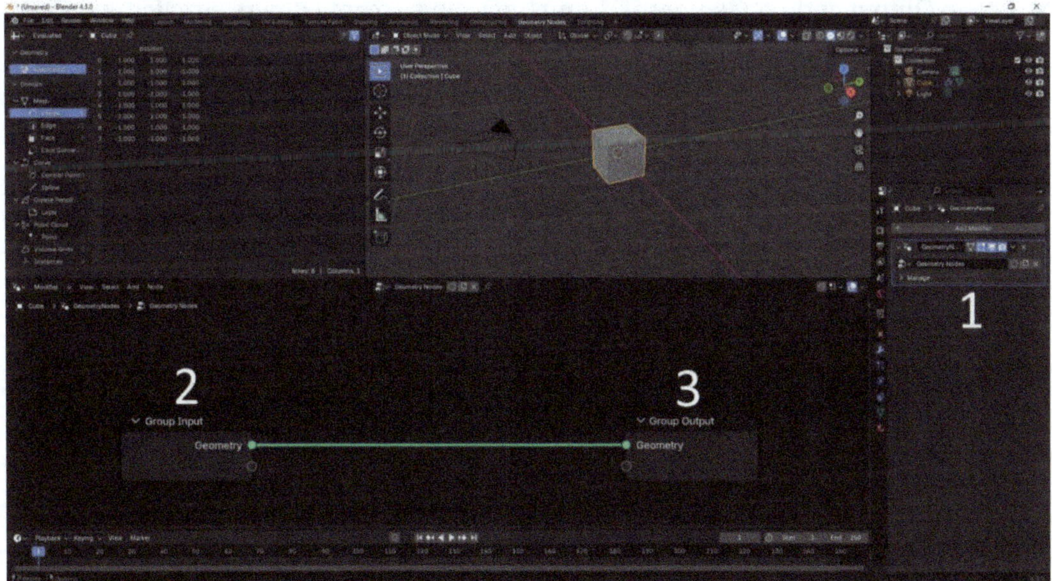

Figure 4-2. *(1) A new geometry node tree added to a mesh object as a modifier under Properties editor ➤ Modifier tab. (2) The Group Input node reads the object data you added the tree to along with other input parameters you might add to the tree. (3) The Group Output node aggregates the final geometry (and other data) produced by the tree*

Click Cube's name in the Outliner and rename it to "round_bumps," then click the tree's name (currently "Geometry Nodes") at the top of the geometry nodes editor and rename it to "round_bumps_tree." Since we want to generate a circular bump from scratch, we don't need the Cube's existing geometry—therefore, we'll delete it by switching the Cube to Edit mode in the viewport, toggle select all with the A key, then X key ➤ Delete ➤ Vertices. We'll also sever the link from the Group Input node's "Geometry" output to the Group Output node's "Geometry" input, by holding down Ctrl-right-click, then moving the mouse cursor across the link.

You can add a new node to the tree with the Add menu, which can be accessed via left-click ➤ Add or Shift-A anywhere within the editor. Alternatively, you can press the spacebar in the editor to bring up the search box, then type in a keyword to look up a node. Let's create a circle by adding a Mesh Circle node (Add ➤ Mesh ➤ Primitives ➤ Mesh Circle). Set the Fill Type to N-Gon and Vertices to 12, which gives the circle a reasonably smooth appearance. We'll leave the Radius at 1m for now (as we'll be calculating it later from input parameters). You can preview the output of any node by clicking to select the node followed by the O key, which creates a link from that node to the Group Output node's "Geometry" input (you can also hold down left-click and drag from the node's output to Group Output node's "Geometry" input). Try this by clicking the Mesh Circle node to select it then the O key. You will see the circle mesh show up in the viewport, as shown on the left of Figure 4-3.

Tip The spacebar is set to bring up the search box by default. You can change what the spacebar does via Edit ➤ Preferences… ➤ Keymap ➤ Preferences ➤ Spacebar Action. You can also look up and customize the current key binding(s) to the search box by entering the term "search" in the search field on the upper right under Edit ➤ Preferences… ➤ Keymap.

Next, we'll extrude the circle upward into a cylinder. Add an Extrude Mesh node (Add ➤ Mesh ➤ Operations ➤ Extrude Mesh), use the mouse cursor to move it over the link between Mesh Circle and Group Output until the link turns white, then click to confirm. You'll see the Extrude Mesh node automatically inserted and linked between those two nodes and the mesh preview in the viewport turn into a cylinder, as shown on the right of Figure 4-3.

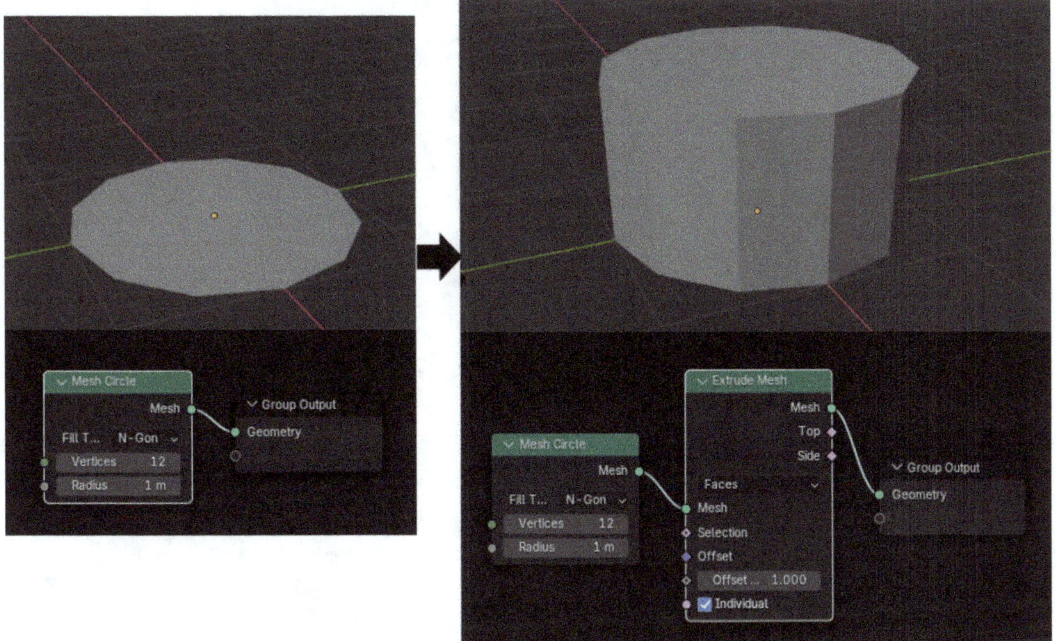

Figure 4-3. *Left: adding a Mesh Circle node with Fill Type=N-Gon, Vertices=12, and Radius=1m. Right: adding an Extrude Mesh node to turn the circle into a cylinder*

Since our goal is to create a 2D array of bumps to bake a normal map from, we need to modify the cylinder so it does not have walls that stand straight up—the reason is that normal maps work by telling the renderer how to change normal directions on a mesh surface (therefore how lights should be reflected differently). If you hover over a cylinder with straight walls and look straight down, the wall normals will be perpendicular to the viewing direction, therefore not picked up during normal map baking by the plane we'll add above it. To make the normal directions intersect the plane above, we must scale the top of the cylinder smaller than the bottom so the walls slant inward. We'll do so by inserting a Scale Elements node (Add ➤ Mesh ➤ Operations ➤ Scale Elements) between the Mesh Circle node and the Group Output node. Since we only want the top of the cylinder scaled, we'll connect the Extrude Mesh node's "Top" output to the "Selection" input of the Scale Elements node and set Scale to 0.6, as shown in Figure 4-4.

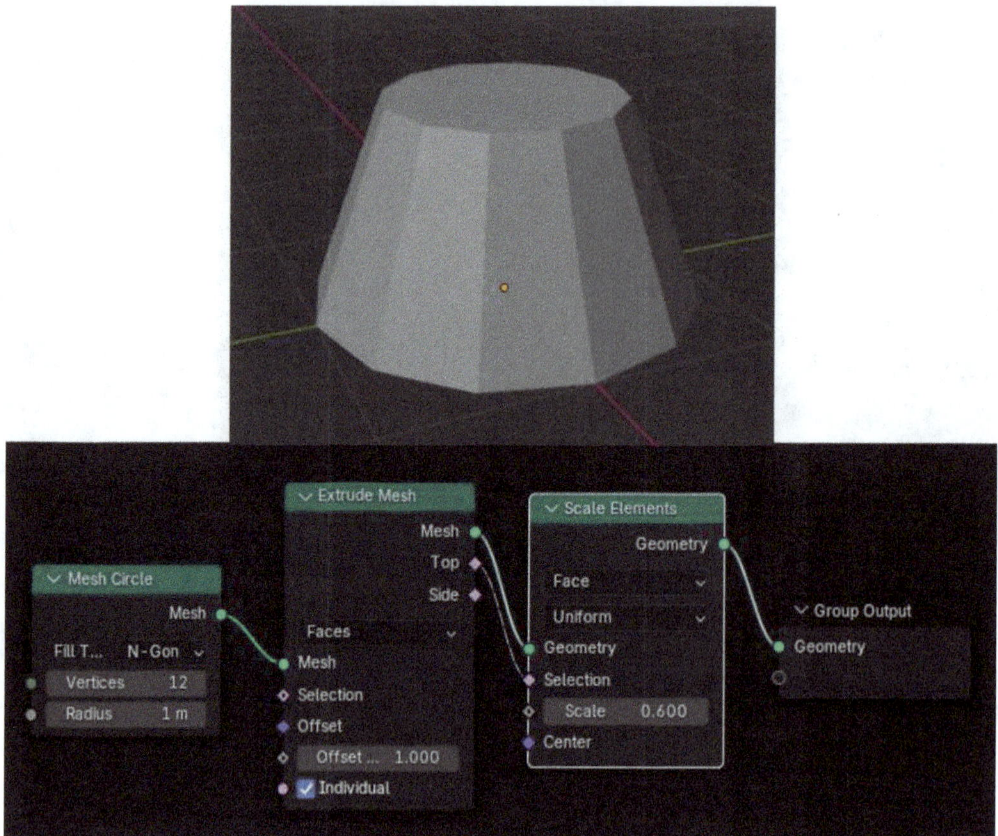

Figure 4-4. *Adding a Scale Elements node to scale the top of the cylinder so it's smaller than the bottom, by connecting the Extrude Mesh node's "Top" output to the Scale Elements node's "Selection" input and setting Scale to 0.600*

Generating a Grid of Circular Bumps

To create a bumpy surface for the grip, we want to populate a 2D array with the circular bump we've just created. We'll start by adding a Grid node (Add ➤ Mesh ➤ Primitives ➤ Grid), which creates a grid mesh, then a Mesh to Points node (Add ➤ Mesh ➤ Operations ➤ Mesh to Points) set to Vertices, and connect the Grid's "Mesh" output to Mesh to Point's "Mesh" input—this will create a point cloud with one point at each of the Grid mesh's vertices. We'll set the Grid node's Size X and Size Y both to 10m and Vertices X and Vertices Y both to 10 for now, which gives us a 10×10 grid, therefore a 2D array of 100 points. In the next section, we'll add user inputs to control the size and density of the grid.

The next step is to add an Instance on Points node (Add ➤ Instances ➤ Instance on Points), which takes a point cloud and duplicates a given "instance" at every point. An instance is a geometric object of any kind, such as a curve, mesh, or another instance. In this case, we want the grid points as the point cloud and the bump as the instance. We'll shrink the bump to fit the grid by setting Mesh Circle's "Radius" to 0.1m and Extrude Mesh's "Offset" to 0.1m, then connect Scale Elements' "Geometry" to Instance on Points' "Instance" and Mesh to Points' "Points" to Instance on Points' "Points"—this will produce a bump at every grid vertex. To give the bumps a plane to sit on, we'll connect both the Grid node's "Mesh" output and Instance on Points' "Instances" output to a Join Geometry node (Add ➤ Geometry ➤ Join Geometry) to combine the two, then with Join Geometry selected, press the O key to link it to Group Output for preview—you'll see the bumpy grid mesh appear in the viewport as shown in Figure 4-5. You may have noticed that since a bump centers at each grid vertex, the bumps along the perimeter of the grid are halfway outside the grid—when we bake the normal map later, we will use a plane above the same size as the Grid node, therefore chopping off the half bumps outside the perimeter.

Creating User Inputs to Control Bump Density

We've verified that the prototype tree generates what we want with hard-coded values, so now is the time to add user inputs to allow custom grid size and bump density. Adding inputs *after* making a tree may seem like an afterthought—but it is the way to go, because using stand-in values (like the 10m X and Y size for the Grid) eliminates the possibility that a bad input could make the tree misbehave, therefore allowing you to debug the tree quicker. Using fixed values also lets you start previewing the node outputs right away. The process of building the tree itself will help you develop a sense of which parameters to expose (and their ranges) to produce valid variations of the generated model.

Remember the Group Input node we've set aside? (If you've deleted it, you can add one back with Add ➤ Group ➤ Group Input.) Press the N key inside the geometry node editor to bring up the Properties shelf, go to the Group tab, and scroll down to the Group Sockets section, where you'll find the list of all input and output sockets for the tree. An input (output) socket has a green dot to the left (right) of its name. Since we are not using the Geometry input socket, we can remove it by clicking the socket then the "-" button, as shown on the left of Figure 4-6. We'll add a Grid Size input for controlling both the X and Y Size of the Grid node, by selecting the socket just before the insertion point (in this case, the Geometry output socket), then clicking the "+" button ➤ Input, as shown in the center of Figure 4-6. Double-click the new socket to rename it from "Socket" to "Grid Size." Next, we'll add a Bump Count Per Axis input socket to control the Grid node's Vertices count for X and Y—for example, a Bump Count Per Axis of 5 means 5×5=25 bumps evenly distributed over the grid.

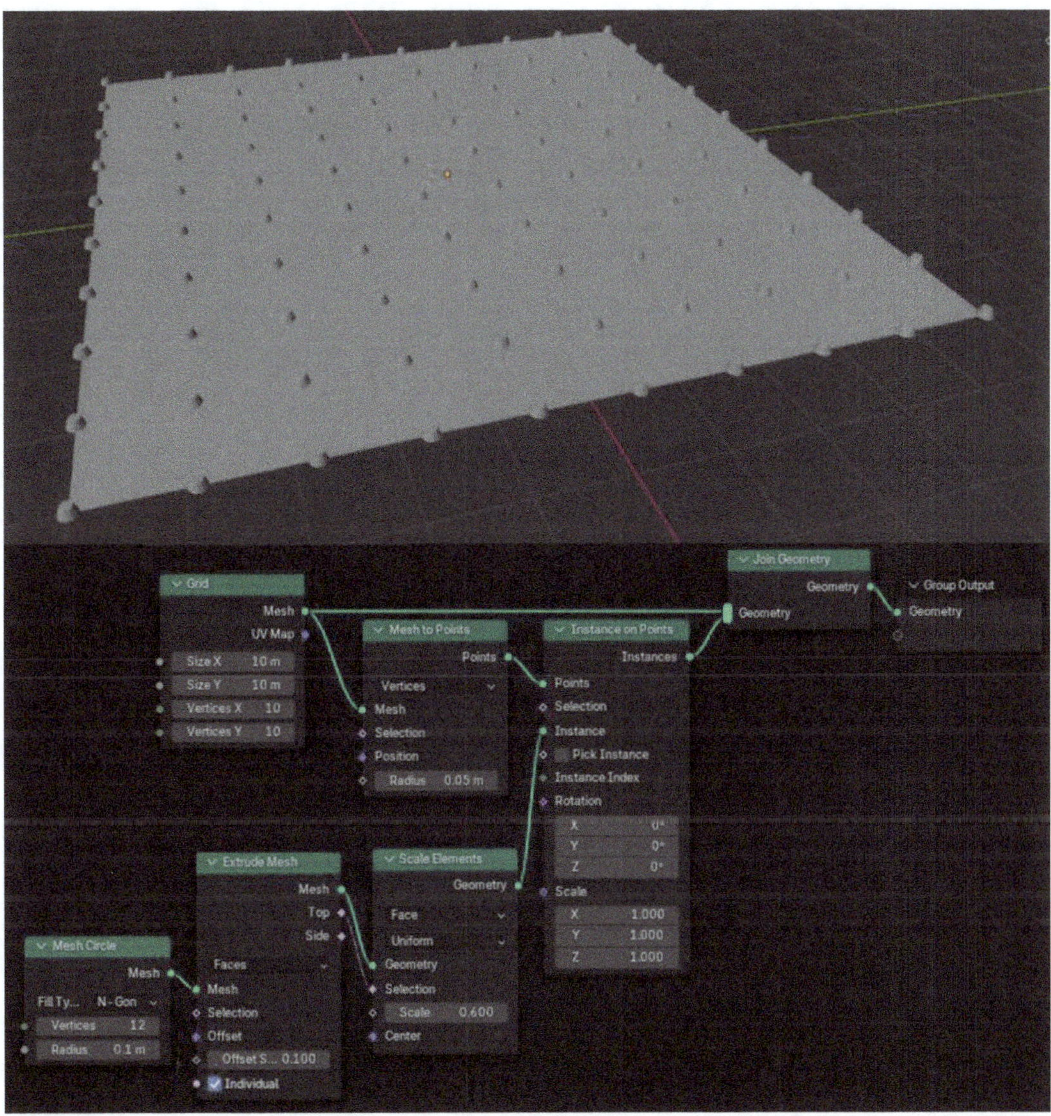

Figure 4-5. *Bump grid mesh generated by distributing Mesh Circle instances (of 0.1m Radius) extruded with Extrude Mesh (with offsets of 0.1m) across a 10m×10m grid with 10 vertices along each axis. The top of the bumps are scaled to 0.6 using the Scale Elements node*

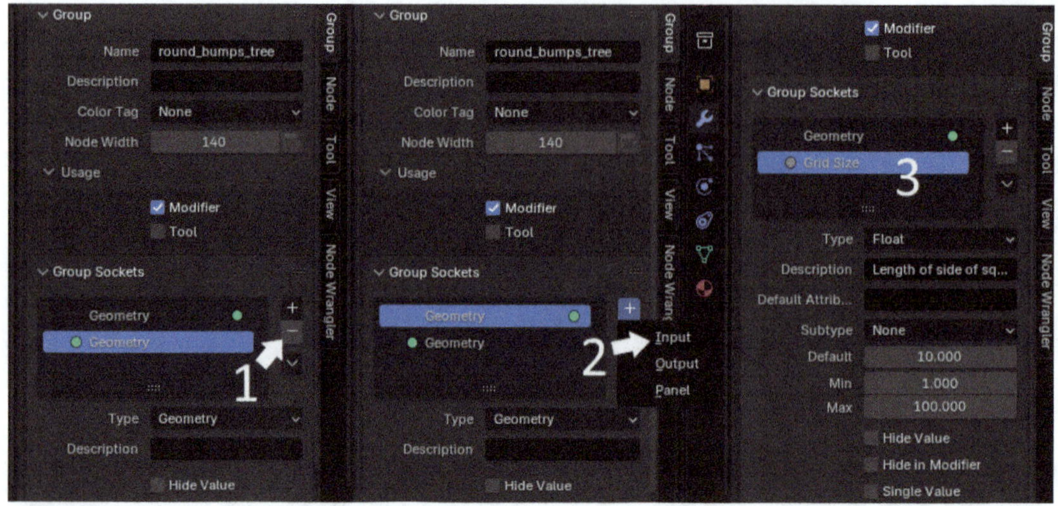

Figure 4-6. *Adding and removing sockets from a geometry node tree. The sockets with dots to the left (right) of their names are input (output) sockets.(1) Click to select a socket in the list, then click the "-" button to remove it. As shown, the Geometry input socket is removed. (2) To add an input socket, click the existing socket right before the insertion point, then click the "+" button ➤ Input. (3) The Grid Size input socket we added to control the X (Y) Size of the Grid node*

Tip If the warning "Node group's geometry input must be the first" appears under a node tree's modifier in the Properties editor ➤ Modifier tab, you need to edit your sockets (N key in the geometry node editor ➤ Group tab ➤ Group Sockets) so the Geometry input socket is before any other input sockets in the list. You can rearrange the order of the sockets by clicking a socket in the list, holding down LMB, and dragging it. If you are not using the Geometry input socket in the tree, you can also remove it.

Next, configure the settings for Grid Size as shown on the right of Figure 4-6, so it has Type as Float, Description as "Length of side of square grid.", and 10, 1, and 100 for Default, Min, and Max, respectively. You'll see a Grid Size float slider appear under the node tree's modifier under Properties editor ➤ Modifier tab. If you hover the cursor over the slider, a tooltip containing the socket's Description string will appear. Right after its creation, the slider will show 0.000—to make it reset to the Default value you entered for the socket, right-click the slider ➤ Reset to Default Value.

Similarly, we'll configure the settings for Bump Count Per Axis so it has Type as Integer, Description as "Number of bumps X/Y.", and 50, 1, and 200 for Default, Min, and Max, respectively. You'll see a Bump Count Per Axis integer slider appear under the node tree's modifier.

The next step is to hook up the slider values to the nodes in the tree they control. Connect the Group Input node's "Grid Size" to both the Grid node's "X Size" and "Y Size," and the Group Input node's "Bump Count Per Axis" to both the Grid node's "Vertices X" and "Vertices Y" inputs. You'll see the bump density immediately change in the viewport. This is not quite enough, however, because we are still using a fixed value for the bumps' radii—if you continue to increase the density, the bumps will start to overlap each other, which we don't want. To fix this, we'll calculate the Mesh Circle "Radius" from the input values using the following steps. First calculate a grid cell's size from Grid Size divided by the number of cells per side, which is Bump Count Per Axis -1:

$$grid\ cell\ size = Grid\ Size \div (Bump\ Count\ Per\ Axis - 1)$$

We want the bump size to be proportional to the cell size, with some slack from bump to bump, so we make the bump diameter 80% of the cell size, then the bump radius is half the bump diameter:

$$bump\ diameter = grid\ cell\ size \times 0.8$$

$$bump\ radius = bump\ diameter\ \div 2$$

We'll use four Math nodes to carry out these calculations. A Math node is by default set to Add. You can change its type by simply selecting it from the dropdown. Change the first Math node to Subtract, then connect Bump Count Per Axis to its first "Value" input and change its second "Value" input to 1, which gives

$$(Bump\ Count\ Per\ Axis - 1)$$

Change the second Math node to Divide, then connect Grid Size to its first "Value" input and the first Math node's output to its second "Value," which gives you

$$Grid\ Size \div (Bump\ Count\ Per\ Axis - 1).$$

Change the third Math node to Multiply, then connect the second Math node's "Value" to its first "Value" and set the second "Value" to 0.8, which gives you

$$grid\ cell\ size \times 0.8.$$

Finally, change the fourth Math node to Divide, and connect the third Math node's "Value" to its first "Value" and change the second "Value" to 2, which gives you

$$\textit{bump diameter} \ \sqrt{2}$$

which is the bump radius.

Connect the fourth Math node's "Value" output to the Mesh Circle node's "Radius" input to complete the tree. The portion of the tree we've constructed in this section is shown on the bottom of Figure 4-7, with the preview of the mesh generated by the tree shown at the top of the same figure.

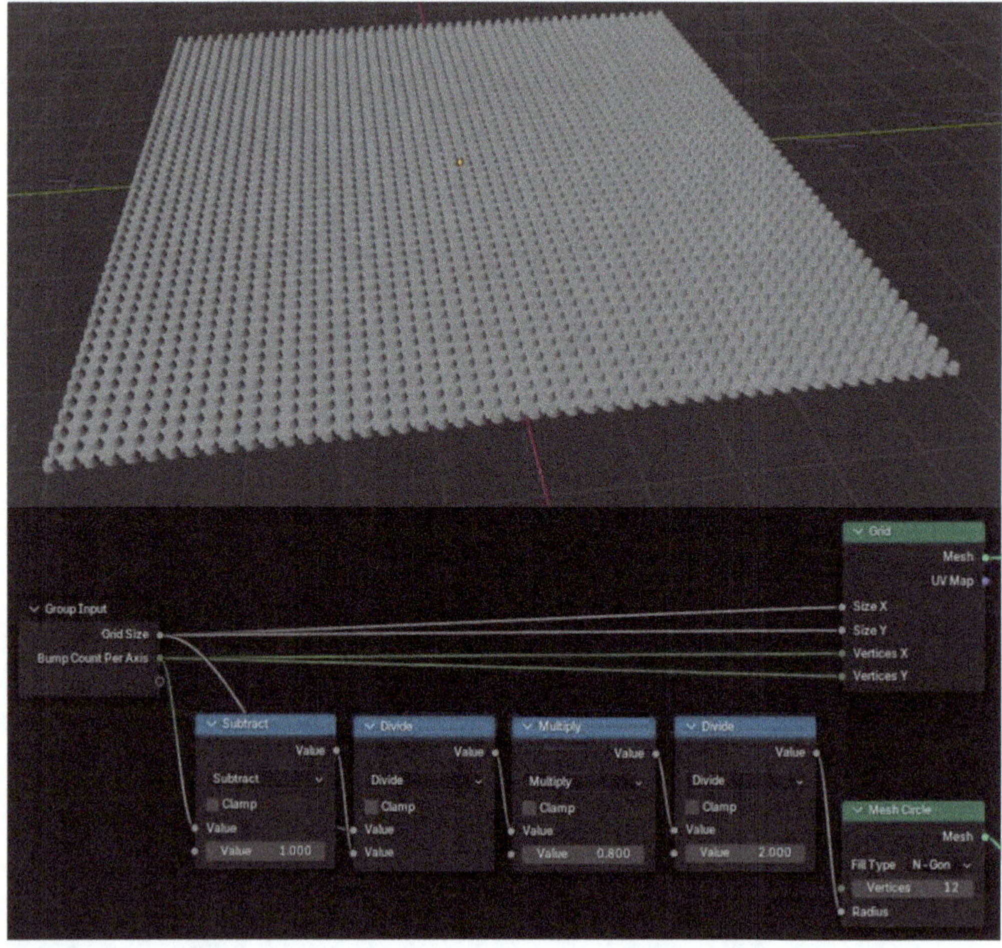

Figure 4-7. *Connecting the Grid Size and Bump Count Per Axis inputs to the tree and adding Math nodes to calculate the bump radius (Mesh Circle "Radius") accordingly. The top shows the preview of the generated mesh with Grid Size and Bump Count Per Axis at default values*

Realizing Instances

Currently, the tree's output in the viewport is still an instance—to turn it into real mesh data, we need to insert a Realize Instances node (Add ➤ Instances ➤ Realize Instances) between Join Geometry and Group Output, as shown in Figure 4-8.

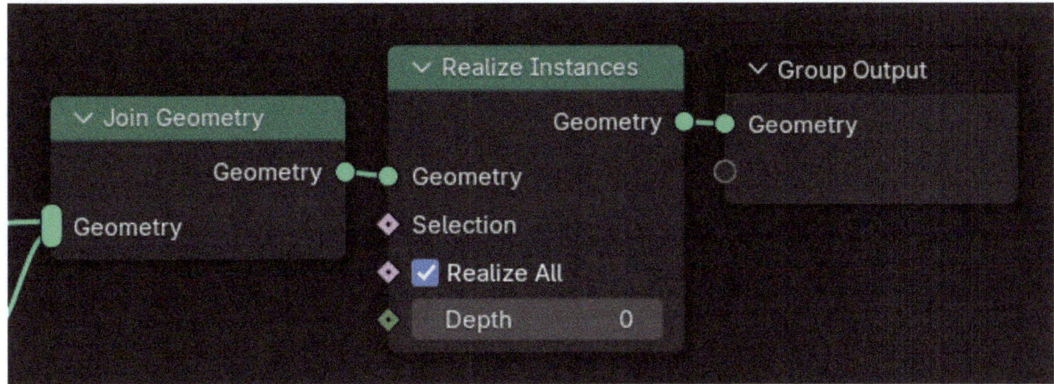

Figure 4-8. *Finalizing the tree by using the Realizing Instances node to turn instanced geometry into real mesh data*

Tip In the geometry node editor, you can hold down MMB and drag to pan and scroll the mouse wheel to zoom in or out.

Baking Normal Map from the Bump Grid Mesh

Before jumping into code, let's recap the process of baking a normal map from a mesh. In the following steps, we'll refer to the mesh we're *baking the normal map from* the "bake-from mesh."

1. Switch the bake-from mesh to Object mode and apply modifiers, to ensure any changes to bake-from mesh's geometry from the modifiers are reflected.

2. Create a new mesh plane object and position it just above the bake-from mesh. Tab the plane into Edit mode. Toggle select all with the A key, then U key ➤ Unwrap ➤ Smart UV Project. Tab back into Object mode.

3. With the plane object still selected, go to Properties Editor ➤ Material tab, click the +New button to create a new material, and make it the active material slot.

4. Switch to the Shading workspace—you're now looking at the shader node tree for the material created in step 3 for the plane object. Create a new Image Texture node (Add ➤ Texture ➤ Image Texture) and select it but not connect it to anything. The Image Texture node will receive the baking.

5. Select the bake-from mesh, then select the plane mesh (the plane mesh is the active object and selected second).

6. Under Properties editor ➤ Render tab, set Scene ➤ Render Engine to Cycles, then under the Bake section, set Bake Type to Normal, Influence ➤ Space to Tangent, check the "Selected to Active" box, set Extrusion to 0.1m, and Output ➤ Target to Image Texture.

7. Under Properties editor ➤ Render tab ➤ Bake, click the Bake button.

The reason you need to unwrap the plane object in step 2 is because otherwise Blender may give you the following error when you click the Bake button:

```
RuntimeError: Error: No active UV layer found in the ↩
    object "round_bumps_plane"
```

Automate Normal Map Baking with Python

We're now ready to automate the steps described above for baking a normal map from a given mesh. The function `bake_normal_map_from_given_mesh` in Listing 4-1 takes the bake-from mesh and the X/Y size of the plane, then bakes and saves the normal map to disk as a `*.png` file.

Listing 4-1. Automatically bake a normal map based on a given mesh and save it to a *.png file (see /Ch4/texture_material_generation.py)

```
def bake_normal_map_from_given_mesh(context, mesh_obj, ↩
    grid_size):
    for obj in context.view_layer.objects:
```

```
    obj.select_set(False)
mesh_obj.select_set(True)
context.view_layer.objects.active = mesh_obj
viewport_co = get_context_override(context, ↩
    'VIEW_3D', 'WINDOW')
with context.temp_override(**viewport_co):
    bpy.ops.object.mode_set(mode='OBJECT')

viewport_co = get_context_override(context, ↩
    'VIEW_3D', 'WINDOW')
with context.temp_override(**viewport_co):
    for m in mesh_obj.modifiers:
        bpy.ops.object.modifier_apply( ↩
            modifier=m.name)

bb = np.array(mesh_obj.bound_box)
z_min, z_max = find_min_max(bb, 2)
plane_loc = Vector(mesh_obj.location)
plane_loc[2] += (0.5*(z_max-z_min) + 0.15)
bm, plane_obj = ↩
    get_placeholder_mesh_obj_and_bm(context, ↩
        mesh_obj.name+"_plane", plane_loc)
grid_size /= 2
segments = floor(grid_size)
bmesh.ops.create_grid(bm, x_segments=segments, ↩
    y_segments=segments, size=grid_size, ↩
    calc_uvs=True)
bmesh.update_edit_mesh(plane_obj.data)
bm.free()
bpy.ops.mesh.select_all(action='SELECT')
bpy.ops.uv.smart_project()
viewport_co = get_context_override(context, ↩
    'VIEW_3D', 'WINDOW')
with context.temp_override(**viewport_co):
    bpy.ops.object.mode_set(mode='OBJECT')
```

```
    plane_mat = create_material(plane_obj, ↩
        plane_obj.name+"_mat")
    nodes = plane_mat.node_tree.nodes
    node_tex_img = nodes.new(type='ShaderNodeTexImage')
    image_block = bpy.data.images.new( ↩
        mesh_obj.name+"_normal_map", 1024, 1024)
    image_block.generated_type = 'BLANK'
    node_tex_img.image = image_block
    rearrange_nodes(nodes)
    node_tex_img.select = True

    mesh_obj.select_set(True)
    plane_obj.select_set(True)
    context.view_layer.objects.active = plane_obj

    context.scene.render.engine = 'CYCLES'
    context.scene.cycles.device = 'GPU'
    context.scene.cycles.bake_type = 'NORMAL'
    context.scene.render.bake.normal_space = 'TANGENT'
    context.scene.render.bake.use_selected_to_active = ↩
        True
    context.scene.render.bake.cage_extrusion = 0.1
    context.scene.render.bake.margin = 0
    bpy.ops.object.bake(type='NORMAL')

    save_image_to_file(script_dir, image_block, ↩
        image_block.name)

    return image_block
```

We start by deselecting all, then select the given mesh_obj, and make it active. We then switch mesh_obj to Object mode using a context override (as if from the viewport), then once mode switch is complete, with another context override, we iterate through mesh_obj's modifiers (mesh_obj.modifiers) and apply them one by one, to get mesh_obj ready as the source for normal map baking.

Next, we'll create a plane mesh object and position it just above mesh_obj. To do so, we compute the location for the plane by calling find_min_max (Listing 4-2) to extract the min and max Z extent of mesh_obj's bounding box. If we offset mesh_obj's Z coordinate plane_loc[2] (which is at its center) by half its Z extent, we get the Z at mesh_obj's top—since we want the plane to sit slightly above, we add another 0.15 ((0.5*(z_max-z_min) + 0.15)). With the plane's location derived, we call get_placeholder_mesh_obj_and_bm (Listing 2-1) to create an object (plane_obj) with blank mesh data and initialize a bmesh instance bm for editing it. Using bm, we then call bmesh.ops.create_grid to add a plane primitive to plane_obj. Note that the size argument for bmesh.ops.create_grid needs to be *half* the grid_size passed in. Since grid_size may not be an integer, we use floor(grid_size) for the number of plane segments. We flush the edits queued on bm to plane_obj's mesh data by calling bmesh.update_edit_mesh(plane_obj.data), then free up bm since we no longer need it. While plane_obj is still in Edit mode, we select all then unwrap with bpy.ops.uv.smart_project() (UV ➤ Unwrap ➤ Smart UV Project). After that, we switch plane_obj back to Object mode.

The next step is calling create_material (Listing 4-3) to create a new material plane_mat for plane_obj along with a basic shader node tree with a Principled BSDF node connected to a Material Output node. We add a new Image Texture node node_tex_img to the tree by calling nodes.new(type='ShaderNodeTexImage'), then create a new 1024×1024 image data block image_block via bpy.data.images.new and set generated type to 'BLANK' for normal map baking. image_block is set as node_tex_img's image (node_tex_img.image = image_block). We clean up the tree by calling rearrange_nodes (Listing 4-5) and select node_tex_img so it's ready to receive the data once we bake.

Next, we select mesh_obj, select plane_obj, then make plane_obj active to establish the source and target objects for baking. We then configure the settings under Properties editor ➤ Render tab, by setting Scene ➤ Render Engine to Cycles (and Device to GPU), Bake Type to Normal, and Influence ➤ Space to Tangent, and check the "Selected to Active" checkbox (by setting the Boolean to True), Extrusion to 0.1m, and Margin Size to 0 px so the map is filled all the way to the edges. With all the settings configured, we call bpy.ops.object.bake(type='NORMAL') to bake the normal map (which is equivalent to pressing the Bake button under Properties editor ➤ Render tab ➤ Bake), followed by save_image_to_file (Listing 4-6) to save the normal map data block to a *.png file, and return that data block.

You can try baking the normal map yourself by opening /Ch4/round_bumps.blend from the downloaded source, which contains the round_bumps object with the geometry node tree round_bumps_tree as described earlier in the chapter, then call Listing 4-1 as follows:

```
bake_normal_map_from_given_mesh(bpy.context, ↩
    bpy.data.objects["round_bumps"], 10)
```

which will bake the normal map and save it to disk as the file `round_bumps_normal_map.png`, shown in Figure 4-9.

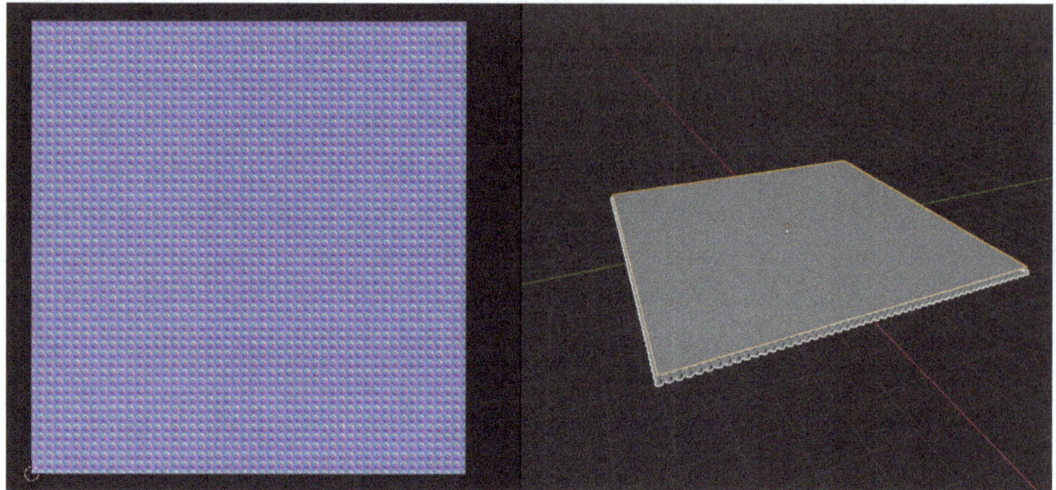

Figure 4-9. *Results of running Listing 4-1 with /Ch4/round_bumps.blend. Left shows the normal map, and right shows the corresponding bump grid mesh with the plane object for baking positioned above it*

Util Functions for Map Baking and Material Creation

In this section, we'll take a closer look at the four utility functions used by `bake_normal_map_from_given_mesh` in Listing 4-1.

Finding the Extent of a Mesh's Bounding Box Along a Given Axis

`find_min_max` in Listing 4-2 takes a numpy array (`np.array`) and a given axis, then returns the minimum and maximum values along that axis.

Listing 4-2. Finding the minimum and maximum along a given axis in a np.array (see /Ch4/material_and_image_utils.py)

```
def find_min_max(points, axis):
    return np.min(points[:, axis]), ↩
        np.max(points[:, axis])
```

When indexing a `np.array`, you use a comma-separated list of values to indicate the index (or range of indices) you want to retrieve from each dimension. The `:` symbol may be used several different ways—for instance, `2:5` means indices 2 to 4, `:6` means everything before index 6, and `3:` means everything after index 3. The `:` symbol by itself means all indices in that dimension.

A two-dimensional array can be thought of as a table with rows and columns. Since `points` is a N×3 array such that each row is one point's (X,Y,Z) coordinates, `points[:, axis]` means all rows of the `<axis>`-th column; therefore, `points[:, 0]` is the X of all points, `points[:, 1]` the Y of all points, and so on (`mesh_obj.bound_box` in Listing 4-1 with which we called Listing 4-2 is the list of corner vertex coordinates of `mesh_obj`'s bounding box, so `axis=2` means to retrieve the min and max Z of the box). Once we obtain the portion of the array to operate on, we can simply call `np.min` and `np.max` to get the minimum and maximum, respectively.

Creating and Assigning a New Material

`create_material` in Listing 4-3 creates (or retrieves) a material by the given name, adds it to the given object's material stack, sets its index as the object's active material index, and sets up its shader node tree.

Listing 4-3. Create a material with a given name, set up its node tree, and assign it to a given object (see /Ch4/material_and_image_utils.py)

```
def create_material(obj, mat_name):
    if bpy.data.materials.find(mat_name) < 0:
        bpy.data.materials.new(mat_name)
    mat = bpy.data.materials[mat_name]
    add_material_to_obj(obj, mat)

    nodes = mat.node_tree.nodes
    bsdf_index = nodes.find('Principled BSDF')
    node_bsdf = nodes.new(type='ShaderNodeBsdfPrincipled') ↩
        if bsdf_index < 0 else nodes[bsdf_index]

    out_index = nodes.find('Material Output')

    node_output = nodes.new( ↩
        type='ShaderNodeOutputMaterial') ↩
            if out_index < 0 else nodes[out_index]
    links = mat.node_tree.links
```

```
    links.new(node_bsdf.outputs['BSDF'], ↩
        node_output.inputs['Surface'])
    return mat
```

The first thing we'll check is whether a material by the given name (`mat_name`) already exists in the blend file by calling `bpy.data.materials.find(mat_name)`—a return value < 0 indicates nothing is found; therefore, we call `bpy.data.materials.new(mat_name)` to create a new material with that name. Either way, we retrieve the material `mat` by name, then call `add_material_to_obj` (Listing 4-4) to add it to the given object `obj`'s stack, and set its index as `obj`'s active material index.

Next, we'll set up `mat`'s shader node tree. We create a Principled BSDF node and a Material Output node if either does not yet exist, then a new link from Principled BSDF's BSDF output to Material Output's Surface input. We finish by returning `mat`.

Adding a Material to an Object and Setting It As Active

Here, we'll take a brief look at the helper function `add_material_to_obj` (Listing 4-4) used in Listing 4-3, which adds a material to a given object's material stack and sets its index as the object's active material index.

Listing 4-4. Add a material to a given object's material stack and set its index as the object's active material index (see /Ch4/material_and_image_utils.py)

```
def add_material_to_obj(obj, mat):
    mat_index = obj.data.materials.find(mat.name)
    if mat_index < 0:
        obj.data.materials.append(mat)
        mat_index = obj.data.materials.find(mat.name)

    obj.active_material_index = mat_index
    mat.use_nodes = True
```

First, we'll check whether the given material (`mat`) is in `obj`'s material stack (`obj.data.materials`) by calling `find` to retrieve its index (`mat_index`)—if not, we'll append it, then call `find` again to get the new index. To wrap up, we set `obj`'s active material index to `mat_index` and enable the use of shader nodes for rendering `mat` by setting `mat.use_nodes` to `True` (which is equivalent to checking the "Use Nodes" box under the shader node editor).

Rearranging Nodes in a Node Tree

`rearrange_nodes` in Listing 4-5 takes a list of nodes from a node tree and lays them out sequentially, one after another, with spacing between adjacent nodes proportional to the nodes' sizes.

Listing 4-5. Lay the given list of nodes out sequentially, with spacing between adjacent nodes proportional to the nodes' sizes (see /Ch4/material_and_image_utils.py)

```
def rearrange_nodes(nodes):
    for i in range(len(nodes)):
        n = nodes[i]
        n.select = False
        if i > 0:
            prev_n = nodes[i-1]
            n.location = prev_n.location
            n.location[0] += (n.width+prev_n.width)*0.5*1.5
```

The function iterates the given list of nodes with a `for` loop and deselects each node (which is useful for our purpose of map baking, since we want only the Image Texture node meant to receive the baking selected). For each node in the list after the first, we copy the previous node's location to the current node, then shift the current node's X coordinate (left-right) by 150% of the average of the two nodes' widths, which has the effect of leaving a gap between the two nodes that is about half of their average width.

Saving an Image Data Block to File

`save_image_to_file` in Listing 4-6 takes a given directory, image data block, and file name (sans the file extension), then saves the block out to a png file.

Listing 4-6. Saving a given image block out to file and form the file path based on the given directory and file name (see /Ch4/material_and_image_utils.py)

```
def save_image_to_file(dir, image_block, name):
    image_block.filepath_raw = dir+'\\'+name+".png"
    image_block.file_format = 'PNG'
    image_block.save()
```

We'll first form the file path by concatenating the given directory (`dir`) with an escaped backslash (for Windows) followed by the given name and ".png" for the extension. After that, we'll assign the path to the image block's path (`image_block.filepath_raw`), set the image block's format (`image_block.file_format`) to `'PNG'`, then call `image_block.save()` to write it out to disk.

Creating Variations of the Bump Grid

You can create variations of the bump grid simply by changing parameters in the node tree. For example, set the Vertices of the Mesh Circle to 3 to make a triangle or 4 to make a square, then use the Rotation ➤ Z value for the Instance on Points node to change the orientation of the shape. The left of Figure 4-10 shows the grid generated with Mesh Circle ➤ Vertices set to 3 and Instance on Points Rotation ➤ Z set to -30 degrees. The right of Figure 4-10 shows the grid generated with Mesh Circle ➤ Vertices set to 4 and Instance on Points Rotation ➤ Z set to 45 degrees.

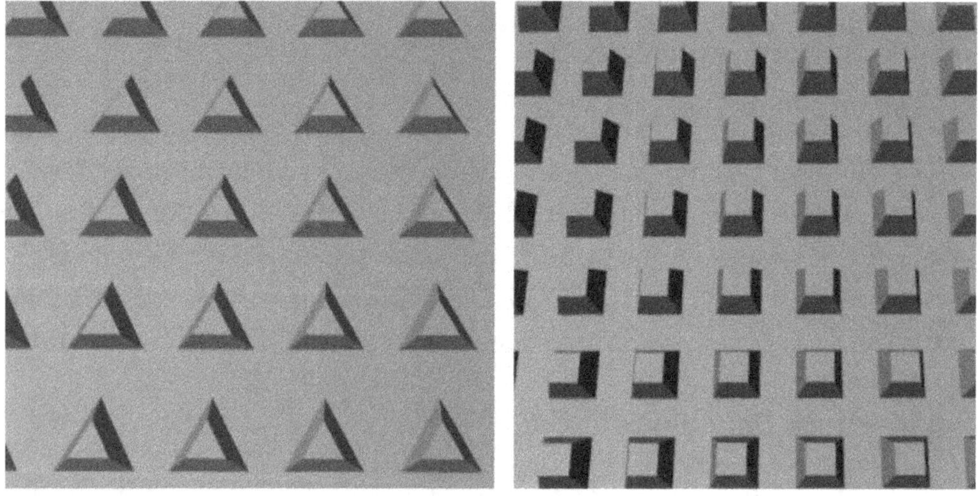

***Figure 4-10.** Variations of the bump grid. Left is generated with Mesh Circle ➤ Vertices set to 3 and Instance on Points Rotation ➤ Z set to -30 degrees. Right is generated with Mesh Circle ➤ Vertices set to 4 and Instance on Points Rotation ➤ Z set to 45 degrees*

Creating a Grid with a Custom Cross-Motif

With the same set up where we divide the grid evenly then derive a radius for the bump based on cell size, we can replace the primitives for the bumps with custom motifs like the cross shown in Figure 4-12 to create more complex designs. To create a square curve, we use a Curve Circle node (Add ➤ Curve ➤ Primitives ➤ Curve Circle) in Radius mode with Resolution = 4 and Radius set to the same value as the Mesh Circle node in Figure 4-7. Since by default the Curve Circle node orients the square like a rhombus, we rotate it with a Transform Geometry node (Add ➤ Geometry ➤ Operations ➤ Transform Geometry) with Rotation 45 degrees around Z so it sits like a square with flat sides at the top and bottom (as (1) in Figures 4-11 and 4-12). To create the cross, we connect the square's diagonal points pairwise—#0 to #2 and #1 to #3 (as (2) and (3) in Figures 4-11 and 4-12). We can access the square's points by index using the Sample Index node (Add ➤ Geometry ➤ Sample ➤ Sample Index), with "Vector" as Data Type, "Point" as Domain, and a Position node (Add ➤ Geometry ➤ Read ➤ Position) as "Value" to indicate the type of value we want to sample is "position" (i.e. X, Y, Z coordinates). In our case, since we want to sample all four of the square's points, we create four Sample Index nodes set to "Vector" and "Point" with Index 0, 2, 1, and 3, then connect one Position node to all four Sample Index nodes' "Value" input, as shown in Figure 4-11. To complete the setup, we add a Curve to Points node (Add ➤ Curve ➤ Operations ➤ Curve to Points) after Transform Geometry to convert the square curve into a list of four points and connect Curve to Points to all four Sample Index nodes.

Next, we use Sample Index #0 and #2 as the Start and End points of one Curve Line node (Add ➤ Curve ➤ Primitives ➤ Curve Line, shown as (2) in Figures 4-11 and 4-12), and Sample Index #1 and #3 as the Start and End points of a second Curve Line node (as (3) in Figures 4-11 and 4-12), then merge both into a cross with a Join Geometry node (4). You can envision now that (1) and (4) combined will create the skeleton of the motif. To add thickness to the cross (5), we connect (4) to a Curve to Mesh node (Add ➤ Curve ➤ Operations ➤ Curve to Mesh) with a Curve Circle in Radius mode with Resolutions = 6 and Radius = 0.08m as its Profile Curve. Similarly, to add thickness to the square, we connect (1) to a Curve to Mesh node with a Curve Circle as its Profile Curve, but this time setting Curve to Mesh to Points mode, with Point1 = (-0.1m, 0m, 0m), Point2 = (0m, 0.1m, 0m), and Point 3 = (0.1m, 0m, 0m), which creates a squared-off profile that tapes down outward (6). Finally, we merge (5) and (6) with a Join Geometry node, turn off shade smooth with a Set Shade Smooth node (Add ➤ Mesh ➤ Write ➤ Set Shade

Smooth) set to Face with "Shade Smooth" unchecked, and turn the instances into real mesh data with a Realize Instances node (Add ➤ Instances ➤ Realize Instances) with "Realize All" checked, which produces the finished cross-motif mesh (7).

You can build out the rest of the tree to generate a 2D grid of cross-motifs by integrating the subtrees from Figures 4-7 and 4-8. I find that a value of 0.95 for the Multiply node in Figure 4-7 (recall that this is a Add ➤ Utilities ➤ Math ➤ Math node set to Multiply) creates nice spacing between motifs, as shown in Figure 4-13. You can then bake a normal map by calling Listing 4-1 with the motif grid and use it to set up the material for the gun's grip, as shown in Figure 4-14.

Note You can find a copy of the complete node tree for this section in the file `/Ch4/cross_motif_grid.blend` in the downloaded source, along with a copy of the baked normal map, `/Ch4/cross_motif_grid_normal_map.png`, and a copy of the blend file after Listing 4.1 is called `/Ch4/cross_motif_grid_after_nomral_map_generation.blend`.

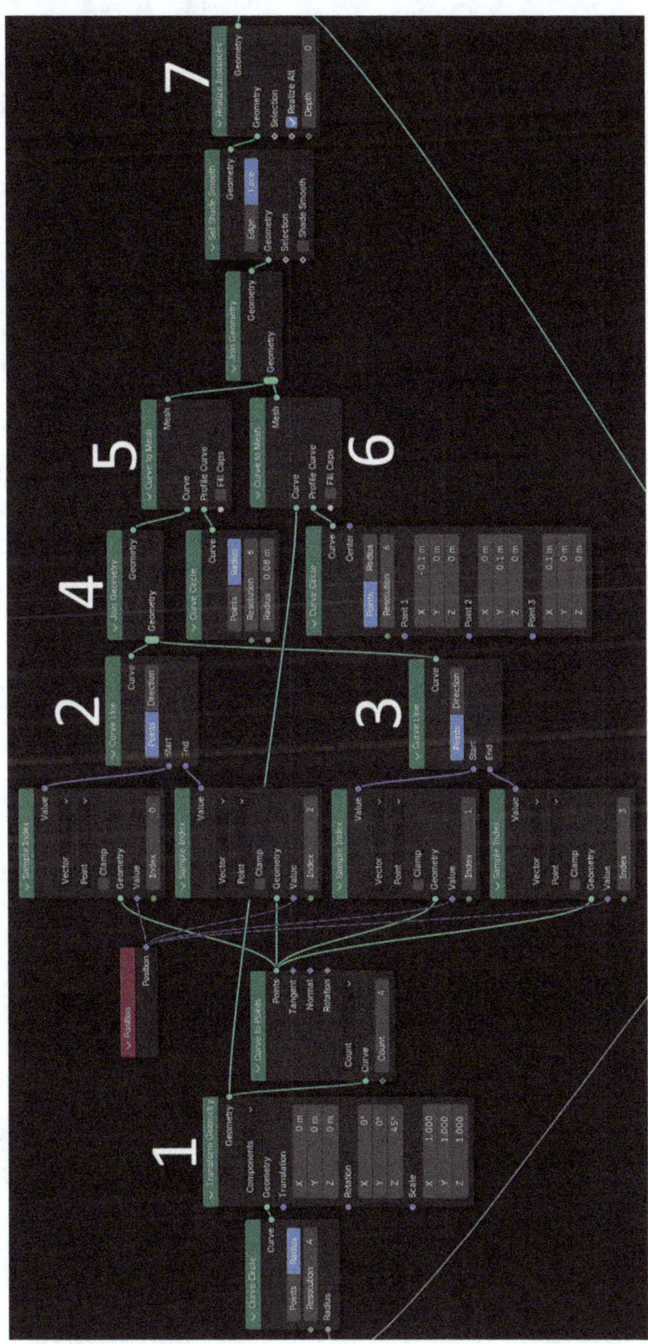

Figure 4-11. *Geometry node tree for generating a single cross-motif*

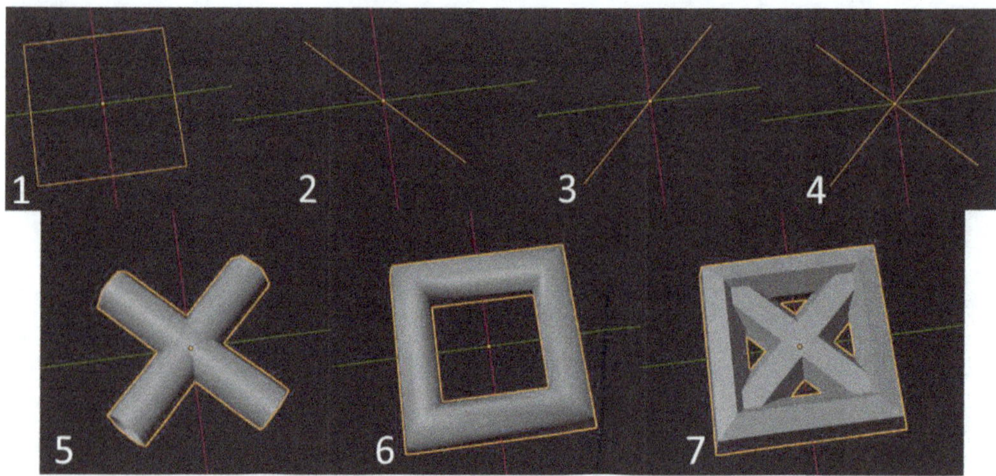

Figure 4-12. *Intermediate stages of generating the cross-motif. (1) to (7) correspond to nodes labeled (1) to (7) in the tree shown in Figure 4-11. (1) is a Curve Circle of four vertices rotated 45 degrees around Z; (2) is a Curve Line from point #0 to #2 of the square in (1) and (3) a Curve Line from point #1 to #3; (4) is Join Geometry of (2) and (3); (5) is (4) with Curve to Mesh; (6) is (1) with Curve to Mesh; (7) is the final realized motif with Shade Smooth disabled*

Figure 4-13. *Cross-motif grid generated by integrating the subtrees from Figures 4-7 and 4-8, with the Multiply node in Figure 4-7 set to 0.95 to make each "bump" fill out 95% of a grid cell*

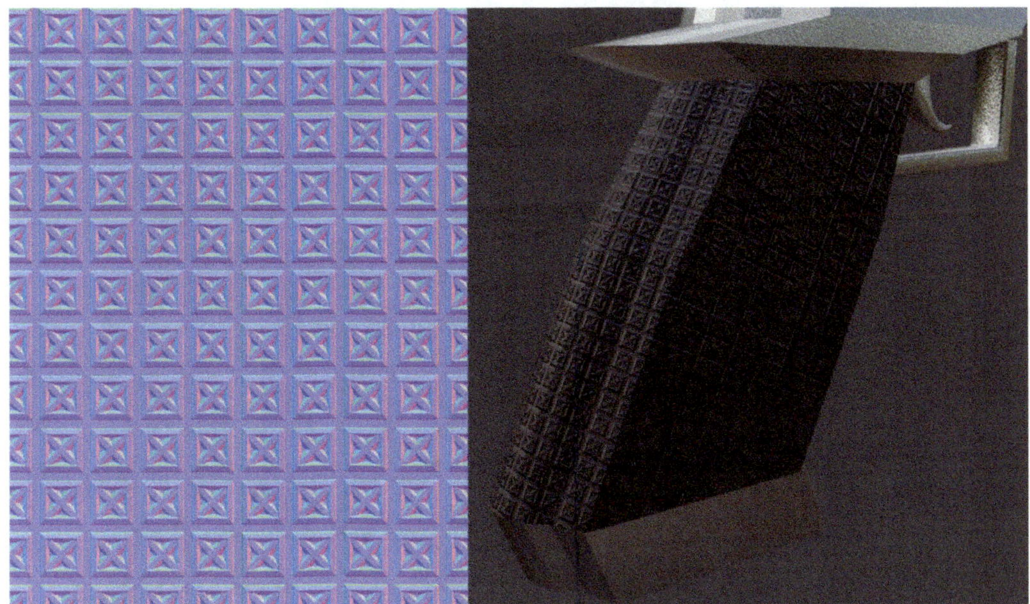

***Figure 4-14.** Normal map baked from the cross-motif grid using Listing 4-1 (left), applied to the grip of a procedural gun generated using the game weapon generator from Chapters 2 and 3 (right)*

Creating Procedural Materials for Gun Parts

In this section, we'll create three metallic materials with different surface characteristics—shiny, brushed, and grid patterned, which are mixed with different colors to make silver, gold, and copper variations. We'll inspect the shader tree for each material followed by Python code to generate it.

Shiny Metal

We can make a basic polished metal by setting the Principled BSDF node's Metallic value to 1 and Roughness to 0, as shown in Figure 4-15. Setting Base Color to different values will then create different colored metals, such as gray for silver, yellow for gold, a rust color for copper, etc., as shown in Figure 4-16.

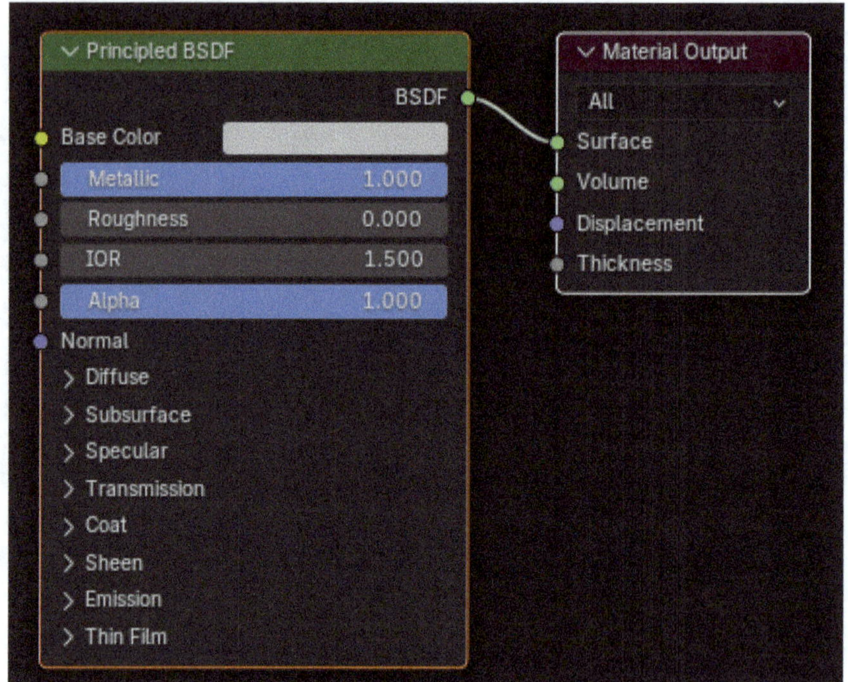

Figure 4-15. *Shader node tree for a silver metallic material. Metallic is set to 1 and Roughness to 0 on the Principled BSDF node, with Base Color set to (0.604, 0.604, 0.604, 1), which is a light gray color*

Generating the Shiny Metallic Material in Python

`create_shiny_metal` in Listing 4-7 configures the settings from Figure 4-15 in a given material `mat`'s node tree (`mat.node_tree`). It starts by looking up the tree's Principled BSDF node `node_bsdf` by name, followed by each of its inputs by name (e.g., Metallic via `node_bsdf.inputs['Metallic']`). Note that the value for each input is set using its `default_value` variable. `color` is passed in as a four-tuple of RGBA values (between 0.0 and 1.0) and assigned directly to Principled BSDF's Base Color (`node_bsdf.inputs['Base Color'].default_value`).

Listing 4-7. Generating the shader node tree for a shiny metallic material with the given color (see /Ch4/texture_material_generation.py)

```
def create_shiny_metal(mat, color):
    nodes = mat.node_tree.nodes
    node_bsdf = nodes['Principled BSDF']
```

```
node_bsdf.inputs['Metallic'].default_value = 1.0
node_bsdf.inputs['Roughness'].default_value = 0.0
node_bsdf.inputs['Base Color'].default_value = color
```

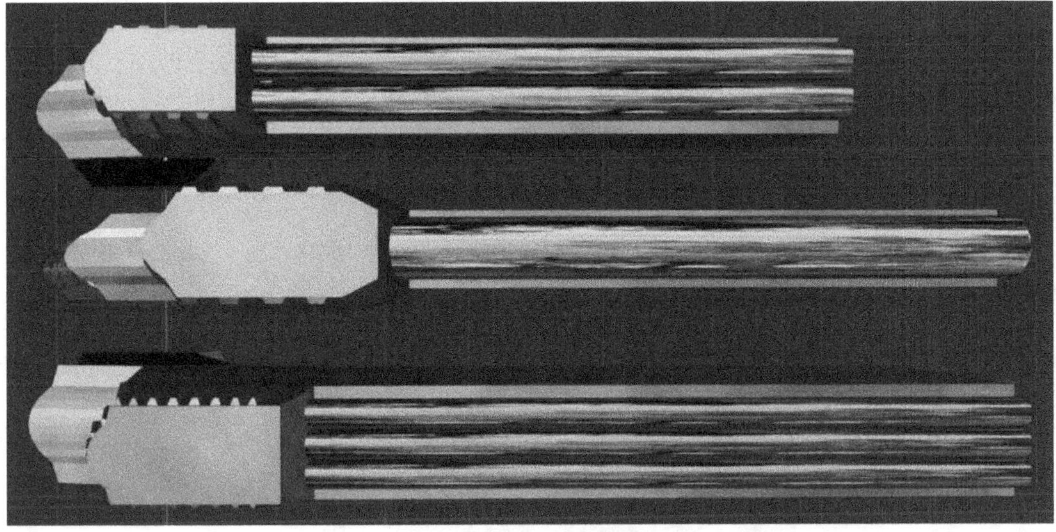

Figure 4-16. *Shiny metallic materials created using Listing 4-7 applied to gun barrels. From top to bottom: silver (color = (0.604, 0.604, 0.604, 1.0)), gold (color = (1.000, 0.829, 0.359, 1.000)), and copper (color = (1.000, 0.383, 0.249, 1.000))*

Brushed Metal

Next, we'll make a brushed metal by using a Noise Texture node to control the Heights input of a Bump node, which is in turn connected to the Normals input of Principled BSDF to create slight unevenness across the surface. Since we're varying the normals of an object with the material, we need to unwrap the object we're applying the material to (in Edit mode, select the portion of the mesh to unwrap, then UV (U Key) ➤ Unwrap). To use the UVs in the shader tree, we'll then add a Texture Coordinate node, select the object unwrapped in the "Object:" dropdown, then connect its "UV" output to the "Vector" input of a Mapping node, as shown in Figure 4-17. The Mapping node's "Vector" output is then linked to the Noise Texture node's "Vector" input. We'll keep Principled BSDF's Metallic value at 1.0 but dial up Roughness slightly to 0.2 to add to the Bump node's effects.

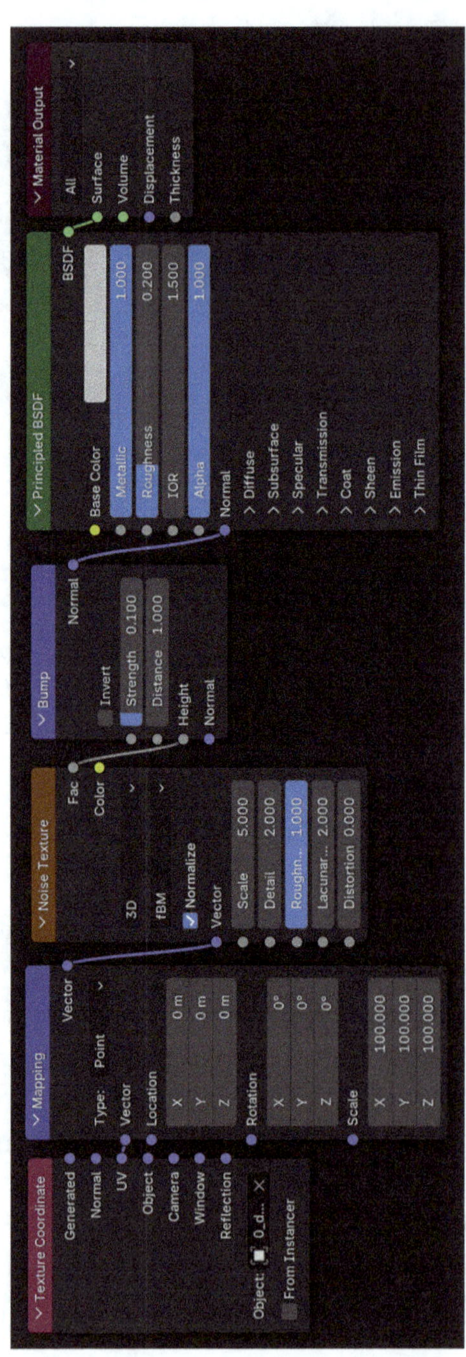

Figure 4-17. *Shader node tree for a brushed silver metallic material. The brushed surface is produced using a Noise Texture as the Height input for a Bump node, which is in turn used as the Normal input for the Principled BSDF node. The silver color is created by setting the Principled BSDF node's Base Color to (0.604, 0.604, 0.604, 1), which is a light gray color*

Generating the Brushed Metallic Material in Python

`create_brushed_metal` in Listing 4-8 generates the shader node tree from Figure 4-17 for a given object (`obj`) and material (`mat`). Just like Listing 4-7, a `color` argument is used to set the Base Color of the Principled BSDF node to create different colored metals, as shown in Figure 4-18.

Listing 4-8. Generating the shader node tree for a brushed metallic material mixed with the given color (see /Ch4/texture_material_generation.py)

```
def create_brushed_metal(obj, mat, color):
    node_tc, node_mapping = ↩
        create_texture_coords_mapping_nodes(obj, mat)
    set_mapping_node_scale(mat, (100,100,100))

    nodes = mat.node_tree.nodes
    node_noise = nodes.new(type='ShaderNodeTexNoise')
    node_noise.noise_dimensions = '3D'
    node_noise.noise_type = 'FBM'
    node_noise.normalize = True
    node_noise.inputs['Roughness'].default_value = 1.0

    links = mat.node_tree.links
    links.new(node_mapping.outputs['Vector'], ↩
        node_noise.inputs['Vector'])

    node_bump = nodes.new(type='ShaderNodeBump')
    node_bump.inputs[0].default_value = 0.1
    links.new(node_noise.outputs['Fac'], ↩
        node_bump.inputs['Height'])

    node_bsdf = nodes['Principled BSDF']
    links.new(node_bump.outputs['Normal'], ↩
        node_bsdf.inputs['Normal'])
    node_bsdf.inputs['Metallic'].default_value = 1.0
    node_bsdf.inputs['Roughness'].default_value = 0.2
    node_bsdf.inputs['Base Color'].default_value = color
```

```
    node_out = nodes['Material Output']
    nodes_to_arrange = [node_tc, node_mapping, ↩
        node_noise, node_bump, node_bsdf, node_out]
    rearrange_nodes(nodes_to_arrange)
```

We'll construct the nodes in Figure 4-17 from left to right, first by calling create_texture_coords_mapping_nodes (Listing 4-9) to create the Texture Coordinate node and the Mapping node to bring in the given object's (obj) UVs, then set_mapping_node_scale (Listing 4-10) to set the mapping scale to 100 in all directions. Next, we'll create the Noise Texture node (of type 'ShaderNodeTexNoise'), set its dimension to '3D', type to 'FBM', check the Normalize box so the output is between 0.0 and 1.0, and set Roughness to 1.0. After that, we link the Mapping node to the Noise Texture node so the given object (obj)'s UVs are used to map it.

Next, we'll create the Bump node (of type 'ShaderNodeBump') and set its Strength (inputs[0]) to 0.1, then connect Noise Texture's "Fac" output to Bump's "Height" input. We assume that the caller had used create_material (Listing 4-3) to create mat before passing it to this function so mat already has a Principled BSDF node; therefore, we simply look it up by name, then connect Bump's "Normal" output to Principled BSDF's "Normal" input. As described in the previous section, we'll again dial Principled BSDF's "Metallic" value to the maximum of 1.0 but increase "Roughness" slightly to 0.2 so it contributes to the unevenness introduced by the Bump node.

We'll copy the passed in color four-tuple of RGBA values directly to Principled BSDF's Base Color. Principled BSDF is already linked to Material Output by create_material (Listing 4-3), so to wrap up the tree, we'll simply call the helper function rearrange_nodes (Listing 4-5) to lay out the nodes sequentially with spacing relative to the nodes' sizes. Figure 4-18 shows examples of brushed metallic materials created with Listing 4-8 applied to various procedural guns produced by the game weapon generator from Chapters 2 and 3, in silver, gold, and copper.

Figure 4-18. *Brushed metallic materials created using Listing 4-8 applied to gun frames. From top to bottom: silver (color = (0.604, 0.604, 0.604, 1.0)), gold (color = (1.000, 0.829, 0.359, 1.000)), and copper (color = (1.000, 0.383, 0.249, 1.000)). The three brushed materials' shiny counterparts are shown on the barrels for comparison*

Creating Subtree with Texture Coordinate and Mapping Nodes

The setup from Figure 4-17 of using a Texture Coordinate node with a Mapping node to bring in UVs of the object to apply the material to is so commonplace across shader trees that it makes sense to write a helper function `create_texture_coords_mapping_nodes` as shown in Listing 4-9 to automate the process.

Listing 4-9. Adding a Texture Coordinate node with a Mapping node to use the given obj's UVs as mapping in the given material's shader tree (see /Ch4/material_and_image_utils.py)

```
def create_texture_coords_mapping_nodes(obj, mat):
    nodes = mat.node_tree.nodes
    node_tc = nodes.new(type='ShaderNodeTexCoord')
    node_tc.object = obj

    node_mapping = nodes.new(type='ShaderNodeMapping')
    links = mat.node_tree.links
    links.new(node_tc.outputs['UV'], ↩
        node_mapping.inputs['Vector'])

    return node_tc, node_mapping
```

To add a Texture Coordinate node, you'll call the material shader tree's `new` method with the node's Enum type `'ShaderNodeTexCoord'`. Assigning the given `obj` to the node's `object` field (`node_tc.object = obj`) is then equivalent to selecting `obj` in the node's "Object:" dropdown in Figure 4-17. Similarly, you'll create a Mapping node (of type `'ShaderNodeMapping'`), then add a link from Texture Coordinate to Mapping by calling the tree's links' `new` method with the "from" socket followed by the "to" socket as arguments—which in this case are the Texture Coordinate node's "UV" output (`node_tc.outputs['UV']`) and the Mapping node's "Vector" input (`node_mapping.inputs['Vector']`).

Tip: Finding the Python Enum Type of a Shader Node

As you've seen in the previous section, to create a new shader node, you have to call the material tree's `new` method with the node's Enum type string (e.g., `'ShaderNodeTexCoord'` for the Texture Coordinate node). Luckily, there is a systematic way to find these Enum strings—through Python Tooltips, which can be enabled under Edit ➤ Preferences... ➤ Interface ➤ Tooltips by checking both the "User Tooltips" and "Python Tooltips" boxes (the former enables tooltips in general and the latter the display of Blender Python API functions corresponding to menu items). Then to find a node's type Enum, you can simply hover over that node's entry under the Add menu in the shader node editor (as shown on the top of Figure 4-19). Alternatively, you can bring up the search box in the shader node editor, type in a search term, then hover over the relevant entry in the search results, as shown on the bottom of Figure 4-19.

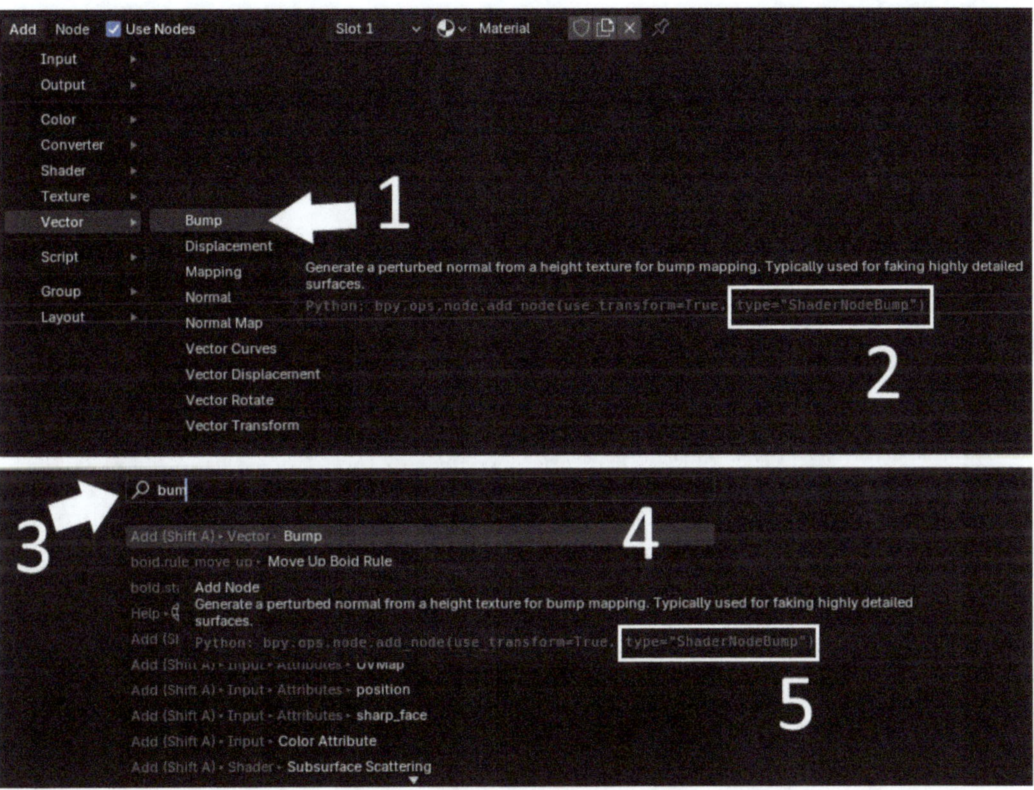

Figure 4-19. *Locating the Enum type string for the Bump node. The first way is to hover over Bump's entry under Add ➤ Vector ➤ Bump (1) in the shader node editor to trigger the tooltip (2), which shows its Enum string 'ShaderNodeBump.' The second way is to type in a search term (e.g., bum) in the search box (3), hover over the relevant entry in the search results (4), then locate the Enum value in the tooltip (5)*

Setting a Material's Mapping Node Scale Values

One of the quickest ways to alter the number of repetitions a texture is tiled across a mesh is by changing the Mapping node's scale values. Taking our grip normal map example from Figure 4-14, if you set the X scale to 4, it will make the motifs shrink to ¼ as wide along X, therefore tile four times as much along that direction. You can write a helper function like `set_mapping_node_scale` in Listing 4-10, which sets the given material `mat`'s Mapping node `scale` to a given three-tuple of values.

Listing 4-10. Setting the Scale X, Y, and Z values of a Mapping node to a given three-tuple (see /Ch4/material_and_image_utils.py)

```
def set_mapping_node_scale(mat, scale):
    nodes = mat.node_tree.nodes
    node_mapping = nodes['Mapping']
    node_mapping.inputs['Scale'].default_value = scale
```

Metal with Surface Grid Pattern

In this section, we'll create a variation of the metallic material which at a distance appears brushed but when zoomed in shows a fine grid surface pattern. The grid is created using a Voronoi Texture as the Height input for a Bump node, which in turn is used as the Normal input for the Principled BSDF node. The cells of the Voronoi Texture become polygons with right angles when you use the F1 feature with Euclidean distance metric and decrease Randomness to 0.0, as shown in Figure 4-20. As with the shiny and brushed materials, we can set Principled BSDF's Base Color to different RGBA values to make silver, gold, copper, and other variations, as shown in Figure 4-21.

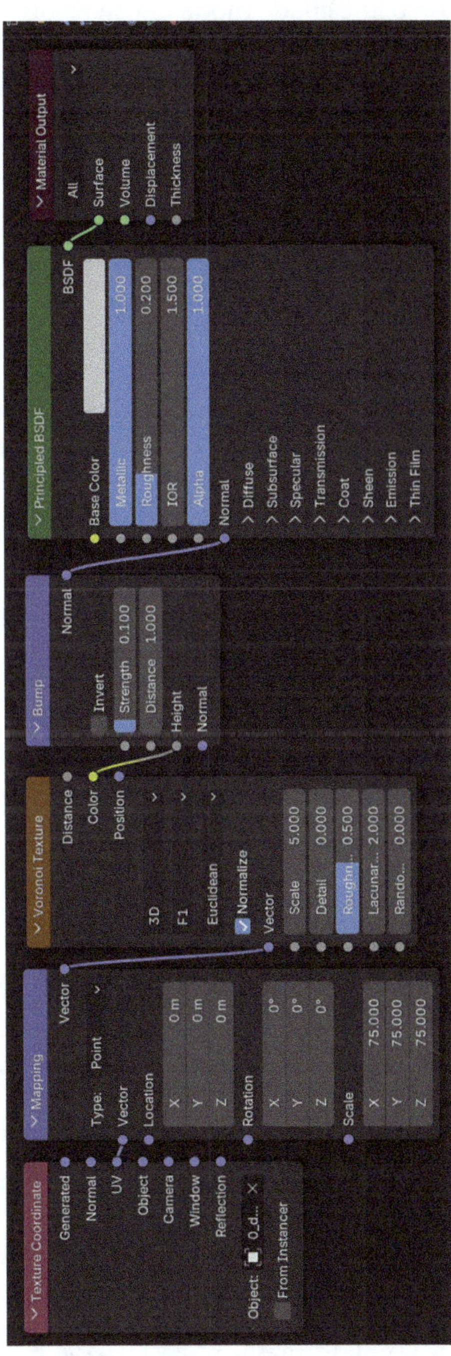

***Figure 4-20.** Shader node tree for a grid-patterned metallic material. The grid is created using a Voronoi Texture as the Height input for a Bump node, which is in turn used as the Normal input for the Principled BSDF node*

Generating the Grid-Patterned Metallic Material in Python

We'll now automate the creation of the shader node tree in Figure 4-20 with the function `create_fine_grid_metal` in Listing 4-11. Similar to the shiny and brushed materials, we'll use a `color` argument to set the Base Color of the Principled BSDF node to create different colored variations of the material as shown in Figure 4-21.

Listing 4-11. Generating a grid-patterned metallic material mixed with the given color (see /Ch4/texture_material_generation.py)

```
def create_fine_grid_metal(obj, mat, color):
    node_tc, node_mapping = ↩
        create_texture_coords_mapping_nodes(obj, mat)
    set_mapping_node_scale(mat, (75,75,75))

    nodes = mat.node_tree.nodes
    node_vor = nodes.new(type='ShaderNodeTexVoronoi')
    node_vor.voronoi_dimensions = '3D'
    node_vor.distance = 'EUCLIDEAN'
    node_vor.feature = 'F1'
    node_vor.normalize = True
    node_vor.inputs['Roughness'].default_value = 0.5
    node_vor.inputs['Randomness'].default_value = 0.0

    links = mat.node_tree.links
    links.new(node_mapping.outputs['Vector'], ↩
        node_vor.inputs['Vector'])

    node_bump = nodes.new(type='ShaderNodeBump')
    node_bump.inputs[0].default_value = 0.1
    links.new(node_vor.outputs['Color'], ↩
        node_bump.inputs['Height'])

    node_bsdf = nodes['Principled BSDF']
    links.new(node_bump.outputs['Normal'], ↩
        node_bsdf.inputs['Normal'])
    node_bsdf.inputs['Metallic'].default_value = 1.0
    node_bsdf.inputs['Roughness'].default_value = 0.2
    node_bsdf.inputs['Base Color'].default_value = color
```

```
node_out = nodes['Material Output']
nodes_to_arrange = [node_tc, node_mapping, ↩
    node_vor, node_bump, node_bsdf, node_out]
rearrange_nodes(nodes_to_arrange)
```

Similar to the brushed metal, we'll build the shader tree from left to right as shown in Figure 4-20, first by calling create_texture_coords_mapping_nodes (Listing 4-9) to create the Texture Coordinate node and the Mapping node to use the given object's (obj) UVs as mapping, then call set_mapping_node_scale (Listing 4-10) to set the Mapping node Scale to 75 uniformly. After that, we'll create the Voronoi Texture node (of type 'ShaderNodeTexVoronoi') and configure its settings—by selecting '3D' as dimension, using the 'F1' feature with 'EUCLIDEAN' as the distance metric for calculation, and checking the Normalize box so output values are in the 0.0 to 1.0 range. To turn the Voronoi cells into rectangular cells, we'll remove randomness by setting Randomness to 0.0 (node_vor.inputs['Randomness'].default_value) and set Roughness to 0.5. At this point, we've finished setting up the Voronoi Texture node, so we'll connect the Mapping node's "Vector" output to the Voronoi Texture node's "Vector" input.

The remaining setup of this material is similar to that of the brushed metal material in Listing 4-8—we'll create the Bump node (of type 'ShaderNodeBump') and set its Strength (inputs[0]) to 0.1, then connect the Voronoi Texture's "Color" output to Bump's "Height" input. We assume that the caller had used create_material (Listing 4-3) to create mat before passing it to this function so mat already has a Principled BSDF node—we retrieve it by name and connect Bump's "Normal" output to Principled BSDF's "Normal" input. We'll again set Principled BSDF's "Metallic" to the maximum at 1.0 and increase "Roughness" to 0.2 and finish by copying the passed in color four-tuple of RGBA values to Principled BSDF's Base Color. Principled BSDF is already linked to Material Output by create_material (Listing 4-3), so we have finished the tree construction at this point. Lastly, we'll call the helper function rearrange_nodes (Listing 4-5) with a list of the nodes in the order we want laid out—rearrange_nodes will then arrange them sequentially with proper spacing. Figure 4-21 shows a close-up example of a material produced by Listing 4-11 on the top and different colored versions at the bottom.

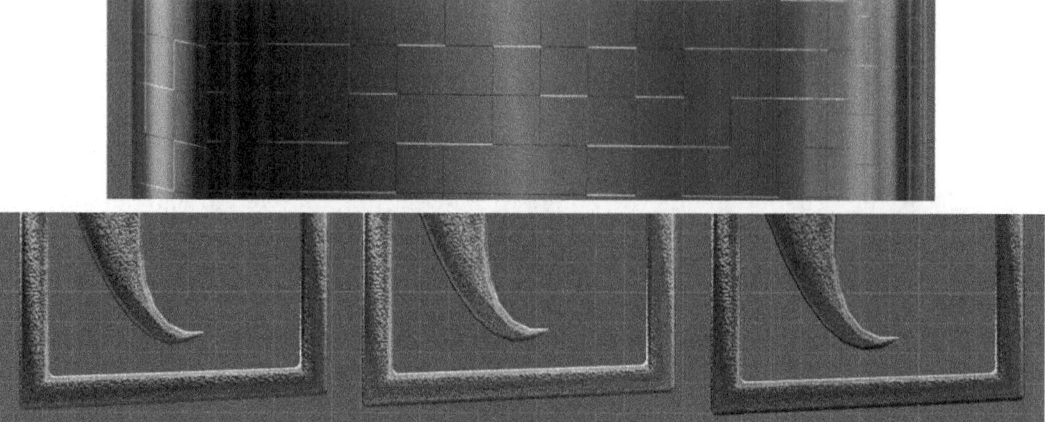

Figure 4-21. *Grid-patterned metallic material created using Listing 4-11 applied to gun triggers. On the bottom, from left to right: silver (color = (0.604, 0.604, 0.604, 1.0)), gold (color = (1.000, 0.829, 0.359, 1.000)), and copper (color = (1.000, 0.383, 0.249, 1.000)). The top shows the silver variation zoomed in to show grid detail*

Rubber with Bump Surface Pattern for Grip

In this section, we'll create the grip material which incorporates the normal maps that we baked from procedural meshes earlier in the chapter.

Building the Shader Node Tree for the Grip Material

We want the grip to resemble a dark colored rubber-like material that is mostly matte with a slight sheen; therefore, we keep the Principled BSDF node's Metallic setting at 0.0, Roughness at 0.5, and increase IOR slightly to 1.5. To incorporate the normal map, we'll use a Texture Coordinate node with a Mapping node to use the gun mesh's UVs for mapping, then create an Image Texture node with the normal map as its image, choose Linear for interpolation, Flat for projection, Repeat for extrapolation, Single Image, and Non-Color for color space. We then link the Image Texture node to a Normal Map node set to Tangent Spaces with Strength 1, which is in turn linked to the Principled BSDF node's "Normal" input. As with the case of the metallic materials created in earlier sections, we'll set Principled BSDF's Base Color to control the underlying color of the material—for example, an RGBA four-tuple (0, 0, 0, 1) for black, (0.086, 0.02, 0.004, 1) for brown, and so on, as shown in Figure 4-22. To wrap up the tree, we connect Principled BSDF's "BSDF" output to Material Output's "Surface" input. The finished tree is shown in Figure 4-23.

Figure 4-22. *Four grip materials created by incorporating the round bump and cross-motif normal maps we baked earlier in this chapter into the shader tree shown in Figure 4-23. The RGBA values (0, 0, 0, 1) are used for black and (0.086, 0.02, 0.004, 1) for brown. From left to right: brown round bumps, black round bumps, brown cross-motif, and black cross-motif*

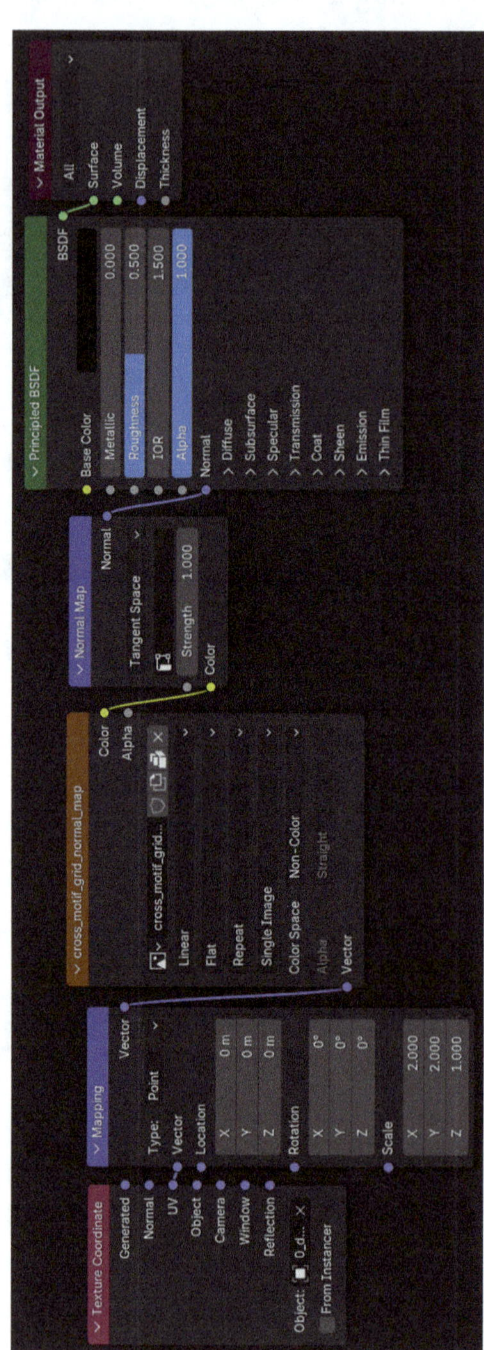

Figure 4-23. *Shader node tree for the gun grip material. An Image Texture node created with a normal map is connected to a Normal Map node, then fed into the Normal input of the Principled BSDF node, with Base Color as black and Roughness = 0.5, for a matte rubber look*

Generating the Grip Material in Python

Let's write some Python code to automate the creation of the shader tree in Figure 4-23. The function `create_grip` in Listing 4-12 will take a material (`mat`) created with `create_material` (Listing 4-3), a `color` for setting Principled BSDF's Base Color, and a path for a normal map file, then construct the tree in Figure 4-23 and apply it to the given object (`obj`).

Listing 4-12. Generate the shader node tree in Figure 4-23 for the gun grip material using the given normal map path and color four-tuple (see /Ch4/texture_material_generation.py)

```
def create_grip(obj, mat, color, normal_map_filepath):
    node_tc, node_mapping = ↩
        create_texture_coords_mapping_nodes(obj, mat)
    set_mapping_node_scale(mat, (2,1,1))

    nodes = mat.node_tree.nodes
    node_tex_img = nodes.new(type='ShaderNodeTexImage')
    image_block = bpy.data.images.load(normal_map_filepath)
    image_block.name = get_name_no_ext(normal_map_filepath)
    image_block.colorspace_settings.name = 'Non-Color'
    node_tex_img.image = image_block

    node_normal_map = nodes.new(type='ShaderNodeNormalMap')
    links = mat.node_tree.links
    links.new(node_mapping.outputs['Vector'], ↩
        node_tex_img.inputs['Vector'])
    links.new(node_tex_img.outputs['Color'], ↩
        node_normal_map.inputs['Color'])
    node_bsdf = nodes['Principled BSDF']
    links.new(node_normal_map.outputs['Normal'], ↩
        node_bsdf.inputs['Normal'])

    node_bsdf.inputs['Metallic'].default_value = 0.0
    node_bsdf.inputs['Roughness'].default_value = 0.5
    node_bsdf.inputs['Base Color'].default_value = color
```

```
node_out = nodes['Material Output']
nodes_to_arrange = [node_tc, node_mapping, ↩
    node_tex_img, node_normal_map, ↩
    node_bsdf, node_out]
rearrange_nodes(nodes_to_arrange)
```

Similar to the brushed metal, we'll construct the shader tree from left to right as shown in Figure 4-23, by calling `create_texture_coords_mapping_nodes` (Listing 4-9) to create the Texture Coordinate and Mapping nodes to employ the given object's (`obj`) UVs as mapping, followed by `set_mapping_node_scale` (Listing 4-10) to set mapping scale to 2 for X, 1 for Y, and 1 for Z (I find that at X=1 the normal maps look stretched horizontally, setting X=2 fixes the issue).

Next, we'll create an Image Texture node (of type `'ShaderNodeTexImage'`) and load the given normal map from disk as an image data block by calling `bpy.data.images.load`. The image block is named to match the name of the normal map file without the extension (which is extracted using the helper function `get_name_no_ext` (Listing 4-13)). To finish setting up the image block, we set its color space to `'Non-Color'` while leaving all other settings at default, then assign the block to the Image Texture node as its image (`node_tex_img.image = image_block`).

Next, we'll create the Normal Map node (of type `'ShaderNodeNormalMap'`), then link the nodes together. Recall that `create_texture_coords_mapping_nodes` (Listing 4-9) already connected the Texture Coordinate and Mapping nodes (the first two nodes of the tree), so we'll start creating links from there. Recall that we create a link by calling the tree links' `new` method (`mat.node_tree.links.new`) with the "from" node's socket and "to" node's socket as arguments. We'll link the Mapping node's "Vector" output to the Image Texture node's "Vector" input, Image Texture's "Color" output to Normal Map's "Color" input, and Normal Map's "Normal" to Principled BSDF's "Normal" input. Again, we assume that the caller had used `create_material` (Listing 4-3) to create the material passed in (`mat`), which means Principled BSDF's "BSDF" output will already be connected to Material Output's "Surface" input.

In the last block of code, we configure the values for the Principled BSDF node, setting Metallic to 0.0, Roughness to 0.0, and Base Color to the RGBA `color` four-tuple passed in. To finish up, we call `rearrange_nodes` (Listing 4-5) with a list of the tree nodes in the order we want laid out—`rearrange_nodes` will then arrange them sequentially with proper spacing.

Tip You can expose the Mapping node scale as an argument for your material generation function to accommodate a wider variety of image textures.

Util Function: Extracting the Name of a File Without the Extension

We'll take a quick look at the util function `get_name_no_ext` (Listing 4-13) we used in `create_grip` (Listing 4-12) to extract the name of the normal map file without the extension. For example, if the given `filepath` is `"C:/documents/round_bumps_normal_map.png"`, `get_name_no_ext` will return the string `"round_bumps_normal_map"`.

Listing 4-13. Return the portion of a file name without the extension (see /Ch4/material_and_image_utils.py)

```
def get_name_no_ext(filepath):
    delimiter = "/" if "/" in filepath else "\\"
    filename_no_ext = ↩
        filepath.split(delimiter)[-1].split(".")[0]
    return filename_no_ext
```

We need to divide `filepath` at the slashes, grab the last portion (which is the file name *with* the extension), then chop off the part after the dot. To do so, we'll use the type of slash present in the given `filepath` as the `delimiter` to call `filepath.split` with, which will return a list of substrings resulting from dividing `filepath` at each occurrence of `delimiter`. The last entry of this list (at index –1) is then the substring *after* the last slash in the path—the file name *with* the extension. We split the file name further by calling `split` again with the dot, which will return the string before and after the dot, the first of which is the name and the second the extension. For example, if `filepath` is `"C:/documents/round_bumps_normal_map.png"`, then

```
delimiter is "/";
filepath.split(delimiter) is ["C:", "documents", ↩
    "round_bumps_normal_map.png"];
filepath.split(delimiter)[-1] is "round_bumps_normal_map.png";
filepath.split(delimiter)[-1].split(".") is ↩
    ["round_bumps_normal_map", "png"];
filepath.split(delimiter)[-1].split(".")[0] is ↩
    "round_bumps_normal_map".
```

Modifying the Game Weapon Generator to Generate and Apply Materials Automatically

In this section, we'll modify the game weapon generator from Chapters 2 and 3 to unwrap various parts of the gun and generate and assign basic materials. These materials' shader trees will in turn be filled out by functions like create_shiny_metal (Listing 4-7), create_brushed_metal (Listing 4-8), create_fine_grid_metal (Listing 4-11), and create_grip (Listing 4-12).

Unwrap and Apply Materials to the Frame and Grip

Recall that the gun model consists of three mesh objects: the grip with the frame, the barrels, and the trigger box with the finger pull. In Listing 4-14, we'll add code to the function generate_gun in gun_generator.py to tackle unwrapping the first object and generating its two required materials, one for the frame and one for the grip.

Listing 4-14. Unwrap and apply material for the grip and frame (see the function generate_gun in /Ch4/gun_generator.py)

```
bpy.ops.mesh.select_all(action='DESELECT')
for f in grip_faces:
    f.select = True
bpy.ops.mesh.select_all(action='INVERT')
bpy.ops.uv.smart_project()
gun_mat = create_material(grip_obj, ↩
    grip_obj.name+"_gun_mat")
bpy.ops.object.material_slot_assign()

bpy.ops.mesh.select_all(action='DESELECT')
for f in grip_faces:
    f.select = True
bpy.ops.uv.smart_project()
grip_mat = create_material(grip_obj, ↩
    grip_obj.name+"_grip_mat")
bpy.ops.object.material_slot_assign()
```

We will insert the code in Listing 4-14 into the function `generate_gun` in `gun_generator.py` right after the grip and frame are generated (the Chapter 4 version of this file already has the code integrated). We'll unwrap the frame and create and assign material to it by calling `create_material` (Listing 4-3), then do the same for the grip.

`create_material` (Listing 4-3) will create a shader tree with only a Principled BSDF and Material Output node—but this is okay, because once the materials for the grip, frame, and other parts of the gun are returned from `generate_gun`, we'll call the functions from the section "Creating Procedural Materials for Gun Parts" to fill out their shader node trees to make them metallic, rubber, etc.

To unwrap the frame, we'll deselect all, select the copy of the grip faces we've saved in `grip_faces` in Chapter 3, then inverse select by calling `bpy.ops.mesh.select_all(action='INVERT')` so everything *but* the grip is selected (shown as (2) in Figure 4-24). We then call `bpy.ops.uv.smart_project()` to unwrap (UV ➤ Unwrap ➤ Smart UV Project) followed by `create_material` (Listing 4-3) to create a basic material named `grip_obj.name+"_gun_mat"`, then `bpy.ops.object.material_slot_assign()` to assign it to the part of the mesh we've just unwrapped. Calling `bpy.ops.object.material_slot_assign()` is equivalent to pressing the "Assign" button with a material selected in the list under Properties editor ➤ Material tab.

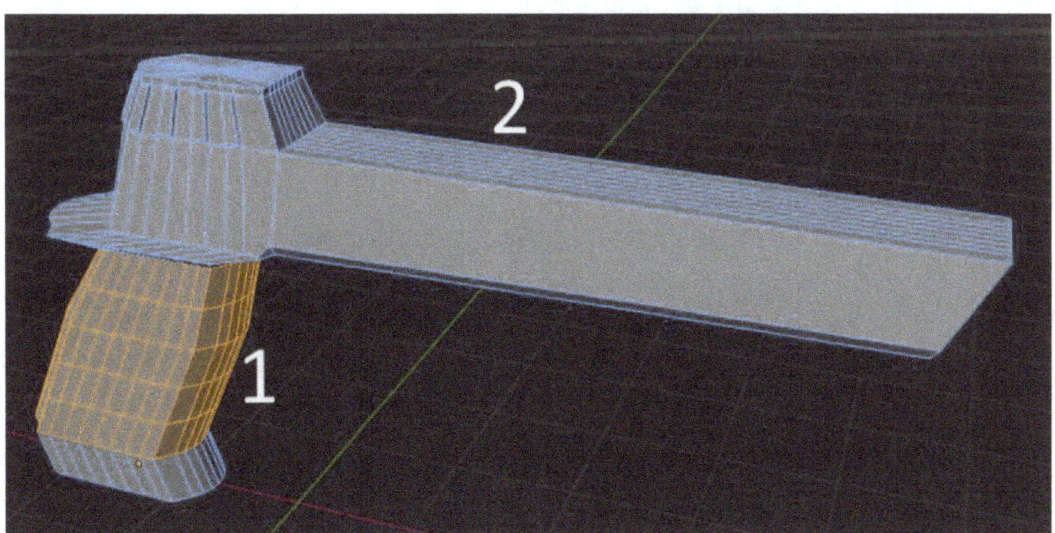

Figure 4-24. *Selecting faces in the grip/frame object to unwrap and assign materials to. (1) shows `grip_faces` in Listing 4-14 selected, which have the material named `grip_obj.name+"_grip_mat"` assigned to it, and (2) shows the inverse selection of `grip_faces`, which has the material named `grip_obj.name+"_gun_mat"` assigned to it*

We'll follow almost identical steps for the grip: deselect all, select the grip faces (but *not* inverse select this time), smart unwrap, then create and assign a material named `grip_obj.name+"_grip_mat"` to the selected portion of the mesh (shown as (1) in Figure 4-24).

Unwrap and Apply Material to the Barrels

In this section, we'll modify the function `generate_gun` in `gun_generator.py` to unwrap and create a material for the barrels. Instead of applying transforms and modifiers *after* all parts of the gun were generated as we did in Chapters 2 and 3, here we apply them right after the creation of each object, before unwrapping, to ensure that the UVs will match the final geometry. The code in Listing 4-15 is inserted in the function `generate_gun` in `gun_generator.py` right after the barrel object is generated, with which we apply the location transform, add and apply a Bevel modifier, then switch to Edit mode, unwrap, and create/assign a new material. You can refer to `/Ch4/gun_generator.py` in the downloaded source, which will contain all the modifications from this chapter.

Listing 4-15. Unwrap and apply material to the barrel object (see the function generate_gun in /Ch4/gun_generator.py)

```
bpy.ops.object.select_all(action='DESELECT')
barrel_obj.select_set(True)
bpy.ops.object.transform_apply(location=True, ↩
    rotation=False, scale=False)
bar_bevel_mod = add_bevel_modifier(barrel_obj, ↩
    width=2, segments=3)
bpy.ops.object.modifier_apply( ↩
    modifier=bar_bevel_mod.name)

bpy.ops.object.shade_smooth()
bpy.ops.object.mode_set(mode='EDIT')
bpy.ops.mesh.select_all(action='SELECT')
bpy.ops.uv.smart_project()
barrel_mat = create_material(barrel_obj, ↩
    barrel_obj.name+"_mat")
```

```
barrel_mat.node_tree.nodes["Principled ↩
    BSDF"].inputs[0].default_value = ↩
        (0, 1, 0, 1)
bpy.ops.object.material_slot_assign()
bpy.ops.object.mode_set(mode='OBJECT')
```

The barrel object has been switched to Object mode in `generate_gun` right before Listing 4-15. Here, we deselect all and select the barrel object (to ensure it is the only thing selected), then apply its location transform and add and apply a bevel modifier, as described in Chapter 3 in the section "Applying Transforms and Adding Modifiers." We then set the object to shade smooth, switch to Edit mode, select all, and call `bpy.ops.uv.smart_project()` to unwrap (UV ➤ Unwrap ➤ Smart UV Project) followed by `create_material` (Listing 4-3) to create a basic material and `bpy.ops.object.material_slot_assign()` to assign it to the mesh (which is still selected). We finish by switching the barrel object to Object mode so we're ready to generate the trigger object after that.

Unwrap and Apply Material to the Trigger

Like the barrel object, we'll apply the trigger object's transform and modifiers before unwrapping it to ensure its UVs will match the final geometry, as shown in Listing 4-16.

Listing 4-16. Unwrap and apply material to the trigger object (see the function generate_gun in /Ch4/gun_generator.py)

```
bpy.ops.object.select_all(action='DESELECT')
trigger_obj.select_set(True)
trigger_bevel_mod = add_bevel_modifier( ↩
    trigger_obj, width=2, segments=3)
trigger_taper_mod = ↩
    add_simple_deform_taper_modifier(trigger_obj)
bpy.ops.object.modifier_apply( ↩
    modifier=trigger_bevel_mod.name)
bpy.ops.object.modifier_apply( ↩
    modifier=trigger_taper_mod.name)
bpy.ops.object.transform_apply(location=True, ↩
    rotation=False, scale=False)
```

```
bpy.ops.object.shade_smooth()
bpy.ops.object.mode_set(mode='EDIT')
bpy.ops.mesh.select_all(action='SELECT')
bpy.ops.uv.smart_project()
trigger_mat = create_material(trigger_obj, ↩
    trigger_obj.name+"_mat")
bpy.ops.object.material_slot_assign()
bpy.ops.object.mode_set(mode='OBJECT')
```

The trigger object has been switched to Object mode in generate_gun right before Listing 4-16. Here, we deselect all and select the trigger object (to ensure it is the only thing selected), add a Bevel modifier, add a Simple Deform modifier (set to taper), then apply both modifiers and the location transform as described in Chapter 3 in the section "Applying Transforms and Adding Modifiers." After that, we set the trigger object to shade smooth, switch it to Edit mode, select all, and call bpy.ops.uv.smart_project() to unwrap (UV ➤ Unwrap ➤ Smart UV Project). We then call create_material (Listing 4-3) to create a material and assign it to the unwrapped portion of the mesh with bpy.ops.object.material_slot_assign(), which is still selected. We finish by switching the trigger object to Object mode.

Since we've moved the code to apply transforms and modifiers in generate_gun to Listings 4-15 and 4-16, we'll remove the part of the code in Listing 3-11. The file /Ch4/gun_generator.py in the downloaded source will have these edits already made for you.

Set Viewport Shading to Material Preview and Return Generated Objects and Materials

There are two final changes we'll make in Listing 4-17 to the function generate_gun in gun_generator.py: the first is to set viewport shading to Material Preview and the second to return all generated mesh objects along with their materials, which we'll in turn pass to functions developed earlier in this chapter like create_shiny_metal (Listing 4-7), create_brushed_metal (Listing 4-8), create_fine_grid_metal (Listing 4-11), and create_grip (Listing 4-12) to fill out their shader node trees.

Listing 4-17. Set viewport shading to Material Preview and return all generated materials and mesh objects (see /Ch4/gun_generator.py)

```
set_viewport_material_preview(context)
return gun_mat, grip_mat, barrel_mat, trigger_mat, ↩
    grip_obj, barrel_obj, trigger_obj
```

We'll call the helper function `set_viewport_material_preview` with the passed-in `context` to set the viewport shading to Material Preview (which we'll look at in Listing 4-18). After that, we'll return the materials followed by the mesh objects.

Setting Viewport Shading to Material Preview

While developing scripts that generate or apply materials, we'll often want to switch to Material Preview in the viewport to check our progress. For convenience, we'll write a helper function `set_viewport_material_preview` (Listing 4-18) to do so which we can reuse in later chapters.

Listing 4-18. Helper function to set viewport shading to Material Preview under the given context (see /Ch4/material_and_image_utils.py)

```
def set_viewport_material_preview(context):
    for a in context.window.screen.areas:
        if a.type == 'VIEW_3D':
            for s in a.spaces:
                if s.type == 'VIEW_3D':
                    s.shading.type = 'MATERIAL'
```

We'll iterate the screen areas under the passed-in context to find the area with type `'VIEW_3D'`, then iterate the nested spaces under that area, until we find a space `s` of type `'VIEW_3D'`, which is the main editor area of the 3D Viewport. We can then set shading to Material Preview via `s.shading.type = 'MATERIAL'`.

Automate Gun Generation with All Materials

We'll now put everything we've developed throughout the chapter together and generate two gun models along with their materials and shader node trees.

Example 1: Black Cross-Motif Grip, Brushed Silver Frame, Shiny Silver Double Barrels, and Trigger with Silver Grid Surface Pattern

Listing 4-19 assumes that you've copied the cross-motif normal map file (/Ch4/cross_motif_grid_normal_map.png) to the directory you are running /Ch4/gun_generator.py from. We'll generate a gun using generate_gun's default parameters (see Listing 2-3) with black cross-motifs on the grip and silver everywhere else with various surface characteristics.

Listing 4-19. Generate a gun with a black grip with cross-motifs, brushed silver frame, shiny silver double barrels, and a trigger with silver grid surface pattern (see /Ch4/gun_generator.py)

```
normal_map_cross_motif_filepath = ↩
    script_dir + "/" + "cross_motif_grid_normal_map.png"
black = (0, 0, 0, 1)
silver = (0.604, 0.604, 0.604, 1.0)

gun_mat, grip_mat, barrel_mat, trigger_mat, grip_obj, ↩
    barrel_obj, trigger_obj = generate_gun(context, ↩
        "0_default_gun", location=(15, 0, 0))

create_grip(grip_obj, grip_mat, black, ↩
    normal_map_cross_motif_filepath)
create_brushed_metal(grip_obj, gun_mat, silver)
create_shiny_metal(barrel_mat, silver)
create_fine_grid_metal(trigger_obj, trigger_mat, silver)
```

Recall in Chapter 2 in the section "Handling Imports for Scripts to Run in the Text Editor," you learned how to derive the absolute path to the current directory you are running the script from and saved it in the variable script_dir in Listing 2-2—here, we'll reuse script_dir to form the path to the cross-motif normal map file by concatenating it with the file name. We'll also create the four-tuple of RGBA values (0, 0, 0, 1) for black and (0.604, 0.604, 0.604, 1.0) for silver, which we'll use to set the Principled BSDF node's Base Color in shader trees later.

Next, we'll generate a gun by calling `generate_gun` with default parameters, then `create_grip` (Listing 4-12) to build the shader tree for the returned grip material (`grip_mat`) with `black` as color and the cross-motif as the normal map. We'll also call `create_brushed_metal` (Listing 4-8) to build the shader tree for the frame material (`gun_mat`), `create_shiny_metal` (Listing 4-7) for the barrel material (`barrel_mat`), and `create_fine_grid_metal` (Listing 4-11) for the trigger material (`trigger_mat`), each with `silver` as its color. The order of these four function calls to build the shader trees for the materials does not matter. The model generated by Listing 4-19 is shown in Figure 4-25.

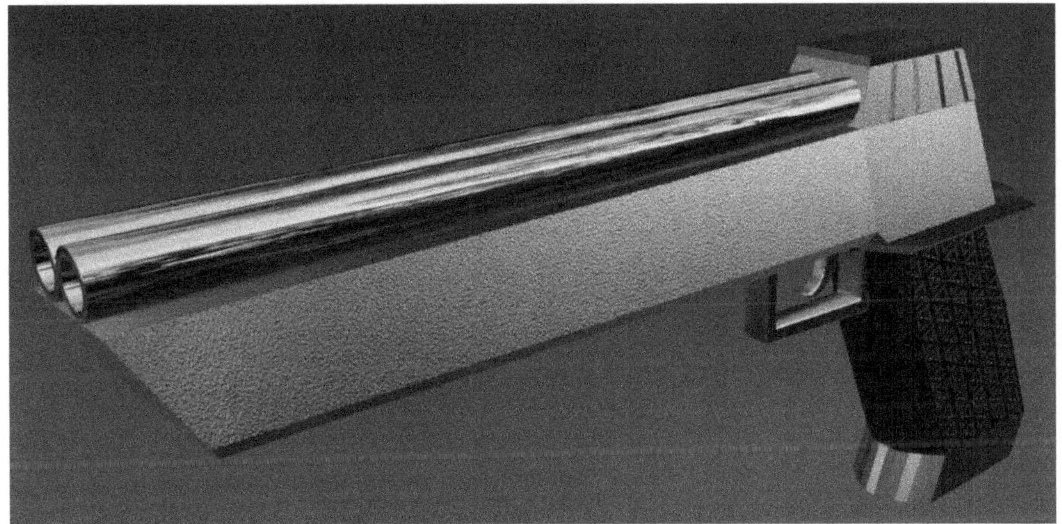

Figure 4-25. *The gun model with all of its materials generated by running Listing 4-19*

Example 2: Brown Round Bump Grip, Brushed Gold Frame, Shiny Copper Triple Barrels, and Trigger with Copper Grid Surface Pattern

In this example, we'll follow the same workflow as Listing 4-19: set up the path to the normal map file, this time the round bumps (`/Ch4/round_bumps_normal_maps.png`), call `generate_gun` to generate the gun and materials, then make four function calls to build the shader trees for the materials, with `brown` for the grip, `gold` for the frame, and `copper` for the barrels and trigger (see Listing 4-20 for the RGBA values for these colors). The generated model is shown in Figure 4-26. The order in which the last four function calls are made in Listing 4-20 does not matter, as you can build or edit the shader trees of any of the materials in any order.

Listing 4-20. Generate a gun with a brown grip with round bumps, brushed gold frame, shiny copper triple barrels, and a trigger with a copper surface grid pattern (see /Ch4/gun_generator.py)

```
normal_map_round_bumps_filepath = script_dir + "/" + ↩
    "round_bumps_normal_map.png"
brown = (0.086, 0.02, 0.004, 1)
gold = (1.000, 0.829, 0.359, 1.000)
copper = (1.000, 0.383, 0.249, 1.000)

gun_mat1, grip_mat1, barrel_mat1, trigger_mat1, ↩
    grip_obj1, barrel_obj1, trigger_obj1 = generate_gun( ↩
        context, "1", location=(20, 0, -55), ↩
        num_cir_segments=56, grip_radius=3, ↩
        num_grip_levels=8, stylize=True, ↩
        side_rib_only=False, num_barrels=3)

create_grip(grip_obj1, grip_mat1, brown, ↩
    normal_map_round_bumps_filepath)
create_brushed_metal(grip_obj1, gun_mat1, gold)
create_shiny_metal(barrel_mat1, copper)
create_fine_grid_metal(trigger_obj1, trigger_mat1, copper)
```

Figure 4-26. *The gun model with all of its materials generated by running Listing 4-20*

More Variations

In `/Ch4/gun_generator.py` in the downloaded source, I've included a function named `test_gen_guns_with_mats` which includes Listings 4-19 and 4-20 as well as additional code to generate three other guns with various material and color combinations. I encourage you to load up the script in the Text Editor and run it, which will produce the five models shown in Figure 4-27 (remember if you switch to the Modeling workspace, you'll have to use Z key ➤ Material Preview to set shading again, since the viewport under the Modeling workspace is separate from the viewport under the Scripting workspace). Try changing the arguments and see what variations will come up.

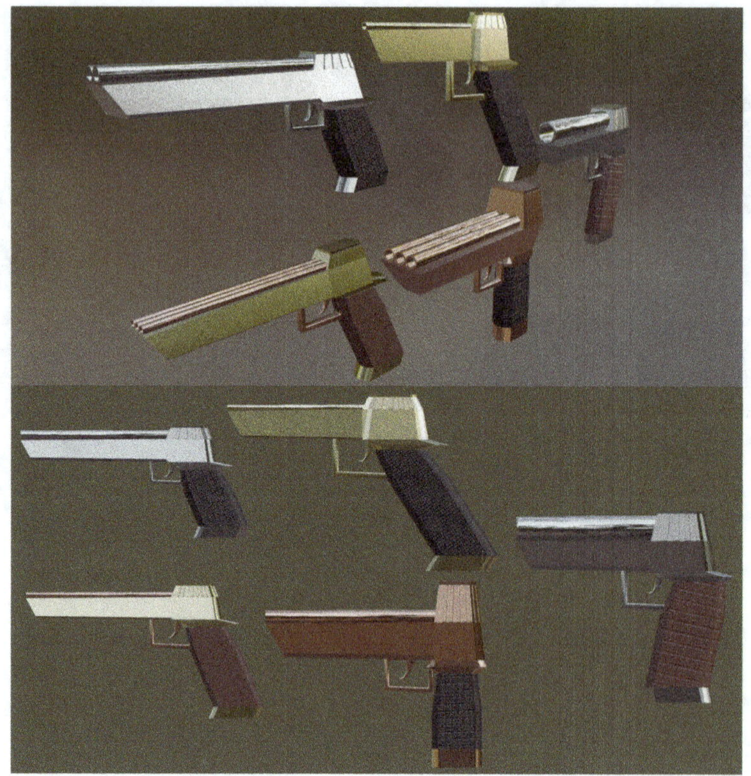

Figure 4-27. *Gun and material variations generated by running the function* `test_gen_guns_with_mats` *in* `/Ch4/gun_generator.py`

You can quickly experiment with new RGBA values for the metallic materials by playing with the shader tree of an existing material. Switch to Object mode, select one of the generated objects (e.g., the grip for a gun), go to Properties editor ➤ Material tab, select a material in the list, then switch to the Shading workspace to access its tree. Click Base Color on the Principled BSDF node to open its color wheel. Picking a new color on the wheel will instantly change the preview on the mesh. Click around to find a color you like, then drag the Value slider to the right of the wheel to find the right level of darkness.

Tip Try using colors like green, blue, etc. for the Principled BSDF node's Base Color to create "non-conventional" metals, like red and green for holiday ornaments.

Summary

In this chapter, you learned how to generate and apply materials to the procedural weapon models from Chapters 2 and 3 using a combination of geometry nodes, Python, and shader nodes. Using a normal map is a great way to emulate 3D surface details without adding extra geometry—in the first part of the chapter, you learned how to write Python code to automatically bake normal maps from grid meshes generated using geometry nodes. Starting with a single circular bump, you quickly extended the concept to create a 2D grid of bumps, before adding user inputs to control the size and spacing of bumps. You then made grids with different primitives like triangles and squares simply by changing tree parameters. Taking the concept further, you built a second geometry node tree to generate a grid of custom cross-motifs. After that, you constructed shader node trees to incorporate the normal maps you baked from the grid meshes to create rubber-like materials for the gun grips.

In addition to the rubber grips, you learned how to create shader trees for three types of metallic materials—shiny, brushed, and grid patterned. You then automated the tree construction in Python and learned that by exposing the Principled BSDF node's Base Color as an argument, you can generate different colored metals on demand, such as yellow for gold, rust for copper, etc. In the final part of the chapter, you modified the gun generator code from Chapters 2 and 3 to unwrap, create, and return materials for the different parts of the gun, which you then fed to the shader tree building functions to turn into metals, rubbers, and so on.

CHAPTER 5

Editing and Generating Meshes with Geometry Nodes

In the section "Baking a Normal Map from a Procedural Mesh" in Chapter 4, you learned the basics of constructing geometry node trees like extruding and transforming primitives, distributing them as instances over another mesh, and sampling the components (or attributes) of an object like the points making up a curve. In addition, you learned how to set up inputs through the Group Input node to allow user control of the tree's generation parameters. In this chapter, we'll continue to build on this trajectory and generate more complex meshes.

In the first half of the chapter, you'll use geometry nodes to generate meshes using built-in textures like Voronoi, Noise, and Gabor in a variety of ways. In the second half of the chapter, you'll use advanced features such as the Repeat block to create `for` loops, Compare nodes to set up Boolean conditions, Mesh Operations like Mesh Boolean to manipulate meshes, and Mesh Topology nodes like Corners of Vertex to derive neighboring geometry.

Running This Chapter's Examples

The source code for this book is available on GitHub via the book's product page, located at `https://link.springer.com/book/9798868817861`. This chapter's examples include both Python scripts (`*.py` files) and `*.blend` files that contain geometry node trees. Navigate to the `/Ch5` folder in the downloaded files, and when prompted by the text,

I. Lupiani, *Procedural Content Generation for Games*, https://doi.org/10.1007/979-8-8688-1787-8_5

open each `*.blend` file with File ➤ Open...(Ctrl-O) and each `*.py` file in the Text Editor under the Scripting workspace. There is an `if __name__ == "__main__"` block already set up at the bottom of each script which invokes the code listings with sample arguments.

Blend Files Overview

Here is an overview of the files supplied in the downloaded source. The usage of each file will be detailed in the text throughout the chapter.

- The folder `/Ch5/tree_setups` contains blend files for the three tree starting points described in the section "Tree Setups": `empty_tree.blend`, `tree_with_object_input.blend`, and `mapping_subtree.blend`.
- The folder `/Ch5/builtin_textures` contains six blend files for the trees described in the section "Generating Meshes from Textures": `/Ch5/cell_plates.blend`, `/Ch5/voxelizer.blend`, `/Ch5/cell_cracks_texture_visualized.blend`, `/Ch5/cell_cracks_and_vines.blend`, `/Ch5/cell_cavities_gemfacets.blend`, and `/Ch5/rock_and_wrinkles.blend`.
- `/Ch5/sliceform.blend` contains all the geometry node trees mentioned in the section "Generating Sliceforms."

Tree Setups

We will use several common starting points for building our geometry node trees throughout the chapter, which are described here. You can continue on or skip to the section "Generating Meshes from Textures" then refer back as prompted by the text.

Empty Tree

First, we'll go over how to create an empty tree to generate geometry from scratch. In a default startup blend file, select the Cube object, go to the Geometry Nodes workspace, then click +New in the node editor to create a new tree. With Cube still selected, tab into Edit mode in the viewport, A to toggle select all, X ➤ Delete ➤ Vertices to delete Cube's existing geometry, and tab back into Object mode. You can optionally delete the Group Input node as well (click then X key).

Tree with Object Input

Create an "Empty Tree" as described above but retain the Group Input node, then sever the link between Group Input and Group Output by holding down Ctrl-RMB and dragging the mouse cursor across the link. Add an object selection dropdown by following these steps: in the node editor, press the N key to summon the Properties shelf, click to select the Geometry input socket, change its Type to Object (the dot to the left of its name will turn orange), and double-click its name to rename it to "Mesh Object." You'll see a dropdown appear in the tree's modifier under Properties editor ➤ Modifier tab, as shown in Figure 5-1.

The trees in this chapter expect a mesh object selected in the dropdown (though the dropdown will let you select *any type* of object). To finish the setup, we link the Group Input node's "Mesh Object" socket to an Object Info node's "Object" input (Add ➤ Input ➤ Scene ➤ Object Info). The Object Info node's "Geometry" output will then give you the object's mesh data.

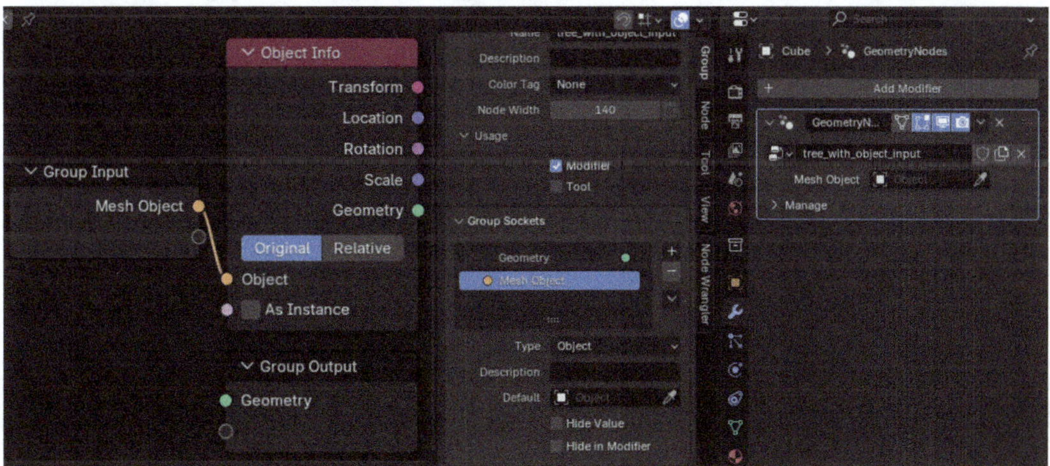

Figure 5-1. *The "Tree with Object Input" setup. The Geometry input socket is renamed to "Mesh Object" with its Type changed from Geometry to Object, which creates an object selection dropdown in the node tree's modifier under Properties editor ➤ Modifier tab*

Mapping Subtree

Since geometry nodes do not have "Texture Coordinate" and "Mapping" nodes like shader nodes, we'll create our own as follows:

1. Get the range of the input vertices' positions using a Bounding Box node (Add ➤ Geometry ➤ Operations ➤ Bounding Box).
    a. If you're using an input mesh object, connect Object Info's "Geometry" output to Bounding Box's "Geometry" input.
    b. If you're using a primitive (e.g., Grid node, Cube node, etc.), connect its "Geometry" output to Bounding Box's "Geometry" input.
2. Add a Map Range node (Add ➤ Utilities ➤ Math ➤ Map Range) and set it to "Vector" and "Linear."
3. Link Bounding Box's "Min" and "Max" to Map Range's "From Min" and "From Max."
4. Add and link a Position node (Add ➤ Geometry ➤ Read ➤ Position) to Map Range's "Vector" input.
5. By leaving Map Range's "To Min" and "To Max" at defaults, we map the input vertices' positions to the normalized range of (0, 0, 0) and (1, 1, 1) as shown in Figure 5-2.

The Map Range node can then be connected to either a built-in Texture node (e.g., Voronoi, Noise, etc.) or an Image Texture node to control their mapping. The span formed by Map Range's "To Min" and "To Max" (i.e., "To Max" minus "To Min") is equivalent to the shader Mapping node's Scale; therefore, we can change this span to manipulate the tiling frequency. For example, leaving "To Min" at 0s and changing "To Max" to (2, 1, 1) has the same effect as setting a shader Mapping node's Scale to (2, 1, 1), which will make the texture tile twice as many times along the X axis.

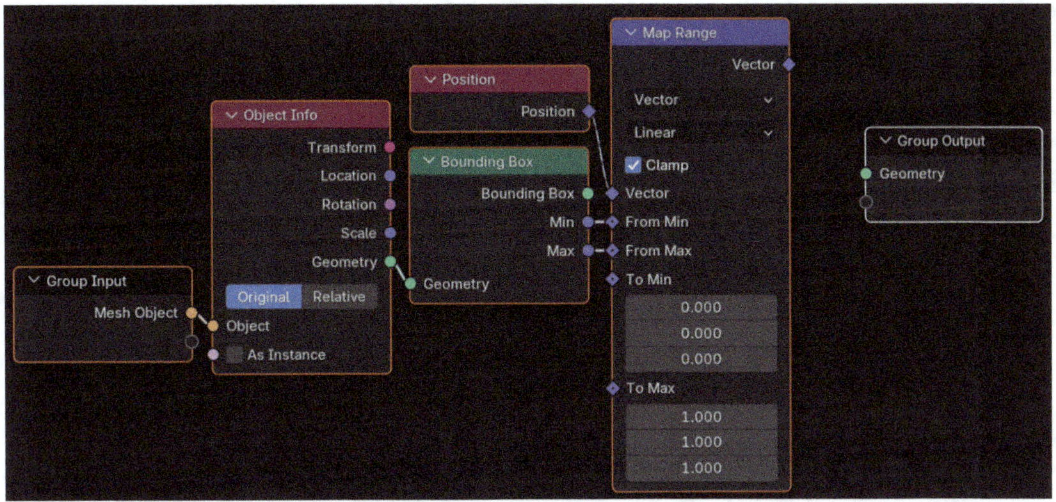

***Figure 5-2.** The "Tree with Object Input" setup with a "Mapping Subtree." You can connect Map Range to a built-in Texture node or Image Texture node to control the tiling frequency. A primitive node (e.g., Cube) may be used instead of the Group Input-Object Info combo*

How to Use the Trees

When prompted by the text to create one of the aforementioned trees, you can either build one from scratch by following the steps, or append the tree from the corresponding blend file in the downloaded source. For example, you can append a copy of "Mapping Subtree" via File ➤ Append... ➤ `mapping_subtree.blend` ➤ Append ➤ NodeTree ➤ `mapping_subtree`. To add the tree to an object, select the object, then under the Properties editor ➤ Material tab, click Add Modifier ➤ Geometry Nodes. In the modifier which appears, click the icon to the left of the +New button and select `mapping_subtree` from the list. If you switch to the Geometry Nodes workspace now, you'll see `mapping_subtree` appear in the node editor, ready to be edited. Note that if you were to append the Empty Tree from `empty_tree.blend`, you would have to delete the existing geometry of the mesh object you are adding the tree to since the tree would not do this for you.

Note The difference between Append and Link is that Append imports a copy of the data that you can edit independently from the original. On the other hand, Link imports a read-only soft copy—any changes made to the original will be automatically reflected in all the blend files that link it.

Generating Meshes from Textures

Remember in Chapter 4 you used geometry nodes to generate bump grids to bake normal maps from, thus creating images from meshes? In this section, we'll flip this around and generate meshes *from* built-in texture nodes like Voronoi, Noise, and Gabor, by offsetting the positions of vertices based on the textures' colors.

The "bunny" mesh that you will see throughout the chapter is created by the author based on the "Stanford bunny," a model originally created in 1994 by Greg Turk and Marc Levoy that is frequently used as a test model in computer graphics literature.

Generating Meshes from Voronoi Texture Nodes

The first texture we'll explore is the Voronoi Texture node. In the Chapter 4 section "Metal with Surface Grid Pattern," you used the Voronoi Texture to alter a shader tree's normals to emulate a grid pattern—here, we'll use Voronoi Texture with default settings (with the exception of Scale) to create organic cell-like divisions on mesh surfaces, as plates, cracks, vines, cavities, and gem-like facets.

Cell Plates

We'll start by generating a box covered by cell plates reminiscent of a sci-fi building. Create an "Empty Tree" as described in that section, add a Cube node (Add ➤ Mesh ➤ Primitives ➤ Cube), and set X=7.5m, Y=5m, and Z=15m to create a rectangular prism. Next, we'll set Cube's vertices X, Y, and Z values (number of verts per axis) to determine its resolution. Since we rely on mapping the Voronoi Texture to the Cube and using the value of the pixel closest to a vertex to decide how to offset it, we want the Cube to have equal or greater resolution as the Voronoi Texture. If the texture has higher resolution, each vertex will correspond to multiple pixels on the texture, causing us to undersample and not capture all the details. The Voronoi Texture is 256 by 256; therefore, we'll set the Cube's' resolution to 256 × 3 per axis. We link a Value node of 256 (Add ➤ Input ➤ Constant ➤ Value) to the first Value of a Multiply node (Add ➤ Utilities ➤ Math ➤ Math set to Multiply), then set the Multiply node's second Value to 3, which gives us 256 times 3. We then link the Multiply node to Cube's vertices X, Y, and Z inputs.

Next, we'll create a "Mapping Subtree" as described in the named section, link Cube's "Mesh" to Bounding Box's "Geometry" socket, then link Map Range to a Voronoi Texture node with default settings, as shown in Figure 5-3. After that, we change Map

Range's "To Max" values to (2, 1, 1) to change the tiling frequency of the texture. Since the X scale is twice that of the Y and Z scales, it will tile twice as many times along X, therefore making the tiles appear elongated along Z.

Note You can access the geometry node tree that generates this section's rectangular prism with Voronoi "plates" in the file `/Ch5/cell_plates.blend`.

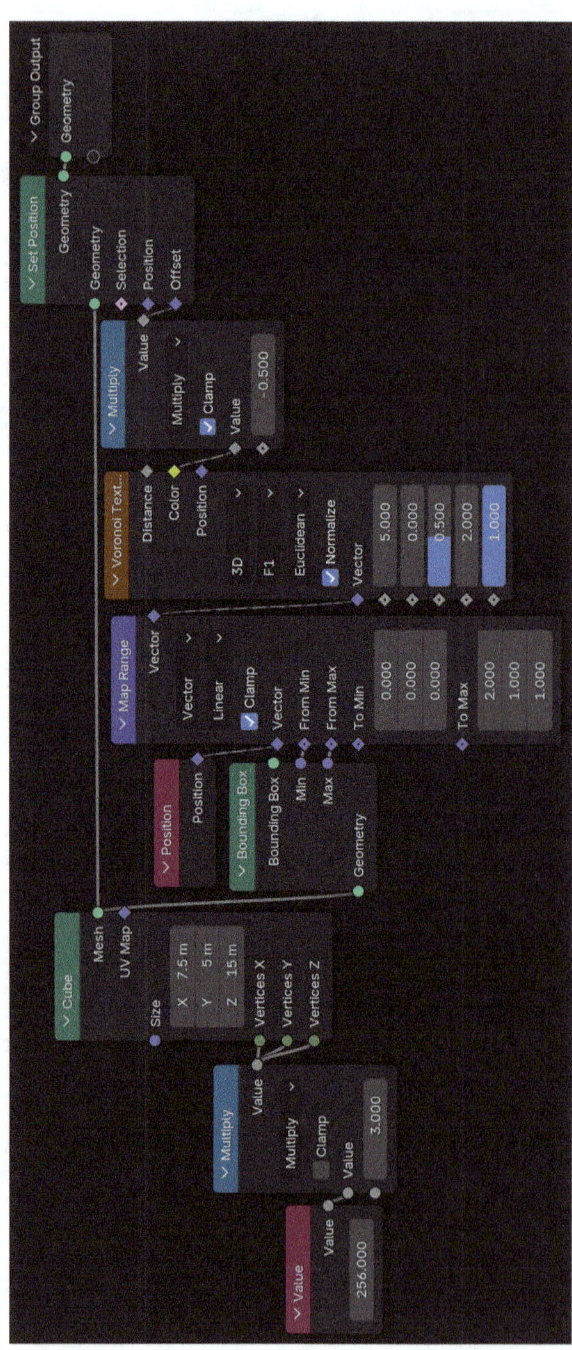

Figure 5-3. *Geometry node tree that generates a rectangular prism with Voronoi cell plates (sci-fi building)*

We're now ready to deform Cube by offsetting its vertices based on the texture's colors. To do so, we link Voronoi Texture's "Color" output to the first Value of a Multiply (Math) node with a second Value of –0.5, which will attenuate Color to 50% and flip its sign (thus flipping the offsets' direction, which is optional). Next, we link Cube to a Set Position node (Add ➤ Geometry ➤ Write ➤ Set Position) from "Mesh" to "Geometry" and link the previous Multiply (Math) node to its "Offset" input, which will offset all of Cube's vertices' positions by the Voronoi color. To finish, we link Set Position to Group Output, which will generate the mesh shown on the left of Figure 5-4. The right of Figure 5-4 shows a variation generated by the same tree with the Voronoi color scaling set to –0.25 (instead of –0.5), which makes the plates less pronounced, and the Map Range node's "To Max" set to (1, 1, 5), which increases the tiling frequency in the Z direction, therefore squashing the plates.

Tip Recall from Chapter 4 that you can add a new node to the tree with the Add menu, which can be accessed via left-click ➤ Add or Shift-A anywhere within the editor. Alternatively, you can *press the spacebar in the editor to bring up the search box, then type in a keyword to look up a node.*

The spacebar is set to bring up the search box by default. You can change what the spacebar does via Edit ➤ Preferences... ➤ Keymap ➤ Preferences ➤ Spacebar Action. You can also look up and customize the current key binding(s) to the search box by entering the term "search" in the search field on the upper right under Edit ➤ Preferences... ➤ Keymap.

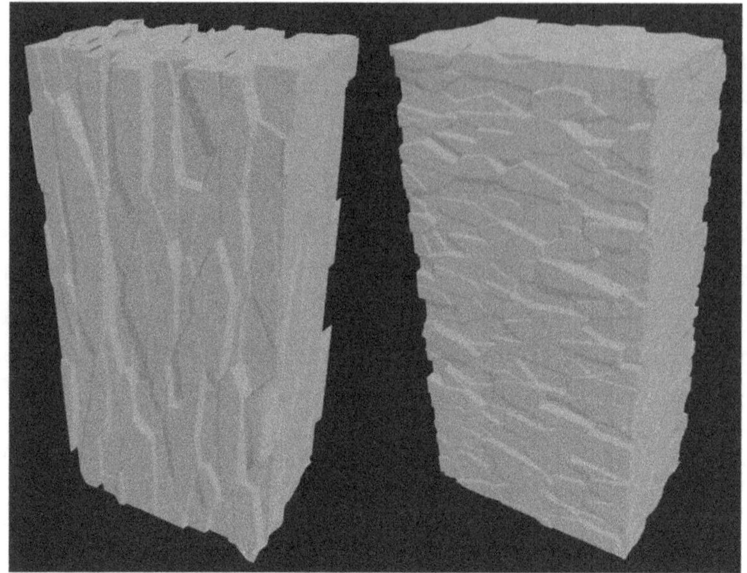

Figure 5-4. *Meshes generated by the node tree in Figure 5-3. Left uses parameter values exactly as shown in Figure 5-3. Right changes the Map Range node's "To Max" to (1, 1, 5) and the Multiply node after Voronoi's second Value to −0.25*

Cell Cracks (or Vines)

Instead of a primitive, which is not terribly exciting, let's try deforming an arbitrary mesh. Beginning with the default startup blend file, import the provided Stanford bunny model via File ➤ Import ➤ STL ➤ `/Ch4/stanford_bunny.stl`, and move stanford_bunny (e.g., G then X to move it along the X axis, LMB to confirm) so it does not overlap with the Cube object. Add a new tree to Cube as described in the "Mapping Subtree" section, with object input, then select stanford_bunny in the "Mesh Object" dropdown in the tree's modifier under Properties editor ➤ Material tab. We're now ready to add Voronoi patterned cracks (or vines) to the bunny via the tree.

The input bunny is triangulated. Since we're deforming it by offsetting its vertices, we need the mesh to have quads of similar or higher resolution than the texture, so it will sample evenly and pick up most of the details. To do so, we link Object Info to a Subdivide Mesh node with Level 1 to increase the resolution (Add ➤ Mesh ➤ Operations ➤ Subdivide Mesh), followed by Mesh to Volume (Add ➤ Mesh ➤ Operations ➤ Mesh to Volume), then Volume to Mesh (Add ➤ Volume ➤ Operations ➤ Volume to Mesh), which will turn the mesh into a voxelized volume, then back into a quad mesh. We change both Mesh to Volume and Volume to Mesh's Resolution type to Size and Voxel Size to 0.02m, while leaving other settings at default. After that, we link Volume to Mesh to Bounding Box.

Next, we'll set Map Range's "To Max" to (4, 2, 2) to increase the tiling frequency, then add a Voronoi Texture node followed by a Color Ramp node (Add ➤ Utilities ➤ Color ➤ Color Ramp). Change Voronoi Texture's feature (second dropdown) to Distance to Edge, and increase its Randomness to 2. Click each of Color Ramp's handles to drag it to the left, until black handle's Pos reads 0.018 and white handle's Pos reads 0.027—this will create an image of white Voronoi cells with black borders, or while plane with black cracks, which we can visualize in a shader node tree, as shown in Figure 5-6. We'll use this image to offset vertices on the bunny so the verts along the dark pixels (the cracks) are insetted. Instead of dragging the Color Ramp handles, you could click a handle to select it (you'll see the color bar across the bottom of the node change to the corresponding color), then type in the desired value in the Pos field to set it.

In the final portion of the tree, we'll use the Color Ramp output to offset the mesh's vertices. We add a Vector Math node set to Multiply (Add ➤ Utilities ➤ Vector ➤ Vector Math) with a Position node as one input (Add ➤ Geometry ➤ Read ➤ Position) and the Color Ramp as the other to create offset vectors from vertex positions multiplied by texture colors. We then insert a Multiply (Math) node set to 0.02 between Color Ramp and Vector Math so we can scale the influence of the texture colors over the offsets—setting this value as positive creates cracks, while setting it as negative creates "vines" since it inverts the colors and makes the cells black and cell borders white, as shown in Figure 5-7. The next step is to use a Set Position node (Add Geometry ➤ Write ➤ Set Position) to apply the offsets to the mesh vertices, by linking Volume to Mesh to Set Position's "Geometry" input and Vector Math to its "Offset" input. Finally, click Set Position then the O key to link it to Group Output to preview the generated mesh, which is shown in Figure 5-7. The complete node tree is shown in Figure 5-8.

Note You can access both the "cracks" and "vines" version of geometry node trees in the file `/Ch5/cell_cracks_and_vines.blend`.

Tip: Build a Voxelizer from Mesh to Volume and Volume to Mesh

Hooking a mesh up to a Mesh to Volume node followed by Volume to Mesh is a quick way to "voxelize" it—in other words, making it "blocky" or pixelated in the 3D sense, as the examples shown in Figure 5-5, where the provided Stanford bunny mesh is voxelized with two different sets of values as summarized in Table 5-1. There is no hard-and-fast rule for finding node values for voxelizing meshes in general since they depend on many factors, such as the poly-count and size of the mesh and the amount of details the mesh has (more details usually require more or smaller voxels). They also depend on the look you are going for. I typically play around with different values until something looks good.

Table 5-1. *Node values used to generate the voxelized bunny meshes in Figure 5-5*

Model	Mesh to Volume	Volume to Mesh
Left in Figure 5-5	Resolution=size, Density=1.2, Voxel Size =0.47m, Interior Band Width =0.1m	Resolution=amount, Voxel Amount=50, Threshold=0.01, Adaptivity=0
Right in Figure 5-5	Resolution=size, Density=0.01, Voxel Size=0.01m, Interior Band Width=0.01m	Resolution=size, Voxel Amount=0.12m, Threshold=0.01, Adaptivity=0

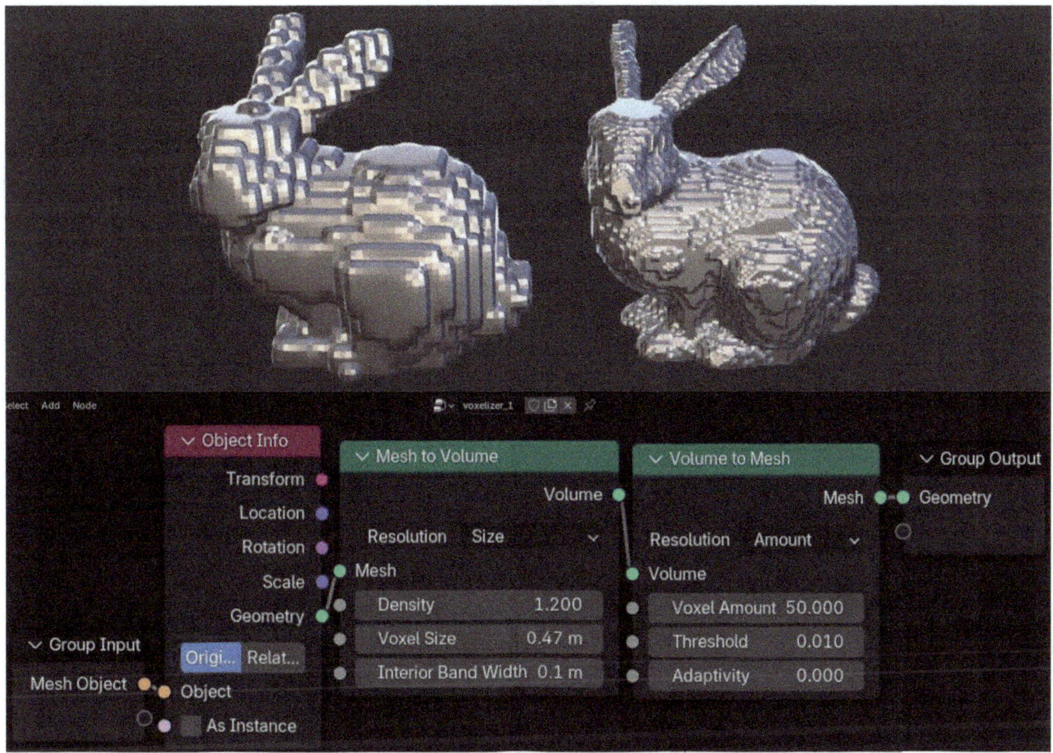

Figure 5-5. *Making a voxelizer by chaining a Mesh to Volume node and a Volume to Mesh node. The node tree at the bottom corresponds to the bunny mesh on the top left. The node values for both bunnies are summarized in Table 5-1*

Note You can access the geometry node trees that generate the two meshes in Figure 5-5 in the file `/Ch5/voxelizer.blend`.

Tip: Dial In and Visualize Textures in the Shader Node Editor

When generating meshes from textures, it's helpful to visualize the textures in the shader node editor and experiment with different settings until you find something you like, then copy the values over to the texture or Color Ramp nodes in the geometry node editor. Figure 5-6 shows the same Voronoi Texture and Color Ramp node combo from Figure 5-8 visualized in the shader node editor. You simply create a plane primitive (viewport in Object mode, Add ➤ Mesh ➤ Plane), then create and assign a material to it. For the "cracks" texture, insert the Voronoi Texture and Color Ramp nodes from Figure 5-8 into the shader tree after Texture Coordinate and Mapping nodes as described in Chapter 4, then link Color Ramp's "Color" output to Principled BSDF's Base Color, as shown in Figure 5-6. You can then experiment with selecting different feature (F1, Distance to Edge, etc.) and other settings for the Voronoi Texture and moving the Color Ramp handles to see what happens.

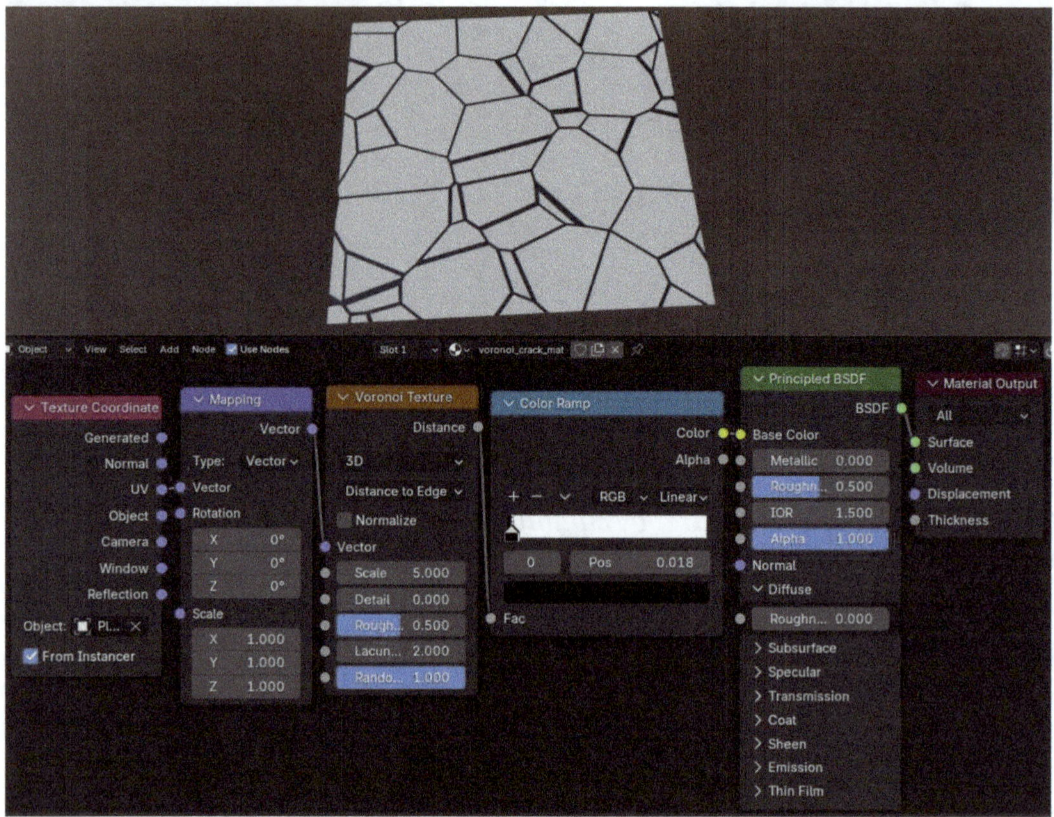

Figure 5-6. *Visualizing the Voronoi "cracks" texture in the shader node editor. As shown, the Color Ramp node has its black handle selected; therefore, Pos=0.018 and a black bar are displayed. Click the white handle to see its Pos value (which is 0.027)*

Note You can access the shader node trees from Figure 5-6 for visualizing the Voronoi "cracks" texture in the file `/Ch5/cell_cracks_texture_visualized.blend`.

Figure 5-7. *Stanford bunny mesh with Voronoi cracks (left) and vines (right) generated by the geometry node tree in Figure 5-8*

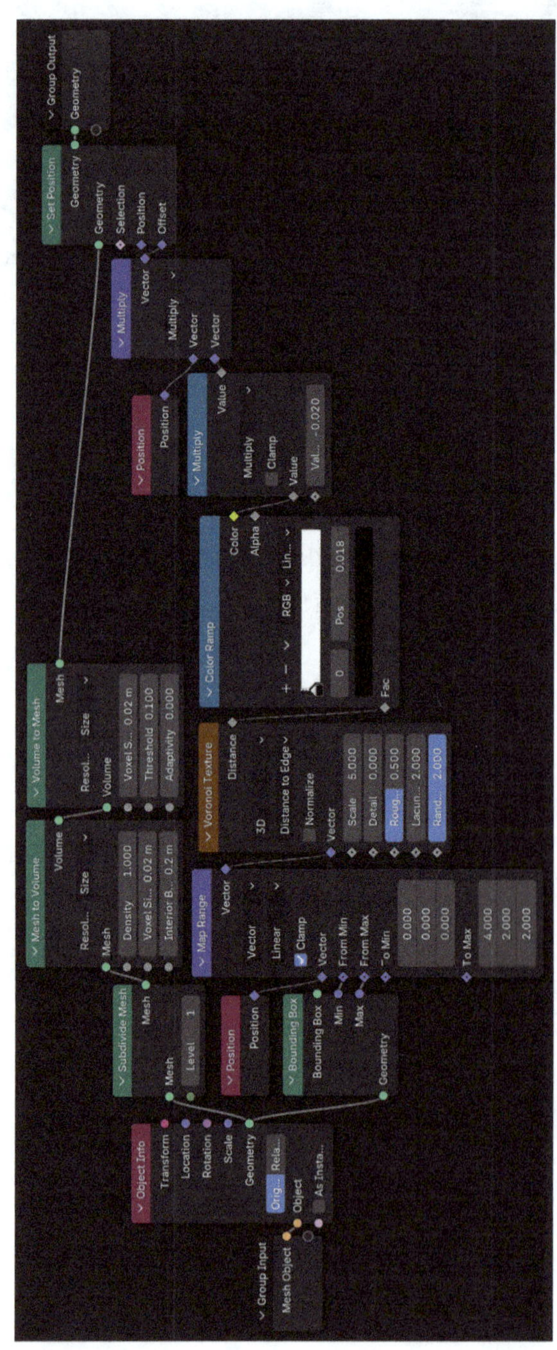

***Figure 5-8.** The geometry node tree that generates the Voronoi cracks on the bunny mesh on the left of Figure 5-7. You can generate the bunny mesh with "vines" on the right of Figure 5-7 by changing the value of the Multiply node in the center from 0.02 to −0.02*

Tip: Copying a Geometry Node Tree to Work Off Of

A quick way to make variations or work off of an existing geometry node tree is to make a copy of it. You can do so by clicking the user count button to the right of the tree's name at the top of the node editor (shown as 1 in Figure 5-9), which will create a copy of the tree with zero user count and name the copy to <tree name>.001. I often select the mesh object with a geometry node tree I like in Object mode, Shift-D to copy it, then rename the object, and copy the node tree this way, which lets me jump off and build another tree without repeating work I've already done. You can also copy the node trees supplied with the chapter examples this way to spin off various experiments.

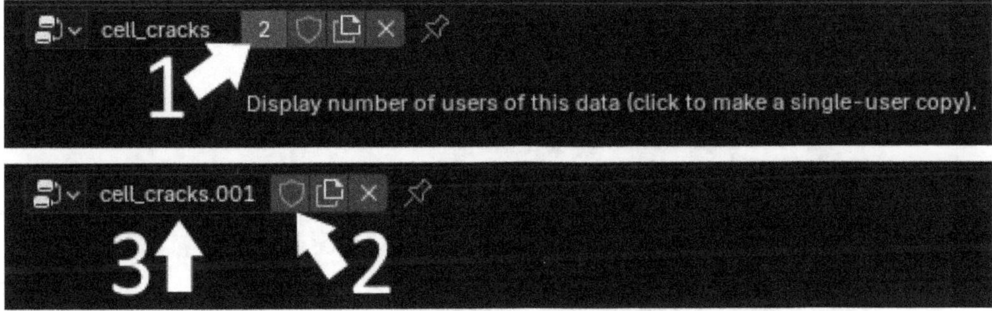

Figure 5-9. *Copying a geometry node tree by clicking the (1) user count button, which creates a copy with (2) zero user count and the name (3) <tree name>.001*

Tip You can resize a node by dragging its left or right border. You can also minimize a node by clicking the "v" at its upper-left corner.

Cell Cavities (or Gem Facets)

It turns out we can make two drastically different variations from the "cracks" node tree in Figure 5-8 with almost no work—by changing the tiling scale (Map Range "To Max"), Color Ramp Pos values, and value of the Multiply (Math) node used to scale the Color Ramp output. Figure 5-10 shows two such variations, which I call "cavities" and "gem facets." The node value changes are listed next to each generated mesh.

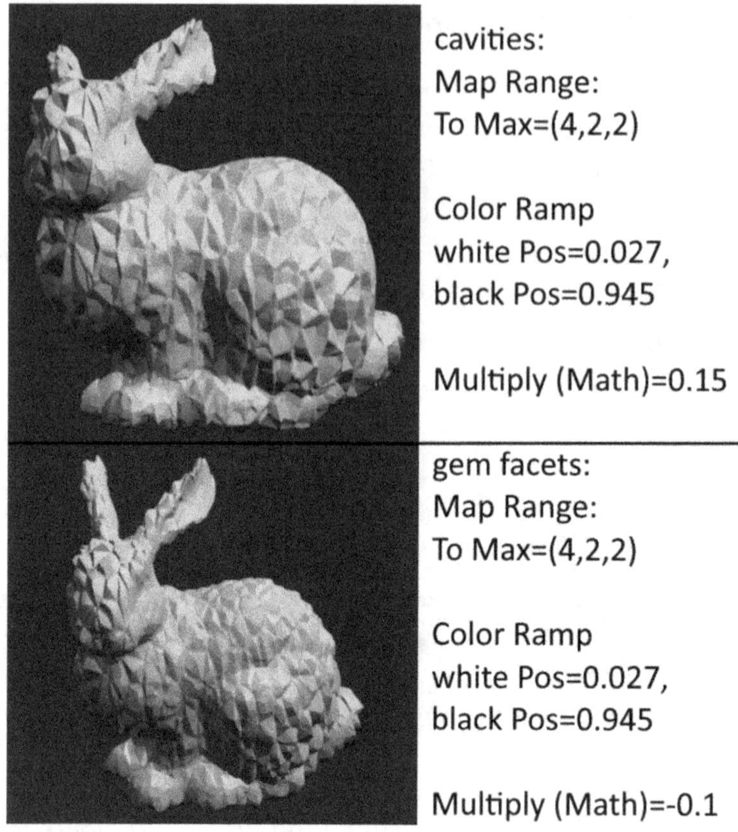

Figure 5-10. *Two more variations (top: cavities, bottom: gem facets) generated by the "cracks" geometry node tree from Figure 5-8 by changing node values. The node values for each variation are shown to its right*

Note You can access both the "cavities" and the "gem facets" versions of the geometry node trees in the file `/Ch5/cell_cavities_gemfacets.blend`.

Generating Meshes from Other Built-In Texture Nodes

So far, we've seen five different examples of using the Voronoi Texture node (with or without a Color Ramp) to generate meshes. In this section, we'll look at what effects we can achieve by trading Voronoi Texture for other built-in texture nodes.

Rock from Noise Texture

Our first experiment is to swap out the Voronoi Texture-Color Ramp combo in the "cracks" tree (Figure 5-8) with a Noise Texture. It turns out by adjusting the tiling frequency (Map Range's "To Max" values) and offsetting scale (value for the Multiply node after Noise Texture), you can make a pretty convincing rock mesh. Shift-click the Voronoi Texture and Color Ramp nodes in the Figure 5-8 tree then X to delete. Add a Noise Texture node (Add ➤ Texture ➤ Noise Texture), link Map Range's "Vector" to Noise Texture's "Vector" input and then Noise Texture's "Fac" output to one of Multiply's Values, and set Multiply's other value to –0.05. Leave the Noise Texture settings at default ("3D," "fBM," with "Normalize" checked), bump Map Range "To Max" to (5, 5, 5), and you'll create the "rock" bunny shown in Figure 5-11. The portion of the tree from Figure 5-8 that's been modified for this exercise is also shown on the bottom of Figure 5-11.

Note Remember that you create Add, Subtract, Multiply, ...etc., by setting a Math node (Add ➤ Utilities ➤ Math ➤ Math) to different types. The Math node has a diverse range of math operations under it, including comparison (Less Than, Greater Than, etc.) and conversion (e.g. To Radians).

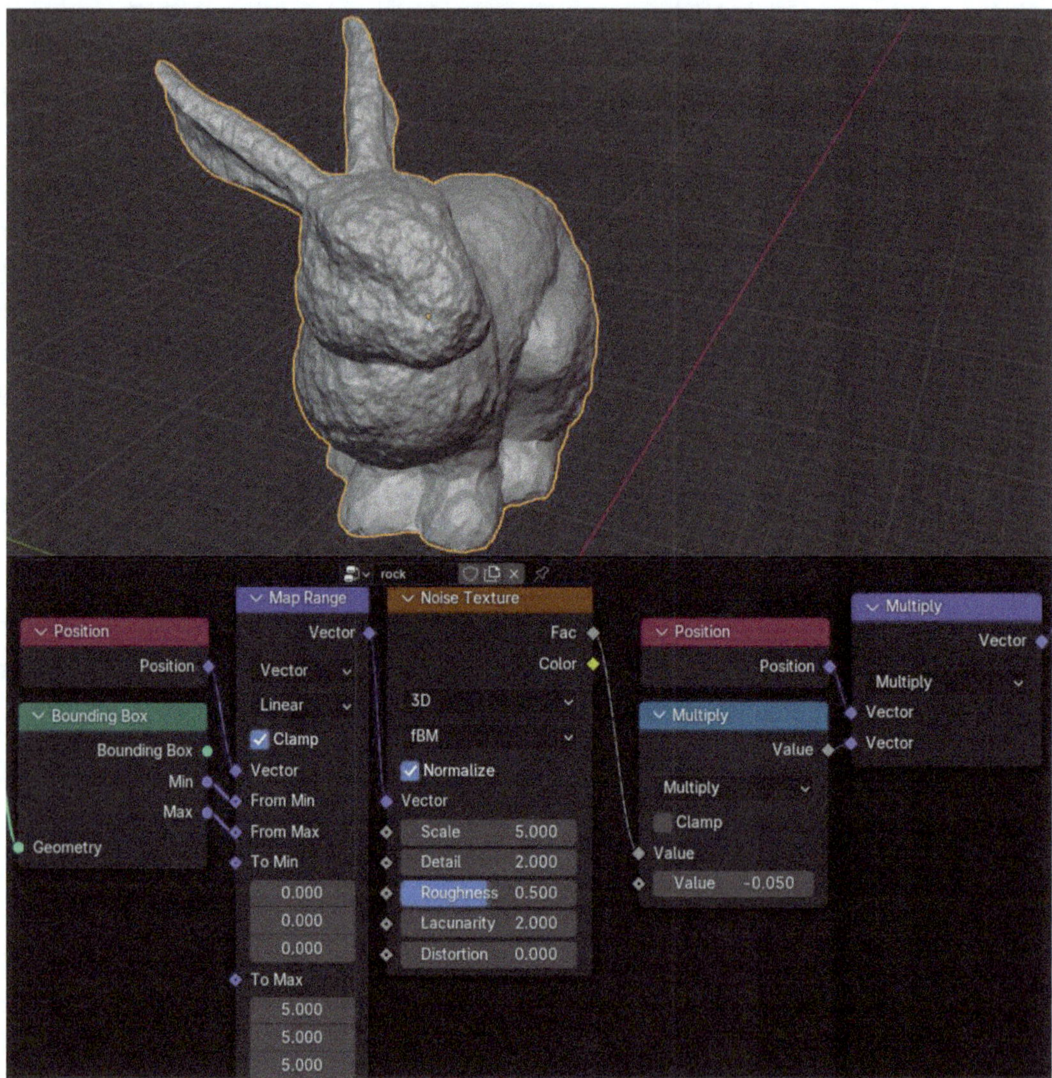

Figure 5-11. *Generating a rock mesh by replacing the Voronoi Texture and Color Ramp combo in Figure 5-8 with a Noise Texture and adjusting tiling frequency (Map Range "To Max") as well as offset scale (Multiply node after Noise Texture)*

Wrinkles/Ripples from Gabor Texture

Our second excursion is to create wrinkles (or ripples) using the Gabor Texture node in place of the Voronoi Texture-Color Ramp combo in the "cracks" tree in Figure 5-8. We'll set the Map Range node's "To Max" (tiling frequency) to (5, 5, 5), the Gabor Texture to 3D mode while leaving other settings at default, and the Multiply node after Gabor Texture to –0.05 as the scale for vertex offsets. This makes a nice fluid ripple effect across the whole mesh, reminiscent of the surface texture of some modern ceramics, as shown in Figure 5-12. The bottom of Figure 5-12 shows the portion of nodes that we swapped out from Figure 5-8 to build this tree.

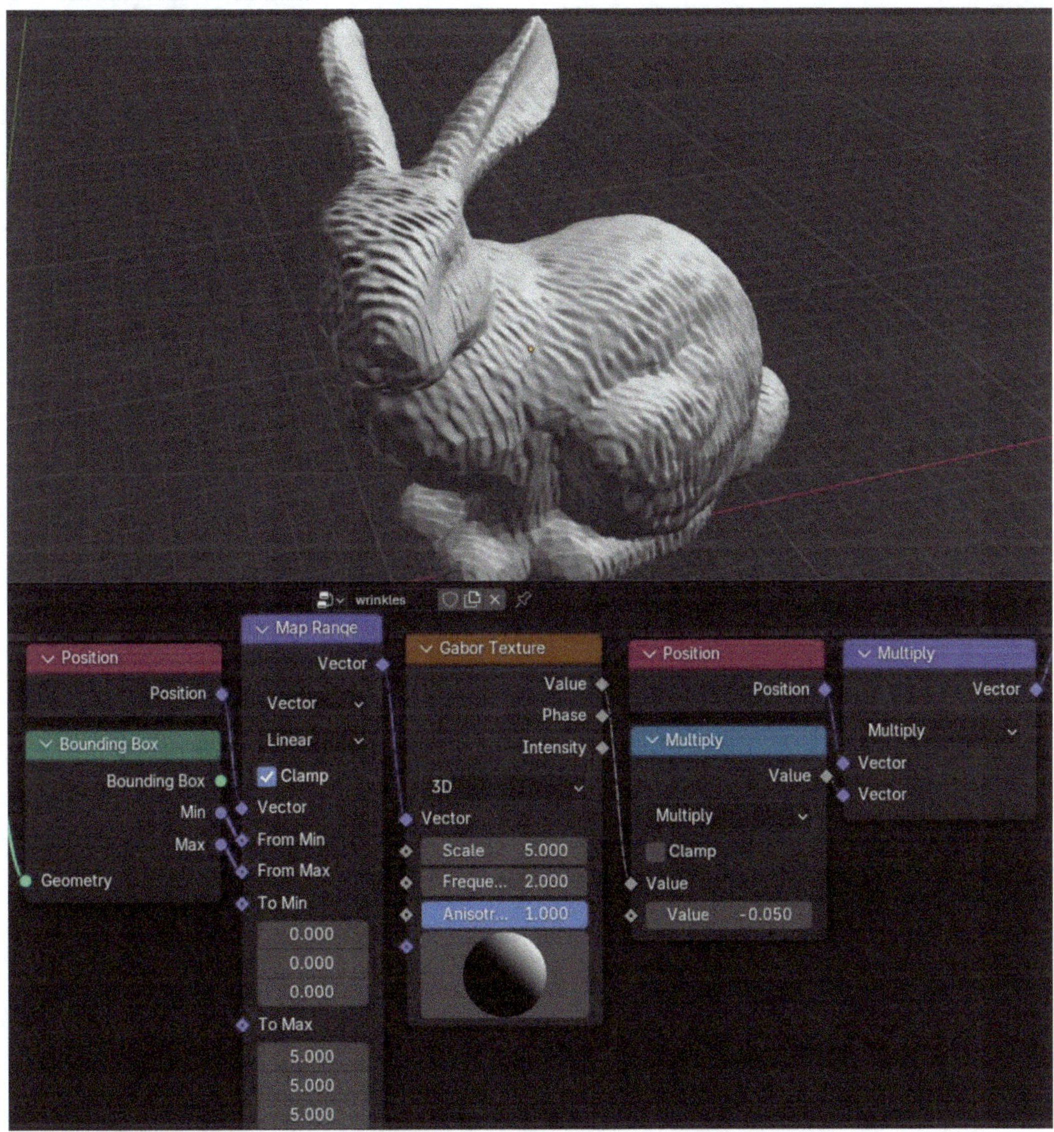

Figure 5-12. *Generating wrinkles (ripples) on meshes with the Gabor Texture node. The node tree is built by replacing the Voronoi Texture and Color Ramp nodes from Figure 5-8 with the Gabor Texture node set to 3D with default settings, adjusting Map Range "To Max" to (5, 5, 5) to increase tiling frequency, and scaling the vertex offsets by −0.05 by setting the Multiply node after Gabor to −0.05*

Tip You can select multiple nodes in the geometry node editor by holding down Shift and clicking. You can delete selected node(s) using the X key.

Note You can access both the "rock" and "wrinkles" geometry node trees in the file `/Ch5/rock_and_wrinkles.blend`.

Generating Sliceforms

From here till the end of the chapter, we'll take on a bigger project—building a sliceform generator. We'll start simple and slice a UV sphere in a single direction with hard-coded parameter values, then gradually build up the tree to automatically recognize two orthogonal directions to slice and allow user control of generation parameters. Along the way, we'll venture into advanced geometry node features such as the Repeat block for creating `for` loops, Compare nodes for creating Boolean conditions for making selections, and Mesh Topology nodes like Corners of Vertex for deriving neighboring geometry.

What Are Sliceforms?

Sliceforms are models made from interlocking two sets of cross-sectional slices of a 3D object that are orthogonal to each other, traditionally used for visualizing mathematical surfaces. When crafted by hand, they are often made of cardstock or wood, like the hemisphere example made by the author in Figure 5-13. Sliceforms can be made such that the slits allowing the two sets of slices to slot together are cut with enough slack to enable the assembled model to flex and in some cases collapse flat, so they are widely used in pop-up greeting cards and pop-up books. Sliceforms cut this way can also have their slices disassembled and put back together, thus making them a suitable medium for 3D puzzles and model kits. In recent years, some designers have favored sliceforms' futuristic looks and utilized them in furniture and even modern architecture, such as the Setas de Sevilla ("Mushrooms of Seville") building in Seville (Figure 5-14). You can take advantage of sliceforms and generate some very cool sci-fi-esque buildings and props for your next game.

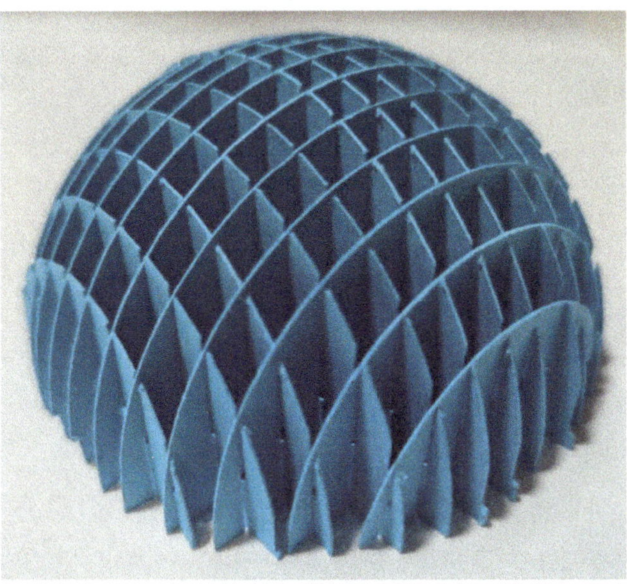

Figure 5-13. *Sliceform model of a hemisphere by the author. Photo also by the author*

Figure 5-14. *Setas de Sevilla ("Mushrooms of Seville"), also known as Las Setas or Metropol Parasol, is a large structure in Seville, Spain, that resembles a sliceform model. Photo by Anual, November 8, 2011* `https://commons.wikimedia.org/wiki/File:Metropolparasolnov2011001.jpg`*, CC BY-SA 3.0, via Wikimedia Commons*

Note You can find all the sliceform-related geometry node trees in the file `/Ch5/sliceform.blend` in the downloaded source.

Tip You can select and copy nodes from one node tree (with Ctrl-C) and paste them to another tree (Ctrl-V) within the same blend file.

Slicing a UV Sphere Horizontally

Let's begin building the node tree that will eventually take an arbitrary mesh as input and generate its sliceform counterpart parametrically. We'll start by adding a UV Sphere node with Radius=5 (Add ➤ Mesh ➤ Primitives ➤ UV Sphere) as our test mesh and repeatedly cut it horizontally to make a vertical stack of slices. To do so, we need to find the line from the top center of the sphere to the bottom center, divide the line evenly and spawn a plane at each tick mark, then use the stack of planes to perform a Mesh Boolean Intersect operation with the sphere to get the cross-sectional slices.

Finding the sphere's top and bottom centers is equivalent to finding its bounding box's top and bottom centers—which is what we'll do. We link UV Sphere to a Bounding Box node, then extract its bottom (index #0) face with a Separate Geometry node set to Face (Add ➤ Geometry ➤ Operations ➤ Separate Geometry) with Selection made via an Equal node (Add ➤ Utilities ➤ Math ➤ Compare, select "Integer" and "Equal") with an Index node as one value (Add ➤ Geometry ➤ Read ➤ Index) and 0 as the other, as shown in Figure 5-15. We extract the top face (index #2) with the same setup except setting the Equal node's other value to 2. The two extracted faces are shown as (3) in Figure 5-16.

We extract the centers of the bottom and top faces by linking both Separate Geometry nodes to Dual Mesh (Add ➤ Mesh ➤ Operations ➤ Dual Meah), which convert the two faces to two meshes, each with a vertex centered at the corresponding face ((4) in Figure 5-16). We cannot use vertices directly as end points of a line; instead, we must convert them to Vectors via the node sequence Dual Mesh ➤ Mesh to Points ➤ Sample Index with Position as Value, to turn each mesh into a list of points, then grab the position (Vector) of the first point in the list. We can then use the two Vectors as the Start and End for a Curve Line ((6) in Figure 5-16).

Note You can find the Mesh to Points node under Add ➤ Mesh ➤ Operations, Sample Index under Add ➤ Geometry ➤ Sample, and Position under Add ➤ Geometry ➤ Read.

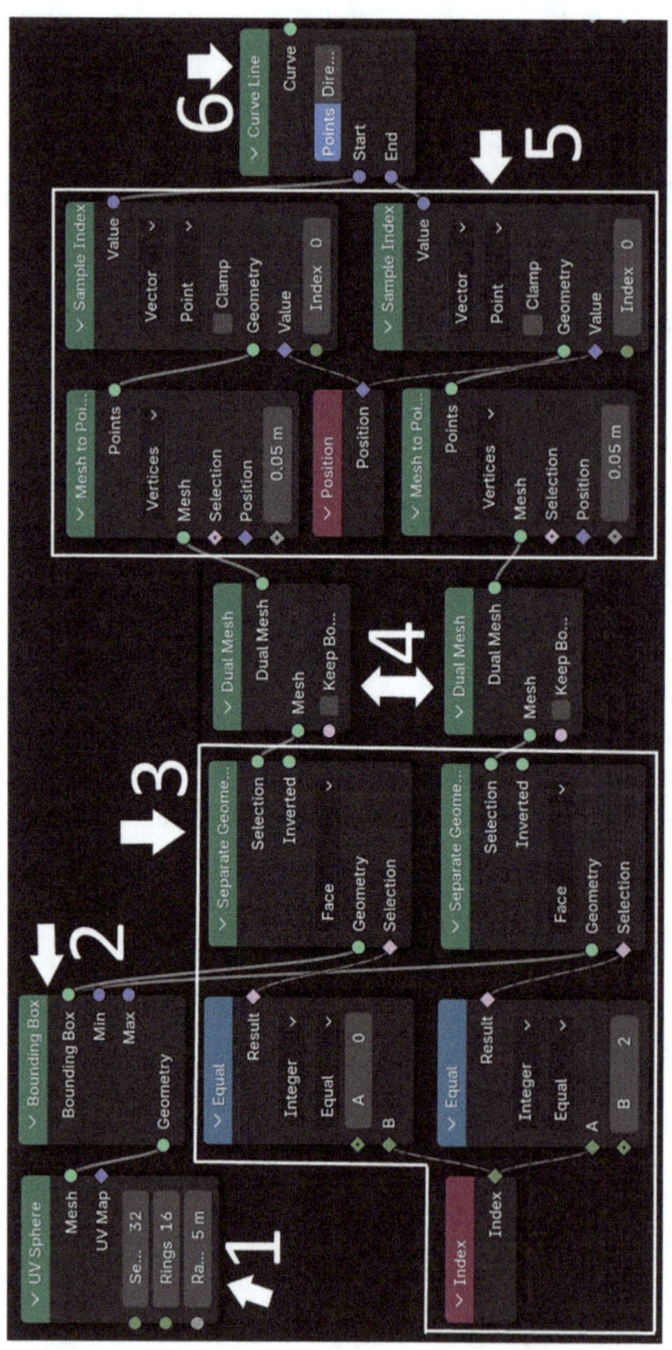

Figure 5-15. *Creating the central curve that will go through the vertical stack of slices. (1) Create a UV Sphere with Radius=5m, take (2) its bounding box and (3) separate the box's faces at indices #0 and #2, (4) Dual Mesh to turn the faces into vertices, convert the vertices into points with (5) Mesh to Points and Sample Index, then (6) create a line from the two points*

Note You can access a copy of the node tree in Figure 5-15 via the object named `1_hardcoded_sph_v_slices` in the file `/Ch5/sliceform.blend` from the downloaded source.

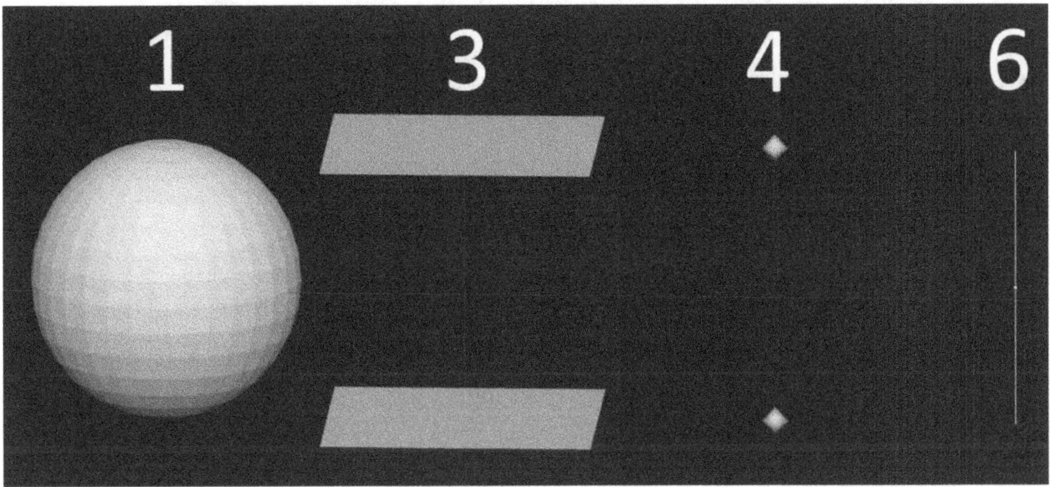

***Figure 5-16.** Steps (1), (3), (4), and (6) of the nodes in Figure 5-15 visualized. (1) is a UV Sphere with Radius=5m; (3) is face #0 and #2 of (1)'s bounding box; (4) is the Dual Mesh of (3), with verts that are (3)'s face centers; (6) is a Curve Line created by linking the two points from (4)*

We'll now create points evenly spaced along the Curve Line we just made, so we can spawn one plane per point to create a stack for the sphere to do Boolean intersection with. For now, we'll use a Value node set to 15 and an Add node to add 2 to it, to create 15 cross-sections ((1) in Figure 5-17)—the reason we add 2 to our intended number of slices is because Curve to Points ((2) in Figure 5-17) will attribute one point at the beginning and one point at the end of the curve, so when you set a count to N, you are getting one point on either end and N-2 points in the middle of the curve, as the example visualized as (2) in Figure 5-18.

The next step is to use the Instance on Points node ((4) in Figure 5-17) to duplicate a Grid across the points from Curve to Points. We want the Grid instance to be large enough to intersect the widest part of the sphere horizontally, so we use the XY dimension of the sphere's bounding box as the Size X and Y for the Grid. We can calculate the size of the Bounding Box by using a Vector Math node (Subtract) to compute the Bounding Box's Max minus Min, which gives you the offset Vector of its longest diagonal, then a Separate

XYZ node to extract its X, Y, and Z components, which are then the X, Y, and Z extents of the box, shown as (3) in Figure 5-17. The reason why we use a Grid node instead of a face from the box as the instance for Instance on Points is because the Grid node has its position coinciding with its origin (center), so we avoid any offset problems. In addition, when we add the orthogonal set of slices later, we need to use slices that are large enough to accommodate both slicing directions, and Grid nodes let us resize easily.

Once we duplicate the Grid instances ((4) in Figure 5-18), we use a Realize Instance node (with Realize All checked) to turn the instances into real mesh data. We then use a Mesh Boolean node (set to Intersect) to find the intersection between the UV Sphere and the realized grid slices, which gives us the circular cross-sections shown as (5) in Figure 5-18.

Note You can find the Value node under Add ➤ Input ➤ Constant. You can create an Add node by adding a Math node under Add ➤ Utilities ➤ Math then setting its type to Add. The Instance on Points node can be found under Add ➤ Instances, while the Mesh Boolean node can be located under Add ➤ Mesh ➤ Operations.

You can access a copy of the node tree that includes everything we've built up to Figure 5-17 via the object named `1_hardcoded_sph_v_slices` in the file `/Ch5/sliceform.blend` from the downloaded source.

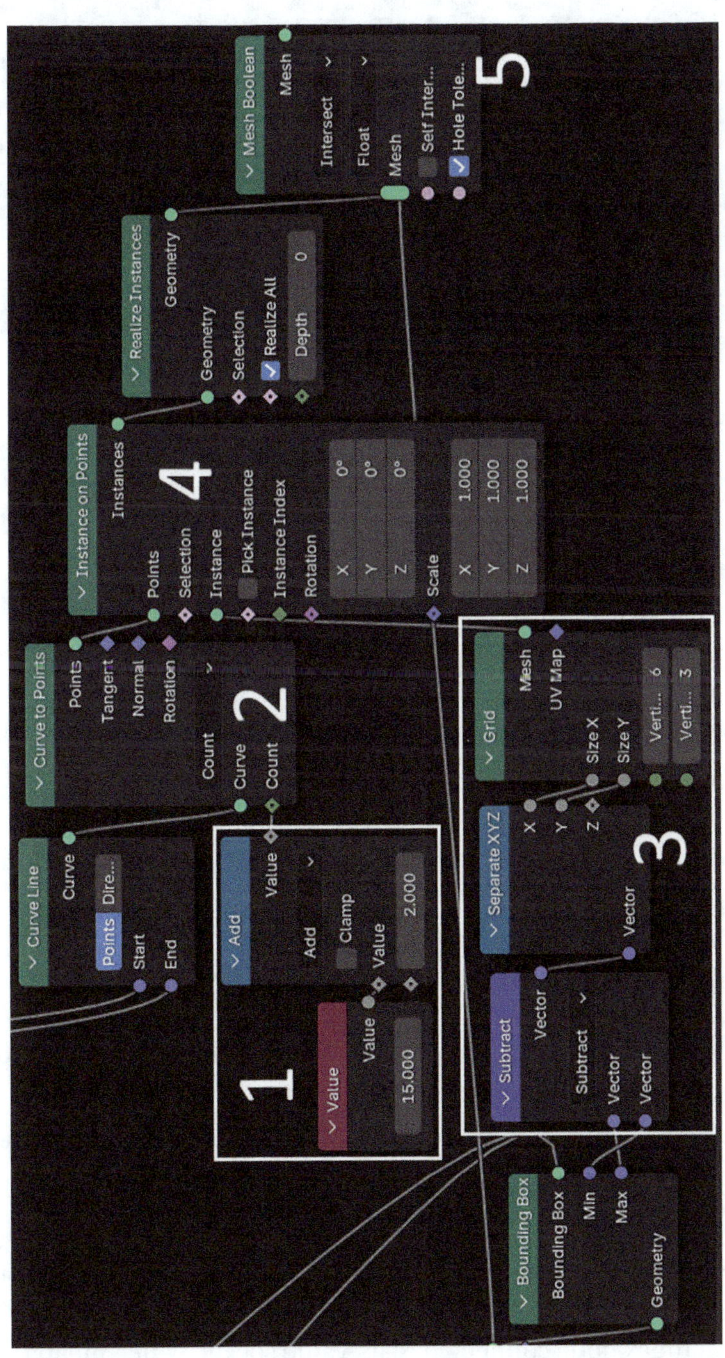

Figure 5-17. *Continuing from Figure 5-15, we use (1) a count of 15+2 points to (2) divide the curve so there are 15 slices plus 2 end points. We use (3) Grid to create a slice instance with XY from the Bounding Box diagonal verts (Max-Min), then (4) use Instance on Points to distribute it along the curve. (5) Mesh Boolean is used to find the intersection between the UV Sphere and the Grids from (4)*

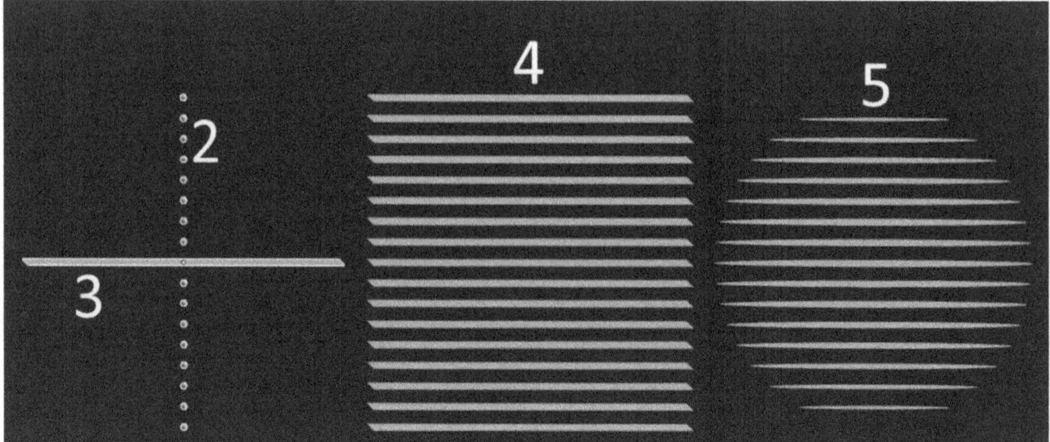

Figure 5-18. *Steps (2), (3), (4), and (5) of the nodes in Figure 5-17 visualized. (2) is the 15+2 points from Curve to Points, (3) is the Grid instance with XY derived from the difference of the Bounding Box diagonal verts, (4) is (3) distributed on (2) using Instance on Points, and (5) is the output of Mesh Boolean: Intersect with the UV Sphere and (4) as inputs*

Deriving Center Axes for Slicing Using Topology Nodes

So far, we've prototyped by creating a 15-slice stack of a UV Sphere primitive, by using the dual meshes of the top (index #2) and bottom (#0) faces of its bounding box to find the line through the slice centers. Instead of hard-coded indices, in this section, we'll generalize the solution by using Topology nodes (Add ➤ Mesh ➤ Topology) to find the top and bottom faces.

Using the Viewer Node to Check Index, Position, etc.

The Topology nodes we'll use is Corners of Vertex and Face of Corner. The best way to see how these two nodes work is by visualizing them through an example. Figure 5-19 shows an abridged version of the sliceform tree with Bounding Box linked to a Viewer node (Add ➤ Output ➤ Viewer). The Viewer node lets you preview various attributes like Index, Position, and so on of a piece of Geometry (instance, curve, mesh, etc.) in the viewport. You link a node from Add ➤ Geometry ➤ Read to the Viewer node's Value socket to control what type of attribute to visualize. In Figure 5-19, the Viewer node has type "Point" and an Index node connected to its Value socket, which means it will display the indices of Bounding Box's vertices. If nothing shows up in the viewport, make sure the "eye" icon at the upper right of the Viewer node is toggled on, and under the Viewport Overlays menu, the Attribute Text box ((2) in Figure 5-19) is checked. The "Color Opacity" slider just above Attribute Text controls the opacity of the preview geometry, which is set to 0 here to make the bounding box shown as a wireframe.

Caution Note that when a Viewer node is enabled ("eye" icon toggled on) in your tree, the Group Output preview is automatically disabled. To return to Group Output preview, simply disable the Viewer node by clicking the "eye" icon.

Accessing a Vertex's Neighboring Face Using Corners of Vertex and Face of Corner

In the viewport preview in Figure 5-19, you can see vertex #0 (lower-left corner closest to you) is where three face corners come together—these face corners are accessible via the Corners of Vertex node (Add ➤ Mesh ➤ Topology ➤ Corners of Vertex). You control which corner is retrieved via Corners of Vertex's "Sort Index" socket—for example, as shown, vertex #0 has face corner #0 coming from the bottom face of the bounding box, face corner #1 from the face on the left side of the box, and face corner #2 from the face closest to you. Vertex #7 (upper right in the back) has face corner #0 from the top face of the box, face corner #1 from the right side of the box, and face corner #2 from the back side of the box.

What we need are the top and bottom *faces* of the box for the vertical stack of slices and left and right faces for the horizontal stack—*not* face corners—therefore, we need to extract the face corners of the first (#0) and last (#7) vertices of the box using Corners of Vertex with Sort Index 0, then use Face of Corner (Add ➤ Mesh ➤ Topology ➤ Face of Corner) to get the corresponding face back.

We're now ready to go back and modify block #3 of Figure 5-15 to use Corners of Vertex and Face of Corner nodes as we've just described. The top and bottom of Figure 5-20 show the extraction of the top and bottom faces of the Bounding Box, respectively. For the top half, we use the Domain Size node to find the number of verts in the box (Point Count, which is 8), Subtract 1 to get the last vertex's index (which is 7), followed by Corners of Vertex with Sort Index=0 to get face corner #0 as shown in Figure 5-19, then Face of Corner to get the top face's index. The bottom half of Figure 5-20 goes through the same process but using the first vertex of the box (at index #0) to extract the bottom face's index.

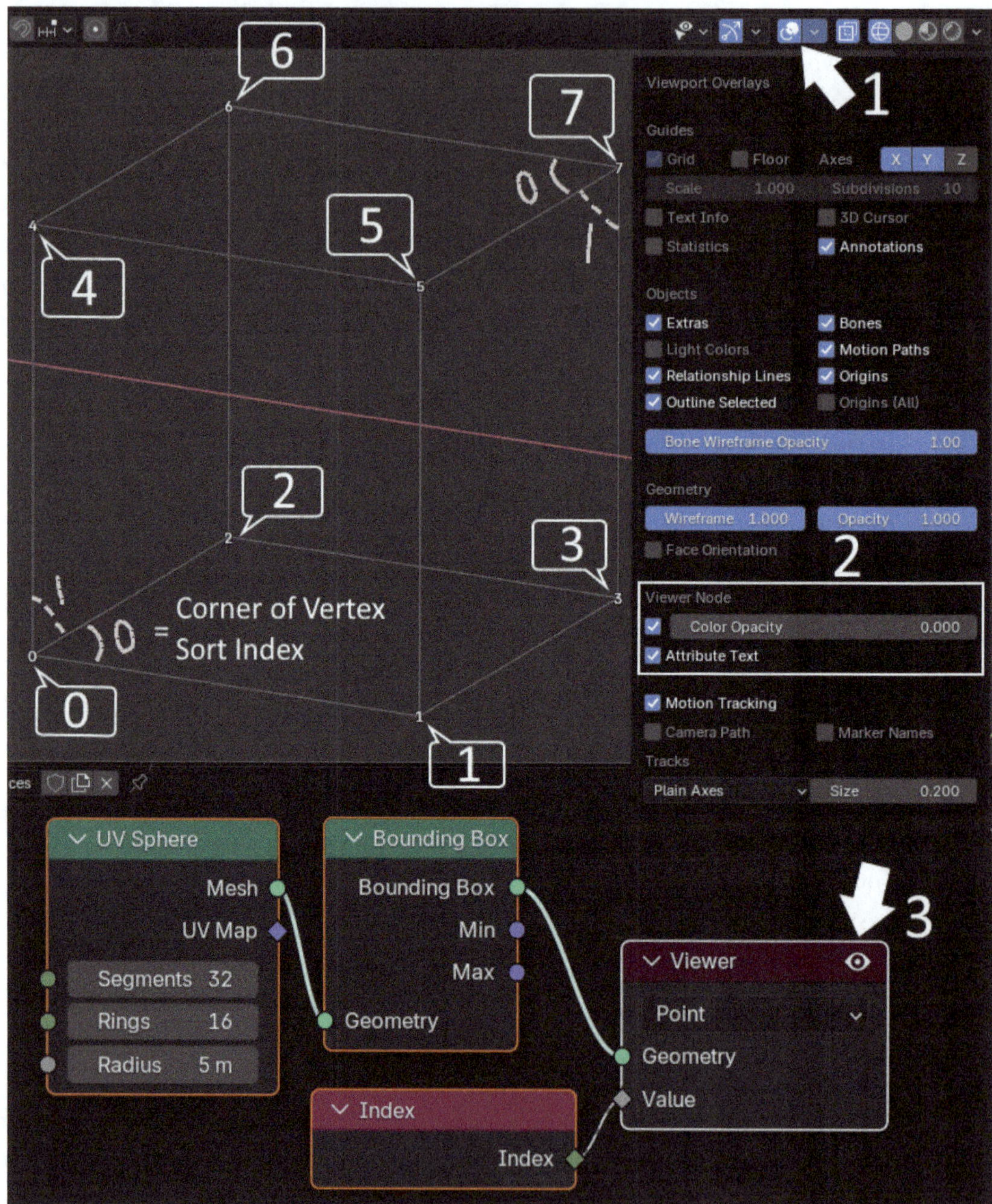

Figure 5-19. *To ensure the Viewer data is displayed, under the (1) Viewport Overlays menu, check the (2) Attribute Text box, and verify (3) the "eye" icon on the Viewer node is toggled on. Two face corners #0 and #1 are shown for vertex #0 and vertex #7, respectively, which can be accessed via the Corners of Vertex node with Sort Index set to the corresponding face corner index*

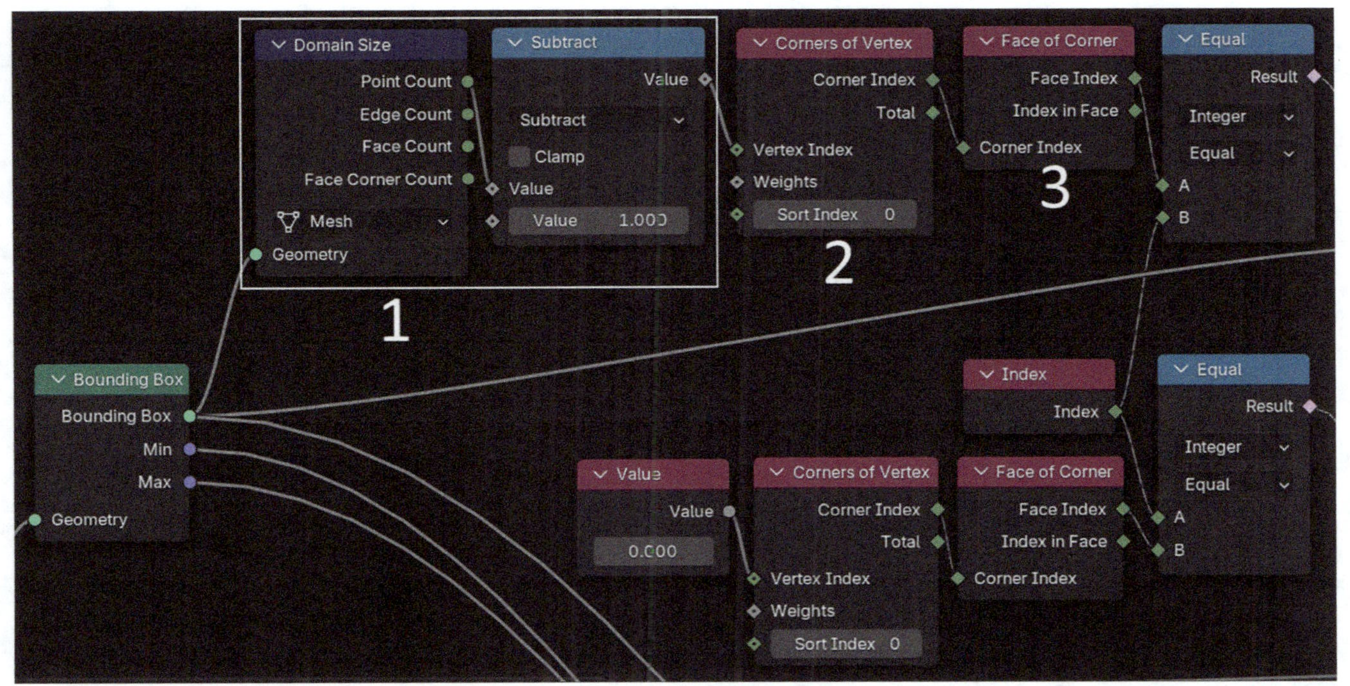

Figure 5-20. *Modifying the sliceform tree to find the top and bottom faces of Bounding Box via Topology nodes. (1) computes the box's last vertex's index via Domain Size: Point Count—Subtract 1, (2) Corners of Vertex node retrieves face corner 0 (Sort Index=0) of that vertex, and (3) Face of Corner gives you the index of the face that corner is a part of*

Note You can access a copy of the node tree that includes everything we've built up to Figure 5-20 via the object named `2_parametric_sph_v_slices` in the file `/Ch5/sliceform.blend` from the downloaded source.

Adding Input to Select Mesh Object to Slice

Let's add an input to our tree for selecting a mesh object to slice. In the node editor, press the N key to call up the Properties shelf, select the Geometry input socket, change its Type to Object, and double-click to rename it to "Mesh Object." You'll see a dropdown appear in the tree's modifier under Properties editor ➤ Modifier tab, as shown in Figure 5-21. To set this input up in the tree, delete the UV Sphere node, link Group Input's "Mesh Object" socket to an Object Info node's "Object" socket (Add ➤ Input ➤ Scene ➤ Object Info), then link Object Info to Bounding Box ("Geometry" to "Geometry") as shown in Figure 5-21.

We'll use the provided Stanford bunny as our test model from here until the end of the chapter. Import it via File ➤ Import ➤ STL ➤ `/Ch4/stanford_bunny.stl`, move the imported `stanford_bunny` object out of the way (e.g., G then X, LMB to confirm), then select it in the Mesh Object dropdown in the tree's modifier. The bunny has more features than the UV Sphere, therefore requiring more slices to capture its detail—we'll change the number of slices from 15 to 20 via the Value node toward the Count for the Curve to Points node (which is in turn for populating the positions of the slices), as shown in Figure 5-22. The resulting bunny slices are shown at the top of Figure 5-21.

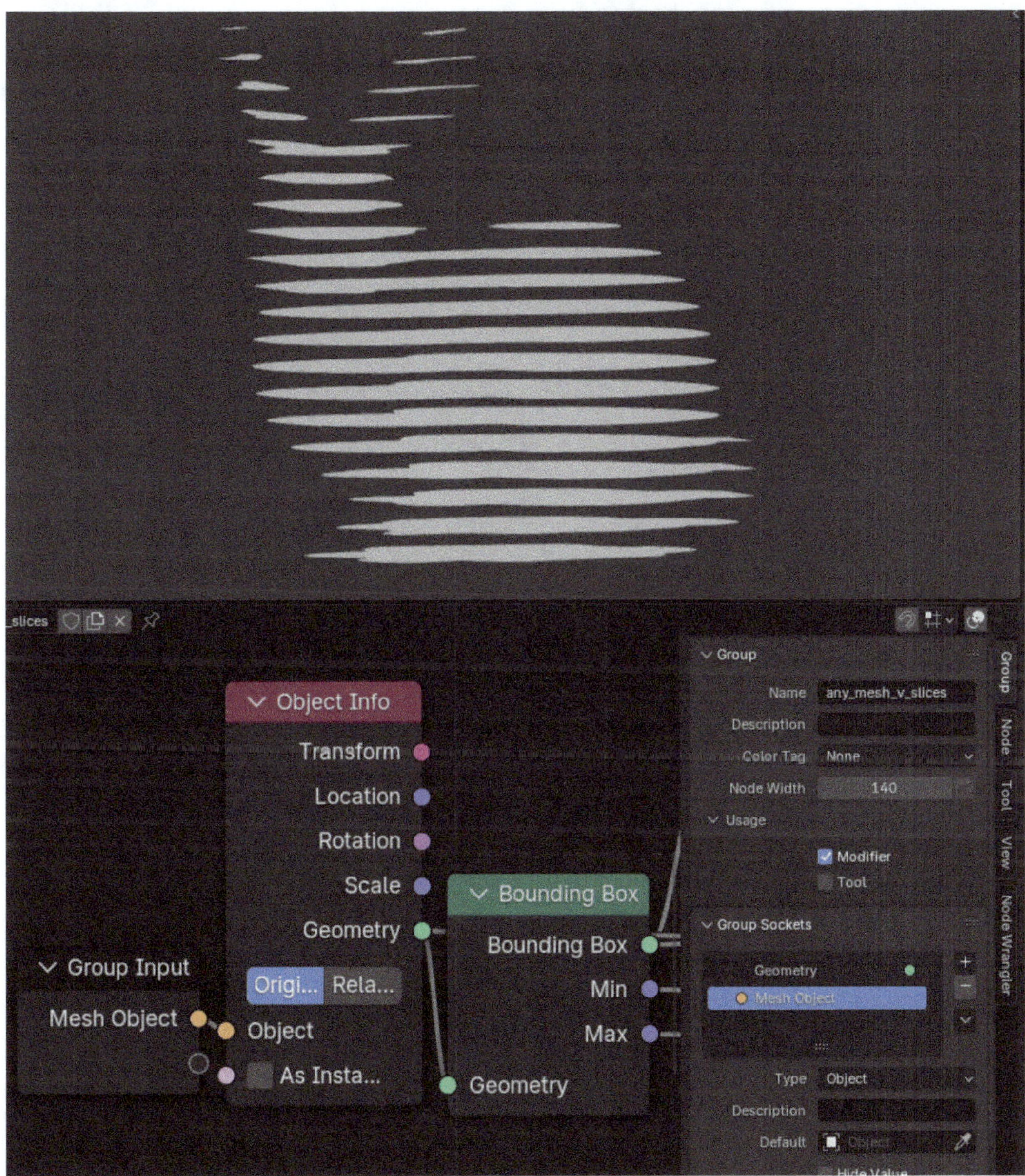

***Figure 5-21.** Adding a Mesh Object input to the sliceform tree and using its value in the tree by linking Group Input's Mesh Object socket to Object Info to Bounding Box. The viewport preview shows the Stanford bunny sliced with our tree so far*

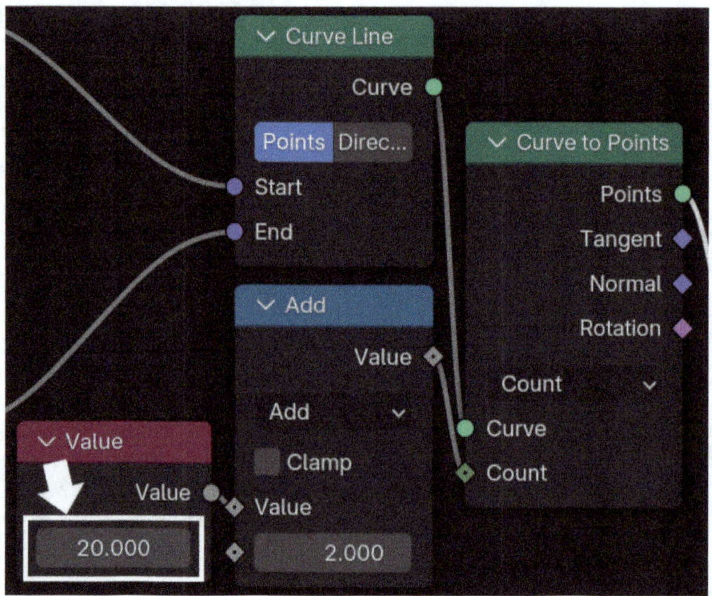

***Figure 5-22.** Changing the number of slices from 15 to 20 to capture more of the Stanford bunny's detail*

Note You can access a copy of the node tree that includes everything we've built up to Figure 5-22 via the object named `3_any_mesh_v_slices` in the file `/Ch5/sliceform.blend` from the downloaded source.

Slicing in the Orthogonal Direction

Now that we've tested slicing horizontally with two meshes, let's try slicing in the orthogonal direction. Recall in the section "Accessing a Vertex's Neighboring Face Using Corners of Vertex and Face of Corner," we found that Sort Index=0 for the Corners of Vertex nodes retrieves the top and bottom faces of the bounding box, while Sort Index=1 gets us the left and right faces—which are what we need as reference for orienting the other set of slices. We don't have a mechanism for selecting both 0 and 1 for Sort Index yet, so we'll change it to 1 for now as shown in Figure 5-23 to slice in the other direction.

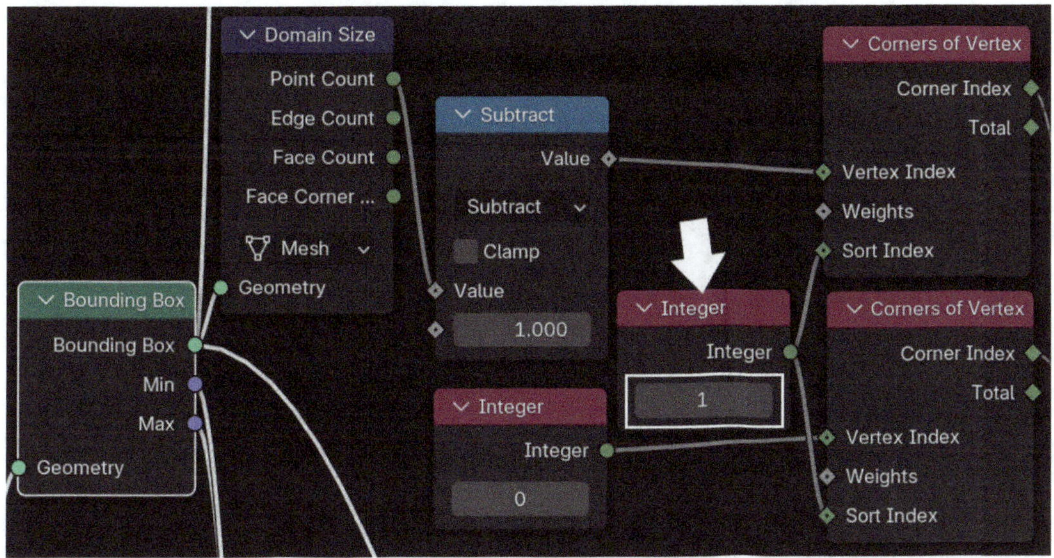

***Figure 5-23.** Changing the Sort Index for the Corners of Vertex nodes to 1 to retrieve the left and right faces of the input mesh's bounding box*

The Instance on Points node retains the instance's rotation when duplicating it across the point cloud. Currently, the Grid used as our slice instance lies on the global XY plane, which doesn't work with the new axis going laterally between the bounding box's left and right faces. Therefore, we need to rotate it 90 degrees around global X, so it is orthogonal to the new axis—to do so, we set up a four-node sequence as shown in Figure 5-24. The Transform Geometry node at the end of the sequence is the one performing the rotation on the Grid, while the three nodes leading up to it are responsible for deriving the rotation Vector. First, we convert 90 degrees to radians using a To Radians node ((1) in Figure 5-24), then link it to a Multiply (Math) node to multiply it by the value used for the Corners of Vertex nodes' Sort Index, which will zero out the rotation when Sort Index=0. We use a Combine XYZ node next to turn the rotation into a Vector (<radians>, 0, 0), at which point it can be fed to the Rotation input of Transform Geometry.

Note You can create a To Radians node from a Math node (Add ➤ Utilities ➤ Math ➤ Math) set to the type To Radians. You can find the Transform Geometry node under Add ➤ Geometry ➤ Operations and the Combine XYZ node under Add ➤ Utilities ➤ Vector.

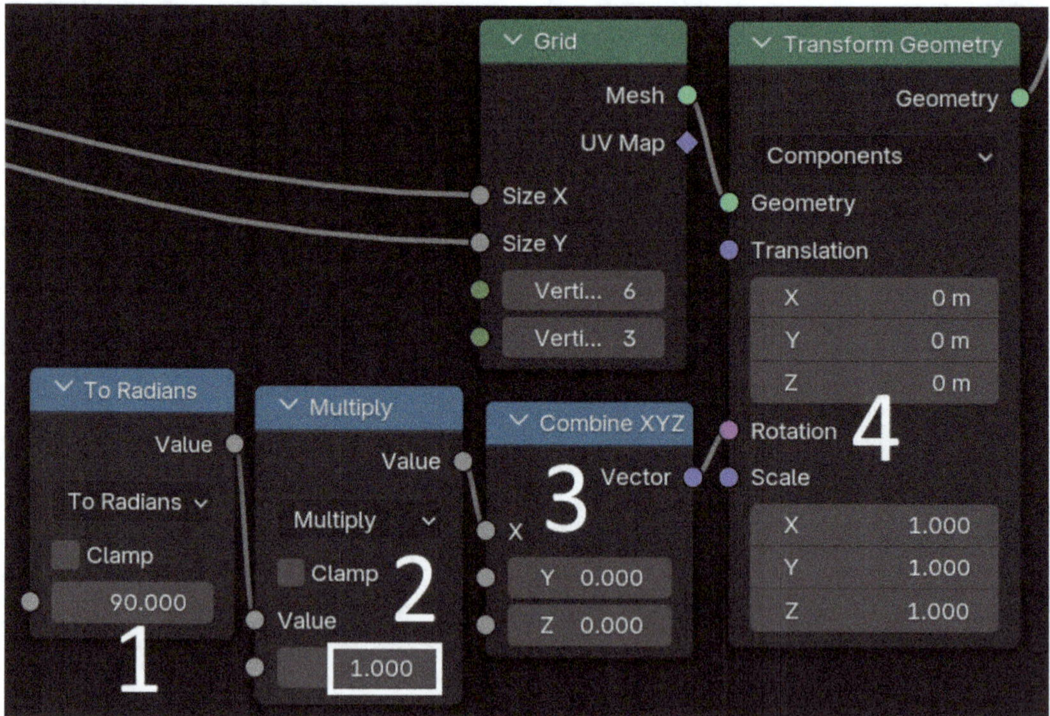

Figure 5-24. *Setting up a 90-degree rotation that is only applied to the Grid instance when the Corners of Vertex nodes' Sort Index is 1. We use a (1) Math node of type To Radians to convert 90 degrees to radians, (2) multiply it by the same value used for Sort Index so rotation is zeroed out when Sort Index=0, (3) convert it from a single value to a Vector, then use it as the (4) Rotation input for Transform Geometry*

Once the Grid instance is rotated properly, you'll see the lateral array of bunny slices show up in the preview; however, you may also notice that some of the slices don't cover the whole cross-section—this is because we previously wired the nodes to use the XY size of the bounding box (see (3) in Figure 5-17); however, in the bunny's case, the XZ size is larger—we can remedy this by using the maximum of the bounding box's X, Y, and Z sizes as the Grid's X and Y Size, which will ensure the slice is large enough to cover either direction we are slicing. After we compute the Bounding Box's diagonal Vector from Max minus Min, we use a Separate XYZ node to divide the Vector into individual values ((1) in Figure 5-25), then compare them pairwise twice (X with Y, then the larger of which with Z) by passing them through two Math nodes set to type Maximum ((2) and (3) in Figure 5-25). The finished bunny slices are shown in Figure 5-26.

Note Separate XYZ is under Add ➤ Utilities ➤ Vector while Math is under Add ➤ Utilities ➤ Math.

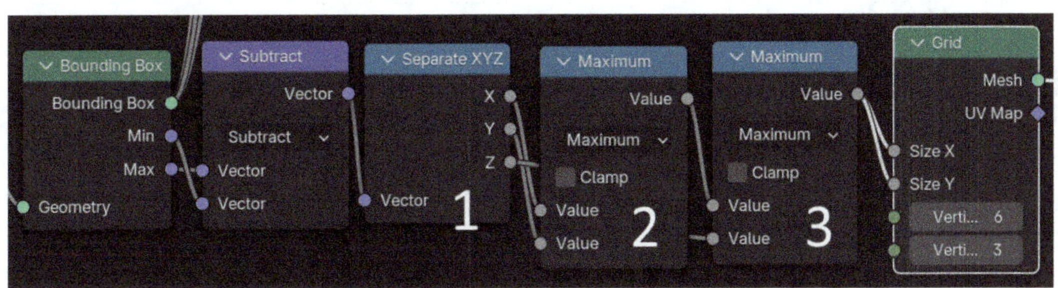

Figure 5-25. *After (1) separating the X, Y, Z sizes of the bounding box, we compare the three values pairwise (X with Y, then the larger of which with Z) using two Math nodes of type Maximum (2 and 3)*

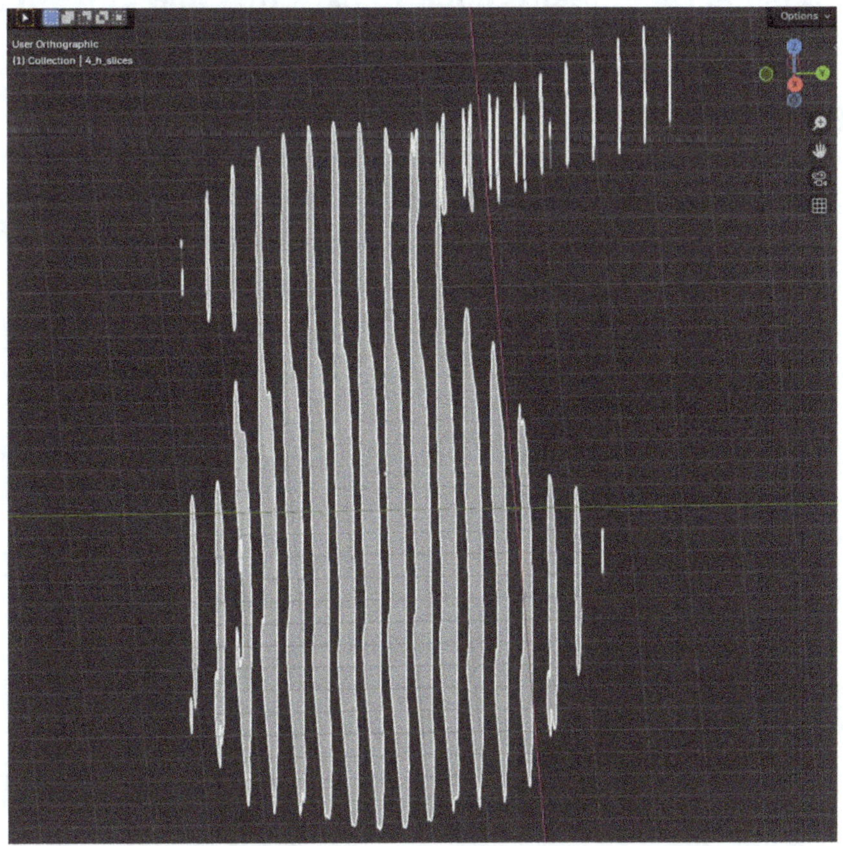

Figure 5-26. *The Stanford bunny sliced parallel to the XZ plane*

Note You can access a copy of the node tree that includes everything we've built up to Figure 5-26 via the object named `4_h_slices` in the file `/Ch5/sliceform.blend` from the downloaded source.

Using a Repeat Block to Slice Both Directions

We've sliced the bunny in the direction parallel to the XY plane (Figure 5-21) as well as parallel to the XZ plane (Figure 5-26), so it seems we've accomplished what we set out to do. The only problem is the tree can only slice one direction at a time. It won't make much sense to duplicate all the nodes, however, just so we can slice both directions in the same tree. Luckily, we can use the Repeat block (Add ➤ Utilities ➤ Repeat) to run the same set of nodes a given number of iterations just like a `for` loop.

Example: Using the Repeat Block to Extrude Each Edge of a Grid an Amount Proportional to Its Index

Before modifying the sliceform tree, let's work through a simple example with a Repeat block to make sense of its mechanism. Create an "Empty Tree" as described in that section, and add a Grid node with Size X and Y=1m and both Vertices X and Y equal to 2 to create a unit square with two verts per side, therefore four verts and four edges total, as shown in Figure 5-27. Our ultimate goal is to extrude all four edges of the Grid; therefore, for starters, we'll set up a tree to extrude the first edge (index #0). To do so, we add an Equal (Math) node set to Integer, then link its two input values A and B to an Index node and 0, respectively, to make a selection for index #0. We connect the Equal node to Extrude Mesh (Add ➤ Mesh ➤ Operations ➤ Extrude Mesh) and set the offset scale to 1 for now, as shown in Figure 5-27, to extrude edge #0 1m in the +Z direction.

Note Grid is under Add ➤ Mesh ➤ Primitives, Equal is a Compare node (Add ➤ Utilities ➤ Math ➤ Compare) set to type Equal, and Index is under Add ➤ Geometry ➤ Read.

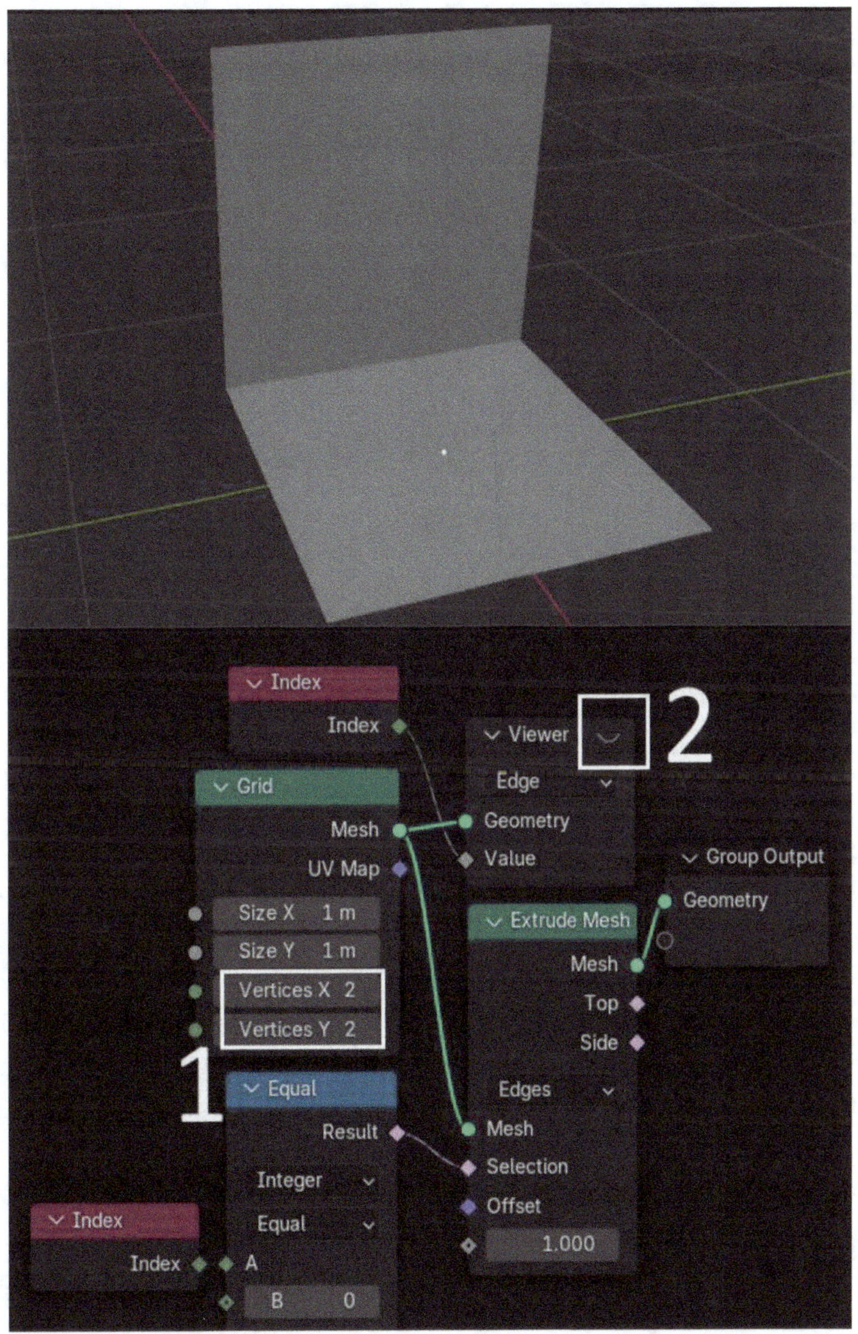

Figure 5-27. *Extruding the first edge (index #0) of a square Grid with (1) two verts per side (therefore four edges total). A (2) Viewer node is setup to display the Grid's Edge indices, which is disabled here so the Group Output preview is shown in the figure*

Suppose we want to extrude each Grid edge an amount proportional to its index, i.e., the first edge (index #0) is extruded 0m, the second edge (index #1) 1m, and so on. To get an idea of how much each edge should be extruded, we'll use a Viewer node ((2) in Figure 5-27) set to type Edge with an Index node linked to its Value socket to display the Grid's edge indices, which are shown in Figure 5-28.

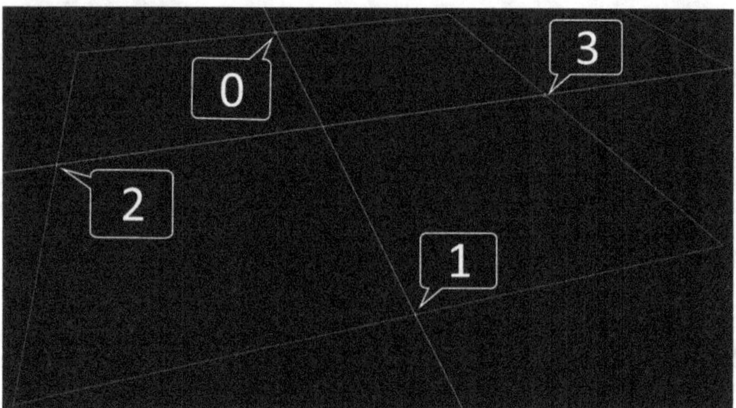

Figure 5-28. *Edge indices of the Grid node displayed by the Viewer node in Figure 5-27*

Instead of duplicating the nodes in Figure 5-27 four times so we can set the edge index (Equal node's B value) and Extrude Mesh's offset scale from 0 to 3, we'll use a Repeat block with four Iterations, then use the iteration number to look up the edge and scale the extrusion.

Let's add a Repeat block (Add ➤ Utilities ➤ Repeat) to the node editor, as shown in Figure 5-29. I call it a "block" as opposed to "node" because it consists of two Repeat nodes—one node on the left representing the beginning of the loop and one on the right representing the end. If you think of a Repeat block with N Iterations as a `for` loop, the left node is the line `for i in range(N)`, the path of wire(s) linking the left and right nodes is the loop body, and the right node is the end of the body. In each iteration, the data flows from the left to the right node, then jumps back to the left node again for the next iteration. You can optionally feed data into the loop through the left node's "Geometry" input socket (which is equivalent to accessing a variable from the code above a `for` loop). You must make at least one path through the Repeat block linking the left and right nodes no matter what you put on that path. You can create as many data paths through a Repeat block as you like by linking empty sockets pairwise between the two Repeat nodes, as shown in Figure 5-29.

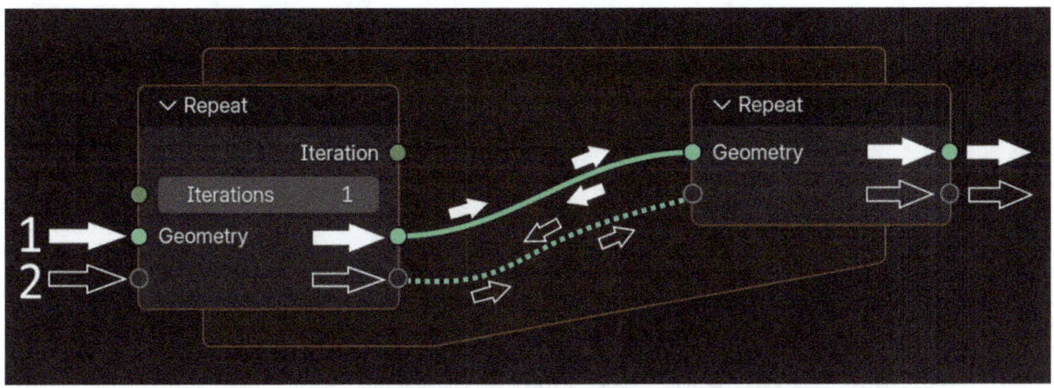

***Figure 5-29.** Data flow of the Repeat block. In each iteration, the data flows from the left to the right node, accumulating edits along the way, before jumping back to the left node for the next iteration. You can create as many data paths as you like by linking the empty sockets pairwise between the two nodes*

Now that we understand how a Repeat block works, let's convert the tree in Figure 5-27 into one iteration of the block and set the block to run a total of four iterations to extrude the Grid's four edges. First, connect Grid to the "Geometry" socket of the Repeat block ((1) in Figure 5-30) to use in the loop through the (1) first data path. For each iteration, we'll use the current iteration number (6) as both the index (7) to look up the edge and the offset scale (8) to extrude that edge. At the end of each iteration, we'll merge the geometry generated so far (from (2) to (3)) with the current iteration's extrusion (from (2), (8), to (3)) using a Join Geometry node, then connect it to the right Repeat node (4) to complete the path back to the left node.

Once all four iterations are complete, the generated geometry flows outward (5) from the right Repeat node, which can in turn be linked to the Group Output node as is in our case (Figure 5-31), or linked to more nodes for further edits. We previously verified the Grid edges' indices using a Viewer node, which are #0, #3, #1, and #2 clockwise as shown in Figure 5-28—now we'll cross-check the Repeat block's output in Figure 5-31 to see if it matches—sure enough, each edge is extruded an amount proportional to its index, where edges with indices #0, #1, #2, and #3 are extruded 0m, 1m, 2m, and 3m, respectively.

Note You can access a copy of the node tree in Figure 5-30 via the object named `repeat_example` in the file `/Ch5/repeat_example.blend` from the downloaded source.

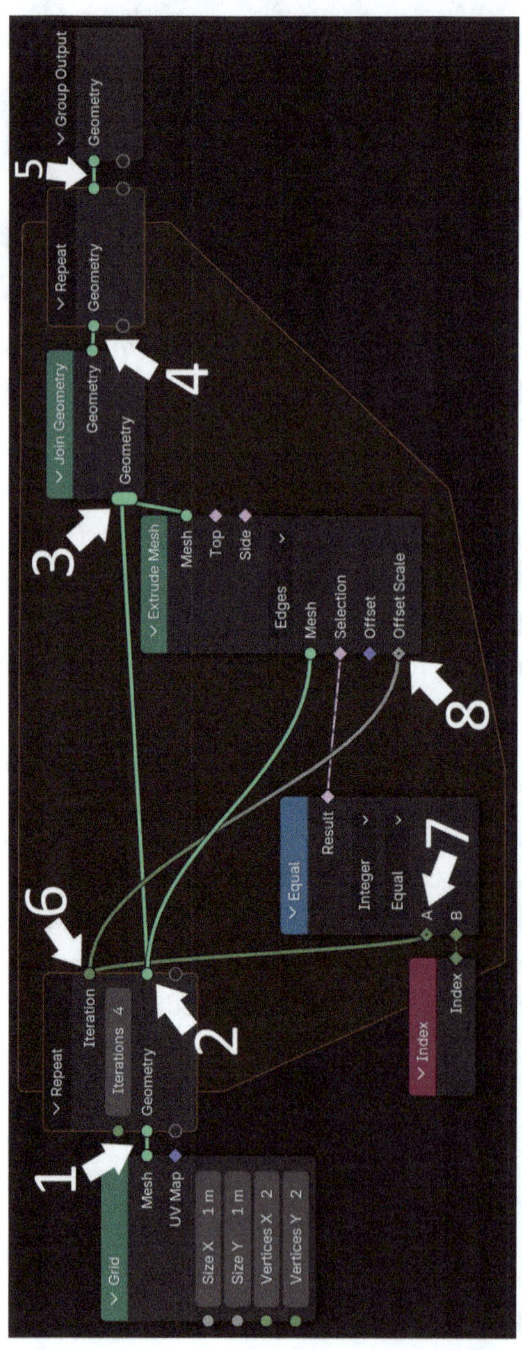

Figure 5-30. *Adapting Figure 5-27 as one iteration through a Repeat block. The Grid (1) is linked as the Geometry input to the block. Each (6) iteration number is used both as the index (7) to look up the edge and (8) offset scale to extrude that edge. At the end of each iteration, a Join Geometry node merges the geometry so far ((2) to (3)) with the current extrusion ((2) to (8) to (3)) and passes it onto the right node to complete the data path back to the left node. Once all iterations are complete (5), data flows out the right side of the right node*

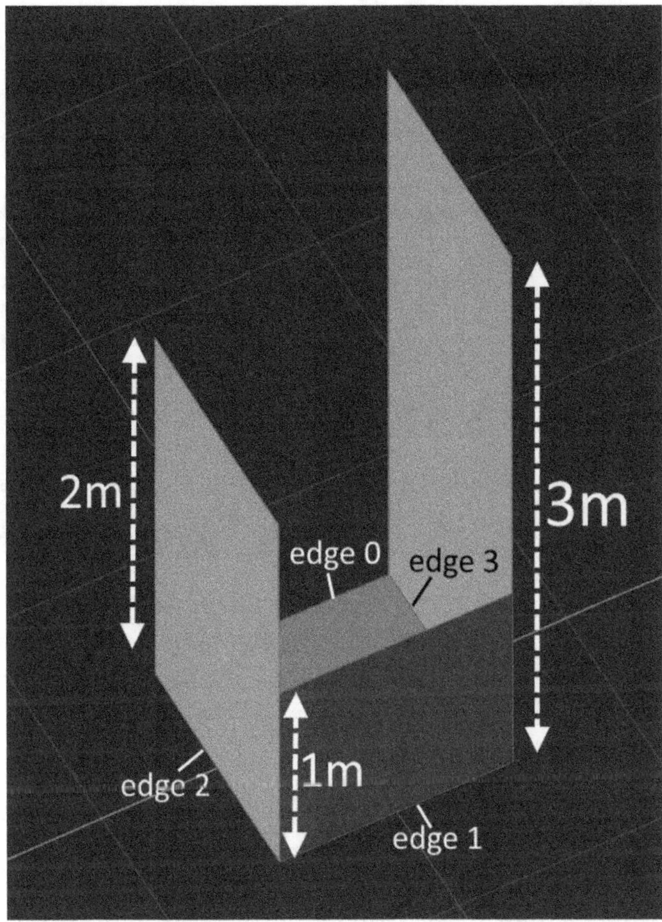

Figure 5-31. *Preview of the Repeat block output from Figure 5-30. Cross-referencing edge indices with Figure 5-28, we verify that each edge's extrusion is scaled by its index*

Modifying the Sliceform Tree to Integrate a Repeat Block

Recall in the section "Deriving Center Axes for Slicing Using Topology Nodes," we found that we can extract the bounding box's faces parallel to the XY plane by setting the Corners of Vertex nodes' Sort Index to 0 and faces parallel to the XZ plane by setting Sort Index to 1. Instead of duplicating the nodes, we can surround them with a Repeat block, set the block to run two Iterations, then use the iteration number to change Sort Index as shown in Figure 5-32—the first iteration (with index #0) will then have Sort Index 0 and second iteration Sort index 1, respectively.

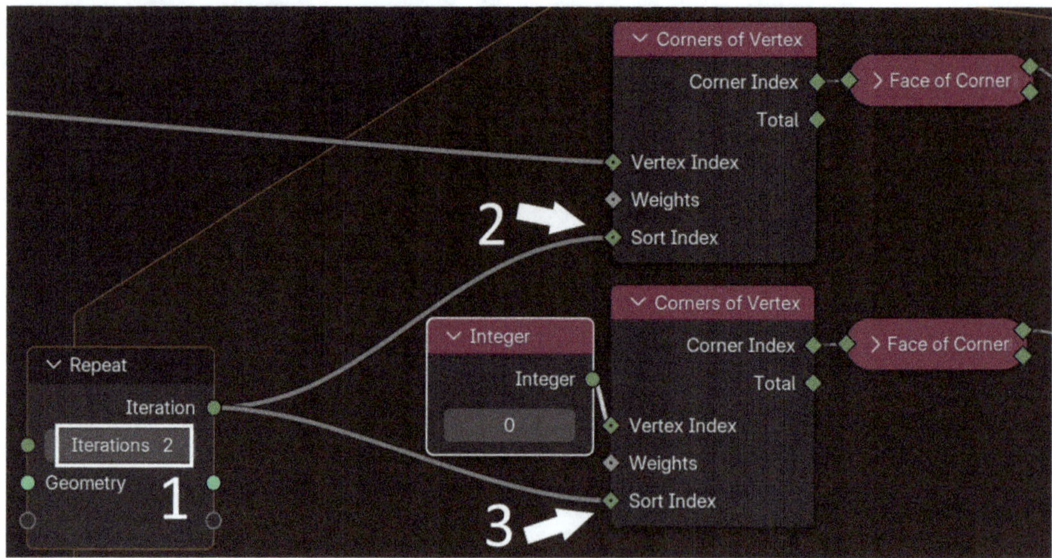

Figure 5-32. *Surrounding the nodes of the sliceform tree with a Repeat block set to run two iterations and use the iteration number to control the Sort Index of the Corners of Vertex nodes to extract the bounding box faces parallel to the XY and XZ planes, respectively*

Recall in the section "Slicing in the Orthogonal Direction," we found that the Grid instance used by Instance on Points for forming the slice stack must already be in the correct rotation relative to the stack direction. Therefore in Figure 5-24, we set up a node sequence to toggle the rotation for the Grid instance based on the Corners of Vertex nodes' Sort Index. When Sort Index is 0, the Grid is already parallel to the XY plane, so no rotation is needed. When Sort Index is 1, however, we need to rotate the Grid 90 degrees around X so it becomes parallel to the XZ plane. Since the Repeat block's iteration number coincides with the Sort Index, we can use it to toggle this rotation by setting it as the Multiply (Math) node's value as shown in Figure 5-33.

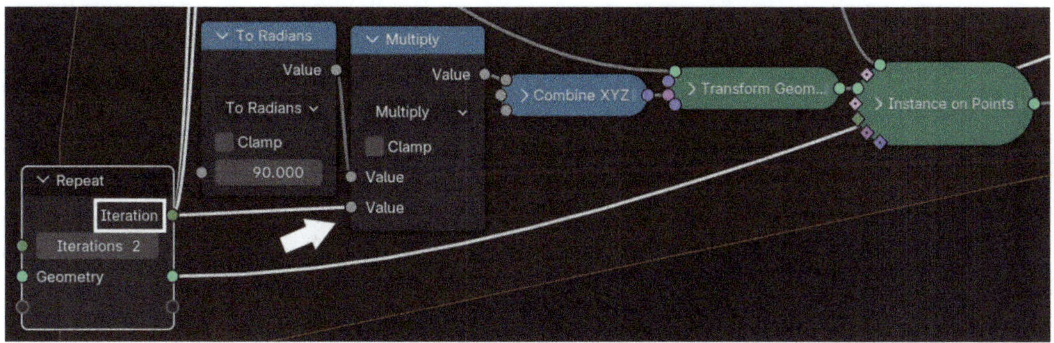

Figure 5-33. *Using the Repeat block's iteration number to control the multiplier of the Grid instance's rotation. When Iteration=0, rotation X=0; when iteration=1, rotation X=radians(90 degrees)*

The last step to integrate the Repeat block is to use a Join Geometry node to merge the geometry produced by the block so far with the current iteration's geometry (output of the Mesh Boolean node), as shown in Figure 5-34. After that, the combined data is passed onto the right Repeat node to complete the path back to the left Repeat node. Note that we did *not* use the left Repeat node's input "Geometry" socket here—this is because we do not want to combine the bounding box nor the original bunny mesh with the generated slices within the block.

With the Repeat block integrated, let's walk through both iterations of the block together. In the first iteration (#0), the Corners of Vertex nodes' Sort Index is 0; therefore, the bounding box's top and bottom are used as reference and the Grid instance for populating the slice stack stays in its original rotation parallel to the global XY plane. At the end of the first iteration, the slices are joined with the geometry so far (which is nothing) and passed back to the beginning of the block. In the second iteration (#1), the Corners of Vertex nodes' Sort Index is 1, so the bounding box's left and right faces are used as reference and the Grid instance is rotated 90 degrees around X to be parallel with the XZ plane. At the end of the second iteration, the geometry so far (the slices parallel to XY) is joined with the current iteration's geometry (slices parallel to XZ). At this point, all iterations are complete, so the combined slices flow out the right of the Repeat block, which are shown in Figure 5-35.

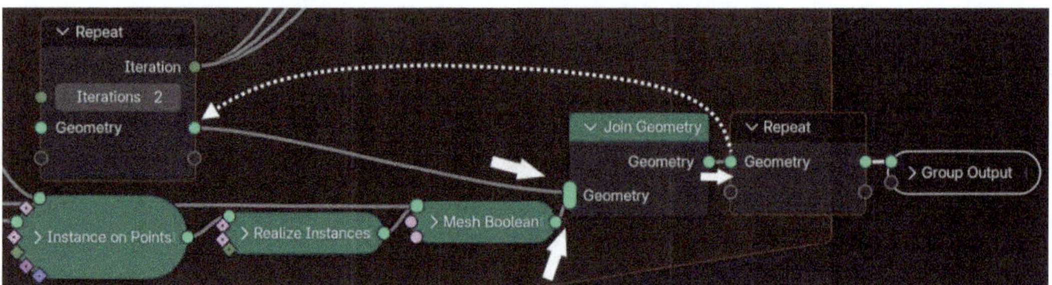

Figure 5-34. *Completing the data path through the Repeat block in the sliceform tree. The dashed arrow shows the data path jumping back to the left node for the next iteration*

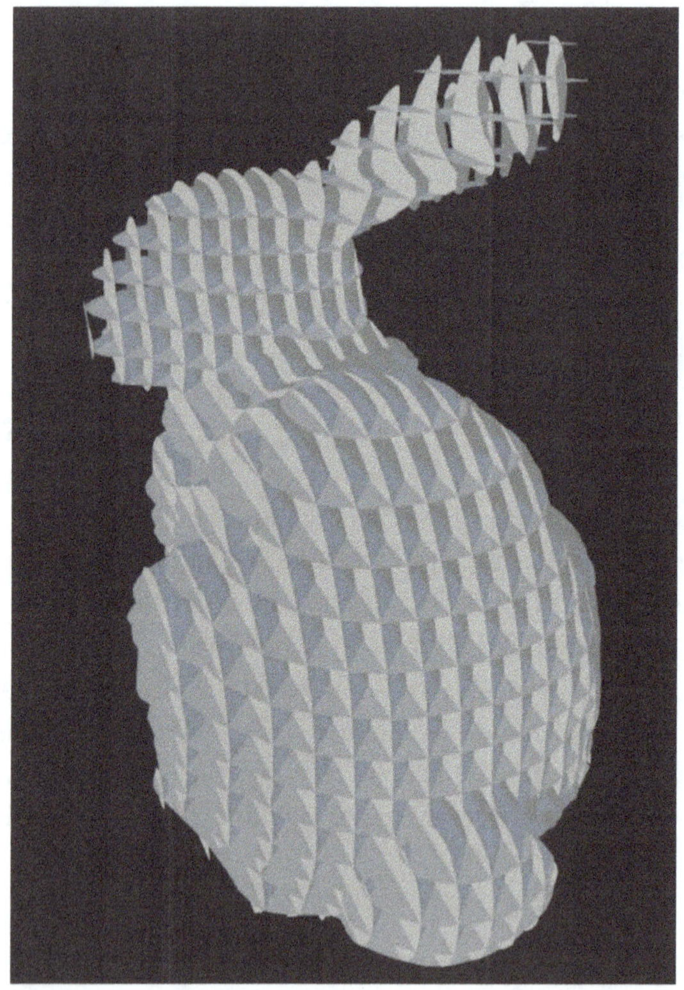

Figure 5-35. *After integrating the Repeat block, the sliceform tree generates both sets of slices at once*

Note You can access a copy of the node tree that includes everything we've built up to Figure 5-35 via the object named `5_repeat_block` in the file `/Ch5/sliceform.blend` from the downloaded source.

Extrude Slices for Thickness

Now that we've got the sliceform tree generating both sets of slices, we can add refinements such as creating slice thickness. We can do so by inserting an Extrude Mesh node between Mesh Boolean and Join Geometry in the Repeat block as shown in Figure 5-36, which will extrude each set of slices before adding them to the geometry accumulated by the block. We'll set Extrude Mesh's offset scale to 0.1 and check the Individual box.

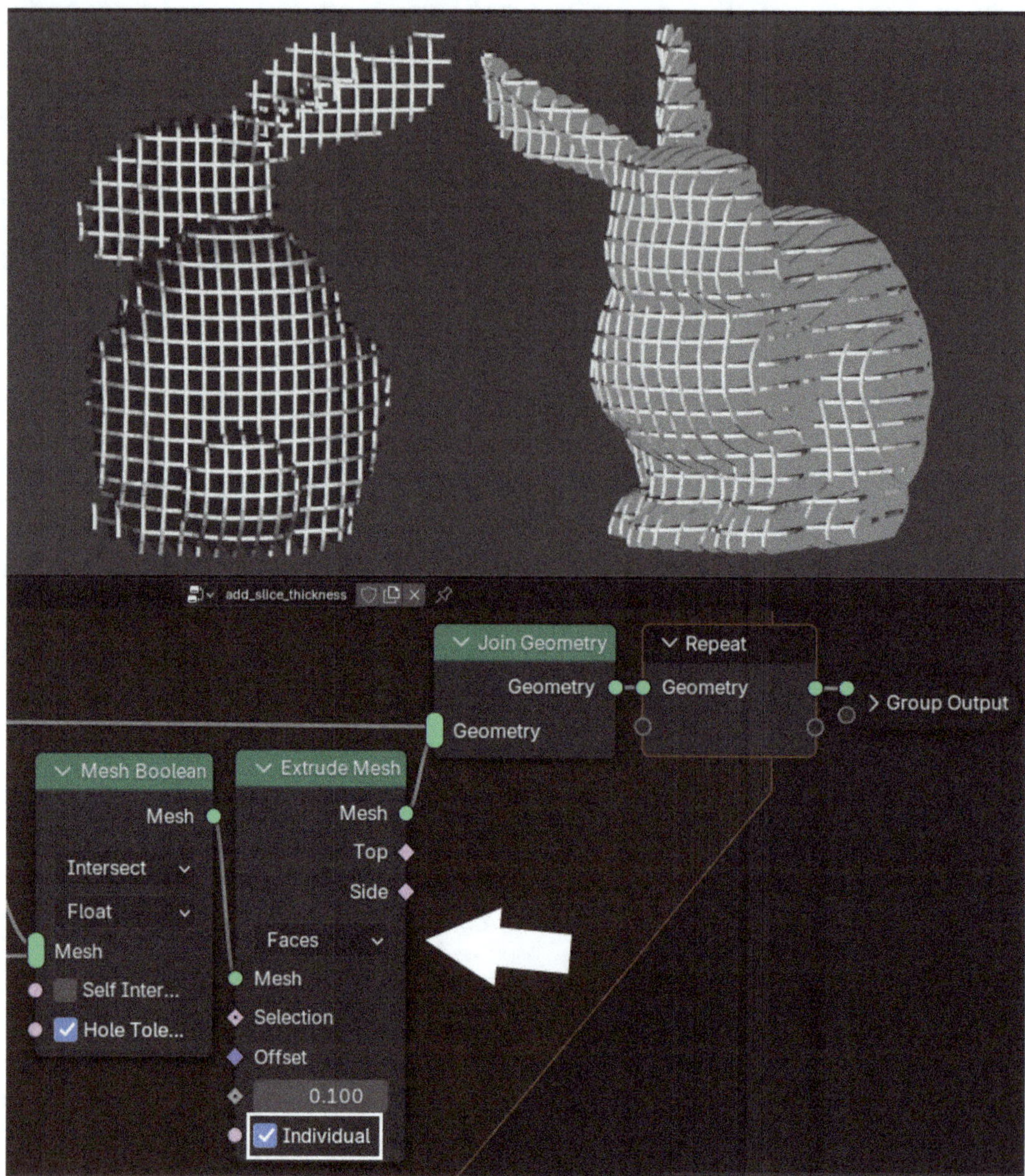

***Figure 5-36.** Using the Extrude Mesh node with a fixed offset scale of 0.1 and the Individual box checked to add thickness to the sliceform slices*

Adding Input for the Number of Slices per Direction

The second refinement we'll make to the sliceform tree is adding a user input to control the number of slices per direction. In the geometry node editor, press the N key to summon the Properties shelf. Under Group Sockets, select "Mesh Object," then click the + button ➤ Input to add a new input socket right after "Mesh Object." Double-click the new socket and rename it to "Slices," set its Type to Integer, then enter the Description "Number of slices to cut in each direction." Set the Default value to 20, Min to 5, and Max to 100. You will see a "Slices" slider show up under the node tree's modifier under the Properties shelf ➤ Modifier tab. The slider will initially show 0 right after its creation—you can reset it to the Default value by right-clicking and selecting "Reset to Default Value."

Next, we'll hook up the Slices value in the node tree itself. Recall that we control the number of slices via the Curve to Points node, which creates the point cloud for Instance on Points to distribute the Grid instances across to create the slice stack. We had previously hardcoded the intended number of slices to 15 for the UV Sphere and 20 for the Stanford bunny, before adding 2 to account for the begin and end points of the curve. Therefore, to incorporate the user input number of slices, we'll link the Group Input node's "Slices" socket to the first Value of the Add node as shown in Figure 5-37, which increments it by 2 then passes it on to the Count for the Curve to Points node.

Note You can access a copy of the node tree that includes everything we've built up to Figure 5-37 via the object named `6_slice_thickness_num_slices` in the file `/Ch5/sliceform.blend` from the downloaded source.

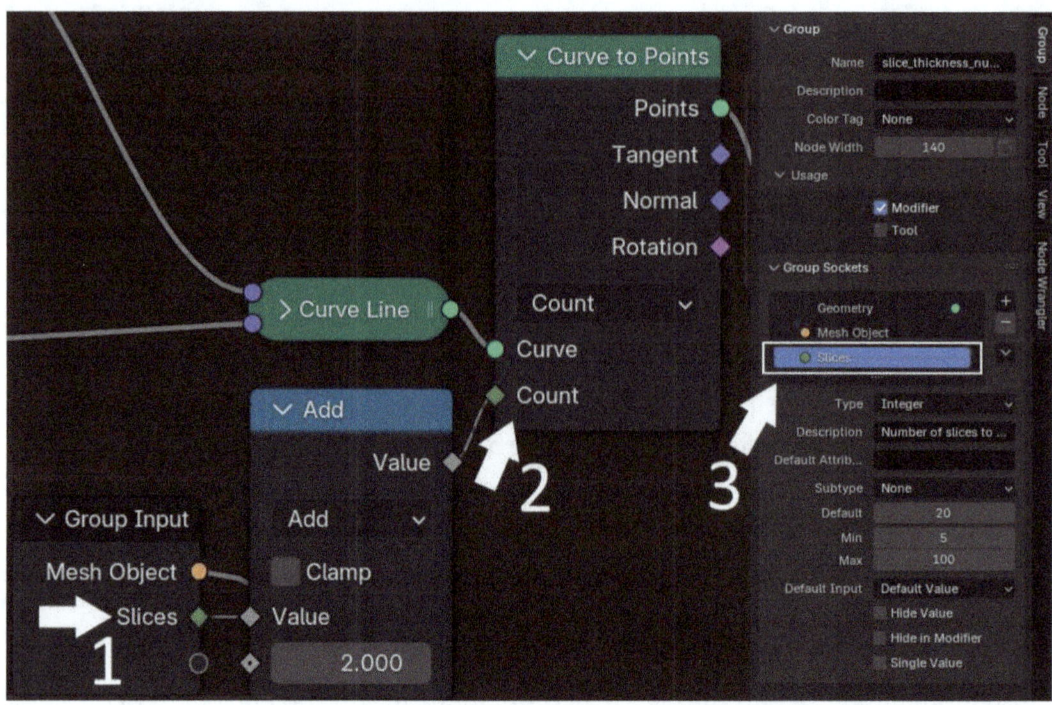

***Figure 5-37.** Incorporating the Slices input in the node tree to control the number of slices per direction. The Group Input node's (1) "Slices" socket is linked to the Add node to replace the previously hard-coded value (20), incremented by 2, then passed on to (2) the Count value for Curve to Points, which creates the point cloud for Instance on Points to distribute the Grid instance to create the slice stack. (3) shows the Slices input socket under Properties shelf ➤ Group Sockets in the node editor.*

Figure 5-38 shows three bunny sliceforms generated with Slices=10, Slices=20, and Slices=30, respectively. Figure 5-39 shows three additional examples of UV Sphere sliceforms generated with Slices=10, Slices=20, and Slices=30.

Note The examples in Figure 5-38 are provided as the objects `bunny_10slices`, `bunny_20slices`, and `bunny_30slices` in the file `/Ch5/sliceform.blend` from the downloaded source. Likewise, the examples in Figure 5-39 are provided as the objects `sphere_10slices`, `sphere_20slices`, and `sphere_30 slices` in the same file.

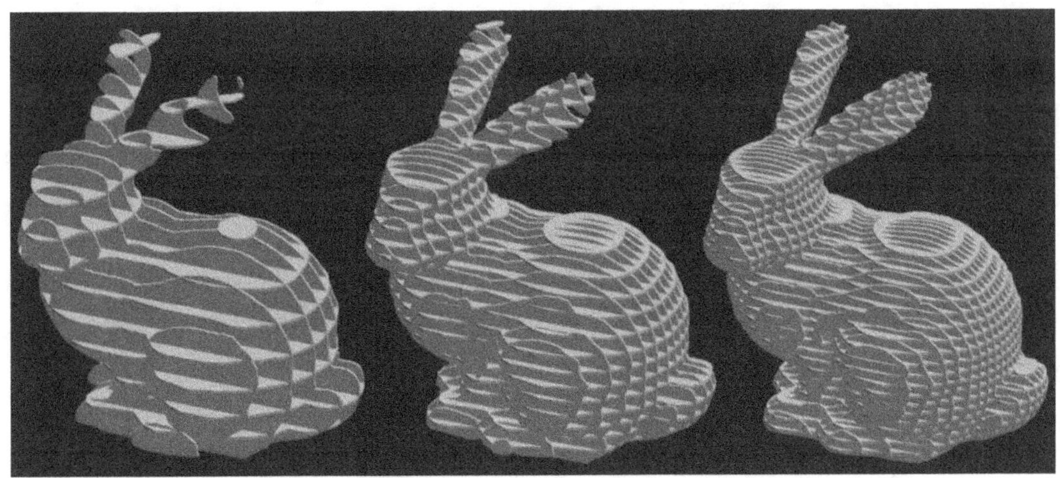

Figure 5-38. *From left to right: sliceform bunnies with Slices=10, Slices=20, and Slices=30*

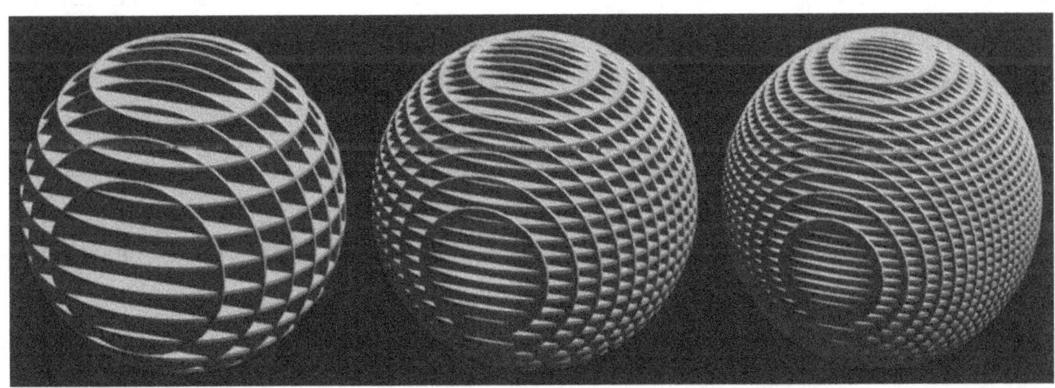

Figure 5-39. *From left to right: sliceform UV Spheres with Slices=10, Slices=20, and Slices=30*

Summary

After picking up geometry node basics in Chapter 4, you delved into more advanced techniques in this chapter, starting with systematically setting up different starting points of trees, including an empty tree for generating a mesh from scratch, a tree that takes a user selected mesh object as input, and your own subtree for controlling tiling frequency of textures to mimic the behavior of a Texture Coordinate and Mapping node combination from shader nodes. In addition, you learned two ways to quickly experiment by modifying off of an existing tree—the first is to append a tree from another blend file which you can edit independently thereafter without affecting the original. The second is to duplicate an object with the tree of interest, then make the tree on the new object a copy by resetting its user count to 0.

In Chapter 4, we used geometry nodes to generate meshes to bake normal maps from; in this chapter, we flipped this concept on its head and used textures to manipulate meshes. Using primitives and the Stanford bunny as our test models, we utilized the Voronoi Texture node to create a variety of effects including cracks, vines, cavities, and gem-like facets. In addition, we used the Noise Texture to create rock-like meshes and the Gabor Texture to create wrinkles and ripples. Along the way, you discovered that you can quickly put together a mesh voxelizer by chaining a Mesh to Volume and a Volume to Mesh node back to back.

In the last part of the chapter, we took on a complex project of building a sliceform generator. We began simple then gradually iterated on the tree with each pass improving on the last. Starting with slicing a primitive in a single direction as proof of concept, we progressed to using the Stanford bunny as the test model, slicing it in the orthogonal direction, then combining the two sets of slices with a Repeat block to avoid duplicating nodes. Along the way, you learned how to use Mesh Topology nodes to access parts of a mesh based on context, how to use Math nodes to create Boolean conditions for making selections, and how to use Viewer nodes to preview mesh attributes such as edge indices in the viewport.

CHAPTER 6

Fractal Terrain Generation

In this chapter, we'll explore terrain generation methods by building a generator in Blender Python with the help of `numpy`. In the first part of the chapter, we'll go over noise-based methods including value noise with uniform sampling, value noise with noise basis functions, fBm, and the diamond-square algorithm. In the second part of the chapter, we'll discuss fractal-based methods, such as hybrid multi fractal, multi fractal, and hetero terrain functions. Whether noise or fractal-based, all the generation methods output a grid of elevation values called a *height map*; therefore, we'll design the generator so that functionalities common between algorithms, such as interpolation, creating mesh data, and adding modifiers, etc., are implemented once and shared among them.

Running This Chapter's Examples

We'll get ready by installing the dependency and downloading the sample code and blend file for this chapter.

Installing Dependency (`numpy`)

This chapter's script imports functions from the third-party Python package `numpy`. Please refer to the Appendix for instructions on how to install `numpy` under Blender Python.

Downloading and Running the Sample Code

The source code and color figures for this book are available on GitHub via the book's product page, located at `https://link.springer.com/book/9798868817861`. Download the files, navigate to the `/Ch6` folder, and open `fractal_terrain_generator.py` in the

I. Lupiani, *Procedural Content Generation for Games*, https://doi.org/10.1007/979-8-8688-1787-8_6

Text Editor under the Scripting workspace. You'll find an `if __name__ == "__main__"` block already set up with calls to the generator at the bottom of the script. Clicking the Run button will generate the terrain meshes matching the provided `*.blend` file, `/Ch6/terrain_demo_final_z_view.blend`.

To duplicate the view in the sample blend file, tab into Object mode in the viewport, then Numpad 7 to switch to the top view, followed by View ➤ Area ➤ Toggle Maximize Area (Ctrl Space Bar). Use the A key to toggle select all, followed by View ➤ Frame All, and the + (–) key or scrolling the mouse wheel to zoom in (out). Use the T key to hide the tool shelf, and click the Show Gizmo and Show Overlays buttons at the upper right corner to turn off the grid and various widgets in the viewport. Under Viewport Shading, change Lighting to MatCap ➤ Studiolight. Figure 6-1 shows this view rotated 90 degrees clockwise to fit the margin of the page. The generator's arguments will be explained in detail throughout the chapter. You can modify the argument values in the sample calls and see how they affect the generated models. The generator code has been tested in Blender 4.2, 4.3, 4.4, and 4.5.2 LTS.

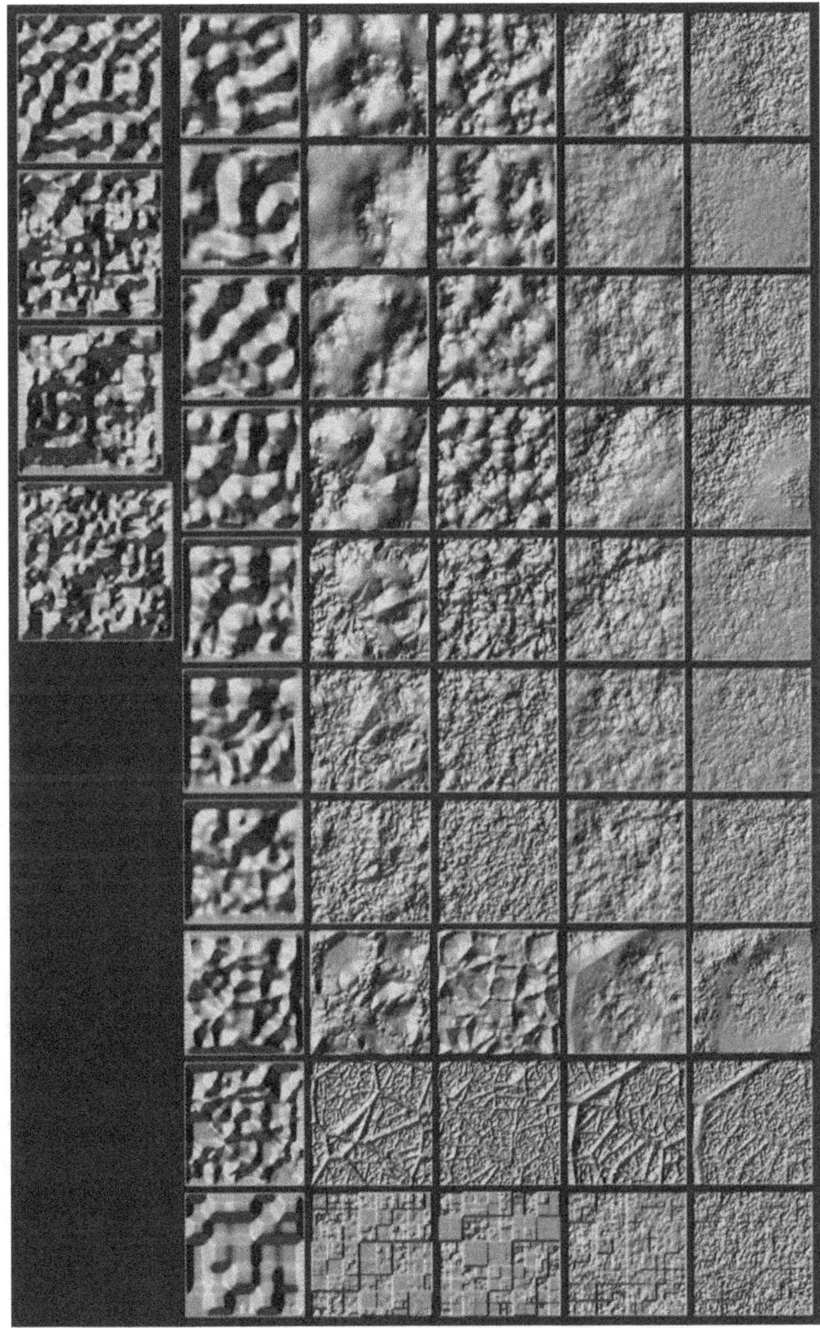

Figure 6-1. *Top view of terrain mesh tiles we'll generate in this chapter. Columns of tiles from left to right: value noise and diamond-square, fBm with basis functions, hybrid multi fractal (three octaves), hybrid multi fractal (four octaves), Blender's multi fractal, and Blender's hetero terrain*

Terrain Generator Design

This chapter centers around the discussion of noise- and fractal-based terrain generation methods, which output grids of elevation values called *height maps*. A height map can correspond to a rectangular or square fictional geographic region, with each grid cell mapping to one unit area. Much like an image, the higher the resolution of a height map, the more detailed terrain it will produce but the more storage and runtime it will require as well.

From Height Map to 3D Mesh

Since a vertex is a point, but a grid cell is a rectangle, to go from a height map to a 3D mesh, we must come up with a way to map one to the other. One way is to define a vertex at each cell center; however, I find it easier to imagine one vertex at each crossing of two grid lines. The good news is since we are generating fictional terrain from scratch, we can control both the data format and the resolution of the height map—therefore, we'll keep things simple and use a one-to-one ratio of vertex to grid point (intersection of two grid lines) throughout the chapter. The grid resolution can then be varied by widening or narrowing the distance between adjacent grid lines. For example, to go from the top-left corner (first row, first column) to the point at the first row, second column, the grid XY coordinates will increase from (0, 0) to (0, 1)—however, when constructing the corresponding vertex, we can translate this to (0, 0) to (0, cell_width), where cell_width is the distance between two vertical grid lines.

Since we'll create the coordinates of *all* terrain vertices based on the height map to generate a mesh, we'll use the Blender Python function `<MESH DATA BLOCK>.from_pydata(verts, edges, faces)`. You create a blank mesh data block first, then use it to call `from_pydata` with the lists of verts, edges, and faces. The list of verts is a nested list with each item denoting the location of one vertex, for example, [[1,2,3], [4, 5, 6], ...]. The edges are specified as a list of vertex-index pairs, with each pair denoting the end points of one edge, for example, [[0, 1], [5, 8]] means there is an edge between vertex #0 and vertex #1 and another edge between vertex #5 and vertex #8—the vertex indices must match the ordering of vertices in the first argument to `from_pydata`. Likewise, each face is given as a list of vertex indices making up its boundary. If empty lists are passed to `from_pydata` for edges and faces, only loose vertices are created. If an empty list is passed for faces but valid vert and edge lists are given, a wireframe mesh is created.

Since we know the ordering of vertices and each vertex's neighbors from the height map, we'll call `from_pydata` with the lists of verts and edges, then use a `bpy` operator to fill in the faces.

Reusing Code Between Terrain Algorithms

You can see a pattern starting to emerge—the XY coordinates for a height map can be created for a chosen dimension the same way regardless of which terrain algorithm is used to fill the Zs. Similarly, the portion of the generator code that converts the height map to verts and edges and constructs the mesh data is identical and can be implemented once and shared among algorithms. This leads to the high-level generator design depicted in Figure 6-2, which is summarized in the following list with the numbered items corresponding to the numbered boxes in Figure 6-2:

1. Generate a blank height map according to the given dimension.
2. **Call one of the noise- or fractal-based terrain algorithms that we'll implement in this chapter to fill in the Z values of the height map.**
3. Use either bilinear or bicubic interpolation to smooth out the elevation between filled grid cells as needed, by interpolating first horizontally then vertically. We'll discuss these interpolation methods in detail later in the chapter.
4. Since we'll be generating terrain meshes as 3D sample "tiles," we'll provide an option to add a tile "border," a.k.a. zeroing out a certain number of rows and columns along the boundary of a tile to keep it tidy. Since the Z values for some vertex locations are altered by this step, we do so before calling `<MESH DATA>.from_pydata()`.
5. We create a new mesh data block and use it to call `<MESH DATA>.from_pydata()` with the vert and edge lists as described in the previous section to form a wireframe terrain mesh.
6. We perform any necessary scaling to the terrain mesh, optionally move it to the desired location, apply transforms, and fill in faces in this step.

7. Lastly, to refine the mesh, we add a Decimate modifier for noise-based methods and/or a Subsurf modifier for both noise and fractal-based methods.

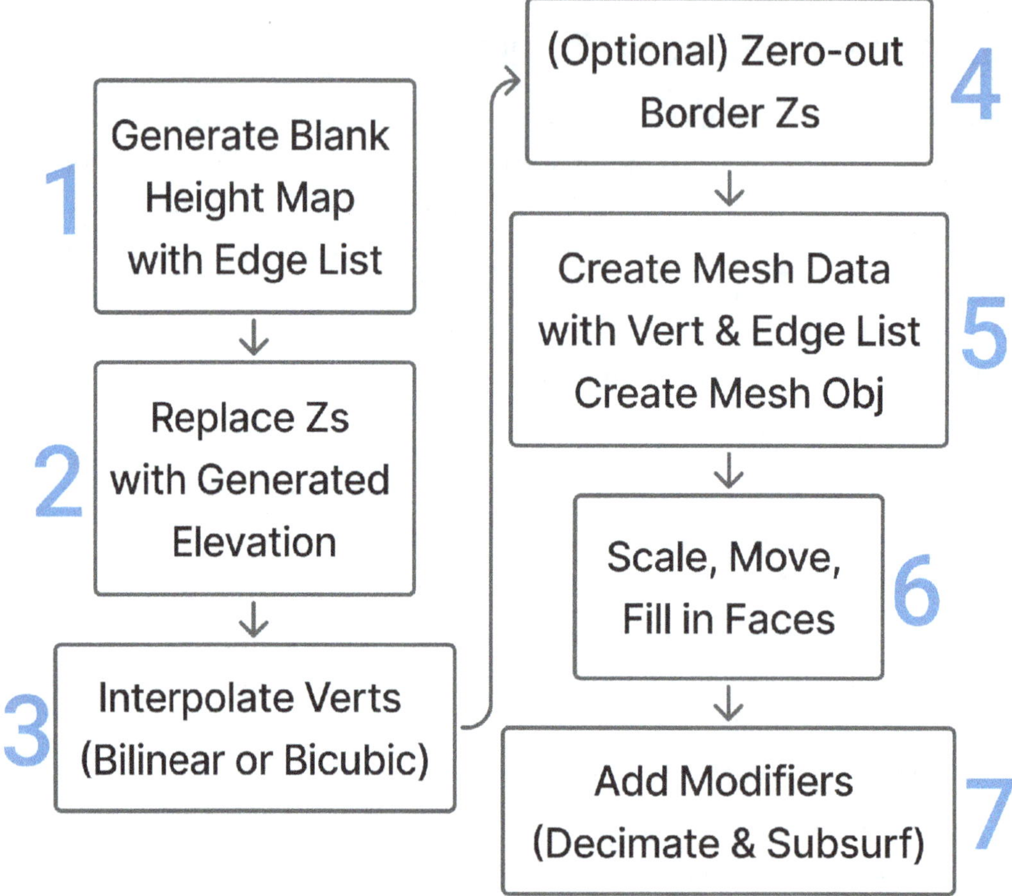

***Figure 6-2.** High-level design of our terrain generator. The numbered boxes correspond to the items in the list above the figure*

From High-Level Steps to Functions

Figure 6-3 translates the steps in Figure 6-2 into functions. For step 2, we'll implement one function per type of noise-based method. All other steps match one to one between Figures 6-2 and 6-3.

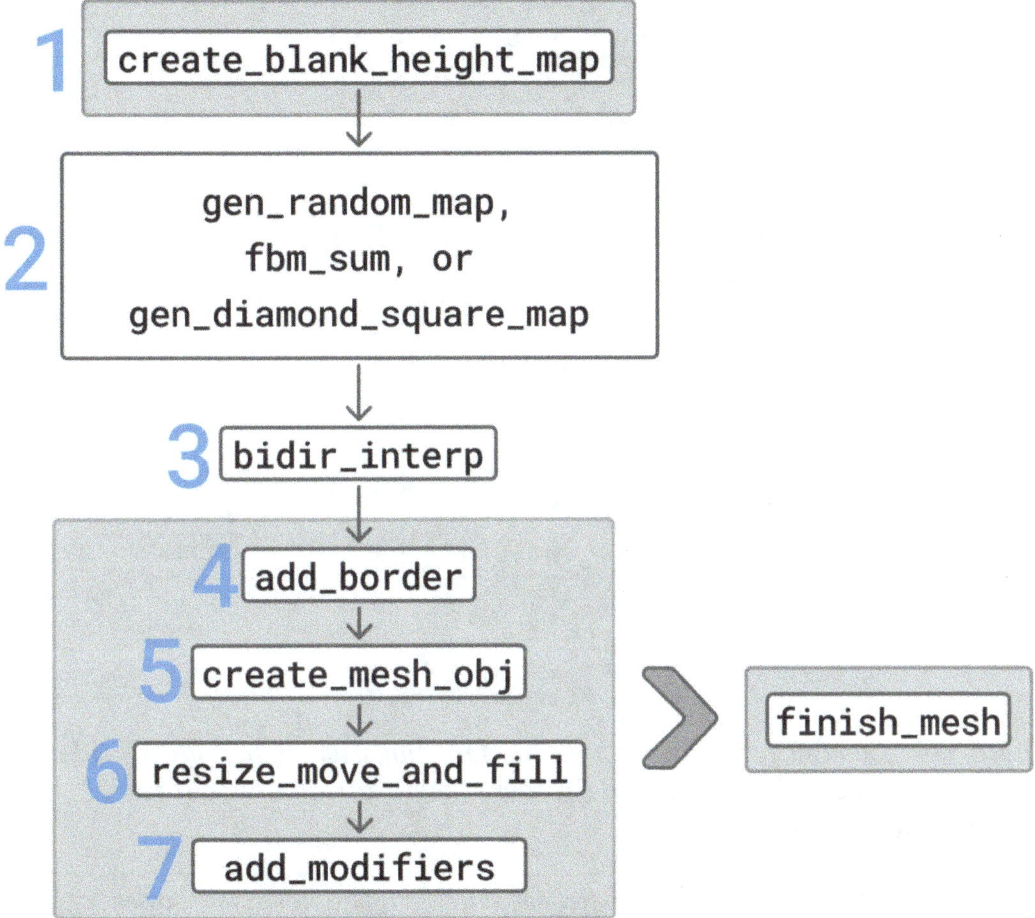

Figure 6-3. *Code structure for noise-based methods (value noise, fBm, and diamond-square) in /Ch6/fractal_terrain_generator.py*

Unlike noise-based methods, which have an explicit interpolation step (#3 in Figure 6-3), fractal-based methods perform implicit Hermit-spline interpolation during Z generation, therefore combining steps 2 and 3 in Figure 6-4. Steps #1 and #4 to #7 are identical between Figures 6-3 and 6-4. To simplify the code, we'll write a function called `finish_mesh` to call functions #4 to #7 in the order as shown under the hood.

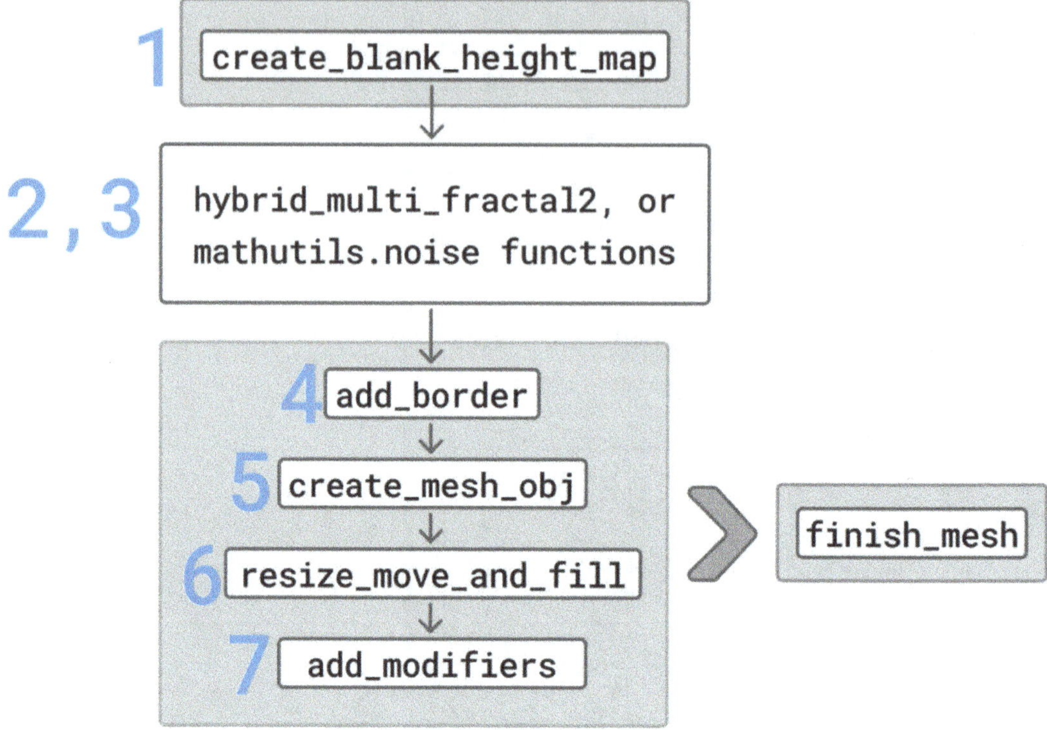

Figure 6-4. *Code structure for fractal-based methods, which include hybrid multi fractal, Blender's multi fractal, and Blender's hetero terrain in /Ch6/fractal_terrain_generator.py*

In the next two sections, we'll discuss noise-based methods (#2 in Figure 6-3) and fractal-based methods (#2 in Figure 6-4), respectively. We'll go over implementation details of #1 and #4 to #7 in both Figures 6-3 and 6-4 at the end of the chapter.

Generating Elevation with Noise Methods

In this section, we'll go over noise-based generation methods, including value noise, which samples a given noise function once at each height map location; fBm, which repeatedly samples at different scales to create a sum; and the diamond-square algorithm, which iteratively fills in grid cells from the average of their corner and diagonal neighbors.

Importing numpy

The following line at the top of /Ch6/fractal_terrain_generator.py imports numpy as np, which we'll use for array manipulation and random sampling throughout the chapter:

```
import numpy as np
```

Value Noise

The first and simplest algorithm we'll discuss is value noise, which is implemented by the function gen_random_map in Listing 6-1. Value noise works by creating a Z value for each height map location by sampling from a given noise function. Each location is sampled independently from one another.

Listing 6-1. Generate Z values using the value noise method with the given noise function (see /Ch6/fractal_terrain_generator.py)

```
def gen_random_map(num_pts, h_min, h_max, noise_basis, ↩
    x, y):
    if noise_basis=='UNIFORM':
        z = np.random.uniform(h_min, h_max, (num_pts,))
        verts = np.stack([x, y, z], ↩
            axis=-1).reshape(num_pts, 3)
        return verts
    else:
        z = np.zeros(num_pts)
        verts = np.stack([x, y, z], ↩
            axis=-1).reshape(num_pts, 3)
        z = np.array( ↩
            [noise.noise([v[0]*0.05, v[1]*0.05, 1], ↩
            noise_basis=noise_basis)*20 for v in verts])
        verts = np.stack([x, y, z], ↩
            axis=-1).reshape(num_pts, 3)
        return verts
```

We assume that prior to calling gen_random_map (Listing 6-1), the generator has called create_blank_height_map (Listing 6-21) to create a blank height map of the given dimension as three column vectors x, y, and z. We'll replace the z column vector in this function, then combine it with the x and y columns passed in to create a N by 3 array (verts) as the list of vertex positions for the terrain mesh, where N is the number of vertices (num_pts) and each row is the XYZ coordinates of one vertex. Later, the generator will call create_mesh_obj (Listing 6-27), which calls from_pydata with this list of verts to create the wireframe terrain mesh. All the terrain generation algorithms in this chapter will integrate with the generator code this way.

In gen_random_map (Listing 6-1), we create the z column vector in one of two ways—if the given noise function type is 'UNIFORM', we call np.random.uniform(h_min, h_max, (num_pts,)), which returns a column vector with num_pts entries uniformly sampled from the range [h_min, h_max). In other words, all numbers in the range ≥ h_min and < h_max have equal chance of getting picked. After that, we simply call np.stack([x, y, z], axis=-1).reshape(num_pts, 3) to combine the newly created z column with the passed in x and y column vectors into a num_pts by 3 array such that each row is the XYZ coordinates of one vertex.

Uniform sampling is not terribly exciting. Luckily, Blender's mathutils.noise module has ten built-in noise functions we can access via the list of Enum strings in Listing 6-2. If noise_basis passed to gen_random_map (Listing 6-1) is not 'UNIFORM', we assume it's one of the strings in Listing 6-2 and use it to call noise.noise. Let's zoom in on the following line of code and examine it bit by bit:

```
z = np.array( ↩
    [noise.noise([v[0]*0.05, v[1]*0.05, 1], ↩
    noise_basis=noise_basis)*20 for v in verts])
```

If you scroll to the top of /Ch6/fractal_terrain_generator.py, you'll see that we've imported the noise module via the line from mathutils import noise; therefore, we can call the noise function under that module with noise.noise. The noise.noise function takes a XYZ position (as a list of three numbers) and returns a single value. Therefore, we create a zero z column vector first with z = np.zeros(num_pts) and combine it with the passed in x and y column vectors to create a num_pts by 3 array of verts. We then iterate through verts using a for loop, calling noise.noise with each vertex v to accumulate a list of z values. After that, np.array is called to turn the list into a column vector. Note that in the for loop, we scaled v[0] and v[1] by 0.05 and the return value of noise.noise by 20—these scale factors are found through experimentation (a.k.a. I tried different values until the terrain looked good). With the z column generated, we combine it with the passed in x and y columns to form the final num_pts by 3 array and return it.

Listing 6-2. List of Enum strings to identify Blender's mathutils.noise functions (see /Ch6/fractal_terrain_generator.py)

```
bl_noise_basis_options = ↩
    ['BLENDER','PERLIN_ORIGINAL','PERLIN_NEW', ↩
    'VORONOI_F1', 'VORONOI_F2','VORONOI_F3','VORONOI_F4', ↩
    'VORONOI_F2F1','VORONOI_CRACKLE','CELLNOISE']
```

As mentioned earlier in the section "Terrain Generator Design," we will implement the functions marked #1 and #4 to #7 in Figures 6-3 and 6-4 and reuse them between different generation methods. Listing 6-3 shows how we put together a value noise generator using this strategy—we call create_blank_height_map (Listing 6-21, #1) to create a blank height map, then gen_random_map (Listing 6-1, #2 in Figure 6-3) to replace the z values using value noise, bidir_interp (Listing 6-24, #3 in Figure 6-3) to interpolate elevation values, and finish_mesh (Listing 6-25, #4 to #7) to add an (optional) border, create the mesh object, resize, move, fill in faces, and add modifiers. We will examine these functions one by one in the last part of the chapter.

Listing 6-3. Generate a terrain mesh object using the value noise method with the given noise function (see /Ch6/fractal_terrain_generator.py)

```
def gen_random_mesh(context, rows, cols, cell_width, ↩
    origin, noise_basis, unit_size=5, h_min=-50, ↩
    h_max=50, chop_border=True):
    elev_type = ElevType.Random
    row_lines, col_lines, num_pts, edges, x, y, z = ↩
        create_blank_height_map(rows, cols, elev_type)

    verts = gen_random_map(num_pts, h_min, h_max, ↩
        noise_basis, x, y)

    bidir_interp(InterpType.Bicubic, verts, row_lines, ↩
        col_lines, 10)
```

```
    z = verts[:,2]
    finish_mesh(context, cell_width, origin, elev_type, ↩
        chop_border, noise_basis, row_lines, col_lines, ↩
        num_pts, edges, x, y, z, False)
```

Listing 6-4 shows a sample call to gen_random_mesh (Listing 6-3) using uniform sampling, with the result shown in Figure 6-5. We can make out some mountain peaks and valleys here and there, but it is nothing sensational. The main problem with value noise is that each vertex's elevation is sampled independently. As a result, the height map tends to look like a field of random bumps. In the real world, terrain in proximity are highly correlated—the few hundred square feet around a mountain peak will most likely have high elevation (Shaker et al., 2016). The value noise method inherently lacks the mechanism to capture this correlation, even with interpolation to neighboring areas.

Listing 6-4. Sample call to gen_random_mesh (excerpt of helper function test_random_fbm_ds()) (see /Ch6/fractal_terrain_generator.py)

```
def test_random_fbm_ds():
    gen_random_mesh(bpy.context, rows=120, cols=120, ↩
        cell_width=1, origin=(0,0,1), ↩
        noise_basis='UNIFORM', unit_size=5, ↩
        h_min=-50, h_max=50, chop_border=True)
    ------------------ SNIPPED ------------------
```

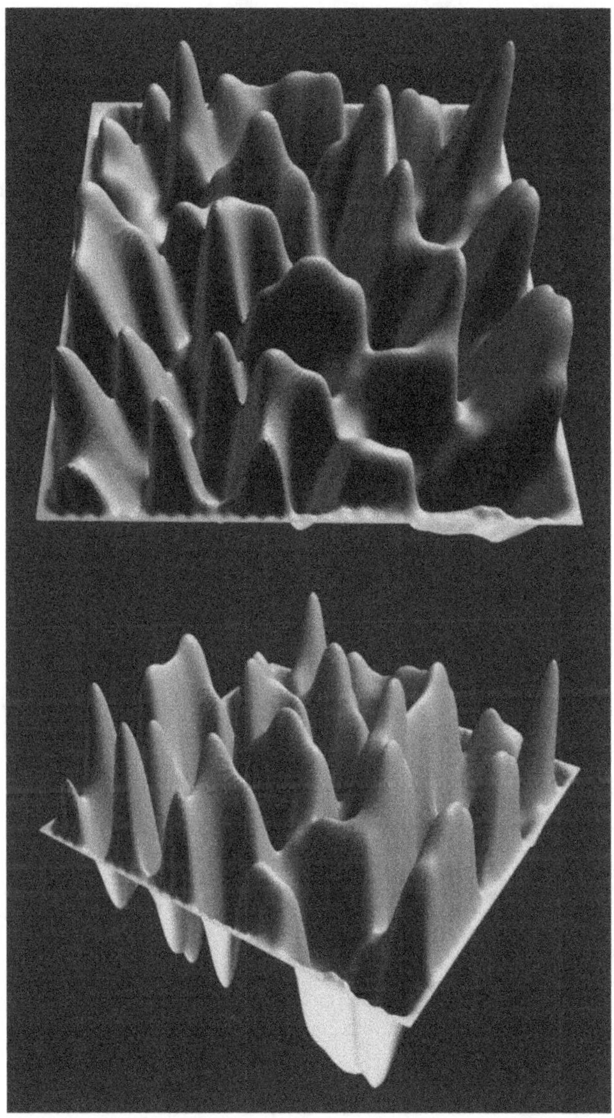

Figure 6-5. *Result of running Listing 6-4, a terrain tile generated using the value noise method with uniform sampling*

Scale and Add to Approximate fBm Random Walk

When you repeatedly zoom in on an image of a real coastline, river, or mountain, you see very similar (although not identical) patterns over and over—this characteristic is called *self-similarity*. Another prominent feature of natural terrain is erosion, which is the accumulation of numerous random surface displacements or faults. Fractional

Brownian motion (fBm) describes a process that mimics erosion, where you start at one point and takes millions of *random walks*, each walk as the sum of many random steps. Taking millions of walks is too slow for our purpose of generating terrain for games; however, there are two simplified algorithms to approximate the effects of fBm, which are scale and add and diamond-square. We'll discuss scale and add in this section and diamond-square in the next.

The scale and add method simulates taking random walks at multiple resolutions by summing scaled outputs of the same noise function at different frequencies. For example, if you use a Perlin noise function called `perlin_noise`, with scale and add, you'll get the following output:

$$perlin\_nosie(f)+\frac{1}{2}perlin\_noise(2f)+\frac{1}{4}perlin\_noise(4f)+\frac{1}{8}perlin\_noise(8f)+\ldots$$

which is a noise mixture that is heavy on the low frequencies (f) and light on the higher frequencies (4f, 8f, etc.).

We can think of frequency as how many repeats of a pattern there are in an interval. The higher the frequency, the more times the pattern repeats, and the smaller the distance between two repeats. With scale and add, each term added to the summation has twice the frequency and half the strength. The first term in the summation is the first *octave*, the second term the second octave, and so on.

Let's work though an example. We'll assume that an interval is an 8 by 8 square portion of a height map with eight row lines and eight column lines, as shown in Figure 6-6. The gray square is our "pattern." #1 in Figure 6-6 shows the first octave where the pattern repeats once every 8 by 8 window. #2 shows the second octave where the pattern repeats twice as often as #1 in each direction, which is once every

$$\frac{8}{2^{2-1}}\,by\,\frac{8}{2^{2-1}}=\frac{8}{2}\,by\,\frac{8}{2}=4\,by\,4$$

window. #3 shows the third octave, where the pattern repeats once every

$$\frac{8}{2^{3-1}}\,by\,\frac{8}{2^{3-1}}=\frac{8}{4}\,by\,\frac{8}{4}=2\,by\,2$$

window.

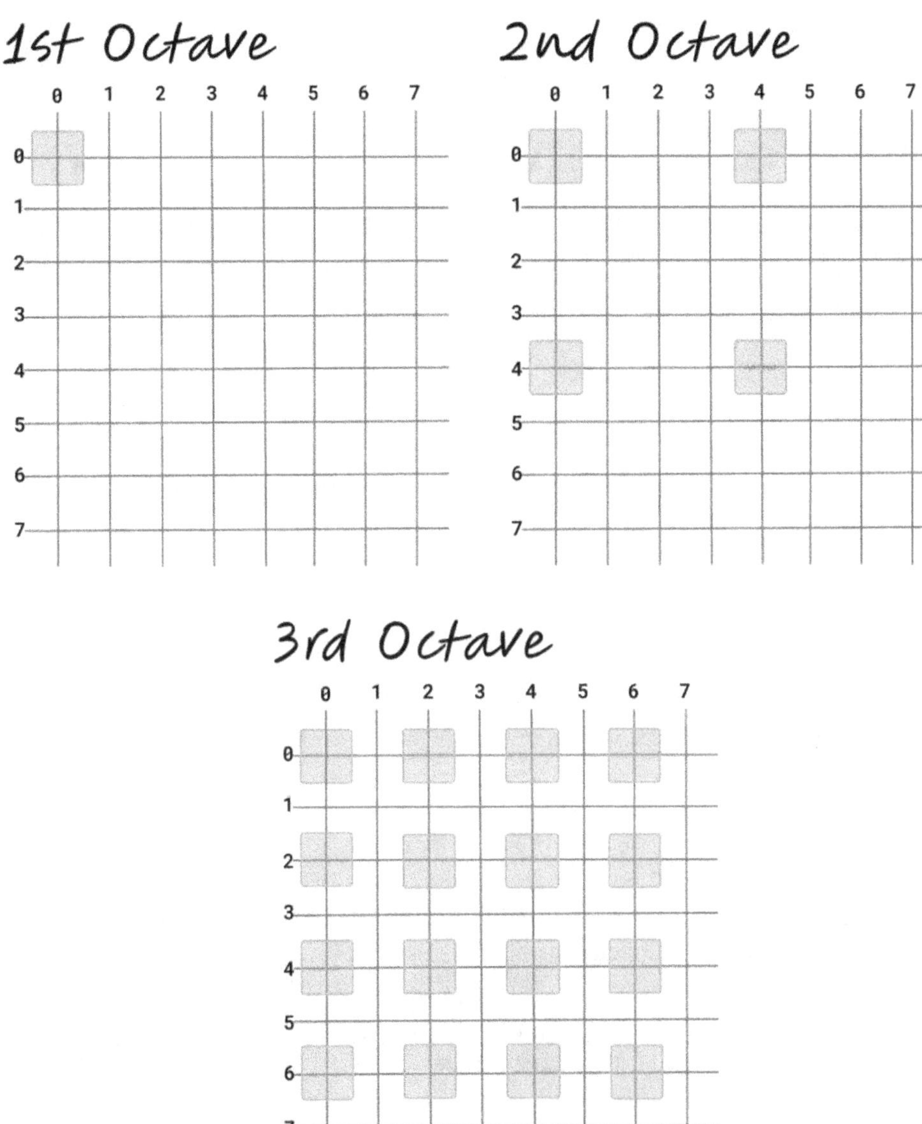

Figure 6-6. *Three octaves of fBm, with step sizes 8, 4, and 2*

Since our height maps are stored as numpy arrays, let's prototype how we can traverse an array properly based on the spacing between repeats in each octave. Head over to the built-in Python console under the Scripting workspace and enter the following three lines to create an array of 8 elements and display its contents. We'll pretend that it represents one dimension of the 8 by 8 interval in Figure 6-6:

```
>>> import numpy as np
>>> a = np.array([i for i in range(8)])
>>> a
array([0, 1, 2, 3, 4, 5, 6, 7])
```

We can use the `::` symbol followed by an integer N to grab every Nth element in a `numpy` array. Let's try this by grabbing every 8th element in `a`, which is equivalent to the frequency of the first octave in Figure 6-6:

```
>>> a[::8]
array([0])
```

Grabbing every 4th element in a then gives us the indices per axis for octave #2, which are rows 0 and 4 and columns 0 and 4:

```
>>> a[::4]
array([0, 4])
```

Grabbing every 2nd element in a then gives us the indices per axis for octave #3, which are rows 0, 2, 4, and 6, as well as columns 0, 2, 4, and 6:

```
>>> a[::2]
array([0, 2, 4, 6])
```

The function `fbm_sum` in Listing 6-5 implements scale and add as we worked out above. We start with a sanity check that both the repeat interval (`unit_size`) and number of octaves (`num_octaves`) are at least 1. If so, we proceed to find the list of factors to scale the frequencies with. For the first octave, we use the full interval, so the factor is 1, or

$$2^{1-1} = 2^0 = 1.$$

With each successive octave, we double the frequency and halve the output. Therefore, the formula for the factors is

$$2^{octave-1}.$$

We accomplish this in Python with the following line of code:

```
div_pow = [int(pow(2, i)) for i in range(0, ↩
    num_octaves)]
```

We proceed to iterating through the list of factors (1, 2, 4, 8, etc.) and generating the height map for each corresponding octave by calling gen_random_map (Listing 6-1) with the given noise function (noise_basis) followed by bidir_interp (Listing 6-24) to smooth, then scaling it with the reciprocal of the octave's factor

$$\frac{1}{2} for\ 2, \frac{1}{4} for\ 4,$$

and so on before adding it to the overall verts array. The spacing between repeats is calculated via floor(unit_size//dp), or the passed in interval divided by the factor for that octave. Since this may not result in integer division, which we need to traverse the height map array with, we force it to be an integer by taking its floor value.

Listing 6-5. Generate Z values using the fBm scale and add method with the given noise function (see /Ch6/fractal_terrain_generator.py)

```
def fbm_sum(verts, interp_type, noise_basis, unit_size, ↩
    h_min, h_max, num_octaves, row_lines, col_lines, ↩
    num_pts, x, y):
    if unit_size < 1 or num_octaves < 1:
        return
    div_pow = [int(pow(2, i)) for i in range(0, ↩
        num_octaves)]
    for dp in div_pow:
        step_size = floor(unit_size//dp)
        if step_size < 1:
            break

        verts_this_oct = gen_random_map(num_pts, ↩
            h_min, h_max, noise_basis, x, y)
        bidir_interp(interp_type, verts_this_oct, ↩
            row_lines, col_lines, step_size)
        verts += (1/dp)*verts_this_oct
```

As we've seen with the value noise implementation, we write a function gen_random_fbm_mesh (Listing 6-6) that calls the shared modules in Figure 6-3 to generate terrain mesh tiles but with fbm_sum (Listing 6-5) as the method for generating Z values. First, create_blank_height_map (Listing 6-21) is called to create a blank height map, then fbm_sum (Listing 6-5) to fill in the Z values and interpolate, then finish_mesh (Listing 6-25) to create and refine the mesh object.

Listing 6-6. Generate a terrain mesh object using the fBm scale and add method with the given noise function (see /Ch6/fractal_terrain_generator.py)

```
def gen_random_fbm_mesh(context, rows, cols, ↩
    cell_width, origin, noise_basis, unit_size=5, ↩
    h_min=-50, h_max=50, num_octaves=4, chop_border=True):
    elev_type = ElevType.Random
    row_lines, col_lines, num_pts, edges, x, y, z = ↩
        create_blank_height_map(rows, cols, elev_type)

    verts = np.zeros((num_pts, 3))
    fbm_unit_size = pow(2, num_octaves-1)*unit_size
    fbm_sum(verts, InterpType.Bicubic, noise_basis, ↩
        fbm_unit_size, h_min, h_max, num_octaves, ↩
        row_lines, col_lines, num_pts, x, y)

    z = verts[:,2]
    finish_mesh(context, cell_width, origin, elev_type, ↩
        chop_border, noise_basis+"_"+str(num_octaves), ↩
        row_lines, col_lines, num_pts, edges, x, y, z, ↩
        False)
```

The code excerpt in Listing 6-7 provides two sample calls to gen_random_fbm_mesh (Listing 6-6) using uniform sampling as the noise function with three and four octaves, respectively. The results of running Listing 6-7 are shown in Figure 6-7. You can see that the terrain smooths out with an increasing number of octaves.

Listing 6-7. Sample calls to gen_random_fbm_mesh using numpy uniform sampling as the noise function with three and four octaves (see /Ch6/fractal_terrain_generator.py)

```
def test_random_fbm_ds():
    ------------------ SNIPPED ------------------
    gen_random_fbm_mesh(bpy.context, rows=120, ↩
        cols=120, cell_width=1, origin=(125,0,1), ↩
        noise_basis='UNIFORM', unit_size=5, h_min=-50, ↩
        h_max=50, num_octaves=3, chop_border=True)
    gen_random_fbm_mesh(bpy.context, rows=120, cols=120, ↩
        cell_width=1, origin=(250,0,1), ↩
        noise_basis='UNIFORM', unit_size=5, h_min=-50, ↩
        h_max=50, num_octaves=4, chop_border=True)
    ------------------ SNIPPED ------------------
```

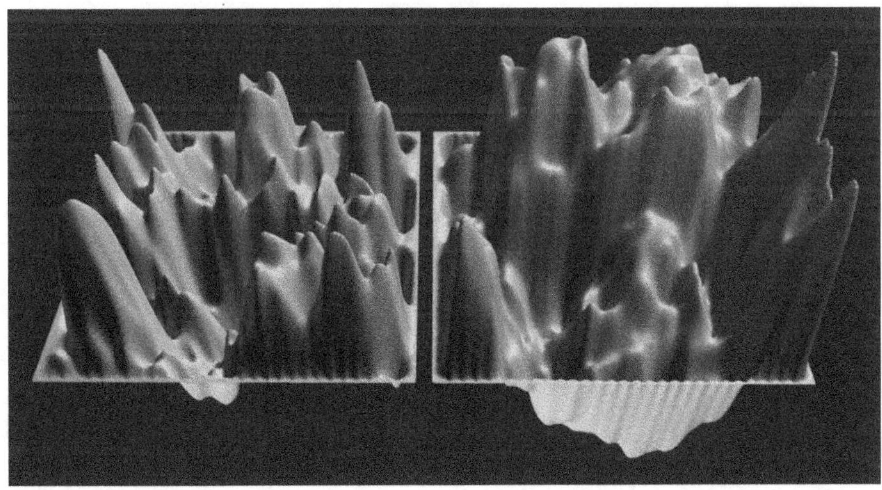

Figure 6-7. *Results of running Listing 6-7, with the first call to gen_random_fbm_mesh() on the left (three octaves) and the second call on the right (four octaves). Both calls use uniform sampling as their noise basis.*

The code excerpt in Listing 6-8 calls gen_random_fbm_mesh (Listing 6-6) repeatedly in a for loop with each of Blender's built-in noise functions under the mathutils.noise module and four octaves. The terrain tiles generated by calling Listing 6-8 are shown in Figure 6-8.

Listing 6-8. Generate terrain mesh tiles by calling gen_random_fbm_mesh (Listing 6-6) in a for loop with all of Blender's noise functions under mathutils.noise (see /Ch6/fractal_terrain_generator.py)

```
def test_random_fbm_ds():
    ------------------ SNIPPED ------------------
    y = 135
    for i in range(len(bl_noise_basis_options)):
        noise_basis = bl_noise_basis_options[i]
        gen_random_fbm_mesh(bpy.context, rows=100, ↩
            cols=100, cell_width=1, origin=(105*i,y,1), ↩
            noise_basis=noise_basis, unit_size=1, ↩
            h_min=-25, h_max=50, num_octaves=4, ↩
            chop_border=True)
    return y
```

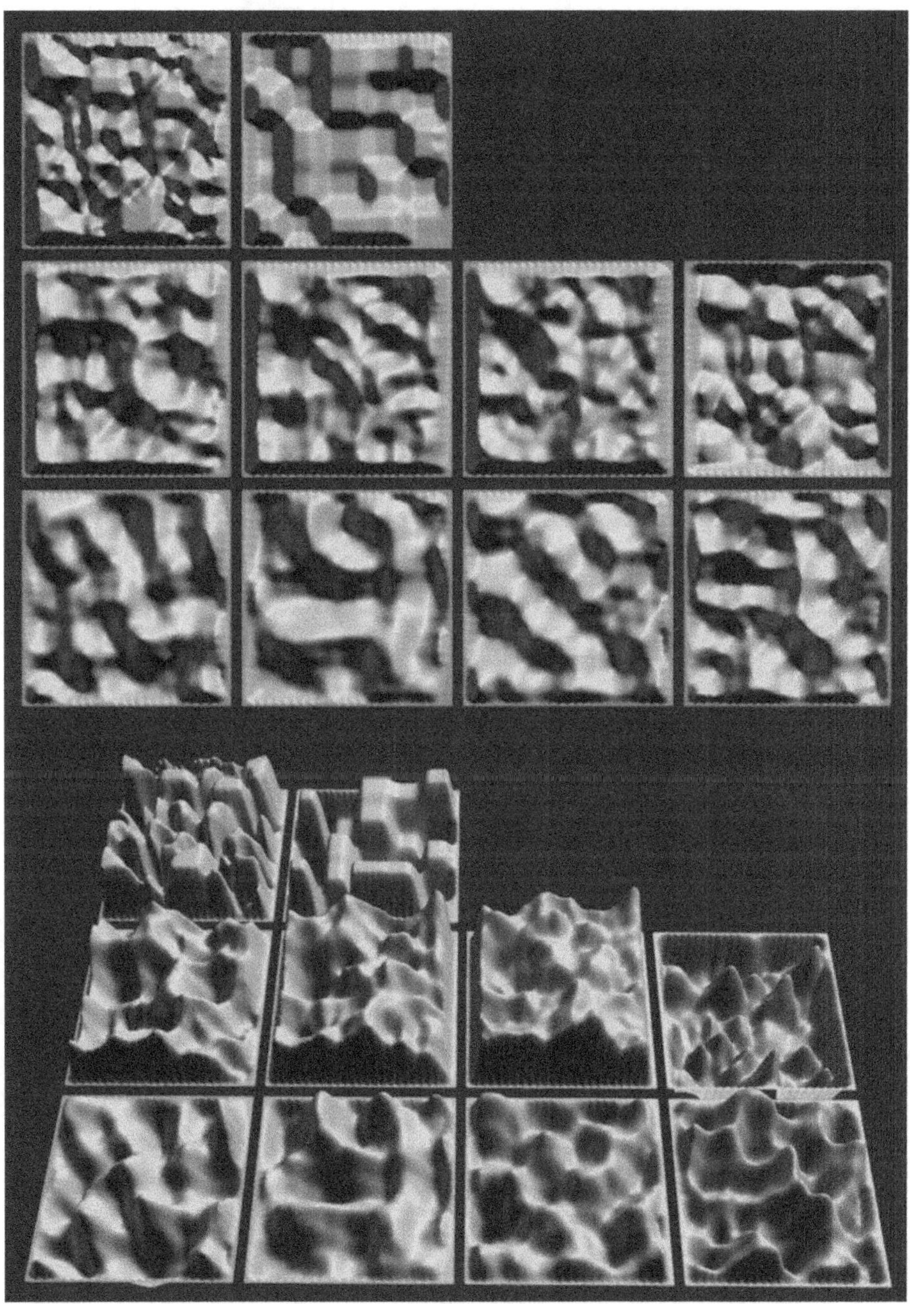

***Figure 6-8.** Results of running Listing 6-8. Ten terrain tiles are generated using fBm scale and add with the following noise basis functions (from left to right, front to back): 'BLENDER', 'PERLIN_ORIGINAL', 'PERLIN_NEW', 'VORONOI_F1', 'VORONOI_F2', 'VORONOI_F3', 'VORONOI_F4', 'VORONOI_F2F1', 'VORONOI_CRACKLE', and 'CELLNOISE'*

Note The Enum strings to call `mathutils.noise.noise()` with for identifying which noise type to use are listed under `bl_noise_basis_options` in Listing 6-2.

Diamond-Square Algorithm

Another way to approximate the effects of fBm is the diamond-square algorithm, which iteratively fills in a height map by alternating the steps of averaging four corner neighbors (diamond step) and four diagonal neighbors (square step) at increasing resolutions (Shaker et al., 2016).

High-Level Overview

Let's go over how the diamond-square algorithm works at a high level before we implement it in Python.

Height Map Size Restriction

Due to the way the neighbors are averaged, diamond-square requires the input height map to be square shaped with side lengths in the following form:

$$2^K + 1, where K\ is\ an\ integer > 0$$

Since we've designed for all other algorithms to take the row and column counts for specifying the height map size, we'll do so with our diamond-square implementation as well—except we'll round *up* the given row count to the next closest `pow(2, K)`, then add 1. For example, if the input row count is 100, then

$$rawK = \log_2(100 - 1) = 6.6293566200796095$$

We need K to be an integer, so we round up K by taking its ceiling:

$$K = ceil(rawK) = 7$$

We can then work backward and compute the new rounded row count like this:

$$row\ count\ rounded\ up\ to\ next\ 2^K = 2^7 = 128$$

Since our convention for this chapter is to use the crossing of grid lines as grid locations, we add 1 to the row count to get the row line count, which gives us a height map dimension satisfying the diamond-square constraint:

$$row\,line\,count = row\,count + 1 = 2^K + 1 = 2^7 + 1 = 128 + 1 = 129$$

The height map size adjustment we've derived above is implemented as part of the function `create_blank_height_map` (Listing 6-21), which is called by `gen_diamond_square_map` (Listing 6-12) before `diamond_square` (Listing 6-11).

Initial Setup

To get ready, we'll create a blank height map of the required size as described above, then fill in the four corner cells each with a randomly sampled number from a uniform distribution. If the side length of the height map is N, then the four corners' coordinates are (0, 0), (0, N-1), (N-1, 0), and (N-1, N-1). We then start the diamond-square iteration with an initial step size of N, which makes the initial sliding window N by N, or the entire height map.

Iteration

In each iteration, we perform one diamond step followed by one square step, then update the range of the uniform distribution we sample noise from with a decay, as detailed below. Like the scale and add method described in the previous section, the step size, or the side length of the sliding window, is halved in each iteration. For example, if the current step size is 33, a step operates on each 33 by 33 window over the entire height map. The next iteration will operate on each 16 by 16 window and so on. If the step size is an odd number, we take the floor of the divided value (i.e., always round down).

Diamond Step

For each window, we use the average of its corners plus a noise to fill its center location. For example, Figure 6-9 shows a diamond step performed on a 4 by 4 window, where we average its four corners (black dots) and add a noise uniformly sampled from a given range to fill the center (gray dot). Figure 6-10 shows the square step right after Figure 6-9 in the same iteration, with Figure 6-11 showing the diamond step of the iteration immediately after.

Square Step

For each diamond centered at the midpoint of a window's edge, we compute the average of its corners, add some noise, then use it to update its center. For example, Figure 6-10 shows one complete square step with four diamond updates. Each diamond's four corners are averaged then incremented by a uniformly sampled noise value to fill that diamond's center (gray dot). Figure 6-11 shows the diamond step for the iteration immediately following Figure 6-10.

Wrapping When Corners Are Out-of-Bounds

Each of the four examples in Figure 6-10 shows a possible boundary case where one of the diamond's corners is out-of-bounds—there are two ways to deal with this, one is to substitute the missing corner with a 0 and the other is to wrap around. Let's work through the four cases in Figure 6-10 and wrap around each one. The height map in Figure 6-10 measures 5 by 5, with valid row and column indices running from 0 to 4.

`diamond_0` has one corner protruding two columns out the left at (2, −2), so we wrap around column-wise from the right as follows. The % symbol means "mod," which gives you the remainder of the division.

$$(row, col \,\%\, number\ of\, columns) = (2, -2 \,\%\, 5) = (2, 3)$$

`diamond_1` has one corner protruding out the top by two rows at (−2, 2), so we wrap around row-wise by staying on the same column as follows:

$$(row \,\%\, number\ of\, rows, col) = (-2 \,\%\, 5, 2) = (3, 2).$$

`diamond_2` has one corner out-of-bound at (2, 6), which is two columns outside the map to the right, so we stay on the same row (2) but wrap around the left column-wise to

$$(row, col \,\%\, number\ of\, columns) = (2, 6 \,\%\, 5) = (2, 1)$$

`diamond_3` has one corner sticking out the bottom two rows below at (6, 2), so we wrap around row-wise from the top as follows:

$$(row \,\%\, number\ of\, rows, col) = (6 \,\%\, 5, 2) = (1, 2)$$

Updates

During either a diamond or square step, we increment the average of the corner values with a noise sampled from a uniform distribution. At the end of each iteration, we decay this distribution to decrease the noise over time. We compute the decay as follows:

$$decay = 2^{-r\_decay\_factor}$$

Or in Python, `decay = pow(2, -r_decay_factor)`, where we use the `pow` function from Python's `math` module (imported with `from math import pow`).

If the distribution has the range `[h_min, h_max)`, or ≥ h_min and < h_max, we decrease both `h_min` and `h_max` by multiplying them with `decay`:

```
h_min *= decay
h_max *= decay
```

Terminating Condition

The loop terminates when the step size is 0, after the entire height map has been filled.

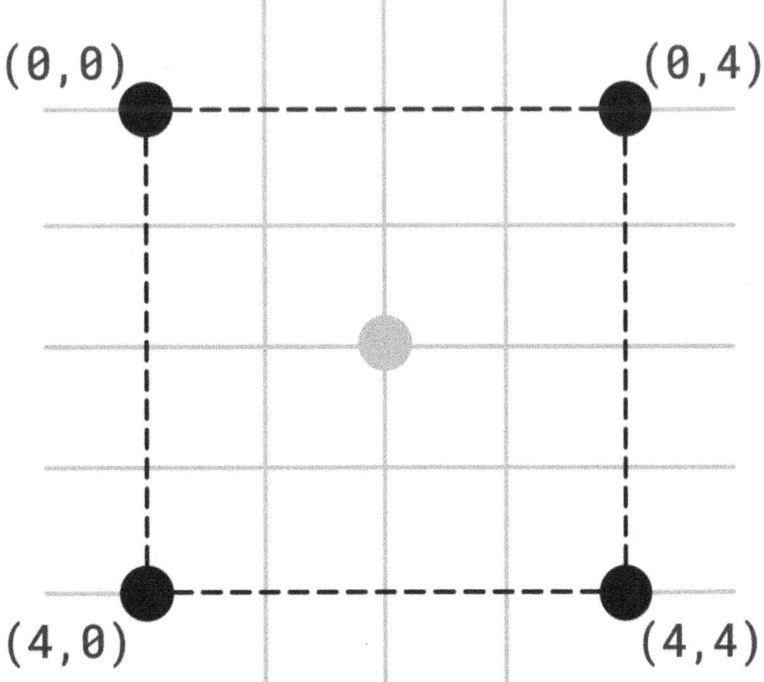

Figure 6-9. *Example of a diamond step of the diamond-square algorithm, where four square corners are summed and averaged to fill the center location*

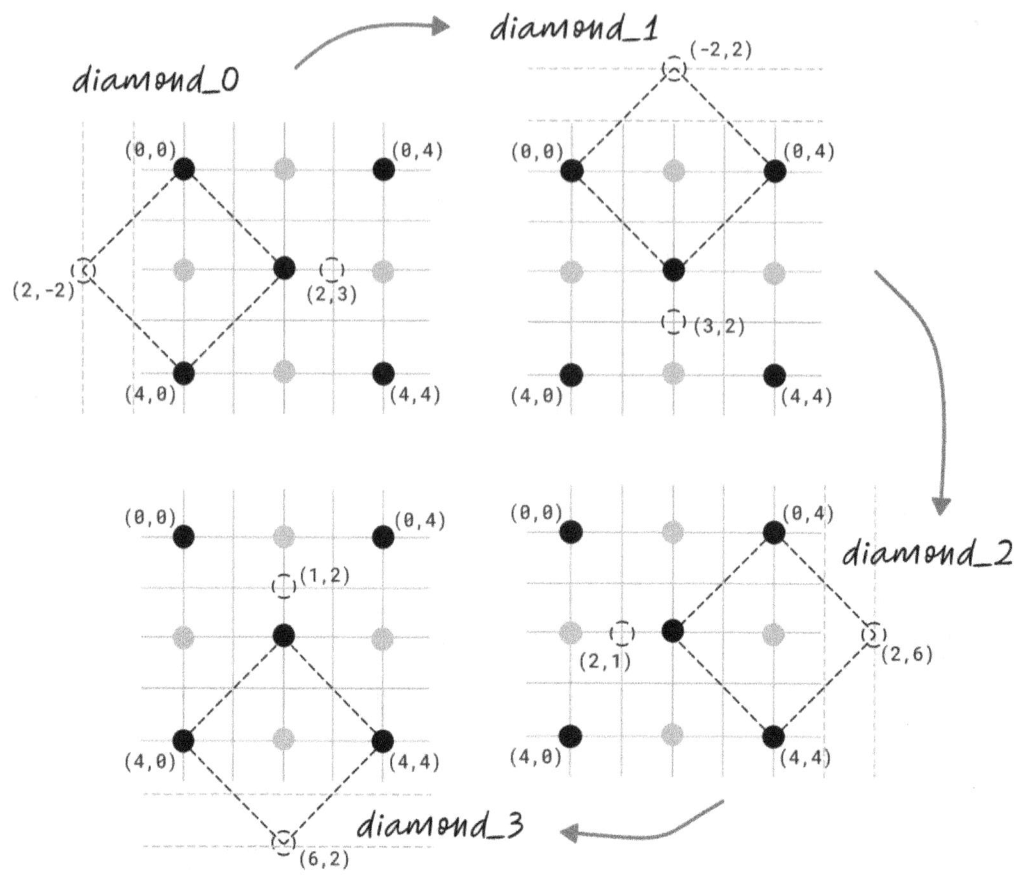

Figure 6-10. *In a square step of the diamond-square algorithm, we update four diamonds centered at the window edges' mid points. The average of each diamond's corners plus a noise sampled uniformly from a given range is used to fill that diamond's center. If any one of a diamond's corners is out-of-bounds, we wrap around the opposite side of the window as shown.*

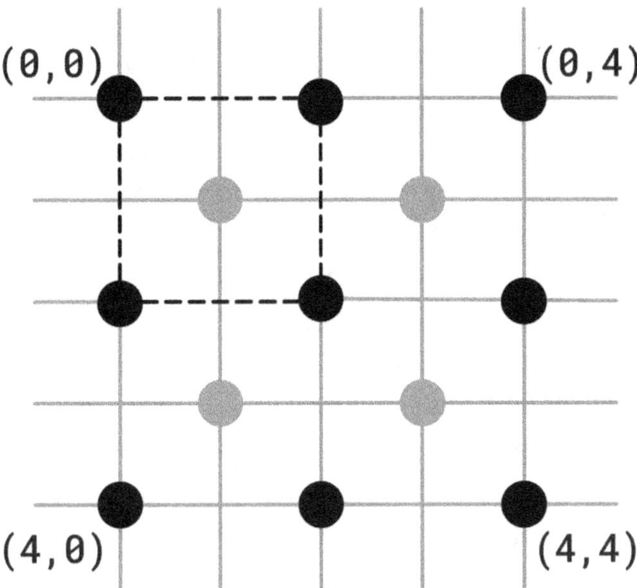

Figure 6-11. *Diamond step of the iteration immediately after the square step in Figure 6-10*

Implementing Diamond-Square in Python

Listing 6-9 shows how the noise added to either a diamond or a square step is generated in Python. We call `np.random.sample()` to draw a sample from a uniform distribution in the range of [0, 1), or ≥0 and <1, then scale the sample and shift it to the given range `[h_min, h_max)`.

Listing 6-9. Generate one sample from a continuous uniform distribution ranging from h_min to h_max (see /Ch6/fractal_terrain_generator.py)

```
def sample_ds_noise(h_min, h_max):
    dsn = (h_max-h_min)*np.random.sample()+h_min
    return dsn
```

Note You can set the seed for numpy's random number generators with `np.random.seed(<SEED VALUE>)`, for example, `np.random.seed(100)`.

In Listing 6-10, we implement one diamond plus one square step. `s` is the current iteration's step size (i.e., the side length of the sliding window to perform a step on), `grid` is the height map, and `h_min` and `h_max` are the range of the uniform distribution we draw the noise from to add to each step. `grid.shape` tells us the row and column line count of the height map. We use a nested loop to iterate through the map, skipping `s` rows or columns to move from window to window. Since we constraint the upper-left corner coordinates to be less than the map height and width with loop conditions, we only need to worry about wrapping around the other three corners of the square (plus its center) in a diamond step. For the square step, we check the corners of the four diamonds that are outside the window for wrapping.

For the diamond step, the four corners of the window in Listing 6-10 are listed clockwise starting at the upper-left corner—upper left, upper right, lower right, and lower left. The expression `hs = s//2` calculates half the window's side length using integer division, i.e., rounding down the divided quotient. The center of the window is the upper-left corner offset by `hs` in both directions. We calculate the new center value by summing the average of the window corners plus a noise generated by a call to `sample_ds_noise` (Listing 6-9).

For the square step, we update the diamonds centered at the window's four edge midpoints one by one starting with the left diamond in clockwise order, as shown in Figure 6-12 and listed in Table 6-1. The variables `r`, `c`, `s`, and `hs` in Table 6-1 correspond to the variables of the same names in Listing 6-10, which are the current iteration's row line, column line, step size, and half step size, respectively. To help you see the relative offsets between diamond corners, the coordinates in Table 6-1 exclude mods for wrap-arounds, which are shown in Listing 6-10 only. For the row wraps, we mod the grid height, and the column wraps the grid width. Each diamond center is updated with the average of that diamond's corners plus a noise generated by a call to `sample_ds_noise` (Listing 6-9). Since we've already calculated the window's center and saved it in the variable `sc` during the diamond step, we reuse this value in the square step whenever possible in the code.

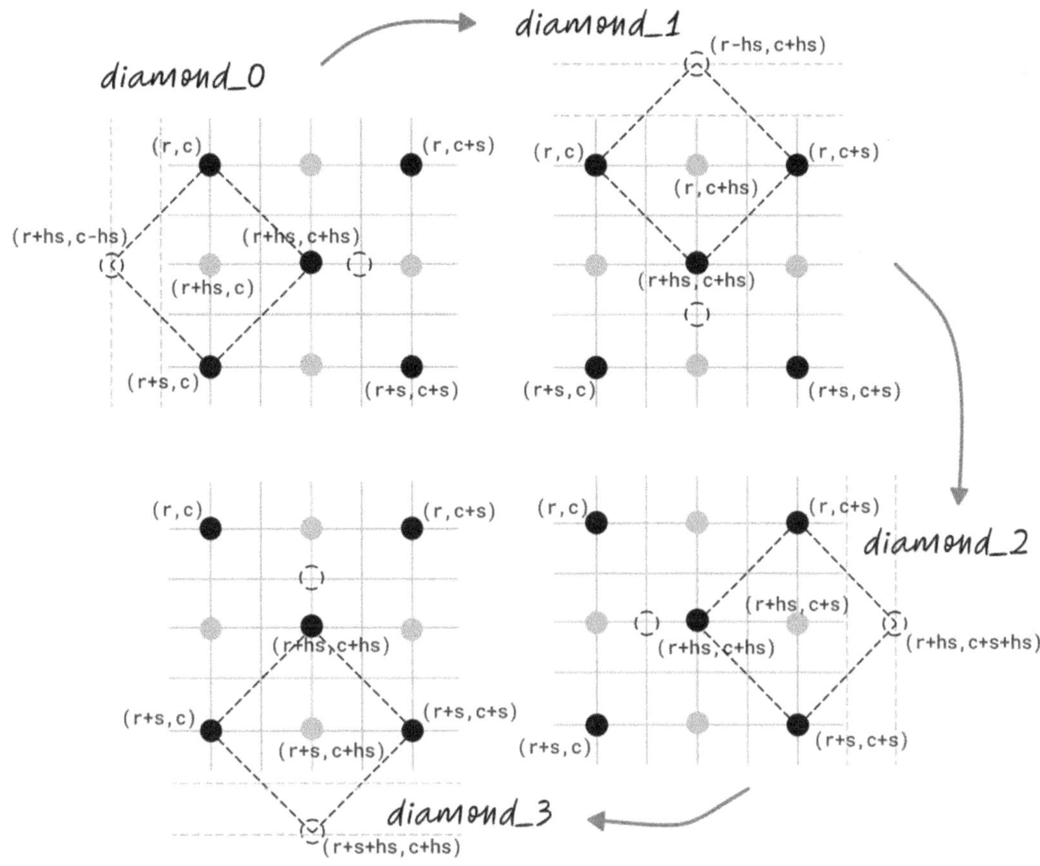

Figure 6-12. *The square step illustrated with the row (r) and column (c) coordinates, step size (s), and half step size (hs) from Listing 6-10. We compose the list of corners for each diamond clockwise starting at the left corner. An out-of-bounds corner is wrapped around the opposite side as shown.*

Table 6-1. *Summary of diamond corners and center coordinates for the square step in Listing 6-10 and Figure 6-12. The variables r, c, s, and hs correspond to the variables in Listing 6-10*

Diamond	Left corner	Top corner	Right corner	Bottom corner	Center
diamond_0	(r+hs, c-hs)	(r, c)	(r+hs, c+hs)	(r+s, c)	(r+hs, c)
diamond_1	(r, c)	(r-hs, c+hs)	(r, c+s)	(r+hs, c+hs)	(r, c+hs)
diamond_2	(r+hs, c+hs)	(r, c+s)	(r+hs, c+s+hs)	(r+s, c+s)	(r+hs, c+s)
diamond_3	(r+s, c)	(r+hs, c+hs)	(r+s, c+s)	(r+s+hs, c+hs)	(r+s, c+hs)

Listing 6-10. Perform a diamond and a square step of the diamond-square algorithm (see /Ch6/fractal_terrain_generator.py)

```
def diamond_square_step(s, grid, h_min, h_max):
    h, w  = grid.shape
    for r in range(0, h, s):
        for c in range(0, w, s):
            r_s = (r+s)%h
            c_s = (c+s)%w
            square = np.array([grid[r][c], grid[r][c_s], ↩
                grid[r_s][c_s], grid[r_s][c]])
            hs = s//2
            sc = np.mean(square) + sample_ds_noise( ↩
                h_min, h_max)
            r_hs = (r+hs)%h
            c_hs = (c+hs)%w
            grid[r_hs][c_hs] = sc

            diamond_0 = np.array([grid[r_hs][(c-hs)%w], ↩
                grid[r][c], sc, grid[r_s][c]])
            grid[r_hs][c] = np.mean(diamond_0) + ↩
                np.random.uniform(h_min, h_max)

            diamond_1 = np.array([grid[r][c], ↩
                grid[(r-hs)%h][c_hs], grid[r][c_s], sc])
            grid[r][c_hs] = np.mean(diamond_1) + ↩
                np.random.uniform(h_min, h_max)

            diamond_2 = np.array([sc, grid[r][c_s], ↩
                grid[r_hs][(c+s+hs)%w], grid[r_s][c_s]])
            grid[r_hs][c_s] = np.mean(diamond_2) + ↩
                np.random.uniform(h_min, h_max)

            diamond_3 = np.array([grid[r_s][c], sc, ↩
                grid[r_s][c_s], grid[(r+s+hs)%h][c_hs]])
            grid[r_s][c_hs] = np.mean(diamond_3) + ↩
                np.random.uniform(h_min, h_max)
```

The function diamond_square in Listing 6-11 implements the loop that drives the diamond-square iterations. We set the initial step size (step) to 1 less than the passed-in row line count, which is a convenience choice to make all subsequent reduction in step size divide cleanly. We repeat the diamond-square step in a while loop until step size is reduced to 0, at which point the entire height map has been filled. As described earlier, in each iteration, we call diamond_square_step (Listing 6-10) to perform a diamond followed by a square step based on the current step size (step), reduce the step size by half, and decay the min and max of the uniform distribution we sample the noise from to distort the corner averages for the diamond and square steps.

Listing 6-11. Loop to drive the diamond-square iterations (see /Ch6/fractal_terrain_generator.py)

```
def diamond_square(n, grid, h_min, h_max, r_decay_factor):
    step = n-1
    while step >= 1:
        diamond_square_step(step, grid, h_min, h_max)
        step = step//2
        decay = pow(2, -r_decay_factor)
        h_min *= decay
        h_max *= decay

    return grid
```

The function gen_diamond_square_map in Listing 6-12 does the initial setup for diamond-square by creating a 2D array based on the row line count passed in, fills its four corners with random noise uniformly sample from the given range, then kicks off the diamond-square iterations by calling diamond_square (Listing 6-11). After the grid of elevation values is fully filled in, it's flattened into a z column vector and returned.

Listing 6-12. Set up and kick off a run of the diamond-square algorithm (see /Ch6/fractal_terrain_generator.py)

```
def gen_diamond_square_map(row_lines, num_pts, ↩
    h_min, h_max):
    n = row_lines
    ds_grid = np.zeros((n,n), dtype=np.float16)
    h_range = h_max-h_min
```

```
    ds_grid[0, 0] = sample_ds_noise(h_min, h_max)
    ds_grid[0, n-1] = sample_ds_noise(h_min, h_max)
    ds_grid[n-1, 0] = sample_ds_noise(h_min, h_max)
    ds_grid[n-1, n-1] = sample_ds_noise(h_min, h_max)

    diamond_square(n, ds_grid, h_min, h_max, 0.3)
    z = ds_grid.flatten()
    return z
```

We put everything together and write a diamond-square generator in Listing 6-13. In gen_ds_mesh, we follow the design in Figure 6-3 and call create_blank_height_map (Listing 6-21) to create a blank height map, gen_diamond_square_map (Listing 6-12) to produce the z values for the height map, bidir_interp (Listing 6-24) to interpolate, and finish_mesh (Listing 6-25) to create the mesh object, perform transforms, and add modifiers.

Listing 6-13. Generate a terrain mesh object using the diamond-square algorithm (see /Ch6/fractal_terrain_generator.py)

```
def gen_ds_mesh(context, rows, cols, cell_width, origin, ↩
    unit_size=10, h_min=-50, h_max=50, chop_border=True):
    elev_type = ElevType.DiamondSquare
    row_lines, col_lines, num_pts, edges, x, y, z = ↩
        create_blank_height_map(rows, cols, elev_type)
    z = gen_diamond_square_map(row_lines, num_pts, ↩
        h_min, h_max)
    verts = np.stack([x, y, z], axis=-1).reshape(num_pts, 3)
    bidir_interp(InterpType.Bicubic, verts, row_lines, ↩
        col_lines, unit_size)
    z = verts[:,2]
    finish_mesh(context, cell_width, origin, elev_type, ↩
        chop_border, 'UNIFORM', row_lines, col_lines, ↩
        num_pts, edges, x, y, z, False)
```

Listing 6-14 shows a sample call to gen_ds_mesh (Listing 6-13), which produces the terrain mesh tile with elevation ranging from –50 to 50 in Figure 6-13.

Listing 6-14. Sample call to gen_ds_mesh (Listing 6-13) (see /Ch6/fractal_terrain_generator.py)

```
def test_random_fbm_ds():
    ------------------ SNIPPED ------------------
    gen_ds_mesh(bpy.context, rows=100, cols=100, ↩
        cell_width=1, origin=(375,0,1), h_min=-50, ↩
        h_max=50, unit_size=5, chop_border=True)
    ------------------ SNIPPED ------------------
```

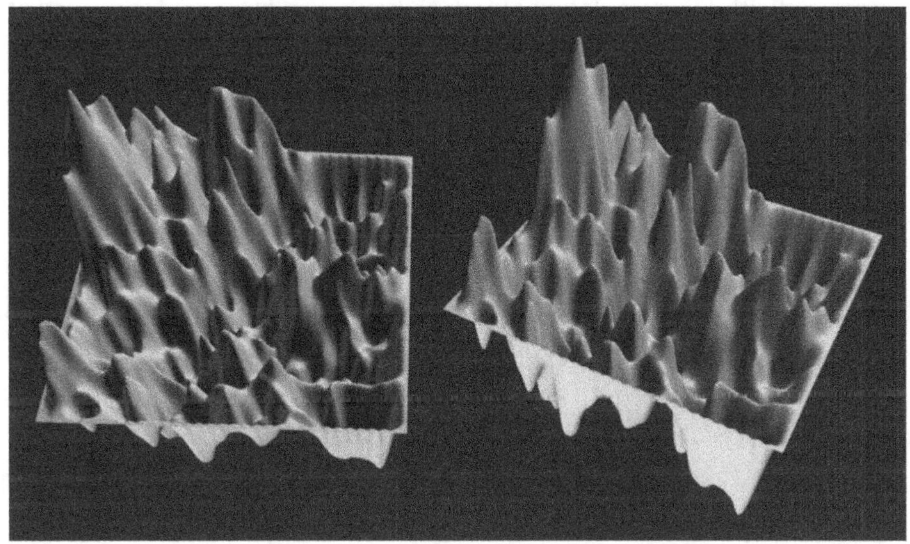

Figure 6-13. *The diamond-square terrain mesh generated by running Listing 6-14*

Generating Elevation with Fractal Methods

Fractal-based methods emulate the self-similarity of real terrain such that the same pattern is observed when you zoom in repeatedly. In this section, you'll implement the hybrid multi fractal algorithm and generate terrain tiles using different noise functions and number of octaves. You'll also learn to use Blender Python's built-in multi fractal and hetero terrain functions to generate meshes to add more tools to your arsenal.

Hybrid Multi Fractal

The idea of using fractals for generating terrain originated from mathematician Benoit Mandelbrot. He discovered that a fBm function produced a curve resembling the skyline of a mountain at fractal dimension 1.2. From there, he deduced if this dimension is increased to 2 and beyond, a terrain surface should begin to emerge (Ebert et al., 2003). Unlike Euclidean mathematics, which only has crisp integral dimensions (e.g., 1D is a line, 2D a surface, 3D a cylinder, etc.), fractal math allows decimal dimensions. Fractal dimension is a measure of the relative details or irregularities at different scale levels (Barnsley et al., 1988). The calculation of fractal dimension is beyond the scope of this book; however, we can use the Koch curve from Chapter 7 as an example—in its construction, we replace each unit segment with one that is 4/3 units long, therefore growing the curve with each iteration while confining it to the same space. It turns out the Koch curve has a fractal dimension of about 1.26. The *higher* the fractal dimension, the *rougher* or *more jagged* a curve or surface.

The earlier fractal-based terrain generation methods use a single fractal dimension throughout. Hybrid multi fractal mixes multiple fractal dimensions, using lower dimensions for smoother plains and valleys and higher dimensions for jagged mountain tops to simulate the results of erosion. The Python implementation of hybrid multi fractal in Listing 6-15 is adapted from F. Kenton Musgrave's version in C from the book *Texturing and Modeling: A Procedural Approach* (Ebert et al., 2003). With scale and add and diamond-square, we approximated a mono-fractal-dimensional fBm by summing the multiresolution layers. `hybrid_multi_fractal2` (Listing 6-15) uses a hybrid approach such that data from layers of different scales are both added and multiplied together. The theoretical underpinning of multi fractals is beyond the scope for this book; however, I encourage you to check out the books in the "References" section to explore further.

Listing 6-15. Generate Z values using the hybrid multi fractal algorithm with the given noise function (see /Ch6/fractal_terrain_generator.py)

```
def hybrid_multi_fractal2(v, H=0.25, lacunarity=2, ↩
    octaves=10, offset=0.7, noise_basis='BLENDER'):
    exp_array = []
    frequency = 1.0
    for i in range(octaves+1):
        exp_array.append(pow(frequency, -H))
        frequency *= lacunarity
```

```
    for i in range(octaves):
        if i == 0:
            altitude = ↩
                (noise.noise(v, noise_basis=noise_basis) ↩
                + offset) * exp_array[0]
            weight = altitude
        else:
            weight = min(weight, 1.0)
            signal = ↩
                (noise.noise(v, noise_basis=noise_basis) ↩
                + offset) * exp_array[i]
            altitude += weight * signal
            weight *= signal

        v = [v[i]*lacunarity for i in range(3)]

    return altitude
```

Let's go over what the arguments are—v is the vertex of which the location is used to compute the noise, H is the fractal dimension of the roughest parts of the terrain, lacunarity controls the gap between neighboring layers (frequencies) in the fBm, octaves is the number of layers in the fBm, and offset is the amount that the terrain as a whole is moved up from sea level (Ebert et al., 2003).

Similar to fbm_sum in Listing 6-5, we'll start by creating an array of scaling factors (exp_array) for the different frequencies up front based on the number of octaves. Each scaling factor is calculated as pow(frequency, -H), or

$$frequency^{-H}$$

Each layer's frequency is lacunarity times the previous layer's frequency.

We compute each octave's (layer's) altitude (signal) by calling the given noise function (noise_basis) on the passed-in vertex (v), shift the altitude by offset, multiply it by the scaling factor for that layer (exp_array[i]), then scale it by the previous layer's altitude (weight), before adding it to the cumulative altitude (altitude) across layers. The very first layer (i == 0) does not have a previous layer, so the last step is skipped. For this algorithm, the passed-in vertex v is also scaled by lacunarity between neighboring octaves. After the altitude has accumulated across all octaves, we return it.

As per tradition, we'll write a generator function gen_hybrid_multi_fractal_mesh (Listing 6-16) to pull everything together and generate terrain mesh tiles on demand based on the hybrid multi fractal method. Listing 6-16 follows the design in Figure 6-4, which calls create_blank_height_map (Listing 6-21) to create a blank height map of the desired size, fills in the map's z values with hybrid_multi_fractal2 (Listing 6-15), then creates mesh data, applies transforms, and adds modifiers with finish_mesh (Listing 6-25).

Listing 6-16. Using the hybrid multi fractal algorithm to generate a terrain mesh tile (see /Ch6/fractal_terrain_generator.py)

```
def gen_hybrid_multi_fractal_mesh(context, rows, ↩
    cols, cell_width, origin, chop_border, noise_basis, ↩
    xy_scale=0.025, lacunarity=3, octaves=5, ↩
    offset=0.25, z_scale=1):
    elev_type = ElevType.HybridMultiFractal
    row_lines, col_lines, num_pts, edges, x, y, z = ↩
        create_blank_height_map(rows, cols, elev_type)
    verts = np.stack([x, y, z], axis=-1).reshape(num_pts, 3)
    verts = verts.tolist()

    z = [hybrid_multi_fractal2([v[0]*xy_scale, ↩
        v[1]*xy_scale, 1], H=0.25, lacunarity=lacunarity, ↩
        octaves=octaves, offset=offset, ↩
        noise_basis=noise_basis)*z_scale for v in verts]
    finish_mesh(context, cell_width, origin, elev_type, ↩
        chop_border, noise_basis, row_lines, col_lines, ↩
        num_pts, edges, x, y, z, True)
```

Testing Hybrid Multi Fractal Generation

Listing 6-17 shows a sample function for testing the hybrid multi fractal implementation, where we set up two for loops with each repeatedly calling gen_hybrid_multi_fractal_mesh (Listing 6-16) using Blender's built-in noise functions under mathutils.noise with a different number of octaves (five and eight, respectively). The two terrain tiles generated by Listing 6-17 are shown in Figures 6-14 and 6-15.

Listing 6-17. Generate terrain mesh tiles by calling `gen_hybrid_multi_fractal_mesh` (Listing 6-16) in `for` loops with Blender's noise functions under `mathutils.noise` (see /Ch6/fractal_terrain_generator.py)

```
def test_hybrid_multi_fractal(y, tile_w):
    spacing = tile_w+5
    y += spacing

    hmf_z_scale = {'BLENDER':15,'PERLIN_ORIGINAL':15, ↩
        'PERLIN_NEW':15, 'VORONOI_F1':15, ↩
        'VORONOI_F2':10, 'VORONOI_F3':5, ↩
        'VORONOI_F4':5, 'VORONOI_F2F1':15, ↩
        'VORONOI_CRACKLE':2.5,'CELLNOISE':10}

    for i in range(len(bl_noise_basis_options)):
        noise_basis = bl_noise_basis_options[i]
        z_scale = hmf_z_scale[noise_basis]
        gen_hybrid_multi_fractal_mesh(bpy.context, ↩
            rows=tile_w, cols=tile_w, cell_width=1, ↩
            origin=(spacing*i,y,1), chop_border=True, ↩
            noise_basis=noise_basis, xy_scale=0.025, ↩
            lacunarity=3, octaves=5, offset=0.25, ↩
            z_scale=z_scale)

    y += spacing
    for i in range(len(bl_noise_basis_options)):
        noise_basis = bl_noise_basis_options[i]
        z_scale = hmf_z_scale[noise_basis]*0.5
        gen_hybrid_multi_fractal_mesh(bpy.context, ↩
            rows=tile_w, cols=tile_w, cell_width=1, ↩
            origin=(spacing*i,y,1), chop_border=True, ↩
            noise_basis=noise_basis, xy_scale=0.05, ↩
            lacunarity=2, octaves=8, offset=0.5, ↩
            z_scale=z_scale)
    return y
```

Figure 6-14. *Results of the first* `for` *loop in Listing 6-17. Ten terrain tiles are generated using five octaves of hybrid multi fractal with the following noise bases (from left to right, front to back): 'BLENDER', 'PERLIN_ORIGINAL', 'PERLIN_NEW', 'VORONOI_F1', 'VORONOI_F2', 'VORONOI_F3', 'VORONOI_F4', 'VORONOI_F2F1', 'VORONOI_CRACKLE', and 'CELLNOISE'*

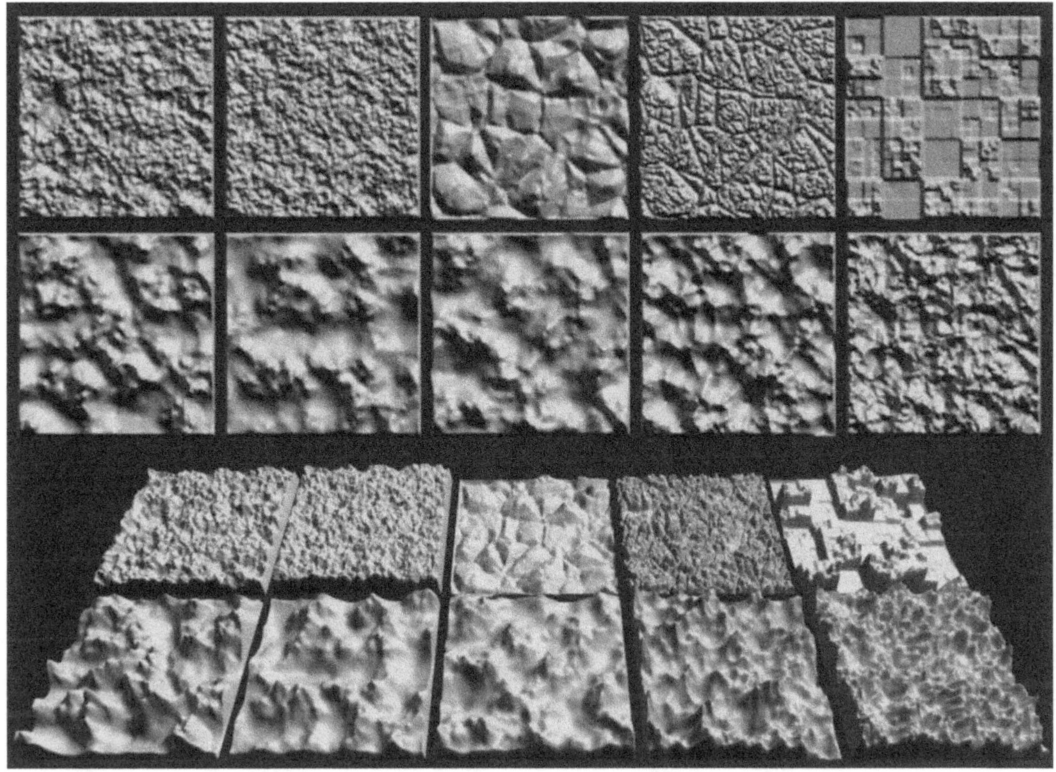

Figure 6-15. *Results of the second* `for` *loop in Listing 6-17. Ten terrain tiles are generated using eight octaves of hybrid multi fractal with the following noise bases (from left to right, front to back): 'BLENDER', 'PERLIN_ORIGINAL', 'PERLIN_NEW', 'VORONOI_F1', 'VORONOI_F2', 'VORONOI_F3', 'VORONOI_F4', 'VORONOI_F2F1', 'VORONOI_CRACKLE', and 'CELLNOISE'*

Using Blender's Built-In Fractal Generation Functions: Multi Fractal and Hetero Terrain

In addition to implementing your own fractal generation methods, gen_bl_fractal_mesh in Listing 6-18 shows how you can call two of Blender's built-in fractal functions under the mathutils.noise module, multi_fractal and hetero_terrain. The Blender Python API documentation does not offer much explanation on how these two methods are implemented; however, multi_fractal typically multiplies the layers of a fBm with a single fractal dimension, whereas hetero_terrain uses mixed fractal dimensions but only adds the layers together as opposed to using a combination of summation and multiplication like we did with *hybrid* multi fractal in the previous section.

Listing 6-18 starts by calling create_blank_height_map (Listing 6-21) to create a blank height map, then either noise.multi_fractal or noise.hetero_terrain to fill in the map's Z values, and finish_mesh (Listing 6-25) to create the mesh object, fill in faces, apply transforms, and add modifiers. In other words, we follow the same generator design in Figure 6-4 as we did with gen_hybrid_multi_fractal_mesh in Listing 6-16. The XY scale factor of 0.01 and other parameter values used with noise.multi_fractal and noise.hetero_terrain in Listing 6-18 are found experimentally.

Listing 6-18. Generate z values using a choice of Blender's built-in multi fractal or hetero terrain functions plus the given noise basis (see /Ch6/fractal_terrain_generator.py)

```
def gen_bl_fractal_mesh(context, rows, cols, cell_width, ↩
    origin, elev_type=ElevType.BlenderMultiFractal, ↩
    chop_border=True, noise_basis='PERLIN_NEW', z_scale=1):

    row_lines, col_lines, num_pts, edges, x, y, z = ↩
        create_blank_height_map(rows, cols, elev_type)
    verts = np.stack([x, y, z], axis=-1).reshape(num_pts, 3)
    verts = verts.tolist()

    match elev_type:
        case ElevType.BlenderMultiFractal:
            z = [noise.multi_fractal( ↩
                (v[0]*0.01, v[1]*0.01, 1), 0.7, 2.0, 8, ↩
                noise_basis=noise_basis)*z_scale for v in ↩
                verts]
```

```
        case ElevType.BlenderHeteroTerrain:
            z = [noise.hetero_terrain( ↩
                (v[0]*0.01, v[1]*0.01, 1), 0.25, 2, 10, ↩
                0.5, noise_basis=noise_basis)*z_scale for ↩
                v in verts]

    finish_mesh(context, cell_width, origin, elev_type, ↩
        chop_border, noise_basis, row_lines, col_lines, ↩
        num_pts, edges, x, y, z, True)
```

Testing Multi Fractal and Hetero Terrain Generation

Similar to how we tested the hybrid multi fractal implementation, we'll write a function `test_bl_fractal_functions` (Listing 6-19) with two `for` loops, the first for testing `multi_fractal` and the second `hetero_terrain`. In each loop, we generate a terrain tile for each of Blender's ten built-in noise functions listed under `bl_noise_basis_options` (Listing 6-2). For convenience, we'll also set up a dictionary containing z scale values for each loop with lookup by noise type. The terrain tiles generated by the first `for` loop in Listing 6-19 are shown in Figure 6-16. The tiles generated by the second `for` loop are shown in Figure 6-17.

Listing 6-19. Generate two groups of terrain mesh tiles, the first using the multi fractal method and the second the hetero terrain method. Each group is generated by calling `gen_bl_fractal_mesh` in a `for` loop with all of Blender's noise functions under `mathutils.noise` (see /Ch6/fractal_terrain_generator.py)

```
def test_bl_fractal_functions(y, tile_w):
    spacing = tile_w+5
    y += spacing
    blmf_z_scale = {'BLENDER':10,'PERLIN_ORIGINAL':10, ↩
        'PERLIN_NEW':10,'VORONOI_F1':10,'VORONOI_F2':5, ↩
        'VORONOI_F3':2.5,'VORONOI_F4':2.5, ↩
        'VORONOI_F2F1':25, 'VORONOI_CRACKLE':2, ↩
        'CELLNOISE':5}
    for i in range(len(bl_noise_basis_options)):
        noise_basis = bl_noise_basis_options[i]
        z_scale = blmf_z_scale[noise_basis]
```

```
        gen_bl_fractal_mesh(bpy.context, rows=100, ↩
            cols=100, cell_width=1,
            origin=(spacing*i,y,1), ↩
            elev_type=ElevType.BlenderMultiFractal, ↩
            noise_basis=noise_basis, z_scale=z_scale)

    y += spacing
    blht_z_scale = {'BLENDER':1,'PERLIN_ORIGINAL':1, ↩
        'PERLIN_NEW':1,'VORONOI_F1':1, 'VORONOI_F2':0.1, ↩
        'VORONOI_F3':0.05, 'VORONOI_F4':0.05, ↩
        'VORONOI_F2F1':15,'VORONOI_CRACKLE':0.05, ↩
        'CELLNOISE':0.5}
    for i in range(len(bl_noise_basis_options)):
        noise_basis = bl_noise_basis_options[i]
        z_scale = blht_z_scale[noise_basis]
        gen_bl_fractal_mesh(bpy.context, rows=100, ↩
            cols=100, cell_width=1, ↩
            origin=(spacing*i,y,1), ↩
            elev_type=ElevType.BlenderHeteroTerrain, ↩
            noise_basis=noise_basis, z_scale=z_scale)
    return y
```

Figure 6-16. *Results of the first for loop in Listing 6-19. Ten terrain tiles are generated using Blender's built-in multi fractal function with the following noise bases (from left to right, front to back): 'BLENDER', 'PERLIN_ORIGINAL', 'PERLIN_NEW', 'VORONOI_F1', 'VORONOI_F2', 'VORONOI_F3', 'VORONOI_F4', 'VORONOI_F2F1', 'VORONOI_CRACKLE', and 'CELLNOISE'*

Figure 6-17. *Results of the second for loop in Listing 6-19. Ten terrain tiles are generated using Blender's built-in hetero terrain implementation with the following noise bases (from left to right, front to back): 'BLENDER', 'PERLIN_ORIGINAL', 'PERLIN_NEW', 'VORONOI_F1', 'VORONOI_F2', 'VORONOI_F3', 'VORONOI_F4', 'VORONOI_F2F1', 'VORONOI_CRACKLE', and 'CELLNOISE'*

Common Functionalities Between Generators

For the rest of this chapter, we'll take a closer look at the functions reused by different terrain generation methods in Figures 6-3 and 6-4.

Selecting Elevation Type

In Listing 6-20, we define an Enum class `ElevType` for identifying which method is used for generating elevation. An `ElevType` instance is passed to `create_blank_height_map` (Listing 6-21) to denote whether to adjust the height map size for diamond-square and to add_border (Listing 6-26) to control the border width for the terrain tiles. By making ElevType inherit from the Python str and Enum types (note the order matters), we force the Enum values to be strings.

@unique is a shorthand for unique(). In Python, a *decorator* is a function that takes other functions or types as arguments (i.e., a higher-order function). unique is a built-in decorator function that takes an Enum type and raises a ValueError if any of its values are duplicates.

Listing 6-20. Enum for identifying which algorithm is used to generate terrain heights (see /Ch6/fractal_terrain_generator.py)

```
@unique
class ElevType(str, Enum):
    Random = "random"
    DiamondSquare = "diamond_square"
    HybridMultiFractal = "hybrid_multi_fractal"
    BlenderMultiFractal = "blender_multi_fractal"
    BlenderHeteroTerrain = "blender_hetero_terrain"
```

Creating Blank Height Map

In Listing 6-21, we implement the function create_blank_height_map which creates a deconstructed blank height map as three column vectors (x, y, and z) based on the requested row and column counts and generation method. The same function also creates the edge list needed for calling <MESH DATA>.from_pydata().

Listing 6-21. Create a blank height map of the given size along with vertex and edge lists for calling <mesh data>.from_pydata() (see /Ch6/fractal_terrain_generator.py)

```
def create_blank_height_map(rows, cols, elev_type):
    if elev_type == ElevType.DiamondSquare:
        rows = 2**ceil(log2(rows-1))
        cols = rows
    row_lines = rows + 1
    col_lines = cols + 1
    num_pts = row_lines*col_lines
```

```
    v_indices = np.arange(0, num_pts, 1).reshape( ↩
        (row_lines, col_lines))
    h_edges = np.zeros((row_lines, cols*2), dtype=np.int32)
    v_edges = np.zeros((rows, col_lines*2), dtype=np.int32)
    for i in range(row_lines):
        h_edges[i][0::2] = v_indices[i][:-1]
        h_edges[i][1::2] = v_indices[i][1:]
        if i < rows:
            v_edges[i][0::2] = v_indices[i]
            v_edges[i][1::2] = v_indices[i+1]
    num_edges = row_lines*cols + rows*col_lines
    edges = np.concatenate((h_edges.flatten(), ↩
        v_edges.flatten())).reshape(num_edges, 2).tolist()

    x = np.arange(0, col_lines, 1)
    x = np.stack([x for i in range(row_lines)]).flatten()
    y = np.arange(0, row_lines, 1).reshape((row_lines, 1))
    y = np.hstack([y for i in range(col_lines)]).reshape( ↩
        (row_lines, col_lines)).flatten()
    z = np.zeros(num_pts)
    return row_lines, col_lines, num_pts, edges, x, y, z
```

Our convention for height maps throughout the chapter has been to use the crossings of grid lines as grid locations, as shown in Figure 6-18. It is easier for humans to envision a grid's dimensions in terms of its side lengths; however, so for Listing 6-21, we take the row and column counts as arguments in the "spreadsheet" sense, then add 1 to get line counts. Recall that for diamond-square, the grid must be a square with side lengths `pow(2, K)+1` with K≥1; therefore, we adapt the passed-in row count accordingly. In any case, the total number of points (`num_pts`) is the product of row line count (`row_lines`) and column line count (`col_lines`).

In the next block, we derive the edge list to use for calling `<MESH DATA>.from_pydata()` in `create_mesh_obj` (Listing 6-27). Each edge is represented by its pair of end point indices, with the "from" vert's index listed first. For example, the height map in Figure 6-18 has vert indices #0 to #5 in the first row, #6 to #11 in the second row, and so on. Therefore, the first row of edges is [(0, 1), (1, 2), (2, 3), (3, 4), (4, 5)], the second row of edges is [(6, 7), (7, 8), (8, 9), (9, 10), (10, 11)], etc. The first column of edges is [(0, 6), (6, 12), (12, 18), (18, 24), (24, 30)], the second column of edges is [(1, 7), (7, 13), (13, 19), (19, 25), (25, 31)], and so on. We generalize this derivation into Python code by first creating a 2D array of size `row_lines` by `col_lines` with the line:

```
v_indices = np.arange(0, num_pts, 1).reshape( ↩
    (row_lines, col_lines))
```

which will serve as the grid line crossing indices in the pattern shown in Figure 6-18 that we'll draw from for forming the edge end point pairs. As we've seen, for each row line, there are `(col_lines-1)` or `cols` number of horizontal edges and for each column line `(row_lines-1)` or `rows` number of vertical edges. Since we need two numbers per edge to denote its end points, we create two arrays, `h_edges` and `v_edges`, each of size two times the number of edges (we'll be arranging them into pairs later). Next, we'll iterate through the row lines and filling in `h_edges` and `v_edges`. For each row line, the following two lines formulate the "from" and "to" end point indices, respectively, by first filling the even-numbered spots (0, 2, 4, etc.) with the first up to the second-to-last vert, then the odd-numbered spots (1, 3, 5, etc.) with the second up to the last vert for that row, like this:

```
        h_edges[i][0::2] = v_indices[i][:-1]
        h_edges[i][1::2] = v_indices[i][1:]
```

The vertical edges are easier, since each "row" of "from" indices matches up with each row of `v_indices` and the "to" indices being the following row. The only thing to look out for is to stop while i+1 is still within range:

```
        if i < rows:
            v_edges[i][0::2] = v_indices[i]
            v_edges[i][1::2] = v_indices[i+1]
```

With both the horizontal and vertical edge pairs formed, we flatten each list then concatenate the two to create the format that `<MESH DATA>.from_pydata()` requires

```
edges = np.concatenate((h_edges.flatten(), ↩
    v_edges.flatten())).reshape(num_edges, 2).tolist()
```

In the final block of code, we create three x, y, and z column arrays so that when arranged side by side, they form a N by 3 array, with each row representing the XYZ coordinates for one vertex for a total of N vertices. The initial z values are zero.

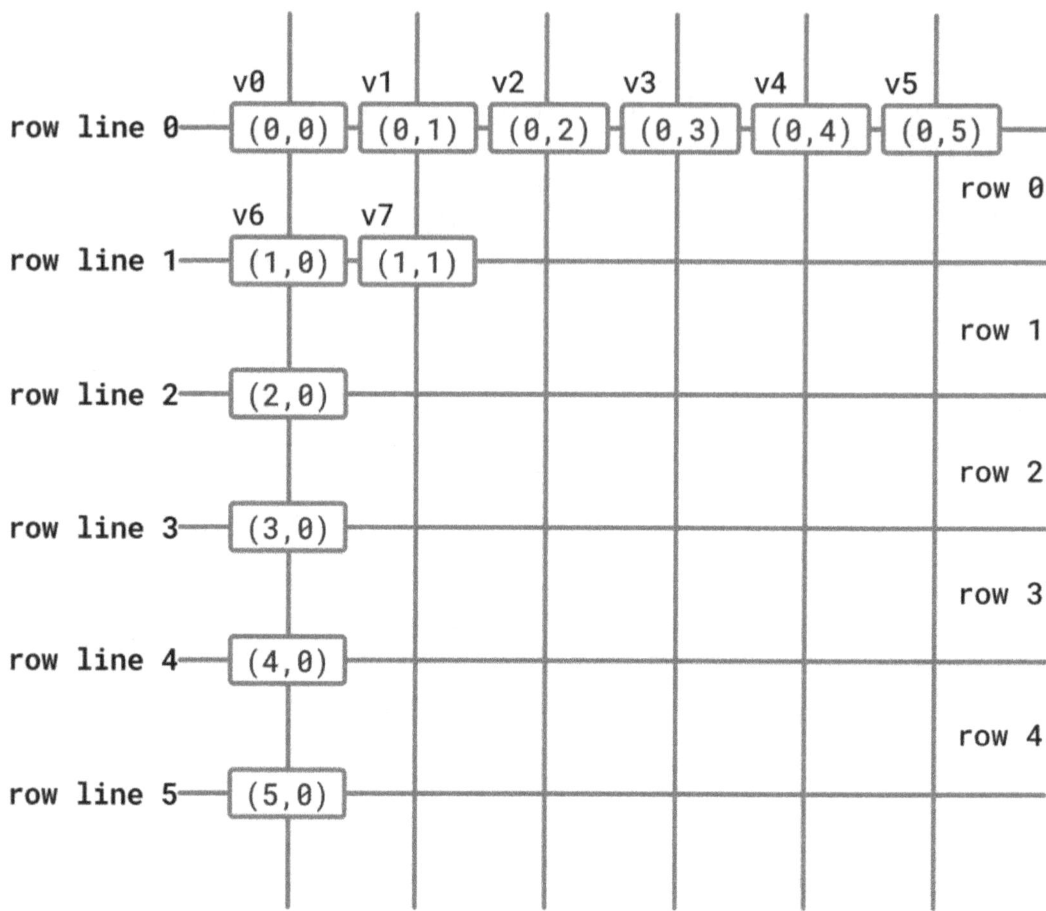

Figure 6-18. *For this chapter, we define a grid location as the intersection of two grid lines. Therefore, for a N row by N column grid, there are N+1 by N+1 grid lines and N+1 by N+1 locations*

Bilinear and Bicubic Interpolations

In this section, we'll implement bilinear and bicubic interpolations in the same function, `bidir_interp` (Listing 6-24). For both bilinear and bicubic interpolations, a point's value is interpolated first horizontally then vertically.

Let's work through an example and see how we derive which neighbors to use for interpolating a given point. Figure 6-19 shows the second octave of the sample 8 by 8 fBm from Figure 6-6, which is blank except for the four points at (0, 0), (0, 4), (4, 0), and (4, 4). Let's pretend we don't know which points are filled but only the step size for that layer, which is 4. To find the closest two horizontal neighbors, we need to first locate the closest *row*, then derive which two *columns* surround the point-in-question. For example, we can find the two rows surrounding (3, 2) by dividing its row index by `step_size` as follows:

$$(row, col) = (3, 2)$$

$$step\_size = 4$$

$$\frac{row}{step\_size} = \frac{3}{4} = 0 \; with \; remainder \; 3 \Rightarrow rq = 0, rr = 3$$

$$r\_sm = surrounding \; row \; with \; smaller \; index = rq \times step\_size = 0 \times 4 = 0$$

$$r\_lg = surrounding \; row \; with \; bigger \; index = r\_sm + step\_size = 0 + 4 = 4$$

Once we know that the two rows surrounding (3, 2) are #0 and #4, we can use (3, 2)'s distance to each row to tell which is closer—which we've already calculated above, since `rr` is the distance from (3, 2) to `r_sm`. We'll compare `rr` to `half_step` to see if it is on or before the halfway point from `r_sm` to `r_lg`—if so, (3, 2) is closer to `r_sm`; otherwise, it is closer to `r_lg`:

$$half\_step = \frac{step\_size}{2} = \frac{4}{2} = 2$$

$$r\_cls = row \; closer = r\_sm \; if \; rr \le half\_step \; else \; r\_lg$$

$$Since \; 3 > 2, \; rr > half\_step, \; r\_cls \; is \; row \; 4$$

Now we know that row 4 is closer to (3, 2) than row 0, the next step is to find which two points on this row we'll interpolate (for the horizontal interpolation). To do so, we find the two closest columns surrounding (3, 2):

$$\frac{col}{step\_size} = \frac{2}{4} = 0 \; with \; remainder \; 2 \Rightarrow cq = 0, cr = 2$$

$$c\_sm = surrounding \; col \; with \; smaller \; index = cq \times step\_size = 0 \times 4 = 0$$

$$c\_lg = surrounding \; col \; with \; bigger \; index = c\_sm + step\_size = 0 + 4 = 4$$

As we did with the rows, we'll compare `cr` to `half_step` to see if it is on or before the halfway point from `c_sm` to `c_lg`—if so, it is closer to `c_sm`; otherwise, it is closer to `c_lg`:

$$c\_cls = col\ closer = c\_sm\ if\ cr \leq half\_step\ else\ c\_lg$$

$$Since 2 \leq 2,\ cr \leq half\_step,\ c\_cls\ is\ col\ 0$$

Therefore, (3, 2) in octave 2 is between rows 0 and 4 but closer to row 4 and between columns 0 and 4 but closer to column 0. I should point out that we could have used `cr < half_step` instead of `cr` ≤ `half_step`—I grouped the equal sign with the left half of the range since with the way we skip indices with `::` in `numpy`, the indices retrieved tend to fall on the left side of each interval, so using ≤ `half_step` as the threshold will favor more filled grid locations.

Bilinear Interpolation

To perform bilinear interpolation, we interpolate horizontally between (4, 0) and (4, 4) first, i.e., row 4 between columns 0 and 4, based on the ratio of (3, 2)'s distance to each of these columns relative to `step_size`:

$$ratio\ to\ c\_sm = dc\_s = \frac{col - c\_sm}{step\_size} = \frac{2-0}{4} = 0.5$$

$$ratio\ to\ c\_lg = dc\_l = \frac{c\_lg - col}{step\_size} = \frac{4-2}{4} = 0.5$$

Therefore, the horizontal interpolation is:

$$(1 - 0.5) \times (value\ of\ (4,0)) + (1 - 0.5) \times (value\ of\ (4,4))$$

Note that we use the ratio to the *other* column as the interpolation weight for *this* column, i.e., the closer column should have a heavier influence in the weighted sum than the further column. Similarly, to interpolate vertically, we'll find the ratio of (3, 2)'s distance to each surrounding row relative to `step_size`:

$$ratio\ to\ r\_sm = dr\_s = \frac{row - r\_sm}{step\_size} = \frac{3-0}{4} = 0.75$$

$$ratio\ to\ r\_lg = dr\_l = \frac{r\_lg - row}{step\_size} = \frac{4-3}{4} = 0.25$$

Therefore, the vertical interpolation is:

$$(1 - 0.75) \times (value\ of\ (0, 0)) + (1 - 0.25) \times (value\ of\ (4, 0))$$

Bicubic Interpolation

To perform bicubic interpolation on the same example from the previous section, we compute both the horizontal and vertical ratios the same way as bilinear interpolation but plug each ratio into the cubic spline formula before multiplying them with the neighbors. The cubic spline formula is as follows:

$$cubic(k) = -2 \times k^3 + 3 \times k^2$$

Therefore, the horizontal interpolation becomes

$$cubic(1-0.5) \times (value\ of\ (4,0)) + cubic(1-0.5) \times (value\ of\ (4,4))$$

The vertical interpolation becomes

$$cubic(1 - 0.75) \times (value\ of\ (0, 0)) + cubic(1 - 0.25) \times (value\ of\ (4, 0))$$

Bilinear interpolation basically draws a straight line between neighbors to fill in the points along that line, therefore doesn't produce the most natural results, since real terrain doesn't have perfectly rigid lines and sharp angles. On the other hand, bicubic interpolation draws a "S"-shaped curve connecting neighbors, which is flat-ish at the top and bottom but sharp in the middle, which looks much closer to how mountain tops and valleys taper off.

Boundary Conditions

Due to the way we slide the `step_size` by `step_size` window around the grid, based on our current derivation, points near the grid border could end up with surrounding row or column indices that are out of the bounds of the grid. For example, for the point (5, 6) in Figure 6-19, we calculate `r_sm` and `r_lg` as follows:

$$\frac{row}{step\_size} = \frac{5}{4} = 1\ with\ remainder\ 1 \Rightarrow rq = 1, rr = 1$$

$$r\_sm = surrounding\ row\ with\ smaller\ index = rq \times step\_size = 1 \times 4 = 4$$

$$r\_lg = surrounding\ row\ with\ bigger\ index = r\_sm + step\_size = 4 + 4 = 8$$

r_lg is 8, which is outside the grid! Fortunately, this is easy to fix. All we need to do is restrict r_lg to at most (number of rows – 1) and c_lg to at most (number of columns – 1).

Implementing Bidirectional Interpolation in Python

Since bilinear and bicubic interpolations are nearly identical, except in the bicubic case we pass the distance ratios through the cubic spline function before multiplying, we can implement both in the same function, then use an Enum argument of type InterpType (Listing 6-22) to select which interpolation to use.

Listing 6-22. Enum denoting the types of interpolation available to use with the bidir_interp function in Listing 6-24 (see /Ch6/fractal_terrain_generator.py)

```
@unique
class InterpType(str, Enum):
    Bilinear = "bilinear"
    Bicubic = "bicubic"
```

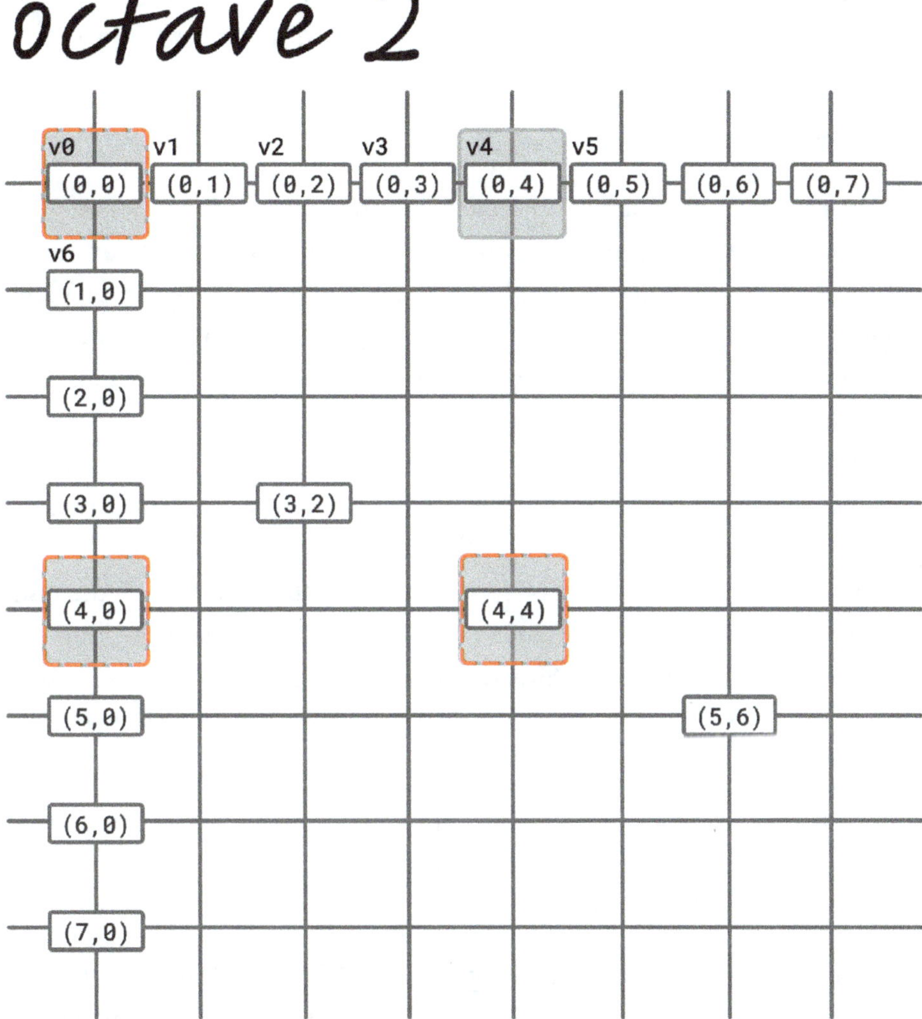

***Figure 6-19.** To perform a bidirectional interpolation, you interpolate horizontally between two filled cells on the closest row, then vertically between two filled cells on the closest column*

We implement the cubic function in Listing 6-23, which is a direct translation to Python from the formula. We use the `pow` function under Python's `math` module, which is imported via `from math import pow`.

Listing 6-23. Cubic function used by the bidir_interp function (Listing 6-24) to perform bicubic interpolation (see /Ch6/fractal_terrain_generator.py)

```
def cubic(x):
    return -2*pow(x, 3) + 3*pow(x, 2)
```

Finally, we implement bilinear and bicubic interpolations in the function bidir_interp (Listing 6-24). The code is almost a one-to-one conversion from the examples we worked through in the previous section; hence, I'll only point out a few implementation-specific items here. Instead of interpolating one point, we iterate through the entire height map, interpolating every point. To confine r_lg to within the boundary of the grid, we call the numpy function np.clip(<item to clip>, <from>, <to>), which makes <item to clip> at least <from> and at most <to>. For r_lg, we call np.clip(r_lg, r_sm, row_lines-1), which confines r_lg to the range [r_sm, row_lines-1]. We clip c_lg in a similar way.

The height map layer (verts) is passed in as a N by 3 numpy array (N is the number of points), whereas our row and column index derivations assumed that the map is a row_lines by col_lines 2D array—therefore, we need to convert the horizontal and vertical neighbors' coordinates to the format used by verts with the following lines:

```
h_sm = r_cls*col_lines + c_sm
h_lg = r_cls*col_lines + c_lg
v_sm = r_sm*col_lines + c_cls
v_lg = r_lg*col_lines + c_cls
```

where h_sm and h_lg are the horizontal neighbors (which are on row r_cls between columns c_sm and c_lg), while v_sm and v_lg are the vertical neighbors (which are on column c_cls between rows r_sm and r_lg).

After both the horizontal interpolation (h_itrp) and vertical interpolation (v_itrp) are calculated, we average the two to get the final interpolation ((h_itrp+v_itrp)*0.5) and set it as the new z value for the point to be interpolated (verts[row*row_lines + col][2]).

Listing 6-24. Perform (choice of) bilinear or bicubic interpolation (horizontal followed by vertical) (see /Ch6/fractal_terrain_generator.py)

```
def bidir_interp(interp_type, verts, row_lines, ↩
    col_lines, step_size):
    half_step = step_size/2
    for row in range(row_lines):
        for col in range(col_lines):
            rq = row//step_size
            rr = row%step_size
            r_sm = step_size*rq
            r_lg = r_sm+step_size
            r_lg = np.clip(r_lg, r_sm, row_lines-1)
            r_cls = r_sm if rr <= half_step else r_lg

            cq = col//step_size
            cr = col%step_size
            c_sm = step_size*cq
            c_lg = c_sm+step_size
            c_lg = np.clip(c_lg, c_sm, col_lines-1)
            c_cls = c_sm if cr <= half_step else c_lg
            h_itrp, v_itrp = 0, 0

            dc_s = 1-((col-c_sm)/step_size)
            dc_l = 1-((c_lg-col)/step_size)
            dr_s = 1-((row-r_sm)/step_size)
            dr_l = 1-((r_lg-row)/step_size)

            h_sm = r_cls*col_lines + c_sm
            h_lg = r_cls*col_lines + c_lg
            v_sm = r_sm*col_lines + c_cls
            v_lg = r_lg*col_lines + c_cls

            match interp_type:
                case InterpType.Bilinear:
                    h_itrp = dc_s*verts[h_sm][2] + ↩
                        dc_l*verts[h_lg][2]
                    v_itrp = dr_s*verts[v_sm][2] + ↩
```

```
                    dr_l*verts[v_lg][2]
            case InterpType.Bicubic:
                h_itrp = cubic(dc_s)*verts[h_sm][2] + ↵
                    cubic(dc_l)*verts[h_lg][2]
                v_itrp = cubic(dr_s)*verts[v_sm][2] + ↵
                    cubic(dr_l)*verts[v_lg][2]
        verts[row*row_lines + col][2] = ↵
            (h_itrp+v_itrp)*0.5
```

Finish Creating the Mesh

As shown in Figures 6-3 and 6-4, we'll write a `finish_mesh` function (Listing 6-25) to call the following four functions under the hood to perform the setup of the terrain mesh—`add_border` (Listing 6-26), which adds an optional border to the mesh tile; `create_mesh_obj` (Listing 6-27), which creates the mesh data block and object; `resize_move_and_fill` (Listing 6-28), which scales the mesh, moves it to the given location, fills in its faces, and applies transforms; and `add_modifiers` (Listing 6-29), which adds a Decimate and/or Subsurf modifier to the mesh. We'll take a closer look at each of these functions next.

Listing 6-25. Finish setting up the terrain mesh object by adding an optional border, scaling and moving it, filling in its faces, and adding a Decimate and/or Subsurf modifier (see /Ch6/fractal_terrain_generator.py)

```
def finish_mesh(context, cell_width, origin, elev_type, ↵
    chop_border, noise_basis, row_lines, col_lines, ↵
    num_pts, edges, x, y, z, is_fractal):
    if chop_border:
        add_border(z, row_lines, col_lines, elev_type)
    verts = np.stack([x, y, z], axis=-1).reshape(num_pts, 3)
    verts = verts.tolist()

    grid_mesh_obj = create_mesh_obj(context, elev_type, ↵
        noise_basis, verts, edges)
    resize_move_and_fill(context, grid_mesh_obj, ↵
        cell_width, origin)
    add_modifiers(is_fractal, grid_mesh_obj)
```

Adding an (Optional) Border

In Listing 6-26, we implement the function add_border, which takes the z array of a height map and zeros out a given width (i.e., number of rows or columns) on all four edges. This is purely optional and meant to create a clean look for demonstration purposes. Feel free to modify this function to create a border at a different height, or variable heights, for example, for stitching two neighboring tiles together at an interpolated height midway between the two.

Listing 6-26. Adding a "border" to a terrain mesh tile by zeroing out a given width of vertices on all sides (see /Ch6/fractal_terrain_generator.py)

```
def add_border(z, row_lines, col_lines, elev_type):
    zero_row = np.zeros(col_lines)
    border = 5 if elev_type == ElevType.Random or ↩
        elev_type == ElevType.DiamondSquare else 1
    zero_border = np.zeros(border)

    for r in range(row_lines):
        i = col_lines*r
        top_border = r < border
        bot_border = r >= row_lines-border
        if top_border or bot_border:
                z[i:(i+col_lines)] = zero_row
        else:
            z[i:(i+border)] = zero_border
            z[(i+col_lines-border):(i+col_lines)] = ↩
                zero_border
```

For convenience, we start by creating an array to represent a "zero row" by calling np.zeros with the number of column lines, which we'll use to replace the appropriate number of rows at the top and bottom of the height map. To keep things simple, we'll hardcode a border width of 5 (rows or columns) for a noise-based mesh tile (ElevType.Random or ElevType.DiamondSquare) and 1 for fractal-based tiles. We'll also create an array (zero_border) to represent a single row of zeros for the left or right border as shown in Figure 6-19 so we can replace that many pixels at the left and right edges with this array. For example, if border is 5, then the top and bottom five rows are zeroed out, along with the first and last five columns of every row, as shown in Figure 6-20.

Next, we'll iterate through the height map row-wise in a `for` loop. Recall that the height map is stored under the hood in a N by 3 array, with each row as a (x, y, z) point—the z array passed in is the column of z values of all points; therefore, the index into the z array at the *beginning* of each row is the row index times the number of column lines (`i = col_lines*r`) and `i+border-1` at the end of that row. If the row index is less than the border width (`r < border`), then we're at a row within the top border. If the row index is the map bottom counting back that many rows or greater (`r >= row_lines-border`), then we're within the bottom border. In either case, we assign the zero row to the whole row in one shot (`z[i:(i+col_lines)] = zero_row`). Otherwise, only the columns up to a border width away counting from the beginning of the row (`i:(i+border)`) or counting back from the end (`(i+col_lines-border):(i+col_lines)`) need to be zeroed out.

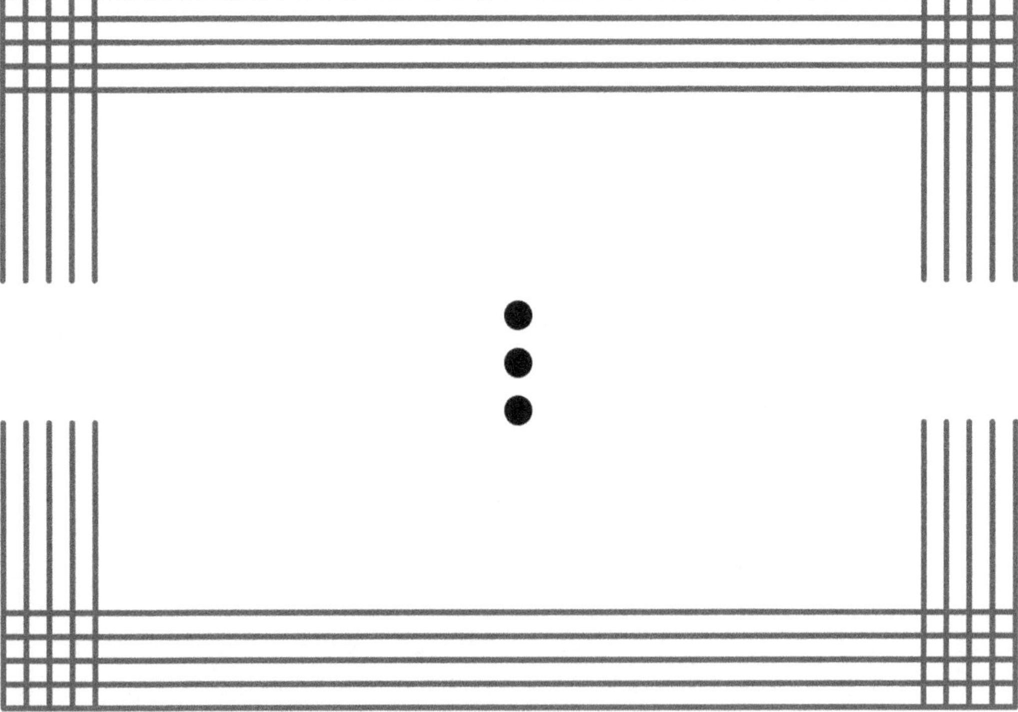

Figure 6-20. *If border width is 5, then the top and bottom five rows are zeroed out, along with the first and last five columns of every row*

Creating Mesh Data and Object

The next helper function create_mesh_obj (Listing 6-27) creates a mesh object based on the list of verts and edges compiled by the previous stages of the pipeline in Figures 6-3 and 6-4 and adds it to the scene collection under the passed-in context.

Listing 6-27. Create a mesh data block, add the given verts and edges to it by calling from_pydata(), then use the block to create a mesh object under the passed-in context's scene collection (see /Ch6/fractal_terrain_generator.py)

```
def create_mesh_obj(context, elev_type, noise_basis, ↩
    verts, edges):
    grid_mesh_data = bpy.data.meshes.new( ↩
        name=elev_type+"_"+noise_basis+"_grid_mesh")
    grid_mesh_data.from_pydata(verts, edges, [])
    grid_mesh_data.update(calc_edges=True)
    grid_mesh_obj = bpy.data.objects.new( ↩
        name=elev_type+"_"+noise_basis+"_grid_obj", ↩
        object_data=grid_mesh_data)
    context.collection.objects.link(grid_mesh_obj)
    return grid_mesh_obj
```

We first create a new mesh data block (grid_mesh_data) by calling bpy.data.meshes.new. Then, we call the following two methods with the list of verts and edges passed in to create a wireframe mesh to add to that data block:

```
grid_mesh_data.from_pydata(verts, edges, [])
grid_mesh_data.update(calc_edges=True)
```

Since we left the faces argument to from_pydata empty, the generated mesh has only verts and edges but no faces, which we'll fill in later. To finish up, we call bpy.data.objects.new with grid_mesh_data to create a mesh object, then context.collection.objects.link to add it to the scene collection under the passed-in context, before returning the object.

Resize, Move, and Fill with Faces

Once `finish_mesh` (Listing 6-25) has called `create_mesh_obj` (Listing 6-27) to create the mesh object, it calls `resize_move_and_fill` in Listing 6-28 to scale and move the object and fill in its faces (remember that we left it as a wireframe in Listing 6-27?).

Listing 6-28. Resize the given mesh object, move it to the specified location, apply transforms, and fill in its faces (see /Ch6/fractal_terrain_generator.py)

```
def resize_move_and_fill(context, grid_mesh_obj, ↩
    cell_width, origin):
    for obj in context.view_layer.objects:
        obj.select_set(False)
    context.view_layer.objects.active = grid_mesh_obj
    grid_mesh_obj.select_set(True)

    c_o = get_context_override(context, 'VIEW_3D', 'WINDOW')
    with bpy.context.temp_override(**c_o):
        bpy.ops.object.mode_set(mode='OBJECT')

    c_o = get_context_override(context, 'VIEW_3D', 'WINDOW')
    with context.temp_override(**c_o):
        bpy.ops.transform.resize( ↩
            value=(cell_width, cell_width, 1))
        bpy.ops.transform.translate(value=origin)
        bpy.ops.object.transform_apply( ↩
            location=True, rotation=False, scale=True)

    c_o = get_context_override(context, 'VIEW_3D', 'WINDOW')
    with bpy.context.temp_override(**c_o):
        bpy.ops.object.mode_set(mode='EDIT')

    c_o = get_context_override(context, 'VIEW_3D', 'WINDOW')
    with bpy.context.temp_override(**c_o):
        bpy.ops.mesh.select_all(action='SELECT')
        bpy.ops.mesh.edge_face_add()
        bpy.ops.object.mode_set(mode='OBJECT')
```

We start by iterating and deselecting the scene objects one by one, before setting the passed-in mesh object (grid_mesh_obj) as active and selecting it. We then switch to Object mode with a context override (as if from the viewport). Once mode switch is complete, with another context override (also from the viewport), we call bpy.ops.transform.resize to scale the mesh object by the given cell_width along XY, bpy.ops.transform.translate to move it to the given location (origin), and apply both transforms via bpy.ops.object.transform_apply. Recall that we must use a separate context override after the mode switch, since transform-related operators require the context to already be in Object mode to run. Scaling by cell_width in XY is like stretching the height map so that each cell is cell_width by cell_width instead of 1 by 1.

Next, we switch the mesh object to Edit mode with a context override (as if from the viewport); then with another override (also from the viewport), we select all with bpy.ops.mesh.select_all(action='SELECT'), fill in the mesh's faces with bpy.ops.mesh.edge_face_add(), then switch it back to Object mode with bpy.ops.object.mode_set(mode='OBJECT').

Adding Modifiers

The last function that finish_mesh (Listing 6-25) calls is add_modifiers (Listing 6-29), which adds a Subsurf modifier to meshes generated with fractal-based methods and both a Decimate and a Subsurf modifier to meshes generated with noise-based methods.

Listing 6-29. Add a Decimate and a Subsurf modifier to a terrain mesh generated using noise methods, or only a Subsurf modifier to a fractal-generated mesh (see /Ch6/fractal_terrain_generator.py)

```
def add_modifiers(is_fractal, grid_mesh_obj):
    if is_fractal:
        subsurf_mod = grid_mesh_obj.modifiers.new( ↩
            grid_mesh_obj.name+"_subsurf_mod", 'SUBSURF')
        subsurf_mod.levels = 1
    else:
        decimate_mod = grid_mesh_obj.modifiers.new( ↩
            grid_mesh_obj.name+"_decimate_mod", 'DECIMATE')
        decimate_mod.decimate_type = 'UNSUBDIV'
        decimate_mod.iterations = 3
```

```
subsurf_mod = grid_mesh_obj.modifiers.new( ↩
    grid_mesh_obj.name+"_subsurf_mod", 'SUBSURF')
subsurf_mod.levels = 2
```

Recall that from a mesh object, we call `modifiers.new` to create and add a modifier to that object's stack with the given name and type. You can refer to the section "Adding a Bevel Modifier to a Mesh Object" in Chapter 3 for a detailed walkthrough on how to find the Enum string for specifying the type of modifier to create (such as `'SUBSURF'`) as well as the Python variables corresponding to a modifier's properties.

For meshes generated with fractal-based methods, we add a Subsurf modifier with Levels Viewport set to 1 (`subsurf_mod.levels = 1`) and all other settings left at default. Otherwise, for meshes generated with noise-based methods, we add a Decimate modifier set to Un-Subdivide (`decimate_mod.decimate_type = 'UNSUBDIV'`) with Iterations = 3, followed by a Subsurf modifier with Levels Viewport set to 2 and all other settings at default.

Summary

In this chapter, you learned to use noise- and fractal-based methods to generate terrain with Blender Python. You implemented each method to output a grid of elevation values (height map), which is in turn passed through shared generator code to create the mesh data and add borders, transforms, and modifiers.

In the first part of the chapter, you formulated a design for the terrain generator to reuse as many components as possible between different types of generation algorithms. Since all types of generation start with a blank height map, this part of the code is shared among them. The different types of generation then fill in the height map with their own Z values, which are in turn passed through common code that creates the mesh data from the height map and adds borders, transforms, and modifiers.

In the second part of the chapter, you found out how to implement both noise- and fractal-based methods to generate Z values for height maps. The noise-based methods generate a Z value at each location then use either bilinear or bicubic interpolation to smooth between them. The noise-based methods you implemented include value noise, fBm, and the diamond-square algorithm. The fractal-based methods emulate the self-similarity of real terrain where the same pattern is observed when a portion of the map is repeatedly zoomed in. You implemented the hybrid multi fractal algorithm and learned to use Blender Python's built-in multi fractal and hetero terrain functions.

In the final part of the chapter, you implemented common functionalities shared between different generation algorithms, such as code for creating a blank height map; for adding an optional border; for creating mesh data and object; for resizing, moving, and filling in faces; and for adding modifiers.

References

Shaker, N., Nelson, M. J., Togelius, J. 2016. Procedural Content Generation in Games. Springer International Publishing Switzerland.

Ebert, D. S., Musgrave, F. K., Peachey, D., Perlin, K., Worley, S., Mark, W. R., Hart., J. C. 2003. Texturing and Modeling: A Procedural Approach. Elsevier Inc.

Barnsley, M. F., Devaney, R. L., Mandelbrot, B. B., Peitgen, H., Saupe, D., Voss, R. F. 1988. The Science of Fractal Images. Springer-Verlag.

CHAPTER 7

L-Systems for Plant Generation

In this chapter, you'll learn how to implement your own L-System interpreter for generating 2D curves and 3D meshes in Blender Python. L-Systems are grammar-based objects composed of a starting string (*axiom*) accompanied by a set of rewriting rules that specify how to substitute symbols. Since characters are replaced simultaneously in each iteration, strings produced by L-Systems are inherently suitable for representing self-repeating structures like trees, which is what we'll focus on in this chapter.

We'll begin by practicing rewriting the Koch curve with pen and paper, then translate the procedure into Python and implement a 2D turtle-graphic class that rewrites L-Systems for a given number of iterations and interprets the expanded string to generate curves. Starting with the simplest case, where the turtle moves one step at a time and turns left or right, we'll gradually build up the system to support skipping (i.e., moving without extending the curve) and branching, which will allow us to generate complex 2D trees. With a 2D turtle at our disposal, we'll explore how to modify existing L-Systems as well as come up with our own, to alter branching patterns of generated trees and affect the density and distribution of their foliage in a systematic way.

In the last part of the chapter, we'll take the turtle from 2D to 3D by converting curves to meshes, then use modifiers to give the trees volume and refine their silhouettes. We'll also discuss strategies for extending the turtle, such as sampling step distance and turn angles instead of using fixed values and embedding rules for placing hand-modeled parts on generated tree branches.

I. Lupiani, *Procedural Content Generation for Games*, https://doi.org/10.1007/979-8-8688-1787-8_7

Running This Chapter's Examples

The source code and color figures for this book are available on GitHub via the book's product page, located at `https://link.springer.com/book/9798868817861`. Navigate to the `/Ch7` folder in the downloaded source to locate the file `L_Systems.py` and open it in the built-in Text Editor under the Scripting workspace to follow along. At the bottom of the script, there is an `if __name__ == "__main__"` block already set up which invokes the code listings with sample arguments. You can experiment by changing the values for these arguments.

Introduction to L-Systems

L-Systems (short for Lindenmayer Systems) are a class of grammar used for describing objects with self-repeating structures. A self-repeating object is one that is made up of smaller copies of itself, with each copy in turn made up of even more scaled down copies, and so on, such that when continuously zoomed in, the topology (patterning) of the object looks the same. For example, the fern shown in Figure 7-1 appears to have the same branching pattern as a whole, at the tip of one major branch, and down a side branch.

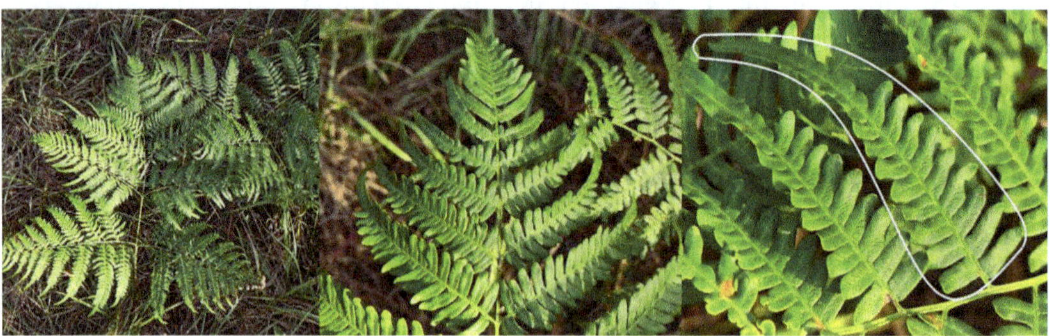

Figure 7-1. *A type of fern with self-repeating structures. Left: the fern as a whole. Middle: the fern zoomed in on one of its major branches, which has the same pattern as the whole plant. Right: the fern zoomed in further on one of its side branches, which has the same pattern as its major branch. Photos taken by the author*

Interestingly, the self-repeating pattern is a form of symmetry, because like other types of symmetries, you could transform the object in some way and make one part of the object coincide with another. For example, a snowflake has six-point rotational symmetry, which means you can rotate it by

$$\frac{360^\circ}{6} = 60^\circ$$

and end up with the same visual. Like we've seen with the fern in Figure 7-1, you're able to zoom in on a self-repeating pattern and have the zoomed-in part of the plant coincide with the plant at a less zoomed level.

Many objects in nature have self-repeating structures, such as trees, flowers, fruits, and vegetables (e.g., the famous "fractal broccoli," Romanesco), which lend themselves well to be described by L-Systems grammars.

What Is an L-System?

An L-System grammar consists of an *axiom* (a starting string) and one or more *rewriting rules*. Each rewriting rule describes how to substitute one character. Starting with the axiom, for each iteration, we examine the current string and see if any of its characters match the left-hand side of a rewriting rule—if so, we replace that character with what is on the right-hand side of the rule. Since each rewriting rule tells how to rewrite a different character, there will only be one rule matching each unique character (if any). If there are multiple characters in the current string with applicable rule(s), we apply all of the rules at the same time—this is called *simultaneous rewriting*. If a character does not match any rule, we leave it unchanged.

Note There are other types of grammars that use *sequential rewriting*—which means you apply one matching rule at a time, one after another, as opposed to applying all matching rules at once.

For an L-System, if the current iteration has a character with no matching rule, we actually assume that there is an unwritten "identity rule" that replaces the character with itself—I find it easier to think of it in terms of leaving the character unaltered, which has the same effect.

After applying rewriting rules for the given number of iterations, you'll end up with a string that is different (and usually longer) than the axiom—let's call this string the *expansion*. The expansion at this point is just a sequence of letters and symbols (from the *alphabet* of the grammar)—which by themselves don't mean much. For an expansion to represent a structure, you must attribute meaning to each symbol so you can *interpret* the string. Although you are allowed to use any symbols or letters in your L-System and assign meaning to them however you like, there are symbols established for Python Turtle interpretations used by many (which we'll go over shortly). It is therefore a good idea to reserve symbols from the turtle-style alphabet and combine them with your own when designing an L-System, so they are easier to comprehend for your users.

Rewriting Strings on Pen and Paper

Next, we'll work through an example of creating an L-System grammar for a 2D curve with a self-repeating structure. The Koch curve is a well-known fractal constructed as follows:

Starting with a horizontal line segment, edit each straight segment per iteration using the following steps:

1. Divide the straight segment into equal thirds.
2. Replace the middle third of the segment with an equilateral triangle whose sides are the same length as the one-third segment. Remove the triangle's bottom edge.

Let's think about how we can translate this process into L-System grammar. Since the Koch curve starts with a straight-line segment, it naturally becomes the axiom—we'll call it *s* (for now). Each iteration describes how you would edit any straight-line segment in the current curve, including the axiom, which translates into the L-System rewriting rule:

$$s \rightarrow \frac{s}{3} \wedge \frac{s}{3}$$

where $\wedge$ is an equilateral triangle with sides $\frac{s}{3}$ and its bottom edge removed. The rule then reads, replace every occurrence of *s* with

$$\frac{s}{3} \wedge \frac{s}{3}$$

Since dividing line segments repeatedly into thirds is cumbersome, to simplify the process, we'll use *s* in place of $\frac{s}{3}$ everywhere on the right-hand side of the rule (i.e., to the right of the arrow), which gives us a longer curve with the same proportion:

Rewriting the curve this way makes the curve four times as long with each iteration (since $\wedge = 2s$); however, since we are deriving an L-System for the purpose of generating meshes, the size does not matter, since we can always scale it postgeneration to our liking. The important thing is to maintain the relative proportion between the parts of the model.

Let's try rewriting three iterations of the Koch curve using the L-System we just derived:

1. Starting with the axiom , we use the rewriting rule and replace it with .
2. Starting with , we replace each with , which becomes .
3. Starting with , we replace each with , which becomes .

The first four iterations of the Koch curve from the above rewriting process are shown in Figure 7-2. To generate the curve, we just need to come up with how to create and in Blender Python, which we'll do shortly with 2D Turtle interpretation, but first, we'll implement a function to rewrite L-System strings.

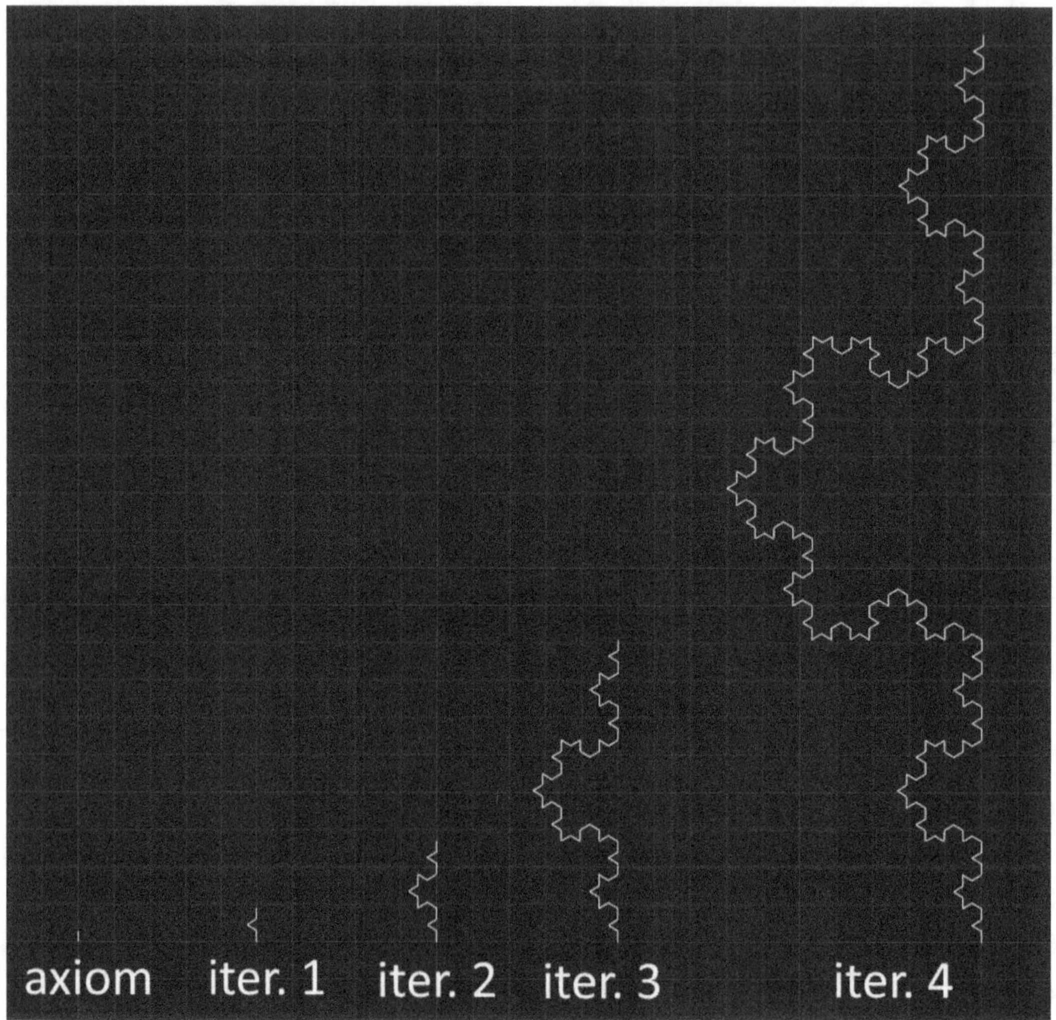

Figure 7-2. *Koch curve L-System rewriting process. From left to right: the axiom (straight-line segment) and iterations 1 to 4*

Rewriting Strings in Python

In this section, we'll write a Python function to perform the L-System rewriting process. Before diving into code, let's think about how we can represent an L-System in Python with a simple example:

axiom: *b*

rewriting rules: *a* ➤ *ab*, *b* ➤ *a*

The axiom is straightforward since we can just store it as a Python string. There are two rewriting rules, each in the format of "replacing the left-hand side string with the right-hand side string." Therefore, a mapping of one string to another. A Python dictionary (of type `dict`) is a natural choice, since it lets us store each rewriting rule as a key-value pair, with the left-hand side string as the key and the right-hand side string as the value. The above L-System then becomes the following in Python:

```
axiom = "b"
rewriting_rules = {"a": "ab", "b": "a"}
```

Using the above construct, we can implement the `rewrite` function (Listing 7-1), which performs the rewriting process for a given number of iterations (`num_iter`) of a passed-in L-System as an `axiom` string and a `rewriting_rules` dictionary.

Listing 7-1. Rewriting a given number of iterations for a passed-in L-System (see /Ch7/L_Systems.py)

```
def rewrite(axiom: str, rewriting_rules: dict, ↩
    num_iter: int):
    str_output = axiom
    for i in range(num_iter):
        str_this_iter = ""
        for c in str_output:
            rewritten = False
            for predecessor, successor in ↩
                rewriting_rules.items():
                if c == predecessor:
                    str_this_iter += successor
                    rewritten = True
                    break
            if not rewritten:
                str_this_iter += c
        str_output = str_this_iter
    return str_output
```

We create a variable str_output to store the current expansion (the rewritten string so far) and assign axiom to it as its initial value. We then set up a for loop to rewrite a total of num_iter iterations. In each iteration, we look at each character c of str_output and see if it matches the left side of any rewriting rule–if so, we use the right side of that rule in place of c in the rewritten string. If not, we copy c verbatim into the rewritten string.

Let's look at the rule-matching portion of the code in more detail. The rules are stored as key-value pairs (rewriting_rules.items()) in the rewriting_rules dictionary, with the line

```
for predecessor, successor in rewriting_rules.items():
```

We break up a key-value pair and assign the key to predecessor (the left side of a rule) and value to successor (the right side), respectively. Instead of overwriting str_output directly as we apply rules, we use a temporary string str_this_iter (that is reset at the start of each iteration) to work out the current expansion. We check each character in str_output (the previous expansion) for a matching rule (c == predecessor)—in which case successor is appended to str_this_iter. If no match is found, we append c to str_this_iter. After str_this_iter is fully formed, we assign it to str_output, thus updating it to the current expansion, and continue.

Note The left side of a rewriting rule (the part before the arrow) is also called the *predecessor* and the right side the *successor*.

Caution The reason we don't overwrite str_output in Listing 7-1 while iterating it (for c in str_output) is because it will cause an error—intuitively, if you imagine checking each character in a string, while modifying that string at the same time—you could lose your place, or read from the wrong memory location (e.g., beyond the end of the string, if the string is shortened). None of which is good!

With rewrite (Listing 7-1) implemented, you can write a simple function like test_rewrite (Listing 7-2) to print out the expansions of an L-System for a few consecutive iterations, to verify that rewrite is behaving correctly.

Listing 7-2. Testing rewriting strings for an L-System (see /Ch7/L_Systems.py)

```
def test_rewrite():
    axiom = "b"
    rewriting_rules = {"a": "ab", "b": "a"}

    for i in range(5):
        print("expansion " + str(i) + ": " + ↩
            rewrite(axiom, rewriting_rules, i))
```

After calling `test_rewrite()`, you should see the following lines printed in the System Console (*Window* ➤ *Toggle System Console*), where expansion 0 is the axiom.

```
expansion 0: b
expansion 1: a
expansion 2: ab
expansion 3: aba
expansion 4: abaab
```

2D Turtle Interpretation of L-Systems in Blender Python

In this section, you'll learn how to generate a curve object in Blender based on a string rewritten from an L-System. Turtle graphics (the `turtle` module) is Python's implementation of the geometric drawing tool first introduced in the programming language Logo. We are *not* going to use the `turtle` module here, but instead write our own in Blender Python using similar conventions as `turtle` for creating polyline drawings, where you can move forward one step in 2D with or without drawing a line, turn left, or turn right.

2D Continuous Drawing with Turns (Pen Stays on Paper)

We'll start with the simplest case, where each time you move forward, you leave a mark, much like drawing without lifting the pen off the page. In turtle convention, F means move forward one unit, + means turn left by rotating in place, and – means turn right.

We'll assume that the turtle always turns by a fixed angle for now. Let's think about how we can use this alphabet = {F, +, −} to create an L-System for constructing the Koch curve. The axiom is a line segment, so we'll simply encode it as F. Recall that the rewriting rule is ⇨ . Since each angle of an equilateral triangle is

$$\frac{180°}{3} = 60°$$

Our turtle always turns 60 degrees. We can draw the successor of the rule using the sequence F, +, F, −, −, F, +, F, as shown in Figure 7-3. Therefore, our new L-System for the Koch curve is

```
turtle_axiom_koch = "F"
turtle_rewriting_rules_koch = {"F": "F+F--F+F"}
```

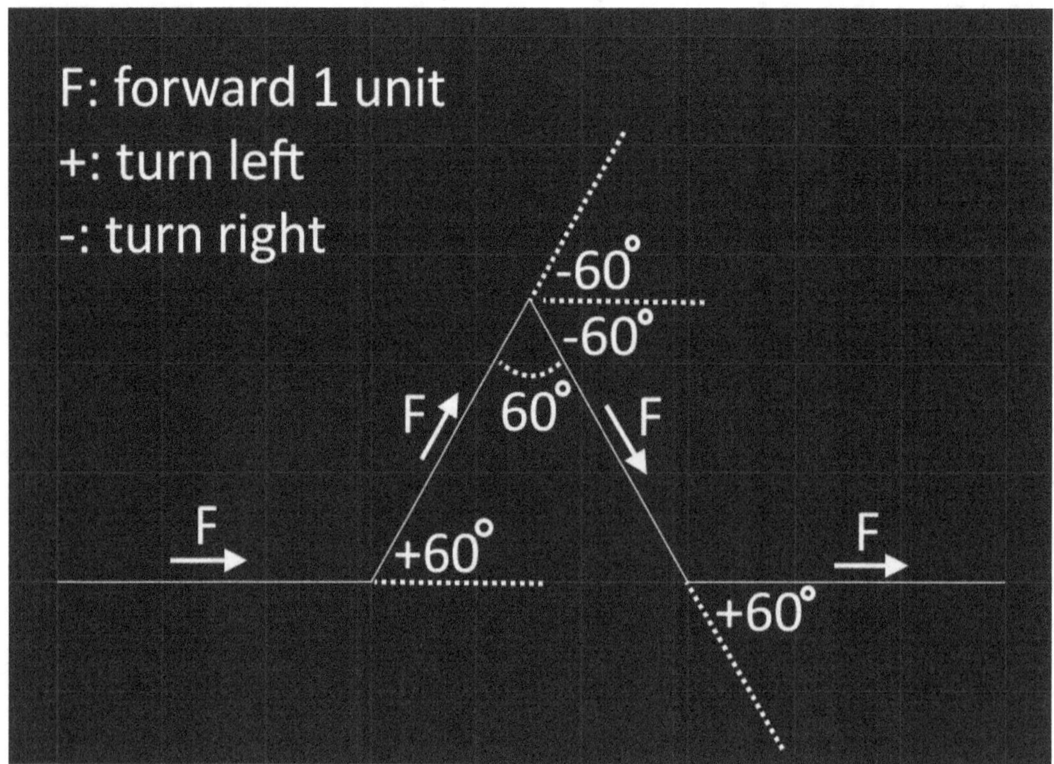

Figure 7-3. *The successor (right-hand side) of the Koch curve rewriting rule visualized*

Implementing a 2D Turtle Class

We're now ready to implement a class turtle_2D in Blender Python for generating curve objects based on L-Systems using the alphabet = {F, +, –}. Listing 7-3 shows the turtle_2D class' __init__ method, which takes as arguments the current context, an L-System (an axiom string and rewriting_rules dictionary), the number of iterations to rewrite (num_iters), the turning angle for + and - (theta), the move forward distance for F (step_dist), the name for the curve object to generate (curve_obj_name), and the location of the first point of the curve (origin, as a Vector). Note that theta is passed in as a list of three values, which correspond to the turn angle for the X, Y, and Z axis, respectively. To generate our Koch curve, we'll turn a fixed angle of 60 degrees per + or – around the turtle's local Z axis (which is the turtle's current heading, as we'll see shortly).

Listing 7-3. Creating a basic 2D turtle system for generating a curve object based on a string rewritten from an L-System for a given number of iterations (see /Ch7/L_Systems.py)

```
class turtle_2D:
    def __init__(self, context, axiom: str, ↩
        rewriting_rules: dict, num_iters: int, ↩
        theta: List[float], step_dist: float, ↩
        curve_obj_name: str, origin: Vector):
        self.cur_str = rewrite(axiom, rewriting_rules, ↩
            num_iters)
        self.theta = theta
        self.step_dist = step_dist

        curve_data = bpy.data.curves.new( ↩
            name=curve_obj_name+"_data", type='CURVE')
        curve_data.dimensions = '3D'
        self.curve_obj = bpy.data.objects.new( ↩
            name=curve_obj_name, object_data=curve_data)
        spline_data = self.curve_obj.data.splines.new( ↩
            type='POLY')
```

```
        spline_data.points[0].co = ↩
            [origin[0], origin[1], origin[2], 0]
        context.collection.objects.link(self.curve_obj)

        self.heading = Vector((0.0, 0.0, 1.0))
        self.lcs = ↩
            self.curve_obj.matrix_local.copy().to_3x3()
```

Since the expansion does not change over time, we only need to derive it once in `__init__` and store it in `self.cur_str` by calling `rewrite` (Listing 7-1) with `axiom`, `rewriting_rules`, and `num_iters`.

`turtle_2D` will generate a curve object based on the expansion, since the turtle-style "drawing" is easily represented by a poly spline. When we venture into 3D later in this chapter, we'll still generate a curve object first, then convert it into a mesh and give it volume. A curve object contains a curve data block, which in turn contains splines; therefore, we'll first create a new curve data block `self.curve_data` by calling `bpy.data.curves.new` with `type='CURVE'` and set its `dimensions` to `'3D'`, then call `bpy.data.objects.new` to create a new curve object `self.curve_obj` with `self.curve_data` as its data block.

Next, we'll create a poly spline under `self.curve_obj.data` by calling `self.curve_obj.data.splines.new(type='POLY')`, which will contain one point with the coordinates (0, 0, 0, 0) at its creation. Notice that a spline point's coordinates contain four numbers, with the first three corresponding to X, Y, and Z. We'll ignore the 4th number and always set it to 0. Since we want the spline to start at the `origin` point passed in, we set the initial point's coordinates to `origin`'s coordinates, plus a 0 as the 4th number (`spline_data.points[0].co = [origin[0],origin[1],origin[2],0]`). At this time, we've finished setting up the curve object, so we link it to the passed-in `context`'s scene collection.

The turtle will continuously update its current heading and local coordinate space as it generates points for the poly spline. Since we're not lifting the pen off the page for now (i.e., the turtle will always lay down a stroke when it moves), we'll have one spline for the entire generation. With each F, the turtle moves along its current heading a distance of `self.step_dist`, then adds a new point to the spline at its new position. With each + or –, the turtle turns in place by rotating its local coordinate space, then updates its heading to the new local unit +Z `Vector`. In other words, the turtle will always head toward its local +Z, no matter how its local coordinate space is oriented. Note that + and – do not contribute new points to the spline, only F does.

We wrap up `__init__` by setting the turtle's initial heading to global unit +Z (`Vector((0.0, 0.0, 1.0))`) so that when we generate trees later in this chapter, the trunk will grow upward toward +Z. We also copy the curve object's local coordinate space to the turtle's local coordinate space (`self.lcs`) as a 3×3 matrix.

Moving the 2D Turtle Forward and Laying Down a Stroke

Next, we'll implement the function `one_step_forward` (Listing 7-4), which will move the turtle a distance of `self.step_dist` forward along its current heading (`self.heading`) and add a point to the spline at the turtle's new position.

Listing 7-4. Move a turtle_2D instance one step forward (F) (see /Ch7/L_Systems.py)

```
class turtle_2D:
    # ---- SNIPPED ----
    def one_step_forward(self):
        spline_data = self.curve_obj.data.splines[-1]
        last spline pt = spline_data.points[-1]
        start_pt = Vector((last_spline_pt.co[0], ↩
            last_spline_pt.co[1], last_spline_pt.co[2]))
        trans_vec = self.heading * self.step_dist
        end_pt = start_pt + trans_vec
        spline_data.points.add(1)
        spline_data.points[-1].co = [end_pt[0], end_pt[1], ↩
            end_pt[2], 0]
```

Since we're not lifting our pen from the page for the entire generation process, the turtle traverses a single spline and is always at the last point added to the spline (`last_spline_pt`). Since a spline point's coordinates have four values, we'll create a `Vector` instance `start_pt` from its first three values, X, Y, and Z, so it is easier to do vector math with. We calculate the forward displacement vector `trans_vec` by multiplying the turtle's heading with the step distance. The turtle's new position (`end_pt`) is then the sum of its last position (`start_pt`) and `trans_vec`. We add a new point to the spline via `spline_data.points.add(1)` and set the new point's coordinates to `end_pt`'s coordinates plus a 0 for the 4th value, which is unused.

Note There is unfortunately no way to specify the coordinates while adding a point to a spline. You must add a new point first, then set the new point's coordinates.

Turning the 2D Turtle and Interpreting an Expansion

Next, we'll implement the method `draw` (Listing 7-5) for the `turtle_2D` class to *interpret* the expansion, which means to generate the curve from the rewritten string of the L-System.

Listing 7-5. Interpret the expansion of an L-System with the alphabet F, +, and – (see /Ch7/L_Systems.py)

```
class turtle_2D:
    # ---- SNIPPED ----
    def draw(self):
        for c in self.cur_str:
            if c == "F":
                self.one_step_forward()
            elif c == "+":
                mat_rot = Matrix.Rotation( ↩
                    radians(-self.theta[2]), 3, 'Y')
                self.lcs.rotate(mat_rot)
                self.heading = self.lcs[2]
                self.heading.normalize()
            elif c == "-":
                mat_rot = Matrix.Rotation( ↩
                    radians(self.theta[2]), 3, 'Y')
                self.lcs.rotate(mat_rot)
                self.heading = self.lcs[2]
                self.heading.normalize()
```

Recall that we've derived the expansion in `__init__` (Listing 7-3) and stored it in `self.cur_str`, so here we simply iterate through `self.cur_str` and read one character `c` at a time. If `c` is F, the turtle calls `self.one_step_forward()` (Listing 7-4) to move one step along its current heading. If `c` is + (–), the turtle rotates left (right) (counterclockwise (clockwise)) relative to its current heading (unit +Z of its local coordinate system), thus making the rotation axis its local Y axis. The amount to turn left (right) is passed in as `theta[2]` in Listing 7-3 since local +Z is the turtle's heading direction. We convert `theta[2]` from degrees to radians and use it to construct a rotation matrix `mat_rot`, which is of type `Matrix` under Blender Python's `mathutils` module. Note that since the turtle's local coordinate system (`self.lcs`) is a 3×3 matrix, we must make `mat_rot` 3×3 as well. We rotate `self.lcs` with `mat_rot` by calling `self.lcs.rotate(mat_rot)`, then update the turtle's heading `self.heading` (a `mathutils.Vector` instance) to the +Z direction of `self.lcs` and normalize it.

Note Recall that the Blender Python module `mathutils` provides 3D math-related types such as `Vector`, `Matrix`, `Euler`, etc. To use the types under `mathutils`, you must explicitly import them into your script (e.g., `from mathutils import Matrix`).

Putting it altogether, we can use the Koch L-System we defined earlier using the turtle alphabet {F, +, –} to create a `turtle_2D` (Listings 7-3 to 7-5) instance and generate a Koch curve object, as shown in Listing 7-6, where we rewrite for four iterations and use a `step_dist` of three Blender units and 60 degrees turn angle for all axes. Running Listing 7-6 will generate a four-iteration Koch curve object like the one shown on the right side of Figure 7-2.

Listing 7-6. Creating a turtle_2D instance with an L-System to generate a Koch curve of four iterations (see /Ch7/L_Systems.py)

```
d = 3
theta_60 = [60.0, 60.0, 60.0]

turtle_axiom_koch = "F"
turtle_rewriting_rules_koch = {"F": "F+F--F+F"}
```

```
def test_2D():
    t_koch_2D = turtle_2D(bpy.context, turtle_axiom_koch, ↩
        turtle_rewriting_rules_koch, 4, theta_60, d,  ↩
        "2D_Koch_4", Vector((100, 100, 0)))
    t_koch_2D.draw()
```

Adding the Ability to Skip (Lift Pen from Paper)

So far, our turtle has no choice but to leave a trail every time it moves. To give our turtle the ability to generate structures beyond continuous line drawings, we'll add another symbol to its alphabet, f, which means to move one unit forward along its current heading but not draw a line. The result is that a new spline is started at the turtle's position *after* the movement.

Being able to lift the pen off the page opens the turtle up to the world of drawings with disjoint parts, such as the "islands and lakes" fractal shown in Figure 7-4, a two-iteration example generated in Blender which we'll implement shortly in Listing 7-7. The L-System formula for "islands and lakes" we'll use in this section is from page 10 of the book *The Algorithmic Beauty of Plants* by Przemyslaw Prusinkiewicz and Aristid Lindenmayer, which is as follows:

```
turtle_axiom_islands_lakes = "F+F+F+F"
turtle_rewriting_rules_islands_lakes = ↩
    {"F": "F+f-FF+F+FF+Ff+FF-f+FF-F-FF-Ff-FFF", ↩
        "f": "ffffff"}
```

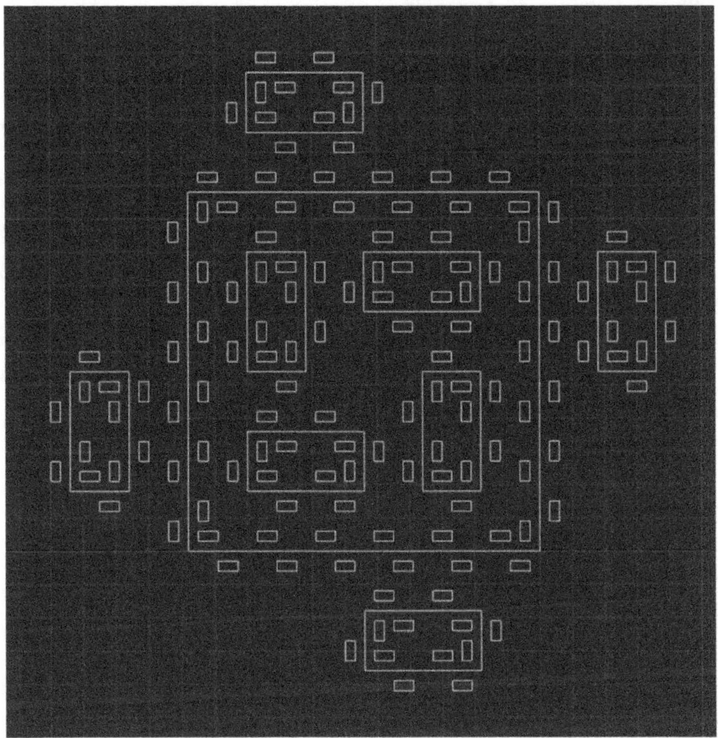

Figure 7-4. *Iteration 2 of the "islands and lakes" fractal from p.10 of the book The Algorithmic Beauty of Plants by Przemyslaw Prusinkiewicz and Aristid Lindenmayer, generated in Blender by the author by running Listing 7-7*

The "islands and lakes" fractal has multiple characters in its axiom, as illustrated in Figure 7-5. The turtle starts at the lower-right corner, then traces out a square counterclockwise, by following the sequence: go forward one step, turn left, go forward one step, turn left, go forward one step, turn left, go forward one step. The turtle always turns left by 90 degrees relative to its current heading in this case.

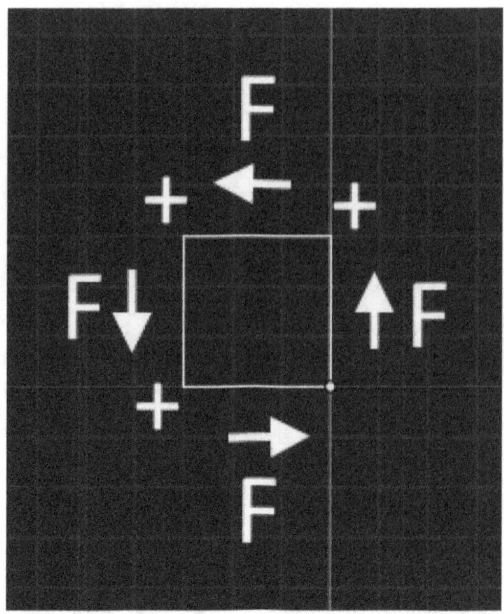

Figure 7-5. *The axiom "F+F+F+F" of the "islands and lakes" fractal visualized. The generation starts at the lower-right corner and traces out a square counterclockwise*

The axiom is a continuous curve. However, the first rewriting rule replaces each segment of the axiom with three disjoint components, which are two rectangles separated by a vertical line, as shown in Figure 7-6. The "islands" (rectangles) of the first rule's successor are constructed using a sequence of F (go forward one step and draw a line), f (forward one step but not leave a line), and + (turn left). When we set the turning angle to 90 degrees, the turtle follows the dashed path on the right of Figure 7-7, with the corresponding sequence of symbols shown in the center of Figure 7-7. By cross-referencing the dashed path with the symbol sequence, you can see that the turtle starts at the bottom center, draws one segment forward, turns left, skips a step, then turns right to trace out a rectangle counterclockwise, before returning to the center and continuing the line at the beginning. After reaching the halfway point, the turtle skips and crosses over to the right, to trace the second rectangle clockwise this time. Lastly, the turtle skips back to the middle and brings the center line to a finish.

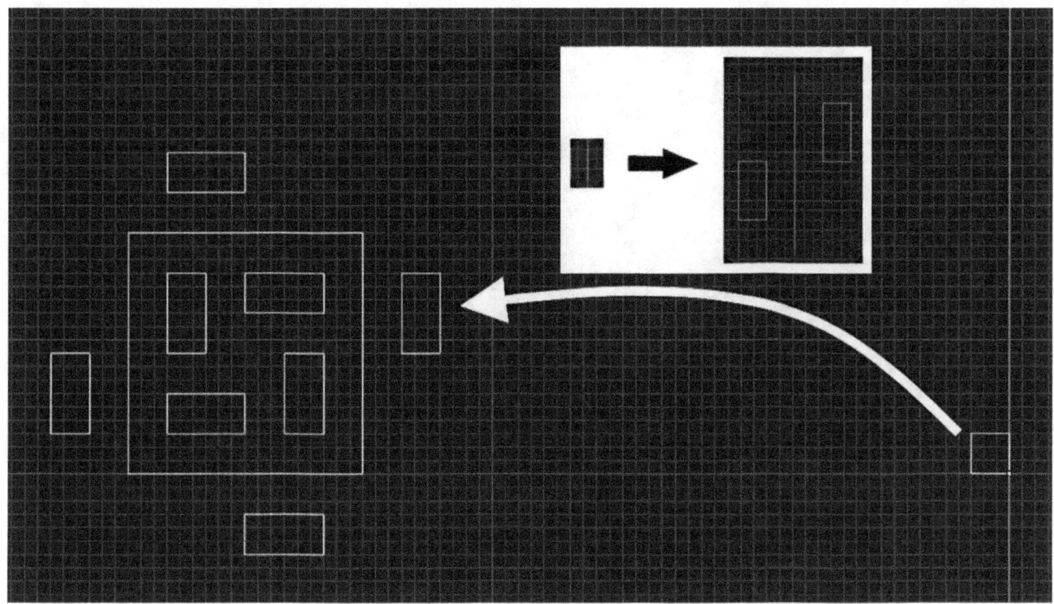

Figure 7-6. *Rewriting one iteration of the "islands and lakes" fractal. The square shown on the right is the axiom. Replacing each of the square's sides with the successor of the rewriting rule in the order the square is drawn, starting at the lower-right corner, going counterclockwise, gives you the first iteration expansion shown on the left.*

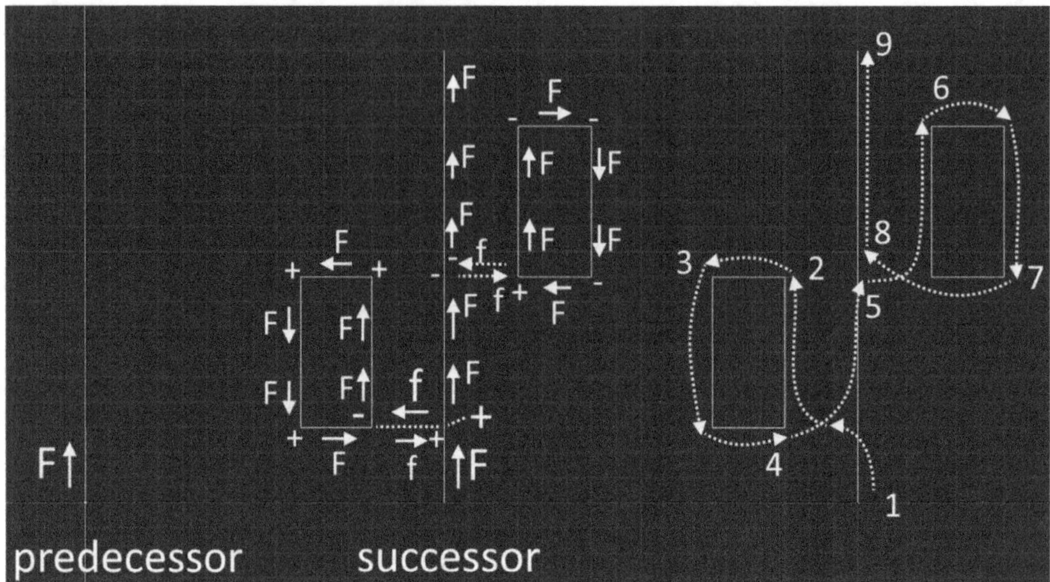

***Figure 7-7.** The rewriting rule "F": "F+f-FF+F+FF+Ff+FF-f+FF-F-FF-Ff-FFF" of the "islands and lakes" fractal visualized. The successor (right-hand side of the rule) follows the dashed path from 1 to 9 shown on the right. The middle shows the successor's sequence of symbols in order, which gets unwieldy quickly*

You can see that the second rewriting rule of "islands and lakes," `"f": "ffffff"`, lengthens the f sequence with each rewrite, which has the effect of widening the spacing between neighboring structures sixfold. Since the first rewriting rule transforms each unit line segment into a structure six times as tall (as shown in Figure 7-7), the second rewriting rule is necessary to keep the rewritten structures from overlapping with each iteration.

Let's add the ability to our turtle to move one step forward without drawing a line. To do this, we'll make the modifications to `turtle_2D` (Listings 7-3, 7-4, and 7-5) as shown in **bold** in Listing 7-7, where we add a check for and interpret the f symbol in the `draw` method and add the option to move but not draw a line in the `one_step_forward` method.

Note Notice that in the downloaded source, the class corresponding to the code in Listing 7-7 is named `turtle_2D_skip` instead of `turtle_2D`, which lets me include complete definitions of both classes without name clashes.

Listing 7-7. Add the ability to the turtle to move forward without leaving a trail (see /Ch7/L_Systems.py)

```
def draw(self):
    for c in self.cur_str:
        if c == "F":
            self.one_step_forward(True)
        elif c == "f":
            self.one_step_forward(False)
        elif c == "+":
            mat_rot = Matrix.Rotation( ↩
                radians(-self.theta[2]),3, 'Y')
            self.lcs.rotate(mat_rot)
            self.heading = self.lcs[2]
            self.heading.normalize()
        elif c == "-":
            mat_rot = Matrix.Rotation( ↩
                radians(self.theta[2]), 3, 'Y')
            self.lcs.rotate(mat_rot)
            self.heading = self.lcs[2]
            self.heading.normalize()

def one_step_forward(self, should_draw: bool=True):
    spline_data = self.curve_obj.data.splines[-1]
    last_spline_pt = spline_data.points[-1]
    start_pt = Vector((last_spline_pt.co[0], ↩
        last_spline_pt.co[1], last_spline_pt.co[2]))
    trans_vec = self.heading * self.step_dist
    end_pt = start_pt + trans_vec

    if should_draw:
        spline_data.points.add(1)
    else:
        spline_data = ↩
            self.curve_obj.data.splines.new(type='POLY')

    spline_data.points[-1].co = ↩
        [end_pt[0], end_pt[1], end_pt[2], 0]
```

We add an argument `should_draw` to `one_step_forward`, which when `True` adds a point to the end of the current spline and when `False` starts a new spline. In either case, the coordinates of the new point are set to the position one step forward along the turtle's current heading.

Adding Branching Capability

Adding the ability to skip ahead without drawing certainly opens up a lot; however, it is not enough to let the turtle draw branching structures like trees. If you take out a pen and doodle tree branches on a piece of paper, you'll most likely draw each branch from the trunk outward. Upon reaching a branch's tip, you move the pen back to the place where the last branch (one you just drew) stemmed from, then find a different spot, and start a new branch—notice the action of backtracking to a previous position. Currently, there is no way for us to mark a position in an L-System rewriting rule for the turtle to backtrack to. Furthermore, skipping or not, the turtle always grows the structure forward. You may be able to get creative and get the turtle back to a previous spot by adding a sequence of 90 degree turns with skips; however, that gets unwieldy quickly.

To mark a place in an L-System rewriting rule's successor for the turtle to backtrack to, we'll introduce the symbols [and]. As the turtle reads an expansion string from left to right, each time it encounters a [, it pushes the turtle's physical location onto a stack (a last-in, first-out container) and continues scanning rightward. When the turtle sees a], it pops the turtle's last recorded location off the top of the stack and starts a new spline from that location (i.e., starting a new "branch"). Let's work through an example. Consider the following L-System from page 25 of the book *The Algorithmic Beauty of Plants* by Przemyslaw Prusinkiewicz and Aristid Lindenmayer, which defines a 2D tree:

```
turtle_axiom_2d_tree1 = "X"
turtle_rewriting_rules_2d_tree1 = ↩
    {"X": "F[+X][-X]FX", "F": "FF"}
```

Note A stack is a LIFO container, which stands for last-in, first-out, meaning that the last item added to the container is the first to be removed. Imagine a stack like a stack of books. Pretend that you cannot pull a book from the middle of the stack, you can only add a new book to the top and take a book from the top.

Let's not worry about how the tree will look for now. We'll look at how the rewriting rule `"X": "F[+X][-X]FX"` is expanded first. The rule reads, replace every `"X"` with the sequence `"F[+X][-X]FX"`. You might have noticed that the letter `"X"` is not part of the L-System's alphabet. This is not an error–`"X"` does not mean anything itself, but is supposed to act like a place marker where further rewriting should occur. If an `"X"` occurs in a final expansion ("final" as in expanded up to the iteration the user specifies), it is ignored when the turtle interprets the expansion to generate the curve.

Note The process in which the turtle uses the expansion string as instructions for procedural generation is called *interpretation*.

Let's try rewriting this L-System and see what we get. Starting with the axiom `"X"`, in the first iteration, we simply apply the first rewriting rule and replace `"X"` with `"F[+X][-X]FX"`. If we pretend this is the final expansion, we can ignore all the X's and simplify the expansion to `"F[+][-]F"`. As mentioned before, each [means "push the turtle's physical location onto the stack," whereas each] means "pop the stack to get the last recorded location and return the turtle to that location." Therefore, the string `"F[+][-]F"` means move forward and draw one unit, record the turtle's location, turn left, return the turtle to the last recorded location, record the turtle's location, turn right, return the turtle to the last recorded location, and move forward and draw one unit. Since the turtle turns left or right in place, and a left turn followed by a right turn cancel each other out, "`[+][-]`" does nothing. So the net effect of `"F[+][-]F"` is that the turtle moves forward and draws two steps, which is not very exciting.

Note When we say "return the turtle to the last recorded location," we mean lift the turtle off the page and drop it at that location (i.e., the movement does not touch the page nor leave a mark).

Let's rewrite for another iteration and see if we can see some branching action from the square brackets. Starting with "F[+X][-X]FX" and applying both rewriting rules, we get the following expansion:

"FF[+**F[+X][-X]FX**][-**F[+X][-X]FX**]FF**F[+X][-X]FX**"

where the first rule applications are in **bold** and the second rule applications are underlined. Let's pretend this is the final expansion and eliminate the X's, so we can get a better idea of what's going on:

"FF[+F[+][-]F][-F[+][-]F]FFF[+][-]F"

We can simplify the string further by crossing out the "[+][-]"s, which do nothing as we've discussed earlier:

"FF[+FF][-FF]FFFF"

Let's step through this expansion now and see what it generates. From left to right, we move the turtle forward and draw two steps (with the two F's), record the turtle's location, then turn *left*, and move forward and draw another two steps. At this point, we've reached the first], so we return the turtle to the previous recorded location (where it was right before turning *left*). Next up in the expansion is [-FF], which is similar to what we just did but with the turtle turning the other way (record turtle location, turn *right*, move/draw two steps, go back). Notice that the movement inside each pair of square brackets gives you one branch—since you move forward, then go back to where you started. After drawing the two branches with [+FF][-FF], the turtle continues on the main branch after the FF at the beginning of the expansion and moves/draws another four steps with FFFF. The turtle's entire movement along this expansion is visualized in Figure 7-8 with a 22.5 degrees turn angle. You can see that the turtle draws the bottom of the trunk, the left branch, the right branch, then grows the trunk taller.

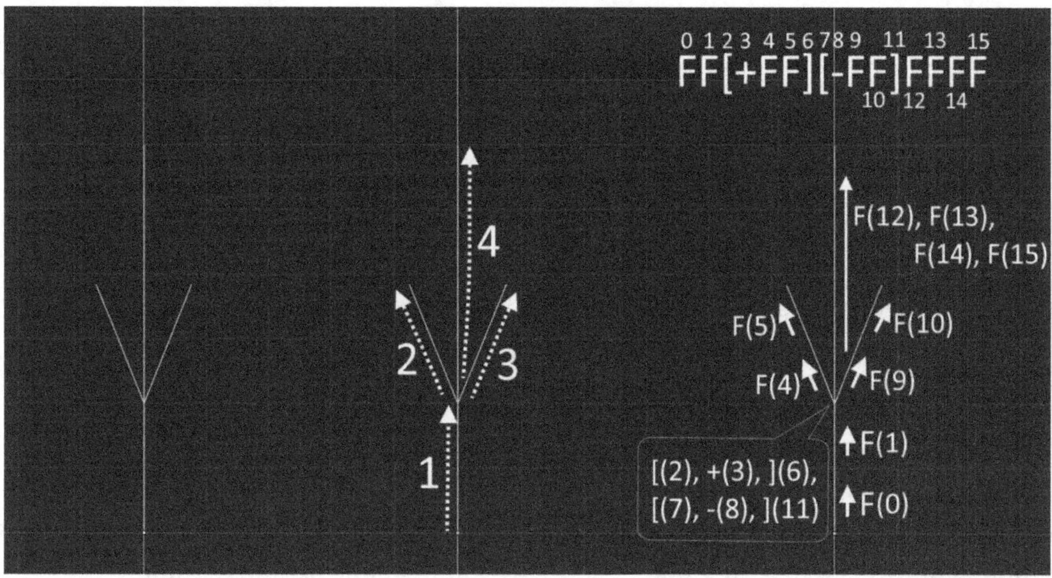

Figure 7-8. *Left: first expansion "FF[+FF][-FF]FFFF" of the branching L-System. Middle: the order of construction of the expansion's branches, marked 1 to 4. Right: the construction symbol by symbol. The number in parentheses after each symbol is its index in the expansion string*

It may not be obvious at first, but after playing with a few existing L-System definitions, expanding them, and drawing them out on paper, you'll start to develop the ability to visualize what structure an L-System will generate in your head. Take our previous example; knowing that forward movement inside a pair of square brackets creates a branch, you can immediately see that the overall structure of the expansion is the following:

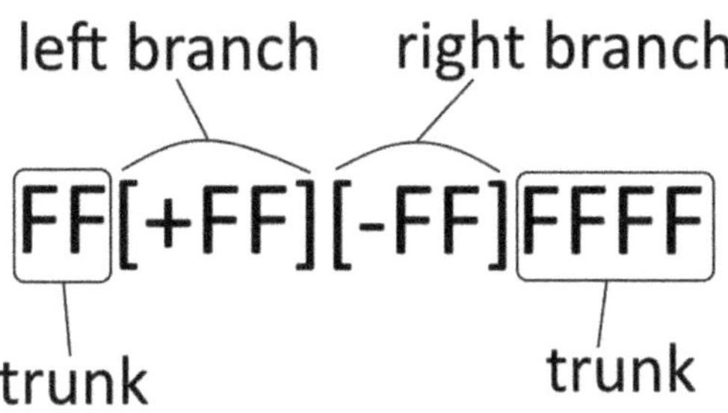

If there are nested square brackets, you've guessed it—it's branching from a branch! Often, knowing either the first or second iteration expansion is enough to know the L-System's overall growth pattern. Due to the nature of simultaneous rewriting, all L-System generated structures are self-similar. In other words, a later iteration will have the same topology, with components made up of the previous iteration. Take our branching example from above, we've derived that the L-System generates a tree with a main trunk going straight up, plus one left branch and one right branch that mirror one another. Even though we only know what the first iteration will look like exactly (Figure 7-8), we know that the second iteration will have the same topology—with the straight trunk in the middle and a branch on either side that mirror one another, except that you take the first iteration structure and use it as the "branch unit" in the second iteration. The first three iterations of this L-System are shown in Figure 7-9. Notice how the generated curves match our intuition, with each iteration having the same branching pattern, but with its "branch units" replaced by copies of the previous iteration.

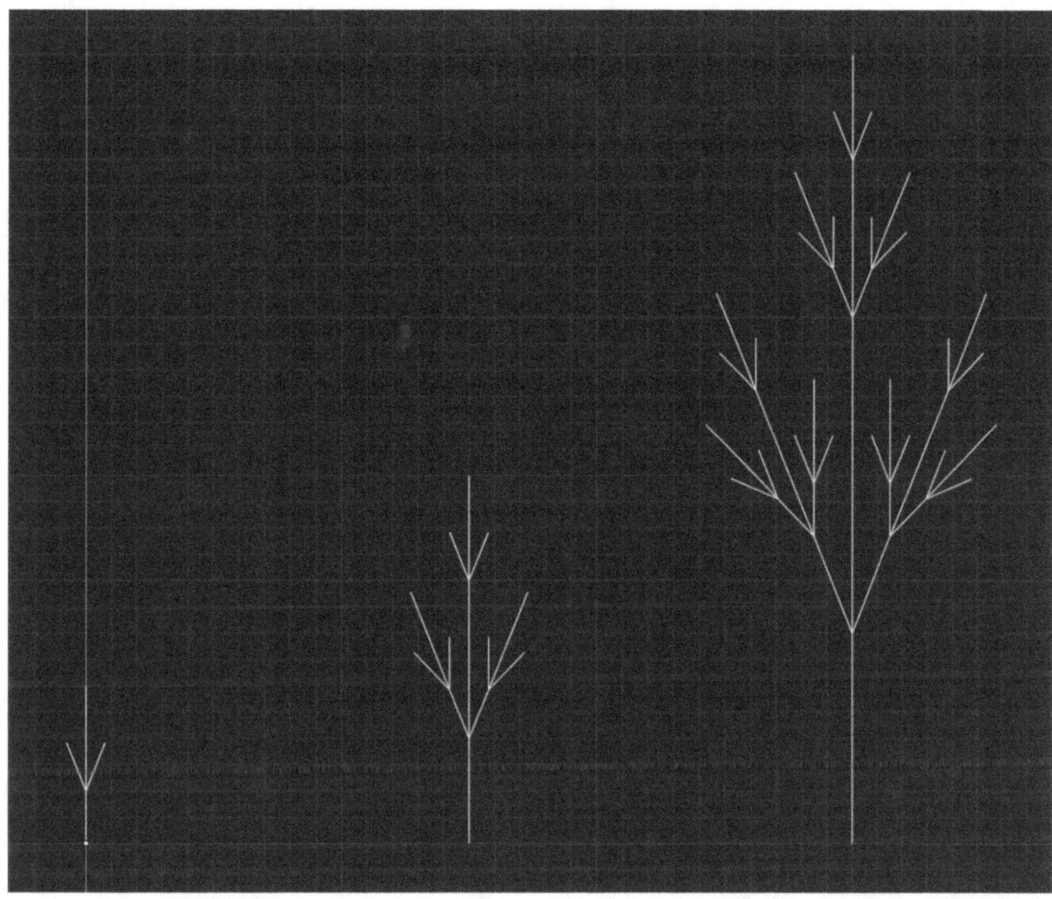

Figure 7-9. *The first three iterations of the branching L-System example generated by the author, shown from left to right. Recall that the L-System has the axiom "X" and the rewriting rules {"X": "F[+X][-X]FX", "F": "FF"} (from page 25 of the book The Algorithmic Beauty of Plants by Przemyslaw Prusinkiewicz and Aristid Lindenmayer). Notice that all three iterations have the same overall branching pattern, with each iteration's "branch units" replaced by copies of the previous iteration.*

Modifying the `turtle_2D` Class to Support [and]

We're now ready to modify the `turtle_2D` class to give it the ability to handle L-Systems with branching. We'll start by adding the stack initialization in the `__init__` method and defining a few other stats to help us keep track of spline and point indices, as shown in Listing 7-8.

Note Take note that in the downloaded source, the class corresponding to the code in Listings 7-8, 7-9, and 7-10 is named `turtle_2D_branching` instead of `turtle_2D`, which lets me include complete definitions of both classes without name clashes.

Listing 7-8. Modify the __init__ method of turtle_2D to give it the ability to handle L-Systems with branching (see /Ch7/L_Systems.py)

```
class turtle_2D:
    def __init__(self, context, axiom: str, ↩
        rewriting_rules: dict, num_iters: int, ↩
        theta: List[float], step_dist: float, ↩
        curve_obj_name: str, origin: Vector):
        # ---- SNIPPED ----
        self.stack = []
        self.prev_popped_pt = []
        self.prev_step_popped = False
        self.last_pt_stats = [0, 0]
```

Python does not have a built-in stack type; however, the `list` class has methods that let you easily use a `list` as a stack, such as `pop()`, which when called without an argument removes and returns the last element in the `list` like popping a stack. The `list` class' append method adds an element to the end of the list, which is analogous to pushing onto a stack. Therefore, we initialize a `stack` member variable as an empty list.

Since we could have "skips" (i.e., moving without drawing) and branching, which both start new splines, plus nested square brackets that branch off of branches, it would become unwieldy quickly if we relied only on notions like "the last spline" or the "last point." Moreover, since the turtle's movement is always relative to its current heading, plus we create rotation matrices using the turtle's local coordinate system, we need to make copies of those in addition to the turtle's location at the time we encounter a [. We create a new member variable `self.prev_popped_pt` to store the record popped from the stack, which contains the turtle's spline index and point index (into that spline), heading, and local coordinate system.

Since we read one symbol at a time in the expansion, if we read a], we pop the stack, but it won't be until the symbol after] that we'll make use of the recorded data. Since] may be few and far between, we create a bool flag `self.prev_step_popped` to signal ourselves the previous symbol in the expansion was a] and we need to unpack the data from `self.prev_popped_pt`. Alternatively, you could add code to keep track of the symbol index you are iterating and what the previous symbol is. I think the `self.prev_step_popped` flag is a little cleaner. Lastly, since the turtle needs to access and record spline and point indices from both the `draw` and `one_step_forward` methods, for convenience, we add a member variable `self.last_pt_stats`, which is a list with two values, the spline index and the point index (into the spline), respectively.

In Listing 7-9, we'll look at how to modify the `draw` method to support [and]. As we iterate the expansion, first thing we check is if `self.prev_step_popped` is `True`—if so, the previous symbol is], and we unpack the spline index (`self.last_pt_stats[0]`), point index (`self.last_pt_stats[1]`), heading (`self.heading`), and local coordinate system (`self.lcs`) from the turtle's last location record, which is stored in the list `self.prev_popped_pt`. Otherwise, these four fields simply carry over from the previous symbol. After unpacking the data, we set the `self.prev_step_popped` flag to `False` and empty the location record by calling `self.prev_popped_pt.clear()`.

Next, we look up the point `last_spline_pt` the turtle will continue from, using the spline index `self.last_pt_stats[0]` and point index `self.last_pt_stats[1]`.

We're now ready to interpret the symbol at hand. If the symbol is a [, we create a copy of the turtle's current location record and push it onto the stack. Recall that the location record is a list of four values, which are spline index, point index, heading, and local coordinate system, in that order. Note that since `self.heading` and `self.lcs` are compound objects, we need to call `copy.deepcopy` to create deep copies of them, so when we edit `self.heading` and `self.lcs` next (e.g., when we rotate due to a + or –), we don't accidentally alter the copies on the stack. We call `self.stack.append` to add the location record (list of four values) to the end of the `self.stack` list, to simulate pushing the record onto the top of the stack. Recall that a pair of square brackets enclosing movement creates a new branch; therefore, we start a new spline here and set its starting point to `last_spline_pt`. We then update the spline and point index (`self.last_pt_stats`) to the new spline's index and 0 (the first point). The new spline is at the last index in the splines list, which is the number of splines minus one (`len(self.curve_obj.data.splines)-1`), since new splines are always added to the end of the list of splines.

If the symbol is a], we check that the stack is not empty (has length > 0), then call `self.stack.pop()` to pop the stack (remove the element from the top) and store the popped location record in `self.prev_popped_pt`. Under the hood, `self.stack.pop()` removes the element from the end of the `self.stack` list. Since we always add to the end of `self.stack`, `self.stack.pop()` will always give you the most recently added record.

Since we've already derived the point `last_spline_pt` that the turtle will continue from, we'll modify the `one_step_forward` method shortly to take it as an additional argument. Here, we change the calls to `one_step_forward` under the checks for the `F` and the `f` symbols accordingly.

Note `copy` is a built-in Python module. To use `copy.deepcopy`, you need to import it via `from copy import deepcopy`.

Listing 7-9. Modify the draw method of turtle_2D to give it the ability to handle L-Systems with branching (see /Ch7/L_Systems.py)

```
class turtle_2D:
    # ---- SNIPPED ----
    def draw(self):
        for c in self.cur_str:
            if self.prev_step_popped:
                self.last_pt_stats[0],self.last_pt_stats[1],↩
                    self.heading,self.lcs=self.prev_popped_pt
                self.prev_step_popped = False
                self.prev_popped_pt.clear()

            last_spline_pt = self.curve_obj.data.splines[ ↩
                self.last_pt_stats[0]].points[ ↩
                    self.last_pt_stats[1]]

            if c == "[":
                self.stack.append([self.last_pt_stats[0], ↩
                    self.last_pt_stats[1], ↩
                    copy.deepcopy(self.heading), ↩
                    copy.deepcopy(self.lcs)])
```

```
            spline_data = ↩
                self.curve_obj.data.splines.new( ↩
                    type='POLY')
            spline_data.points[-1].co = last_spline_pt.co
            self.last_pt_stats = ↩
                [len(self.curve_obj.data.splines)-1, 0]
        elif c == "]":
            if len(self.stack) > 0:
                self.prev_popped_pt = self.stack.pop()
                self.prev_step_popped = True
        elif c == "F":
            self.one_step_forward(True, last_spline_pt)
        elif c == "f":
            self.one_step_forward(False, last_spline_pt)
    # ---- SNIPPED ----
```

Next, we'll modify the one_step_forward method in Listing 7-10 so it takes the last_spline_pt we've already derived in Listing 7-9 as an additional argument. In the case where the turtle moves and draws one step, we make one_step_forward use self.last_pt_stats[0] as spline index to look up spline data and update the point index self.last_pt_stats[1] to the end of the spline points list at len(spline_data.points) - 1.

In the case where the turtle moves but does not draw, a new spline is created with the turtle's location postmovement as its first point. Therefore, we update self.last_pt_stats[0] with the spline index len(self.curve_obj.data.splines)-1, which is the index of the last spline at (number of splines minus 1), since new splines are always added to the end of the list. The point index self.last_pt_stats[1] is set to 0.

Listing 7-10. Modify the one_step_forward method of turtle_2D to give it the ability to handle L-Systems with branching (see /Ch7/L_Systems.py)

```
class turtle_2D:
    # ---- SNIPPED ----
    def one_step_forward(self, should_draw: bool, ↩
        last_spline_pt):
        start_pt = Vector((last_spline_pt.co[0], ↩
            last_spline_pt.co[1], last_spline_pt.co[2]))
```

```
if should_draw:
    spline_data = self.curve_obj.data.splines[ ↩
        self.last_pt_stats[0]]
    trans_vec = self.heading * self.step_dist
    end_pt = start_pt + trans_vec
    spline_data.points.add(1)
    spline_data.points[-1].co = [end_pt[0], ↩
        end_pt[1], end_pt[2], 0]
    self.last_pt_stats[1] = len(spline_data.points)-1
else:
    spline_data = self.curve_obj.data.splines.new( ↩
        type='POLY')
    trans_vec = self.heading * self.step_dist
    end_pt = start_pt + trans_vec
    spline_data.points[-1].co = [end_pt[0], ↩
        end_pt[1], end_pt[2], 0]
    self.last_pt_stats = [ ↩
        len(self.curve_obj.data.splines)-1, 0]
```

Generating 2D Branching Tree Variations

With the branching ability implemented for the turtle, in this section, we'll work through a few additional examples of L-Systems that generate 2D trees. One of the best ways to learn how to translate your own designs into L-System definitions is to experiment by changing an existing L-System in different ways and see what effect each modification has on the generated model. We'll start by modifying the branching L-System example from the previous section, which is reproduced in Listing 7-11. To generate this tree, you can create an instance of the modified turtle_2D class from Listings 7-8, 7-9, and 7-10 (or turtle_2D_branching in the downloaded source), then call the instance's `draw()` method with 22.5 degrees turn angles and 7 iterations. The results of calling Listing 7-11 are shown in Figure 7-10.

Listing 7-11. Generating the branching tree example with 22.5 degrees turn angles and 7 iterations (see the function trees_2D_variations() in /Ch7/L_Systems.py)

```
turtle_axiom_2d_tree1 = "X"
turtle_rewriting_rules_2d_tree1={"X":"F[+X][-X]FX", "F":"FF"}

theta_22_5 = [22.5, 22.5, 22.5]
t_2D_tree1_7iters = turtle_2D_branching( ↩
    bpy.context, turtle_axiom_2d_tree1, ↩
    turtle_rewriting_rules_2d_tree1, 7, ↩
    theta_22_5, 1, "2D_Tree1_7iters", Vector((0, 100, 0)))
t_2D_tree1_7iters.draw()
```

Figure 7-10. *The original branching tree example* `turtle_axiom_2d_tree1` *with the axiom* `"X"` *and rewriting rules* `{"X": "F[+X][-X]FX", "F": "FF"}` *generated with 22.5 degrees turn angles and 7 iterations. The L-System definition is from page 25 of the book The Algorithmic Beauty of Plants by Przemyslaw Prusinkiewicz and Aristid Lindenmayer.*

Since the [+X] and [-X] create branches to the left and right, respectively, we can think of the F's as the "main" (nonside shooting) branches and the second rewriting rule "F": "FF" as scaling these branches twice as long each iteration. Intuitively, if we change the rule so the lengthening ratio is 3 instead of 2, we'll expect the tree to get taller, with the side branches more spread out. Let's see if this is the case. We'll create a new L-System with the rule "F": "FFF" instead of "F": "FF" and generate this tree using the branching version of turtle_2D (or turtle_2D_branching in the downloaded source), again with 22.5 degrees turn angles and 7 iterations, as shown in listing 7-12, and see if the outcome matches our intuition.

Listing 7-12. Generating the longer-forward segments variation of the branching tree with 22.5 degrees turn angles and 7 iterations (see the function trees_2D_variations() in /Ch7/L_Systems.py)

```
turtle_axiom_2d_tree1_3Fs = "X"
turtle_rewriting_rules_2d_tree1_3Fs = ↩
    {"X": "F[+X][-X]FX", "F": "FFF"}

t_2D_tree1_3Fs_7iters = turtle_2D_branching(
    bpy.context, turtle_axiom_2d_tree1_3Fs, ↩
    turtle_rewriting_rules_2d_tree1_3Fs, 7, ↩
    theta_22_5, 1, "2D_Tree1_3Fs_7iters", ↩
    Vector((-700, 100, 0)))
t_2D_tree1_3Fs_7iters.draw()
```

The call generates the tree shown on the right of Figure 7-11, which indeed is taller and has more spread-out branches than the original, as we expected.

Tip Generate the variations of an L-System (e.g., with rewriting rules modified) with the same turning angles, step distance, and number of iterations as the original, so it is easier to see the effects the modifications have on the generated models.

Figure 7-11. *Left: the original branching tree example* `turtle_rewriting_rules_2d_tree1`*. Right: the modified version* `turtle_rewriting_rules_2d_tree1_3Fs` *with the rewriting rule* `"F": "FF"` *replaced by* `"F": "FFF"`

Next, we'll see how we can influence the branching pattern. As we've learned so far, movement enclosed by square brackets creates branching. Let's see if we can make the tree branch toward the left more. We'll make each left branch grow another left branch from its tip, by changing the successor of the first rewriting rule from "F**[+X]**[-X]FX" to "F**[+X+X]**[-X]FX". Since we added more branching, in addition to the left leaning, we also expect the tree to look fuller. Let's see if this is the case, by generating this tree using the branching version of `turtle_2D` (or `turtle_2D_branching` in the downloaded source), with 22.5 degrees turn angles and 7 iterations, as shown in Listing 7-13, which produces the tree on the right of Figure 7-12. Compared side by side with the original, you can see that this tree has a lot more branches, and the additional branches lean toward the left, as we anticipated.

Listing 7-13. Generating the longer left branches variation of the branching tree with 22.5 degrees turn angles and 7 iterations (see the function trees_2D_variations() in /Ch7/L_Systems.py)

```
turtle_axiom_2d_tree1_longer_L_branches = "X"
turtle_rewriting_rules_2d_tree1_longer_L_branches = { ↩
    "X": "F[+X+X][-X]FX", "F": "FF"}

t_2D_tree1_longer_L_branches_7iters = turtle_2D_branching( ↩
    bpy.context, turtle_axiom_2d_tree1_longer_L_branches, ↩
    turtle_rewriting_rules_2d_tree1_longer_L_branches, 7, ↩
    theta_22_5, 1, "2D_Tree1_longer_L_branches", ↩
    Vector((-250, 100, 0)))

t_2D_tree1_longer_L_branches_7iters.draw()
```

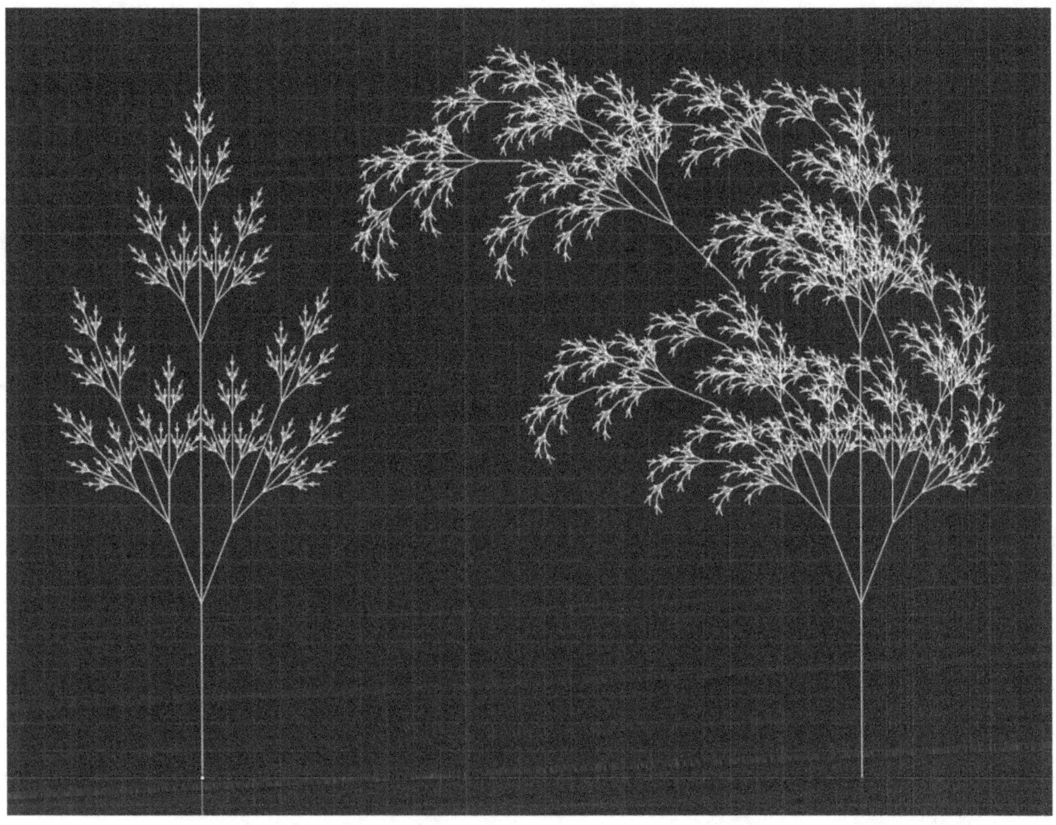

***Figure 7-12.** Left: the original branching tree example* `turtle_rewriting_rules_2d_tree1`*. Right: the modified version* `turtle_rewriting_rules_2d_tree1_longer_L_branches` *with the rewriting rule* `"X": "F[+X][-X]FX"` *replaced by* `"X": "F[+X+X][-X]FX"`

What if we want additional branches, but don't want the branches to bend one way or another? In that case, we add a branch between two branches, rather than have it grow from the tip of another branch. To accomplish this, we insert a movement enclosed by square brackets at the same level as other brackets, as opposed to adding it inside an existing pair of brackets. For example, we can change the successor of the first rewriting rule from `"F[+X][-X]FX"` to `"F[+X][-X]`**`[--X]`**`FX"`, adding the `[--X]` after `[-X]`. After `[-X]` grows a right branch, `[--X]` will grow another branch that's an additional right turn relative to it. As we've also added more branching with this modification, we expect the tree to be fuller. Let's generate the tree, using the branching version of `turtle_2D` (or `turtle_2D_branching` in the downloaded source), with 22.5 degrees turn angles and 7 iterations, as shown in Listing 7-14.

Listing 7-14. Generating the variation of the branching tree with additional right-pointing branches with 22.5 degrees turn angles and 7 iterations (see the function trees_2D_variations() in /Ch7/L_Systems.py)

```
turtle_axiom_2d_tree1_multi_R_branches = "X"
turtle_rewriting_rules_2d_tree1_multi_R_branches = ↩
    {"X": "F[+X][-X][--X]FX", "F": "FF"}

t_2D_tree1_multi_R_branches_7iters = turtle_2D_branching( ↩
    bpy.context, turtle_axiom_2d_tree1_multi_R_branches, ↩
    turtle_rewriting_rules_2d_tree1_multi_R_branches, 7, ↩
    theta_22_5, 1, "2D_Tree1_multi_R_branches", ↩
    Vector((-400, 100, 0)))
t_2D_tree1_multi_R_branches_7iters.draw()
```

The tree generated from Listing 7-14 is shown on the right of Figure 7-13, which is fuller than the original, with the added branches pointing to the right. Comparing the two tree variations in Figures 7-12 and 7-13, the tree in Figure 7-12 appears not only left leaning but also drooping, vs. the tree in Figure 7-13, which grows toward the right but with its branches looking straight.

Figure 7-13. *Left: the original branching tree example `turtle_rewriting_rules_2d_tree1`. Right: the modified version `turtle_axiom_2d_tree1_multi_R_branches` with the rewriting rule `"X": "F[+X][-X]FX"` replaced by `"X": "F[+X][-X][--X]FX"`*

Next, we'll experiment with nesting square brackets. When you nest square brackets, you grow branches with the inner pairs of brackets, then go back to where you started. You can imagine this would produce a flatter structure in general, with more branches side by side than tip to tip. Let's try this by modifying the previous L-System, by enclosing the portion of the first rewriting rule's successor before FX with square brackets, as shown in Listing 7-15. With "F[+X][-X][--X]FX", you grow the FX from the *tip* of the F at the beginning of the string, vs. with "[F[+X][-X][--X]]FX", you grow the FX from the *root* of that F. Therefore, you can imagine the structure generated with "[F[+X][-X][--X]]FX" will be flatter and shorter.

Let's generate this tree with nested brackets using the branching version of `turtle_2D` (or `turtle_2D_branching` in the downloaded source), with 22.5 degrees turn angles and 7 iterations as shown in Listing 7-15 to confirm our suspicion.

Listing 7-15. Generating the variation of the branching tree where the branching pattern is nested, with 22.5 degrees turn angles and 7 iterations (see the function trees_2D_variations() in /Ch7/L_Systems.py)

```
turtle_axiom_2d_tree1_nested_R_branches = "X"
turtle_rewriting_rules_2d_tree1_nested_R_branches = ↩
    {"X": "[F[+X][-X][--X]]FX", "F": "FF"}

t_2D_tree1_nested_R_branches_7iters = turtle_2D_branching( ↩
    bpy.context, turtle_axiom_2d_tree1_nested_R_branches, ↩
    turtle_rewriting_rules_2d_tree1_nested_R_branches, 7, ↩
    theta_22_5, 1, "2D_Tree1_nested_R_branches", ↩
    Vector((-550, 100, 0)))

t_2D_tree1_nested_R_branches_7iters.draw()
```

The tree generated by calling Listing 7-15 is shown on the right of Figure 7-14. You can see that the tree plateaus after reaching a certain height and develops branches that accumulate laterally, almost like a part of a dandelion seed head.

***Figure 7-14.** Left: the original branching tree example* `turtle_rewriting_rules_2d_tree1`*. Right: the modified version* `turtle_rewriting_rules_2d_tree1_nested_R_branches` *with the rewriting rule* `"X": "F[+X][-X][--X]FX"` *replaced by* `"X": "[F[+X][-X][--X]]FX"`

I've collaged the original branching tree example `turtle_rewriting_rules_2d_tree1` with the three variations we've derived throughout this section in Figure 7-15 so you can compare them side by side, which are the left leaning tree (`turtle_rewriting_rules_2d_tree1_longer_L_branches`), the tree with additional right-pointing straight branches (`turtle_rewriting_rules_2d_tree1_multi_R_branches`), and the "dandelion" tree (`turtle_rewriting_rules_2d_tree1_nested_R_branches`).

You can see that the three variations are wildly different in terms of height and branching patterns, even though they all stem from the same L-System with minor modifications to its rewriting rules.

Figure 7-15. *The original branching tree example with three of its variations, each generated with 22.5 turn angles and 7 iterations by calling the modified* `turtle_2D` *with branching ability (or* `turtle_2D_branching` *in the downloaded source). From left to right:* `turtle_rewriting_rules_2d_tree1`*,* `turtle_rewriting_rules_2d_tree1_longer_L_branches`*,* `turtle_rewriting_rules_2d_tree1_multi_R_branches`*, and* `turtle_rewriting_rules_2d_tree1_nested_R_branches`

Note The sample code in this section (Listings 7-11, 7-12, 7-13, 7-14, and 7-15) are collected into one function named `trees_2D_variations()` in the script file `/Ch7/L_Systems.py` in the downloaded source.

3D Turtle Interpretation of L-Systems in Blender Python

Now that you're well versed in generating 2D trees with L-Systems, we'll kick it up a dimension and go 3D. In this section, we'll continue to build on our turtle implementation and add support to handle rewriting L-Systems encoding symbols representing 3D rotations and movements, as well as generating 3D meshes from their expansions.

Adding Symbols to the Alphabet for Pitching, Rolling, and Turning Around

So far, our turtle sets off with an initial heading of `Vector((0.0, 0.0, 1.0))` (the global +Z unit vector) and turns either left or right relative to its current heading by rotating around its local Y axis. As a result, the turtle generates 2D curves on a plane parallel to the XZ plane, with the curves' Z offset dependent upon the initial position for the turtle specified by the user.

To enable the turtle to move in 3D, we will add five symbols to our alphabet: & to pitch down, ^ to pitch up, \\ to roll left, / to roll right, and | to turn around, as shown in Listing 7-16. Here, the turtle class is renamed to `turtle_3D`, with everything inside the `draw` method that is identical to the 2D implementation marked as `# ---- SNIPPED ----`.

Since the turtle rotates around local Y to turn left or right (with + or –), it will rotate around local X to pitch down or up (with & or ^) and rotate around local Z to roll left or right (with \\ or /). Since turning around is just turning left or right 180 degrees, the turtle will rotate around Y to turn around (with |) just as it will with + or –. Notice that the symbol for rolling left is encoded as double backslashes because the first backslash serves as an escape character.

Listing 7-16. Adding the ability for the turtle to traverse in 3D (see /Ch7/L_Systems.py)

```
class turtle_3D:
    # ---- SNIPPED ----
    def draw(self):
        for c in self.cur_str:
            # ---- SNIPPED ----
            if c == "[":
                # ---- SNIPPED ----
            elif c == "]":
                # ---- SNIPPED ----
            elif c == "F":
                # ---- SNIPPED ----
            elif c == "f":
                # ---- SNIPPED ----
```

```
elif c == "+":
    # ---- SNIPPED ----
elif c == "-":
    # ---- SNIPPED ----
elif c == "&":
    mat_rot = Matrix.Rotation( ↩
        radians(self.theta[0]), 3, 'X')
    self.lcs.rotate(mat_rot)
    self.heading = self.lcs[2]
    self.heading.normalize()
elif c == "^":
    mat_rot = Matrix.Rotation( ↩
        radians(-self.theta[0]), 3, 'X')
    self.lcs.rotate(mat_rot)
    self.heading = self.lcs[2]
    self.heading.normalize()
elif c == "\\":
    mat_rot = Matrix.Rotation( ↩
        radians(-self.theta[2]), 3, 'Z')
    self.lcs.rotate(mat_rot)
    self.heading = self.lcs[2]
    self.heading.normalize()
elif c == "/":
    mat_rot = Matrix.Rotation( ↩
        radians(self.theta[2]), 3, 'Z')
    self.lcs.rotate(mat_rot)
    self.heading = self.lcs[2]
    self.heading.normalize()
elif c == "|":
    mat_rot = Matrix.Rotation( ↩
        radians(180), 3, 'Y')
    self.lcs.rotate(mat_rot)
    self.heading = self.lcs[2]
    self.heading.normalize()
```

Converting from Curve to Mesh

Recall that we've already added the ability for the turtle to skip (move without drawing) and branch in 2D. The good news is the same implementation will also work in 3D; therefore, we can reuse the turtle class' `__init__` and `one_step_forward` methods as they are.

Up to this point, the turtle has been generating curve objects in Blender, which is not super exciting. In Listing 7-17, we'll implement the method `pipe` for the `turtle_3D` class in which the turtle converts the curve object to a mesh and uses modifiers to refine it.

Listing 7-17. Convert the turtle-generated curve to mesh and add modifiers (see /Ch7/L_Systems.py)

```
class turtle_3D:
    # ---- SNIPPED ----
    def pipe(self, context, subsurf_level=1, ↩
        solidify_thickness=1, apply_modifiers=True):
        for obj in context.view_layer.objects:
            obj.select_set(False)
        context.view_layer.objects.active = self.curve_obj
        self.curve_obj.select_set(True)

        context_override = get_context_override(context, ↩
            'VIEW_3D', 'WINDOW')
        with bpy.context.temp_override(**context_override):
            bpy.ops.object.mode_set(mode='OBJECT')

        context_override = get_context_override(context, ↩
            'VIEW_3D', 'WINDOW')
        with bpy.context.temp_override(**context_override):
            bpy.ops.object.convert(target='MESH')

        context_override = get_context_override(context, ↩
            'VIEW_3D', 'WINDOW')
        with bpy.context.temp_override(**context_override):
            bpy.ops.object.mode_set(mode='EDIT')

        context_override = get_context_override(context, ↩
            'VIEW_3D', 'WINDOW')
```

```
with bpy.context.temp_override(**context_override):
    bpy.ops.mesh.select_all(action='SELECT')
    bpy.ops.mesh.remove_doubles()
    bpy.ops.mesh.normals_make_consistent( ↩
        inside=False

self.mesh_obj = context.view_layer.objects[ ↩
    self.curve_obj.name]
context_override = get_context_override(context, ↩
    'VIEW_3D', 'WINDOW')
with bpy.context.temp_override(**context_override):
    skin_mod = self.mesh_obj.modifiers.new( ↩
        "skin_mod", 'SKIN')
    skin_mod.branch_smoothing = 1

    solidify_mod = self.mesh_obj.modifiers.new( ↩
        "solidify_mod", 'SOLIDIFY')
    solidify_mod.offset = 0
    solidify_mod.thickness = solidify_thickness

    weld_mod = self.mesh_obj.modifiers.new( ↩
        "weld_mod", 'WELD')

    subsurf_mod = self.mesh_obj.modifiers.new( ↩
        "subsurf_mod", 'SUBSURF')
    subsurf_mod.levels = subsurf_level
    subsurf_mod.render_levels = subsurf_level
    subsurf_mod.subdivision_type = 'CATMULL_CLARK'
context_override = get_context_override(context, ↩
    'VIEW_3D', 'WINDOW')
with bpy.context.temp_override(**context_override):
    bpy.ops.object.mode_set(mode='OBJECT')

if apply_modifiers:
    context_override = get_context_override( ↩
         context, 'VIEW_3D', 'WINDOW')
    with bpy.context.temp_override( ↩
        **context_override):
```

```
            bpy.ops.object.modifier_apply( ↩
                modifier=skin_mod.name)
            bpy.ops.object.modifier_apply( ↩
                modifier=solidify_mod.name)
            bpy.ops.object.modifier_apply( ↩
                modifier=weld_mod.name)
            bpy.ops.object.modifier_apply( ↩
                modifier=subsurf_mod.name)
    context_override = get_context_override(context, ↩
        'VIEW_3D', 'WINDOW')
    with bpy.context.temp_override(**context_override):
        bpy.ops.object.transform_apply(location=True, ↩
            rotation=True, scale=False)
        bpy.ops.object.origin_set( ↩
            type='ORIGIN_GEOMETRY', ↩
            center='MEDIAN')
```

The pipe method takes the current context, the number of levels for the Subsurf modifier (subsurf_level), the thickness for the Solidify modifier (solidify_thickness), and a bool for controlling whether the modifiers should be applied (apply_modifiers).

To begin, we set the curve object as the active object and select it. We then switch it to Object mode with a context override as if from the viewport, and with another context override, call bpy.ops.object.convert(target='MESH') to convert it to a mesh (Right-click ➤ Convert To ➤ Mesh). The reason we used separate context overrides for the two operator calls is because the context for the bpy.ops.object.convert call must be made from a viewport context already in Object mode; therefore, we create a new override after the mode switch is complete.

Next, we switch the mesh to Edit mode with a context override (viewport), and after which, with another override (viewport), we select all, remove doubles, and recalculate outside normals (Mesh ➤ Normals (Alt N) ➤ Recalculate Outside (Shift N)) with bpy.ops.mesh operators. Again, here we create a new override after the mode switch to Edit is complete, since bpy.ops.mesh operators require the viewport context to be already in Edit mode.

Blender gives the converted mesh object the same name as the curve object. Therefore, we can retrieve a reference to the mesh object using self.curve_obj.name and store the reference in self.mesh_obj to refer to later.

Even though we have a mesh now, it is still a stick figure with only vertices and edges. With a context override (as if from the viewport), we add a Skin modifier by calling `self.mesh_obj.modifiers.new` with type `'SKIN'` and set its Branch Smoothing value to 1.000 (`skin_mod.branch_smoothing = 1`) to create a solid shape (Properties Editor ➤ Modifier tab ➤ Add Modifier ➤ Generate ➤ Skin). To give the mesh additional thickness, we add a Solidify modifier by calling `self.mesh_obj.modifiers.new` with type `'SOLIDIFY'` and set its Offset to 0 and Thickness to the passed-in `solidify_thickness` value (Properties Editor ➤ Modifier tab ➤ Add Modifier ➤ Generate ➤ Solidify). To close up small gaps or holes formed by the previous modifiers, we add a Weld modifier by calling `self.mesh_obj.modifiers.new` with type `'WELD'` and leave its settings at default (Properties Editor ➤ Modifier tab ➤ Add Modifier ➤ Generate ➤ Weld). Finally, for additional smoothing, we add a Subdivision Surface modifier by calling `self.mesh_obj.modifiers.new` with type `'SUBSURF'`, set both its Levels Viewport and Render to the passed-in `subsurf_level` value via `subsurf_mod.levels` and `subsurf_mod.render_levels`, and click the Catmull-Clark button (`subsurf_mod.subdivision_type = 'CATMULL_CLARK'`).

After the modifiers are set up, we switch the mesh object to Object mode with a context override (viewport); then if the argument `apply_modifiers` is `True`, we use another override (viewport) to apply the four modifiers we created earlier, one by one, in the order they are created, by calling `bpy.ops.object.modifier_apply` with each modifier's name, which is equivalent to clicking the blue downward arrow on the upper right corner of each modifier and Apply (Properties Editor ➤ Modifier tab ➤ Apply (Ctrl A)), as shown in Figure 7-16.

Lastly, with a context override (viewport), we apply both the mesh object's Location and Rotation transforms by calling `bpy.ops.object.transform_apply` (viewport Ctrl A ➤ Location, and Ctrl A ➤ Rotation) and set its origin to geometry via `bpy.ops.object.origin_set` with `type='ORIGIN_GEOMETRY'` (Object ➤ Set Origin ➤ Origin to Geometry).

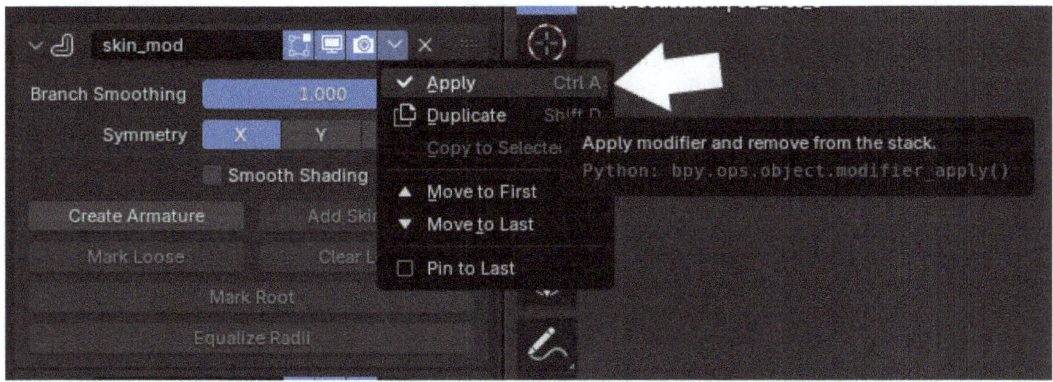

Figure 7-16. *Applying a modifier by clicking on the blue downward arrow at the upper right corner ➤ Apply under the modifier's entry, under the Properties Editor ➤ Modifier tab.*

Generating a 3D Tree

With the `turtle_3D` class implemented, we'll write a `test_3D_tree()` function as shown in Listing 7-18 to define an L-System for a 3D tree and create a `turtle_3D` instance to generate it, with 22.5 degrees turn angles, step distance of 10, for 3 iterations.

Listing 7-18. Test 3D tree generation (see /Ch7/L_Systems.py)

```
def test_3D_tree():
    turtle_axiom_3d_tree = "F"
    turtle_rewriting_rules_3d_tree = { ↩
        "F": "F[-&\F][\++&F][/--^F]||F[--&/F][++^\F][+&F]"}

    t_3D_tree = turtle_3D(bpy.context, ↩
        turtle_axiom_3d_tree, ↩
        turtle_rewriting_rules_3d_tree, 3, theta_22_5, ↩
        10, "3D_Tree_3", Vector((-100, 200, 0)))
    t_3D_tree.draw()
    t_3D_tree.pipe(bpy.context, subsurf_level=1, ↩
        solidify_thickness=2, apply_modifiers=False)
```

To generate the 3D tree mesh, we'll first call the `draw` method on the `turtle_3D` instance to generate the curve object, followed by the `pipe` method to convert the curve to a mesh object, add modifiers, and apply transforms. In this example, we add a Subsurf modifier with 1 level for both preview and render and a Solidify modifier with 2m thickness. The result of running Listing 7-18 is shown in Figure 7-17.

Figure 7-17. *3D L-System tree mesh generated by running Listing 7-18*

Extending Your L-System

In this section, we'll discuss a few ways that you could extend your `turtle_3D` implementation to produce richer and more varied structures.

Sample Parameter Values from Ranges

One of the simplest ways to increase the variations your turtle can generate is to sample ranges of values for the step distance and turn angles instead of using fixed numbers. For example, you can modify the turtle_3D class' __init__ method to expect a List type for both theta and step_dist, like this:

```
class turtle_3D_sample_ranges:
    def __init__(self, context, axiom: str, ↩
        rewriting_rules: dict, num_iters: int, ↩
        theta: List, step_dist: List, ↩
        curve_obj_name: str, origin: Vector):
```

We'll set up theta so it encodes a minimum and maximum turn angle around each of the three axes, like this:

```
[[<min_angle_X>, <max_angle_X>], [<min_angle_Y>, ↩
    <max_angle_Y>], [<min_angle_Z>, <max_angle_Z>]]
```

For example, a theta value of [[30, 60], [20, 40], [50, 70]] specifies a turn angle between 30 and 60 degrees around the X axis (for pitching down with & or up with ^).

The step_dist is encoded in a similar manner, as a list of two numbers, indicating the minimum and maximum values for each F or f. For example, a step_dist value of [10, 30] will move the turtle between a distance of 10 and 30 Blender units for each step.

We'll import the uniform method from Python's random module, which, when given a range specified by two floating point numbers, returns a value between the two, inclusive of the minimum and maximum:

```
from random import uniform
```

In the draw method, instead of using a fixed angle, you'll call uniform to sample between the min and max angles for an axis to construct the rotation matrix. For example, for + (turning left), which is a rotation around the local Y axis, you'll call uniform with the list of two values at self.theta[1], like this:

```
elif c == "+":
    angle_deg = uniform(self.theta[1][0], self.theta[1][1])
    mat_rot = Matrix.Rotation(radians(-angle_deg), 3, 'Y')
```

You'll also sample from `self.theta[1]` for – (turning right) and | (turning around), which are also rotations around the local Y axis. The turtle rotates around the local X axis for & and ^ (pitching down and up); therefore, you'll sample from `self.theta[0]`. The turtle rotates around local Z for \\ (roll left) and / (roll right) so you'll sample from `self.theta[2]`.

In the `one_step_forward` method, you'll also call `uniform` to sample from the list of two `self.step_dist` values in the calculation of the step displacement vector, like this:

```
trans_vec = self.heading * uniform(self.step_dist[0], ↩
    self.step_dist[1])
```

With these simple modifications, you can now use the same L-System definition to generate different trees for the same number of iterations. Listing 7-19 shows two examples of using our modified turtle class from this section and the 3D L-System tree definition from Listing 7-18 in combination with different ranges of `theta` and `step_dist` values for the same number of iterations (3). The results are shown in the center and right of Figure 7-18, respectively, with the center sampling from `theta_ranges_1` and `dist_range_1` and the right sampling from `theta_ranges_2` and `dist_range_2`. Compared to the original tree (shown on the left in Figure 7-18), you can see that the variations produced using ranges of `theta` and `step_dist` values are quite different.

Listing 7-19. Create tree variations by sampling from ranges of theta and step_dist values (see /Ch7/L_Systems.py)

```
def test_3D_tree_sample_range():
    turtle_axiom_3d_tree = "F"
    turtle_rewriting_rules_3d_tree = { ↩
        "F": "F[-&\F][\++&F][/--^F]||F[--&/F][++^\F][+&F]"}

    theta_ranges_1 = [[30, 60], [20, 40], [30, 60]]
    dist_range_1 = [10, 30]
    t_3D_tree_1 = turtle_3D_sample_ranges(bpy.context, ↩
        turtle_axiom_3d_tree, ↩
        turtle_rewriting_rules_3d_tree, 3, ↩
        theta_ranges_1, dist_range_1, ↩
        "3D_Tree_3_sample_ranges_1", ↩
        Vector((-300, 200, 0)))
```

```
t_3D_tree_1.draw()
t_3D_tree_1.pipe(bpy.context, subsurf_level=1, ↩
    solidify_thickness=2, apply_modifiers=False)

theta_ranges_2 = [[15, 45], [20, 40], [15, 45]]
dist_range_2 = [5, 25]
t_3D_tree_2 = turtle_3D_sample_ranges(bpy.context, ↩
    turtle_axiom_3d_tree, ↩
    turtle_rewriting_rules_3d_tree, 3, ↩
    theta_ranges_2, dist_range_2, ↩
    "3D_Tree_3_sample_ranges_2", ↩
    Vector((-500, 200, 0)))
t_3D_tree_2.draw()
t_3D_tree_2.pipe(bpy.context, subsurf_level=1, ↩
    solidify_thickness=2, apply_modifiers=False)
```

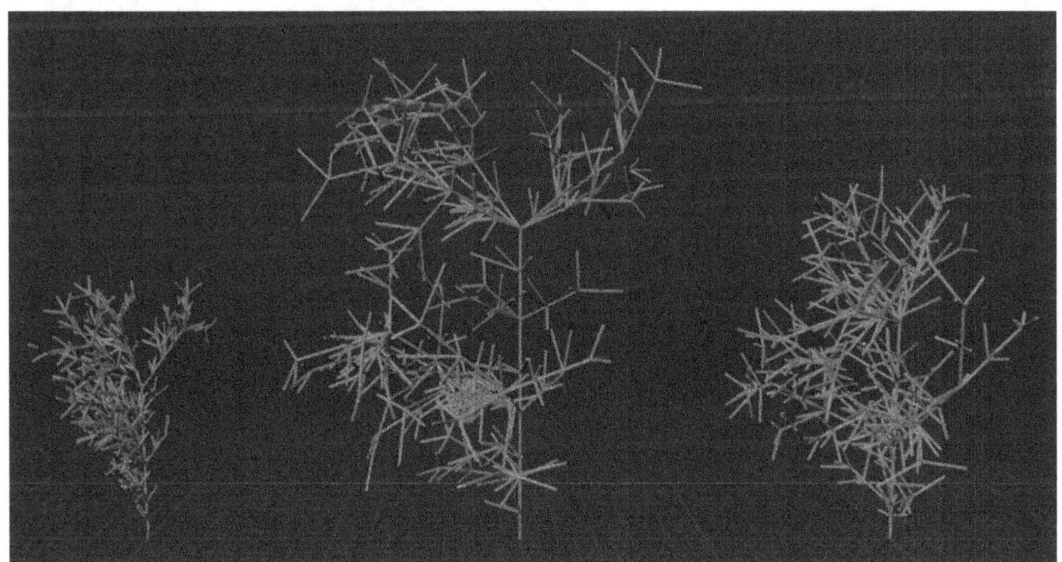

Figure 7-18. *Different trees generated from the same L-System for the same number of iterations, by sampling from different ranges of `theta` and `step_dist`. Left is the original 3D tree produced by Listing 7-18, and the center and right are variations based on the same L-System produced by Listing 7-19 (the center samples from `theta_ranges_1` and `dist_range_1`, whereas the right samples from `theta_ranges_2` and `dist_range_2`).*

Selectively Firing Rules Based on Conditions

Another way to create more variations with your L-System is to define multiple rules with the same predecessor, each with a different condition for being selected. For example, you might define different branching rules to simulate growth stages of a tree, such that initially it strives for height (by moving forward with F along the main trunk and main branches), but once it gets tall enough, it focuses on developing foliage (by rewriting with many lateral branches with nested brackets with F and turns).

Placing Prefab Mesh Parts

An L-System turtle need not always generate all parts of a mesh from scratch, you can very well combine generated meshes with prefab mesh parts and incorporate logic of how and where these parts are attached in the rewriting rules themselves. For example, you can hand model a library of leaf meshes (or generate them ahead of time from a separate PCG system and store them), then introduce a new symbol for each leaf model to your L-System, and use it wherever you want an instance of that leaf placed.

To create more variations, you can employ parameter sampling (dice rolling) that we've discussed earlier to decide whether to place a leaf. Depending on how you've defined the rule, this could mean whether the turtle chooses to interpret the leaf symbol when it encounters one, or if the rule gets selected during rewriting.

You could also modify your L-System interpreter such that prefab parts are only placed if certain conditions are met. For example, you might create a set of leaf meshes for different maturity levels of a tree. Before the tree reaches a certain height or number of branches, the turtle will choose the young leaf mesh to place, then once the tree gets old enough, an old leaf mesh. A similar strategy could be used to simulate flowering stages. For example, you could have a series of hand-modeled flower meshes, like green bud, developed bud, partially open flower, fully open flower, flowering starting to wilt, and wilted flower. You could then establish conditions on when to choose each. The various prefab flowers could mix once the tree reaches blooming season, so simultaneously there are some buds coming, some flowers about to blossom, some open, and some that have wilted and turned into prefab fruit. Such an effect will make the tree look more realistic since in nature flowers are not perfectly synchronized.

Summary

In this chapter, you learned how to use L-Systems to represent self-repeating structures and wrote your own turtle-style interpreter in Blender Python to generate curves and meshes. We started with an overview of L-Systems, which are grammar-based objects each consisting of a starting string called the *axiom* accompanied by a set of *rewriting rules* that tell how to substitute a given character (the *predecessor*) with a new substring (the *successor*). Starting with the axiom, in each iteration, we apply any applicable rewriting rule by simultaneously replacing all characters in the current string that match the predecessor of the rule. The nature of simultaneous rewriting lends L-Systems well to represent self-repeating structures, such as fractals and trees. We worked through a concrete example of rewriting the Koch curve on pen and paper (a well-known fractal resembling a snowflake) before translating the procedure into Python.

The second part of the chapter took you through implementing a turtle-graphic style L-System interpreter in Blender Python to generate 2D curves, starting with the simplest alphabet which allowed the turtle to move forward one step and turn left or right. We gradually built on this system and added abilities for the turtle to skip (move without drawing) and branch, which enabled us to generate complex 2D trees.

Starting with an existing L-System tree definition from the book *The Algorithmic Beauty of Plants* by Przemyslaw Prusinkiewicz and Aristid Lindenmayer, we systemically experimented with modifying rewriting rules in different ways to create categories of tree variations, such as using brackets enclosing movements to create left leaning foliage, or nested pairs of brackets to create a dandelion bulb-like structure.

In the final part of the chapter, we extended the 2D turtle implementation to 3D, by adding support for the turtle to roll, pitch, and turn around. We then wrote code to convert the Blender curve objects to meshes and added modifiers to create volume and refine the mashes' silhouettes. Last but not least, we discussed several ideas of how to extend the turtle implementation to create more variations, such as sampling parameter values like step distance and turn angles from given ranges. We also discussed using conditions to select among rewriting rules with the same predecessor, to simulate different branching patterns at different growth stages of a tree's life. Instead of generating meshes entirely from scratch, you could employ a library of hand-modeled leaf or flower meshes and indicate where to place these meshes on generated branches in the rewriting rules.

CHAPTER 8

GIS-Based Generation Part 1: Skylines from Building Footprint Data

In the next two chapters, we'll venture into the side of PCG where we generate meshes from real-world Geographic Information System (GIS) data. In this chapter, we'll write a Blender Python script that generates city meshes from building footprint data (a form of GIS data). We'll start with an introduction to what building footprint is, what a dataset consists of, and how we can inspect and plot its contents to gain insight. After that, we'll go over where and how to source building footprint data and how to edit them in the open source GIS software QGIS to convert them into the formats we can work with in Blender Python. Once we're familiar with the composition and limitation of building footprints, we'll formulate a design for a generator and start implementing it in Python. Using a top-down approach, we'll compose a series of functions, each doing a unit of work at a finer granularity than the last. Finally, we'll test the generator with two provided building footprint datasets and produce skyline meshes of Battery Park, NYC, and Havana, Cuba.

Running This Chapter's Examples

The skyline generator we'll implement in this chapter utilizes several third-party open source Python packages to read and plot GIS data. In this section, we'll go over how to set them up under Blender Python.

I. Lupiani, *Procedural Content Generation for Games*, https://doi.org/10.1007/979-8-8688-1787-8_8

Installing Dependencies

As we'll see shortly, the input GIS data for the skyline generator comprises a shapefile (`*.shp`) with polygons that outline building footprints and a spreadsheet (`*.xlsx`) containing corresponding roof heights. We will use `pip` to install the open source Python packages `pyshp` for parsing shapefiles, `pandas` for reading spreadsheets, and `matplotlib` for plotting shapes, so we can anticipate what the buildings will look like before implementing the generator. Before proceeding, please refer to the Appendix for instructions on how to install these packages under Blender Python.

Downloading and Running the Sample Code

The source code and color figures for this book are available on GitHub, located at `https://link.springer.com/book/9798868817861`. Download the code, navigate to the `/Ch8` folder, and open `skyline_generator.py` in the Text Editor under the Scripting workspace. Scroll to the bottom of the script, where you'll find an `if __name__ == "__main__"` block already set up with calls to the generator. Clicking the Run button at the top of the Text Editor will generate two skyline meshes, Battery Park in New York City and Havana in Cuba. Each city's building footprints come in a pair of two files, a `*.shp` file and a `*.xlsx` file. In addition to the `*.shp` and `*.xlsx` files, the generator takes a handful of other arguments, which will be explained in detail throughout the chapter. You can experiment by changing the values of these arguments.

Introduction to Building Footprint Data

Building footprint is a type of GIS (Geographic Information System) data that describes the shape and dimension of buildings. In this section, we'll discuss what to expect from a building footprint dataset and how to inspect its contents using the Python libraries `pyshp` and `matplotlib` with the provided Battery Park dataset as an example. After you are comfortable with the sample files, we'll go over how to download your own datasets and edit them in the open source GIS software QGIS to convert them to suitable formats for generating meshes in Blender Python.

Composition of Building Footprint Data

A building footprint dataset contains descriptions of buildings over a municipal area like a county or a city. When you download a dataset, it is usually in the `*.csv` format, which you open in GIS software such as QGIS to isolate an area of interest like a neighborhood to export out as a shapefile (`*.shp`) containing curves outlining the building cross-sections and a spreadsheet (`*.xlsx`) with corresponding building heights, ground elevation, etc. These two files are what we'll use to generate building meshes. In the next three sections, we'll write Python code to inspect and visualize the contents of the provided `*.shp` and `*.xlsx` files.

Note The provided building footprint dataset of Battery Park, NYC (/Ch8/qgis_battery_park.shp and /Ch8/qgis_battery_park.xlsx), is downloaded from NYC OpenData (`https://data.cityofnewyork.us/City-Government/Building-Footprints-Map-/3g6p-4u5s`).

The provided building footprints of Havana, Cuba (/Ch8/havana.shp and /Ch8/havana.xlsx), is downloaded from Google Research Open Buildings (CC By 4.0). Both datasets are edited by the author in QGIS 3.20.2-Odense.

Reading and Inspecting Contents of a Shapefile (*.shp) with pyshp

Building footprint datasets are *not* standardized and can be highly inconsistent in terms of scale and the type of data they carry. Although we know a shapefile contains outlines of building cross-sections, we don't know what units the file uses until we look through its contents. In general, whenever you are able, it's always a good idea to look through the input data your Blender Python code will be using ahead of time, to ensure its correctness, as well as to get a sense of what output to expect, which will make debugging that much easier.

The function `read_shp_file` in Listing 8-1 shows how you can parse a shapefile using `pyshp`. You import `pyshp` by adding the line `import shapefile` to the top of a script, then call `shapefile.Reader` with the path to a shapefile (`shp_filepath`) to get an object `shp_file` back loaded with the content of the file. You then access the list of shape polygons via `shp_file.shapes()`, with each as a sequence of points.

We extract the name of the shapefile *without* the extension next, which will come in handy for naming the preview plot as well as the mesh we'll be generating later in the chapter. To do so, we use whichever slash (forward "/" or back "\\") is present in shp_filepath as the delimiter to call split with (Python string's built-in method), which gives us the list of strings from dividing it at the slashes—the last of which (at index –1) is the file name *with* the extension, which we further split at the dot into two strings (before and after the dot), and the first of which is then the part of the file name *without* the extension. For example, if shp_filepath is "C:\\Ch8\\qgis_battery_park.shp", the delimiter is "\\", and shp_filepath.split(delimiter) returns the list ["C:", "Ch8", "qgis_battery_park.shp"]. The string at index –1 is then "qgis_battery_park.shp", which when split at the dot gives you the strings ["qgis_battery_park", "shp"], the first of which is "qgis_battery_park", which is the name of the shapefile *without* the extension.

To wrap up Listing 8-1, we return the loaded shapefile object, list of shapes, and the file name without the extension.

Listing 8-1. Using the pyshp module to parse the shapefile at the given file path

```
import shapefile
def read_shp_file(shp_filepath: str):
    shp_file = shapefile.Reader(shp_filepath)
    shapes = shp_file.shapes()

    delimiter = "/" if "/" in shp_filepath else "\\"
    shp_filename = shp_filepath.split( ↩
        delimiter)[-1].split(".")[0]

    return shp_file, shapes, shp_filename
```

Note See the Appendix on how to install the third-party Python library pyshp under Blender Python.

The backslash is a special character which must be prepended with another backslash ("escaped") in a Python string.

Plotting the Polygons in a Shapefile with matplotlib

With a shapefile loaded, next we'll write a function `plot_shp_file` as shown in Listing 8-2 to create a 2D plot to preview the shape polygons.

Listing 8-2. Create a 2D polygon plot given a bounding box, list of shape curves, and plot name

```
import matplotlib.pyplot as plt
from matplotlib.patches import Polygon

def plot_shp_file(bbox, shapes, shp_filename):
    fig, axes = plt.subplots()
    x_min, y_min, x_max, y_max = bbox
    axes.set_xlim(x_min, x_max)
    axes.set_ylim(y_min, y_max)
    axes.set_title(shp_filename)

    for shape in shapes:
        points = shape.points
        polygon = Polygon(points, edgecolor='green', ↩
            facecolor='lightgreen')
        axes.add_patch(polygon)
    plt.show()
```

The first line in Listing 8-2 `import matplotlib.pyplot as plt` imports the `pyplot` submodule from `matplotlib` as the shorthand `plt`, which we'll be using to create the plot. The second line imports the `Polygon` function we'll use to draw the individual shape polygons in the plot. The function `plot_shp_file` takes the bounding box of the shapes (more on this shortly) as well as the list of shapes and shape file name without the extension returned by Listing 8-1 as arguments. We call `plt.subplots()` to create the plot window and XY axes then use the bounding box (`bbox`) to set the extent of the axes, and the shape file name without the extension to set the plot title.

With the plot window set up, we iterate through the list of shapes and call `Polygon` to draw each as a polygon with green edges and light green faces, then `axes.add_patch` to add the polygon to the plot. After all the polygons are added, we call `plt.show()` to display the plot. The choice of edge and face colors here are arbitrary.

We can now call Listings 8-1 and 8-2 back to back in a helper function like check_shp_file (Listing 8-3) to parse a shapefile, then plot its shapes. Note that the shapefile object shp_file loaded by read_shp_file (Listing 8-1) has a member variable shp_file.bbox that gives you the bounding box of the shapes, which we can use to call plot_shp_file (Listing 8-2).

Listing 8-3. Helper function to read and plot a given shapefile as 2D polygons

```
def check_shp_file(shp_filepath: str):
    shp_file, shapes, shp_filename = ↩
        read_shp_file(shp_filepath)
    plot_shp_file(shp_file.bbox, shapes, shp_filename)
```

Assuming you've saved this chapter's downloaded files to the folder C:\\Ch8\\, you can call Listing 8-3 with

```
check_shp_file("C:\\Ch8\\qgis_battery_park.shp")
```

which will create the plot shown in Figure 8-1.

Note See the Appendix on how to install the third-party Python library matplotlib under Blender Python.

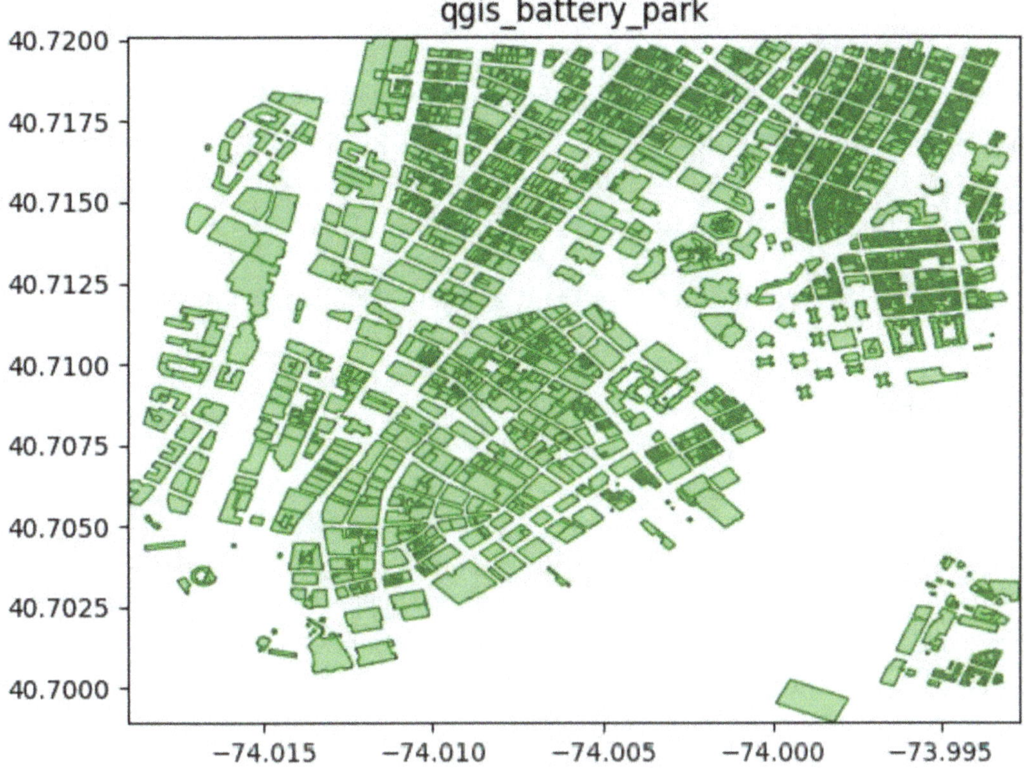

Figure 8-1. *Shape polygons from the provided shapefile /Ch8/qgis_battery_park.shp plotted by running Listing 8-3*

Inspecting the Contents of a Spreadsheet (*.xlsx) Accompanying a Shapefile with `pandas`

Unfortunately, building footprint datasets are *not* standardized across the board; therefore, you cannot make assumptions about how many fields nor the type of fields present in the spreadsheet accompanying a shapefile. Most datasets have fields describing roof heights, shape areas, perimeters of shapes, etc.; however, they are often inconsistently named (e.g., "shape_area" vs. "area"). Therefore, the only way to know which fields are applicable and their names is to preview the spreadsheet. Since we'll be using `pandas` later to extract fields such as the roof height for generating the skyline meshes, we'll use it here to preview the spreadsheet as well.

After adding the line `import pandas as pd` to the top of a script, you'll be able to call functions under `pandas` via the shorthand `pd`. You can then write a helper function like `read_spreadsheet_pandas` in Listing 8-4, where you call `pd.read_excel` to load a spreadsheet at a given file path (`xslx_filepath`) into an object (`wb`). `wb.head()` will then return the first few rows of the sheet, which you can display in the System Console (Window ➤ Toggle System Console) via `print(wb.head())`.

Listing 8-4. Helper function to read and preview the first few lines of a spreadsheet

```
import pandas as pd
def read_spreadsheet_pandas(xlsx_filepath: str):
    wb = pd.read_excel(xlsx_filepath)
    print(wb.head())
```

You can call Listing 8-4 with the provided spreadsheet `/Ch8/qgis_battery_park.xlsx` in the `if __name__ == "__main__":` block at the bottom of `/Ch8/skyline_generator.py` as shown below, which will print the lines in Figure 8-2 to the System Console (Window ➤ Toggle System Console):

```
if __name__ == "__main__":
    read_spreadsheet_pandas( ↩
        script_dir+"/qgis_battery_park.xlsx")
```

```
       bin  cnstrct_yr  doitt_id  feat_code  groundelev  ...     time_lstmo   lst
0  3001592        1899     31218       2100          55  ...  00:00:00.000  Cons
1  1005645        1930     79482       2100          36  ...  00:00:00.000  Cons
2  1002184        1920    426267       2100           9  ...  00:00:00.000  Cons
3  1077207        1930     37237       2100          19  ...  00:00:00.000  Cons
4  1003296        1915    708848       2100          21  ...  00:00:00.000  Cons

[5 rows x 12 columns]
```

Figure 8-2. *The first few rows of the provided spreadsheet /Ch8/qgis_battery_park.xlsx displayed in the System Console by calling Listing 8-4 (cropped to fit page width)*

`script_dir` is a variable containing the current directory path the script is running from. The value of `script_dir` is derived in a block of code at the top of `/Ch8/skyline_generator.py` (see the section "Deriving the Script's Current Directory" at the end of this chapter to find out how).

Downloading and Preprocessing Building Footprint Data

Now that you know what to expect in a prepared dataset, in this section, we'll go over how to source, download, and preprocess building footprint datasets of your own using the open source GIS software QGIS. The QGIS screenshots throughout the section are taken in version 3.20.2-Odense.

Where to Download Building Footprint Data

Building footprint data is widely available as free downloads. The following is a list of suggested sources. Depending on the outlet, the data may come in different formats, such as csv, geojson, etc., and may require different types of preprocessing. Discussing the differences between these data types and how to deal with them is sadly beyond the scope of this chapter. However, it is my hope that with the skills you build from working through this chapter, you'll be able to explore further on your own.

- Local government websites, for municipal areas like cities, counties, etc.
    - For example, the provided dataset of the NYC Battery Park neighborhood is downloaded from NYC OpenData (`https://data.cityofnewyork.us/City-Government/Building-Footprints-Map-/3g6p-4u5s`).
- Building footprint data of all 50 states plus DC by Microsoft in geojson format (`https://github.com/microsoft/USBuildingFootprints`).
- Google Research Open Buildings (`https://sites.research.google/gr/open-buildings/`).

Editing Building Footprint Data in QGIS

Let's download the NYC building footprint data, then edit it in QGIS and export the shapefile (`*.shp`) and spreadsheet (`*.xlsx`) for the Time Square area, which you can use later as an additional test set for the skyline generator. Download the latest stable version of QGIS from `https://qgis.org/download/` for your OS and follow the installation directions. The steps illustrated in this section are based on QGIS 3.20.2-Odense for Windows.

Downloading Building Footprint Data from NYC OpenData

Go to the building footprint data page on the NYC OpenData site (`https://data.cityofnewyork.us/City-Government/Building-Footprints-Map-/3g6p-4u5s`) and click the triple-dot icon on the upper right ➤ Download Building Footprints ➤ All Data ➤ CSV for Excel, as shown in Figure 8-3. At the time of writing, this downloads the file "`Building_Footprints_20250115.csv`," which is about 525MB.

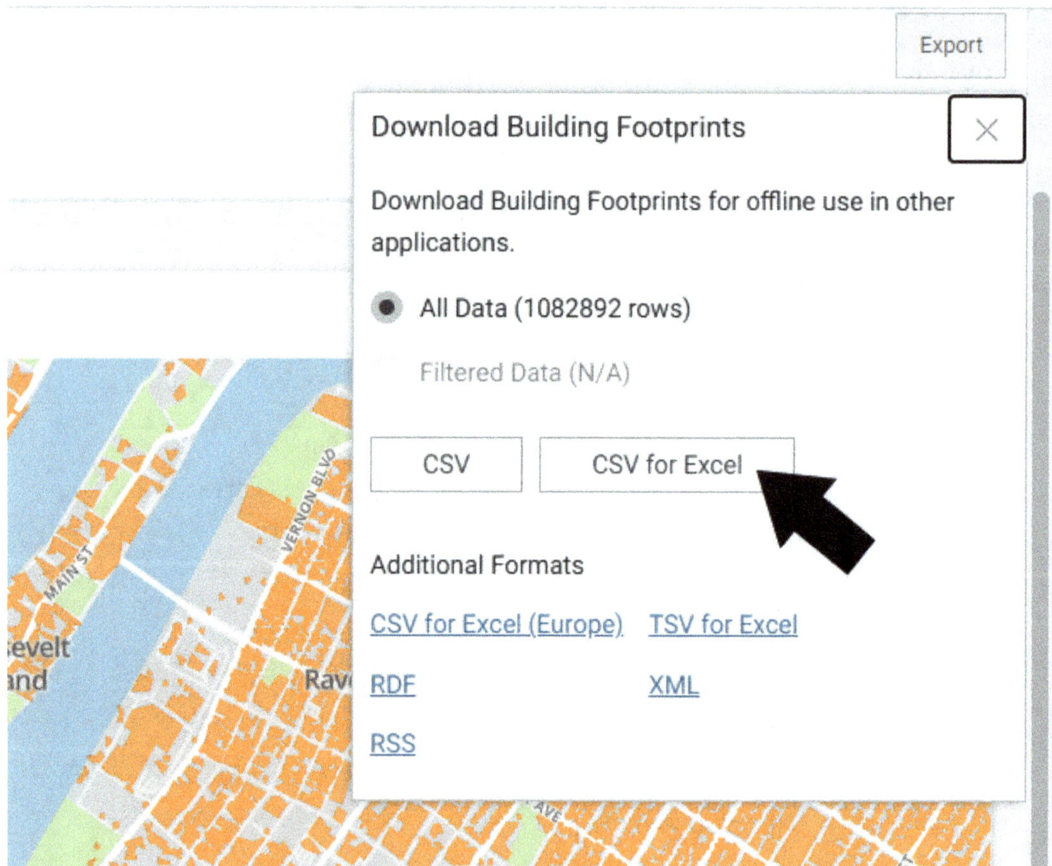

***Figure 8-3.** Download building footprint data from NYC OpenData*

Importing Downloaded *.csv File in QGIS as Delimited Text

Open QGIS and create a new project with Project ➤ New (Ctrl-N), then import the downloaded *.csv file via the following steps:

1. Layer ➤ Add Layer ➤ Add Delimited Text Layer.
2. Click the "..." button to the right of the File name field (shown as (1) in Figure 8-4).
3. In the file open dialog that appears, select the downloaded Building_Footprints_20250115.csv file.
4. Leave all autopopulated settings at default. The Layer name will be the file name without the extension, File format will be CSV, and Geometry Definition with well-known text (WKT) should be selected.
5. Click the Add button to add the layer.

It will likely take a few minutes to load the layer after you click Add since the *.csv file contains buildings over a large area. Be patient and let it whirl. Once the layer appears, the Add button will be grayed out. Click Close (or the X at the upper right) to close the dialog. The layer will look like Figure 8-5.

If the footprint data is over a large area (as is in our case), the shapes may resemble dots when first loaded since the layer is zoomed to fit by default. If this is the case, you can simply scroll the mouse wheel to zoom in (or View ➤ Zoom In) until shapes begin to emerge, as shown in Figure 8-6. You can also select 1:5000 from the Scale dropdown at the bottom of the window.

Selecting an Area of Interest (Time Square)

For this exercise, we'll select Time Square as our area of interest. While you can certainly try and locate it by holding down MMB while dragging to pan around the map (or View ➤ Pan Map, then holding down LMB while dragging), for a large map like ours, it is much quicker to locate an area based on (latitude, longitude). We can find the (latitude, longitude) pair for Time Square by searching for it on Google Maps (map.google.com) and right-clicking its pin on the map to open the context menu, to find the (latitude, longitude) = (40.75785, -73.98556) as shown in Figure 8-7.

With the (latitude, longitude) pair handy, you can either enter them in the Coordinate box in QGIS at the bottom of the window (careful to preserve the degree symbols) and press Enter, or move the mouse cursor while watching the Coordinate values change until you are approximately at the right location.

Now we'll select an area to export. Summon the selection tool via Edit ➤ Select ➤ Select Features by Polygon, then create a polygon to enclose the desired region by clicking to lay down one vertex at a time, moving clockwise around the perimeter of the intended area. Once you've laid down the last vertex, right-click to confirm. The selection will turn yellow as shown in Figure 8-8.

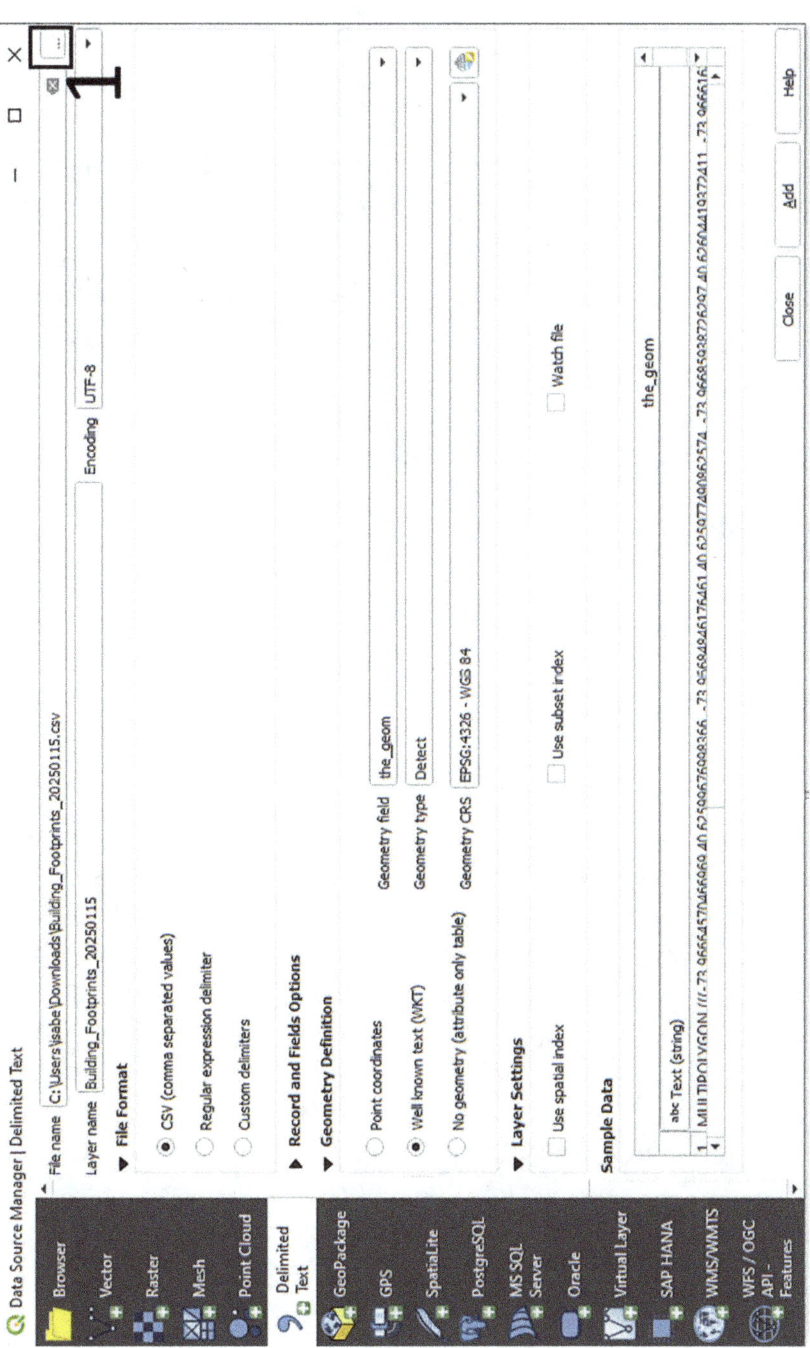

Figure 8-4. *Adding the downloaded building footprint file in QGIS via Add ➤ Add Layer ➤ Add Delimited Text Layer. (1) is the button to call up the file open dialog.*

Figure 8-5. *The NYC building footprint data Building_Footprints_20250115.csv first loaded as a layer in QGIS*

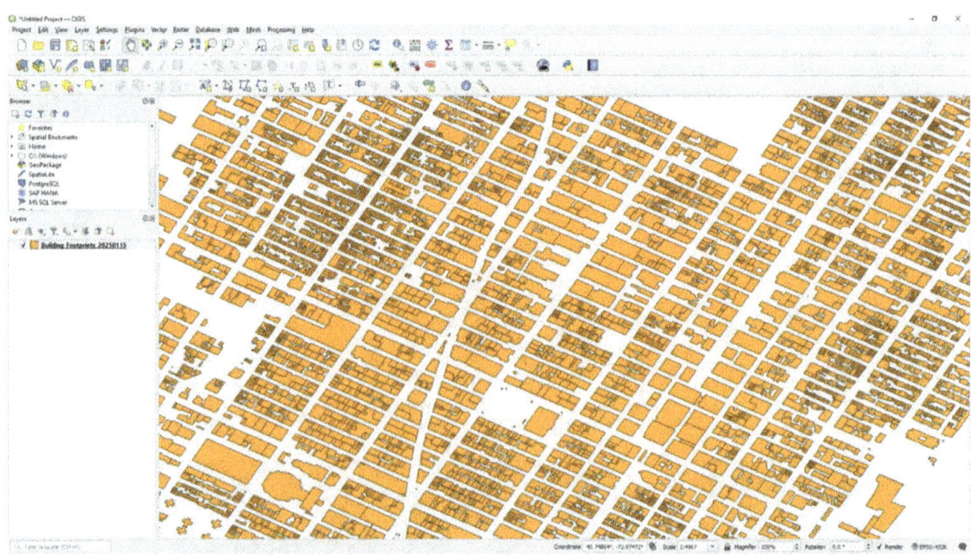

Figure 8-6. *Initially, the layer is too zoomed out to make out individual building footprints; however, if you scroll the mouse wheel (or View ➤ Zoom in) to zoom in, you'll start to see the shapes emerge.*

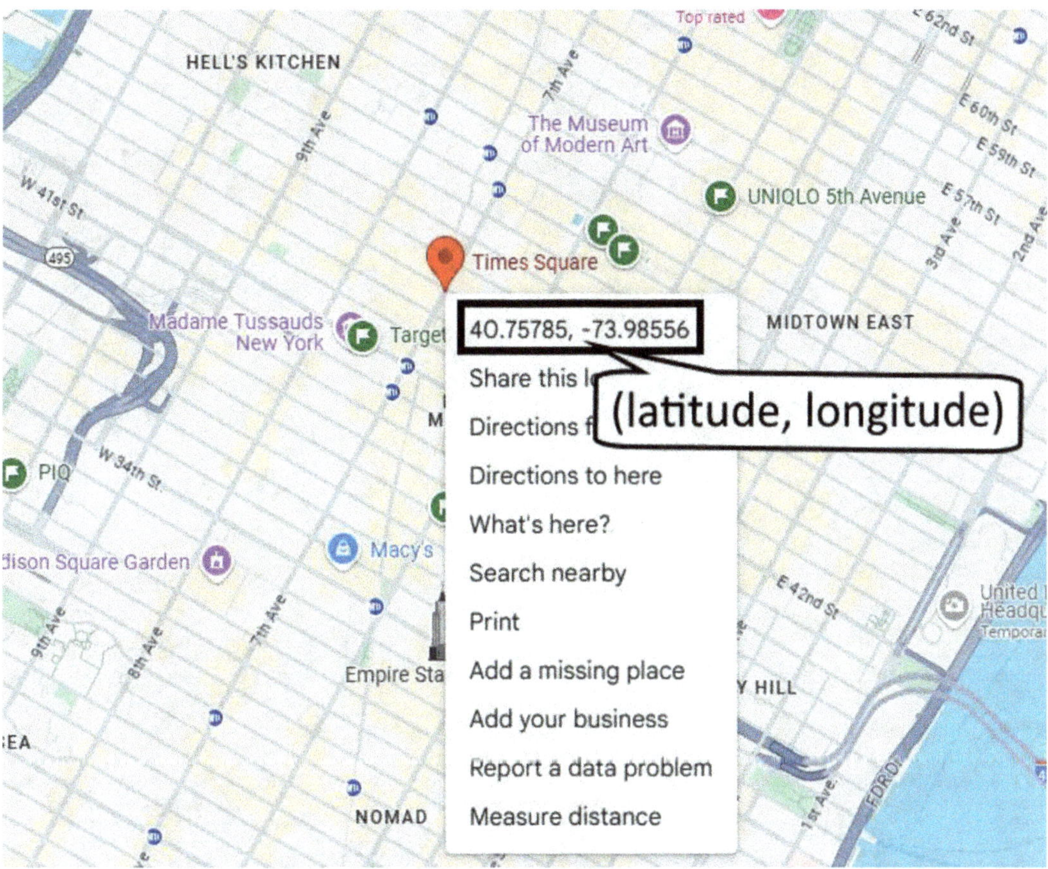

Figure 8-7. Finding the (latitude, longitude) of Time Square by searching for it on Google Maps, then right-clicking its pin on the map

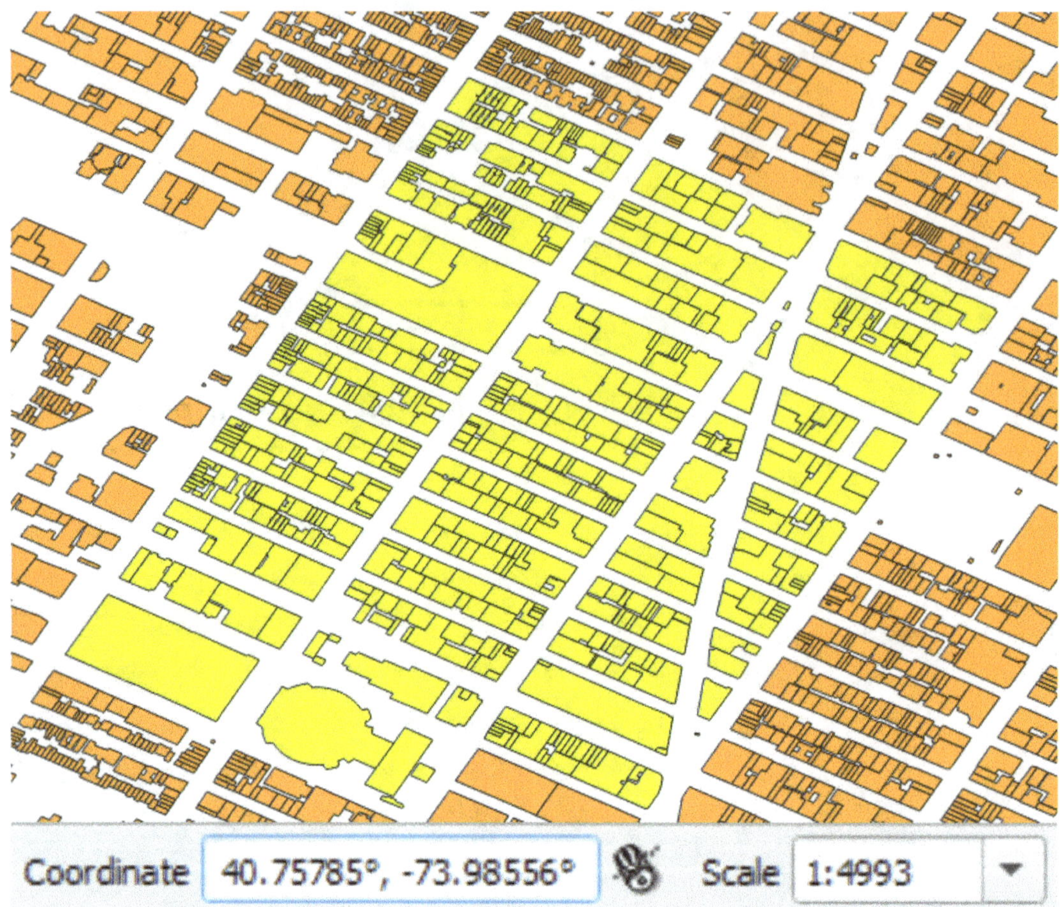

Figure 8-8. *Enter the (latitude, longitude) pair in the Coordinate box at the bottom of the window in QGIS to jump to an area, then use Edit ➤ Select ➤ Select Features by Polygon to select it. The selection will turn yellow as shown. The Coordinate and Scale in the figure are enlarged for readability.*

Exporting Selection as Shapefile (*.shp) and Spreadsheet (*.xlsx)

We can now export the selection as a shapefile (`*.shp`) containing building outlines as polycurves and a spreadsheet (`*.xlsx`) with the corresponding roof heights, etc. (the field types depend on what is present in the source csv file). We can initiate the dialog to export both types of files by right-clicking the layer name ➤ Export ➤ Save Selected Features As... as shown in Figure 8-9, which will bring up the "Save Vector Layer as..." dialog shown in Figures 8-10 and 8-11.

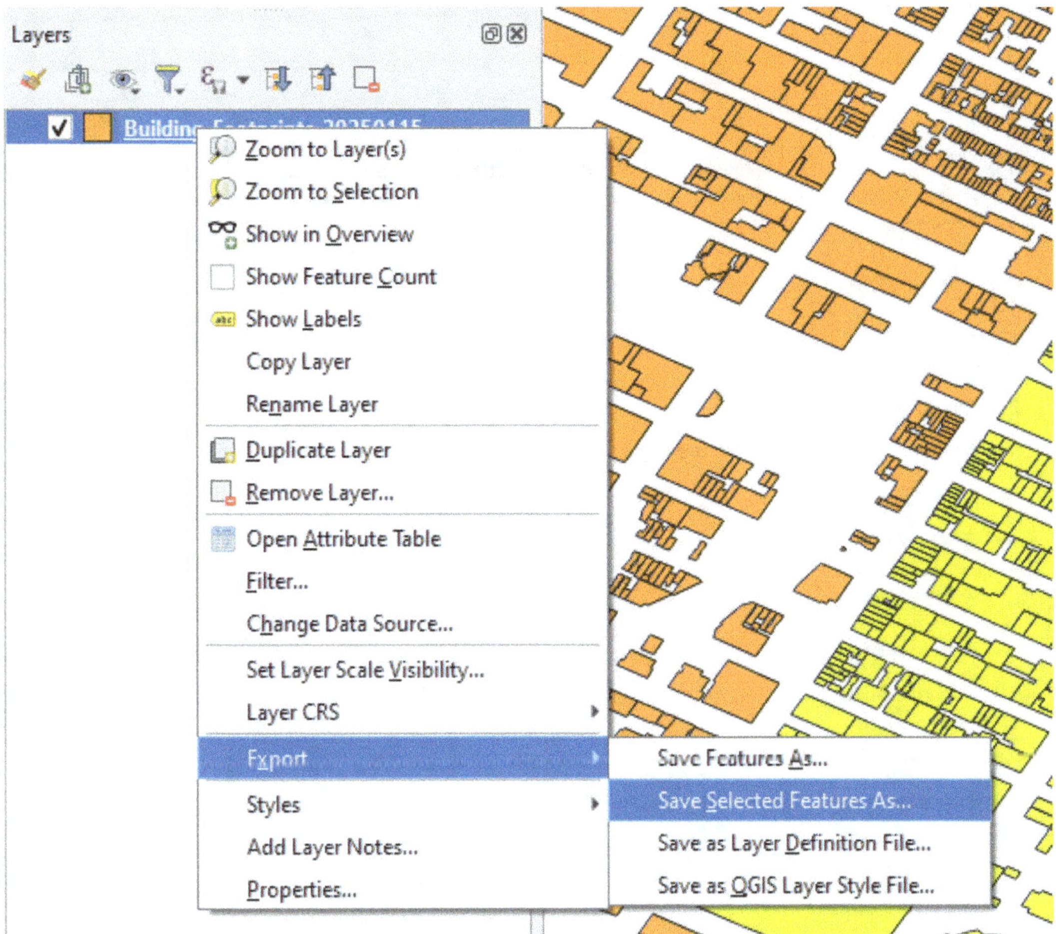

Figure 8-9. *Right-click the layer name, then Export ➤ Save Selected Features As... to bring up the "Save Vector Layer as..." dialog for exporting the selection to different file formats*

To export the selection as a shapefile (*.shp), set the Format to "ESRI Shapefile" and CRS to "EPSG:4326 - WGS 84," as shown in Figure 8-10, and leave the other settings at default.

To export the selection as a spreadsheet (*.xlsx), set the Format to "MS Office Open XML spreadsheet [XLSX]" and CRS to the same setting as the shapefile, as shown in Figure 8-11, while leaving other settings at default. You should name the shapefile and spreadsheet consistently. For example, I named the two files `time_square.shp` and `time_square.xlsx`, so it's easy to tell that the two files come as a pair.

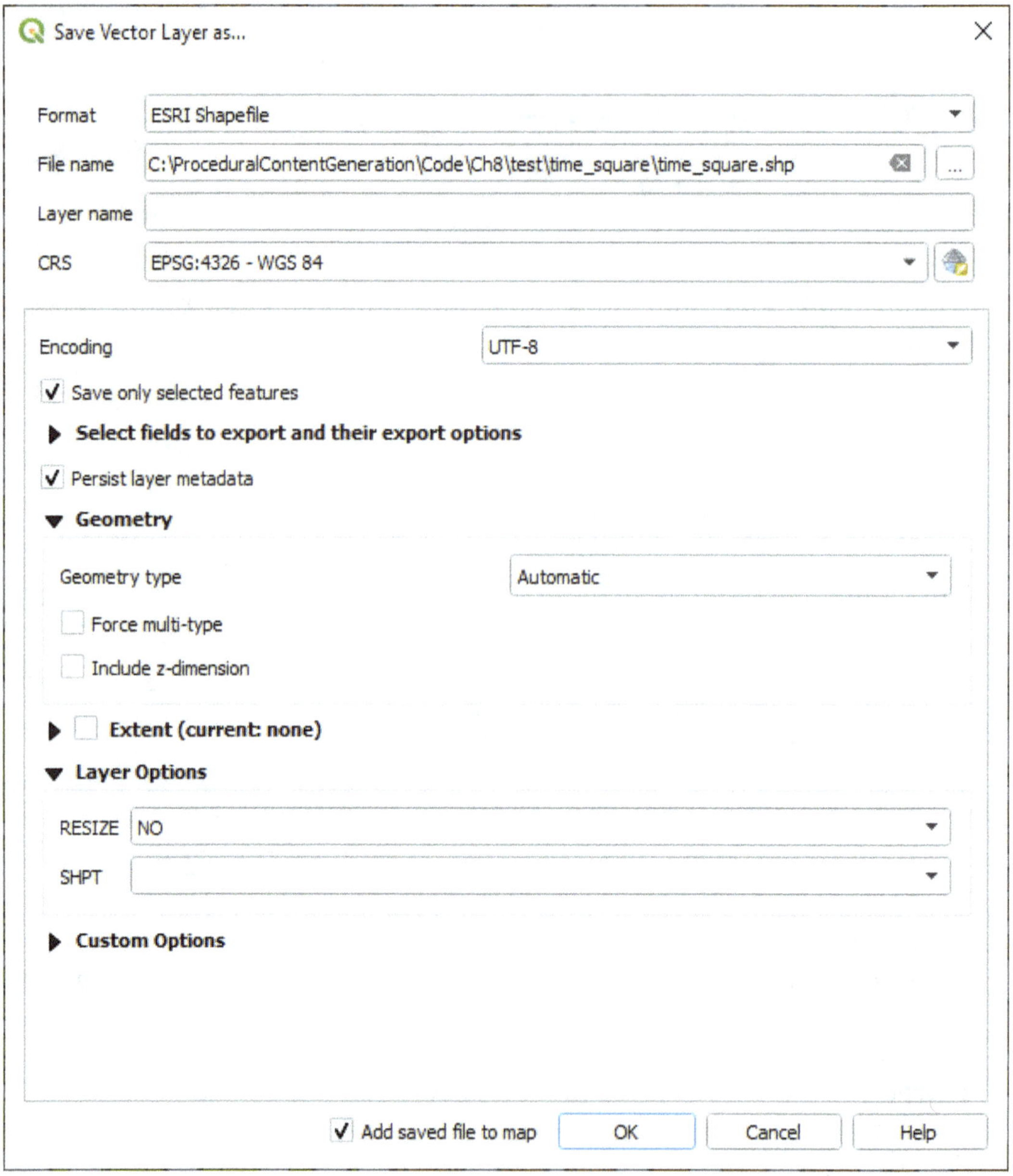

Save Vector Layer as...

Format	ESRI Shapefile
File name	C:\ProceduralContentGeneration\Code\Ch8\test\time_square\time_square.shp
Layer name	
CRS	EPSG:4326 - WGS 84

Encoding: UTF-8

☑ Save only selected features

▶ **Select fields to export and their export options**

☑ Persist layer metadata

▼ **Geometry**

Geometry type: Automatic

☐ Force multi-type

☐ Include z-dimension

▶ ☐ **Extent (current: none)**

▼ **Layer Options**

RESIZE: NO

SHPT:

▶ **Custom Options**

☑ Add saved file to map | OK | Cancel | Help

Figure 8-10. *The "Save Vector Layer as..." dialog set to export the current selection as a shapefile (*.shp)*

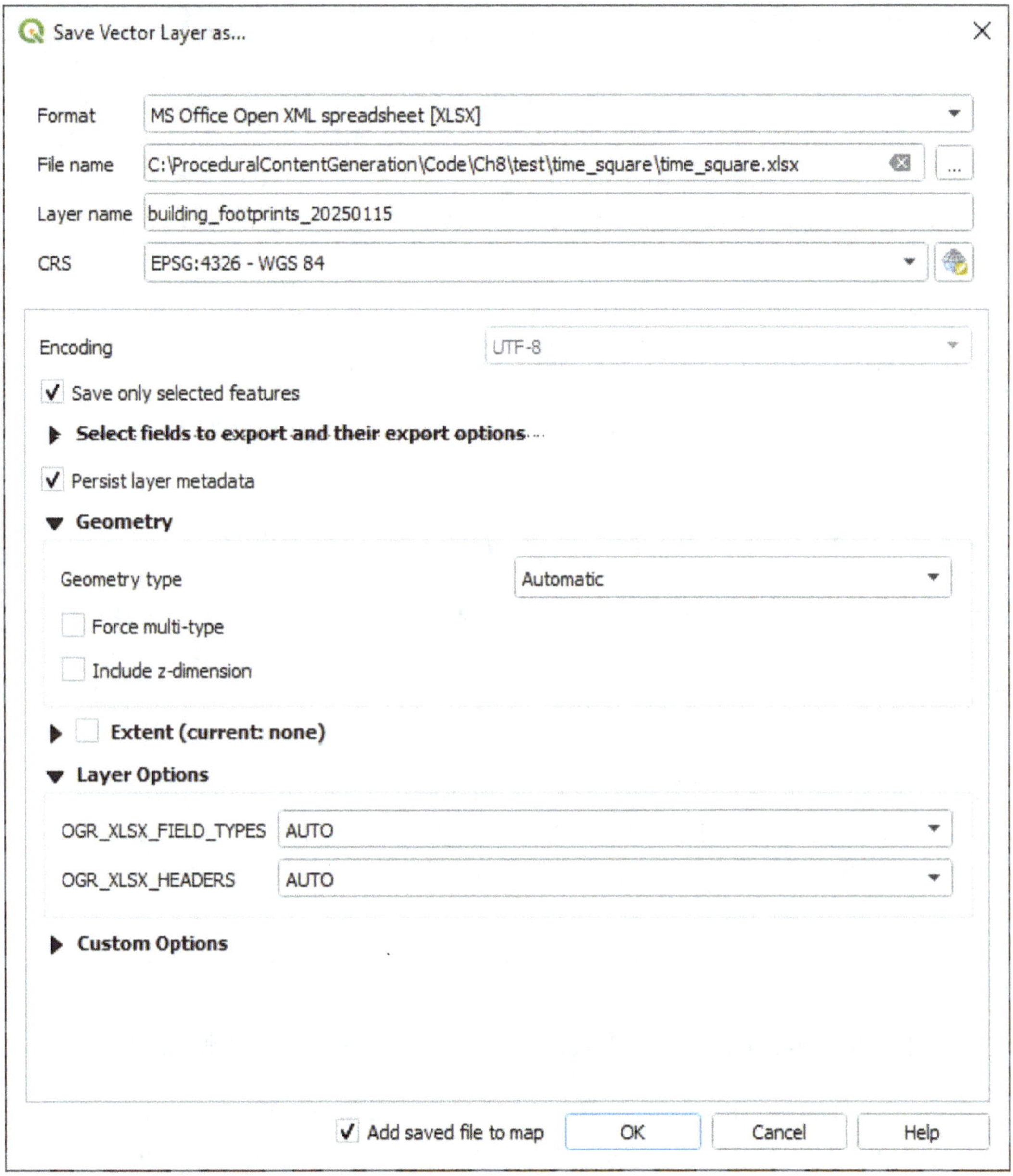

Save Vector Layer as...

Format: MS Office Open XML spreadsheet [XLSX]

File name: C:\ProceduralContentGeneration\Code\Ch8\test\time_square\time_square.xlsx

Layer name: building_footprints_20250115

CRS: EPSG:4326 - WGS 84

Encoding: UTF-8

☑ Save only selected features

▶ **Select fields to export and their export options**

☑ Persist layer metadata

▼ **Geometry**

Geometry type: Automatic

☐ Force multi-type

☐ Include z-dimension

▶ ☐ **Extent (current: none)**

▼ **Layer Options**

OGR_XLSX_FIELD_TYPES: AUTO

OGR_XLSX_HEADERS: AUTO

▶ **Custom Options**

☑ Add saved file to map | OK | Cancel | Help

Figure 8-11. *The "Save Vector Layer as..." dialog set to export the current selection as a spreadsheet (*.xlsx)*

Generating Skyline Meshes from Building Footprints

You started the chapter by writing Python code to inspect and visualize the provided building footprint files to learn their structures. You then tried downloading your own dataset, editing it in QGIS, and exporting an area of interest as a shapefile (*.shp) and an accompanying spreadsheet (*.xlsx). In the next few sections, we'll use the shapefile and spreadsheet to generate skyline meshes in Blender Python.

Formulating a Design for the Generator

Let's pause for a moment and contemplate the steps we'll take to generate the building meshes.

Converting Shape Polycurves to Wireframe Meshes

To start, we'll use `pyshp` to read the shapefile and `pandas` to read the spreadsheet into memory, then access the shapefile's geojson layer to get to the points making up the shape curves, with which we can create initial wireframe meshes of the footprints.

Note GeoJSON (*.geojson) is an open format for encoding GIS data that is beyond the scope of this book. All you need to know is that it stores data in a hierarchy that can be accessed with keys like a multidimensional Python dictionary.

Filling in Wireframes and Extruding Based on Roof Heights

Once we have the wireframes for the footprints, we fill them in with faces then extrude them along +Z to the corresponding building heights. Recall that the contents of the spreadsheets are inconsistent and sometimes missing roof heights, in which case we sample the numbers from a range of either user-specified or programmer-entered values.

Moving Building Meshes Based on Elevation

Once an individual building mesh is generated, we move it to the correct elevation based on the corresponding value in the spreadsheet. As is with the case of roof heights, elevations are sometimes missing from a spreadsheet, in which case we sample from a range of either user-specified or programmer-entered values.

Scaling

As we've seen in the section "Reading and Inspecting Contents of a Shapefile (`*.shp`) with `pyshp`," the scales of shapes can vary wildly from one shapefile to the next; as a result, some scaling is usually needed. We can derive baseline scale factors from cross-referencing shape curves with their perimeter values in the spreadsheet. In addition, multipliers can be exposed to users to tune the look of the meshes. Next, we'll consider the possible types of scale factors and how each can be derived or specified.

XY (Footprint) Scale

The first type of scale factor is for building cross-sections. Since we are orienting the footprints on the global XY plane and extruding upward toward +Z, we'll call this XY scale, which can be calculated by dividing the first building footprint's perimeter value in the spreadsheet by the measured length of its corresponding polycurve in the shapefile (we'll only do this once with the first building and assume that the ratio is the same across all buildings). If the shape perimeter is missing in the spreadsheet, we'll estimate the XY scale from a user-supplied "target length" and the longer side of the city's bounding box.

Roof Height Scale

The roof height scale can be either a stand-alone multiplier optionally specified by the user or the same value as the XY scale.

Ground Elevation Scale

The ground elevation scale can be either a stand-alone multiplier optionally specified by the user or the same value as the XY scale.

Implementing the Generator in Blender Python

We're now ready to implement the plan from the previous section in Blender Python. We'll take a top-down approach and break the generation into a series of functions, with each function performing a unit of the previous function's work. The first function gen_skyline (Listing 8-5) serves as the entry point to the generator, which gathers the paths to the shapefile and spreadsheet along with other user-specified parameter values such as the range to sample missing roof heights and scale multipliers (we'll get into the nitty-gritty of the individual arguments as they come in context).

gen_skyline starts by calling read_shp_file to load the shapefile (discussed in Listing 8-1), followed by pd.read_excel to read the spreadsheet (discussed in Listing 8-4). The data returned by these two functions are in turn passed to create_buildings_mesh (Listing 8-6) to generate the building meshes.

Listing 8-5. Entry point to the skyline generator, where given the paths to a shapefile and corresponding spreadsheet and other user parameters, generate the buildings as one mesh object (see /Ch8/skyline_generator.py)

```
def gen_skyline(shp_filepath: str, wb_filepath: str, ↩
    target_len: float, context, elev_scale, roof_h_key, ↩
    gnd_elev_key, shp_len_key, location=(0,0,0), ↩
    rand_roof_h_range=(30,60), rand_gnd_elev_range=(10,30)):

    shp_file, shapes, shp_filename = read_shp_file( ↩
        shp_filepath)
    wb = pd.read_excel(wb_filepath)
    create_buildings_mesh(context, shp_filename, ↩
        target_len, shapes, shp_file.bbox, wb, 0.1, ↩
        elev_scale, roof_h_key, gnd_elev_key, ↩
        shp_len_key, location, rand_roof_h_range, ↩
        rand_gnd_elev_range)
```

Generating All Buildings

create_buildings_mesh (Listing 8-6) takes the shapefile and spreadsheet that have been read into memory by Listing 8-5 and generates a mesh object containing all buildings. Our plan of attack is to make a single mesh data block for the whole shapefile and a bmesh instance bm for editing it, then call add_shape_from_geojson (Listing 8-8) on each shape to add the respective building mesh to bm, and during which calculate the scale factors for the city by cross-referencing curve lengths from the shapefile with their perimeter values in the spreadsheet.

Listing 8-6. Create building meshes from a given shapefile and spreadsheet pair (see /Ch8/skyline_generator.py)

```
def create_buildings_mesh(context, shp_file_name, ↩
    target_len: float, shapes, bbox, wb, scale, ↩
    elev_scale, roof_h_key, gnd_elev_key, ↩
    shp_len_key, location, rand_roof_h_range, ↩
    rand_gnd_elev_range):
    x_min, y_min, x_max, y_max = bbox
    x_span = x_max-x_min
    y_span = y_max-y_min
    num_shapes = len(shapes)
    mesh_data = bpy.data.meshes.new( ↩
        name=shp_file_name+"_data")
    mesh_obj = bpy.data.objects.new( ↩
        name=shp_file_name, object_data=mesh_data)
    context.collection.objects.link(mesh_obj)
    bm = bmesh.new()

    roof_h_min, roof_h_max = rand_roof_h_range
    roof_heights = wb[roof_h_key] if roof_h_key ↩
        in wb.keys() else get_sample(num_shapes, ↩
        roof_h_max, roof_h_min)
    gnd_elev_min, gnd_elev_max = rand_gnd_elev_range
    ground_elevs = wb[gnd_elev_key] if gnd_elev_key in ↩
        wb.keys() else get_sample(num_shapes, gnd_elev_max, ↩
        gnd_elev_min)
    scale_factor = 1

    for i in range(num_shapes):
        shp_geojson = shapes[i].__geo_interface__
        height = roof_heights[i]*scale
        elev = ground_elevs[i]*scale*elev_scale
```

```
        if i == 0:
            perimeter = add_shape_from_geojson(context, ↩
                bm, i, shp_geojson, location, ↩
                x_min, y_min, height, elev)
            shp_len0 =  wb[shp_len_key][0] if shp_len_key ↩
                in wb.keys() else -1
            xy_scale = shp_len0/perimeter*scale ↩
                if shp_len0 > 0 else ↩
                    target_len/max(x_span, y_span)
        else:
            add_shape_from_geojson(context, bm, i, ↩
                shp_geojson, location, x_min, y_min, ↩
                height, elev)

    bm.to_mesh(mesh_data)

    for obj in context.view_layer.objects:
        obj.select_set(False)
    context.view_layer.objects.active = mesh_obj
    mesh_obj.select_set(True)

    context_override = get_context_override(context, ↩
        'VIEW_3D', 'WINDOW')
    with bpy.context.temp_override(**context_override):
        bpy.ops.object.mode_set(mode='OBJECT')

    context_override = get_context_override(context, ↩
        'VIEW_3D', 'WINDOW')
    with context.temp_override(**context_override):
        bpy.ops.transform.resize(value=(xy_scale, ↩
            xy_scale, 1))
        bpy.ops.transform.translate(value=location)
        bpy.ops.object.transform_apply(location=True, ↩
            rotation=False, scale=True)
```

We'll begin by setting up metadata and a mesh object for accumulating building geometry. First, we infer the corners of the city bounding box (bbox) so we can use the lower-left corner (x_min, y_min) as the city's origin. We also derive the sides of bbox (x_span and y_span) from the differences of the extreme X and Y values, which will help us calculate the scale factor later. After that, we create a new mesh data block (mesh_data) and use it to set up a new mesh object (mesh_obj) for the city. We also create a bmesh instance bm intended for accumulating the building geometry by calling bmesh.new() but *not* associate it with mesh_data yet—reason being we'll pass bm to helper functions later to queue up edits for each building; then once we're done with all buildings, we transfer the geometry from bm to mesh_data in one shot by calling bm.to_mesh(mesh_data).

In the next block of code, we set up lists of roof heights and ground elevations for generating buildings. We prefer using the "real" values from the spreadsheet whenever possible and only generate random values in their absence. We check the presence of roof heights with the passed-in roof_h_key and elevations with gnd_elev_key in wb.keys(), which is the list of all keys (column names) in the spreadsheet. In the event that a key is missing, we call get_sample (Listing 8-7) to sample from the ranges passed in. For example, for the roof heights, this is done via the line get_sample(num_shapes, roof_h_max, roof_h_min), where the min and max are extracted from the passed-in range (roof_h_min, roof_h_max = rand_roof_h_range). Since we provided default values for both the roof and elevation ranges in the function signature, the function will always have values to fall back on for sampling when needed. We'll finish the setup by creating a default scale_factor of 1.

Next, we'll iterate through the shapes and accumulate building geometry created from each shape on bm. We access each shape's geojson (shp_geojson = shapes[i].__geo_interface__), which contains the lists of polygons comprising that shape with each polygon as a list of 2D points (XY coordinates). We also adjust the roof height (height) and ground elevation (elev) based on the passed-in scale factors, before calling add_shape_from_geojson (Listing 8-8) to generate the building geometry. If this is the first shape (with i == 0), add_shape_from_geojson will also compute and return the shape's perimeter, which we'll use to derive the factor for scaling the buildings horizontally (xy_scale), which is as follows—first, we look up the corresponding perimeter length from the spreadsheet with the following line:

```
shp_len0 = wb[shp_len_key][0] if shp_len_key in wb.keys() ↩
    else -1
```

which reads, if shp_len_key is present in the spreadsheet's column names (wb.keys()), retrieve the first row of that column (wb[shp_len_key][0]), which is the perimeter of the first shape; otherwise, use −1 for shp_len0. On the next line (reproduced below), we check if shp_len0 is greater than 0—if so, it means the value is both present in the spreadsheet and valid; we'll divide it by the curve length (perimeter) returned by add_shape_from_geojson (Listing 8-8) and multiply it by the passed-in scale. If shp_len0 is invalid, we ballpark xy_scale by dividing the passed-in target length for the city (target_len) by the longer side of the bounding box (max(x_span, y_span)). target_len is how long you want the city mesh to measure when it's generated (if the city is a rectangle, it's the longer of its two sides).

```
xy_scale = shp_len0/perimeter*scale ↩
    if shp_len0 > 0 else ↩
        target_len/max(x_span, y_span)
```

We assume that the scale (as in the ratio between the shape curve length and the corresponding perimeter length from the spreadsheet) is uniform across the footprint dataset; therefore, we only estimate it once from the first shape. For all remaining shapes, we simply call add_shape_from_geojson (Listing 8-8) to create the building geometry to add to bm. Once we iterate through all buildings, we call bm.to_mesh(mesh_data) to transfer the geometry from bm to mesh_data, the mesh data block we created at the beginning that's set up with the city mesh object (mesh_obj).

Next, we'll finish up by applying transforms to mesh_obj. We deselect all objects in the scene, then set mesh_obj as active and select it. We then switch mesh_obj to Object mode with a context override (as if from the viewport), and after mode switch to Object is complete, with another override, we scale mesh_obj horizontally by calling bpy.ops.transform.resize with (xy_scale, xy_scale, 1), which applies xy_scale in the X and Y directions but leaves Z alone. We also call bpy.ops.transform.translate to move mesh_obj to the location passed in and finish with bpy.ops.object.transform_apply to apply location and scale transforms.

Sampling Random Values from a Given Range

We write a helper function get_sample (Listing 8-7) to sample from a given range when either the roof height or elevation is missing from the spreadsheet. Given a range from min to max, we calculate the span as max-min. The call to np.random.random_sample(num_items) gives us num_items numbers from 0 to 1 (including 0, excluding 1), which when multiplied by span map into the range 0 to span. Adding min back remaps the numbers into the range min to (min+span), which is equal to min to (min+max-min), therefore min to max.

Listing 8-7. Return the given number of random values sampled from a given range (see /Ch8/skyline_generator.py)

```
def get_sample(num_items, max, min):
    span = max-min
    return np.random.random_sample(num_items)*span+min
```

Generating a Single Building

In add_shape_from_geojson (Listing 8-8), we'll handle the generation of one building mesh. As discussed earlier, we'll take the first building as an example and compute the ratio of its curve's length from the shapefile to its perimeter value from the spreadsheet to derive the XY scale for buildings across the dataset.

Listing 8-8. Generate a single building mesh from the given geojson structure (see /Ch8/skyline_generator.py)

```
def add_shape_from_geojson(context, bm, idx, shp_geojson, ↩
    location, x_min, y_min, height, elev):
    polygons = shp_geojson['coordinates']
    mesh = bpy.data.meshes.new(name=str(idx))
    verts = []
    edges = []

    num_polygons = len(polygons)
    loop_ref_edge_indices = []
    for i in range(num_polygons):
        p = polygons[i]
        num_verts_in_p = len(p)
        if num_verts_in_p < 3:
            continue
```

```
        vert_idx_start_for_p = len(verts)
        verts.extend([(p[i][0]-x_min, p[i][1]-y_min, 0) ↩
            for i in range(num_verts_in_p)])

        for j in range(num_verts_in_p-1):
            edge_ends = [vert_idx_start_for_p+j, ↩
                vert_idx_start_for_p+j+1]
            edges.append(edge_ends)

        edges.append( ↩
            [vert_idx_start_for_p+num_verts_in_p-1, ↩
            vert_idx_start_for_p])
        loop_ref_edge_indices.append(vert_idx_start_for_p)

    mesh.from_pydata(verts, edges, [])
    mesh.update(calc_edges=True)

    perimeter = calc_perimeter(mesh) if idx==0 else 0

    if num_polygons == 1:
        extrude_single_polygon(mesh, height, elev)
        bm.from_mesh(mesh)
    elif num_polygons == 2:
        extrude_two_polygons(mesh, height, elev, len(edges))
        bm.from_mesh(mesh)
    else:
        extrude_multiple_polygons(context, mesh, ↩
            loop_ref_edge_indices, height, elev)
        bm.from_mesh(mesh)
    bpy.data.meshes.remove(mesh)

    if idx == 0:
        return perimeter
```

We can access the list of polygons comprising the shape under the shape's geojson as shp_geojson['coordinates'], which is a nested list with each polygon as a list of points and each point as [X, Y]. To create a mesh from this structure, we'll call bpy.data.

meshes.new to create a mesh data block, then iterate through the polygons to create a list of vertices and a list of edges, with which to call mesh.from_pydata followed by mesh.update(calc_edges=True) to create wireframe geometry under mesh.

Let's take a closer look at this process. For each polygon, we first check if it's valid (with at least three points); if so, we proceed to create vertices from it and add the vertices to the list we have so far (verts) with this line:

```
verts.extend([(p[i][0]-x_min, p[i][1]-y_min, 0) ↩
    for i in range(num_verts_in_p)])
```

We use the passed-in (x_min, y_min) as mesh's origin (recall that mesh is one building—since we're making the city a single mesh object and adding buildings to it one by one, we want all the buildings to share the same origin). Each polygon point p[i] is in the form [X, Y]; therefore, to convert it to 3D, we subtract (x_min, y_min) and add a 0 for Z to get (p[i][0]-x_min, p[i][1]-y_min, 0). The line

```
[(p[i][0]-x_min, p[i][1]-y_min, 0) ↩
    for i in range(num_verts_in_p)]
```

creates a list of 3D coordinates in the format we just described for every point in the polygon. This sort of shorthand where you embed a for loop inside a list construction is called *list comprehension* in Python. Finally, extend will append all the points from the list we just made to verts, the list with which we're accumulating all the vertices for the footprint. With the verts constructed, next we'll create an edge from each adjacent pair of vert indices (which is the format we need to ultimately call mesh.from_pydata with). To do so, we begin with the index of the first vert added by *this polygon*, which is vert_idx_start_for_p = len(verts)—note that we placed this line right *before* verts.extend so len(verts) is the number of verts *before* this polygon is added; in other words, one passed the index of the last vertex *before* this polygon, therefore the index of the first vertex of this polygon. We iterate through vert indices from this value up to and include the second-to-last vert of this polygon, forming adjacent pairs (e.g., (0, 1), (1, 2), etc.), and after the loop, add another pair from the last vert index (vert_idx_start_for_p+num_verts_in_p-1) to the first (vert_idx_start_for_p). For each polygon, we also record the index of one of its edges in loop_ref_edge_indices, which we'll use later to select the shape's edge loops for extrusion. After iterating through all polygons, we call mesh.from_pydata with the list of verts and list of edges followed by mesh.update(calc_edges=True) to create the shape wireframe under mesh.

After making the shape wireframe, we calculate its perimeter length then use its ratio to the corresponding value in the spreadsheet to determine the scale factor. For example, if the mesh's perimeter is 3.5m, and the shape's length is 350m in the spreadsheet, then the scale is

$$350 / 3.5 = 100.$$

We assume there is a uniform ratio between every building's curve perimeter from the shapefile to its length in the spreadsheet; therefore, we only compute the ratio once per shapefile from the first shape.

Next, we delegate the tasks of filling in the wireframe, extruding it to roof height, and moving the building to the right elevation to three helper functions in Listings 8-10, 8-11, and 8-12, *based on the number of polygons in the shape*. After the appropriate helper function is called to edit `mesh`, we call `bm.from_mesh(mesh)` to append `mesh`'s geometry to `bm` (the `bmesh` instance passed in), after which we no longer need `mesh`, so we remove it.

To summarize, we create one mesh data block per shapefile with a `bmesh` instance `bm` for editing it. We then iterate through the shapes, call Listing 8-8 on each shape to create the corresponding building mesh, and append it to `bm`. Once `bm` has all the building meshes queued on it, we transfer them all from `bm` to the original shapefile-level mesh data block in one shot.

Calculating Shape Perimeter

As mentioned earlier, we only calculate shape perimeter once per shapefile (of the first shape only); therefore, it's cleaner to write a helper function and only call it when index is zero. Given a `mesh` (which is assumed to be a 2D wireframe), `calc_perimeter` in Listing 8-9 creates a `bmesh` instance `bm` to iterate through its edges and accumulate their lengths to find the `perimeter`.

Listing 8-9. Given a 2D wireframe mesh, calculate its perimeter by going around its list of edges (see /Ch8/skyline_generator.py)

```
def calc_perimeter(mesh):
    bm = bmesh.new()
    bm.from_mesh(mesh)
    bm.edges.ensure_lookup_table()
```

```
    perimeter = 0
    for e in bm.edges:
        perimeter += e.calc_length()

    bm.free()
    return perimeter
```

Note that here we create a blank `bmesh` instance `bm` with `bmesh.new()`, then call `bm.from_mesh(mesh)` to associate `bm` with `mesh`'s data, thus allowing edits to `mesh` through `bm`. We call `bm.edges.ensure_lookup_table()` to ensure that `bm`'s internal edge indices are up to date before iterating through its edges, calculating the length of each (`e.calc_length()`) and accumulating it in `perimeter`. Afterward, we no longer need `bm`; therefore, we destroy it by calling `bm.free()`, before returning `perimeter`.

Extruding One Shape

In the next three sections, we'll look at how to fill in and extrude 2D wireframe meshes created by `add_shape_from_geojson` (Listing 8-8). The wireframes can be divided into three categories—a single polygon, two nested polygons (one inside the other), and multiple polygons enclosed by one larger polygon. A polygon here refers to one closed edge loop. Unless the source of the building footprint data indicates otherwise, there are multiple ways to interpret what the nested polygons represent, such as roof inset detail, roof outset detail, courtyards, tower, etc. Here, I choose the interpretation of courtyards, i.e., the inner shapes are cut away before extrusion.

Type 1: Single Polygon

In `extrude_single_polygon` (Listing 8-10), we extrude the first and simplest case—a shape made of a single edge loop going around its perimeter.

Listing 8-10. Extrude a 2D wireframe mesh made up of a single loop to the given height, then move the mesh to the given elevation along +Z (see /Ch8/skyline_generator.py)

```
def extrude_single_polygon(mesh, height, elev):
    bm = bmesh.new()
    bm.from_mesh(mesh)
    bmesh.ops.edgeloop_fill(bm, edges=bm.edges)
```

```
bm.faces.ensure_lookup_table()
bmesh.ops.solidify(bm, geom=bm.faces, thickness=height)
bm.verts.ensure_lookup_table()
bmesh.ops.translate(bm, vec=Vector((0,0,elev)), ↩
    verts=bm.verts)
bm.to_mesh(mesh)
bm.free()
```

We start by creating a blank bmesh instance bm with bmesh.new(), then call bm.from_mesh(mesh) to associate bm with the given mesh so we can edit mesh through bm ((1) in Figure 8-12).

To fill the edge loop with face(s), we call bmesh.ops.edgeloop_fill ((2) in Figure 8-12). We then call bm.faces.ensure_lookup_table() to refresh bm's internal face indices since new face(s) are added, before calling bmesh.ops.solidify with bm.faces and the given building height as thickness to extrude the face(s) to that height ((3) in Figure 8-12).

Since new verts are added during the extrusion, we call bm.verts.ensure_lookup_table() to refresh bm's internal vert indices, before calling bmesh.ops.translate to move them along +Z to the given elevation elev ((4) in Figure 8-12). Finally, we transfer the edits from bm to mesh via bm.to_mesh(mesh), then destroy bm with bm.free() since we no longer need it.

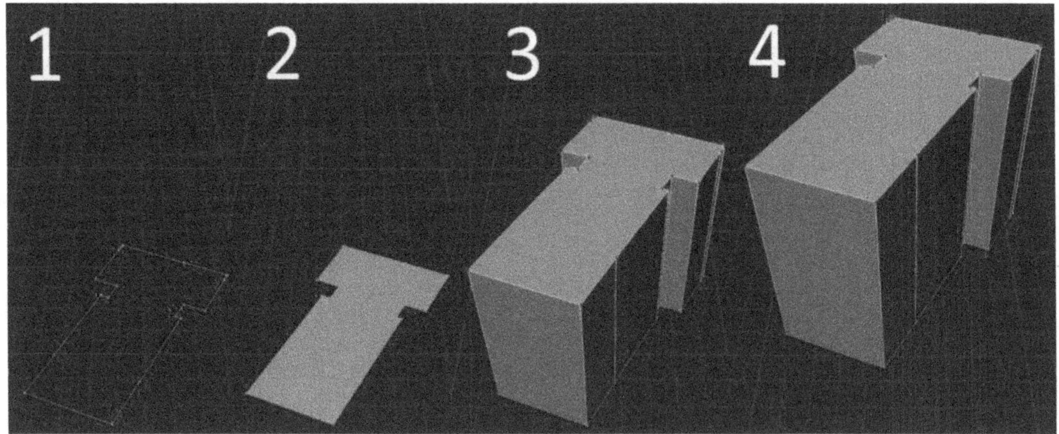

Figure 8-12. *Intermediate steps of extruding shape #1250 from the provided /Ch8/ qgis_battery_park.shp file by calling `extrude_single_polygon` (Listing 8-10). (1) Create a `bmesh` instance for editing `mesh`, and select the edge loop. (2) Fill in the edge loop with face(s) by calling `bmesh.ops.edgeloop_fill`. (3) Extrude face(s) to roof height with `bmesh.ops.solidify` (4) Move `mesh` to correct elevation with `bmesh.ops.translate`*

Type 2: Two Nested Polygons

In `extrude_two_polygons` (Listing 8-11), we deal with the case where the shape consists of two polygons, one nesting inside the other.

Listing 8-11. Given a 2D wireframe mesh made up of two nested loops, extrude it to the given height and move it to the given elevation along +Z (see /Ch8/ skyline_generator.py)

```
def extrude_two_polygons(mesh, height, elev, num_shp_edges):
    bm = bmesh.new()
    bm.from_mesh(mesh)

    top = bmesh.ops.extrude_edge_only(bm, edges=bm.edges)
    bm.edges.ensure_lookup_table()
    bmesh.ops.translate(bm, vec=Vector((0,0,height)), ↩
        verts=[v for v in top["geom"] if isinstance(v, ↩
        bmesh.types.BMVert)])
```

```
bmesh.ops.bridge_loops(bm, edges=[e for e in ↩
    top["geom"] if isinstance(e, bmesh.types.BMEdge)])

bm.edges.ensure_lookup_table()
bmesh.ops.bridge_loops(bm, ↩
    edges=bm.edges[:num_shp_edges])

bm.verts.ensure_lookup_table()
bmesh.ops.translate(bm, vec=Vector((0,0,elev)), ↩
    verts=bm.verts)

bm.to_mesh(mesh)
bm.free()
```

We create a blank bmesh instance bm with bmesh.new(), then call bm.from_mesh(mesh) to associate bm with the given mesh so we can edit mesh through bm. Next, we extrude the two edge loops by calling bmesh.ops.extrude_edge_only (shown as (1) in Figure 8-13. Note that the two sets of loops overlap postextrusion). bmesh.ops operators return a dictionary containing data describing the geometry they create, with the geometry's verts, edges, etc., stored under the dictionary's "geom" key. Here, we save the data returned by bmesh.ops.extrude_edge_only in the variable top, which gives us access to the extruded loops' verts, edges, etc., in top["geom"].

Since new edges are added by the extrusion, we follow with a call to bm.edges.ensure_lookup_table() to refresh bm's internal edge indices. After that, we move the top set of loops to the given height along +Z (with Vector((0,0,height))) using bmesh.ops.translate, then call bmesh.ops.bridge_loops to add faces between them to form the roof ((2) and (2b) in Figure 8-13). Note that we specify the geometry for bmesh.ops.translate to edit by passing in the list of verts, which we get by filtering top["geom"] with type bmesh.types.BMVert using the line

```
verts=[v for v in top["geom"] if isinstance(v, ↩
    bmesh.types.BMVert)]
```

Similarly, we filter top["geom"] to get only the edges (of type bmesh.types.BMEdge) of the top loops to pass to bmesh.ops.bridge_loops to edit.

Bridging the roof created new geometry; therefore, we call `bm.edges.ensure_lookup_table()` to refresh `bm`'s internal edge indices. At this point, the building is bottomless; therefore, we fill in the bottom by calling `bmesh.ops.bridge_loops` ((3) and (3b) in Figure 8-13). The number of edges in the original footprint is passed in as `num_shp_edges`. Since edge indices are in the order of their creation (i.e., edges created first have smaller indices), and the bottom loops are created first, the first `num_shp_edges` edges are part of the bottom loops (from indices `0` to `num_shp_edges-1`). Therefore, calling `bmesh.ops.bridge_loops` with `bm.edges[:num_shp_edges]` bridges the bottom loops.

At this point, the building mesh is fully formed. We call `bm.verts.ensure_lookup_table()` to refresh vert indices, then call `bmesh.ops.translate` to move the building to the correct elevation along +Z with `Vector((0,0,elev))` ((4) in Figure 8-13). Since we're moving the building as a whole, we simply pass `bm.verts` (all of `bm`'s verts) to `bmesh.ops.translate`.

Woot—we're done. To finish up, we'll transfer mesh data from `bm` to `mesh` via `bm.to_mesh(mesh)` and clear `bm` with `bm.free()` since we no longer need it.

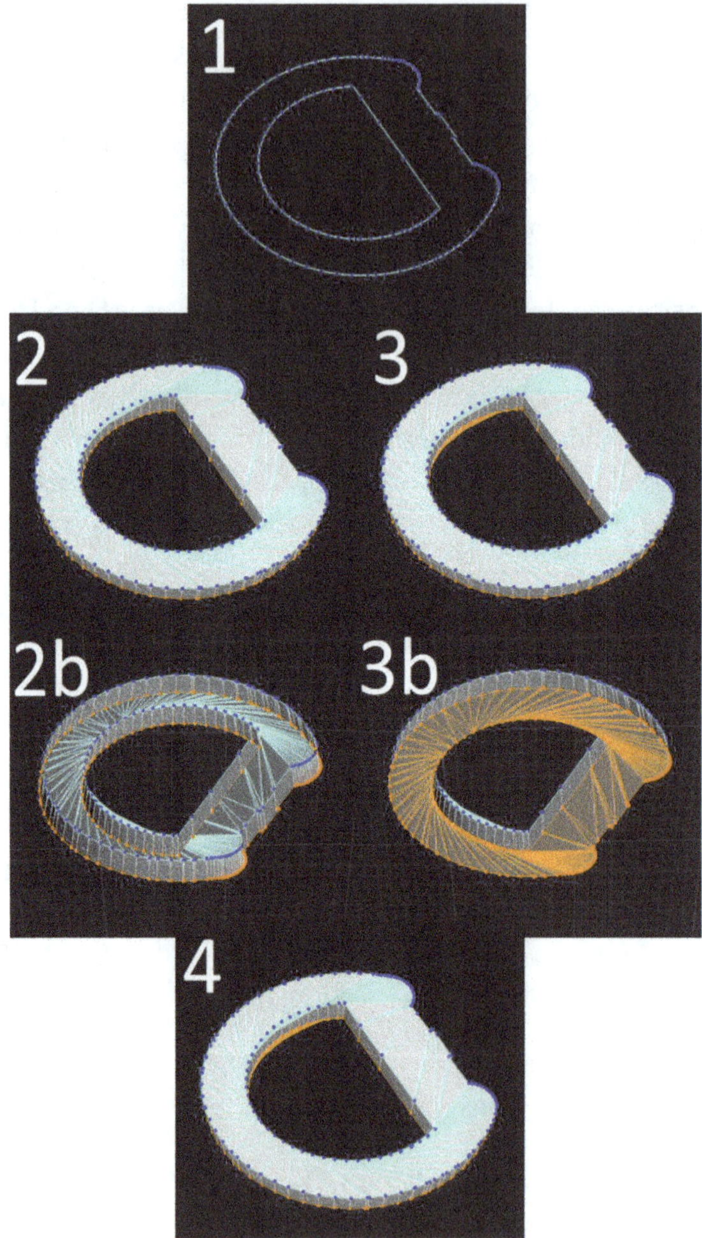

Figure 8-13. *Intermediate steps of extruding shape #479 from the provided /Ch8/ qgis_battery_park.shp file by calling* `extrude_two_polygons` *(Listing 8-11). (1) The two sets of edge loops of the mesh immediately postextrusion. (2) The extruded loops translated to the correct building height along +Z, then bridged to form the roof (2b shows the bottom view). (3) The bottom loops bridged (3b shows the bottom view). (4) The mesh translated to the correct elevation along +Z*

Type 3: Multiple Polygons Enclosed by One Larger Polygon

In `extrude_multiple_polygons` (Listing 8-12), we deal with the case where the shape consists of one larger polygon enclosing multiple smaller nonoverlapping polygons. Here, we treat the inner polygons as cutaways (e.g., courtyards) though other interpretations are possible.

Listing 8-12. Given a 2D wireframe mesh made up of one loop enclosing multiple nonoverlapping smaller loops, extrude the mesh to the given height and move it to the given elevation along +Z (see /Ch8/skyline_generator.py)

```
def extrude_multiple_polygons(context, ↩
    mesh, loop_ref_edge_indices, height, elev):
    temp_obj = bpy.data.objects.new(name="temp", ↩
        object_data=mesh)
    context.collection.objects.link(temp_obj)
    for obj in context.view_layer.objects:
        obj.select_set(False)
    context.view_layer.objects.active = temp_obj
    temp_obj.select_set(True)
    context_override = get_context_override(context, ↩
        'VIEW_3D', 'WINDOW')
    with bpy.context.temp_override(**context_override):
        bpy.ops.object.mode_set(mode='EDIT')
    bm = bmesh.from_edit_mesh(temp_obj.data)
    bm.edges.ensure_lookup_table()

    for i in loop_ref_edge_indices:
        bm.edges[i].select = True
    bpy.ops.mesh.loop_multi_select(ring=False)
    bpy.ops.mesh.fill()

    bm.faces.ensure_lookup_table()
    bm.normal_update()
    top = bmesh.ops.extrude_face_region(bm, geom=bm.faces)
```

```
bmesh.ops.translate(bm, vec=Vector((0,0,height)), ↩
    verts=[v for v in top["geom"] if isinstance(v, ↩
    bmesh.types.BMVert)])
bm.normal_update()

bm.verts.ensure_lookup_table()
bmesh.ops.translate(bm, vec=Vector((0,0,elev)), ↩
    verts=bm.verts)

bmesh.update_edit_mesh(temp_obj.data)
context_override = get_context_override(context, ↩
    'VIEW_3D', 'WINDOW')
with bpy.context.temp_override(**context_override):
    bpy.ops.object.mode_set(mode='OBJECT')
context.collection.objects.unlink(temp_obj)
context.view_layer.update()
bpy.data.objects.remove(temp_obj)
```

For the previous two categories of buildings, we used a bmesh instance to edit the passed-in mesh directly. For this category, we'll use a different strategy, by creating a temp object (temp_obj) from the passed-in mesh, edit it with bmesh, flush the edits from the bmesh instance (bm) back to mesh, then dispose of temp_obj. Due to our choice to interpret the inner loops as cutaways, the only operators in Blender that will reliably bridge the loops this way are bpy.ops.mesh.loop_multi_select followed by bpy.ops.mesh.fill(). It ends up being a cleaner implementation to create a temp object which allows us to call these two bpy.ops operators then transfer the edits back to the passed-in mesh.

Let's break down the code block by block. In the first block, we create a temp mesh object (temp_obj) with the name "temp" and the passed-in mesh as its mesh data by calling bpy.data.objects.new and link it to the scene collection under the passed-in context via context.collection.objects.link. We then iterate through the scene objects, deselecting them one by one, before setting temp_obj as active and selecting it. With a context override (as if from the viewport), we switch temp_obj to Edit mode so we can create a bmesh instance (bm) for editing it, then call bm.edges.ensure_lookup_table() to prepare for iteration through its edges next.

In the second block of code, we select all the edge loops ((1) in Figure 8-14), fill in the space between the inner loops and the enclosing loop, then extrude (2) and move the faces to the passed-in roof `height` along +Z (3, with bottom view shown in 3b). Recall in `add_shape_from_geojson` (Listing 8-8) we accumulated the list of edge indices with one from each loop in `loop_ref_edge_indices`; here, we simply iterate it to select the edges one by one, then call `bpy.ops.mesh.loop_multi_select(ring=False)` to select all the loops these edges are a part of in one shot. After that, we call `bpy.ops.mesh.fill()` to add faces between the loops (in Edit mode, Face ➤ Fill). Since new faces are added by `fill()`, we follow up with `bm.faces.ensure_lookup_table()` to refresh `bm`'s internal face indices and update normals (`bm.normal_update()`). We then call `bmesh.ops.extrude_face_region` to extrude all of `bm`'s faces, which has the same effect as A to select all, E to extrude, then LMB to confirm and leave the extrusion in place. As discussed in the previous section, `bmesh.ops` operators return a dictionary containing data describing the geometry they create, with the geometry's verts, edges, etc., stored under the dictionary's "geom" key. Here, we assign the data returned by `bmesh.ops.extrude_face_region` to the variable `top`, which gives us access to the extrusion's verts, edges, etc., in `top["geom"]`. We filter `top["geom"]` to get the verts in the extrusion (of type `bmesh.types.BMVert`) to pass to `bmesh.ops.translate` with the line

```
verts=[v for v in top["geom"] if isinstance(v, ↩
    bmesh.types.BMVert)]
```

Since the faces are extruded then moved up, both the top and bottom of the mesh will already be filled in. We update normals via `bm.normal_update()` then call `bm.verts.ensure_lookup_table()` to account for the verts added during the extrusion. To finish constructing the mesh, we call `bmesh.ops.translate` with all of `bm`'s verts to move the whole mesh to the passed-in elevation (`elev`) along +Z with `Vector((0,0,elev))`. We then flush the edits queued on `bm` to `mesh`, at which point we no longer need `temp_obj`; therefore, we switch it back to Object mode with a context override (as if from the viewport) to unlink it from the scene collection, update the view layer, then delete `temp_obj` from the blend file via `bpy.data.objects.remove(temp_obj)`.

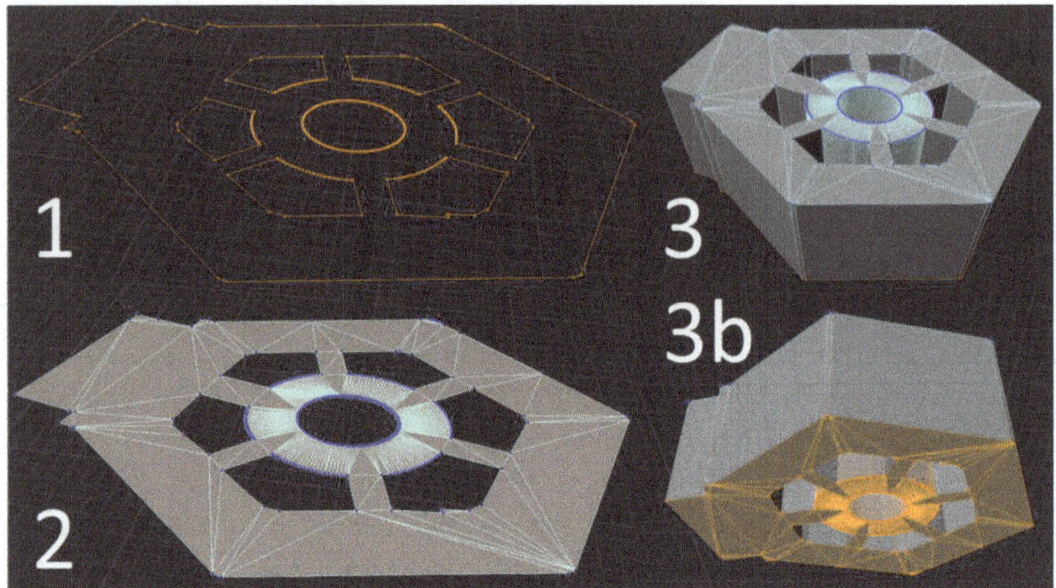

***Figure 8-14.** Intermediate steps of extruding shape #307 from the provided /Ch8/qgis_battery_park.shp file by calling `extrude_multiple_polygons` (Listing 8-12). (1) Select all edge loops. (2) Fill in the space between the inner loops and the enclosing loop, then extrude the faces in place. (3) Grab and move the extrusion to roof height along +Z; (3b) shows the bottom view.*

Testing Skyline Generation with the Provided Datasets

Our skyline generator is complete. Let's call `gen_skyline` (Listing 8-5) to generate some cities. At the bottom of `/Ch8/skyline_generator.py`, there is already an `if __name__ == "__main__"` block set up with two calls to `gen_skyline` (Listing 8-5), each with one of the provided building footprint datasets, as shown in Listing 8-13.

Listing 8-13. Main block in /Ch8/skyline_generator.py with sample calls to gen_skyline (Listing 8-5)

```
if __name__ == "__main__":
    start = timeit.default_timer()

    gen_skyline(script_dir+"/qgis_battery_park.shp", ↩
        script_dir+"/qgis_battery_park.xlsx", 100.0, ↩
        bpy.context, 1, "heightroof", "groundelev", ↩
        "shape_len")
```

```
gen_skyline(script_dir+"/havana.shp", ↩
    script_dir+"/havana.xlsx", 200.0, bpy.context, ↩
    1, "", "", "", (-170,0,0), (40,100), (10,30))

end = timeit.default_timer()
print("Runtime: " + str(end-start))
```

Let's take a closer look at the main block. Right away, you'll notice that there are two calls to `timeit.default_timer()` surrounding `gen_skyline` calls—these are to take timestamps right before and after the generation so we can measure the runtime by subtracting the two and display it in the System Console (Window ➤ Toggle System Console) with a `print` statement. We'll look at `timeit.default_timer()` in more detail shortly.

The first `gen_skyline` call uses the Battery Park, NYC, dataset (`/Ch8/qgis_battery_park.shp` and `/Ch8/qgis_battery_park.xlsx`) with a `target_len` of 100.0 Blender units and an `elev_scale` of 1. Recall that `target_len` is used to derive the XY scale factor should the derivation by cross-referencing curve length with the perimeter from the spreadsheet fails. `script_dir`, which is the current directory of the script, is used to form the absolute file path to the `*.shp` and `*.xlsx` files. You'll see how to find `script_dir` in the next section. The roof heights, ground elevation, and shape perimeter values are all present in this dataset's spreadsheet, so we pass their keys to `gen_skyline` and leave the sampling range values at default. The skyline generated by this call is shown in Figure 8-15.

The second `gen_skyline` call uses the Havana, Cuba, dataset (`/Ch8/havana.shp` and `/Ch8/havana.xlsx`), with a `target_len` of 200.0 Blender units and an `elev_scale` of 1. The roof heights, ground elevation, and shape perimeter values are all missing in this dataset's spreadsheet, so we pass zero-length strings as their keys, along with a roof height range of 40 to 100 and a ground elevation range of 10 to 30. `(-170,0,0)` is used as the location for the city mesh object so it does not overlap the Battery Park mesh in the viewport. The Havana mesh generated by this call is shown in Figure 8-16.

You can find a copy of both meshes generated by Listing 8-13 in `/Ch8/skyline_demo.blend` from this chapter's downloaded files.

Note You'll find the attribution of the two provided building footprint datasets in the earlier section "Composition of Building Footprint Data."

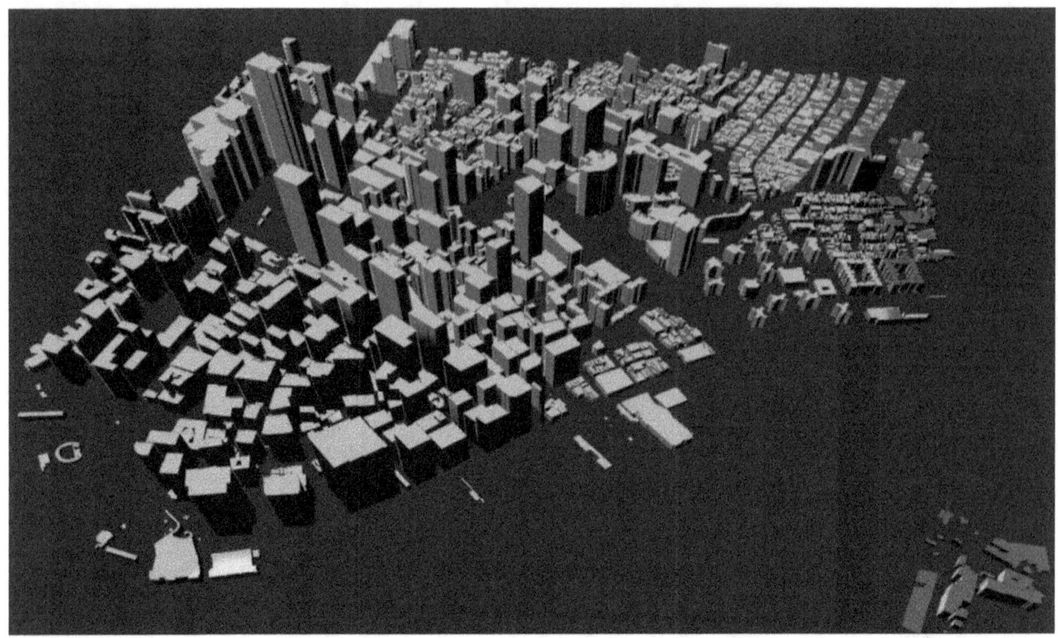

***Figure 8-15.** The Battery Park, NYC, mesh generated by running Listing 8-13*

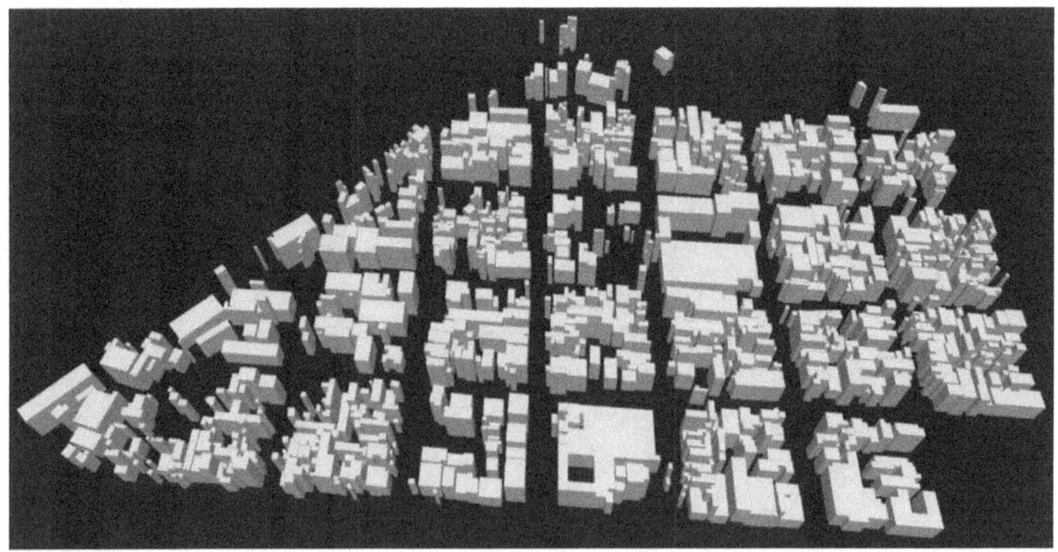

***Figure 8-16.** The Havana, Cuba, mesh generated by running Listing 8-13*

Deriving the Script's Current Directory

Recall in Listing 2-2 (Chapter 2, section "Handling Imports for Scripts to Run in the Text Editor") we wrote a snippet to add the directory that a script is running out of in the Text Editor to the list of locations Blender Python scans for imports. In Listing 8-14, we create a shortened version of Listing 2-2 that stops once it finds the script's current directory (`script_dir`). Assuming that we have the `*.shp` and `*.xlsx` files in the same directory as `/Ch8/skyline_generator.py`, we can simply concatenate `script_dir` with a slash followed by the file name as shown in Listing 8-13 to form the absolute path to these files to pass to `gen_skyline` (Listing 8-5). For a detailed explanation of Listing 8-14, please refer to Listing 2-2.

Listing 8-14. Snippet at the top of in /Ch8/skyline_generator.py that derives the path to the script's current directory

```
import os
script_dir = ""
if bpy.context.space_data and bpy.context.space_data.text:
    script_filepath = bpy.context.space_data.text.filepath
    if script_filepath:
        script_dir = os.path.dirname(script_filepath)
```

Estimating Runtime with `timeit`

When developing scripts meant to generate large amounts of data, as is the case of our skyline generator, it's usually a good idea to keep an eye on runtime, which will tell you if and where improvements could be made. For example, if there are several operators that could potentially achieve the same effect, such as `bpy.ops.mesh` vs. `bmesh.ops` operators—is one slower than the other? Moreover, from runtime, you can estimate how large a dataset your script can realistically handle. You can quickly measure runtime with the built-in Python module `timeit`, by calling `timeit.default_timer()` immediately before and after a block of code in question, as shown in Listing 8-15. The runtime is then the difference between the two timestamps, which you can display in the System Console (Window ➤ Toggle System Console) with a `print` statement.

Listing 8-15. Example of measuring runtime by taking timestamps with timeit.
default_timer()

```
import timeit
start = timeit.default_timer()
gen_skyline("C:\\Ch8\\qgis_battery_park.shp", ↩
    "C:\\Ch8\\qgis_battery_park.xlsx", 100.0, bpy.context, ↩
    1, "heightroof", "groundelev", "shape_len")
end = timeit.default_timer()
print("Runtime: " + str(end-start))
```

Summary

In this chapter, you learned how to implement a skyline generator in Blender Python that produces city meshes from GIS building footprint data. You started by analyzing the composition of a building footprint dataset and wrote Python code to inspect and plot its contents for further insight. You then found out where to source building footprint datasets as well as how to edit them in the open source GIS software QGIS to convert them into shapefiles (`*.shp`) containing footprints as polycurves (lists of points) and roof heights in corresponding spreadsheets (`*.xlsx`) that are suitable to work with under Blender Python.

With your newfound knowledge on footprints, you formulated a high-level design for a generator, which converts polycurves from shapefiles to wireframe meshes, fills in the wireframes, extrudes them based on roof heights, and moves them into place according to the elevations from the spreadsheet. You then implemented the generator in Blender Python using a top-down design, by writing a series of functions, each doing a unit of work for the previous at a finer granularity.

The first function serves as the entry point to the generator, loading given footprint files and filling in any missing data (e.g., roof heights) by sampling from user-supplied ranges before passing the buck to the second function, which creates a city mesh object and a master `bmesh` instance for editing it, plus handling postgeneration scaling and transform application. The third function iterates through the shapes and calls the appropriate helper function to create the building geometry to add to the city mesh via the master `bmesh` instance. The fourth level, which is at the finest granularity, consists of three functions, each handling a different type of footprint shape—single polygon, two nested polygons, and multiple polygons enclosed by a larger polygon. After finishing the generator, you tested it with the two provided datasets from the downloaded source and generated the skylines of Battery Park, NYC, and Havana, Cuba.

CHAPTER 9

GIS-Based Generation Part 2: Terrain from Digital Elevation Models (DEM)

A Digital Elevation Model (DEM) is a type of GIS data that encodes the surface relief of an area on Earth or other planets. In this chapter, I'll show you how to write a DEM-based terrain generator using a combination of Blender Python, geometry nodes, and shader nodes. In the first half of the chapter, we'll go over the composition of DEMs, how to plot and convert them into PNG files for visualization, and how to analyze their contents to locate the band containing the elevation data. In addition, we'll look at how to filter and subsample the elevation points, calculate scale factors, and convert the points into a format usable in Blender.

In the second half of the chapter, we'll formulate a design and implement the terrain generator. We'll divide the generation into several stages: the first stage transforms the elevation points sampled from the DEM into vertices, the second stage triangulates the mesh using a geometry node based voxelizer, and the third stage applies a material generated from the same DEM to the mesh. To drive the concept home, we'll make use of two provided DEMs throughout the chapter, one of Colorado Springs (courtesy of USGS) and the other of the Mars crater (from the HiRISE project by the University of Arizona). By the end of the chapter, you'll have generated terrain meshes based on both DEMs.

I. Lupiani, *Procedural Content Generation for Games*, https://doi.org/10.1007/979-8-8688-1787-8_9

Running This Chapter's Examples

The terrain generator we'll implement in this chapter takes input DEM models stored in TIFF (Tag Image File Format) files with the extension `*.tif` and IMG (Raw Image) files with the extension `*.img`. In this section, we'll go over how to set up dependencies and download source code to parse and visualize these files in Blender Python.

Installing Dependencies

We'll install the Python module `rasterio` to parse the TIFF (`*.tif`) and IMG (`*.img`) files, `matplotlib` to plot and visualize the DEMs, and `numpy` to implement utility functions. Before proceeding, please refer to the Appendix for directions on how to install these third-party modules under Blender Python.

Downloading and Running the Sample Code

The source code and color figures for this book are available on GitHub via the book's product page, located at `www.apress.com/979-8-8688-1786-1`). Download the files, navigate to the `/Ch9` folder, and open `dem_terrain_generator.py` in the Text Editor under the Scripting workspace. You'll find an `if __name__ == "__main__"` block already set up with calls to the generator at the bottom of the script. Simply click the Run button to generate the terrain meshes based on the two provided DEM models, Colorado Springs, Colorado, United States, and Mars crater. The generator's arguments will be explained in detail throughout the chapter. You can modify the argument values in the sample calls and see how they affect the generated model.

`/Ch9/dem_terratin_generator.py` imports utility functions for material creation from the file `/Ch9/material_and_image_utils.py`. These imports have been set up for you. For more info on how to set up imports for scripts run out of the Text Editor, please refer to the section in Chapter 2 "Handling Imports for Scripts to Run in the Text Editor." The script `material_and_image_utils.py` is also used in Chapter 4.

Attribution to the Provided DEM Models

Here is the detailed attribution to the two provided DEM models. The first is `/Ch9/USGS_13_n39w106_20230602.tif`, which is the dataset "USGS 1 Arc Second n39w106 20230602" downloaded from US Geological Survey (USGS) at `https://www.sciencebase.gov/catalog/item/64800f24d34eac007b56a827`. This model contains the elevation profile of an area in Colorado Springs, Colorado, United States.

The second is `/Ch9/DTEEC_041878_1460_041021_1460_G01.IMG`, which is the model "Crater with Steep Gullied Slopes" downloaded from the HiRISE project (High Resolution Imaging Science Experiment) of the University of Arizona's LPL (Lunar & Planetary Laboratory) at `https://www.uahirise.org/dtm/ESP_041878_1460`. This model contains the elevation profile of the Mars crater.

Introduction to Digital Elevation Models (DEM)

A *Digital Elevation Model* (DEM) is a type of Geographic Information System (GIS) data that encodes the surface relief of a piece of terrain. DEMs are "bare earth" models that depict terrain elevation after all surface objects such as trees, buildings, etc., have been stripped away. Traditionally, DEMs are derived from topographic maps. In more recent years, most practitioners have shifted toward deriving DEMs from lidar point clouds.

Note Light detection and ranging (lidar) data is a type of GIS data in the form of point clouds that are usually gathered by vehicles with sensors picking up reflections of pulsed laser beams. Lidar data over large areas are often collected aerially by a plane, whereas smaller areas are scanned by cars.

Composition of a DEM

Like many types of GIS data, a DEM is stored as a *raster*, which is similar to a multichannel image, as shown in Figure 9-1. A raster consists of one or more "bands" of the same dimension. Each band is a 2D table of numbers, with each cell corresponding to a unit area over a geographic location. The resolution of a raster can be calculated by dividing the area of the geographic region it covers by the number of band cells. For example, if a raster covers a 600 square mile area in New Mexico, United States, and each band in the raster is 20 by 10 and therefore has

$$20 \times 10 = 200\,cells$$

then each cell (or pixel) covers a

$$600 \div 200 = 3\, square\, mile\, area.$$

As we'll see later in this chapter, a DEM usually consists of a single band with a 2D table of decimal numbers representing the elevation of the area it maps to. Other types of GIS data like satellite imagery could also be stored in a raster, but with multiple bands, each representing a different section of the electromagnetic spectrum.

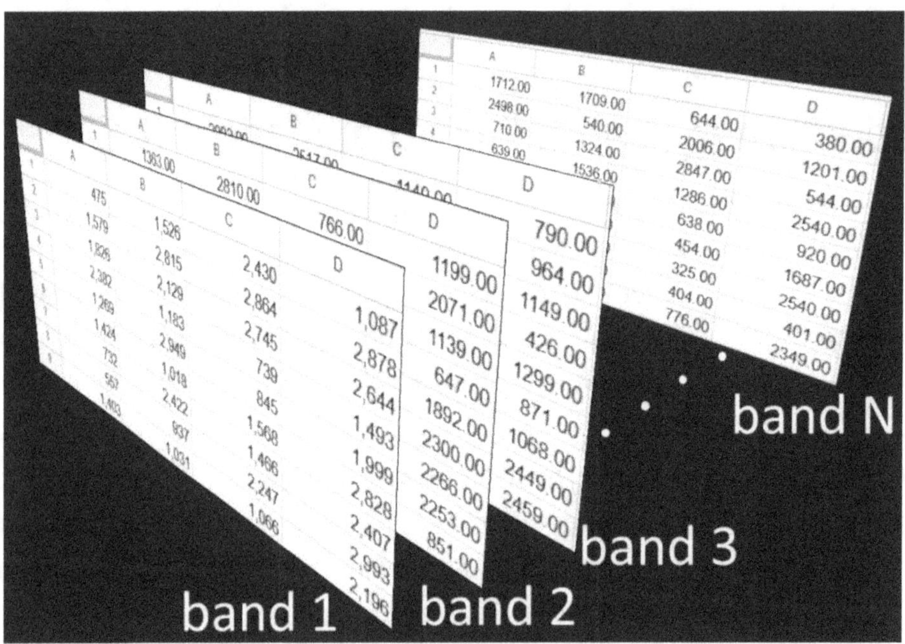

***Figure 9-1.** Like a multichannel image, a DEM is stored in a raster with one or more "bands," each containing a 2D table of numbers. All the bands in a raster have the same dimension.*

Inspecting the Contents of a DEM

Since DEMs can be intuitively thought of as multichannel images, one of the best ways to inspect their contents is visually. Even if you aren't sure how many bands are in a file or the type of data each band holds, you can try plotting each one to see what comes up.

While some image editors (Blender's Image Editor included) will open TIFF and IMG files, DEM files don't encode data the same way as images. If you try opening the DEM file in one of these editors, it may open but would likely not display correctly.

For example, the provided USGS DEM file (TIFF) shows incorrectly as a white image in Blender's Image Editor. Therefore, in this section, we'll write our own Python function to display and convert DEM files.

Importing rasterio, matplotlib, and numpy

The following three lines at the top of /Ch9/dem_terrain_generator.py imports rasterio as the shorthand ri (which we'll use to read the DEM file), the submodule matplotlib.pyplot as plt (which we'll use to plot), and numpy as np (which we'll use to convert the band to 8-bit):

```
import rasterio as ri
import matplotlib.pyplot as plt
import numpy as np
```

Plot a Given Band in a DEM File

Given the path to a DEM file and the band number, the function plt_dem_image in Listing 9-1 reads the DEM with rasterio, plots the given band with matplotlib, and saves the plot to a *.png file on disk in script_dir, the same directory the active script is running out of in the Text Editor. You can subsequently open the PNG file in any image editor.

Listing 9-1. Plotting a given band of a DEM file with matplotlib and saving the figure to disk as a *.png file (see /Ch9/dem_terrain_generator.py)

```
def plt_dem_image(dem_filepath:str, band_num:int):
    dem_file = ri.open(dem_filepath)
    band = dem_file.read(band_num)

    eight_bit = (band*(255/np.max(band))).astype(np.uint8)
    plt.imshow(eight_bit)
    plt.axis('off')

    dem_filename_no_ext = get_name_no_ext(dem_filepath)
    plt.savefig(script_dir+"/"+dem_filename_no_ext+ ↩
        "_plt_color.png", bbox_inches='tight', ↩
        transparent=True, pad_inches=0)

    plt.show()
```

We start by calling `ri.open` with the path to the DEM file and use the returned object `dem_file` to call `read()` with a band number to access a given band. Since `plt` can only plot 8-bit images (i.e., images with pixel values ranging from 0 to 255), we convert the band to 8-bit on the next line by scaling it with `(255/np.max(band))` and setting it as type `np.uint8`, which is the unsigned 8-bit integer type in `numpy`. Note that `np.max(band)` gives you the maximum value of `band`, therefore dividing `band` by `np.max(band)` maps `band` to the range of 0 to 1, which when further multiplied by 255 moves to the range of 0 to 255.

Next, we'll create the plot by calling `plt.show` with the 8-bit version of the band (`eight_bit`). We don't need the plot axes to show on an image so we call `plt.axis('off')` to turn them off. Instead of calling `plt.show()` next to display the image like we normally would, we save the plot to the disk first—this is because calling `plt.show()` then `plt.savefig` would make the image show up blank, so we must reverse the order. To form the path to save the plot, we derive the part of the DEM file's name without the extension using `get_name_no_ext` (Listing 4-13), then append it with `*.png` and prepend it with `script_dir` to create a file path to the same directory as the script. We then call `plt.savefig` with this path to save the plot with zero padding (`bbox_inches='tight'` and `pad_inches=0`) and transparency enabled (`transparent=True`), after which we call `plt.show()` to display the plot on screen.

Note You can find `get_name_no_ext` (Listing 4-13) in the Chapter 4 section "Util Function: Extracting the Name of a File Without the Extension."

You can refer to the Chapter 8 section "Deriving the Script's Current Directory" for an explanation on how to find `script_dir`, the directory in which the active script in the Text Editor resides.

Plot the Provided DEM Files

Listing 9-2 shows how we can call `plt_dem_image` (Listing 9-1) to plot the two provided DEM files. Since these two files are under the same folder as `dem_terrain_generator.py`, we can form their paths using `script_dir`. We plot band #1 for both files, which contains the elevation data we'll need to generate the terrain later. Note that the bands in a DEM file use 1-based indexing, i.e., the first index is at 1, not 0. The resulting plots are shown in Figures 9-2 and 9-3.

Listing 9-2. Plotting the two provided DEM files (see /Ch9/dem_terrain_generator.py)

```
def plot_provided_dems():
    plt_dem_image( ↩
        script_dir+"/USGS_13_n39w106_20230602.tif", 1)
    plt_dem_image(script_dir ↩
        +"/DTEEC_041878_1460_041021_1460_G01.IMG", 1)
```

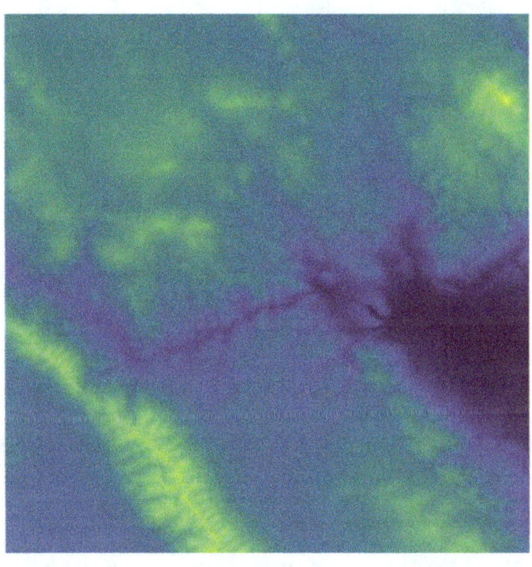

Figure 9-2. *The provided DEM file /Ch9/USGS_13_n39w106_20230602.tif plotted by calling plt_dem_image (Listing 9-1)*

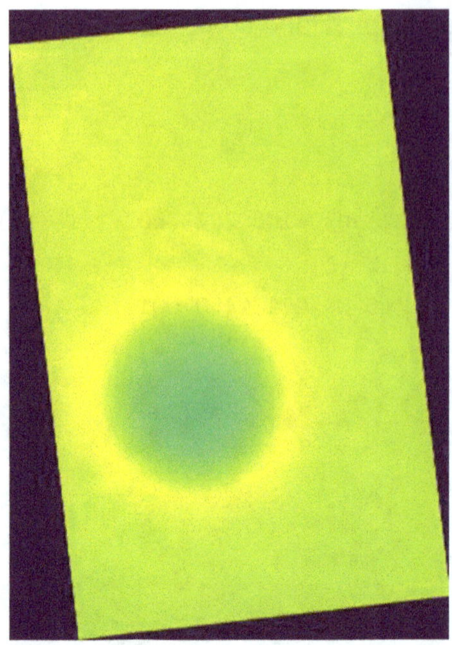

Figure 9-3. *The provided DEM file /Ch9/DTEEC_041878_1460_041021_1460_G01.IMG plotted by calling `plt_dem_image` (Listing 9-1)*

Converting DEM Data Point to (X, Y, Z) Coordinate in Blender

Once we locate the band with elevation data, we need to find out how to convert it into a format usable in Blender. The elevation points are stored in a 2D table analogous to a spreadsheet. If you think of the real-world location coordinates of each cell as the (X, Y) coordinate of a vertex, then the number stored in that cell is the elevation, or Z coordinate of the vertex. Not every cell in a DEM band contains valid data, however, so we must prune the invalid cells before converting them to 3D points. Finally, since DEM sets usually contain many cells, converting the cells to 3D points one to one will create too dense of a mesh; therefore, we subsample the 3D points before using them as vertex positions. `elev_band_to_XYZ` (Listing 9-3) implements these steps in Python, which we'll take a closer look at next.

Listing 9-3. Filtering, subsampling, and converting elevation data to (X, Y, Z) coordinates (see /Ch9/dem_terrain_generator.py)

```
def elev_band_to_XYZ(context, dir:str, ↩
    dem_filepath:str, target_len:float, ↩
    sample_step=1000, verbose=True):
    dem_file = ri.open(dem_filepath)
    num_rows, num_cols = dem_file.height, dem_file.width
    band1 = dem_file.read(1)

    mask_has_data = band1!=dem_file.nodata
    z = band1[mask_has_data]
    row_indices, col_indices = np.where(mask_has_data)

    x, y = ri.transform.xy(dem_file.transform, ↩
        row_indices, col_indices)
    points = np.stack([x,y,z], axis=-1).reshape(len(x), 3)

    x_min, x_max = find_min_max(points, 0)
    y_min, y_max = find_min_max(points, 1)
    z_min, z_max = find_min_max(points, 2)
    xy_scale = target_len/max(x_max-x_min, y_max-y_min)
    points_subsampled = points[::sample_step] if ↩
        sample_step > 0 else points

    if verbose:
        print("\n" + get_name_no_ext(dem_filepath) + ":")
        print("band1.shape = " + str(band1.shape))
        print("points.shape = " + str(points.shape))
        print("points_subsampled.shape " + ↩
            str(points_subsampled.shape) + "\n")
```

As we've done in `plt_dem_image` (Listing 9-1), we call `ri.open` with the path to the DEM file to get the parsed object `dem_file`, which we use to access everything about the DEM, such as the number of rows and columns under it (`dem_file.height` and `dem_file.width`).

We call `dem_file.read(1)` to retrieve the first band, which contains the elevation. During parsing, the invalid cells in `dem_file` are populated with the value `dem_file.nodata`; therefore, we can prune the band such that only *valid* cells remain with the expression `band1[mask_has_data]`, where `mask_has_data` is the Boolean condition `band1!=dem_file.nodata`, which reads, "Cells in `band1` with values *other than* `dem_file.nodata`." To find the (row, column) indices of these cells, we call `np.where` with the same condition. We'll step through how `np.where` works in the next section.

The next step is to convert the cells' (row, column) indices to their real-world XY counterparts, by calling `ri.transform.xy` with the DEM model's *coordinate reference system* (`dem_file.transform`) along with the cells' row and column indices:

```
x, y = ri.transform.xy(dem_file.transform, ↩
    row_indices, col_indices)
```

Earth is spherical, but papers and screens are flat. As a result, all maps are approximated by projecting from a spherical to a planar surface. A coordinate reference system (CRS) describes the inverse of this projection, i.e., how the 2D coordinates in your GIS data relate to the real locations on Earth. The above call to `ri.transform.xy` takes the `dem_file`'s CRS (`dem_file.transform`) and converts the given row and column indices to their corresponding XY coordinates on Earth (we used Earth as an example here, but DEMs can encode data for other planets too, like the provided DTEEC Mars crater model).

At this point, we've compiled a list of Earth locations in the arrays `x` and `y` with their corresponding elevation in the array `z`. To use them as vertex positions in Blender, we need to combine the three separate arrays into a single array of (X, Y, Z) coordinates. To do so, we make the following call to `np.stack`:

```
points = np.stack([x,y,z], axis=-1).reshape(len(x), 3)
```

For example, if `x = [1, 2, 3, 4, 5]`, `y = [6, 7, 8, 9, 10]`, and `z = [11, 12, 13, 14, ,15]`, the above call will combine them into a 5 by 3 array that looks like the following, where `x` becomes the first column, `y` the second column, and `z` the third column:

```
[[1, 6, 11],
 [2, 7, 12],
 [3, 8, 13],
 [4, 9, 14],
 [5, 10, 15]]
```

With the points formatted, next we'll scale and subsample them. Currently, the points have (X, Y, Z) coordinates in Earth scale, which depending on the units used by the DEM (km, mile, m, etc.) may be very large (or very small) relative to the Blender unit for length. You can find and change the units used by your copy of Blender under the Properties editor—Scene tab—Units, as shown in Figure 9-4. By default, Blender uses meters for length. To scale the points, we let the users specify a target length (`target_len`) for the longer side of the mesh that the points will generate as vertex positions. We then call `find_min_max` (Listing 4-2) to find the minimum and maximum of each direction, which we use to derive the X and Y spans covered by the points. After that we divide `target_len` by the longer side to find the scale factor (`xy_scale`). Usually, a DEM consists of a massive number of points, which if used one to one would generate too dense of a mesh. We can easily subsample the points array by skipping every `sample_step` items with the following line:

```
points_subsampled = points[::sample_step] if ↩
    sample_step > 0 else points
```

Since `sample_step` is a user-specified parameter, we do some simple error checking by allowing the subsampling only if `sample_step` is greater than 0.

Finally, we add a block of code to optionally display the intermediate shapes of the points array in the System Console (Window—Toggle System Console) so we can follow how the dimension of the array changes after we filter, reformat, and subsample it.

Note You can learn more about how coordinate reference systems (CRS) work in the QGIS documentation at `https://docs.qgis.org/3.40/en/docs/gentle_gis_introduction/coordinate_reference_systems.html`.

You can find the helper function `find_min_max` (Listing 4-2) under the Chapter 4 section "Finding the Extent of a Mesh's Bounding Box Along a Given Axis."

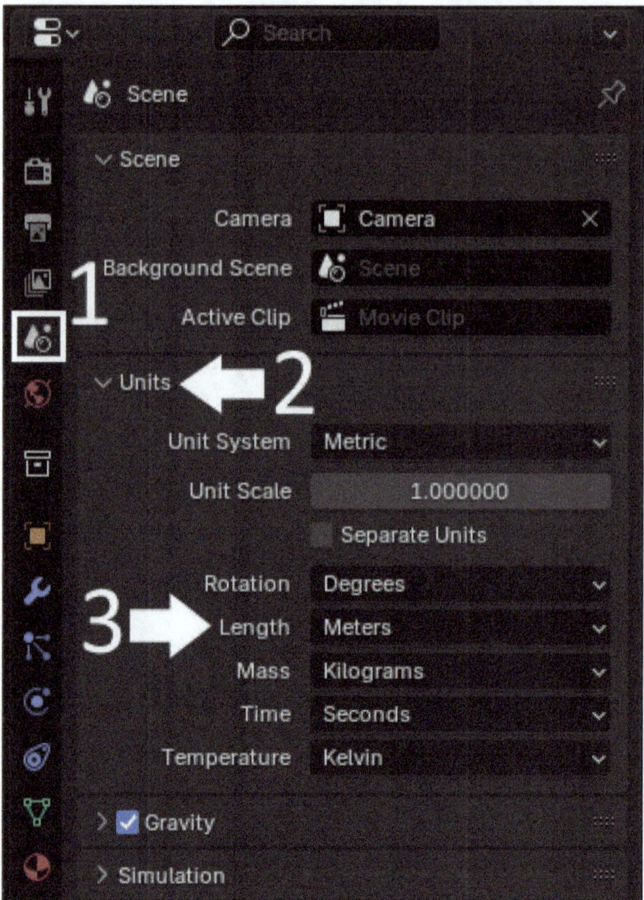

Figure 9-4. *You can find which units your copy of Blender is set to use under the (1) Properties editor—Scene tab—(2) Units. By default, (3) Meters are used for Length.*

A Closer Look at np.where

Listing 9-3 used `np.where` to extract array indices based on different conditions. In this section, we'll take a closer look at how `np.where` works. When faced with an unfamiliar API function, other than consulting documentation, I find the best way to learn its usage is to create a simple example and analyze its output. One such example is shown in Listing 9-4, where I construct a list of points and use `np.where` to extract the row and column indices that satisfy a given Boolean condition.

Listing 9-4. Create a simple example to test np.where's behavior (see /Ch9/dem_terrain_generator.py)

```
def test_np_where():
    points = np.array([(9,-2),(11,7),(0,12),(3,7),(-5,1)])
    print("points = " + str(points))

    row_indices, col_indices = np.where(points < 5)
    print("row_indices = " + str(row_indices))
    print("col_indices = " + str(col_indices))

    matches = list(zip(row_indices.tolist(), ↩
        col_indices.tolist()))
    print("np.where(points < 5) = " + str(matches))
```

Running Listing 9-4 will display the following results in the System Console (Window—Toggle System Console):

```
points = [[ 9 -2]
[11  7]
[ 0 12]
[ 3  7]
[-5  1]]
row_indices = [0 2 3 4 4]
col_indices = [1 0 0 0 1]
np.where(points < 5) = [(0, 1), (2, 0), (3, 0), (4, 0), ↩
    (4, 1)]
```

Looking at `points` printed in the System Console, you can see it's stored as a 2D array with five rows and two columns. With the following line, we extract the row and column indices where items in `points` are less than 5:

```
row_indices, col_indices = np.where(points < 5)
```

Having the row and column indices in two separate arrays is difficult to decipher; therefore, we call Python's built-in function `zip` to cross-reference the two, forming pairs by taking an item from each array at corresponding indices. For example, from the printed output in the System Console, the two arrays are

```
row_indices = [0 2 3 4 4]
col_indices = [1 0 0 0 1]
```

At each index (0, 1, etc.), zip takes an item from each array to make a pair, for example, at index 0, this is (0, 1); at index 1, this is (2, 0); and so on. Note that because row_indices and col_indices are numpy arrays, we must call to_list() to convert them to Python lists before using them to call zip.

Lastly, let's verify that the index pairs from zip lead us to items in points that are less than 5. The first pair is (0, 1); at this position, points have the entry –2, which is < 5. The second pair is (2, 0); at this position, points have the entry 0, which is also < 5, and so on.

Note Recall that the result of print statements is displayed in the System Console (Window—Toggle System Console).

Analyzing Data Shapes of the Two Provided DEMs

print_data_shapes in Listing 9-5 shows sample calls to elev_band_to_XYZ (Listing 9-3) with the two provided DEMs, with target_len=100.0, and a sample_step of 1000 for the USGS set and sample_step of 100 for the DTEEC (Mars crater) set. Again, we use script_dir (described in the section "Plot a Given Band in a DEM File") to form the path to the two DEM files.

Listing 9-5. Calling elev_band_to_XYZ (Listing 9-3) with the two provided DEMs (see /Ch9/dem_terrain_generator.py)

```
def print_data_shapes():
    elev_band_to_XYZ(bpy.context, script_dir, ↩
        script_dir+"/USGS_13_n39w106_20230602.tif", ↩
        100.0, 1000, True)
    elev_band_to_XYZ(bpy.context, script_dir, ↩
        script_dir+ ↩
            "/DTEEC_041878_1460_041021_1460_G01.IMG", ↩
        100.0, 100, True)
```

Calling Listing 9-5 prints the following lines to the System Console (Window—Toggle System Console):

```
USGS_13_n39w106_20230602:
band1.shape = (10812, 10812)
points.shape = (116899344, 3)
points_subsampled.shape (116900, 3)

DTEEC_041878_1460_041021_1460_G01:
band1.shape = (7680, 5536)
points.shape = (33924352, 3)
points_subsampled.shape (339244, 3)
```

Let's do a little math to verify that the shapes printed by Listing 9-5 make sense. For the USGS dataset, we see that `band1` is a 10812 by 10812 square table—which matches the shape of the image we plotted from this set in Figure 9-2. As described in the previous section, we use the CRS-transformed (row, column) indices of each band cell as its (X, Y) coordinates and the cell's content as its Z coordinate to make a 3D point, which makes a total of

$$10812 \times 10812 = 116899344$$

points, matching the shape of the `points` array at (116899344, 3). Lastly, since we specified a `sample_step` of 1000 for this set, consequently

$$116899344 \div 1000 \cong 116900$$

points are sampled.

For the DTEEC dataset (Mars crater), `band1` is 7680 by 5536, which is a rectangle, matching our expectation from the image plotted for the set in Figure 9-3. You'll notice that Figure 9-3 is taller than it is wide, which makes sense since the band has more rows than columns. From `band1`'s size, we expect

$$7680 \times 5536 = 42516480$$

3D points; however, `points` have shape (33924352, 3), implying it only contains 33924352 points, which means some data cells must have contained `nodata` (see Listing 9-3) and were therefore pruned. Finally, since we specified a `sample_step` of 100 for this dataset, we expect

$$33924352 \div 100 \cong 339244$$

points to be sampled, which matches the shape of `points_subsampled`.

Formulating a Design for the Terrain Generator

In this section, we'll lay out the high-level workflow for the terrain generator. In the previous sections, you plotted the DEM using `plt_dem_image` (Listing 9-1) and identified the band containing the elevation data, then filtered, transformed with CRS, and subsampled the elevation points with `elev_band_to_XYZ` (Listing 9-3). The next step is to reshape the points array into a (number of points) by 3 array, i.e., one (X, Y, Z) point per row, so we can use the array as vertex positions with Blender Python's `<mesh>.from_pydata` to populate a mesh data block (as we did in Chapter 8). At this point, the mesh only has vertices, so we need to connect the verts and fill in the faces. It turns out we can reuse the geometry node voxelizer we put together in Chapter 5, which subsamples as well as generates the edges and faces. We'll use Blender Python to create the voxelizer node tree so we can have a terrain generator that is automated end to end (input to output) in Python.

Taking advantage of the fact that the elevation data can be easily interpreted as an image, we'll also write some code to convert it to a grayscale image and save it as a PNG file, which we'll in turn use as an image texture to create a material to apply to the generated terrain mesh to accentuate its ridges and valleys. A visual summary of the overall workflow we've discussed in this section is shown in Figure 9-5.

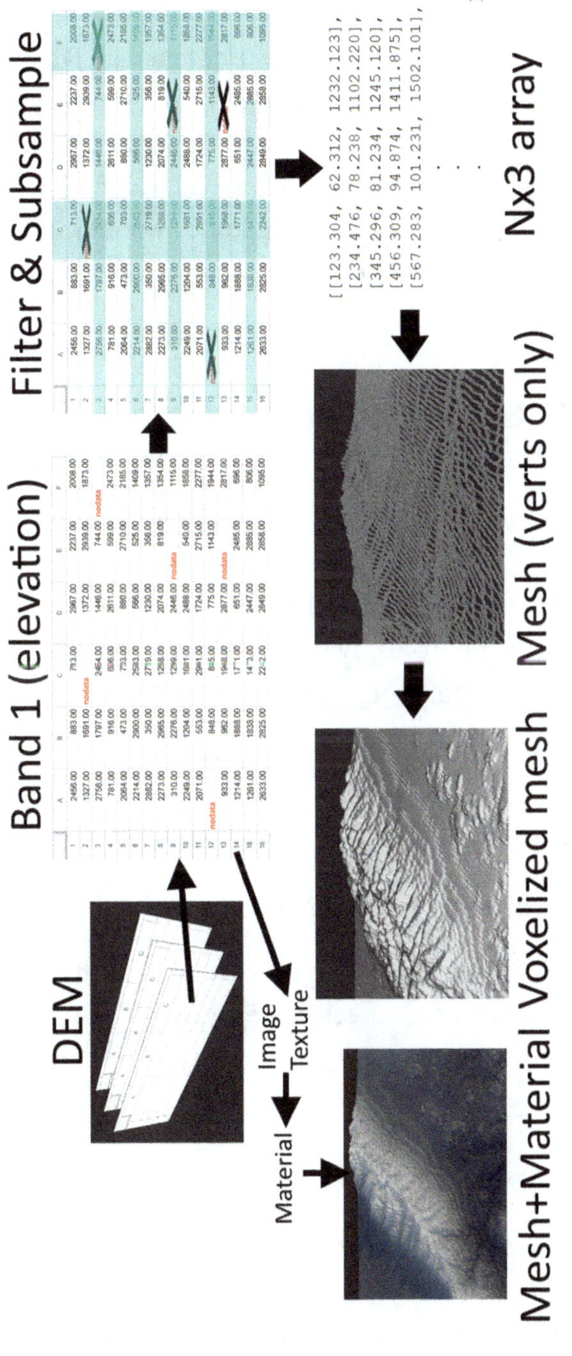

***Figure 9-5.** High-level workflow of our proposed DEM terrain generator*

Implementing the Terrain Generator with Blender Python, Geometry Nodes, and Shader Nodes

With a high-level design in hand, for the rest of the chapter, we'll implement the terrain generator in Blender Python with help from geometry and shader nodes. We'll break the generation into a series of stages. The first stage serves as an entry point where we parse and filter the DEM. The second stage creates a terrain mesh from the subsampled elevation points with numpy, bpy functions, and geometry nodes. The third stage converts the elevation points into a grayscale image, which is subsequently used by the fourth stage to create a material for the mesh.

Generating a Terrain Mesh from a DEM

gen_dem_mesh (Listing 9-6) is the entry point to the generator, which reads the DEM file, processes the elevation data, and kicks off the rest of the generation process.

Listing 9-6. Generate a terrain mesh object from the given DEM at the given subsampling rate and optionally apply the DEM as a grayscale image texture to the mesh (see /Ch9/dem_terrain_generator.py)

```
def gen_dem_mesh(context, dir:str, dem_filepath:str, ↩
    target_len:float, sample_step=1000, location=(0,0,0), ↩
    z_scale=0.000015, voxel_size=0.1, add_mat=True):

    ---- SNIPPED (see elev_band_to_XYZ in Listing 9-3)----

    dem_filename_no_ext = get_name_no_ext(dem_filepath)
    terrain_obj, geo_nodes_mod = mesh_from_points( ↩
        context, dem_filename_no_ext, points_subsampled, ↩
        (x_min,y_min,z_min), location, xy_scale, ↩
        z_scale, voxel_size)

    if add_mat:
        row_indices_no_data, col_indices_no_data = ↩
            np.where(band1==dem_file.nodata)
        band1[row_indices_no_data, col_indices_no_data] = ↩
            z_min
```

```
dem_img_blk = create_grayscale_image_from_array( ↩
    band1, num_rows, num_cols, ↩
    dem_filename_no_ext, dir)
mat_name = dem_filename_no_ext + "_mat"
apply_mod_and_add_mat(context, terrain_obj, ↩
    geo_nodes_mod, dem_img_blk, mat_name)
```

The first half of the function is copied from `elev_band_to_XYZ` in Listing 9-3 (minus the `print` statements), in which we parse the DEM file, then filter, scale, and subsample the elevation points. The reason we duplicate the code from Listing 9-3 instead of calling it as a function is because too many of the variables in Listing 9-3 would have to be returned.

`gen_dem_mesh` calls `mesh_from_points` to generate the terrain mesh from the subsampled elevation points, which is discussed next in Listing 9-7. If the user wishes to add a material to the mesh by passing in `add_mat` as `True`, the function proceeds with the next block of code, which fills in the invalid cells in `band1` with the minimum of its Z (elevation) values and calls `create_grayscale_image_from_array` (discussed in Listing 9-9) to convert it to a grayscale image then uses it as an image texture to create a material to apply to the mesh with the function `apply_mod_and_add_mat` (Listing 9-11).

Note See the earlier section "Converting DEM Data Point to (X, Y, Z) Coordinate in Blender" for a walkthrough on how to filter arrays with Boolean conditions using `np.where`.

Meshing from Points Using Python and Geometry Nodes

In this section, we'll examine `mesh_from_points` (Listing 9-7), the helper function called by `gen_dem_mesh` (Listing 9-6) to create a mesh from the array of subsampled elevation points. Our high-level strategy is to create a mesh data block, call `<MESH BLOCK>.from_pydata` to add vertices to it converted from elevation points, then create a geometry node tree to voxelize the mesh and fill it in with edges and faces.

Listing 9-7. Create a mesh object from a given array of points (see /Ch9/dem_terrain_generator.py)

```
def mesh_from_points(context, dem_name, points, mins,
    location, xy_scale, z_scale, voxel_size):
    terrain_mesh_data = bpy.data.meshes.new( ↩
        name=dem_name+"_data")
    offset = np.full(points.shape, mins)
    verts = np.subtract(points, offset)
    verts_z_scale = verts*z_scale
    verts = np.stack([verts[:,0],verts[:,1]*-1, ↩
        verts_z_scale[:,2]],axis=-1).reshape(len(points),3)
    terrain_mesh_data.from_pydata(verts, [], [])
    terrain_mesh_data.update(calc_edges=True)
    terrain_obj = bpy.data.objects.new(name=dem_name, ↩
        object_data=terrain_mesh_data)
    context.collection.objects.link(terrain_obj)

    for obj in context.view_layer.objects:
        obj.select_set(False)
    context.view_layer.objects.active = terrain_obj
    terrain_obj.select_set(True)

    co = get_context_override(context, 'VIEW_3D', 'WINDOW')
    with bpy.context.temp_override(**co):
        bpy.ops.object.mode_set(mode='OBJECT')

    co = get_context_override(context, 'VIEW_3D', 'WINDOW')
    with context.temp_override(**co):
        bpy.ops.transform.resize(value=(xy_scale, ↩
            xy_scale, xy_scale))
        bpy.ops.transform.translate(value=location)
        bpy.ops.object.transform_apply(location=True, ↩
            rotation=False, scale=True)

    geo_nodes_mod = create_voxelizer_node_tree( ↩
        terrain_obj, voxel_size)

    return terrain_obj, geo_nodes_mod
```

In the first block of code, we create a mesh data block via `bpy.data.meshes.new`, populate it with vertices converted from the subsampled elevation points passed in, then tie it to a new mesh object and add it to the scene. Recall that locations of vertices in a mesh are relative to the mesh's origin, for example, if the origin is at global coordinates (1, 2, 3) and a vertex has location (0, 2, 5), then the vertex's global coordinates are (1, 2, 3) + (0, 2, 5) = (1, 4, 8). Since we want the lower-left corner of the terrain to be the mesh origin, we use the passed-in three-tuple `mins` as the mesh's location, which are the X, Y, and Z minimums of the elevation points derived by `gen_dem_mesh` (Listing 9-6). Consequently, we subtract `mins` from the elevation points to turn them into vertex locations so they are relative to `mins`. To do so, we create a `numpy` array `offset` in the same dimension as the elevation points array but filled it with the point `mins` (`offset = np.full(points.shape, mins)`). Subtracting `offset` from `points` (`verts = np.subtract(points, offset)`) will then subtract the two arrays elementwise, i.e., the pairs at the same indices from both arrays subtract. We also scale the points in the Z direction by multiplying them with the passed-in `z_scale` with the line `verts_z_scale = verts*z_scale`, which scales the points elementwise by multiplying each point by that number. Since the Y axis of the DEM points in the opposite direction of Blender's global Y, we correct it by isolating the Y coordinates of all points, multiplying them by −1, then reassembling the X, Y, Z columns back into a N by 3 array, where N is the total number of points:

```
verts = np.stack([verts[:,0],verts[:,1]*-1, ↩
    verts_z_scale[:,2]],axis=-1).reshape(len(points),3)
```

The expression `verts[:K]` grabs the Kth column of the `verts` array. With `verts` properly formatted and offset, we can now use it to call `from_pydata` followed by `update(calc_edges=True)` to fill the mesh block with verts but leave edges and faces blank. After that, we create a mesh object by calling `bpy.data.objects.new` and pass in the mesh block as its data, then link it to the scene collection under the passed-in context via `context.collection.objects.link(terrain_obj)`. The mesh generated up to this point is shown as (1) in Figure 9-6.

Next, we apply the passed-in `xy_scale` and `location` to the mesh object. To do so, we iterate the view layer objects and deselect them one by one, before setting the terrain object as active and selecting it. We then switch it to Object mode with a context override (as if from the viewport); then once mode switch is complete, with another override (viewport), call `bpy.ops.transform.resize` to scale the object uniformly by `xy_scale` in all directions followed by `bpy.ops.transform.translate` to move it to the given `location`. Before leaving the override scope, we call `bpy.ops.object.transform_apply` with `location=True` and `scale=True` to apply both the scaling and movement.

So far, we've only filled the mesh data with vertices. To add edges and faces, we'll pass the mess through a voxelizer created with geometry nodes, by calling `create_voxelizer_node_tree`, which is discussed in the next section in Listing 9-8. The state of the mesh at the end of Listing 9-8 is shown as (2) in Figure 9-6.

Figure 9-6. *Intermediate and final states of the mesh generated by `mesh_from_points` (Listing 9-7). (1) Mesh data filled in with vertices created from subsampled DEM elevation points, via `<MESH BLOCK>.from_pydata()`. (2) The same terrain mesh after voxelization by the geometry node tree we'll create next in Listing 9-8*

Create a Voxelizer Using Geometry Nodes from Python

In this section, we'll implement the helper function create_voxelizer_node_tree (Listing 9-8) to build a voxelizer from geometry nodes to add to the given terrain mesh object.

Listing 9-8. Create a voxelizer from geometry nodes (see /Ch9/dem_terrain_generator.py)

```
def create_voxelizer_node_tree(terrain_obj, voxel_size):
    geo_nodes_mod = terrain_obj.modifiers.new( ↩
        name=terrain_obj.name+"_geo_nodes_mod", ↩
        type='NODES')
    node_group = bpy.data.node_groups.new( ↩
        terrain_obj.name+"_geo_nodes_mod", ↩
        'GeometryNodeTree')
    geo_nodes_mod.node_group = node_group

    node_group.interface.new_socket( ↩
        name="Geometry", in_out="INPUT", ↩
        socket_type="NodeSocketGeometry")
    node_group.interface.new_socket( ↩
        name="Geometry", in_out="OUTPUT", ↩
        socket_type="NodeSocketGeometry")

    input_node = node_group.nodes.new('NodeGroupInput')

    pts_to_vol_node = node_group.nodes.new( ↩
        'GeometryNodePointsToVolume')
    pts_to_vol_node.resolution_mode = 'VOXEL_SIZE'
    pts_to_vol_node.inputs['Density'].default_value = 1.000
    pts_to_vol_node.inputs['Voxel Size'].default_value = ↩
        voxel_size
    pts_to_vol_node.inputs['Radius'].default_value = 0.6

    vol_to_mesh_node = node_group.nodes.new( ↩
        'GeometryNodeVolumeToMesh')
    vol_to_mesh_node.resolution_mode = 'GRID'
    vol_to_mesh_node.inputs['Threshold'].default_value = 0.1
```

```
output_node = node_group.nodes.new('NodeGroupOutput')

input_node.location = Vector((0, 0))
pts_to_vol_node.location = ↩
    Vector((input_node.width*1.5, 0))
vol_to_mesh_node.location = ↩
    Vector((pts_to_vol_node.location[0]+ ↩
        pts_to_vol_node.width*1.5, 0))
output_node.location = ↩
    Vector((vol_to_mesh_node.location[0]+ ↩
        vol_to_mesh_node.width*1.5, 0))

node_group.links.new(input_node.outputs['Geometry'], ↩
    pts_to_vol_node.inputs['Points'])
node_group.links.new( ↩
    pts_to_vol_node.outputs['Volume'], ↩
    vol_to_mesh_node.inputs['Volume'])
node_group.links.new( ↩
    vol_to_mesh_node.outputs['Mesh'], ↩
    output_node.inputs['Geometry'])

return geo_nodes_mod
```

The job of this function is to build the geometry node tree shown in Figure 9-7. We start by adding a new tree to the passed-in `terrain_obj` as a modifier by calling `terrain_obj.modifiers.new` with `type='NODES'` (Properties editor—Modifier tab—Add Modifier—Geometry Nodes). After that, we create a new node group by calling `bpy.data.node_groups.new` then assign it to the modifier via the line `geo_nodes_mod.node_group = node_group`. From this point on, all the nodes added to this node group will also be added to the tree.

Next, we'll add a Geometry input socket to the node group we've just created using the line

```
node_group.interface.new_socket( ↩
    name="Geometry", in_out="INPUT", ↩
    socket_type="NodeSocketGeometry")
```

followed by a Geometry output socket with the next line

```
node_group.interface.new_socket( ↩
    name="Geometry", in_out="OUTPUT", ↩
    socket_type="NodeSocketGeometry")
```

which have the same effects as going under the Properties shelf (N key in Geometry Node editor)—Group tab—Group Sockets—clicking the + button—Input (Output).

We're now ready to add the nodes to the tree via the node group. We'll add them one by one in the order shown in Figure 9-7. The first is a Group Input node, which we'll add via `node_group.nodes.new('NodeGroupInput')`. The second is a Points to Volume node (of type `'GeometryNodePointsToVolume'`), with its Resolution set to Size, Density to 1.000, Voxel Size to the passed-in `voxel_size`, and Radius to 0.6. Note that Resolution, which is a dropdown in the node's UI, is set via the `resolution_mode` member variable directly on the node instance, whereas the next three sliders Density, Voxel Size, and Radius are set via `inputs[<NAME>].default_value` on the node, for example, `pts_to_vol_node.inputs['Density'].default_value` for the Density slider.

The third node we'll add is a Volume to Mesh node (of type `'GeometryNodeVolumeToMesh'`), with its Resolution set to Grid and Threshold set to 0.1. The last node to add is a Group Output node, which is of type `'NodeGroupOutput'`.

With all four nodes added to the tree, we'll adjust spacing between nodes. Both shader and geometry nodes have locations stored as 2D `Vector` instances with X going left-right (right is positive). You access a node's location via `<NODE>.location`, where `<NODE>.location[0]` is its X coordinate (e.g., `pts_to_vol_node.location[0]`) and `<NODE>.location[1]` its Y coordinate. We'll lay out the nodes in a row from left to right with the first node (Group Input) at `Vector((0, 0))`. Each subsequent node's location is derived by offsetting the previous node by 1.5 times its width. For example, the first node Group Input is at (0, 0); if Group Input is 10 units wide, then the second node's location is

$$(0,0)+(10\times1.5,0)=(15,0)$$

To finish up, we'll link the neighboring nodes pairwise from left to right. We call `node_group.links.new` with the output socket of the "*from* node" followed by the input socket of the "*to* node" to create a link between them. For example, the following line links the Group Input node's "Geometry" output socket to the Points to Volume node's "Points" input socket:

```
node_group.links.new(input_node.outputs['Geometry'], ↩
    pts_to_vol_node.inputs['Points'])
```

The output sockets are stored under `<NODE>.outputs` (e.g., `input_node.outputs`) in a dictionary-like container. You look up a socket using its name as the key (e.g., `input_node.outputs['Geometry']`). We create two more links, from Points to Volume's "Volume" to Volume to Mesh's "Volume" and Volume to Mesh's "Mesh" to Group Output's "Geometry," as shown in Figure 9-7, and return the completed node tree.

The advantage of using a voxelizer tree to generate edges and faces is the resulting mesh will consist of mostly quads, therefore have a clean topology, as the example shown in Figure 9-8, which is generated with the provided USGS DEM.

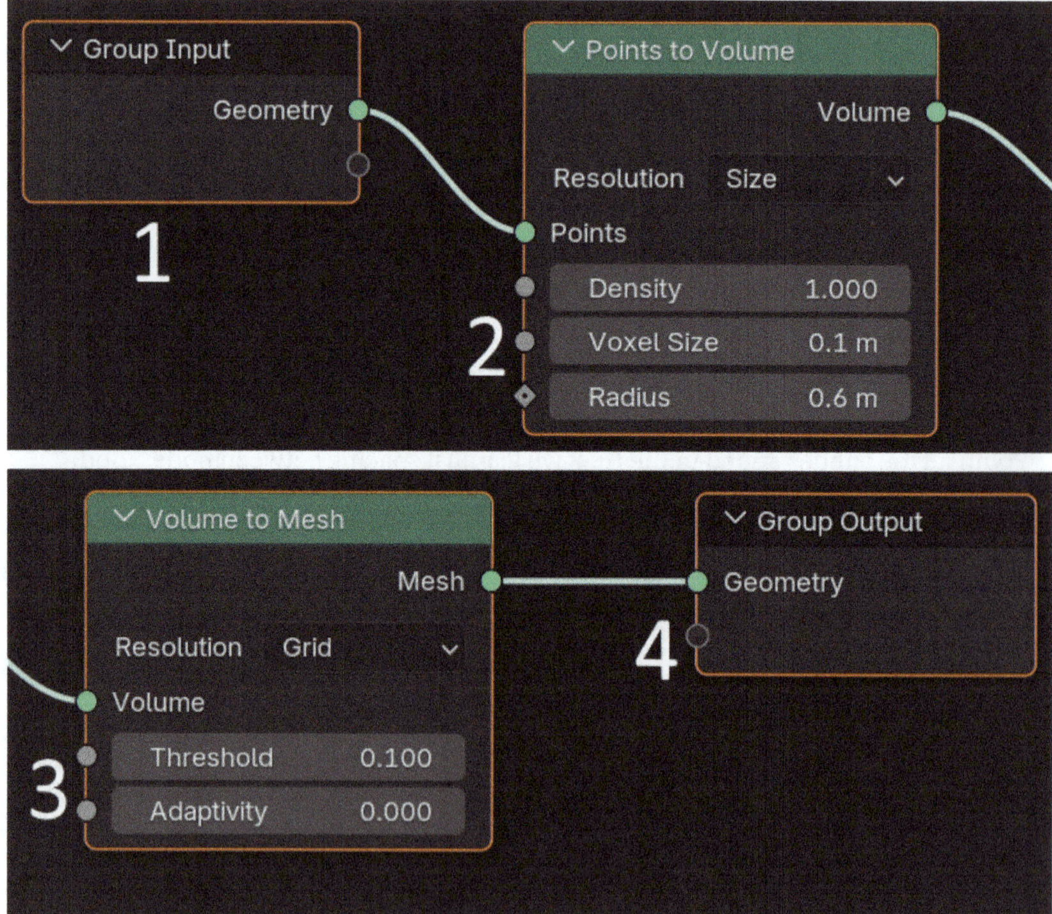

Figure 9-7. *Geometry node tree generated by running Listing 9-8. The node graph is cut in half then collaged vertically. The order of nodes is marked 1 to 4. The sequence of the Points to Volume node followed by Volume to Mesh forms a quick-and-dirty voxelizer.*

Tip You can find the Points to Volume node in the Geometry Node editor under Add—Point—Points to Volume and the Volume to Mesh node under Add—Volume—Operations—Volume to Mesh.

Note Remember that to use the `Vector` type in a script, you must import it via `from mathutils import Vector`. You pass a two-tuple (three-tuple) of numbers to initialize a `Vector` instance for a 2D (3D) point, for example, `Vector ((1, 2))`. Note the nested pairs of parentheses—the inner pair belongs to the tuple.

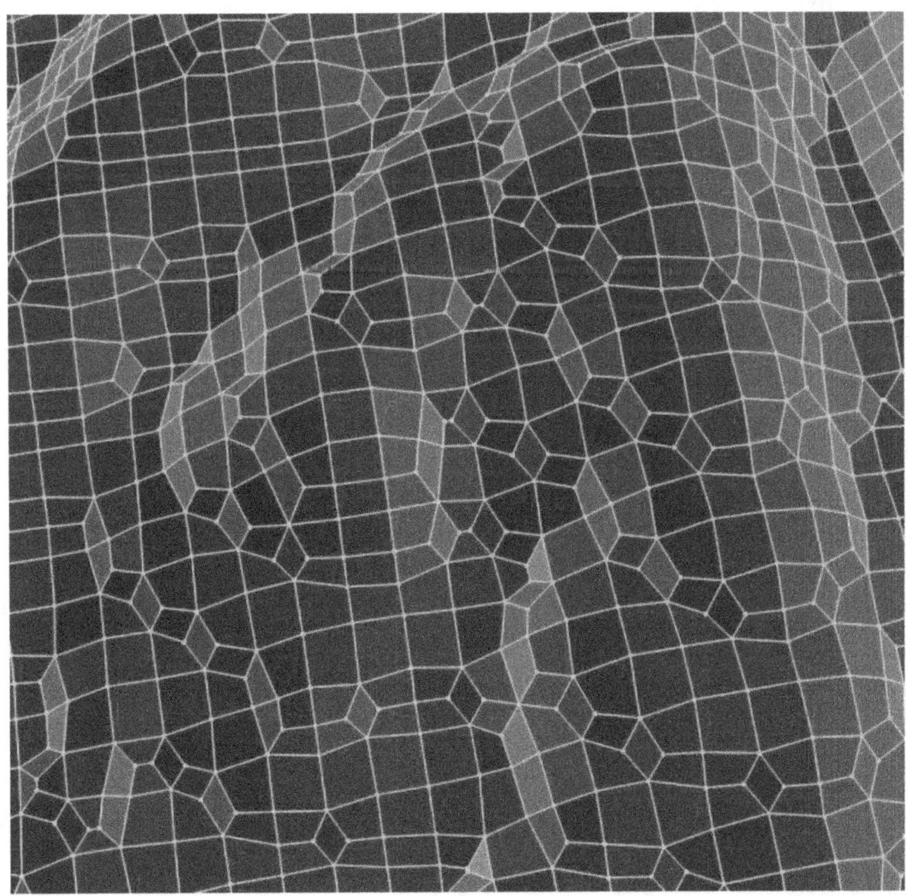

Figure 9-8. *Close-up view of a voxelized mesh generated from the provided USGS DEM using `create_voxelizer_node_tree` (Listing 9-8). The resulting mesh is mostly quads with a clean topology.*

Creating Grayscale Image from Elevation Points

With the terrain mesh generated, in this section, we'll write a function `create_grayscale_image_from_array` (Listing 9-9) to create a grayscale image from the DEM elevation points prior to subsampling, which we'll use later as an image texture to create a material for the terrain mesh.

Listing 9-9. Create a grayscale image data block from the elevation points (see /Ch9/dem_terrain_generator.py)

```
def create_grayscale_image_from_array(intensities, h, w, ↩
    name, dir):
    max = intensities.max()
    min = intensities.min()
    span = max-min
    normed_its = (intensities-min)*(1.0/span)

    image_block = bpy.data.images.new(name, w, h)
    alpha = np.ones(normed_its.shape)
    normed_its_arr = [normed_its, normed_its, normed_its, ↩
        alpha]
    image_block.pixels = np.stack( ↩
        normed_its_arr, axis=-1).reshape(h, w, 4).ravel()
    image_block.update()
    save_image_to_file(dir, image_block, "grayscale")
    return image_block
```

Blender encodes grayscale images with each pixel as a list of four decimal numbers from 0 to 1 (inclusive) that corresponds to its RGBA values—red, green, blue, and alpha. We want to use the elevation points array passed in (`intensities`) as pixels values, but it is not yet in the range of 0 to 1; therefore, we normalize it as follows: we find the maximum and minimum of the array, then the difference between the two gives us the span:

```
max = intensities.max()
min = intensities.min()
span = max-min
```

We then subtract the minimum from intensities, then divide it by the span to map it to the range of 0 to 1:

```
normed_its = (intensities-min)*(1.0/span)
```

Using the passed-in h and w, which are the number of rows and columns in the elevation data, we create a new image data block with the following line:

```
image_block = bpy.data.images.new(name, w, h)
```

Note that for bpy.data.images.new, the width of the image is passed before the height.

Since we're creating a grayscale image, we'll use normed_its as the R, G, and B channel values. We'll create an array that is the same dimension as normed_its but filled with ones as the values for the alpha channel to make the image fully opaque, with this line:

```
alpha = np.ones(normed_its.shape)
```

Next, we'll combine the four individual pixel channel arrays into one. We concatenate the four channels into one list as follows:

```
normed_its_arr = [normed_its, normed_its, normed_its, ↩
    alpha]
```

Then convert the list with np.stack into a h by w by 4 array, where h is the height (number of rows) and w the width (number of columns) of the image, then assign it to the image data block's pixels variable, like this:

```
image_block.pixels = np.stack( ↩
    normed_its_arr, axis=-1).reshape(h, w, 4).ravel()
```

After that, we call image_block.update() to force the image block to refresh, call save_image_to_file (Listing 9-10, discussed next) to save the block to disk as a PNG file, then return the image block. The grayscale image generated from the provided USGS DEM by running Listing 9-9 is shown in Figure 9-9. The grayscale image generated from the provided DTEEC DEM (Mars crater) is shown in Figure 9-10.

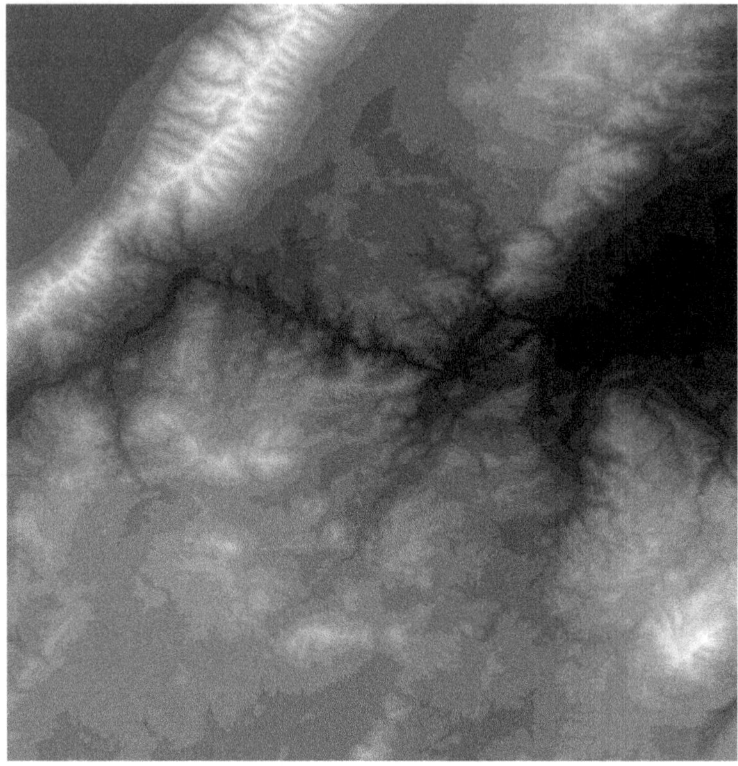

Figure 9-9. *Grayscale PNG image file generated from the provided USGS DEM by running* `create_grayscale_image_from_array` *(Listing 9-9)*

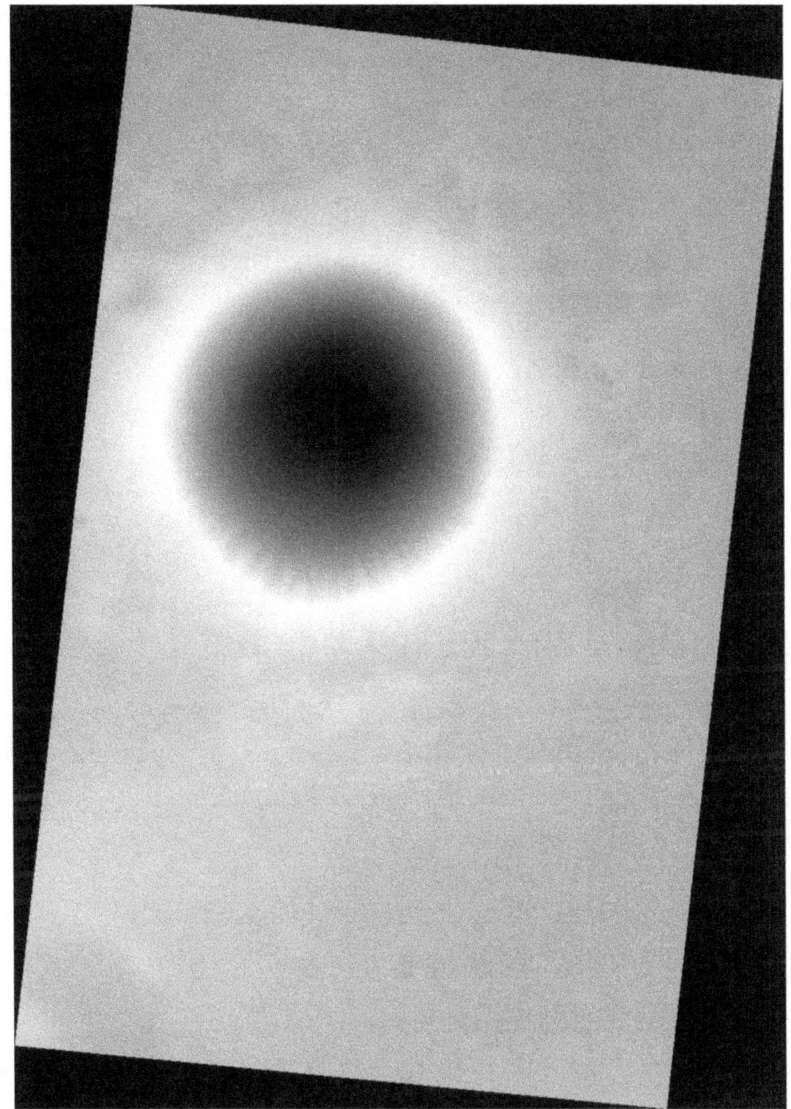

Figure 9-10. *Grayscale PNG image file generated from the provided DTEEC DEM (Mars crater) by running* `create_grayscale_image_from_array` *(Listing 9-9)*

Helper Function: Saving Image Data Block to File

Recall in Chapter 4 we wrote a helper function that saves a given image data block to disk as a PNG file. The Chapter 4 version of this function used the image block's name as the PNG file's name—here in Listing 9-10, we modify it slightly so we can insert a "trailing name," i.e., a string after the image block name but before the file extension. This is so we can distinguish between the colored image output by `plt_dem_image` (Listing 9-1) and the grayscale image output by `create_grayscale_image_from_array` (Listing 9-9). For instance, for the provided USGS DEM file, these two images are `USGS_13_n39w106_20230602_plt_color.png` and `USGS_13_n39w106_20230602_grayscale.png`, respectively.

Listing 9-10. Save the given image data block to disk as a PNG file with the given trailing name (see /Ch9/dem_terrain_generator.py)

```
def save_image_to_file(dir, img_blk, trailing_name):
    img_blk.filepath_raw = ↩
        dir+"/"+img_blk.name+"_"+trailing_name+".png"
    img_blk.file_format = 'PNG'
    img_blk.save()
```

Applying Modifiers and Adding Material

Up to this point, we have generated a terrain mesh object along with a grayscale image created from the elevation points. Now, we'll write a function `apply_mod_and_add_mat` (Listing 9-11) to unwrap the terrain mesh and create a material to apply to it by using the grayscale image as an image texture.

Listing 9-11. Apply modifiers then unwrap and add material to the given terrain mesh object (see /Ch9/dem_terrain_generator.py)

```
def apply_mod_and_add_mat(context, terrain_obj, ↩
    geo_nodes_mod, txt_img_blk, mat_name):
    for obj in context.view_layer.objects:
        obj.select_set(False)
    context.view_layer.objects.active = terrain_obj
    terrain_obj.select_set(True)

    co = get_context_override(context, 'VIEW_3D', 'WINDOW')
    with bpy.context.temp_override(**co):
        bpy.ops.object.mode_set(mode='OBJECT')
```

```
    bpy.ops.object.modifier_apply( ↩
        modifier=geo_nodes_mod.name)

    unwrap_and_add_mat(context, terrain_obj, ↩
        terrain_obj.name+"_top_uvs", txt_img_blk, mat_name)
```

In `mesh_from_points` (Listing 9-7), we generated the terrain mesh from the subsampled elevation points with a combination of `bpy` code and a geometry node tree built in Python. Since a geometry node tree is added to a mesh object as a modifier (regardless of whether the tree is created by hand or via Python), we must apply the modifier prior to unwrapping to ensure the UVs account for the geometry edited by the node tree. To apply the geometry node modifier, we iterate through the view layer objects to deselect them one by one, then set the terrain mesh (`terrain_obj`) as active and select it. With a context override (as if from the viewport), we then switch `terrain_obj` to Object mode, before calling `bpy.ops.object.modifier_apply` with the geometry node modifier's name (`geo_nodes_mod.name`) to apply it.

With the modifier applied, next we call the helper function `unwrap_and_add_mat` (discussed next in Listing 9-12) to unwrap `terrain_obj` and apply a material to it incorporating the grayscale image as an image texture.

A side-by-side comparison of the terrain generated from the provided USGS DEM with and without the grayscale image as texture is shown in Figure 9-11. The comparison for the provided DTEEC DEM (Mars crater) is shown in Figure 9-12.

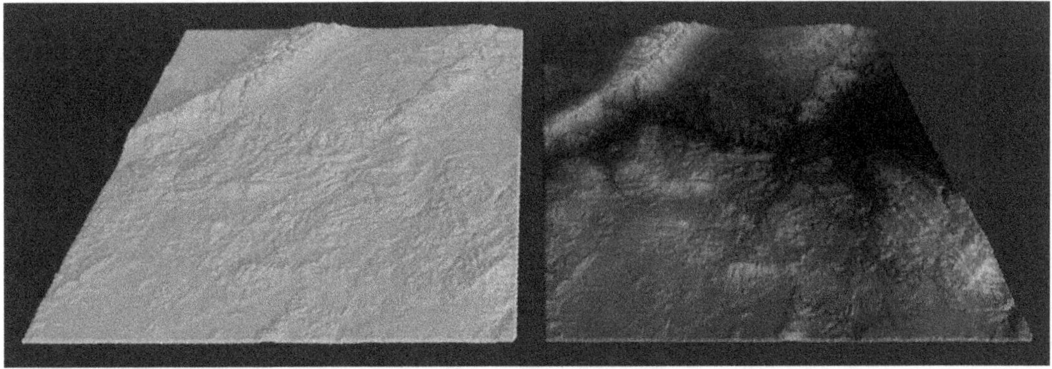

Figure 9-11. *Applying the grayscale image created from the elevation points as a texture to the generated terrain. Left: terrain mesh generated from the provided USGS DEM without a material. Right: the same terrain after a material with the grayscale image texture is applied*

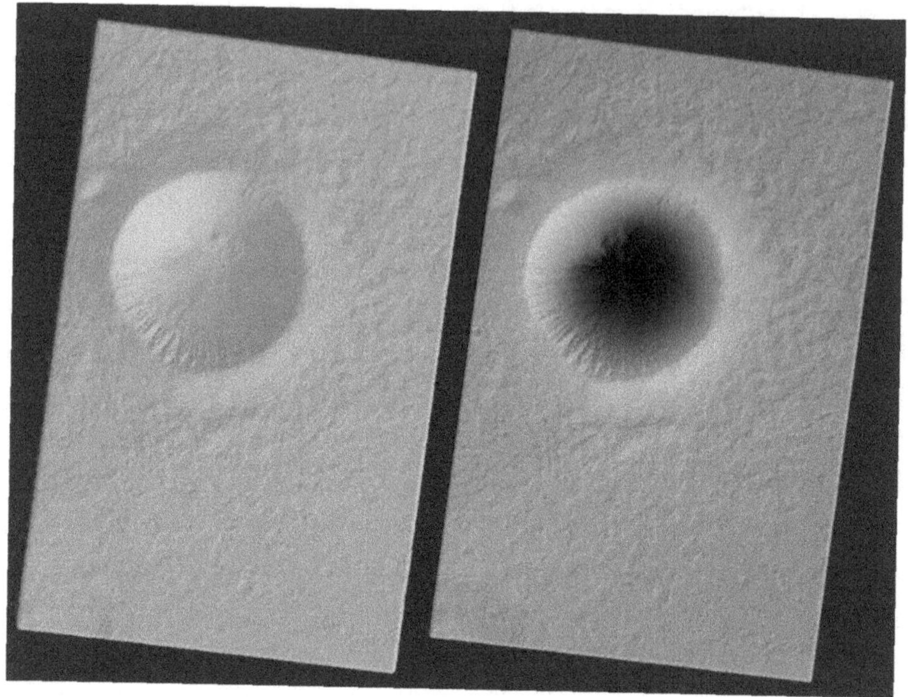

***Figure 9-12.** Left: terrain mesh generated from the provided DTEEC DEM (Mars crater) without a material. Right: the same mesh after a material with the grayscale image texture is applied*

Helper Function: Unwrapping and Applying Material

In this section, we'll take a closer look at the helper function `unwrap_and_add_mat` (Listing 9-12), which is called by `apply_mod_and_add_mat` (Listing 9-11) to unwrap the terrain mesh by projecting from the top view, before adding a material to it with the DEM as a grayscale image texture.

Listing 9-12. Unwrap the given terrain mesh by projecting from the top view and add a material created using the given image data block (see /Ch9/dem_terrain_generator.py)

```
def unwrap_and_add_mat(context, obj_to_unwrap, ↩
    uv_map_name, txt_img_blk, mat_name):
    mesh_to_unwrap = obj_to_unwrap.data
    uv_map_idx = mesh_to_unwrap.uv_layers.find(uv_map_name)
    if uv_map_idx < 0:
```

```
    mesh_to_unwrap.uv_layers.new(name=uv_map_name)
    uv_map_idx = mesh_to_unwrap.uv_layers.find( ↩
        uv_map_name)

uv_map = mesh_to_unwrap.uv_layers[uv_map_name]
uv_map.active_render = True
mesh_to_unwrap.uv_layers.active_index = uv_map_idx

viewport_co = get_context_override(context, ↩
    'VIEW_3D', 'WINDOW')
with bpy.context.temp_override(**viewport_co):
    bpy.ops.object.mode_set(mode='EDIT')

viewport_co = get_context_override(context, ↩
    'VIEW_3D', 'WINDOW')
with bpy.context.temp_override(**viewport_co):
    bpy.ops.mesh.select_all(action='SELECT')
    bpy.ops.view3d.view_selected(use_all_regions=False)

viewport_co = get_context_override(context, ↩
    'VIEW_3D', 'WINDOW')
with bpy.context.temp_override(**viewport_co):
    bpy.ops.view3d.view_axis(type='TOP')

for a in context.window.screen.areas:
    if a.type=='VIEW_3D':
        for s in a.spaces:
            if s.type=='VIEW_3D':
                s.region_3d.update()
                s.shading.type = 'MATERIAL'

viewport_co = get_context_override(context, ↩
    'VIEW_3D', 'WINDOW')
with bpy.context.temp_override(**viewport_co):
    bpy.ops.uv.project_from_view(camera_bounds=False, ↩
        correct_aspect=True, scale_to_bounds=True)
```

```
context.scene.render.engine = 'CYCLES'
create_mat_with_img_texture(obj_to_unwrap, ↩
    mat_name, txt_img_blk)
bpy.ops.object.material_slot_assign()

viewport_co = get_context_override(context, ↩
    'VIEW_3D', 'WINDOW')
with bpy.context.temp_override(**viewport_co):
    bpy.ops.object.mode_set(mode='OBJECT')
```

The grayscale image is 2D, whereas the terrain mesh occupies approximately the same XY space but has a third dimension (Z) added—in other words, the grayscale image aligns roughly with the terrain in XY; therefore, to apply the grayscale image as an image texture, we unwrap the terrain by projecting from the top view.

The function starts by using the given UV map name (`uv_map_name`) to look up the UV map index to unwrap into (on `obj_to_wrap`'s mesh data), which is the slot under Properties editor—Data tab—UV Maps. If a slot by that name not yet exists, a new slot is created with that name.

Next, we'll configure the UV map's settings. We retrieve a reference to the UV map by looking it up by name among the UV layers stored on the object's mesh data (`mesh_to_unwrap.uv_layers[uv_map_name]`), through which we set Active Render to True (which is the same as toggling on the "camera" icon under Properties editor—Data tab—UV Maps). We also select this UV map as active by assigning its index to `mesh_to_unwrap.uv_layers.active_index`, so it will be the slot the UV goes to next time we unwrap.

To get ready to unwrap, we switch `obj_to_wrap` to Edit mode with a context override (as if from the viewport). Then once mode switch is complete, with a new override (viewport), we select all and adjust view to frame selected (`bpy.ops.view3d.view_selected`). With the next override (viewport), we switch to the top view via `bpy.ops.view3d.view_axis(type='TOP')`. Note that for the view change to take effect immediately, we must force a viewport update by iterating through the nested screen hierarchy under the passed-in context, locate the space `s` under the viewport, and call `s.region_3d.update()`. For convenience, we also set viewport shading to Material Preview at the same time, via `s.shading.type = 'MATERIAL'`.

With the view correctly oriented, in the next block, we call `bpy.ops.uv.project_from_view` with a context override (as if from the viewport) to unwrap by projecting from view, then set the render engine to Cycles (Properties editor—Render tab—Render

Engine—Cycles). After that, we call the next helper function create_mat_with_img_texture (Listing 9-13) to create a material using the passed-in image block as texture, then call bpy.ops.object.material_slot_assign() to assign the material to the part of the mesh we've just unwrapped (which is the mesh as a whole). Calling bpy.ops.object.material_slot_assign() is equivalent to pressing the "Assign" button with a material selected in the list under Properties editor—Material tab. We finish the function by switching obj_to_unwrap to Object mode using an override (as if from the viewport).

Helper Function: Creating a Material Shader Tree with an Image Texture Node

We delegate the task of creating a material with a given image block as texture to the helper function create_mat_with_img_texture (Listing 9-13).

Listing 9-13. Create a material and add the given image data block to its shader tree as an Image Texture node (see /Ch9/dem_terrain_generator.py)

```
def create_mat_with_img_texture(obj, mat_name, ↩
    txt_img_block):
    mat = create_material(obj, mat_name)
    node_tc, node_mapping = ↩
        create_texture_coords_mapping_nodes(obj, mat)

    nodes = mat.node_tree.nodes
    node_tex_img = nodes.new(type='ShaderNodeTexImage')
    node_tex_img.image = txt_img_block

    node_bsdf = nodes['Principled BSDF']
    links = mat.node_tree.links
    links.new(node_mapping.outputs['Vector'], ↩
        node_tex_img.inputs['Vector'])
    links.new(node_tex_img.outputs['Color'], ↩
        node_bsdf.inputs['Base Color'])

    node_out = nodes['Material Output']
    nodes_to_arrange = [node_tc, node_mapping, ↩
        node_tex_img, node_bsdf, node_out]
    rearrange_nodes(nodes_to_arrange)
```

In Listing 9-13, we start by calling two functions we've developed in Chapter 4; the first is `create_material` (Listing 4-3), which creates (or retrieves) a material by a given name, adds it to a given object's material stack as the active material, and sets up its shader tree (with a Principled BSDF and a Material Output node). The second is `create_texture_coords_mapping_nodes` (Listing 4-9), which adds a Texture Coordinate node and a Mapping node to a material's shader tree so the object's UVs can be used to map the material. Once these two functions are called, the tree will look like Figure 9-13 minus the Image Texture node on the upper right; therefore, to complete the tree, all that's left to do is create an Image Texture node with the image block passed in as its image, then insert it in the tree between the Mapping and the Principled BSDF nodes, which is the underlined portion of the code in Listing 9-13.

Let's take this step by step. We create the Image Texture node by calling `nodes.new( type='ShaderNodeTexImage')`. To insert the Image Texture node into the tree, we need access to the Mapping node (`node_mapping`) previously returned by `create_texture_coords_mapping_nodes` (Listing 4-9) and the Principled BSDF node, which we look up by name. To link the nodes, we call the `new` method on the tree's links, once to connect the Mapping node (Vector) to Image Texture (Vector) with the line `links.new(node_mapping.outputs['Vector'], node_tex_img.inputs['Vector'])`, then a second time to create the link from Image Texture (Color) to Principled BSDF (Base Color).

To finish the tree, we call another helper function from Chapter 4, `rearrange_nodes` (Listing 4-5), which, when passed a list of a tree's nodes, lays them out in order with proper spacing based on the nodes' sizes.

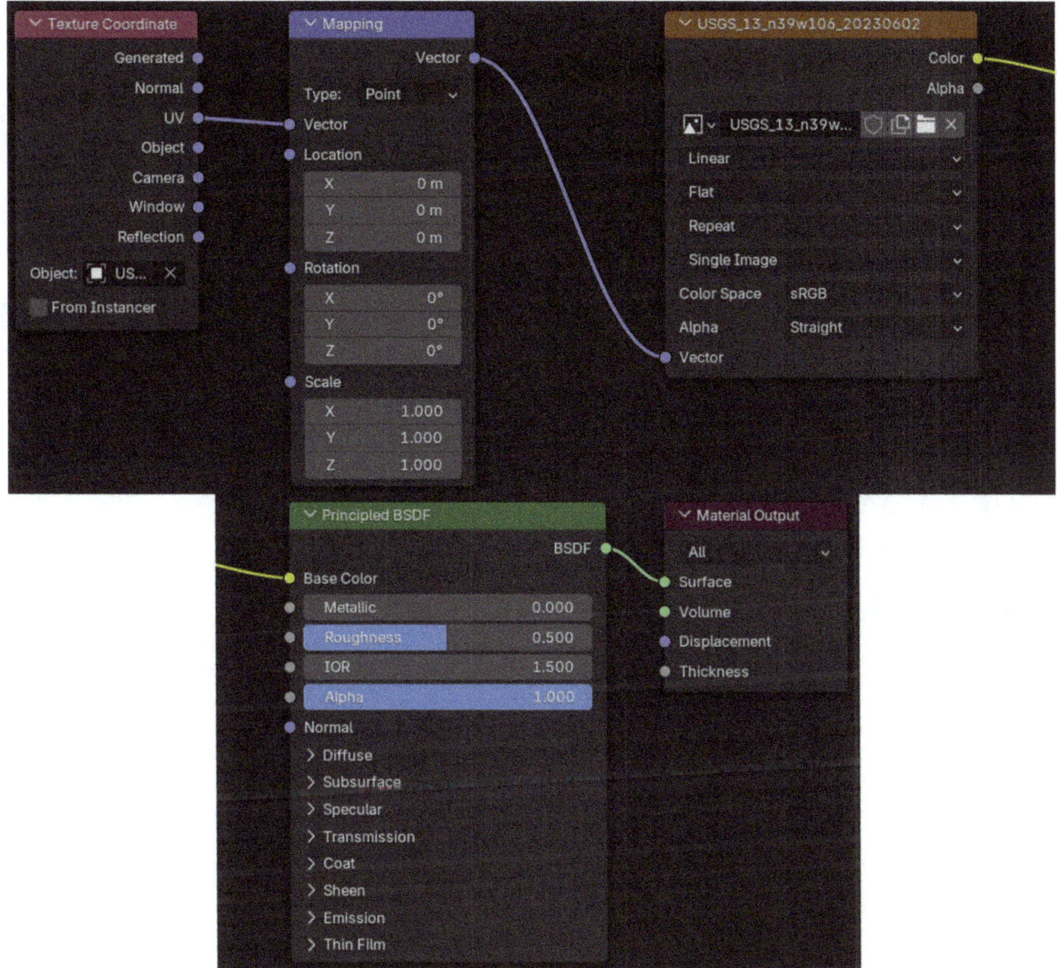

***Figure 9-13.** Shader node tree generated by `create_mat_with_img_texture` (Listing 9-13) with the provided USGS DEM. The screenshot of the tree is cut in half then collaged vertically for space. The Image Texture node on the upper right of the figure connects to the Principled BSDF node on the lower left.*

Testing Terrain Generator with Provided DEMs

We've completed the implementation of our terrain generator—phew! Let's try it out by generating two terrain meshes using the provided DEMs. The function `gen_provided_dems` in Listing 9-14 shows two sample calls to `gen_dem_mesh` (Listing 9-6) with their key parameter values summarized in Table 9-1 for comparison.

Listing 9-14. Call gen_dem_mesh (Listing 9-6) with the two provided DEMs to generate terrain mesh objects (see /Ch9/dem_terrain_generator.py)

```
def gen_provided_dems(add_mat:bool):
    start = timeit.default_timer()

    gen_dem_mesh(bpy.context, script_dir, ↩
        script_dir+"/USGS_13_n39w106_20230602.tif", ↩
        100.0, voxel_size=0.2, add_mat=add_mat)

    gen_dem_mesh(bpy.context, script_dir, ↩
        script_dir+ ↩
            "/DTEEC_041878_1460_041021_1460_G01.IMG", ↩
        100.0, 100, location=(-75,0,0), z_scale=1, ↩
        add_mat=add_mat)

    end = timeit.default_timer()
    print("Runtime = " + str(end-start))
```

Table 9-1. *Summary of key parameter values of calls to* gen_dem_mesh *in Listing 9-14*

DEM	target_len	sample_step	z_scale	voxel_size
USGS	100.0	1000	0.000015	0.2
DTEEC (Mars)	100.0	100	1	0.1

We set `target_len` for both meshes to 100.0m for easy comparison and `add_mat` to `True` to generate materials for both. Since the USGS DEM has more points than the DTEEC DEM, we set its `sample_step` and `voxel_size` larger while its `z_scale` smaller. If the source you obtained the DEM from provides the units and scale used for the model, you can calculate parameter values for the generator. Otherwise, you'll have to experiment with different values until you find a good set, like I did with the two provided DEMs.

Using the same approach from Chapter 8 for measuring runtime, we call `timeit.default_timer()` to take a timestamp right before and after the two calls to `gen_dem_mesh` (Listing 9-6), the difference of which then gives a good approximation of the time it takes to generate the two meshes. The runtime is printed to the System Console (Window—Toggle System Console) via the `print` statement.

The terrain mesh generated by the first call to `gen_dem_mesh` is shown in Figure 9-14, while the second call is shown in Figure 9-15.

Tip Blender uses meters as the default unit for length. See Figure 9-4 on how to change this.

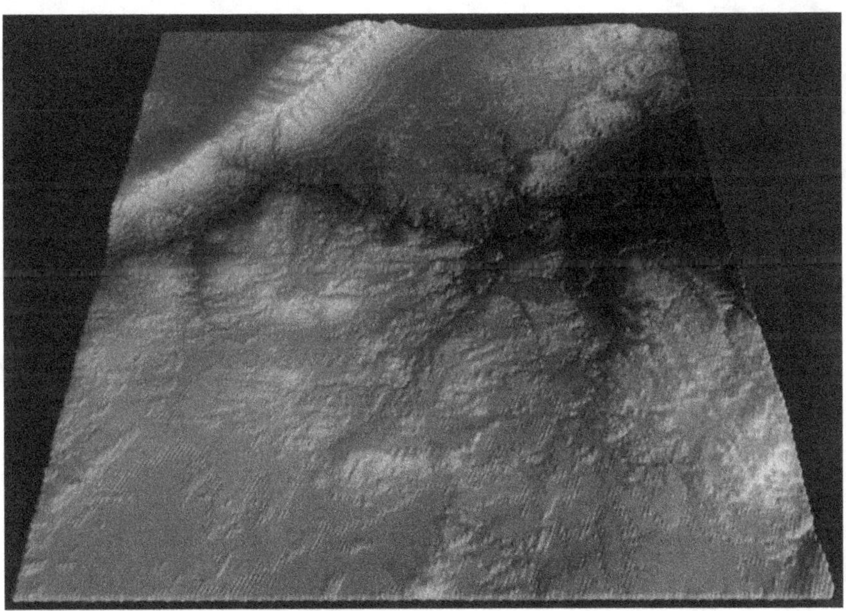

Figure 9-14. *Terrain mesh generated by the first call to* `gen_dem_mesh` *in Listing 9-14*

Figure 9-15. *Terrain mesh generated by the second call to* `gen_dem_mesh` *in Listing 9-14*

Summary

In this chapter, you learned what DEMs are, how to plot and analyze their contents, and how to procedurally generate terrain meshes from them. A DEM is a type of "bare earth" GIS model that encodes terrain heights after surface objects like trees and buildings have been removed. Modern DEMs are typically derived from lidar point clouds and stored in a raster format containing multiple bands, with each band encoding a 2D table of numbers, resembling a channel in an image. A DEM file usually has a `*.tif` or `*.img` extension.

In the first half of the chapter, you wrote Python code to plot and convert DEM bands to PNG images to visualize their contents and identify which band has the elevation points. You also learned to filter, subsample, scale, and convert the elevation points from a DEM into a format suitable for denoting vertex positions in Blender.

In the second half of the chapter, you formulated a design for a generator that produces terrain meshes based on DEM data, then implemented it using a combination of Blender Python, geometry nodes, and shader nodes. You divided the generator into several stages. The first stage preps and converts the elevation points into vertex positions, from which the second stage creates and triangulates mesh data using `bpy` functions and a voxelizer built from geometry nodes. The third stage creates a grayscale image from the elevation points and saves it out to a PNG file, which is in turn used by the fourth stage as an image texture to create a material for the mesh. Throughout the chapter, you used two provided DEMs to practice image and mesh syntheses. The first DEM (courtesy of USGS) covers part of the Colorado Springs, CO, United States, area, while the second DEM (courtesy of HiRISE by the University of Arizona) depicts the Mars crater.

CHAPTER 10

Import Generated Geometry into Unreal Engine 5

In this chapter, you'll learn how to export a mesh from Blender and import it into Unreal Engine 5 (UE5) as a Static Mesh. The first part of the chapter will take you through exporting a model manually, from setting the scene units, postprocessing the mesh, configuring relevant settings for glTF 2.0 and FBX, to cleaning up post-export. The second part of the chapter will show you how to automate the export steps in Blender Python and modify the code from Chapter 4 to generate and export a model in one go. The third part of the chapter will show you how to import a model in UE5 as a Static Mesh and instantiate it in a level.

Running This Chapter's Examples

Before we start, let's set up the dependency and download the chapter source.

Installing Python Dependency

This chapter's scripts import functions from the third-party Python package `numpy`. Please refer to the Appendix for instructions on how to install or update numpy.

Note `numpy` and other third-party Python packages need to be installed under each version of Blender on your system separately.

I. Lupiani, *Procedural Content Generation for Games*, https://doi.org/10.1007/979-8-8688-1787-8_10

Downloading and Running the Sample Code

The source code and color figures for this book are available on GitHub via the book's product page, located at `https://link.springer.com/book/9798868817861`. Download the files, navigate to the `/Ch10` folder, and open each `*.py` in the Text Editor under the Scripting workspace as prompted by the chapter text.

The file `/Ch10/export_utils.py` contains functions for postprocessing meshes as well as exporting them to both glTF and FBX formats. `/Ch10/gun_generator.py` is a version of the weapon generator from Chapter 4 which has been modified to make use of `/Ch10/export_utils.py`. If you open `gun_generator.py` in the Text Editor under the Scripting workspace, you'll find an `if __name__ == "__main__"` block already set up at the bottom of the script. Clicking the Run button will generate a sample gun mesh, postprocess it, and export it to `test_gun.glb` (binary glTF format). We will go through how the code works in detail throughout the chapter.

The following is a summary of the sample files under the `/Ch10` folder, with each file's dependencies organized as sub-bullets under it:

- export_utils.py
    - material_and_image_utils.py
- gun_generator.py
    - mesh_editing_utils.py
    - material_and_image_utils.py
    - texture_material_generation.py
    - export_utils.py
    - cross_motif_grid_normal_map.png (normal map referenced by gun_generator.py for creating materials)
    - round_bumps_normal_map.png (normal map referenced by gun_generator.py for creating materials)
- test_gun.glb (sample copy of glTF binary file exported by running gun_generator.py)

Exporting Meshes by Hand

In this section, we'll go over how to manually export mesh objects in Blender to either glTF 2.0 or FBX format for the purpose of importing them as static meshes in Unreal Engine 5. Once you're familiar with how to export by hand, in the second part of the chapter, we'll implement the same steps in Blender Python and create our own custom export script.

Export Workflow

Figure 10-1 shows the overall workflow to export a mesh in Blender to either FBX or glTF 2.0 format. This section will describe each of the numbered steps in Figure 10-1.

Step #1: Configure Scene Units

In **step #1**, we navigate to the Properties editor ➤ Scene tab, click to expand the Units section, and set the Unit System to Metric, Unit Scale to 1, and Length unit to Meters.

Steps #2 to #6: Postprocess Mesh (Optional)

Steps #2 to #6 perform a series of postprocessing steps to get a mesh ready for export to either FBX or glTF format. Some or all of these steps may be optional depending on the state of the mesh, for example, if a mesh's modifier stack is empty, there's no need to apply modifiers. Since UE5's renderer requires meshes to only have triangles, in **step #2**, we triangulate each mesh, for example, by adding a Triangulate modifier (Properties editor ➤ Modifier tab ➤ Add Modifier ➤ Generate ➤ Triangulate, or in Object mode, Object ➤ Modifiers ➤ Add Modifier ➤ Generate ➤ Triangulate), as shown in Figure 10-2.

Step #3 applies each object's modifiers (with an object selected, in Object mode, under Properties editor ➤ Modifier tab, select each modifier and click the "v" button ➤ Apply (Ctrl-A)).

In **step #4**, we apply each mesh object's transforms (with the object selected, in Object mode, Ctrl-A ➤ All Transforms, or Object ➤ Apply ➤ All Transforms).

For **step #5**, if a model consists of multiple objects, we join them into a single object. In Object mode, select the pieces either by shift-clicking each one, or use the A key to toggle select all (if the pieces are the only objects in the scene). Then Ctrl-J (or Object ➤ Join) to join. Blender will by default name the joined object after the last object selected. We'll rename the joined object to something more descriptive.

In **step #6**, we scale each object to the appropriate size. The scaling factor will depend on what you intend to use the mesh for in UE5 and its relative size to other assets. For example, when scaled to a length of 0.36m along X, the gun models we generated in Chapter 4 appear proportional to the player character in UE5's Third Person starter project.

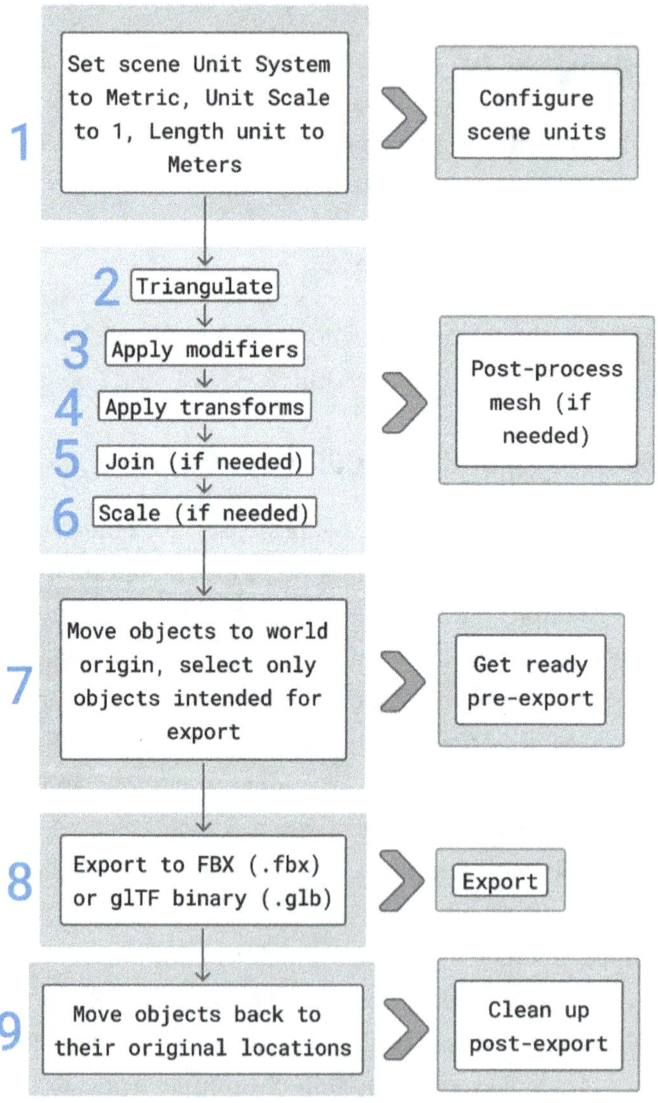

Figure 10-1. *High-level workflow for exporting static meshes to glTF or FBX. The steps marked 1 to 9 in this figure are implemented by the functions with the corresponding numbering in Figure 10-7*

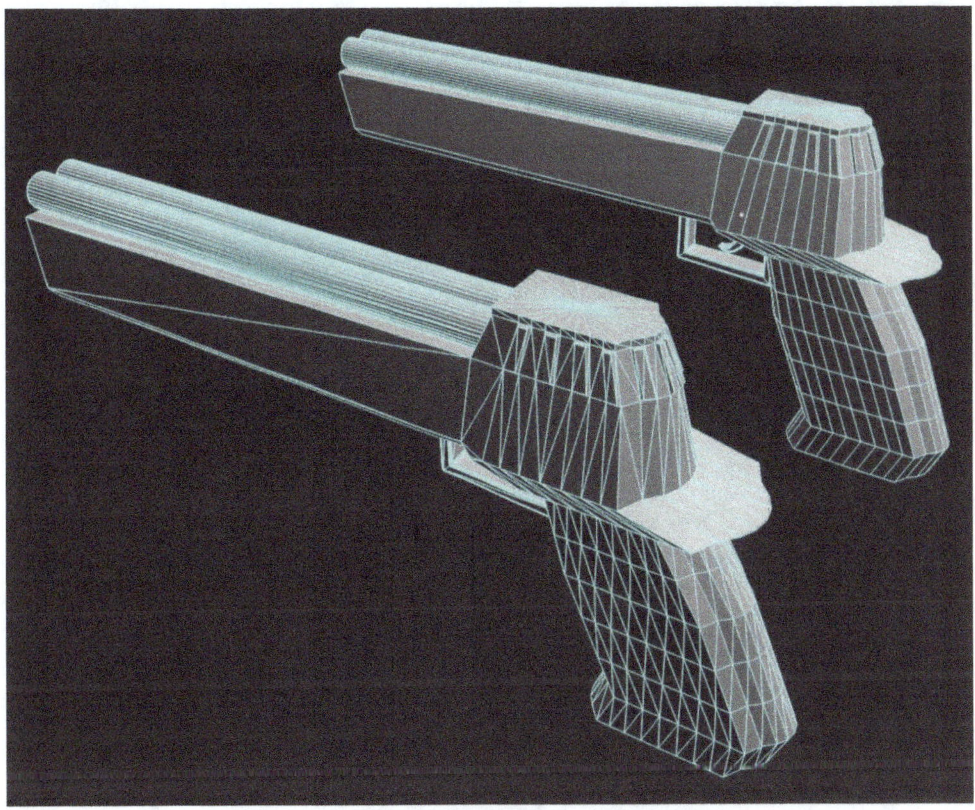

Figure 10-2. *A gun generated using Chapter 4's version of the weapon generator (back-right) and the same gun triangulated using the Triangulate modifier with default settings (front-left) for comparison*

Step #7: Select and Move Objects to World Origin

Blender uses the world origin as an object's origin when exporting to either FBX or glTF 2.0. For **step #7**, we first set each object's origin to the desired spot (e.g., Object ➤ Set Origin ➤ Origin to Center of Mass (Volume)), then move the object such that its origin aligns with Blender's world origin. This way, when the exported file is imported in UE5, the mesh's origin will match its origin in Blender, as shown in Figure 10-3. Note that Blender uses a right-handed coordinate system with +Z up, whereas UE5 uses left-handed with +Z up, as shown in Figure 10-4—therefore, after a Blender mesh is imported into UE5, its Y axis is flipped.

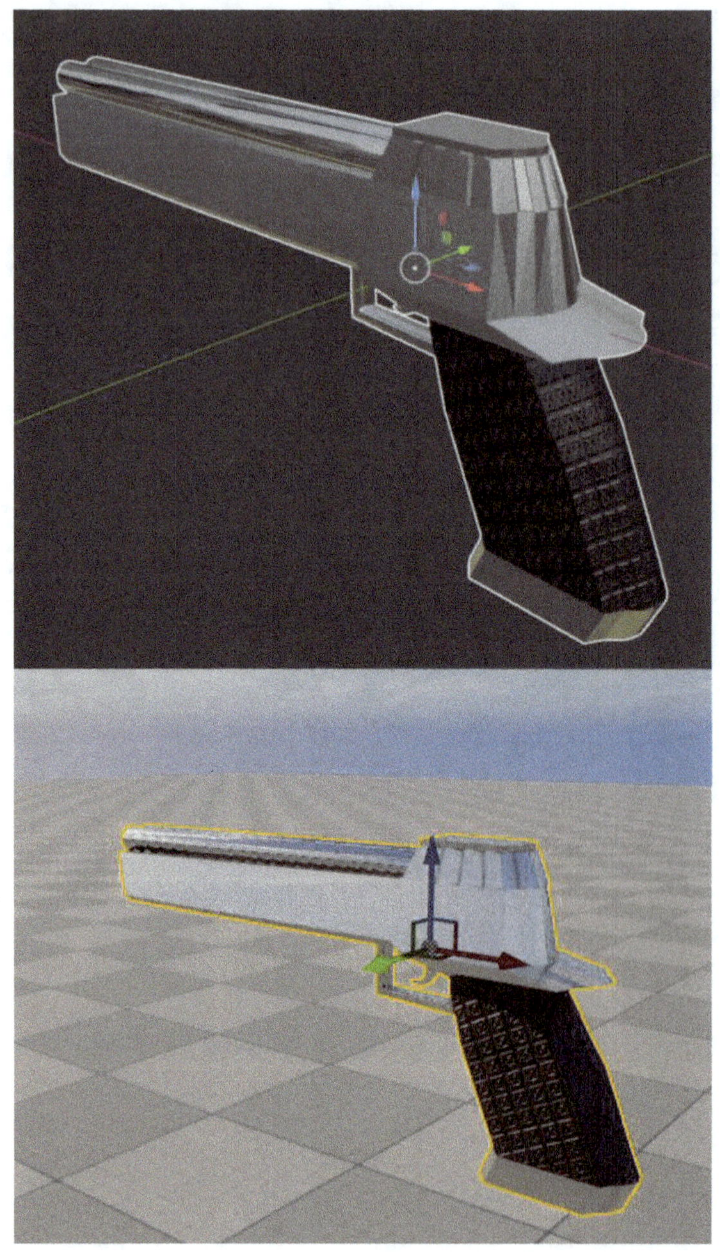

Figure 10-3. *Top: gun mesh generated using Chapter 4's weapon generator with its origin set to Center of Mass (Volume) and moved to Blender's world origin. Bottom: the gun exported as a *.glb file then imported into UE5 as a static mesh. Comparing top to bottom, you can see that Blender has a right-handed coordinate system with Z up, whereas UE5 is left-handed with Z up; therefore, the mesh's Y axis is flipped*

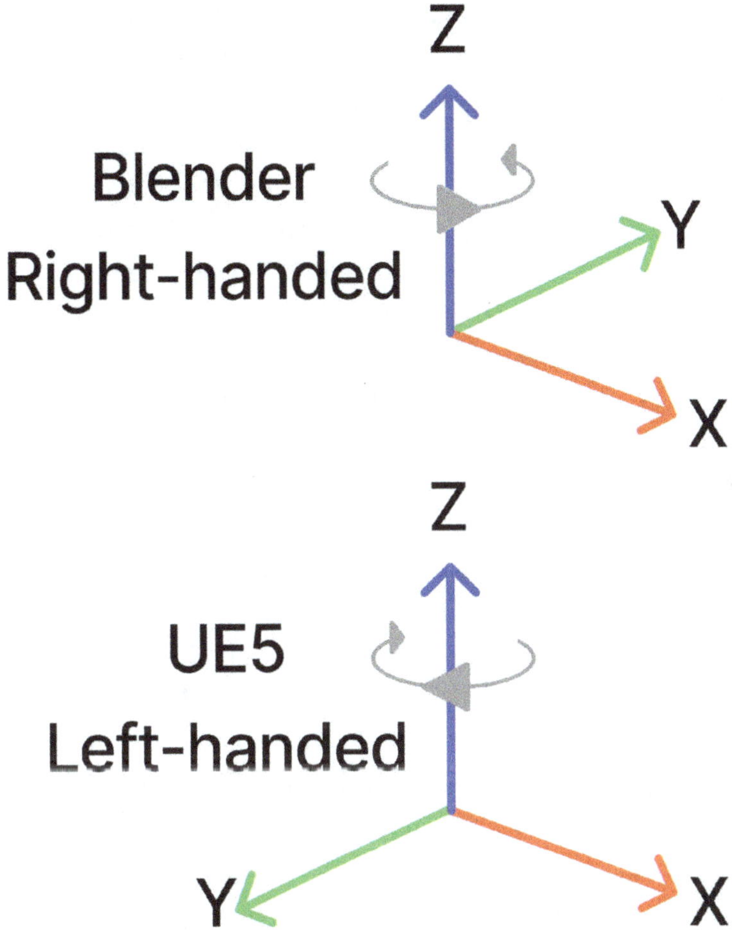

Figure 10-4. *Top: Blender's coordinate system is right-handed with Z up. Bottom: UE5's coordinate system is left-handed with Z up*

Step #8: Export to glTF 2.0 or FBX

After the first seven steps, the meshes are ready to export. We shift-click each object or use the A key to toggle select all (if only those intended for export are in the scene). To export mesh objects with materials from Blender to be used as static meshes in UE5, we can export the meshes either as a *.glb (glTF binary) or *.fbx (FBX) file. *.glb is the recommended format since it will preserve the material setup for a mesh when imported into UE5 much better than *.fbx. Later in this chapter in the section "Automating the Export

Process in Python," we'll work through an example where we modify the weapon generator from Chapter 4 to generate a gun model, postprocess it, then export it to a *.glb file, which, when imported into UE5, can be directly dragged into the level with all materials intact and ready to go. If you were to export the same model as a *.fbx file and import it in UE5, you would find that some of the materials are broken and need to be manually repaired.

To export selected mesh objects to a `*.glb` file with all of their materials, go to File ➤ Export ➤ glTF 2.0 (.glb/.gltf), then set format to glTF Binary (.glb), check "Remember Export Settings" to save the export settings to the blend file, and click "Selected Objects" to limit export to only those selected in the scene, as shown in Figure 10-5. Even though both Blender and UE5 use Z up, I've found through experimentation that you must check the +Y Up box (4 in Figure 10-5) to export in the correct orientation. Click to expand "Mesh" and check "Apply Modifiers," then click to expand "Materials" and select "Export," set Images to "JPEG Format (.jpg)," and slide Image Quality to 100. If the mesh does not have animation, you can uncheck the "Animation" box. Leaving all other settings at default, enter a file name in the bottom center of the dialog, then click the "Export glTF 2.0" button to export.

To export selected mesh objects to a `*.fbx` file with their materials, go to File ➤ Export ➤ FBX (.fbx), then in the dialog that opens, set Path Mode to Copy and click the "Embed Textures" button to its right to include a copy of the models' materials in the same file, as shown in Figure 10-6. After that, we set Batch Mode to "Off," check "Selected Objects" so only the selected objects in the scene are exported. Next, click to expand "Transform" and set Up to "Z Up," which will automatically set Forward to "-X forward" (if not, set it manually). Uncheck "Apply Transform" since it is still an unstable feature in Blender 4.4. To wrap up, click to expand "Geometry," check "Apply Modifiers," and uncheck "Animation" if exporting a mesh without animation. Leaving all other settings at default values, enter a file name in the bottom center of the dialog, then click the "Export FBX" button to export.

Step #9: Move Objects Back to Their Original Locations (Optional)

After exporting, you can optionally move the objects back to their original positions, so they don't all sit at the world origin overlapping one another. To set an object's position, click to select it in the viewport or Outliner, use the N key to summon the Properties shelf, then under the Item tab ➤ Location, enter the X, Y, and Z coordinates of the object. It is tedious to write down objects' original locations and set them back one by one post-export. Fortunately, it is not hard to write a Python script to do the same as you'll see later in this chapter. Alternatively, you could duplicate the blend file before moving the objects.

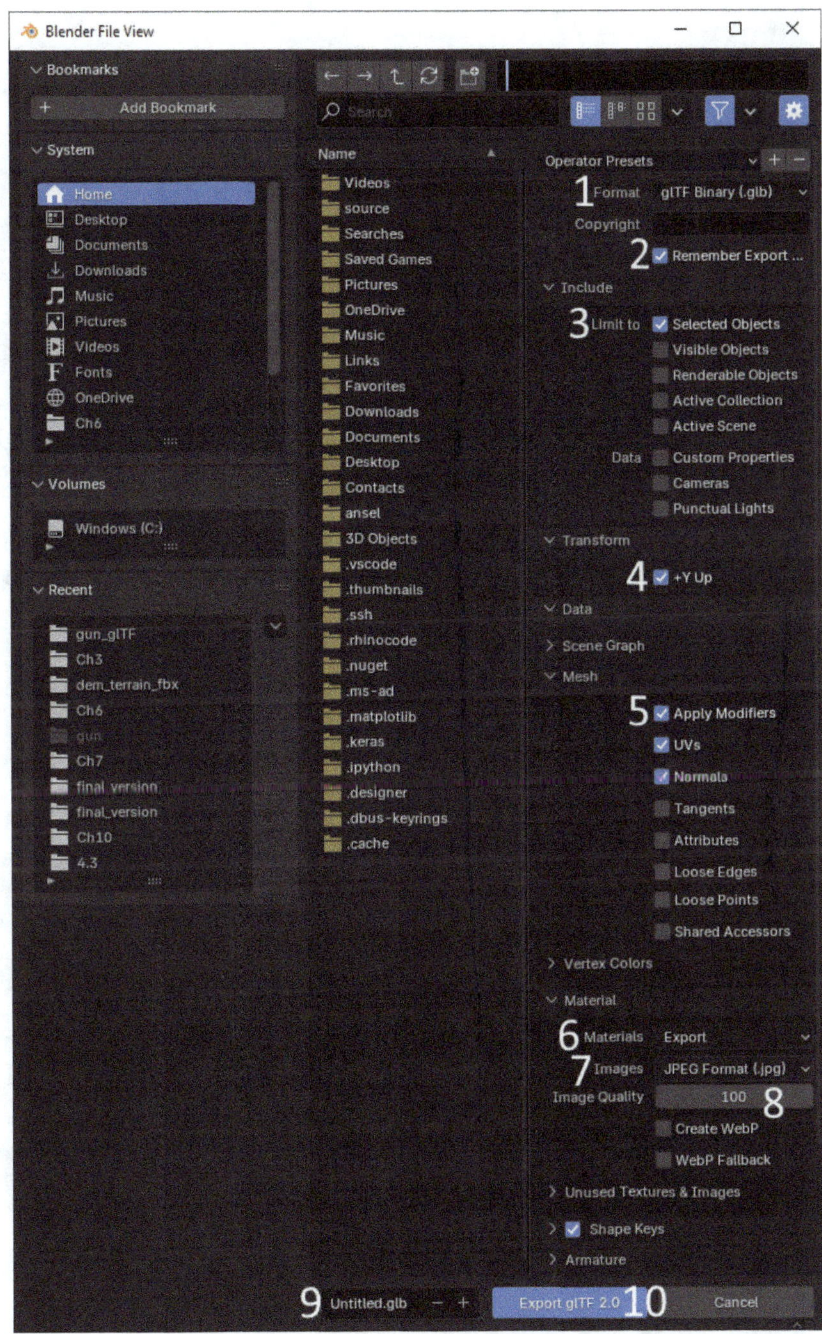

Figure 10-5. *File ➤ Export ➤ glTF 2.0(.glb/.gltf). (1) Set Format to glTF Binary (.glb). (2) Check "Remember Export Settings." (3) Check "Selected Objects." (4) Check "+Y Up." (5) Check "Apply Modifiers." (6) Set Materials to "Export," (7) Images to JPEG Format (.jpg), and (8) Image Quality to 100. (9) Enter file name, and (10) click Export glTF 2.0 to export*

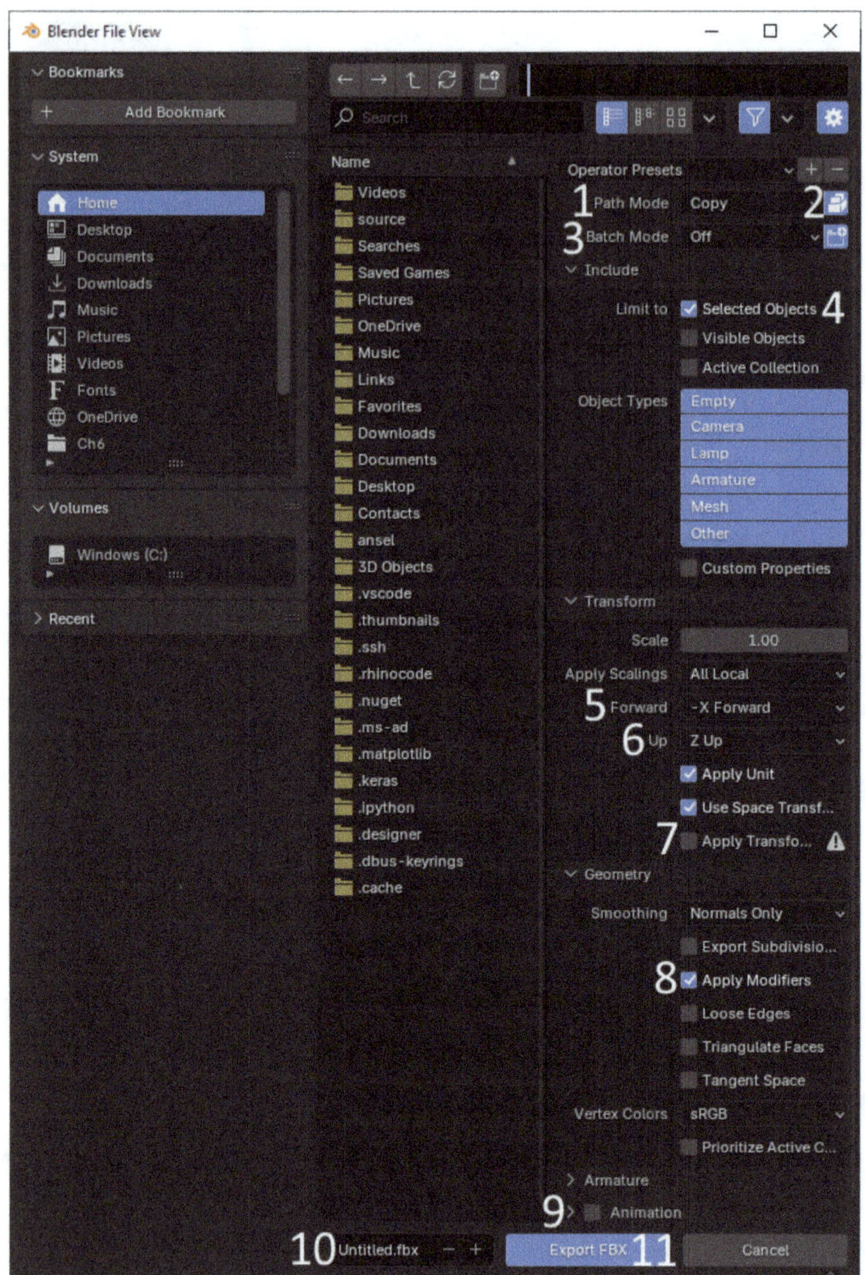

Figure 10-6. *File ➤ Export ➤ FBX(.fbx). (1) Set Path Mode to Copy and click the (2) Embed Textures button to its right. (3) Set Batch Mode to Off. (4) Check "Selected Objects." (5) Set Forward to –X Forward and (6) Up to Z Up. Uncheck (7) Apply Transform. Check (8) Apply Modifiers. Uncheck (9) Animation. (10) Enter file name, and (11) click Export FBX to export*

Automating the Export Process in Python

Now that you're familiar with how to manually export static meshes to glTF and FBX, we'll automate the process in Blender Python. We'll create functions to postprocess the meshes (triangulate, apply transforms, join, etc.), get them ready for export (set units, moving them to world origin), export to the desired format, and restore the meshes to their original locations. After we're done implementing the export utilities in Python, we'll modify the weapon generator from Chapter 4 to fully automate the process of generating a model with materials and exporting it to a *.glb file to be directly imported into UE5.

Export Workflow in Python

Figure 10-7 shows the overall architecture of our static mesh export script in Blender Python. Each function is shown with its listing as well as its corresponding number in Figure 10-1. The helper routines each gray-box function makes use of are shown to their left. In a moment, we'll dive into each function and explain its inner working. It may be helpful to refer to Figure 10-7 again after you've finished reading the code explanations to tie it altogether.

Step #1: Configure Scene Units

`set_length_units` (Listing 10-2) sets the scene Unit System to Metric, Unit Scale to 1, and Length unit to Meters (implements #1 in Figure 10-1).

Steps #2 to #6: Postprocess Mesh (Optional)

`post_process_objs_for_export` (Listing 10-1) performs postprocessing including joining meshes, triangulating, applying modifiers and transforms, and scaling to desired target lengths (implements #2 to #6 in Figure 10-1). It uses the helper function `get_dim_XYZ` (Listing 10-3) to derive the joined mesh's dimension for the purpose of calculating scale factor based on the given target length.

Steps #7 to #8: Select and Move Objects to World Origin, Export to glTF 2.0 or FBX

The two functions `export_gltf` (Listing 10-9) and `export_fbx` (Listing 10-10) export a list of static meshes to glTF binary (`*.glb`) and FBX (`*.fbx`) files, respectively (they implement #7 to #9 in Figure 10-1).

Both `export_gltf` and `export_fbx` call the helper function `get_ready_for_export` (Listing 10-4) to move the objects so their origins align with Blender's world origin (#7 in Figure 10-1).

After exporting to file, both `export_gltf` and `export_fbx` call the helper function `move_objs_post_export` (Listing 10-7) to move the objects back to their original locations.

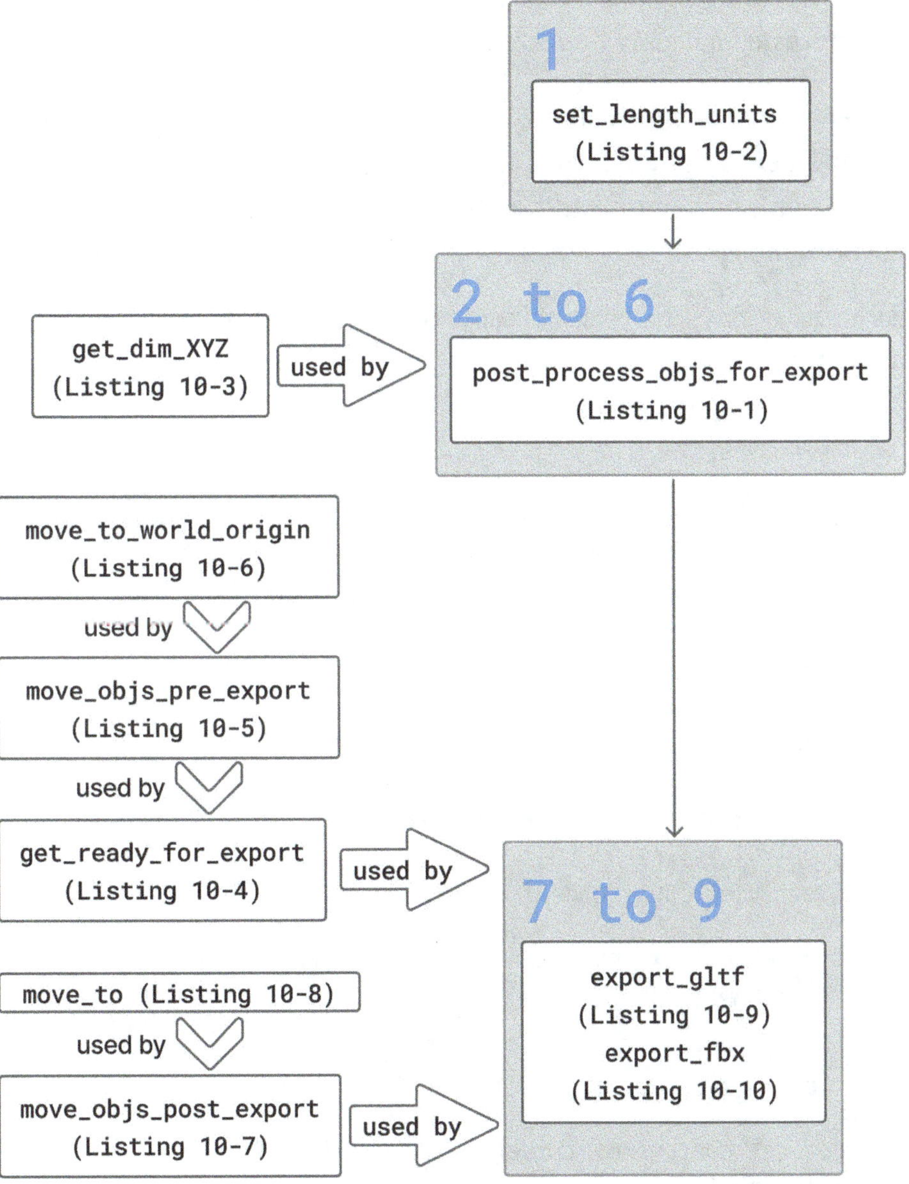

Figure 10-7. *This chapter's Python workflow for static mesh export to glTF/FBX. The functions marked 1 to 9 in this figure implement their conceptual counterparts in Figure 10-1*

Postprocess Meshes (Triangulate, Apply Transforms and Modifiers, Set Origin, Join, and Scale)

The first export utility function we'll write is `post_process_objs_for_export` in Listing 10-1, which postprocesses and joins a given list of meshes into one so it's ready to export.

Listing 10-1. For each mesh object in the given list, add a Triangulate modifier, apply all modifiers and transforms, and set origin to Center of Mass (Volume). Then join the objects into one and scale it based on the given target length (see /Ch10/export_utils.py)

```
def post_process_objs_for_export(context, objs_to_join, ↩
    target_length=-1):
    if len(objs_to_join) < 1:
        return None

    for obj in context.view_layer.objects:
        obj.select_set(False)

    filtered_objs_to_join = []
    for obj in objs_to_join:
        if obj.type != 'MESH':
            continue

        filtered_objs_to_join.append(obj)
        obj.select_set(True)
        context.view_layer.objects.active = obj

        c_o = get_context_override(context, 'VIEW_3D', ↩
            'WINDOW')
        with bpy.context.temp_override(**c_o):
            bpy.ops.object.mode_set(mode='OBJECT')

        c_o = get_context_override(context, 'VIEW_3D', ↩
            'WINDOW')
        with bpy.context.temp_override(**c_o):
            tri_mod = obj.modifiers.new( ↩
                obj.name+"_tri_mod", 'TRIANGULATE')
```

```
        for m in obj.modifiers:
            bpy.ops.object.modifier_apply( ↩
                modifier=m.name)

        bpy.ops.object.transform_apply( ↩
            location=True, rotation=True, scale=True)
        bpy.ops.object.origin_set( ↩
            type='ORIGIN_CENTER_OF_VOLUME', ↩
            center='MEDIAN')
    obj.select_set(False)

if len(filtered_objs_to_join) < 1:
    return None

context.view_layer.objects.active = ↩
    filtered_objs_to_join[-1]
name_of_joined_obj = filtered_objs_to_join[-1].name

for obj in filtered_objs_to_join:
    obj.select_set(True)
c_o = get_context_override(context, 'VIEW_3D', 'WINDOW')
with bpy.context.temp_override(**c_o):
    bpy.ops.object.join()

if context.view_layer.objects.find( ↩
    name_of_joined_obj) < 0:
    return None

joined_obj = ↩
    context.view_layer.objects[name_of_joined_obj]

if target_length > 0:
    x_dim, y_dim, z_dim = get_dim_XYZ(joined_obj)
    scale_factor = target_length/max(x_dim, y_dim)

    c_o = get_context_override(context, 'VIEW_3D', ↩
        'WINDOW')
    with bpy.context.temp_override(**c_o):
        bpy.ops.transform.resize( ↩
```

```
                value=(scale_factor, scale_factor, ↩
                    scale_factor))
            bpy.ops.object.transform_apply( ↩
                location=False, rotation=False, ↩
                scale=True)
    return context.view_layer.objects[name_of_joined_obj]
```

We start with a sanity check—if the number of objects passed in (`objs_to_join`) is less than 1, there is nothing to do, so we simply return. The code is divided into three parts—in the first part, we pick out the mesh objects, triangulate, and apply all modifiers and transforms. In the second part, we join the mesh objects into one. In the third part, we compute the target length's ratio to the larger of the joined mesh's XY sizes, then scale it accordingly. We'll walk through each part in detail.

We kick off the first part of the code by deselecting all, then iterate through the passed-in objects (`objs_to_join`) in a `for` loop. For each object (`obj`), we check if it is a mesh; if so, we save a reference to it in the list to join later (`filtered_objs_to_join`). We set `obj` as active and select it so we can switch it to Object mode with a context override (as if from the viewport). Since UE5 requires meshes to be triangulated, we add a Triangulate modifier, before applying all of `obj`'s modifiers via calls to `bpy.ops.object.modifier_apply`, and applying all transforms with `bpy.ops.object.transform_apply(location=True, rotation=True, scale=True)`. When exporting to either FBX or glTF, Blender ignores the object's origin and uses the world origin instead. Therefore, to use the object's origin in UE5, we must move the object so its origin aligns with Blender's world origin right before exporting. We won't move the object just yet. Instead, we'll call `bpy.ops.object.origin_set(type='ORIGIN_CENTER_OF_VOLUME',center='MEDIAN')` to set the object's origin to Center of Mass (Volume), so when it's joined or moved later, it will have the correct point of reference. Note that we must deselect the object at the end of each iteration (`obj.select_set(False)`) so the subsequent iteration does not accidentally apply operator calls to the wrong object.

Remember that while iterating, we accumulated a list of mesh objects to be joined (`filtered_objs_to_join`). If this list ends up being empty, meaning the list of objects passed in (`objs_to_join`) doesn't contain any meshes; there's nothing more to do, so we simply return. Otherwise, we proceed to join the meshes. When joining meshes with Ctrl-J, Blender defaults the joined object's name to the *last* object selected—in other words, if the join is successful, there should be an object with that name in the scene afterward. We set the last object in the list to join as active and grab its name (`filtered_` `objs_to_join[-1].name`), then select the rest of the objects one by one, and with a context override (as if from the viewport), call `bpy.ops.object.join()` to join them. Afterward, we check if the view layer contains an object with the name we expect—if not, the join failed, so we return. Otherwise, we retrieve a reference to the joined object, so we can scale it next.

In the final part of the code, we scale the joined mesh based on the given `target_length`. We start by calling the helper function `get_dim_XYZ` (Listing 10-3) to derive the joined mesh's dimension along X, Y, and Z (more on this shortly). We then divide `target_length` by the larger of the X and Y dimensions to find the `scale_factor`. Then with a context override (as if from the viewport), we call `bpy.ops.transform.resize` to scale the joined mesh uniformly with `scale_factor` and `bpy.ops.object.transform_apply` with `scale=True` to apply the scaling right after. At this point, we're done—so we return the joined mesh.

Setting Units

The helper function `set_length_units` (Listing 10-2) configures the following three options under Properties editor ➤ Scene tab ➤ Units: Unit System to Metric, Unit Scale to 1, and Length to Meters, which are shown in Figure 10-8 (in the same figure, all other settings are left at default).

Listing 10-2. For the scene under the passed-in context, set the Unit System to Metric, Unit Scale to 1, and Length unit to Meters (see /Ch10/export_utils.py)

```
def set_length_units(context):
    context.scene.unit_settings.system = 'METRIC'
    context.scene.unit_settings.scale_length = 1
    context.scene.unit_settings.length_unit = 'METERS'
```

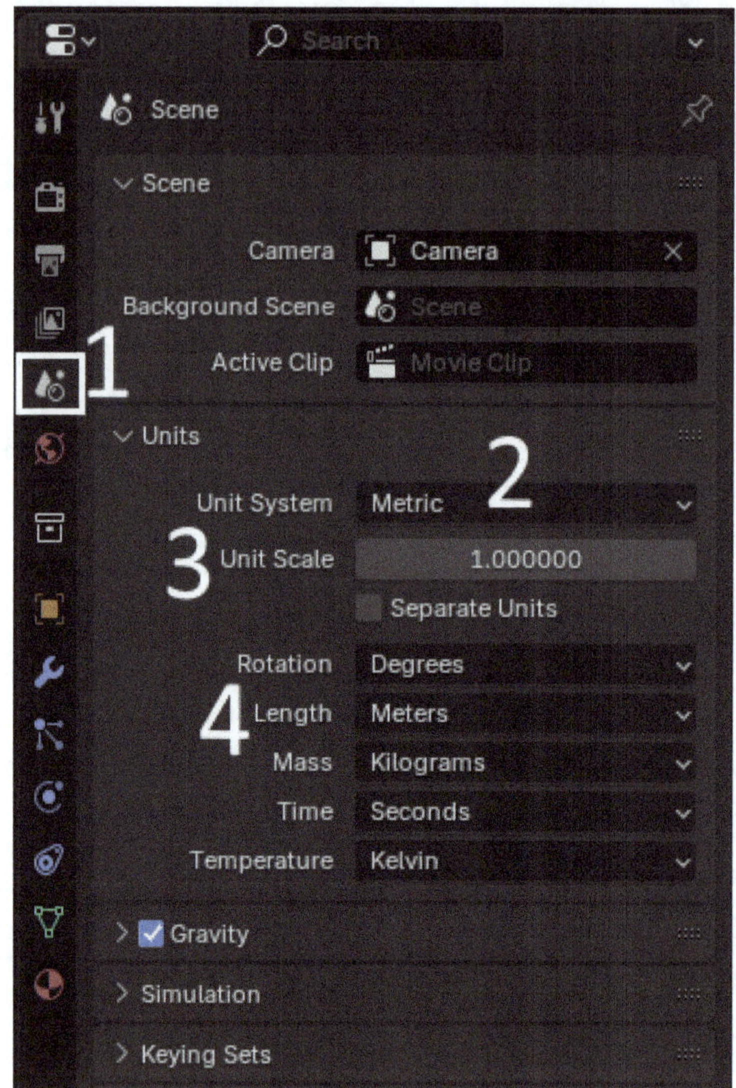

Figure 10-8. *You can configure the scene units under the (1) Properties editor ➤ Scene tab. For exporting this chapter's sample gun mesh, we set the (2) Unit System to Metric, (3) Unit Scale to 1, and (4) Length to Meters*

Finding Mesh Dimension per Axis by Dissecting Its Bounding Box

Since we designed for the caller of `post_process_objs_for_export` (Listing 10-1) to specify a length to scale a mesh to (`target_length`), we write a helper function `get_dim_XYZ` (Listing 10-3) to calculate a mesh's dimension along X, Y, and Z from its bounding box. We then divide target_length in Listing 10-1 by the larger of the X and Y sizes returned by Listing 10-3 to find the scale factor.

Listing 10-3. Given a mesh object, analyze its bounding box to find its size along X, Y, and Z (see /Ch10/export_utils.py)

```
def get_dim_XYZ(obj):
    bbox = [[v[0], v[1], v[2]] for v in obj.bound_box]
    bbox_verts = np.array(bbox).reshape(len(bbox), 3)
    x_min, x_max = find_min_max(bbox_verts, 0)
    y_min, y_max = find_min_max(bbox_verts, 1)
    z_min, z_max = find_min_max(bbox_verts, 2)
    return (x_max-x_min), (y_max-y_min), (z_max-z_min)
```

A mesh object obj's bounding box can be accessed via obj.bound_box, which is a nested bpy_prop_array of size 8 by 3 containing the XYZ coordinates of the eight corner vertices of the box (each row is the coordinates of one vertex). We start by creating a nested Python list (bbox) from the bpy_prop_array, then convert the list to a numpy array of size 8 by 3 (bbox_verts), so we can use the helper function find_min_max to find the minimum and maximum per axis (we implemented find_min_max in Listing 4-2 in material_and_image_utils.py). The difference between the maximum and minimum per axis is then the size for that axis (e.g., x_max-x_min is the span of the obj along X).

Moving Objects to World Origin and Selecting Them

As we discussed earlier, an export to either FBX or glTF ignores a mesh object's origin and uses Blender's world origin instead. Therefore, for a mesh to have the same origin in UE5, we must move it so its origin coincides with Blender's world origin prior to export. Since we don't necessarily want the objects to stay at (0, 0, 0) post-export, we'll save their original locations in a list so we can move them back. This comes in handy when you have multiple objects in a scene and want to export them in one *.glb or *.fbx file, but don't want them to stay overlapped at (0, 0, 0) after export.

In Listing 10-4, we implement the function get_ready_for_export, which moves a list of mesh objects to the world origin while recording their original locations. It is assumed that the caller had already performed any postprocessing necessary on the meshes (e.g., joining and triangulation) by calling post_process_objs_for_export (Listing 10-1) before calling Listing 10-4.

Listing 10-4. Get the given list of mesh objects ready for export by moving them to the world origin while recording their original locations, switching to Object mode, and selecting them (see /Ch10/export_utils.py)

```
def get_ready_for_export(context, objs_to_export, ↩
    obj_orig_locs):
    if len(objs_to_export) < 1:
        return

    move_objs_pre_export(context, objs_to_export, ↩
        obj_orig_locs)

    for obj in context.scene.objects:
        obj.select_set(False)

    context.view_layer.objects.active = objs_to_export[0]
    objs_to_export[0].select_set(True)
    c_o = get_context_override(context, 'VIEW_3D', 'WINDOW')
    with bpy.context.temp_override(**c_o):
        bpy.ops.object.mode_set(mode='OBJECT')

    for obj in objs_to_export:
        obj.select_set(True)
```

Since Python passes containers by reference, we have the caller of `get_ready_for_export` pass in the list for recording object locations (`obj_orig_locs`), which we in turn pass to `move_objs_pre_export` (Listing 10-5) to modify in place. This setup is more efficient than creating and returning the list at each level of execution since only one list is created at the top level.

Since we intend for only selected objects to be exported, we deselect all, set the first object from the given list as active and select it, then with a context override (as if from the viewport) switch to Object mode. The choice of the first object is arbitrary—we just needed a mesh object so we could switch to Object mode. After that, we select the remainder of the given list by calling `select_set(True)` on each object.

Note Pass-by-reference means passing the memory location of an object to a function instead of a copy of that object. The function can then modify the same instance of the object that the caller has.

Moving Objects to World Origin Pre-export

move_objs_pre_export (Listing 10-5) is a helper function called by get_ready_for_export (Listing 10-4) which simply iterates through and calls move_to_world_origin (Listing 10-6) on each object to export and accumulates their original locations in the passed-in list (obj_orig_locs).

Listing 10-5. Move the given list of objects to the world origin, while recording their original locations in the passed-in list (see /Ch10/export_utils.py)

```
def move_objs_pre_export(context, objs_to_export, ↩
    obj_orig_locs):
    for obj in objs_to_export:
        obj_orig_locs.append( ↩
            move_to_world_origin(context, obj))
```

Listing 10-6 shows the implementation of move_to_world_origin, which moves a given object (obj_to_move) to the world origin. We start by deselecting all, then set obj_to_move as active and select it. We then call deepcopy (imported via from copy import deepcopy) to make a hard copy of obj_to_move's location, i.e., a copy of the mathutils.Vector instance that can be independently edited from the original, not just a copy of its memory address. With a context override (as if from the viewport), we switch to Object mode. Once mode switch is complete, with another override (viewport), we move obj_to_move to the world origin by calling bpy.ops.transform.translate with a Vector equal to the displacement from the object's current location (obj_orig_loc) to (0, 0, 0), then immediately after apply this transform via bpy.ops.object.transform_apply with location=True (which is equivalent to Ctrl-A in Object mode ➤ Location). We finish by returning the hard copy of the object's original location (obj_orig_loc).

Listing 10-6. Move the given object to the world origin (see /Ch10/export_utils.py)

```
def move_to_world_origin(context, obj_to_move):
    for obj in context.scene.objects:
        obj.select_set(False)
    context.view_layer.objects.active = obj_to_move
    obj_to_move.select_set(True)
    obj_orig_loc = deepcopy(obj_to_move.location)
```

```
    c_o = get_context_override(context, 'VIEW_3D', 'WINDOW')
    with bpy.context.temp_override(**c_o):
        bpy.ops.object.mode_set(mode='OBJECT')

    c_o = get_context_override(context, 'VIEW_3D', 'WINDOW')
    with context.temp_override(**c_o):
        bpy.ops.transform.translate( ↩
            value=Vector((0,0,0))-obj_orig_loc)
        bpy.ops.object.transform_apply( ↩
            location=True, rotation=False, scale=False)

    return obj_orig_loc
```

Restoring Object Locations Post-export

As we discussed, if there are multiple objects in the scene to be exported at once, it's nice to have the option of returning them to their original locations post-export so they don't all sit at the world origin overlapping one another. We've designed the export workflow so that `get_ready_for_export` (Listing 10-4) calls `move_objs_pre_export` (Listing 10-5) to move the objects (`objs_to_export`) to world origin while accumulating their original locations in a list (`obj_orig_locs`). `move_objs_post_export` in Listing 10-7 reverses the action of `move_objs_pre_export` (Listing 10-5) by moving `objs_to_export` back to their original locations (`obj_orig_locs`). Python's built-in function `zip` takes two lists and returns the pairs formed by taking the first items from both lists, second items from both lists, and so on. Therefore, `zip(objs_to_export, obj_orig_locs)` gives us the list `[(obj #0, obj #0's original location), (obj #1, obj #1's original location), ...]`.

Listing 10-7. Move the list of given objects back to their original locations (see /Ch10/export_utils.py)

```
def move_objs_post_export(context, objs_to_export, ↩
    obj_orig_locs):
    for obj, loc in zip(objs_to_export, obj_orig_locs):
        move_to(context, obj, loc)
```

In Listing 10-8, we implement the `move_to` function called by `move_objs_post_export` (Listing 10-7) to move a single mesh object (`obj_to_move`) to a given `location`. We deselect all, set `obj_to_move` as active and select it, then with a context override (as if from the viewport) switch to Object mode since transforms could only be applied in Object mode. Once mode switch is complete, with another override (viewport), we move `obj_to_move` to `location` by calling `bpy.ops.transform.translate`—here, the displacement `Vector` is just `location`, since `obj_to_move` is currently at the world origin, and `location - Vector((0, 0, 0))` is just `location`. We call `bpy.ops.object.transform_apply` with `location=True` immediately after to apply the transform (which is equivalent to Ctrl-A in Object mode ➤ Location).

Listing 10-8. Move a given object to the given location (see /Ch10/export_utils.py)

```
def move_to(context, obj_to_move, location):
    for obj in context.scene.objects:
        obj.select_set(False)
    context.view_layer.objects.active = obj_to_move
    obj_to_move.select_set(True)

    c_o = get_context_override(context, 'VIEW_3D', 'WINDOW')
    with bpy.context.temp_override(**c_o):
        bpy.ops.object.mode_set(mode='OBJECT')

    c_o = get_context_override(context, 'VIEW_3D', 'WINDOW')
    with context.temp_override(**c_o):
        bpy.ops.transform.translate(value=location)
        bpy.ops.object.transform_apply( ↩
            location=True, rotation=False, scale=False)
```

Exporting to glTF Format

Recall that we designed the export workflow in Python such that mesh postprocessing steps are grouped together in `post_process_objs_for_export` (Listing 10-1), then the "export to file" function is called, followed by `move_objs_post_export` (Listing 10-7) to restore objects to their original locations. There are two possible "export to file" functions, `export_gltf` (Listing 10-9) to export to `*.glb` (glTF binary), which we'll look at here, and `export_fbx` (Listing 10-10) to export to `*.fbx` which we'll look at in the next section.

export_gltf (Listing 10-9) performs an export to *.glb in three steps: calling get_ready_for_export (Listing 10-4) to move the objects to world origin and select them, bpy.ops.export_scene.gltf to export the objects to *.glb file on disk (File ➤ Export ➤ glTF 2.0 (.glb/.gltf)) with settings in Figure 10-5, then move_objs_post_export (Listing 10-7) to return the objects to their original locations. The glTF export settings under File ➤ Export ➤ glTF 2.0 (.glb/.gltf) that correspond to the argument values of bpy.ops.export_scene.gltf in export_gltf (Listing 10-9) are summarized in Table 10-1. For additional arguments to bpy.ops.export_scene.gltf, see https://docs.blender.org/api/current/bpy.ops.export_scene.html#bpy.ops.export_scene.gltf under the current version of the Blender Python documentation.

Note that although both Blender and UE5 use +Z up, I've found that *when exporting to glTF 2.0, checking the "+Y Up" box will produce correct orientation in the exported model.* Since for this chapter's example we're exporting the gun as a static mesh without any animation, we use export_animation=False. To ensure that the gun's materials are exported with the mesh in the same *.glb file, we use export_materials='EXPORT', export_image_format='JPEG', and export_jpeg_quality=100 to export the materials as JPEG images at the maximum quality. As we'll see shortly, the resulted *.glb file can be directly imported into UE5 with all the materials set up and ready to instantiate in a level.

Listing 10-9. Export selected meshes with their materials to a *.glb file (binary glTF) (see /Ch10/export_utils.py)

```
def export_gltf(context, fp, objs_to_export):
    obj_orig_locs = []
    get_ready_for_export(context, objs_to_export, ↩
        obj_orig_locs)

    bpy.ops.export_scene.gltf(filepath=fp, ↩
        export_format='GLB', will_save_settings=True, ↩
        use_selection=True, export_extras=True, ↩
        export_yup=True, export_apply=True, ↩
        export_texcoords=True, export_normals=True, ↩
        export_materials='EXPORT', ↩
        export_image_format='JPEG', ↩
```

```
        export_jpeg_quality=100, ↩
        export_animations=False)

    move_objs_post_export(context, objs_to_export, ↩
        obj_orig_locs)
```

Table 10-1. *Summary of arguments to bpy.ops.export_scene.gltf in the export_gltf function in Listing 10-9*

Argument to bpy.ops.export_scene.gltf	Setting under File ➤ Export ➤ glTF 2.0 (.glb/.gltf)
export_format='GLB'	Format: select "glTF Binary (.glb)."
will_save_settings=True	Check the "Remember Export Settings" box (saves settings to blend file).
use_selection=True export_extras=True	Under "Include," in the "Limit to" section, check the "Selected Objects" box; in the "Data" section, check the "Custom Properties" box.
export_yup=True	Under "Transform," check the "+Y Up" box *(Note: although both Blender and UE5 use +Z up, I've found that checking "+Y Up" will produce the correct orientation in the exported model).*
export_apply=True export_texcoords=True export_normals=True	Under "Mesh," check the "Apply Modifiers" box, check the "UVs" box, and check the "Normals" box.
export_materials='EXPORT' export_image_format='JPEG' export_jpeg_quality=100	Under "Material," for "Materials," select "Export"; for "Images," select "JPEG Format (.jpg)," and set "Image Quality" to 100.
export_animations=False	Uncheck the "Animation" box, since we're exporting the gun mesh as a static mesh without any animation.

Exporting to FBX Format

Similar to `export_gltf` (Listing 10-9), `export_fbx` (Listing 10-10) performs the export to `*.fbx` in three steps: call `get_ready_for_export` (Listing 10-4) to move the objects to world origin and select them, `bpy.ops.export_scene.fbx` to export the objects to `*.fbx` file on disk (File ➤ Export ➤ FBX (.fbx)) based on settings shown in Figure 10-6, then move_objs_post_export (Listing 10-7) to return the objects to their locations pre-export. The FBX export settings under File ➤ Export ➤ FBX (.fbx) that correspond to the argument values of bpy.ops.export_scene.fbx in export_fbx (Listing 10-10) are summarized in Table 10-2. For additional arguments to bpy.ops.export_scene.fbx, see https://docs.blender.org/api/current/bpy.ops.export_scene.html#bpy.ops.export_scene.fbx under the current version of the Blender Python documentation.

Note that to ensure the materials are exported with the mesh in a single *.fbx file, we use the options path_mode='COPY' and embed_textures=True. Since both Blender and UE5 use +Z up, we use axis_forward='-X' and axis_up='Z' to ensure that the exported model will have the correct orientation. At the time of writing, the Apply Transform setting (under Transform) is unstable in Blender 4.4; therefore, we uncheck it by setting bake_space_transform=False. Since for this chapter's example we're exporting the sample gun as a static mesh without any animation, we also set bake_anim=False to uncheck the Animation box.

Note that the export_fbx function is provided here as an additional example, since I recommend exporting to glTF rather than FBX for UE5, reason being that UE5 will *not* import some materials correctly from FBX and will require manually editing. At the time of writing, UE5.5.4 and UE5.6 will both import the test_gun.glb file (glTF binary) created by running test_gun_export_gltf (Listing 10-11) perfectly with all materials intact without any manual tweaking.

Listing 10-10. Export selected meshes with their materials to a *.fbx file (see /Ch10/export_utils.py)

```
def export_fbx(context, fp, objs_to_export):
    obj_orig_locs = []
    get_ready_for_export(context, objs_to_export, ↩
        obj_orig_locs)

    bpy.ops.export_scene.fbx(filepath=fp, ↩
        path_mode='COPY', embed_textures=True, ↩
        batch_mode='OFF', use_selection=True, ↩
        bake_space_transform=False, ↩
        use_mesh_modifiers=True, bake_anim=False, ↩
        axis_forward='-X', axis_up='Z')

    move_objs_post_export(context, objs_to_export, ↩
        obj_orig_locs)
```

***Table 10-2.** Summary of arguments to bpy.ops.export_scene.fbx in the export_fbx function in Listing 10-10*

Argument to bpy.ops. export_scene.fbx	Setting under File ➤ Export ➤ FBX (.fbx)
path_mode='COPY' embed_textures=True	Under "Path Mode," select "Copy" and click the button to the right (Embed Textures) to ensure it is toggled on (blue) so the materials are exported together with the mesh in the same *.fbx file.
batch_mode='OFF'	Select "Off" for Batch Mode.
use_selection=True	In the "Include" section, under "Limit to," check the "Selected Objects" box.
axis_forward='-X' axis_up='Z' bake_space_ transform=False	In the "Transform" section, for "Forward," select "-X forward"; for Up, select "Z Up" and *uncheck* the "Apply Transform" box since it is an experimental/unstable setting.
use_mesh_ modifiers=True	In the "Geometry" section, check the "Apply Modifiers" box.
bake_anim=False	Uncheck the "Animation" box, since we're exporting the gun mesh as a static mesh without any animation.

Modifying the Game Weapon Generator to Export to *.glb File

Time to put it altogether. We'll modify the version of `gun_generator.py` from Chapter 4 by adding the function `test_gun_export_gltf` (Listing 10-11), which generates a sample gun with materials and calls `post_process_objs_for_export` (Listing 10-1) to postprocess it and then `export_gltf` (Listing 10-9) to export it out to a glTF binary file (`test_gun.glb`).

Listing 10-11. Generate a gun mesh with default proportions with black cross-motif material on the grip, shiny silver barrels, brushed silver frame, and grid-patterned silver trigger box, then export everything (mesh + materials) to a glb file (binary glTF) (see /Ch10/gun_generator.py)

```
def test_gun_export_gltf(context):
    normal_map_cross_motif_filepath = ↩
        script_dir+"/cross_motif_grid_normal_map.png"
    black = (0, 0, 0, 1)
    silver = (0.604, 0.604, 0.604, 1.0)

    gun_mat, grip_mat, barrel_mat, trigger_mat, grip_obj, ↩
        barrel_obj, trigger_obj = generate_gun(context, ↩
            "0_default_gun", location=(5, 10, 0))
    create_grip(grip_obj, grip_mat, black, ↩
        normal_map_cross_motif_filepath)
    create_brushed_metal(grip_obj, gun_mat, silver)
    create_shiny_metal(barrel_mat, silver)
    create_fine_grid_metal(trigger_obj, trigger_mat, ↩
        silver)

    set_length_units(context)
    gun_objs = [grip_obj,barrel_obj,trigger_obj]
    joined_gun = post_process_objs_for_export(context, ↩
        gun_objs, 0.36)
    joined_gun.name = "test_gun"
    glb_filepath = script_dir+"/"+joined_gun.name+".glb"
    export_gltf(context, glb_filepath, [joined_gun])
```

The block of code in Listing 10-11 before `set_length_units` should look familiar—it is the first block of code from the function `test_gen_guns_with_mats` in the same `gun_generator.py` file, which we've gone over in Listing 4-19. It generates a gun model with black cross-motif grip, shiny silver double barrels, brushed frame, and a silver grid-patterned trigger box. We generate this same model here to demonstrate how we can export it to glTF using the functions we've written in this chapter. To do so, we call `set_length_units` (Listing 10-2) to ensure that the scene is set to Metric with Meters as the Length unit, then `post_process_objs_for_export` (Listing 10-1) to join the gun meshes into one object, triangulate it, apply all modifiers and transforms, and scale it to a target length of 0.36m along the barrels, which when imported into UE5 looks about right as a handgun in proportion to UE5's sample third-person player character, as we'll see shortly. We finish by calling `export_gltf` (Listing 10-9) to export it out to a glTF binary file named `test_gun.glb` in the directory that `gun_generatory.py` is run from.

Listing 10-12. Sample call to test_gun_export_gltf (Listing 10-11) (See /Ch10/gun_generator.py)

```
if __name__ == "__main__":
    test_gun_export_gltf(bpy.context)
```

As an example, the Chapter 10 version of `gun_generator.py` has already been modified to call `test_gun_export_gltf` (Listing 10-11) in the `if __name__ == "__main__"` block, as shown in Listing 10-12. Please refer to the section "Downloading and Running the Sample Code" for more detail on how to download this chapter's source code and setup the dependency. Once you do, you can open `/Ch10/gun_generator.py` in the Text Editor under the Scripting workspace and click the Run button to see the result of calling `test_gun_export_gltf` (Listing 10-11). Since the gun is scaled to 0.36m barrel wise, it may be hard to find due to its small size—while it is still selected post-run (or click to select it in the Outliner), you can use View ➤ Frame Selected to zoom and focus on it.

Import Meshes in Unreal Engine 5

In this section, we'll import the `test_gun.glb` file generated in the previous section in UE5 as a static mesh (a copy of `test_gun.glb` is also included in this chapter's downloaded source files). Please refer to `https://www.unrealengine.com/en-US/download` for instructions on how to download and install Unreal Engine. The screenshots in this section are based on UE5.5.4, although the same import steps have been verified in UE5.6 as well.

Create a Project

If you do not have a UE5 project yet, go ahead and create one. The figures for the remainder of this section are based on the Games ➤ Third Person starter project in UE5.5.4 with the following options: Blueprint, Target Platform as Desktop, Quality Preset as Maximum, and the Starter Content box checked, as shown in Figure 10-9. Go ahead and save the project to a directory that is convenient and give it a name with no spaces as UE5 does not allow it.

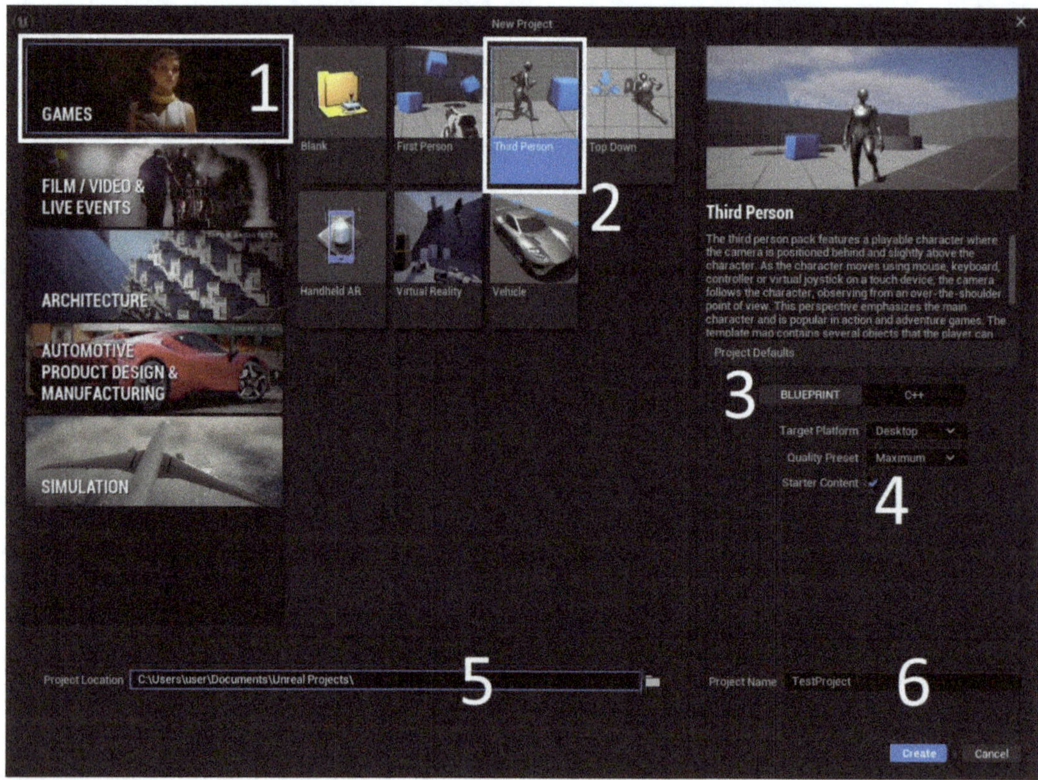

***Figure 10-9.** If you do not have a UE5 project yet, you can create a (1) Games ➤ (2) Third Person starter project, with the settings (3) Blueprint, Target Platform as Desktop, Quality Preset as Maximum, and (4) the Starter Content box checked. Choose (5) a directory that is convenient to save the project to and give it (6) a name without any spaces as UE5 does not allow it*

Import Content

Once you've created the Third Person starter project and opened it, the UE5 editor will load the ThirdPersonMap level automatically. If you are using your own project, go ahead and open a level or create a new level. Then click the "Quickly add to the project" button followed by "Import Content..." (1 and 2 in Figure 10-10) to open the import dialog (Figure 10-11).

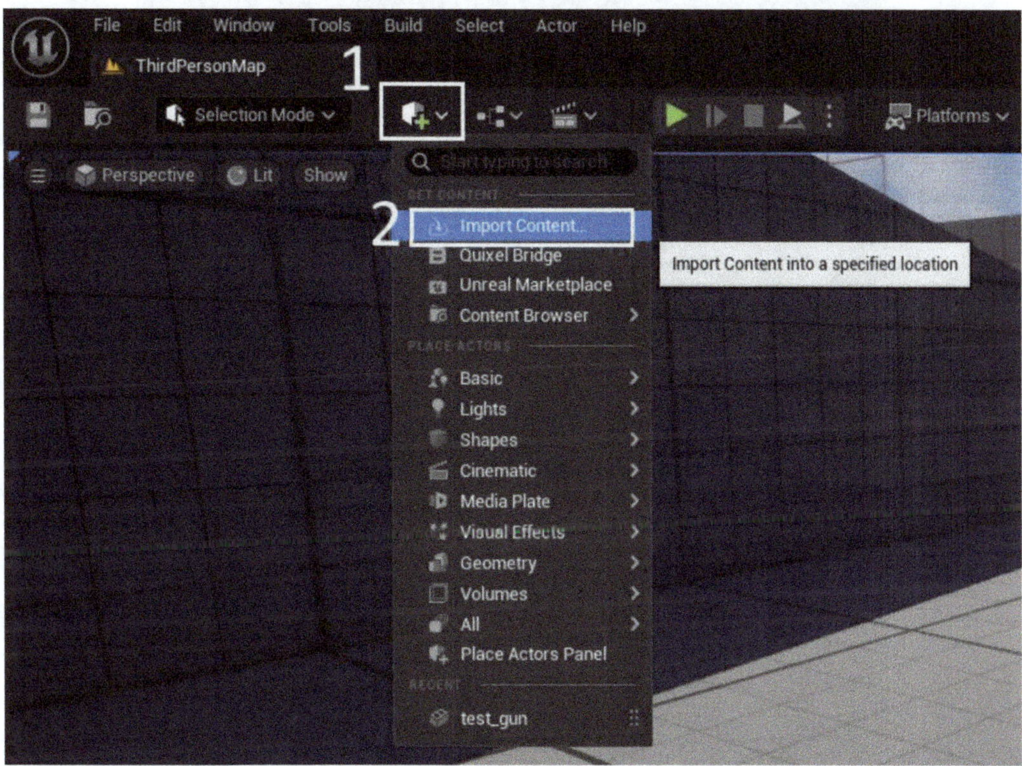

Figure 10-10. *To import contents to a project, click the (1) "Quickly add to the project" button, then (2) Import Content...to open the import dialog*

In the import dialog, click to select the Content folder (top, 1 in Figure 10-11), then right-click ➤ New Folder to create a new folder under Content (e.g., MyContent). With the new folder selected, click OK to set it as the destination for saving imported content, as shown on the bottom of Figure 10-11. Upon clicking OK, a file open dialog will appear, through which you'll navigate to and select the "test_gun.glb" file that you've either generated by running `test_gun_export_gltf` (Listing 10-11) or downloaded with the chapter's source files. Selecting "test_gun.glb" will automatically trigger the "Import Content" dialog to open with glTF import as context, as shown in Figure 10-12. Ensure that the "Default GLTF Assets Pipeline (InterchangeGenericAssetsPipeline)" option is selected, leave all other settings at default, and click "Import." Once the import is complete, you'll see six files appear in the Content Drawer under the "MyContent" folder (or the folder you've created in Figure 10-11), as shown in Figure 10-13.

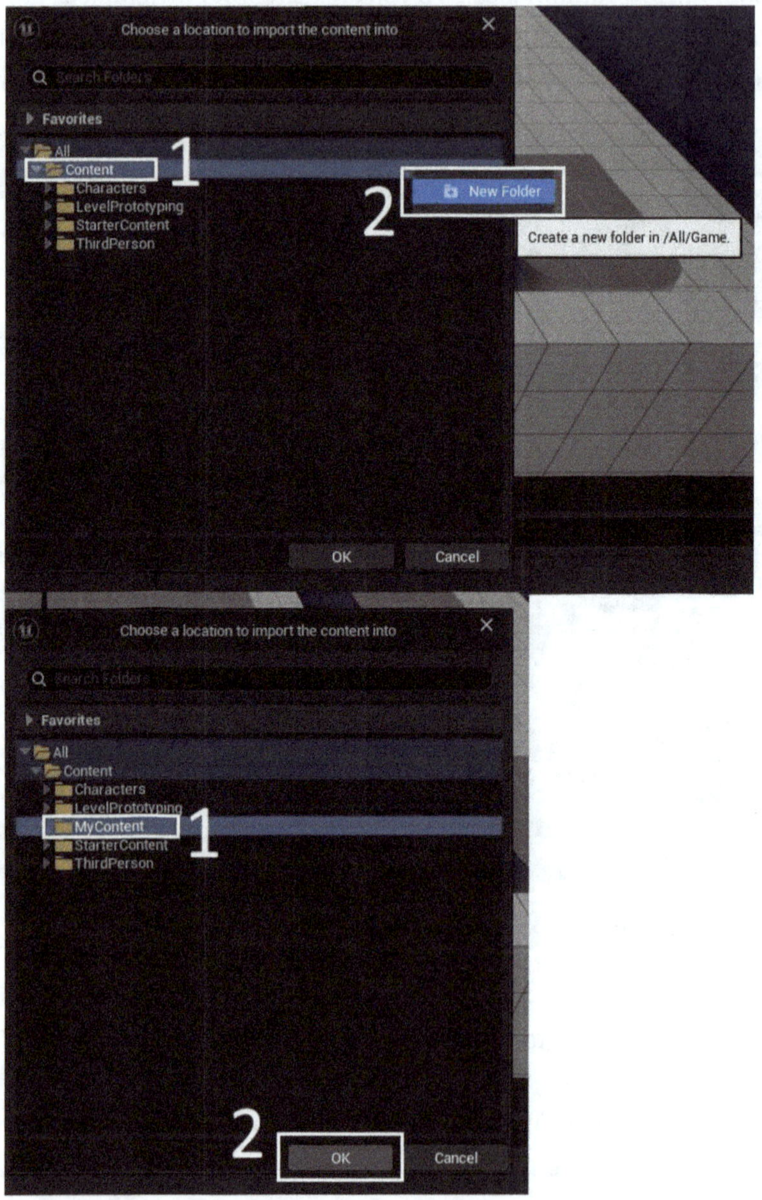

Figure 10-11. *The dialog after Figure 10-10. Click the Content folder (top, 1), right-click ➤ New Folder (top, 2) to create a folder under it, e.g., MyContent (bottom, 1), then with the new folder selected, click OK (bottom, 2) to save imported contents to this folder*

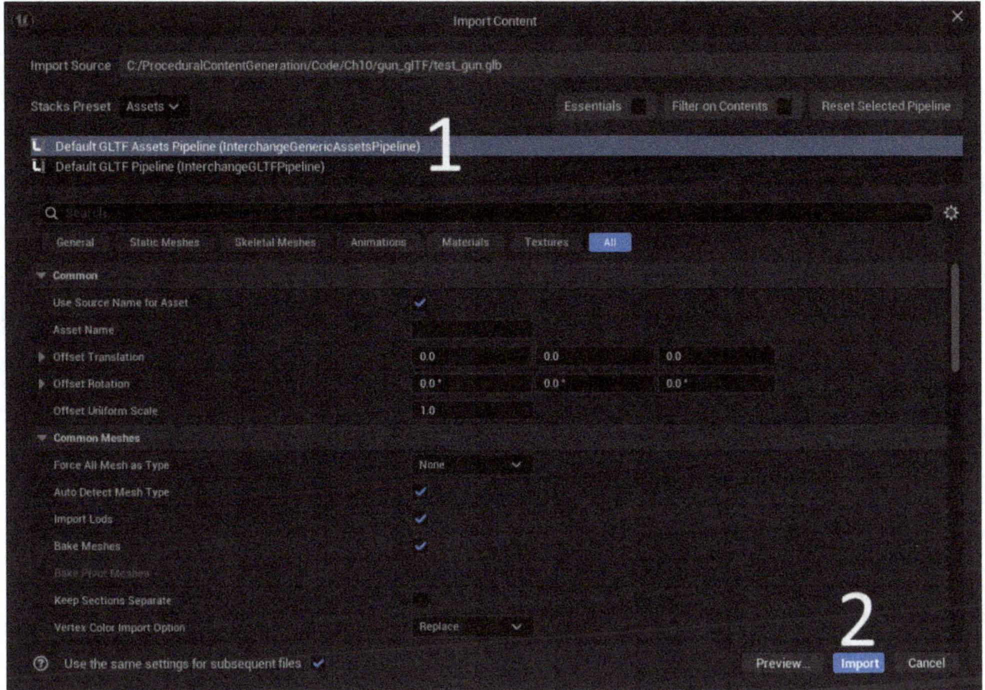

***Figure 10-12.** The "Import Content" dialog triggered by selecting the "test_gun.glb" file after Figure 10-11. Proceed by selecting (1) "Default GLTF Assets Pipeline (InterchangeGenericAssetsPipeline)" and clicking (2) Import*

Look more closely at the six files imported (2 to 7 in Figure 10-13) and verify that they are the following: 0_default_gun_barrel_mat, 0_default_gun_grip_mat, 0_default_gun_gun_mat, 0_default_gun_trigger.mat, cross_motif_grid_normal_map, and test_gun. The first four files are the materials for the barrels, grip, frame, and trigger, respectively, which are imported into Unreal as Material Instances. The fifth file is the normal map used by the grip material, which is imported as a Texture. The sixth file is the gun mesh itself, which is brought into UE5 as a Static Mesh.

Double-clicking the imported test_gun Static Mesh in the Content Drawer will open the editor window shown in Figure 10-14, which allows you to edit various properties of the mesh, including its materials and collision.

Note In UE5.6, importing the "test_gun.glb" file will create a folder named test_gun under MyContent, with three additional folders (Materials, StaticMeshes, and Textures) nested under it. The same six files are created but with the first four (2 to 5 in Figure 10-13) under test_gun/Materials, the test_gun Static Mesh (7 in Figure 10-13) under test_gun/StaticMeshes, and the normal map (6 in Figure 10-13) under test_gun/Textures.

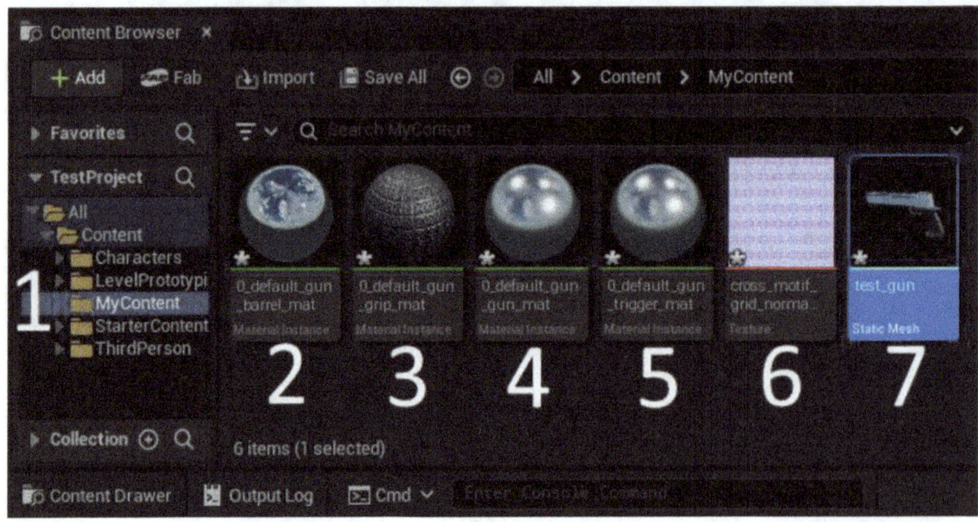

Figure 10-13. Once test_gun.glb is imported, six new files (2 to 7) will appear in the Content Drawer under the (1) MyContent folder (created in Figure 10-11) in UE5.5.4. 2 to 5 are the materials for the barrels, grip, frame, and trigger, respectively. 6 is the normal map for the grip material as a Texture and 7 the gun mesh itself as a Static Mesh

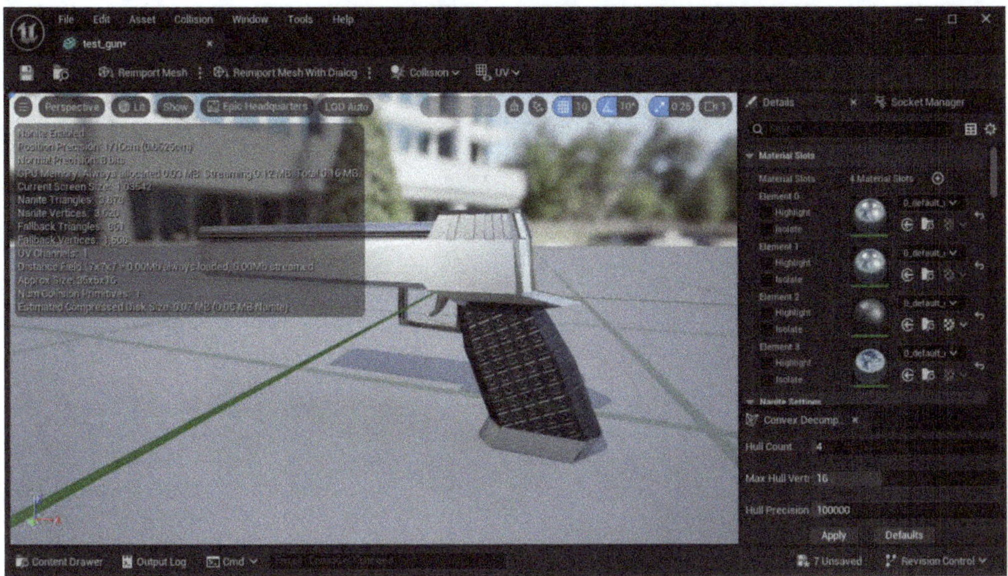

Figure 10-14. *When you double-click the test_gun Static Mesh in the Content Drawer, an editor will open as shown. You can edit various properties of the mesh in this editor, such as its collision and materials*

To create an instance of the gun in the level, drag the test_gun Static Mesh from the Content Drawer to the viewport as shown in Figure 10-15 (in UE5.6, this is under MyContent/test_gun/StaticMeshes). UE5 will default the instance's name to the name of the Static Mesh. You can double-click the instance's name in the Outliner to auto-zoom and frame it in the viewport. Upon its creation, the instance's origin will sit on the ground. You can drag one of its axes handles to move it around.

Editing objects in UE5 is beyond the scope of this book; however, here are a few tips to get you started: with an object selected, you can use the R, E, and W keys to switch between the scale, rotate, and move widgets. In the viewport, holding down MMB while moving the mouse pans the camera in a similar way as holding Shift-MMB and moving the mouse in Blender. You can also simulate what some call the "Maya" style camera movement in UE5 by holding down Alt-LMB while moving the mouse, which is equivalent to holding down MMB while moving the mouse in Blender. Being a game engine, UE5 also provides a "game style" camera movement with Alt-Shift-LMB while moving the mouse, where the viewpoint is fixed with the camera moving and rotating around it.

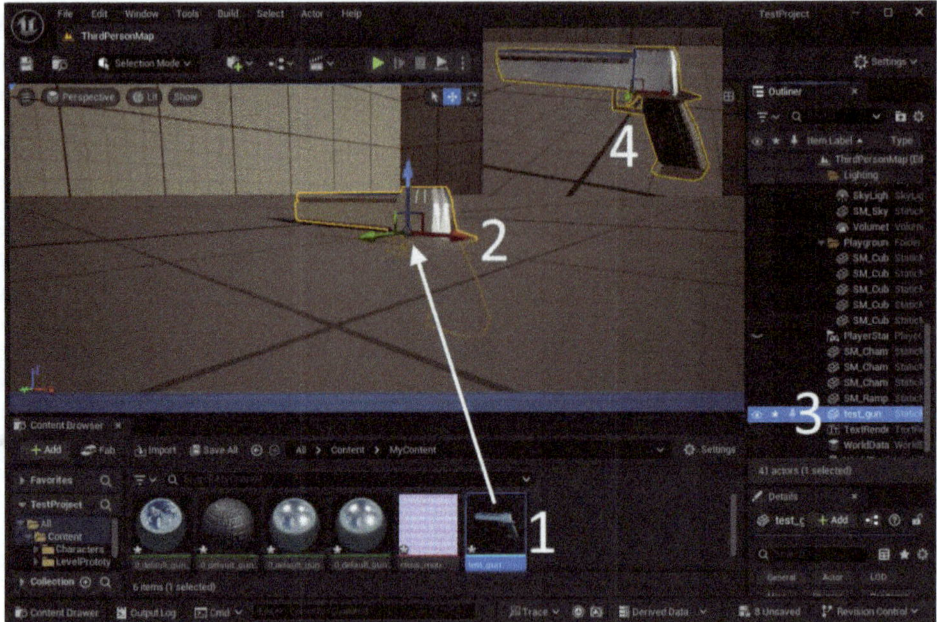

Figure 10-15. *(1) Drag the test_gun Static Mesh into the viewport to (2) instantiate it in the level (notice the origin of the mesh sits on the ground by default). You can (3) double-click the instance's name (which by default is the same as the Static Mesh's name) to zoom and frame it in the viewport. After locating the instance, you can (4) drag any axis of its movement widget to move it*

Recall that we set the gun's origin to Center of Mass (Volume) and moved it to coincide with Blender's world origin prior to export, so when imported into UE5, the Static Mesh has the same origin but with its Y axis flipped, due to conversion from a right-handed Z up coordinate system (Blender) to a left-handed (UE5) Z up system. If you'd prefer the Static Mesh to have a different origin in UE5, for example, centered on the grip as a mounting point instead, you can offset the mesh accordingly from the world origin before exporting out of Blender.

Summary

In this chapter, you learned how to prep and export a mesh from Blender to glTF 2.0 and FBX formats with materials embedded, both by hand and in Blender Python. You also found out how to modify the gun generator from Chapter 4 to integrate the code from this chapter, so it could generate a mesh and export it in one go. At the end of the chapter, you tried your hand at importing the exported gun into UE5 as a Static Mesh and instantiating it in a level.

The export process entailed setting the scene units to Metric and Length to Meters, then triangulating the meshes, applying modifiers and transforms, and optionally joining mesh pieces and scaling the model to the desired length. After that, you'd select the meshes and move them so their origins (or other desired reference points) align with Blender's world origin, since the world origin becomes an object's origin in the exported file. The relevant settings for glTF 2.0 or FBX are configured next so the meshes export with their materials in one file. Finally, objects are restored to their original locations pre-export.

APPENDIX

Installing Third-Party Python Packages for Blender 4.4.3+ on Windows 10 and 11

In this Appendix, we'll go over how to install third-party Python packages for Blender 4.4.3+ on Windows 10 and 11. Note that each version of Blender installed on your system comes with a separate copy of Python; therefore, you must repeat the package installations for each Blender version (e.g., `pyshp` installed for Blender 4.4 will not carry over to Blender 4.5).

Using Blender Python's pip to Install Packages

In this section, we'll look at how to install third-party packages to Blender 4.4.3+ on Windows 10 and 11 in general, using the pip version shipped with Blender.

Starting Command Prompt as Administrator

Due to Windows security, you must run pip in a Command Prompt window opened with "Run as administrator." To do so, in the search box to the right of the Windows button, type in "com" to locate Command Prompt, then right-click ➤ Run as administrator (which will look like Figure A-1 on Windows 11). When prompted "Do you want to allow

I. Lupiani, *Procedural Content Generation for Games*, https://doi.org/10.1007/979-8-8688-1787-8

this app to make changes to your device?", click Yes to proceed. A Command Prompt window will appear with the prompt "C:\Windows\System32>," assuming that C drive is the main partition containing Windows 10 or 11.

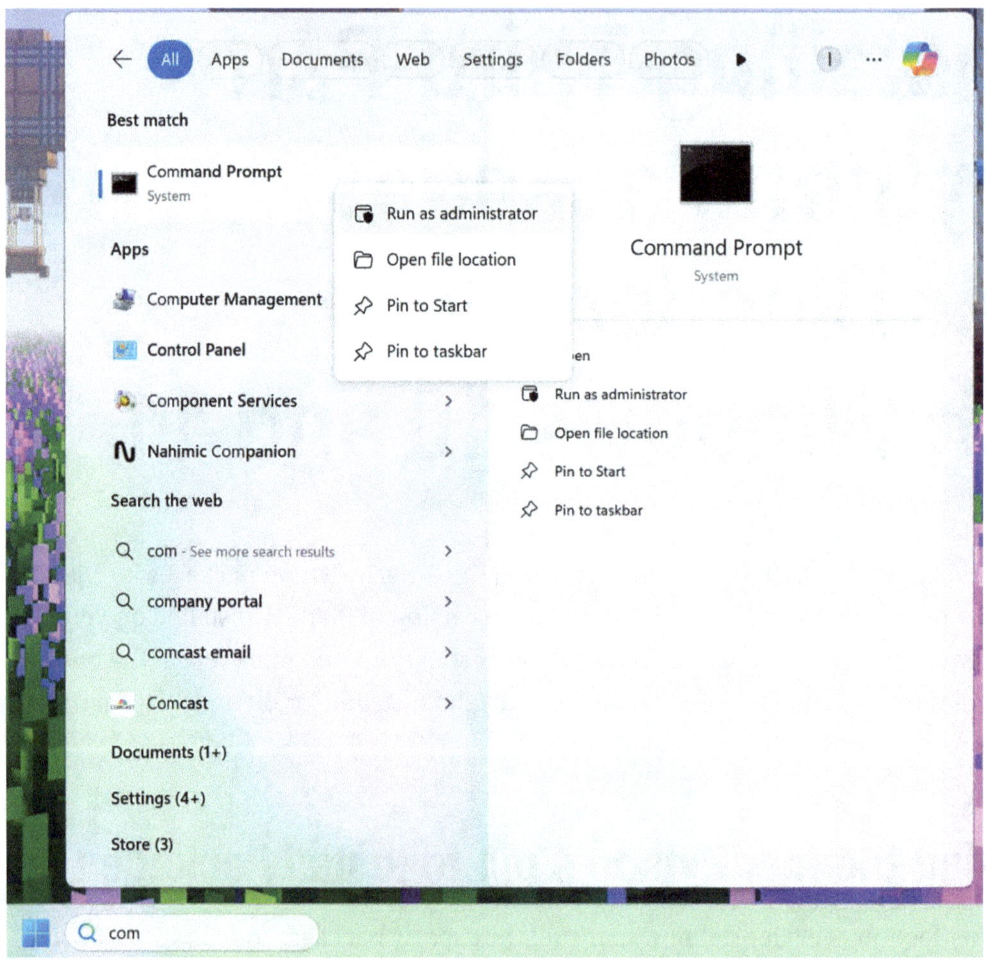

Figure A-1. *Type in "com" in the search box next to the Windows button, then right-click Command Prompt ➤ Run as administrator*

Finding and Copying the Path to python.exe Under Blender

To use the version of pip shipped with Blender, you must find the path to python.exe under Blender 4.4.3+. In the File Explorer, navigate to

C:\Program Files\Blender Foundation\Blender 4.4\4.4\python\bin

Right-click python on Windows 11 (or left-click followed by shift-right-click python.exe on Windows 10), then click "Copy as path," which will copy the path "C:\Program Files\Blender Foundation\Blender 4.4\4.4\python\bin\python.exe" to the clipboard.

Update the Version of pip Shipped with Blender

Before installing per-chapter dependencies, we'll perform a one-time update on the version of pip shipped with Blender. To do so, start Command Prompt using "Run as administrator," then enter the following command at the prompt:

"C:\Program Files\Blender Foundation\Blender 4.4\4.4\python\bin\python.exe" -m pip install --upgrade pip

The first part of the command is the path to python.exe under Blender 4.4.3+. Make sure to surround the path with double quotes as shown (if you've copied and pasted the path as described in the previous section, it should paste with double quotes included).

If successful, you should see output similar to the following:

```
C:\Windows\System32>"C:\Program Files\Blender Foundation\Blender 4.4\4.4\
python\bin\python.exe" -m pip install --upgrade pip
Requirement already satisfied: pip in c:\program files\blender foundation\
blender 4.4\4.4\python\lib\site-packages (24.0)
Collecting pip
  Using cached pip-25.1.1-py3-none-any.whl.metadata (3.6 kB)
Using cached pip-25.1.1-py3-none-any.whl (1.8 MB)
Installing collected packages: pip
  Attempting uninstall: pip
    Found existing installation: pip 24.0
    Uninstalling pip-24.0:
      Successfully uninstalled pip-24.0
```

```
  WARNING: The scripts pip.exe, pip3.11.exe and pip3.exe are installed in
'C:\Program Files\Blender Foundation\Blender 4.4\4.4\python\Scripts' which
is not on PATH.
  Consider adding this directory to PATH or, if you prefer to suppress this
warning, use --no-warn-script-location.
Successfully installed pip-25.1.1
```

Use pip to Install Third-Party Packages

To install a third-party Python package, you will start Command Prompt with "Run as administrator," then enter the following command at the prompt (but replace the word <package> with the name of the actual package you want to install):

"C:\Program Files\Blender Foundation\Blender 4.4\4.4\python\bin\python.exe" -m pip install --upgrade <package>

The first part of the command is the path to python.exe under Blender 4.4.3+. Make sure to surround the path with double quotes (if you've copied and pasted the path as described in the section "Finding and Copying the Path to python.exe under Blender," it should paste with double quotes included). Use --upgrade even if you are installing <package> for the first time. The command will install <package> to C:\Program Files\Blender Foundation\Blender 4.4\4.4\python\lib\site-packages. After installing new package(s), ensure that you close and relaunch Blender. ***A copy of the pip logs from the author's own installations of the per-chapter dependencies are provided at the end of this Appendix.***

Chapter 4

For Chapter 4, run the following command in Command Prompt opened with "Run as administrator" to install numpy, which at the time of writing is version numpy-2.2.6. This can be skipped if you've already installed numpy for Chapter 6, 8, 9, or 10. Be sure to close and relaunch Blender after installing numpy.

```
"C:\Program Files\Blender Foundation\Blender 4.4\4.4\python\bin\python.exe"
-m pip install --upgrade numpy
```

Note For Blender 4.5.2 LTS users on Windows 10 and 11, you may need to run the following command twice for pip to install the latest version of numpy, which at the time of writing is numpy-2.3.2:

"C:\Program Files\Blender Foundation\Blender 4.5\4.5\python\bin\python.exe" -m pip install --upgrade numpy

Chapter 6

For Chapter 6, run the following command in Command Prompt opened with "Run as administrator" to install `numpy`, which at the time of writing is version `numpy-2.2.6`. This can be skipped if you've already installed `numpy` for Chapter 4, 8, 9, or 10. Be sure to close and relaunch Blender after installing `numpy`.

```
"C:\Program Files\Blender Foundation\Blender 4.4\4.4\python\bin\python.exe"
-m pip install --upgrade numpy
```

Chapter 8

For Chapter 8, in a Command Prompt window opened with "Run as administrator," run the following command to install `pyshp-2.3.1`, `pandas-2.2.3`, `numpy-2.2.6`, and `matplotlib-3.10.3`. You can skip `numpy` if you've already installed it for Chapter 4, 6, 9, or 10. The package `openpyxl` is required by `pandas`, whereas `PyQt5` is required by `matplotlib`. Be sure to close and relaunch Blender after installing the new package(s):

```
"C:\Program Files\Blender Foundation\Blender 4.4\4.4\python\bin\python.exe"
-m pip install --upgrade pyshp; pandas; numpy; openpyxl; PyQt5; matplotlib
```

IMPORTANT for Windows 11 users: After installing the packages, in the File Explorer, navigate to C:\Program Files\Blender Foundation\Blender 4.4\4.4\python\lib\site-packages and ***change the permission for each of the following files: shapefile (shapefile.py) and six (six.py)***, by following the steps listed in the section "Changing File Permissions on Windows 11."

Instead of installing all packages with a single command, you can also install one package at a time, like the following:

```
"C:\Program Files\Blender Foundation\Blender 4.4\4.4\python\bin\python.exe"
-m pip install --upgrade pyshp
```

```
"C:\Program Files\Blender Foundation\Blender 4.4\4.4\python\bin\python.exe"
-m pip install --upgrade pandas
```

```
"C:\Program Files\Blender Foundation\Blender 4.4\4.4\python\bin\python.exe"
-m pip install --upgrade numpy
```

```
"C:\Program Files\Blender Foundation\Blender 4.4\4.4\python\bin\python.exe"
-m pip install --upgrade openpyxl
```

```
"C:\Program Files\Blender Foundation\Blender 4.4\4.4\python\bin\python.exe"
-m pip install --upgrade PyQt5
```

```
"C:\Program Files\Blender Foundation\Blender 4.4\4.4\python\bin\python.exe"
-m pip install --upgrade matplotlib
```

Chapter 8 Troubleshooting for Blender 4.5.2 LTS on Windows 10

For Blender 4.5.2 LTS users on Windows 10, if you run into errors running the Chapter 8 code, follow the steps in this section to resolve them. First, run the following two commands in a Command Prompt window opened with "Run as administrator":

```
"C:\Program Files\Blender Foundation\Blender 4.5\4.5\python\bin\python.exe"
-m pip install --upgrade pytz
```

```
"C:\Program Files\Blender Foundation\Blender 4.5\4.5\python\bin\python.exe"
-m pip install --upgrade six
```

Then locate the file `six.py` inside the following directory:

```
C:\Program Files\Blender Foundation\Blender 4.5\4.5\python\lib\site-
packages\pip\_vendor\urllib3\packages
```

Right-click `six.py`, then click Properties. In the window that opens, go to the Security tab, under Group or user names, click ALL APPLICATION PACKAGES to select it, then click the Edit button. In the next window that opens (titled Permissions for six.py), check the "Allow" box for Full control, Modify, and Write. Click Apply then OK to close the window, followed by Apply then OK to close the previous window. Next, copy `six.py` to the following directory:

```
C:\Program Files\Blender Foundation\Blender 4.5\4.5\python\lib\
site-packages
```

Chapter 9

For Chapter 9, in a Command Prompt window opened with "Run as administrator," run the following command to install `numpy-2.2.6`, `matplotlib-3.10.3`, and `rasterio-1.4.3`:

```
"C:\Program Files\Blender Foundation\Blender 4.4\4.4\python\bin\python.exe"
-m pip install --upgrade numpy; PyQt5; matplotlib; rasterio
```

`numpy` can be skipped if you've already installed it for Chapter 4, 6, 8, or 10. `PyQt5` and `matplotlib` can be skipped if you've already installed them for Chapter 8 (`PyQt5` is a dependency of `matplotlib`). Be sure to close and relaunch Blender after installing the new package(s).

Instead of installing all packages with a single command, you can also install one package at a time, like the following:

```
"C:\Program Files\Blender Foundation\Blender 4.4\4.4\python\bin\python.exe"
-m pip install --upgrade numpy
```

```
"C:\Program Files\Blender Foundation\Blender 4.4\4.4\python\bin\python.exe"
-m pip install --upgrade PyQt5
```

```
"C:\Program Files\Blender Foundation\Blender 4.4\4.4\python\bin\python.exe"
-m pip install --upgrade matplotlib
```

```
"C:\Program Files\Blender Foundation\Blender 4.4\4.4\python\bin\python.exe"
-m pip install --upgrade rasterio
```

Chapter 10

For Chapter 10, run the following command in a Command Prompt window opened with "Run as administrator" to install `numpy`, which at the time of writing is version `numpy-2.2.6`. This can be skipped if you've already installed `numpy` for Chapter 4, 6, 8, or 9. Be sure to close and relaunch Blender after installing `numpy`.

```
"C:\Program Files\Blender Foundation\Blender 4.4\4.4\python\bin\python.exe"
-m pip install --upgrade numpy
```

Changing File Permissions on Windows 11

This section shows how to grant Full control permission of a file to a user on Windows 11, which is required for some files added by third-party Python packages.

Right-click the file in question, then click Properties. In the window that opens, go to the Security tab, then click "Advanced," as shown in Figure A-2.

In the next window "Advanced Security Settings for <filename>" (Figure A-3), click "Change permissions," which opens the window shown in Figure A-4.

Click "Add." The window titled "Permission Entry for <filename>" (Figure A-5) will appear. Click "Select a principal" to open the "Select User or Group" window (Figure A-6), then type your username in the box and click OK. The username here is the name of the user folder under C:\Users, which is usually a five-letter string. Clicking OK will bring you back up a level to the previous window, with your Windows sign-in name now appearing after "Principal" (Figure A-7).

Check the "Full control" box (Figure A-8), then click "OK." This will bring you back up a level to "Advanced Security Settings for <filename>," with your Windows sign-in name now appearing in the Permission entries section (Figure A-9), with Type "Allow" and Access "Full control." Click Apply, then click OK. Make sure you click Apply first!

In the last window that remains (<filename> Properties), click OK to close it.

Note For Blender 4.5.2 LTS users on newer versions of Windows 11, the process to change file permission has simplified. If this applies to you, congrats! You can follow these steps instead: Right-click the file in question, then click Properties. In the window that opens, go to the Security tab, under Group or user names, click ALL APPLICATION PACKAGES to select it, then click the Edit button. In the next window that opens, check the "Allow" box for Full control, Modify, and Write. Click Apply then OK to close the window, followed by Apply then OK for the previous window.

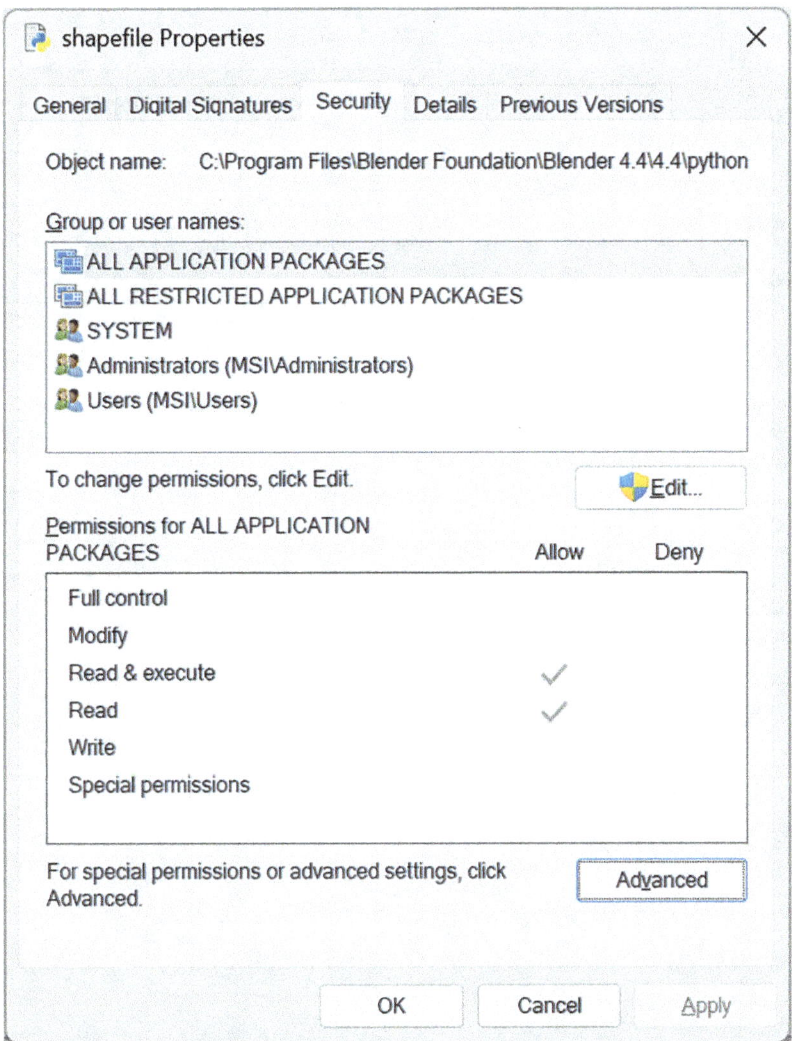

Figure A-2. *The window that opens after right-clicking a file ➤ Properties. Click "Advanced" to continue*

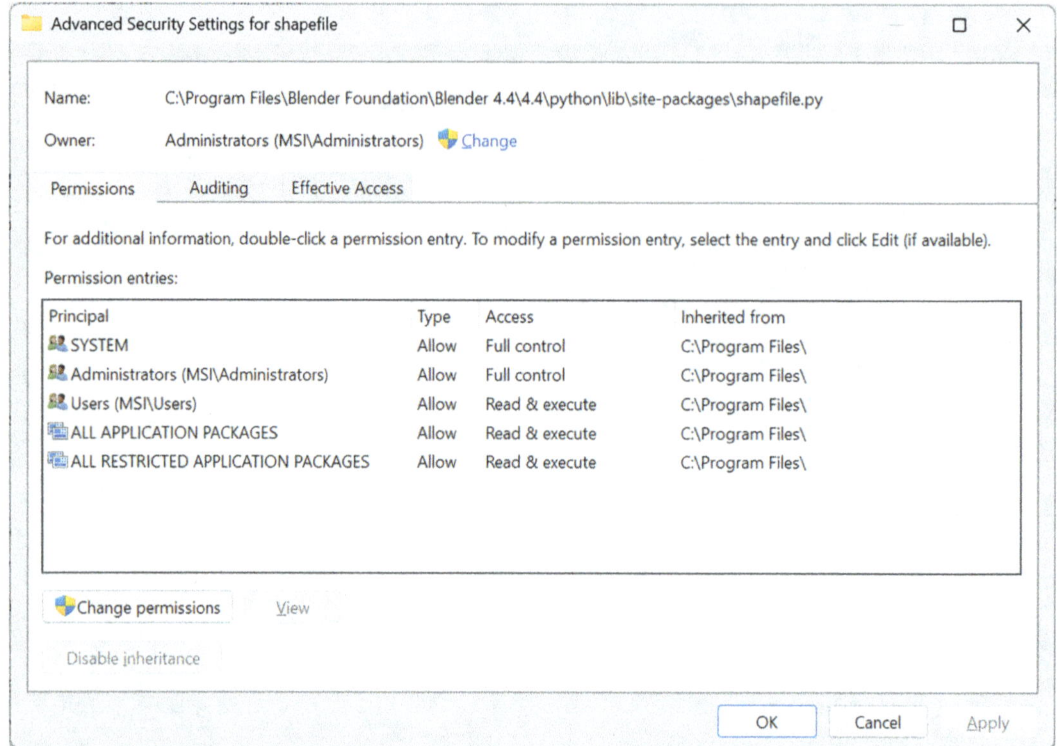

Figure A-3. *The window that opens after clicking "Advanced" in Figure A-2. Click "Change permissions" to proceed*

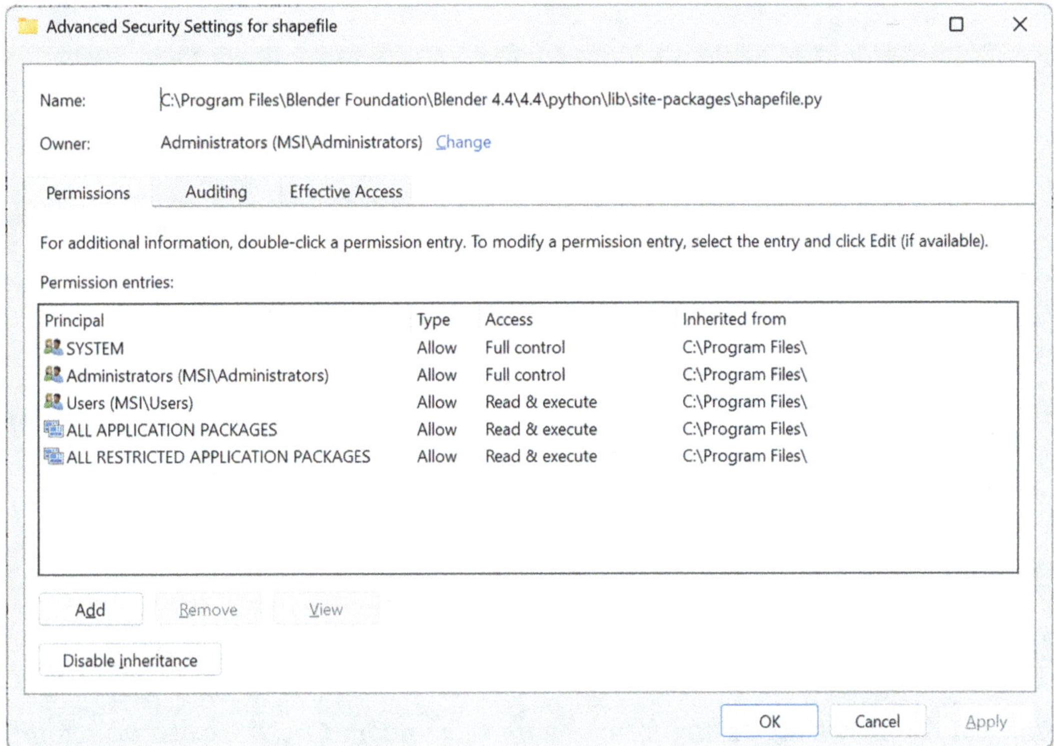

Figure A-4. *"Advanced Security Settings for <filename>" window. Click "Add" to proceed*

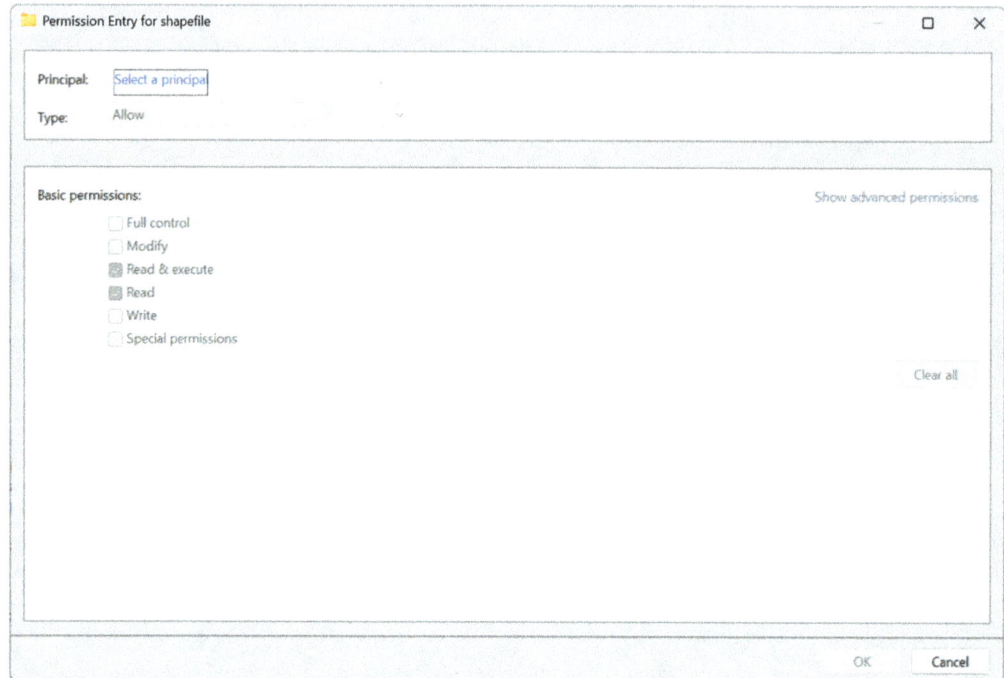

Figure A-5. *"Permission Entry for <filename>" window. Click "Select a principal" to proceed*

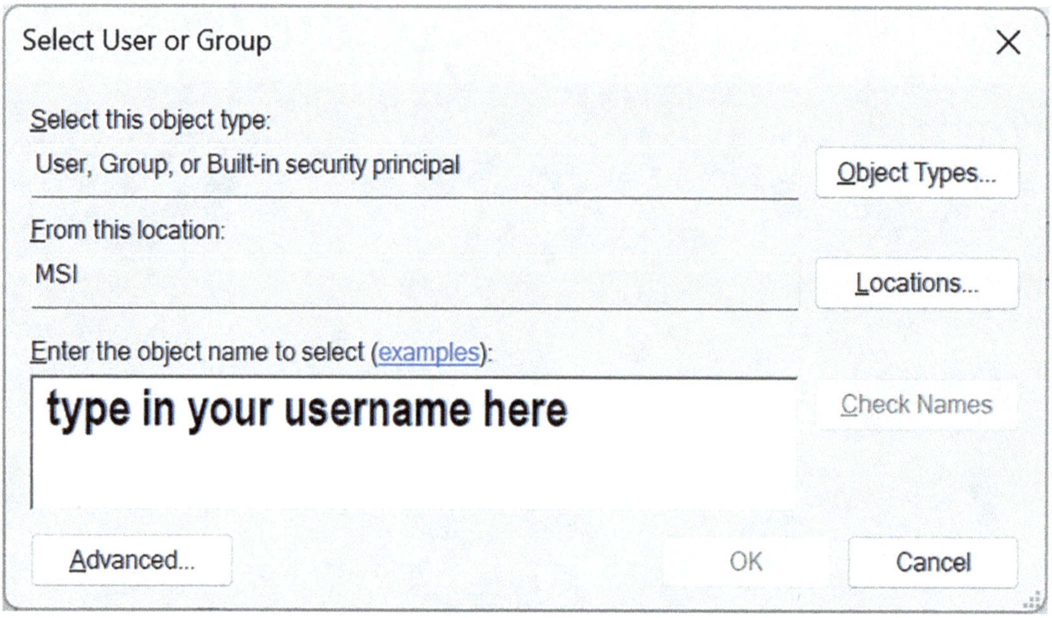

Figure A-6. *"Select User or Group" window. Type in your username (name of the user folder under C:\Users) in the box, then click OK*

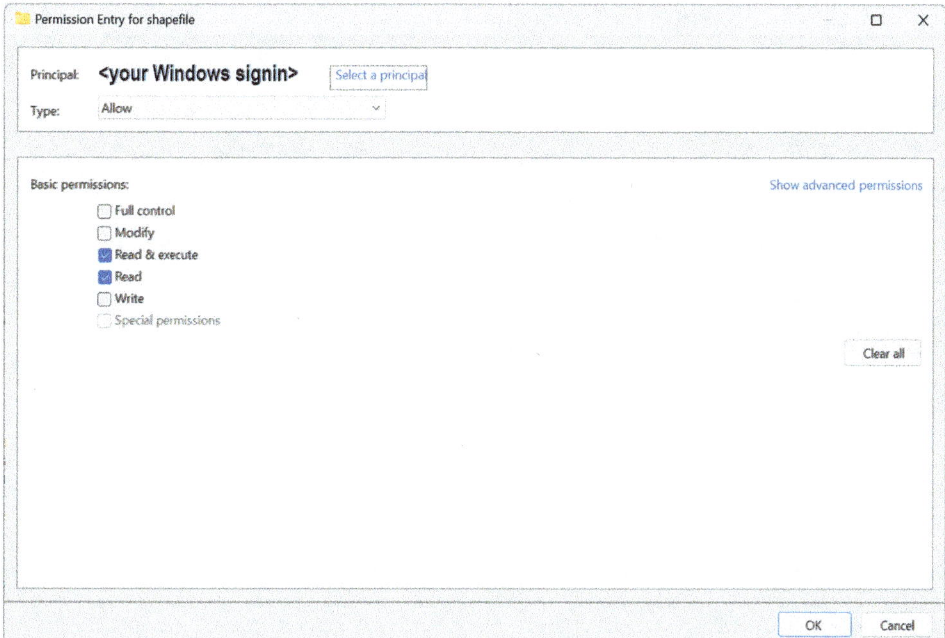

***Figure A-7.** Your Windows sign-in name should now appear under Principal at the top of the "Permission Entry for <filename>" window*

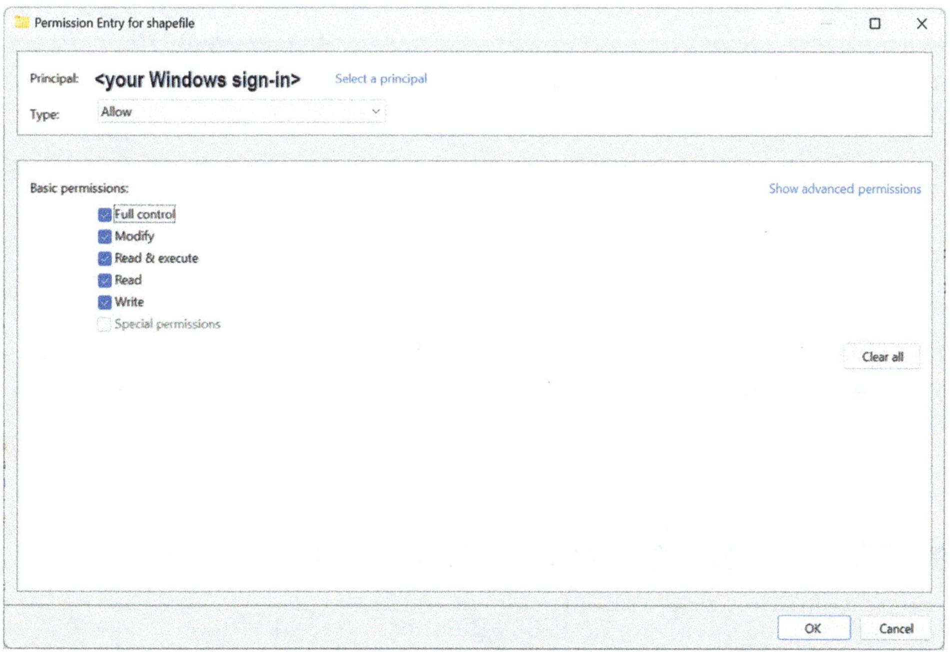

***Figure A-8.** Click the "Full control" box, then click OK*

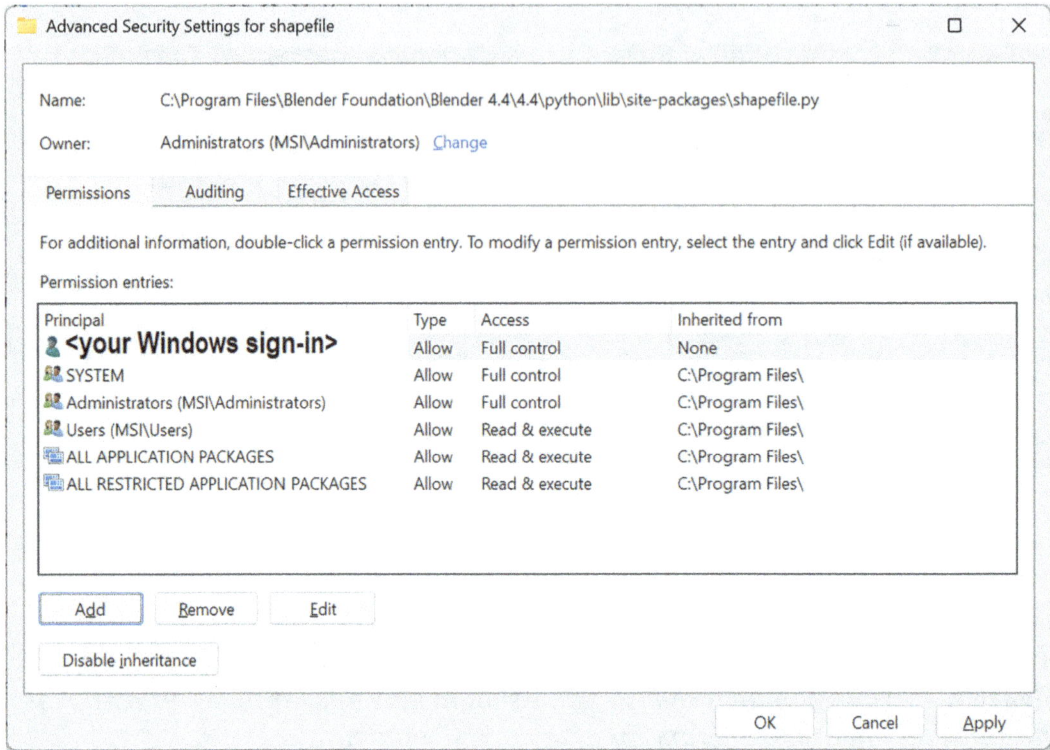

Figure A-9. *Verify your Windows sign-in name now appears in the Permission entries list for the file, with Type "Allow" and Access "Full control," then click Apply, followed by OK*

pip Log Transcript

This section provides sample copies of the logs following each tool installation or update described in this Appendix. As a reminder, the logs are produced based on Blender 4.4.3+ on Windows 11, in Command Prompt windows opened with "Run as administrator." The logs are merely provided as additional data for troubleshooting.

Updating pip Shipped with Blender 4.4.3+

C:\Windows\System32>"C:\Program Files\Blender Foundation\Blender 4.4\4.4\python\bin\python.exe" -m pip install --upgrade pip

```
Requirement already satisfied: pip in c:\program files\blender foundation\
blender 4.4\4.4\python\lib\site-packages (24.0)
Collecting pip
  Using cached pip-25.1.1-py3-none-any.whl.metadata (3.6 kB)
Using cached pip-25.1.1-py3-none-any.whl (1.8 MB)
Installing collected packages: pip
  Attempting uninstall: pip
    Found existing installation: pip 24.0
    Uninstalling pip-24.0:
      Successfully uninstalled pip-24.0
  WARNING: The scripts pip.exe, pip3.11.exe and pip3.exe are installed in
  'C:\Program Files\Blender Foundation\Blender 4.4\4.4\python\Scripts'
  which is not on PATH.
  Consider adding this directory to PATH or, if you prefer to suppress this
warning, use --no-warn-script-location.
Successfully installed pip-25.1.1
```

Installing pyshp

C:\Windows\System32>"C:\Program Files\Blender Foundation\Blender 4.4\4.4\python\bin\python.exe" -m pip install --upgrade pyshp

```
Collecting pyshp
  Using cached pyshp-2.3.1-py2.py3-none-any.whl.metadata (55 kB)
Using cached pyshp-2.3.1-py2.py3-none-any.whl (46 kB)
Installing collected packages: pyshp
Successfully installed pyshp-2.3.1
```

Installing pandas

C:\Windows\System32>"C:\Program Files\Blender Foundation\Blender 4.4\4.4\python\bin\python.exe" -m pip install --upgrade pandas

```
Collecting pandas
  Using cached pandas-2.2.3-cp311-cp311-win_amd64.whl.metadata (19 kB)
```

```
Requirement already satisfied: numpy>=1.23.2 in c:\program files\blender
foundation\blender 4.4\4.4\python\lib\site-packages (from pandas) (1.26.4)
Collecting python-dateutil>=2.8.2 (from pandas)
  Using cached python_dateutil-2.9.0.post0-py2.py3-none-any.whl.metadata
(8.4 kB)
Collecting pytz>=2020.1 (from pandas)
  Using cached pytz-2025.2-py2.py3-none-any.whl.metadata (22 kB)
Collecting tzdata>=2022.7 (from pandas)
  Using cached tzdata-2025.2-py2.py3-none-any.whl.metadata (1.4 kB)
Collecting six>=1.5 (from python-dateutil>=2.8.2->pandas)
  Using cached six-1.17.0-py2.py3-none-any.whl.metadata (1.7 kB)
Using cached pandas-2.2.3-cp311-cp311-win_amd64.whl (11.6 MB)
Using cached python_dateutil-2.9.0.post0-py2.py3-none-any.whl (229 kB)
Using cached pytz-2025.2-py2.py3-none-any.whl (509 kB)
Using cached six-1.17.0-py2.py3-none-any.whl (11 kB)
Using cached tzdata-2025.2-py2.py3-none-any.whl (347 kB)
Installing collected packages: pytz, tzdata, six, python-dateutil, pandas
Successfully installed pandas-2.2.3 python-dateutil-2.9.0.post0 pytz-2025.2
six-1.17.0 tzdata-2025.2
```

Updating numpy

C:\Windows\System32>"C:\Program Files\Blender Foundation\Blender 4.4\4.4\python\bin\python.exe" -m pip install --upgrade numpy

```
Requirement already satisfied: numpy in c:\program files\blender
foundation\blender 4.4\4.4\python\lib\site-packages (1.26.4)
Collecting numpy
  Using cached numpy-2.2.6-cp311-cp311-win_amd64.whl.metadata (60 kB)
Using cached numpy-2.2.6-cp311-cp311-win_amd64.whl (12.9 MB)
Installing collected packages: numpy
  Attempting uninstall: numpy
    Found existing installation: numpy 1.26.4
    Uninstalling numpy-1.26.4:
      Successfully uninstalled numpy-1.26.4
```

```
  WARNING: The scripts f2py.exe and numpy-config.exe are installed in 'C:\
Program Files\Blender Foundation\Blender 4.4\4.4\python\Scripts' which is
not on PATH.
  Consider adding this directory to PATH or, if you prefer to suppress this
warning, use --no-warn-script-location.
Successfully installed numpy-2.2.6
```

Installing openpyxl

C:\Windows\System32>"C:\Program Files\Blender Foundation\Blender 4.4\4.4\python\bin\python.exe" -m pip install --upgrade openpyxl

```
Collecting openpyxl
  Using cached openpyxl-3.1.5-py2.py3-none-any.whl.metadata (2.5 kB)
Collecting et-xmlfile (from openpyxl)
  Using cached et_xmlfile-2.0.0-py3-none-any.whl.metadata (2.7 kB)
Using cached openpyxl-3.1.5-py2.py3-none-any.whl (250 kB)
Using cached et_xmlfile-2.0.0-py3-none-any.whl (18 kB)
Installing collected packages: et-xmlfile, openpyxl
Successfully installed et-xmlfile-2.0.0 openpyxl-3.1.5
```

Installing PyQt5

C:\Windows\System32>"C:\Program Files\Blender Foundation\Blender 4.4\4.4\python\bin\python.exe" -m pip install --upgrade PyQt5

```
Collecting PyQt5
  Using cached PyQt5-5.15.11-cp38-abi3-win_amd64.whl.metadata (2.1 kB)
Collecting PyQt5-sip<13,>=12.15 (from PyQt5)
  Using cached PyQt5_sip-12.17.0-cp311-cp311-win_amd64.whl.metadata
(492 bytes)
Collecting PyQt5-Qt5<5.16.0,>=5.15.2 (from PyQt5)
  Using cached PyQt5_Qt5-5.15.2-py3-none-win_amd64.whl.metadata (552 bytes)
Using cached PyQt5-5.15.11-cp38-abi3-win_amd64.whl (6.9 MB) Using cached
PyQt5_Qt5-5.15.2-py3-none-win_amd64.whl (50.1 MB) Using cached PyQt5_
sip-12.17.0-cp311-cp311-win_amd64.whl (59 kB)
```

```
Installing collected packages: PyQt5-Qt5, PyQt5-sip, PyQt5 -------------
------------- ------------- 2/3 [PyQt5] WARNING: The scripts pylupdate5.
exe, pyrcc5.exe and pyuic5.exe are installed in 'C:\Program Files\Blender
Foundation\Blender 4.4\4.4\python\Scripts' which is not on PATH. Consider
adding this directory to PATH or, if you prefer to suppress this warning,
use --no-warn-script-location. Successfully installed PyQt5-5.15.11 PyQt5-
Qt5-5.15.2 PyQt5-sip-12.17.0
```

Installing matplotlib

C:\Windows\System32>"C:\Program Files\Blender Foundation\Blender 4.4\4.4\python\bin\python.exe" -m pip install --upgrade matplotlib

```
Collecting matplotlib
  Using cached matplotlib-3.10.3-cp311-cp311-win_amd64.whl.metadata (11 kB)
Collecting contourpy>=1.0.1 (from matplotlib)
  Using cached contourpy-1.3.2-cp311-cp311-win_amd64.whl.metadata (5.5 kB)
Collecting cycler>=0.10 (from matplotlib)
  Using cached cycler-0.12.1-py3-none-any.whl.metadata (3.8 kB)
Collecting fonttools>=4.22.0 (from matplotlib)
  Using cached fonttools-4.58.1-cp311-cp311-win_amd64.whl.metadata (108 kB)
Collecting kiwisolver>=1.3.1 (from matplotlib)
  Using cached kiwisolver-1.4.8-cp311-cp311-win_amd64.whl.metadata (6.3 kB)
Requirement already satisfied: numpy>=1.23 in c:\program files\
blender foundation\blender 4.4\4.4\python\lib\site-packages (from
matplotlib) (2.2.6)
Collecting packaging>=20.0 (from matplotlib)
  Using cached packaging-25.0-py3-none-any.whl.metadata (3.3 kB)
Collecting pillow>=8 (from matplotlib)
  Using cached pillow-11.2.1-cp311-cp311-win_amd64.whl.metadata (9.1 kB)
Collecting pyparsing>=2.3.1 (from matplotlib)
  Using cached pyparsing-3.2.3-py3-none-any.whl.metadata (5.0 kB)
Requirement already satisfied: python-dateutil>=2.7 in c:\program files\
blender foundation\blender 4.4\4.4\python\lib\site-packages (from
matplotlib) (2.9.0.post0)
```

```
Requirement already satisfied: six>=1.5 in c:\program files\blender
foundation\blender 4.4\4.4\python\lib\site-packages (from python-
dateutil>=2.7->matplotlib) (1.17.0)
Using cached matplotlib-3.10.3-cp311-cp311-win_amd64.whl (8.1 MB)
Using cached contourpy-1.3.2-cp311-cp311-win_amd64.whl (222 kB)
Using cached cycler-0.12.1-py3-none-any.whl (8.3 kB)
Using cached fonttools-4.58.1-cp311-cp311-win_amd64.whl (2.2 MB)
Using cached kiwisolver-1.4.8-cp311-cp311-win_amd64.whl (71 kB)
Using cached packaging-25.0-py3-none-any.whl (66 kB)
Using cached pillow-11.2.1-cp311-cp311-win_amd64.whl (2.7 MB)
Using cached pyparsing-3.2.3-py3-none-any.whl (111 kB)
Installing collected packages: pyparsing, pillow, packaging, kiwisolver,
fonttools, cycler, contourpy, matplotlib
   -------------------- ------------------- 4/8 [fonttools]  WARNING:
The scripts fonttools.exe, pyftmerge.exe, pyftsubset.exe and ttx.exe are
installed in 'C:\Program Files\Blender Foundation\Blender 4.4\4.4\python\
Scripts' which is not on PATH.
  Consider adding this directory to PATH or, if you prefer to suppress this
warning, use --no-warn-script-location.
Successfully installed contourpy-1.3.2 cycler-0.12.1 fonttools-4.58.1
kiwisolver-1.4.8 matplotlib-3.10.3 packaging-25.0 pillow-11.2.1
pyparsing-3.2.3
```

Installing rasterio

```
C:\Windows\System32>"C:\Program Files\Blender Foundation\Blender 4.4\4.4\
python\bin\python.exe" -m pip install --upgrade rasterio
Collecting rasterio
  Downloading rasterio-1.4.3-cp311-cp311-win_amd64.whl.metadata (9.4 kB)
Collecting affine (from rasterio)
  Downloading affine-2.4.0-py3-none-any.whl.metadata (4.0 kB)
Collecting attrs (from rasterio)
  Downloading attrs-25.3.0-py3-none-any.whl.metadata (10 kB)
```

```
Requirement already satisfied: certifi in c:\program files\blender
foundation\blender 4.4\4.4\python\lib\site-packages (from rasterio)
(2021.10.8)
Collecting click>=4.0 (from rasterio)
  Downloading click-8.2.1-py3-none-any.whl.metadata (2.5 kB)
Collecting cligj>=0.5 (from rasterio)
  Downloading cligj-0.7.2-py3-none-any.whl.metadata (5.0 kB)
Requirement already satisfied: numpy>=1.24 in c:\program files\blender
foundation\blender 4.4\4.4\python\lib\site-packages (from rasterio) (2.2.6)
Collecting click-plugins (from rasterio)
  Downloading click_plugins-1.1.1-py2.py3-none-any.whl.metadata (6.4 kB)
Requirement already satisfied: pyparsing in c:\program files\blender
foundation\blender 4.4\4.4\python\lib\site-packages (from rasterio) (3.2.3)
Collecting colorama (from click>=4.0->rasterio)
  Downloading colorama-0.4.6-py2.py3-none-any.whl.metadata (17 kB)
Downloading rasterio-1.4.3-cp311-cp311-win_amd64.whl (25.5 MB)
   ---------------------------------------- 25.5/25.5 MB 26.4 MB/s
eta 0:00:00
Downloading click-8.2.1-py3-none-any.whl (102 kB)
Downloading cligj-0.7.2-py3-none-any.whl (7.1 kB)
Downloading affine-2.4.0-py3-none-any.whl (15 kB)
Downloading attrs-25.3.0-py3-none-any.whl (63 kB)
Downloading click_plugins-1.1.1-py2.py3-none-any.whl (7.5 kB)
Downloading colorama-0.4.6-py2.py3-none-any.whl (25 kB)
Installing collected packages: colorama, attrs, affine, click, cligj,
click-plugins, rasterio
   ---------------------------------- ----- 6/7 [rasterio]  WARNING: The
script rio.exe is installed in 'C:\Program Files\Blender Foundation\Blender
4.4\4.4\python\Scripts' which is not on PATH.
  Consider adding this directory to PATH or, if you prefer to suppress this
  warning, use --no-warn-script-location.
Successfully installed affine-2.4.0 attrs-25.3.0 click-8.2.1 click-
plugins-1.1.1 cligj-0.7.2 colorama-0.4.6 rasterio-1.4.3
```

Index

A

B

I. Lupiani, *Procedural Content Generation for Games*, https://doi.org/10.1007/979-8-8688-1787-8

C

D

E

F

G

H

I, J, K

L

M

N

O

P, Q

R

S

T

U

V, W, X, Y, Z

GPSR Compliance
The European Union's (EU) General Product Safety Regulation (GPSR) is a set of rules that requires consumer products to be safe and our obligations to ensure this.

If you have any concerns about our products, you can contact us on

ProductSafety@springernature.com

In case Publisher is established outside the EU, the EU authorized representative is:

Springer Nature Customer Service Center GmbH
Europaplatz 3
69115 Heidelberg, Germany

www.ingramcontent.com/pod-product-compliance
Lightning Source LLC
LaVergne TN
LVHW081345060526
838201LV00050B/1712
* 9 7 9 8 8 6 8 8 1 7 8 6 1 *